A Poverty of Rights

A Poverty of Rights

Citizenship and Inequality in
Twentieth-Century Rio de Janeiro

Brodwyn Fischer

STANFORD UNIVERSITY PRESS

STANFORD, CALIFORNIA

2008

This book was published with the assistance of Northwestern University

Stanford University Press,
Stanford California
©2008 by the Board of Trustees of the
Leland Stanford Junior University

Library of Congress Cataloging-in-Publication Data

Fischer, Brodwyn M.
 A poverty of rights : citizenship and inequality in twentieth-century Rio de Janeiro / Brodwyn Fischer.
  p. cm.
 Includes bibliographical references and index.
 ISBN 978-0-8047-5290-9 (cloth : alk. paper)
  1. Poor—Civil rights—Brazil—Rio de Janeiro—History—20th century. 2. Equality—Brazil—Rio de Janeiro—History—20th century. 3. Rio de Janeiro (Brazil)—Politics and government—20th century. 4. Rio de Janeiro (Brazil)—Social conditions—20th century. 5. Brazil—Politics and government—20th century. I. Title.

HC189.R4F57 2008
323.3'2942098153—dc22   2007025421

Printed in the United States of America on
acid-free, archival-quality paper

Typeset at Stanford University Press in 10/12 Sabon

To My Family

Acknowledgments

This book has taken shape over more years than I care to count, and the debts accumulated in the process are many. These lines cannot do more than hint at my deep thanks to everyone who has helped this project along its many paths.

Those thanks must begin with the people who nurtured the early interests that would lead me eventually to write this book, long before I had ever set foot in Brazil. In very different ways, Nancy Koehn, Jorge Domínguez, Jim Brennan, Emilio Kourí, and John Womack, Jr., helped to shape undergraduate affinities for old documents, social history, and Latin American studies into intellectual passions that have so far stood the test of time. In the year after my college graduation, a Michael Rockefeller traveling fellowship allowed me to spend a year pursuing those passions in Mexico City. I owe thanks to the fellowship board, and more still to the Unión de Mujeres from the neighborhood of Ixtlahuacan, who welcomed me into their homes, told me about their lives, and helped me begin to see just how important water pipes, sewer lines, and property ownership could be in shaping women's ideas of cities and their place within them. To Carmen Retana in particular, I owe enormous gratitude, for her friendship, her intelligence, and her extraordinary patience, commitment, and generosity.

This book took its first form as a doctoral dissertation at Harvard, where I received financial support from Harvard University, from the Jacob Javits Fellowship Program, and from the Mellon Foundation. My advisers in Harvard's history department, Jack Womack and John Coatsworth, were in appropriate measures kind, insightful, and exacting. I am grateful to Professor Womack for his inexhaustible curiosity, his commitment to getting to the heart of things, and his uncanny instinct for knowing what is important, and why; without his intelligence, insight, and loyalty I would likely never have become a historian. Professor Coatsworth's unflagging optimism and simple insistence that all my archival digging be done for a clear purpose saved me from the twin perils of narrowness and baroque irrelevance. Without his constant support and incisive queries, this book could never have been written. I would also likely have given up on the whole enterprise had it not been for the companionship and inspiration of my friends from graduate school, especially José Orozco, Kathryn Burns, Aurora Gómez, Elizabeth Boggs, Graciela Márquez, Ana Romo, Laura Gotkowitz, Michel Gobat, and Emilio Kourí. Felo Matos Rodríguez was another constant and much-valued friend and colleague throughout.

As my interest in Rio and urban poverty deepened, Alma Guillermo-prieto, Sandra Lauderdale-Graham, Pablo Piccato, and Teresa Meade all offered welcome advice, and Michael Conniff generously shared both his encouragement and his research notes. Thomas Skidmore opened his archives to me, and welcomed me to his home for multiple conversations, some of which I only came fully to understand years later. Elizabeth Leeds has repeatedly shared her extensive knowledge of Rio and its favelas, and put me in contact with some of her many friends in Rio. I was also lucky enough to meet Sueann Caulfield at this stage; over many years since, her infectious love of Brazil, her long familiarity with Rio and its archives, and her savvy about Brazilian historiography have helped me in more ways than I can name.

Over several years, my graduate research in Brazil was funded by the Fundación MAPFRE América, the Jens Aubrey Westengard Fund, the Harvard Graduate Society, the Frederick Sheldon fund, the FLAS program, the Fulbright program, the Mellon Foundation, and the Social Science Research Council. I am grateful to all for the research they made possible.

I would never have gotten far in Brazil without Sabrina Wilson's gift for language instruction, and my first exploratory trip would have been lonely indeed without Joel Wolfe's kind tips, Daryle Williams's friendly company and advice, and Kathryn Burns's precious list of old friends. In Rio, I am especially thankful to Monica Grin, who introduced me to the city and a few of its intellectual circles. I owe much of my initial enchantment with Rio to Monica's friendship, hospitality, and intellectual energy. Through her, I met Wanderley Guilherme dos Santos, who welcomed me to many meals and is probably unaware of the favor he did me by showing me—subtly, ironically, and kindly—the scope of my ignorance about Brazil. That first trip also introduced me to Gilberto Hochman, whose intelligence, advice, help, and friendship I have valued ever since. I am also grateful to Jaime Benchimol, Nísia Trinidade Lima, Lícia Valladares, and José Murilo de Carvalho for their willingness to meet and share their work with a student at such an early stage of her research.

The year I spent doing the core research for my dissertation was both productive and joyful. Throughout that year, and the many since then, the staff of Rio's Arquivo Nacional has helped me enormously; I am especially grateful to Sátiro Nunes for his aid in locating documents and facilitating reproduction. My thanks also go to the staffs of the Arquivo da Cidade, the Biblioteca Nacional, the now-extinct Arquivo Judiciário, the archives of Rio's 20th Vara Criminal, the library of the Serviço de Obras Sociais, the Fundação Getúlio Vargas, and the Casa Rui Barbosa.

I could probably never have understood the things I found in the archives—and I certainly would not have enjoyed digging them out so much—had I not happened upon such a lovely group of friends and colleagues in Brazil. Maria da Conceição Ferreira Pinto, "Dona Filinha," welcomed me to her home in Chapeu Mangueira and spent long hours showing me around the neighborhood and recounting her many memories of community life and activism. In the Arquivo Nacional, I was lucky enough to share research discoveries and lunch breaks with Sueann Caulfield, Kirsten Schultz, Barbara Sommer, Álvaro Nascimento, Olívia Gomes da Cunha, Marcos Bretas, Alessandra Silveira, and Tânia Salgado Pimenta. I am especially grateful to Marcos for his help in gaining access to police logbooks, and to Sueann, Olívia, and Álvaro for the many conversations and collaborations that have followed from those early encounters. Sidney Chalhoub furnished constant inspiration in written form, and offered incisive questions and kind encouragement during our encounters in Campinas and in the old AN reading room. Martha Abreu, in all her generosity and radiance, became a valued adviser and dear friend even as she finished her dissertation and became a mother; my thanks to her and to Zé Carlos for many happy visits to their home in Itaipú. Miriam Chaves's energy, spirit, and humor made the whole year more enjoyable. Finally, no account of my time in Brazil would be complete without mention of Keila Grinberg; over the years, from Brazil to the United States and back, Keila has been an inspiration, a kindred spirit, and a great friend. She and Flávio Limoncic have done more than anyone else to make Rio feel like a second home to me, and I cannot thank them enough.

As I returned to the United States, married, and began to write my dissertation in a little log cabin in Etna, NH, I enjoyed the company and encouragement of many people; my special thanks to John Watanabe, Annelise Orleck, Judy Byfield, Leo Spitzer, Agnes Lugo-Ortiz, Diane Miliotes, Michael Ermarth, and Marysa Navarro. Participants in the Boston Area Latin American History workshop and the University of Michigan conference on honor, status, and the law provided especially helpful comments on my work in progress. As I finished the dissertation and moved on to my first job at Amherst College, many generous colleagues shared their insights, enthusiasm, and friendship. John Servos, Margaret Hunt, Marni Sandweiss, Jerry Dennerline, Frank Couvares, Martha Saxton, Kim Brandt, Catherine Epstein, Javier Corrales, and Durba Ghosh merit particular thanks.

Due in part to life events, but mostly to my own stubborn ideas, the road from dissertation to book has been a very long one, and many people have helped me along the way. I received support for new research and writing from Amherst College, Northwestern University, and Northwestern's Alice Kaplan Center for the Humanities. The staffs of the ALERJ library, the Biblioteca Nacional, Rio's various civil varas, the Carlos Lacerda Archives in Brasília, the Fundação Oswaldo Cruz, the Arquivo da Cidade, the Instituto Pereira Passos, and the University of Michigan libraries all provided invaluable assistance. Nathan Wright helped me to create the statistical models for Part III of the book. Without the miracle team of Lu Pinheiro, Gabrielle Moreira, and Viviane Jorge, I would never have been able to bring together the story of Rio's favela struggles in the 1940s and 1950s. Eliane Athayde kindly took the time to tell me about her experiences with the Pastoral das Favelas, and Pedro Strozenberg met with me on various occasions to talk about Rio's poor communities, both past and present. Participants in the Favela Tem Memória project helped bring me into contact with a number of residents and activists in Rio's favelas; my thanks especially to Marcelo Monteiro, and also to Abdias José Nascimento dos Santos, Lúcio de Paula Bispo, and Odília dos Santos Gama for taking so much time to share their memories and life stories.

Both the dissertation and its revisions received valuable feedback from any number of friends and colleagues. Sessions at the University of San Diego, the ANPUH meetings at the Universidade Federal Fluminense, the AHA meetings in Chicago, the LASA meetings in Miami and Las Vegas, the American Bar Foundation, the University of Chicago history workshop, and the Kaplan Center for the Humanities were especially helpful. Silvia Lara and Joseli Mendonça organized a terrific seminar on Brazil's legal history at Campinas in 2004, and their comments—along with those of Alexandre Fortes, John French, Claudio Batalha, and Michael Hall—were very important to my revisions of Part II. Olívia Gomes da Cunha and Flávio Gomes generously arranged two presentations at the IFCS, one as part of the since-released compilation, *Quase-Cidadão*; comments and questions from Martha Abreu, Paulo Lins, and Luis Antonio Machado were especially appreciated. Jeremy Adelman, Dain Borges, and John French all took time to read through my dissertation soon after its completion; their critiques, insights, and support—then, and since—have been invaluable, and have helped to shape critical aspects of this book. Elizabeth Leeds, Barbara Weinstein, Ângela de Castro

Gomes, Claudio Lomnitz, Tamar Herzog, Zephyr Frank, Amy Chazkel, and Bryan McCann also read portions of the manuscript and offered valuable comments and advice along the way.

Northwestern University has been my academic home since 2001, and my colleagues there have everything to do with this book's completion. Frank Safford has been an exemplary mentor, offering valuable comments, guidance, and encouragement since the day we first met. Joe Barton has taken the time to talk about everything under the sun, and he, Mary Weismantel, and Jorge Coronado have been terrific co-conspirators in our Rockefeller Humanities project. Ben Schneider and Michael Hanchard took the time for many worthwhile conversations. In the history department, my thanks go out to all of my colleagues, but especially to Henry Binford, Ethan Shagan, Ben Frommer, Peter Carroll, Dylan Penningroth, Kate Masur, and Francesca Bordogna. I am also grateful to department chairs Ed Muir, Sara Maza, Jock McLane, and Nancy MacLean for their support and decency over the years.

A number of friends from Hyde Park and the University of Chicago were important sources of inspiration, advice, and company during this book's completion: Claudio Lomnitz, Elena Climent, Dain Borges, Julia Scott, Tamar Herzog, Steve Pinkus, Susan Stokes, Alison Winter, Adrian Johns, Amy Kim, Erica Dudley, and Richard Neer have helped to make Chicago home, even through busy and difficult times. As I put the final touches on the introduction and conclusion and waited for the press wheels to turn, Erin Goodman and Edwin Ortiz, along with the rest of the staff at Harvard's David Rockefeller Center for Latin American Studies, made me feel welcome in my sabbatical perch. Ken Maxwell, Merilee Grindle, Jorge Domínguez, and Biorn Mayberry-Lewis helped the conclusion along with terrific questions, as did many other participants in the DRCLAS Tuesday seminar and the Boston Area History workshop. As good fortune would have it, Alma Guillermoprieto, Aurora Gómez, and César Hernández were also back in Cambridge during those months; I have been acquainted with all of them practically since this book's inception, and Aurora, especially, has been a fellow traveler all the way; it seemed only right to share with them its ending.

Norris Pope at Stanford University Press has been a kind and patient supporter of this book since our first encounter; my many thanks to him and to John Feneron for their help in bringing the book through to completion. Joseph Love and José Moya were insightful, exacting, and very generous readers of the manuscript; it is a better book thanks to them, though some of their questions will have to await further projects for the responses they deserve.

I come now to the most difficult of these lines, because they concern people whose main role in this book has been to shape its author. My mother, Connie Dickinson, is everywhere in these pages. Her hardest times allowed me to know the difference between poverty and degradation, and to see the importance of small and practical things; the stubbornness I both learned and inherited from her left me little choice but to push ahead through this project's worst moments; and her love of books made me know from the beginning that I would one day write one. My father, Mark Fischer, is also here throughout; to him I owe my initial interest in Latin America, the love of music that is inseparable from my affinity for Brazil, and whatever patience and meticulousness I could muster to sustain me through some of this project's toughest stages. As important as any of that was his constant love, pride, and support, discernable even from half a world away. I am grateful also to Corinn Castro, for the generosity and love she's shown toward us grown-up "kids" since joining our family. Linda Jacobs became my family by choice, nearly thirty years ago; without her example, I might never have dreamed of work in other languages and distant places, and without her love, challenge, and encouragement I could not have become the person and scholar I am. I am thankful to my brothers, and especially Dylan Fischer, for putting up with me through childhood and recognizing what we share as adults. Marie Martin has also known me since childhood, and I am very grateful for her constant support and encouragement. Elena del Pino, my mother-in-law, has been a model of maternal love and human elegance since I've known her, and she and the entire Kourí family have welcomed me with more generosity and support than I could ever have hoped for.

My last words go out to the family that has taken shape along with this book. In friendship, companionship, and marriage, Emilio Kourí has allowed this project to creep into every nook and cranny of our lives. He has inspired me, challenged me, and shown me patience and love far greater than I deserve. Over the last seven years, with two children, two books, two moves, and two new jobs, it has been sometimes hard to remember the rambling times in Mexico City, Coatepec, Cambridge, Rio, and Etna, which gave rise to it all. Emilio's willingness to share with me the sacrifices and joys of this new life have shown me as nothing else could have that those times were no thin enchantment.

Without our daughters, Sofía and Lucía, this book would surely have been written more quickly and less painfully. But I like to think also that it would contain far less light, and wisdom. For that, this book is dedicated to them, and to their loving father.

Contents

Part IV: Owning the Illegal City

Tables

Photographs, Maps, and Figures

Political Parties Represented in Rio de Janeiro's City Council, 1947–64

ATD   Democratic Labor Alliance; brought together left-leaning members of various parties, including the PSD, the PDC, the POT, and some dissidents from the UDN.

ED   Democratic Left, an anti-Vargas party that would become the PSB in 1947.

PCB   Brazilian Communist Party, banned in 1947; its members were purged from the government in 1948. Thereafter, communists were elected under the standard of the PRT.

PDC   Christian Democratic Party

PL   Liberating Party

POT   Labor-Oriented Party, extinct after 1951

PR   Republican Party

PPB   Proletarian Party of Brazil

PRP   Party of Popular Representation

PRT   Republican Labor Party (a vehicle for communists after official ban in 1947).

PSB   Brazilian Socialist Party

PSD   Social Democratic Party. The PSD was, along with the PTB, born of the Vargas regime during the re-democratization of the 1940s, though factions within the party eventually broke with Vargas, and some even allied themselves with the archrival UDN. Presidents Dutra and Kubitschek were both members.

PSP   Social Progressive Party

PST   Social Labor Party

PTB   Trabalhista Party. The PTB was a vehicle for popular currents of the Vargas regime, and was the party of both Vargas and João Goulart.

PTN   National Labor Party

UDN   National Democratic Union. This was the most conservative of the major parties in the postwar period, anticommunist and anti-Vargas. Jânio Quadros was elected president from the UDN in 1960. Carlos Lacerda was the party's most prominent Carioca member. The UDN supported the military coup in 1964.

A Note on Historical Context

This book was written for many different audiences, and each of its interwoven stories attempts to give necessary historical context to the non-specialist. Nevertheless, a few initial signposts are in order, beginning with the city where this story unfolds. Rio de Janeiro was Brazil's national capital between 1763 and 1960, when the national government moved to the futuristic metropolis of Brasília. As the capital, Rio was the site of the presidential palace, the national legislature, the country's highest courts, its military forces, and all of its national ministries. Because of its status as Federal District, Rio was governed until 1960 by a presidentially appointed prefect rather than by an elected mayor, and the National Congress and the president regularly took an active interest in the city's affairs. While Rio did have an elected city council for most of the period studied here, the council was never endowed with much concrete power. After 1960, the city of Rio de Janeiro became the state of Guanabara, with the right to elect its own governor, and with new autonomy in governing its own affairs.

Rio de Janeiro was Brazil's second largest city for most of the twentieth century, and it was also, along with São Paulo, one of the strongest magnets for the waves of rural migration that crested in Brazil during the 1950s, 1960s, and 1970s. Rio's industrial development lagged far behind São Paulo's, however, and its employment base was divided among public service, industry, tourism, and a large (and largely informal) service sector. Unlike São Paulo, Rio was never an especially notable hotbed of working-class radicalism, but the city's urban poor had a particularly strong physical, cultural, and even political presence. Their shantytowns, or *favelas*, often abutted the city's most valuable residential and industrial neighborhoods; their music, samba, became Rio's anthem and Brazil's national emblem; and their proximity to the seats of power allowed them to play the political game with particular skill and intensity.

A bit of background about Brazil's national political trajectory may also be useful. This book treats a tumultuous period of Brazilian history, in which the central political figure was unquestionably Getúlio Dornelles Vargas, the president and dictator who dominated Brazilian politics from 1930 to 1954. Vargas originally came to power as the leader of the 1930 "revolution" that put an end to Brazil's First Republic, which itself had followed the demise, in 1889, of the country's nineteenth-century empire. Vargas, first serving as provisional president, and then elected to that office in 1934, went on to lead a 1937 coup against his own constitutional order, creating the so-called Estado Novo, or New State, in which he acted as dictator until a 1945 coup. During these years, Vargas's regime revolutionized many aspects of Brazilian society, and most especially the relationship between the national state and the urban working classes. It also flirted with fascism; repressed workers who sought to organize independently of the state; and brutally abused political dissidents, especially communists.

In 1946, a new constitution paved the way for a chaotic eighteen years of democracy, in which popular political participation skyrocketed and political tensions frequently threatened to explode. In the initial years after Vargas's ouster, the conservative General Eurico Gaspar Dutra served as elected president; by the end of Dutra's term, Vargas had reinvented himself as a democratic populist and was elected Brazil's president once more in 1950. In August 1954, under the weight of a mounting political scandal and military calls for his resignation, Vargas committed suicide, achieving in the process an unparalleled political martyrdom. For the next ten tumultuous years—through the developmentalist optimism of President Juscelino Kubitschek, the dramatic resignation of President Jânio Quadros, and the radical flirtations of President João Goulart— Vargas's legacy continued to shape Brazilian politics. In 1964, a military coup ended the democratic experiment and gave rise to more than twenty years of military rule. That coup, and especially the 1968 crackdown that followed it, effectively shut down many forms of overt social struggle and protest, especially those involving legal rights. For that reason, this book's story does not, for the most part, extend beyond 1964.

A Poverty of Rights

Introduction

Ah, minha irmã . . . o Getúlio adiantou nosso povo. O Getúlio
começou a lei, com Getúlio tinha lei, irmã. Não existia lei antes do
Getúlio não, irmã. . . . O povo, a gente era bicho. Olha aqui: não foi
a Princessa Isabel que nos libertou não. Ela assinou, irmã, mas não fez
nada, não, irmã. Ela assinou a libertação, mas quem nos libertou do
jugo da escravatura, do chicote, do tronco, foi Getúlio, Getúlio Dorneles Vargas.

Oh, my sister . . . Getúlio moved our people forward. Getúlio started
the law, with Getúlio there was law, sister. Before Getúlio there was
no law, no sister . . . the people, we were animals. Look here. It wasn't
Princess Isabel who liberated us, no. She signed, sister, but she didn't do
anything, no, sister. She signed the liberation, but the person who liberated us from the yoke of slavery, from the whip, from the stocks, was
Getúlio, Getúlio Dorneles Vargas.

—Cornélio Cancino, great-grandson of an Angolan-born slave, interviewed
at the age of 82 by Ana Lugão Rios in Juiz de Fora, Minas Gerais, 9 May
1995, excerpt transcribed in Lugão Rios and Mattos, *Memórias*, p. 129

This is a book about the formation of poor people's citizenship rights in
twentieth-century Rio de Janeiro. It seeks to tell how people with scarce
education, little money, and less power carved a place for themselves in
a mostly unwelcoming capital city, and used that position to gain a foothold in a rapidly changing legal terrain. And it explains also how their
hard-won place in both the city and the city of laws fell short of full entitlement, ensuring that a poverty of rights would help to define modern
urban destitution.

The intertwining histories of urbanization and citizenship are among
the metanarratives of Brazil's twentieth-century history, and the incomplete enfranchisement of the urban poor has long been among the central contradictions of Brazilian democracy. In the 1920s, when this book
begins, Brazil was a mostly rural country, a republic of few enfranchised

citizens and unevenly effective laws, governed from the cities but existing mainly in a vast countryside only just emerging from slavery, where local and informal power was often far more consequential than elections, laws, and constitutions. By the early 1960s, when this story ends, Brazil was a largely industrialized society, a chaotic democracy where most urban adults voted, and where citizenship entailed social and economic as well as political rights. Many of Brazil's fertile agricultural regions had been mechanized and modernized, and many of its arid backlands had fallen victim to cyclical and deadly droughts; refugees from both processes had flooded the cities, attracted not only by the perceived abundance of industrial and bureaucratic work but also, as this book will show, by the promise of citizenship.

This process made cities the principal laboratories of a grand experiment, in which political leaders—and most especially Getúlio Vargas, who governed Brazil from 1930 to 1945, and again from 1951 until 1954—sought to transform Brazilian society by exchanging social and economic rights for popular support. Nowhere was the experiment more encompassing than in Rio de Janeiro, Brazil's national capital until 1960, and the place—along with São Paulo—where the period's most critical political and legal innovations were first and most completely implemented. These experiments revolutionized Brazilian law, extending both its reach and its grasp and connecting legal institutions ever more closely to Brazilian daily life. At their best, the Vargas-era innovations forged an idealized form of Brazilian citizenship, creating a wide array of political, social, and economic rights that gave working people hope in the possibilities of law and politics. Yet that citizenship mostly excluded rural people, and it extended only partially to the urban poor, thus also helping to create an urban underclass whose position in Brazilian society was often akin to that of undocumented immigrants: people for whom neither economic prosperity nor citizenship was fully attainable, who built their lives with a patchwork of scanty rights and hard-won tolerance, and whose access to theoretically public benefits and guarantees was scarce or nonexistent. In the end, the reality of this poverty of rights did much to corrode the promise of both the city and the citizenship it had represented.

In exploring why and how rights poverty was born of the promise of expanded citizenship, this book traces the history of Rio de Janeiro's urban poor, a frustratingly vague and heterogeneous social group that was far more familiar to mid-twentieth-century Brazilians than it is to modern scholars. Most histories of post-1930 Brazil have focused on people whose political and social importance has long been recognized in Europe and the United States: class-conscious workers, Afro-descendants, foreign immigrants, women. To some extent, such interest is richly warranted, both historically and historiographically. The organized working classes of certain Latin American cities or regions did emerge as dominant political forces at critical twentieth-century historical junctures—in São Paulo, Buenos Aires, Córdoba, Santiago de Chile, or the state of Veracruz, Mexico, to name just a few examples—and they assumed a critical role in the so-called populist pacts that governed many of Latin America's largest countries in the mid-twentieth century. Communists, anarchists, socialists, and union activists were often at the vanguard of the strikes and social movements that showed Brazil's poor at their most heroic, and the rhetoric that such activists employed, and prolifically recorded, nearly always lionized the working class. Though political movements forged on the basis of race, ethnicity, or gender have been historically weaker than those of the working classes, such shared identities have nevertheless deeply and subtly shaped not only the historical experiences of poor people throughout Brazil and Latin America but also the very nature of Latin American law, politics, and culture.

Yet, despite this, the fact remains that in Rio—as in other places, from Mexico City to Caracas to Lima to Salvador—neither race nor gender nor working-class identities were generalized and powerful enough to define the relationship between the urban poor and their surrounding society for most of the twentieth century. Too few people really belonged to the organized working class; too many racial and regional identities competed with one another on too many planes; too many cultural, economic, and personal ties bound the very poor to patrons, employers, and protectors from other social categories; and too many migrants streamed constantly into a city for which they held great hopes. Poor people in Rio did understand themselves in part as women and men, light-skinned and dark, native or foreign, working-class or not. But they also understood themselves in less specific and segmented terms, simply as poor people trying to get by in the city. It is difficult to delve into the history of poor people's politics or identities without understanding why that broader characterization had meaning for them, and why they so often privileged it above all others.

Contemporaries had many words for the urban poor, each less exact than the one before. They might be *o povo* or *o povão*, *trabalhadores* or *miseráveis*; among the less charitable, they were commonly labeled *marginais*. They often called themselves simply "poor families" or "poor workers." Unlike the working class in its strictest Marxist definition, this group was not defined by the type of work its members performed, though most of them did work long hours for most of their lives. The urban poor could include the lower ranks of Marx's classic working class, but the term also encompassed washerwomen and domestic servants, street vendors and odd-jobbers, cobblers, tailors, and workers fallen into the ranks of the perennially unemployed. Nor could the urban poor be accurately categorized by the labels of gender or identity politics; while they were disproportionately Afro-Brazilian or of rural origin, and while female-headed families were common among them, the urban poor included men and women, young and old, black and white, natives as well as migrants from Europe, the Middle East, and every Brazilian region. And while the group's composition shifted constantly with changing patterns of migration and labor, its heterogeneity persisted; in the 1960s, exactly as in the 1920s, whites made up roughly a third of Rio's shantytown population, and urban poverty could not be soldered to any one economic category, ethnic label, or racial identity. The only thing that held all of Rio's poor together was the daily reality of making do with scarce resources in the city—hardly the sort of bonding that scholars or activists are taught to recognize as historically or politically significant.

And yet, in Brazil as in the rest of Latin America, the heterogeneous urban poor arguably comprised the most important social group to develop in the twentieth century. They never coalesced politically around an autonomous vision of revolutionary change or came together in mass activism along the lines traced by the U.S. civil rights movement. But they did form the numerical majority or plurality in many Brazilian cities, and their shared experience of scarce earnings, political exclusion, social discrimination, and residential segregation helped them to forge a common identity and even sometimes a common agenda, which transformed everything from everyday discourse to social geography to popular culture to municipal and national politics. Any understanding of the ways in which Rio's urban poor came to relate to one another, to their city, or to the Brazilian nation must begin with the recognition that poor people's heterogeneity did not obstruct some other, more "natural" path toward common identity and collective action; it was instead the defining feature of a loose grouping whose main concerns centered on the uneven incorporation of poor and rural people into Brazil's economic, social, cultural, and political modernities.

In documenting how poor people's shared experience of the city helped to forge twentieth-century Brazilian citizenship, this book takes as a point of departure the notion that urban poverty was shaped by poor people's relationships with legal rights and institutions, and vice versa. The link between citizenship and poverty in Brazil is neither original nor surprising. Sociological and anthropological studies of Rio's urban poor written from the 1940s through the 1970s generally recognized scarce access to legal rights as an important component of poverty. The shantytowns that such studies often focused on were partially defined by their illegality;

early shantytown surveys usually asked about residents' access to identification documents and social security guarantees, and a few pioneering studies even explored poor people's interactions with civil and criminal law.[1] More recently, a number of historical works have focused on poor people's legal relationships under slavery and during Brazil's First Republic (1889–1930), positing that access to legal rights and guarantees fundamentally shaped the experiences of slavery, abolition, and early urbanization.[2] A handful of pioneering histories have highlighted the experience of the urban poor in Brazil's criminal justice and labor law systems after 1930, and since the late 1980s any number of works have traced Rio's modern wave of violence and lawlessness to the weakness of poor people's citizenship.[3] Read together, all of these studies make a convincing case that weak legal status has always been an important component of Brazilian urban poverty.

Yet these fragmented arguments about the importance of legal relationships in poor people's lives have not consolidated into a full-blown historical argument about the connections between law, poverty, and citizenship in modern urban Brazil. In part, this is because of the relatively subtle nature of Brazil's legal inequities. Arguments about the links between law and social stratification are much easier to make in contexts such as the segregated U.S. South, or South Africa under apartheid, where scattered experiences from any number of legal fields reveal clear, consistent, and deliberate discrimination against an easily defined group. In the Brazilian case, no such clarity existed. With only a few significant exceptions—most notably the prohibition of illiterate suffrage and the exclusion of rural and domestic workers from the labor code—twentieth-century Brazilian laws are written in a relatively universal language: there is no discrimination on the basis of race, ethnicity, or place of birth; the law applies to everyone; and the rights and benefits of citizenship are available freely to all. Gender discrimination—present in civil, criminal, and family codes well into the twentieth century—was another important exception to this rule, yet even it diminished greatly with the Vargas-era legal reforms. For this reason, Brazil, along with most other regions of Latin America, was long held up as the antithesis of the Jim Crow South, a vastly unequal society by historical legacy rather than by legal design.

Like so many other components of the myth of Latin American racial democracy, this notion does not hold up under close examination. Most poverties of rights in twentieth-century Brazil originated not in outright discrimination but rather in an unusually radical misfit between Brazilian law and the people and communities it governed. Legal inequality thus has to be sought not in the letter of Brazil's laws but instead in the assumptions that underlay them, and in the processes that enforced them.

Critically, even in the mid-century era of popular democracy, Brazilian statutes habitually sought to eliminate perceived social and cultural imperfections by simply outlawing customs and practices that were intimately woven into the fabric of poor people's lives. Just as significantly, in governing the distribution of most Vargas-era benefits and guarantees of citizenship, Brazilian laws required bureaucratic agility, legal knowledge, and material resources that the very poor simply did not possess. The result was a doubly weak enfranchisement. Most poor people could lay only uneven claim to the social and economic rights that Getúlio Vargas and his successors touted as key to social justice and mobility; and they also frequently found their homes, jobs, and family structures relegated to a legal no-man's land, where basic guarantees of property, liberty, and privacy did not apply. Vulnerability and weak access to legality, rather than any more overt discrimination, were at the heart of Brazilian rights poverty.

Understood in that sense, poverties of rights came to shape much of what it meant to be poor in Rio de Janeiro. Between the 1920s and the 1960s, laws and legal institutions expanded to touch every imaginable aspect of poor people's lives. Their work conditions often depended on their ability to access labor rights; their access to social welfare, education, and housing was contingent upon the legal status of their families and jobs; their ability to establish a permanent home depended on building codes, sanitary laws, and property rights; and their personal freedom hinged on their ability to prove to the police and criminal courts that they were respectable citizens rather than burdensome vagabonds. In myriad arenas, Rio's poor people, like those elsewhere in Latin America, were constantly struggling for basic legal recognition, which was rightly understood as one of the most critical components of survival and social mobility.

Ubiquitous though it was, this tenacious quest for rights has never been the focus of much historical attention. Scholars and activists have often bemoaned the relative weakness of popular political movements in places like Rio, citing the absence of full-fledged revolutionary struggles as evidence of populist cooptation, incomplete modernization, or political apathy. Certainly, the daily rights negotiations of Rio's urban poor don't qualify as revolutionary. Most of them were founded on the optimistic belief that the rights of citizenship, as already set forth by the Brazilian government, were worth fighting for. Poor people normally negotiated their rights on a small scale, as individuals, families, or at most communities; aside from occasional labor activism, only their struggle for property rights ever reached the status of a broad-based social movement. And the cumulative achievements of decades of such dispersed struggles might seem, to outsiders, sparse; Rio's urban poor never have achieved full rights, and their weak citizenship has become a deeply entrenched component of Brazil's economy and politics, where both wealth and power are frequently built on the legal vulnerabilities of those with few resources. Nearly half a century after this book's story ends, rights poverty is still a defining element of most poor people's lives, and of Brazilian society as a whole.

Yet an account that measured the value of poor people's struggles solely by their failure to achieve full and equal citizenship would significantly miss the mark. The question at stake from the 1930s through the 1960s was not, for the most part, whether or not the very poor would have full rights. It was, rather, whether or not they would have any meaningful part in Brazil's republic of laws. The codes that governed Rio as a city and Brazil as a nation left precious little room for poor urban people to legally exist as such. Even after 1930, when Brazilian citizenship came for the first time to be worth something concrete to the urban popular classes, rights extended mainly to formally recognized workers and their families, and the burdens imposed by the expansion of legal regulation fell especially heavily on the shoulders of the very poor. Had the issue been left up to some legislators, urban poor people who could not find a place for themselves in the proper working or bureaucratic classes would have been forcibly sent back to the countryside, or to agricultural colonies in the Amazon or the Brazilian far west. At the very least, the urban poor would have been forced from Rio's so-called noble zones, pushed to distant suburbs with few trappings of urban convenience or comfort. Rio's shantytowns would all have been burned to the ground, and poor people who were perceived as socially dangerous would have been sent for indefinite "regeneration" within the criminal justice system, even if they had never committed a crime. Had any of these things come fully to pass, the phrase "rights destitution" rather than "rights poverty" would have properly described the state of the very poor, and both the city and citizenship itself would have evolved in radically different directions.

Seen in the light of those alternatives, rights poverty emerges as a compromise rather than a defeat. Urban poor people's citizenship, like the wood-and-zinc shacks of Rio's shantytowns, was mostly assembled from scraps. Yet it was relatively rare for even the poorest urban families to remain entirely without rights, as they often had been before 1930, and might well have remained if they had stayed in the countryside. By managing to claim some degree of urban permanence, most families began to build a legal existence, establishing a critical foothold in the city of laws. The fact that poor people's citizenship remained so incomplete and fragmented, and that a common poverty of rights came to define the urban poor as clearly as material lack did, has arguably prevented the full consolidation of Brazilian democracy. Poor people have often used laws, but few have come to believe in them, and without that belief the rule of law has never become a dominant praxis. Yet all the same, the fact that poor people in Rio and in other cities managed to gain access to some law, where before there had been none, cannot be lightly dismissed.

This contradictory reality perhaps explains the nostalgia with which Getúlio Vargas's extensions of citizenship rights are often remembered, even among poor people who never fully enjoyed their benefits. Vargas did not create, and probably never seriously sought, a society where citizenship did not depend on social status. But his government did add legal protections and guarantees to the arsenal of tools with which the very poor might fight for a decent existence, making it sometimes possible for such people to negotiate their public lives on the basis of rights rather than of patronage or charity. It is difficult to understand the nature of poor people's lives and struggles in twentieth-century Rio de Janeiro without recognizing the significance and magnitude of that transformation.

STRUCTURE, METHOD, AND RELEVANT BACKGROUND

This book examines the history of rights poverty in modern Rio de Janeiro in four parts, each of which explores interactions between the urban poor and a particular field of Brazilian law during the middle decades of the twentieth century. Part I (chapters 1 and 2) focuses on the long history of urban planning and regulatory law in Rio, beginning in the late nineteenth century and running through the early 1960s. It introduces readers to the city's urban evolution, highlights Rio's historically skewed distribution of public resources, and chronicles the social and political significance of broad and largely ineffective bans on the sorts of living arrangements that allowed the very poor to remain within the city. Part II (chapters 3 and 4) focuses on the development of labor and social welfare laws during the Vargas era (1930–1954), exploring the limited degree to which poor people in Brazil's national capital were able to make that legislation's extraordinary promise meaningful, and emphasizing the role of documentary requirements and other bureaucratic hurdles in weakening poor people's access to social and economic rights. Part III (chapters 5 and 6) zeroes in on the frequently conflictual relationship between the urban poor and Rio's criminal justice system from the late 1920s through the early 1960s. It argues that Vargas-era reforms of criminal law and practice often served to strip Rio's poorest populations of significant civil rights, thus eroding their already weak moral faith in justice so dispensed. Part IV (chapters 7 and 8) turns to the only component of the rights struggle that became a full-fledged social movement: a battle for rights of property and possession that pitted thousands of shantytown residents and other illegal squatters against private owners and civil courts between the 1930s and the late 1950s. These land battles resulted in surprising victories, to which the many shantytowns still located on Rio's prime industrial and residential lands bear witness. But while settlers achieved de facto permanence, they never won effective land rights; the result was a state of perpetual ambiguity that serves as an apt metaphor for poor people's place in Brazil's city of laws.

This narrative structure is somewhat unorthodox. The four parts run parallel to one another, rather than progressing chronologically; with the exception of Part I, each begins in the late 1920s, just before Vargas's 1930 revolution, and ends in the late 1950s or early 1960s, at the point when Rio ceased to be Brazil's national capital, and when a military coup quickly truncated Brazil's democratic dynamic. Each of the four parts is relatively autonomous, and could easily be read as an independent historical essay. The reader may well wonder why this book has been conceived of in such a form, which offers so little in the way of chronological progress or satisfying narrative climax.

The answer has to do mostly with the nature of the Brazilian legal field. As in most other countries governed by civil law, Brazil's statutes are usually conceived within comprehensive legal codes rather than bubbling piecemeal from common practice. While everyday laws frequently modify the codes, each is understood as an idealized and rational legal universe, which ought not be tainted by precedent or by haphazard law-making.[4] Each area of the law—criminal, civil, commercial, family, labor, electoral, and so forth —has a separate code, and most are governed by their own courts and even enforced through their own chains of command.

All of this grants a great deal of autonomy to each body of law. Even during the first Vargas period (1930–1945), when nearly every Brazilian legal code was either newly invented or significantly changed, no single group of lawmakers was responsible for transformations across the legal spectrum. Each of the codes was influenced by the same material and political constraints, and each sought to resolve similar debates about the nature of citizenship and its proper role in a vastly unequal society. But jurists rather than politicians wrote most codes, and each was molded by philosophical, legal, and historical debates particular to its own field. Due to this, and due to the notably heterogeneous ways in which each code was translated into practice, any attempt to crowd so many such singular histories into a chronological narrative would simply sow confusion.

My hope is that the independent exploration of each of these four legal fields will not only clarify each strand of my story, but will also serve to emphasize what they all have in common. The trajectories explored here are united by the similarly paradoxical ways in which rights poverty emerged from processes that expanded either citizenship's meaning or the law's reach. In each of these four case studies, legal change in the 1920s through the 1960s entailed an ambitious expansion of the law's scope and relevance. In each, this form of legal modernization allowed some poor people, at some times, to use rights to navigate Brazilian society more effectively. And yet, everywhere, poor people's access to citizenship was curtailed by laws and processes that outlawed critical aspects of their daily existence, clashed with less formal systems of value and practice, or required material and bureaucratic resources that most poor people could not lay hands on. The informal world thus created became a functional part of Brazil's economy and politics, no longer an incidental side effect of legal modernization but rather a building block of power relations in nearly every public arena. The resulting poverties of rights are all the more striking because they emerged at once from so many disparate processes, and poor people's general experience of citizenship was shaped by the commonalities and intersections among all of them.

In Rio, as elsewhere, poor people have typically left few deliberate records of their lives, and the documents others have recorded about them are generally both incomplete and opaque. For that reason, I have taken seriously the historian's role as scavenger, utilizing material from an unusually broad and eclectic spectrum of documentary and testimonial sources. These include civil and criminal court cases; juridical writings; legal codes; ministerial records; legislative debates; statistics; photographs; oral histories; samba lyrics; dozens of daily newspapers; early academic works on shantytowns and urban poverty; and the public archives of presidents, prefects, governors, and bureaucrats. All of this material is complemented by deep secondary literatures on urban poverty, social and racial inequality, Rio's urban history, and Brazilian politics and citizenship.

Despite their richness, each of these sources presents surprising and exasperating gaps. Ministerial and presidential archives disappear or thin out after 1945 (many, it is said, were lost or burned when the capital moved to Brasília). Most municipal records for the period between 1945 and 1960 are lost or not yet organized, and the court cases for these years have been destroyed or are held in judicial archives that are only patchily available for research. The secondary literature for Rio, while extraordinary for the period before 1930, weakens considerably after that year, leaving critical aspects of the city's general evolution relatively unchronicled. Oral histories, both my own interviews and the many conducted and published by other researchers, are necessarily personal and inconstant, and are particularly sparse for the first Vargas period. Most of the people still alive to tell their tales in the 1980s and 1990s were too young to have played any real part in this book's most significant events, and their memories tended to downplay the importance of earlier decades in favor of the heroic and often-recounted histories of the 1960s and 1970s.

In light of these circumstances, I cast my net widely, using the strengths of each body of evidence to counterbalance the omissions and biases of the others. As might be expected, reference to such varied sources has also required a spectrum of historical methodologies, ranging from quantitative to qualitative techniques, close readings to broad syntheses, and micro- to macrohistories. At the risk of disappointing some readers, but in the hope of writing a book that would be both accessible and enduring, I have not devoted much space to overt theoretical analysis. Debates about popular agency, race relations, the links between law and society, the evolution of urban space, and the form and meaning of citizenship are all present here. But this book seeks to contribute to them through the story it tells rather than through abstract theoretical discussions.

The history of rights poverty among Rio's urban poor is a subtle and elusive one, and I make no claims to capturing it completely. My hope is rather to bring the story into sharper focus, and to argue that any understanding of the nature of citizenship, the experience of poverty, or the function of law in modern Brazil must begin with an exploration of the historical interactions among them. Rights poverty is not incidental to Brazil's modern history but is rather at its very core. This book aims to begin to understand how, and why, that came to pass.

PART I

Rights to the Marvelous City

Musicians and residents of the Morro da Favela greet a visitor, city photographer Augusto Malta, 1920. Courtesy of the Arquivo Geral da Cidade do Rio de Janeiro.

"A favela vai abaixo"

A favela vai abaixo

Minha cabocla, a Favela vai abaixo
Quanta saudade tu terás deste torrão
Da casinha pequenina de madeira
que nos enche de carinho o coração

Que saudades ao nos lembrarmos das
* promessas*
que fizemos constantemente na capela
Pra que Deus nunca deixe de olhar
por nós da malandragem e pelo morro
* da Favela*
Vê agora a ingratidão da humanidade
O poder da flor sumítica, amarela
quem sem brilho vive pela cidade
impondo o desabrigo ao nosso povo da
* Favela*

Minha cabocla, a Favela vai abaixo
Ajunta os troço, vamo embora pro Bangú
Buraco Quente, adeus pra sempre meu
* Buraco*
Eu só te esqueço no buraco do Caju

Isto deve ser despeito dessa gente
porque o samba não se passa para ela
Porque lá o luar é diferente
Não é como o luar que se vê desta Favela
No Estácio, Querosene ou no Salgueiro
meu mulato não te espero na janela
Vou morar na Cidade Nova
pra voltar meu coração para o morro da
* Favela*

The Favela's Coming Down

My *cabocla*, the favela is coming down
Oh, how you will miss this great lump of soil
and the little wooden house
that fills our hearts with love

What nostalgia when we remember the
  promises
that we constantly made in the chapel
so that God would never stop looking out
for us from the world of *malandragem* and for
  the Favela hill
Look now at the ingratitude of humanity
at the power of the fleeting yellow flower
that thrives throughout this city without
  brilliance
imposing homelessness on the people of Favela

My *cabocla*, the favela is coming down
Gather our stuff, we'll go to Bangú
Buraco Quente, farewell forever my
  buraco
I will only forget you in the *buraco* of Cajú

All of this must be born of those people's spite
because samba doesn't grace them
because elsewhere the moonlight is different
It isn't like the moonlight that you see from
  this Favela
in Estácio, Querosene, or in Salgueiro
I won't be there waiting for you at the window,
  my *mulato*
I'm going to live in the Cidade Nova
where I can turn my heart toward the Morro
  da Favela

—Sinhô (J. B. da Silva), 1927

⇌

"A favela vai abaixo" was one of the runaway hits of Rio de Janeiro's 1928 carnival season. Recorded by Francisco Alves—a bohemian son of Portuguese bar owners, who worked as a shoeshiner, a factory laborer, and a chauffeur before rising to fame as "the Midas of song"—the tune encapsulated elements that were already allowing samba music to become the edgy rage of flapper-era Rio.[1] Its composer, known as Sinhô, had grown up in the Cidade Nova, a decadent lower-class neighborhood adjacent to some of the city's first shantytowns, or *favelas*.[2] He had cut his musical teeth in the home of the famous *Bahiana* Tia Ciata, a place widely recognized as a hothouse of Afro-Brazilian culture, and the cradle of modern samba.[3] The song's infectious rhythm betrayed samba's Afro-Brazilian origins, and its lyrics touched on themes at once racy and already consecrated in samba's embryonic cannon: *malandragem* (rascalry), racial mixture, and samba's reputed ability to grace a people's soul.[4] At the same time, the music's smooth orchestration, and Alves's lilting voice and precise diction, showcased the hybridity that was already allowing samba to cross over from shantytowns and bohemian bars to the commercial mainstream of Brazilian culture.[5]

But lost in Alves's jaunty, melodious rendition—and largely hidden from a modern audience accustomed to associating samba with quaint visions of life in Rio's old-time shantytowns—was a message that's very romanticism was unmistakably political. "A favela vai abaixo" was among the very first sambas to focus on the favelas, which were quickly becoming prime settlements for the city's very poor.[6] It also appeared just as a prominent French urban planner, Alfred Agache, was elaborating a "master plan" for Rio's development, one that sought to wipe all of Rio's shantytowns—and their residents—from the central city map.[7] In this context, what might easily have been taken for moony idealization became also a precise negation of the degrading images that were pushing city officials to destroy Rio's favelas. In the language of the chroniclers and city officials who advised Agache, the shantytowns were aesthetic and moral "leprosies" that stained the gorgeous cityscape, home to the "miserable" poor whose destitution left no room for community or family, and whose unhealthy shacks harbored nests of criminality and moral perversion.[8] In Sinhô's rendition, the general derogatory label "favela" gives way to a specific and beloved place; the original Morro da Favela, a quarry-pocked hill above the city's central railroad station that, according to popular legend, harbored the returning soldiers who had constructed the city's first shantytown.[9] That shantytown, far from dissolute, is home to love, religion, and memory. And the will to destroy it, far from suggesting "civilization," indicated instead greed and ingratitude toward the poor people whose souls were uniquely capable of evoking the samba. For all its cheerful rhythm and romantic poetics, "A favela vai abaixo" was a radical manifesto, turning upside down the precepts justifying the visible poor's expulsion from Rio de Janeiro's central cityscape.

More celebrated and public than any more conventional form of protest, "A favela vai abaixo" was in fact only a particularly lyrical salvo in an ongoing struggle over the rights of Rio de Janeiro's very poor to the city they lived in. Since the late nineteenth century, when Rio plunged into a period of vertiginous growth and quick social and physical transformation, federal and municipal authorities had assumed increasingly centralized powers to regulate public health, construct public works, set municipal building standards, and distribute or subcontract a growing array of public services. At the same time, the city's heterogeneous poor population—composed of ex-slaves and freedpersons, rural migrants, Spanish and Portuguese immigrants, and Rio natives, who were known as *Cariocas*—had found themselves mostly left out of these authorities' modernizing visions, deprived of public resources, and obliged to create their own urban world in the suburbs, swamps, hills, and backyards of the "civilized" city. By the 1920s, the clash between islands of carefully regulated urbanity and a growing expanse of improvised cityscape had begun to intensify. Public authorities envisioned a comprehensive urban development plan—given force through the ambitious use of legal instruments such as building codes, zoning restrictions, and sanitary regulations—that would showcase Rio's beauty and sophistication and leave no crevices of unregulated growth. At the same time, many poor and working-class residents rejected the premises of such a road map, laying haphazard but stubborn claim to Rio's spaces and resources, and fiercely rejecting the premise that a city's fate should be determined by a comprehensive, top-down plan.

Alfred Agache's 1927 hire as the municipal government's master planner brought all of these tensions to the surface, initiating a modern age in which Rio's future would be determined neither by exclusionary central planning, nor by poor Cariocas' desire to occupy the city core, but rather by the permanent, unresolved clash between the two. By mid-century, 25 years of central planning had left scant space for Rio's very poor in the legally sanctioned city. Most of their homes were technically banned by the building code, many of their neighborhoods were constantly threatened, and their access to "public" services was largely subject to the whims of politicians and local bosses. At the same time, the very poor stubbornly inhabited and shaped the living city; if they could not claim formal rights—to services, to a voice in planning, to legality itself—they did unveil, with their very presence, what many of them saw as the illegitimate bases upon which those rights were constructed. By the mid-1960s, it was clear that this standoff not only endured but had also produced a functional ambiguity integral to Rio's urban fabric. Thanks to this ambiguity, the very poor, while deprived of rights, were able to ward off expulsion and lay claim to land and community in Rio's very heart. Politicians and bureaucrats found enormous power in the ability to distribute services and legal tolerance as favors rather than entitlements. And city planners could continue to view the illegal city as a temporary contingency of rapid development, one that produced no permanent claims and would leave no lasting mark.

Yet the sustained distance between plan and practice exacted its price. A paucity of rights—which required the poor to claim public goods as supplicants, rather than citizens—became a permanent and deepening feature of Carioca poverty. At the same time, evident impotence left city plans and legal implements destitute of popular legitimacy, sources of arbitrary power rather than effective instruments of social policy and mediation. Rights to the city were a privilege, and thus became impoverished. The two chapters that follow trace this evolution, first placing it in the context of the city's longer history, and then unraveling the social and political trajectories of urban legal change after 1930.

CHAPTER ONE

The City of Hills and Swamps

⁓

SPACE, NATURE, AND THE COLONIAL CITY

From its founding in 1565, Rio was a city forged by a stunning and challenging geography. Nestled on the jagged edges of the Bahia de Guanabara, one of South America's largest ports, the city's breathtaking setting lent itself more easily to rapturous odes than to large-scale settlement. Three distinct mountain massifs, with peaks as high as 1,024 meters, surrounded and interrupted the city, forming narrow valleys where their tentacular ridges cascaded down toward the bay. Lower hills and rocky outcroppings rose from these same valleys and jutted abruptly from the water, creating countless discrete enclaves of gently sloping land and protected sea. At the time of the city's founding, rivers riddled its territory, and the lower reaches of its valleys were covered with lakes and marshes. Exuberant tropical vegetation draped the hills and mountains. Such dramatic overlappings of mountain, river, marsh, and sea proved formidable barriers to continuous settlement; steep slopes impeded communication from one narrow valley to the next; rivers claimed their banks as flood plains in the rainy season; marshes harbored mosquitoes and rendered vast expanses of lowlands uninhabitable; and the sea could turn wild and eat away at the very city it sustained.

Settlers could hardly claim seamless possession of such unruly landscape. Early on, defensive exigencies exacerbated natural ones, and settlers clung together, briefly in a tiny beach enclave near the Pão de Açucar and then, from 1567, to the slopes of the now-flattened Morro do Castelo in central Rio. Over the following two centuries, as Rio grew from a small and relatively insignificant village to a great port city and the seat of the viceroyal government, urban residents ventured only tentatively from the small-lake-dotted plain bounded by the hills of Castelo, Santo

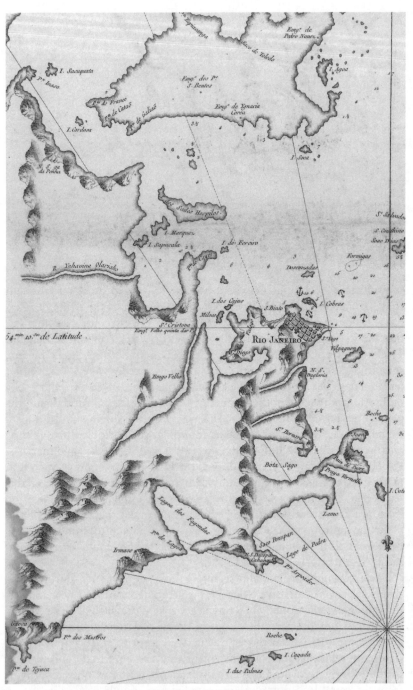

Rio and Guanabara Bay, 1785. Courtesy of Harvard Map Collection.

Antônio, São Bento, and Conceição. As the city grew, its center gradually descended from the flanks of the Morro do Castelo toward the port's small docks and warehouses.[10]

The uneven archipelago of dry land jutting up from the valley's lakes and marshes quickly proved inadequate for an increased population and intensified commercial traffic. Settlers responded by creating land from water, filling wetlands with earth.[11] At first such efforts were haphazard and individual; but by the mid-seventeenth century, public authorities had begun to take an active role, authorizing the full drainage of lakes and the leveling of small hills. By the late eighteenth century, some of Rio's best-known landmarks had arisen from such machinations, among them the Passeio Público and the Largo da Carioca, which housed the fountain that dispensed much of the city's potable water through the mid-nineteenth century. Outside such public spaces, however, the creation of so much territory clouded an already ambiguous system of property rights, rendering its administration difficult. A system of ownership and land use that was founded on sixteenth-century *sesmaria* grants and on presumed municipal jurisdiction was incapable of neatly defining the rights and obligations of occupants living on land that they themselves had created.[12]

The economic surge brought to the city by Brazil's early-eighteenth-century gold and diamond boom—Rio, among the chief exits for mineral exports, was also the main port of entry for African slaves and European consumer goods—propelled its promotion to capital of the viceroyalty in 1763. With commercial and bureaucratic expansion came influxes of fortune seekers, businessmen, slaves, and bureaucrats. By 1799, Rio was home to more than 43,000 inhabitants, more than a third of whom were enslaved.[13] After 1808, the arrival of some 15,000 members and followers of the Portuguese royal court, fleeing the Napoleonic Wars, accelerated this growth; and the early coffee boom in Rio's hinterlands cemented it. By 1849, the city probably held around 206,000 souls, and by 1872 its population stood at 274,972 (see table 1).[14]

In the short term, responses to this population boom varied widely. Settlers rendered land from marshes; houses and shacks pressed ever closer together; the poor improvised spaces in backyards, swamps, and hills; royal governors summarily expelled all classes of residents to make room for the royal court.[15] In the long term, though, growth implied exodus from the colonial cradle. First snatching up rural land along colonial highways, and later filling the space between those spidery pathways through the familiar techniques of drainage, landfill, and leveling, settlers gradually expanded the city to the west, northwest, and south, creating in the process such neighborhoods as the Cidade Nova, São Cristóvão, Glória, Catete, and Botafogo.[16] While some of this settlement was made

TABLE 1

Population of Rio de Janeiro, 1799–1970

Census year	Total population	Census year	Total population
1799	43,376	1906	805,335
1808	54,255	1920	1,147,599
1821	112,695	1940	1,759,277
1838	137,078	1950	2,375,280
1849	205,906	1960	3,300,431
1872	274,972	1970	4,251,918
1890	522,651		

SOURCES: Recenseamentos Gerais do Brasil; Mary Karasch, *Slave Life in Rio de Janeiro, 1808–1850* (Princeton, N.J.: Princeton University Press, 1987).

possible by large-scale public works—examples include the channeling of the Saco de São Diogo into the Mangue Canal, which helped create the Cidade Nova, or the draining of Carioca Lake to create the Largo do Machado—most expansion was more haphazard, an incremental filling in of lots and open spaces by individuals hoping to lay claim to lands rendered from sweat, dirt, and garbage. The resulting patchy geography, as in the old city core, created a knot of confusion about everything from the definition of inhabitable land to ownership boundaries, occupancy rights, and jurisdictional responsibilities. In the colonial centuries, ownership and use rights were among the few public goods that municipal governors were authorized to distribute. Yet the peculiarities of Rio's geographical expansion rendered the precise administration of territory impossible, setting an early precedent for the approximate relationship between legal and use rights that would characterize the twentieth-century city.

IMPERIAL INEQUITIES

After Independence in 1822, changes in size, demography, technology, and administrative ambition further complicated Rio's inconstant social and legal geography. In the wake of Brazil's mid-nineteenth-century coffee boom and the gradual abolition of slavery, new groups began to fuel Rio's quick population growth. Slaves, freedmen, and other landless rural people came to the city in search of work and fuller freedom.[17] Migrants from Portugal and, later, from Italy, Spain, and the Middle East swelled their ranks. At the same time, the steady emancipation of Rio's remaining slaves—and the practice of allowing some of those who were still enslaved to pay their masters for the right to live and work independently—transformed, cut, or loosened many of the ties that had ordered Rio's social world.[18] By 1890, Rio's total population was 522,651, nearly 500,000 more than it had been in 1808. Among this population, nearly 30 percent were foreign-born, and 26 percent were migrants from other Brazilian states; 37.2 percent were of African descent.[19] Many of these Afro-Brazilians would have been freed from slavery in 1888, in Rio or in the provinces. Many more would have been born free or lived in Rio as freed men and women for years or decades before official abolition. In 1872, the last census before abolition, only 17.8 percent of Rio's population was enslaved, down from 41.5 percent in 1849.[20] Of the total 1890 population with declared professions, 20.9 percent worked in manufacturing, 20.7 percent in commerce, 6.3 percent in transportation, and 32 percent in domestic service (all broadly defined). The remaining workers ran the gamut from agriculture to civil service to the professions.[21]

The ways in which Rio's social geography expressed its marked social differences became more complex as the city expanded and its demography became more intricate. Above all, physical growth, technological progress, and widening elite ambitions for social engineering transformed the degree to which public authority and large-scale private enterprise influenced patterns of urban social inequality. While some settlers could push the city's boundaries informally as before—first claiming land abutting on highways and other transportation routes, then using drainage, leveling, and landfill to create continuous territory between them—the effective integration of many new districts required more purposeful intervention. Tunnels had to be drilled, massive swamps drained, and streetcar and train tracks laid; none of this could be done without public orchestration and financing.[22] New technologies, too, mandated increased public coordination; by the late nineteenth century, electricity, sewers, piped water, improved pavement, and new public transportation systems had become part and parcel of "urban" life, yet such services could not be acquired haphazardly or individually. And, finally, the influence of European racial and social ideologies, along with the very fact of socioeconomic diversification, helped to convince many elite Cariocas that new forms of social regulation—of criminality, of public health, of entertainment, even of architecture and urban design—were necessary to make Rio a fully "civilized" city.[23] The power to apportion or concession public works, public services, and public social regulation made Rio's governors and bureaucrats referees in the rough, competitive jockeying that would determine which Cariocas enjoyed newly complex and valuable rights to the city. Their decisions laid the foundations for a strikingly bifurcated form of urban growth, both deepening and broadening colonial inequities.

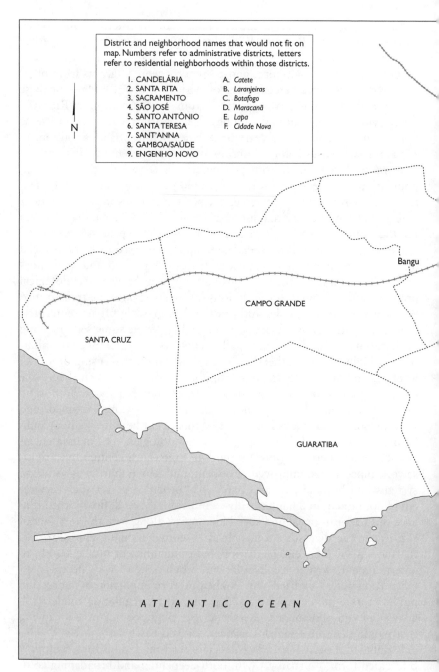

District and neighborhood names that would not fit on
map. Numbers refer to administrative districts, letters
refer to residential neighborhoods within those districts.

1. CANDELÁRIA   A. *Catete*
2. SANTA RITA   B. *Laranjeiras*
3. SACRAMENTO   C. *Botafogo*
4. SÃO JOSÉ   D. *Maracanã*
5. SANTO ANTÔNIO   E. *Lapa*
6. SANTA TERESA   F. *Cidade Nova*
7. SANT'ANNA
8. GAMBOA/SAÚDE
9. ENGENHO NOVO

N

Bangu

CAMPO GRANDE

SANTA CRUZ

GUARATIBA

ATLANTIC OCEAN

Rio's neighborhoods and railroad lines, early twentieth century.

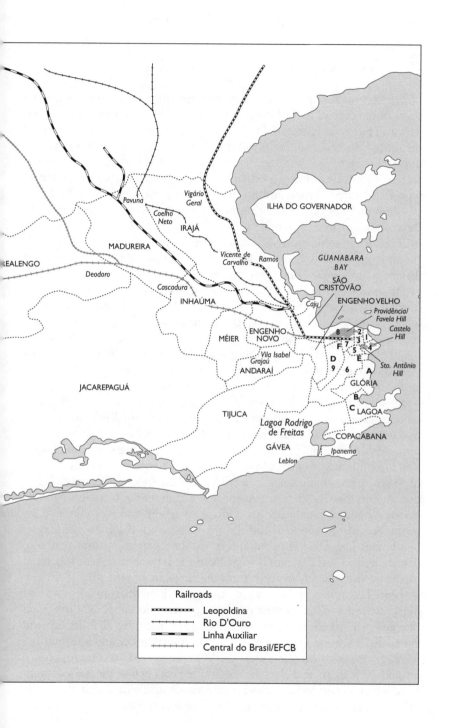

ILHA DO GOVERNADOR

GUANABARA
BAY

Vigário
Geral

Pavuna

Coelho
Neto

IRAJÁ

MADUREIRA

REALENGO

Deodoro

Cascadura

INHAÚMA

Vicente de
Carvalho

Ramos

SÃO
CRISTÓVÃO

Caju

ENGENHO VELHO

Providência/
Favela Hill

Castelo
Hill

MÉIER

ENGENHO
NOVO

8

7

2
3
5

1
4

F

E

Vila Isabel

Grajaú

ANDARAÍ

D
9

6

A

Sto. Antônio
Hill

GLÓRIA

JACAREPAGUÁ

B

C LAGOA

TIJUCA

Lagoa Rodrigo
de Freitas

COPACABANA

GÁVEA

Ipanema

Leblon

Railroads

Leopoldina
Rio D'Ouro
Linha Auxiliar
Central do Brasil/EFCB

SERVICES AND CITIZENSHIP IN REPUBLICAN RIO

The technical trappings of modernity spread across Rio's central districts in the second half of the nineteenth century, impulsed by both private and public initiatives. In 1854, gas lanterns began to replace the fish-oil lamps that had traditionally illuminated Carioca streets; in 1905, they in turn began to give way to electric light.[24] In 1863, sewage pipes began to eliminate the need for so-called "tigers," generally slaves or prisoners who had hauled human and household waste for disposal in the bay.[25] In 1876, pipes began to bring running water to private homes, replacing the colonial system of public fountains and spouts.[26] During these same decades, more sophisticated paving techniques gradually smoothed Rio's rough stone roads and sidewalks, tramlines facilitated travel over short distances, and new parks, theaters, and shopping districts drew Cariocas of all classes and both sexes to newly alluring public spaces.[27] The Rio of the early nineteenth century—a city of cramped, often putrid streets, where quotidian public life was the domain of vendors, washerwomen, servants, and slaves, and where public celebration was a mark of low social class and racial degradation—had begun to give way to a sophisticated, modern capital where some streets, at least, aspired to the bustle and glamour of London or Paris's elite districts.[28]

Even in the most central neighborhoods, though, the veneer of urban modernization spread only unevenly. In the midst of Rio's downtown, two *morros* (hills) that had marked the boundaries of colonial settlement now signaled the limits of its so-called progress. In the words of chronicler Luiz Edmundo, writing about turn-of-the-century Rio, the *morros* of Santo Antônio and Castelo were "two hamlets of affliction and destitution" in the city's heart.[29] According to Edmundo, Castelo's colonial mansions had degenerated into tenements in the wake of elite exodus to the beachfront suburbs, and the spaces between the erstwhile luxurious homes had filled with miserable wooden shacks.[30] Santo Antônio, despite its privileged location steps from the lyric theater, was inhabited by the destitute, many of them rural migrants, most probably of African descent. The *morro*'s houses were "improvised, made from leftovers and rags, tattered and sad as their residents";[31] its children were "dirty" and "ragged" or "skeletal";[32] its mothers were "destitute, abandoned, and exhausted by bone-grinding work";[33] its food, music, and spiritual life were infused with African influence.[34] On the Morro do Castelo, photographs show lights and electric lines in the years before the hill's demolition, which occurred in 1920–21, and residents claimed that there was at least some water piped to public repositories there.[35] But the same pictures show muddy, unpaved streets, navigated by women balancing water cans on their heads, and lined with dilapidated colonial mansions whose dark cubicles were surely not lighted, drained, or piped. On Santo Antônio, too, there may have been some services at the hill's foot, but in the shantytown above, the modern city ended; the streets were not paved or lighted, water did not run, and waste was not piped away; no street-cars eased the winding journey up the hill, and no public spaces were beautified for local promenades.[36] In both places, the streets delineated on early-twentieth-century city maps ended at the hills' bases.

Santo Antônio and Castelo were exceptional. Few of the central districts' tenements and shacks were so concentrated as they were on those hills, and few of the city's many embryonic shantytowns were so central. But tenements, rooming houses, and backyard shacks without access to established public services riddled Rio's central districts in the late nineteenth and early twentieth centuries, and there was hardly a hill in urbanized Rio that did not hold a smattering of shacks that would evolve into a modern favela.[37] The net of service provision cast by the municipal government and the companies it granted concessions to was always woven unevenly, leaving points and patches of lack even in the urbanized center.

Outside the city's central districts, tramlines—and, to a lesser extent, passenger rail routes—exercised a seemingly magnetic pull on the expansion of public services.[38] Tramlines, or *bondes*, appeared as early as the 1860s, powered first by animal traction and later by electricity. The first routes, built and controlled by private companies—many of which were also contracted by the city to provide other basic services—ran from the center to already well-heeled and well-populated regions: Glória and Catete to the south, Santa Teresa to the southwest, and São Cristóvão to the northwest.[39] The city granted many later concessions for tram service to nearly uninhabited regions in the near north and south, without any requirement that lines be extended also to less profitable but more populated suburban regions. Land developers and speculators, many of whom also had a financial interest in the tram companies, gained title to many of the old agricultural lands in these new areas, subdividing them and gradually selling them off.[40] By the second decade of the twentieth century, fully serviced southern residential districts such as Jardim Botânico, Laranjeiras, Gávea, Copacabana, Ipanema, and Leblon had already begun to fill with wealthy foreigners and Cariocas. To the north, speculation combined with industrialization to create the middle- and working-class neighborhoods of Andaraí, Tijuca, Vila Isabel, Grajaú, and Maracanã.[41]

Trams not only allowed residence and work in distant enclaves but also spearheaded other types of urban modernization. In the southern beachfront neighborhoods, and along the lines traced by the *bondes* that led toward them, speculators, in conjunction with city officials, began to create models of tropical urbanism. They filled in swamplands, blasted tunnels, laid out roads, and brought in piped water, drainage, electricity, and pavement. The sumptuous houses and beachfront *palacetes* built on these lands quickly became the beacons of a new ideal of tropical elegance, centered on the natural beauty of the mountains and the sea and the belle époque exaggeration of the residential architecture. As in the urban core, however, this rush of urbanization was never continuous or complete. It tended to concentrate around the tramlines and the increasingly valuable lands immediately surrounding them, ignoring vast tracts of swampy or mountainous terrain—stretches of which gradually began to fill with rough streets lined with humble houses or even wooden shacks, whose presence marked the boundaries of the sunny modernity sold by developers of the southern tramway *bairros*.

The northern and remote southern industrial regions served by the tramways underwent a different, though equally discontinuous, transformation.[42] Here, industrialists, taking advantage of cheap land and easy transportation, often sought to conquer Rio's topography and extend the city's domain themselves, building model factories, often with worker "villas" or vast worker shanty settlements surrounding them.[43] Small-time commerce flourished around these industrial outposts, which gradually became full-fledged middle- and working-class neighborhoods; as such districts grew, land speculators poured in to sell cheap, simple row houses or vacant lots to working-class families eager to escape the squalor of inner-city tenements. City officials and private utilities rushed to bring services to the areas adjacent to the tramlines, but many poorer paths and alleyways, located on the most difficult terrain, remained unserved. Likewise, even the main thoroughfares contained tenements, shacks, and rooming houses that remained unequipped to take advantage of city services. Here, too, the myriad urban conveniences that spread in the wake of the tramlines extended their reach selectively, leaving interstices of abject lack in the urbanized terrain.

Beyond the reach of tramlines, though, urban modernity itself became the interstice. Far to the north and the west, in flat, swampy areas with few vistas attractive enough to lure the sorts of residents who populated the beachfront suburbs, only Rio's four major railways allowed for efficient residential and economic integration with the central city before the age of the automobile. Unlike the *bondes*, Rio's rail services were not designed initially for human transportation. The first rail line, the Estrada de Ferro Dom Pedro II (later the Central do Brasil), began in

1858 as a short track from Rio's Praça da República to the distant and then-rural enclave of Nova Iguaçu. Quickly extended to the neighboring states of Minas Gerais and São Paulo, the Central initially transported mostly agricultural and commercial cargo. Along the way, it began to add passenger stations in the more distant reaches of Rio de Janeiro's municipal territory. Stations at the already populated northern neighborhoods of São Cristóvão and Deodoro soon joined those at Cascadura and Engenho Novo, which had been inaugurated along with the original line in 1858, and others quickly followed. Another railway line, called the Rio D'Ouro and inaugurated to transport materials to a dam-construction project in 1883, followed a similar trajectory, adding passenger service to such northwestern suburbs as Irajá, Pavuna, Vicente de Carvalho, and Coelho Neto by the end of the nineteenth century. The Leopoldina Railway—running north and east from Rio de Janeiro city, around Guanabara Bay, through Rio de Janeiro state and into the neighboring states of Espírito Santo and Minas Gerais—inaugurated passenger service in 1886 to such northern regions as Ramos and Vigário Geral. A final line, called the Estrada de Ferro Melhoramentos do Brasil (later the Linha Auxiliar), veered north from the Central after 1893, serving the areas between that line and the Rio D'Ouro.

These tracks ran through distant, often semi-rural areas, far even from the northern industrial suburbs. The rapidly growing commercial and industrial center of Madureira, for instance, stood almost 18 kilometers northwest of Rio's central train station, and the still rural agricultural enclave of Santa Cruz lay 55 kilometers to the southwest.[44] Sections of the railways, most notably on the Rio D'Ouro line, straddled narrow stretches of landfill in order to avoid the surrounding swamplands. Accommodations on the trains were generally miserable; the historian Noronha Santos, writing in the early 1930s, characterized the experience of riding on them at peak hours as a "martyrdom."[45] Service schedules never managed to meet the needs of passengers, many of whom commuted daily to work in Rio's industrial, commercial, or touristic regions.

The railways' poor service may have impeded middle- and upper-class settlement of these distant reaches, or perhaps it was symptomatic of it; in any case, disdain and lack fed on one another, and the urban development of suburban regions was left to scattered industrialists, small-time speculators, petty businessmen, and—mostly—to the poor and lower-middle-class people who increasingly called these areas home. Lima Barreto, in his 1911 novel *Triste fim de Policarpo Quaresma*, described the mishmash of urbanity and suburbanity that grew up around the railway stations. He noted the crooked, irregular, mostly unpaved streets and sidewalks, as well as homes in a kaleidoscope of styles—everything from "wattle-and-daub huts" to overcrowded rooming houses to "bourgeois" residences with "lacy summits"—that "surged forth as if they had been seeds planted by the wind."[46] Lima Barreto could just have easily pointed out additional variations in the urban landscape—the orderly villas constructed around the few textile and cement factories that pioneered suburban industrialization, or the vast lowlands that remained populated by agriculturists, or the swamps where settlers began to erect houses on stilts early in the twentieth century.[47] In Rio's suburban landscapes, the lifelines of urban development traced by the railway lines cut through vast and varied expanses of haphazard, chaotic, unregulated city building, whose vistas contrasted sharply with Rio's central commercial districts and prosperous tramcar *bairros*.[48]

In these suburban reaches, few urban conveniences existed, and those that did stuck close to the railway lines, in narrow regions dwarfed by most districts' immense territory. A municipal building survey published in 1933 sheds some light on the cumulative impact of more than half a century of service distribution.[49] By this date, as table 2 demonstrates, Rio's central and near-suburban residential and industrial neighborhoods enjoyed considerably more complete access to urban conveniences than did the northern and western suburbs. This imbalance was not necessarily out of proportion with regional population distribution: the number of streets served by electricity (distributed by a private company) and piped water (subcontracted under the responsibility of the federal government) seems actually to have corresponded relatively well to local population size.[50] But suburban neighborhoods were much larger and more dispersed than the central districts, and their poorest residents tended to make their homes far from the relatively well-served areas around the railway stations, on innumerable sparsely settled side streets and rough paths where land could be bought cheaply or occupied illegally, and where city officials were less likely to prohibit rustic dwellings. Other suburban services were entirely out of proportion to local population size, most notably pavement (undertaken by municipal authorities and land developers), public transportation (provided by private companies under municipal concession), and sewer lines (mostly laid and maintained by a private company under federal concession).[51] In the central districts and streetcar *bairros*, service destitution was an exceptional and immeasurable gap in the terrain of urban modernization. In the poorer railway *subúrbios*, the gap nearly enveloped the whole.

The social meaning of this pattern emerges strikingly when the percentage of illiterate adults and whites resident in each neighborhood in 1940 is correlated with the percentage of its streets that enjoyed urban services in 1933. A half-century of decisions about urban service provi-

TABLE 2

Percentage of Building Types, City Services, and Population Subsets by Neighborhood, 1933–1940

(percent)

	Illiterate	Male	White	Non-brick	With sewers	With water	With electricity	With pavement	With transport
Candelária	6.8	62.1	85.0	1.7	100.0	100.0	100.0	100.0	40.7
São José	15.5	61.2	88.4	2.7	82.5	78.9	80.7	96.5	28.0
Santa Rita	13.7	62.5	84.2	4.8	94.0	94.0	92.0	98.0	26.0
São Domingos	12.8	58.2	87.7	0.6	100.0	100.0	100.0	100.0	23.5
Sacramento	12.8	62.7	87.9	1.3	100.0	100.0	100.0	100.0	44.8
Ajuda	10.5	59.6	84.2	4.2	91.6	91.6	97.2	94.4	66.7
Santo Antônio	11.2	58.2	84.6	5.9	100.0	100.0	100.0	100.0	45.2
Santa Tereza	14.6	49.3	79.1	12.1	85.0	85.7	91.4	80.7	20.0
Glória	13.1	45.8	78.4	8.8	81.2	81.2	92.1	88.1	20.8
Lagoa	15.3	44.6	73.8	7.0	70.9	89.5	93.0	90.7	30.2
Gávea	23.6	46.1	65.3	29.4	53.9	83.0	63.1	68.1	10.6
Copacabana	14.2	42.2	78.8	7.5	74.1	93.8	83.9	87.5	25.0
Sant'Anna	14.9	60.8	85.9	8.0	100.0	100.0	100.0	100.0	87.5
Gamboa	22.2	56.1	69.4	37.7	93.8	93.8	81.5	87.7	20.0
Espírito Santo	18.6	53.7	78.9	19.6	96.9	96.9	91.8	83.5	18.6
Rio Comprido	18.7	47.6	71.3	21.7	94.9	96.2	91.1	84.8	21.5
Engenho Velho	11.1	46.8	82.1	7.0	98.7	98.7	94.9	94.9	21.5
São Cristóvão	17.3	51.2	75.3	24.1	100.0	100.0	89.0	64.1	18.6
Tijuca	19.2	44.8	71.5	23.8	74.1	83.4	72.8	79.5	11.9
Andarahy	14.1	46.0	80.5	15.8	74.5	92.4	91.1	63.7	10.8
Engenho Novo	18.5	48.9	71.1	27.7	89.2	89.8	83.7	47.0	10.2
Meyer	17.0	47.2	73.8	19.5	79.1	98.1	62.0	38.6	12.0
Inhaúma	13.4	48.8	77.3	14.4	43.2	83.2	47.4	25.3	14.2
Piedade	17.3	49.7	70.3	20.0	0.0	67.3	28.6	7.8	4.1
Penha	19.3	50.4	72.3	20.4	0.0	50.8	32.4	13.4	10.0
Irajá	21.4	49.8	69.7	27.1	0.8	48.4	33.3	6.6	7.8
Pavuna	23.6	49.7	58.9	38.1	0.0	12.9	10.2	5.9	2.3
Madureira	22.5	49.8	59.5	24.6	0.0	31.7	20.6	2.8	3.5
Anchieta	27.2	50.6	53.4	40.4	0.0	10.8	5.0	3.6	1.8
Jacarepaguá	24.3	52.2	61.7	47.8	0.0	74.7	16.5	5.2	3.0
Realengo	23.1	52.9	62.7	43.7	0.0	16.3	15.2	7.7	1.8
Campo Grande	34.5	51.4	58.3	62.2	0.0	15.1	7.3	13.5	6.1
Guaratiba	36.0	51.6	52.3	79.4	0.0	9.3	1.0	7.2	16.5
Santa Cruz	33.6	51.8	51.0	60.4	0.0	28.4	9.2	11.3	5.0
Islands (total)	25.3	54.9	67.4	40.0	0.0	35.4	38.4	34.1	9.6
TOTAL	19.0	49.7	71.1	26.0	31.7	57.5	43.9	33.7	10.8

SOURCES: Instituto Brasileiro de Geografia e Estatística, *Recenseamento Geral do Brasil, 1 Setembro 1940* (Rio de Janeiro, 1951); Ministerio do Trabalho, Indústria e Comércio, Departamento de Estatística e Publicidade, *Estatística Predial do Distrito Federal, 1933* (Rio de Janeiro, 1935).

sion both reflected and reinforced the marginalization of Rio's poorest residents, the majority of whom were Afro-Brazilian. Illiteracy showed a strong inverse correlation with sewer service, water pipes, electricity, and pavement, and a modest negative correlation with public transportation routes.[52] Whiteness—itself strongly correlated with literacy—showed an even stronger positive correlation with the same services.[53] The presence of shacks and other "rustic" dwellings on Rio's streets correlated strongly with illiteracy, negatively with whiteness, and negatively also with all city services.[54] In apportioning public resources, politicians and businessmen had etched an uneven patchwork of urban modernity onto Rio's cityscape, making of the modernized city a discontinuous enclave of privilege.

Legislating the Republic's Urban Divide

At the same time that patchy urban services etched their geographies of inequality, legislation in the areas of public health and urban planning began to give deeper legal foundation to social inequities. The process began with a public health scare. In the mid-1850s, just as gas lamps began to glimmer on Rio's central streets, a deadly wave of cholera steeled the imperial government's resolution to add public health to the list of improvements vital to the city's modernization. The sanitary campaigns unleashed over the following three-quarters of a century transformed Rio's physical and social landscapes in ways at least as fundamental as the installation of city services. The campaigns did fight disease, but they also altered Carioca habits of building and inhabitance and did much to drive the city's poorest residents from the central districts. More significantly still, the sanitary campaigns did much to alter the relationship between urban regulatory law and Rio's everyday social realities. In the campaigns' wake, authorities would habitually approach Rio's urban problems with expansive laws that mandated drastic and quite unachievable transformations. Such unenforceable laws had enormous power all the same, instantly rendering vulnerable all the structures and living habits they deemed illegal, and creating oases of legally sanctioned urbanity that closely matched the archipelago of modernity traced by the expansion of city services.

At the time of the 1850s outbreak, little was known about the epidemiology of cholera, yellow fever, plague, and other dread diseases that periodically ravaged Rio; doctors debated endlessly whether they were spread by specific contagious agents or were due to atmospheric conditions caused by putrid or festering organic matter.[55] Even without causal certainty, though, doctors and city officials—soon to be merged in the newfangled figure of the professional hygienist—quickly intuited that the spread of dread diseases had something to do with sanitary conditions in the crowded *cortiços* and *estalagens*, ramshackle tenements which by then housed a quickly expanding proportion of the freedpersons, rural migrants, foreign immigrants, and slaves-for-hire who made up much of Rio's independent poor population.[56]

The officials' initial efforts, spearheaded by the newly formed Junta Central de Higiene, were partial, ineffectual, and aimed mainly at the *cortiços*' sanitary and moral reform.[57] By the time a sustained wave of yellow fever hit the capital in the 1870s, a more radical view began to prevail, one that equated poverty not only with disease but also with moral danger, and advocated drastic intervention.[58] In the name of public hygiene—which city councilman and Junta chief José Pereira Rego defined as the "mirror" that "reflected the conquests" of a people "on the road toward civilization"—*cortiços*, always equivocally defined, could not be sanitized and had eventually to be eliminated.[59] Successive regulations (1873, 1876) banned new construction of *cortiços* in the central districts, and a more comprehensive sanitary code enacted in 1890 empowered "hygienic inspectors" to summarily shut down any *cortiço* or *estalagem* found to endanger public health.[60]

In 1892, the hygienist Cândido Barata Ribeiro became Rio's first prefect, or mayor, setting the precedent for a series of technical professionals who would use the new office's concentrated powers to remold the central city.[61] On his watch, anti-*cortiço* prohibitions escalated into a series of violent demolitions, culminating most famously in the destruction of the Cabeça de Porco (pig's head) tenement in January 1893.[62] Once home to as many as 4,000 people, the rambling *cortiço* was ripped down by municipal workers in front of an assembled delegation of notables, even as residents emerged from the ruins to beg fruitlessly for the chance to remove their belongings.[63] After the dust settled, Prefect Barata Ribeiro reportedly allowed some of those residents to lug the scraps of their homes up the jagged hill that rose behind the *cortiço*, thus founding the shantytown that would inspire the term "favela."[64]

Social and racial prejudice often infused the anti-*cortiço* campaign's high-minded justifications and emerged especially clearly in hygienists' descriptions of the tenements' evils. In 1877, for example, Cândido Barata Ribeiro, the future prefect, claimed that the *cortiços* fed "the lubricity of vice, which shamelessly flaunts itself, wounding the eyes and ears of serious society, and feed also that ragged and repugnant misery, which makes of laziness a throne."[65] Such prejudices also emerged in officials' selective definition of the "public" interests that mandated the *cortiços'* destruction; yellow fever, for instance, which sickened mainly white and immigrant populations, received far greater attention than did the deadlier tuberculosis, which hit hardest in the poorest and most heavily Afro-Brazilian communities.[66] The campaign also smacked frequently of corruption, since the most spectacular demolitions generally occurred in areas subsequently targeted for highly profitable real-estate development, undertaken by companies in which city officials often had a direct interest.[67] Both the campaign's prejudice and its corruption found parallels around the world and set precedents for subsequent Carioca urban policy.[68]

More uniquely significant than the mixed motives of the *cortiços'* destruction, though, was the fact that it was achieved on the basis of legislation so vague and unrealistic that it became, in practice, an instrument of aleatory power. Laws might ban *cortiços* and *estalagens*, but up to 25 percent of the Carioca population lived in collective housing in the late nineteenth century, and healthier alternatives were virtually nonexistent.[69] Proposed affordable-housing projects rarely came to fruition, and the cost and inconvenience of transportation made suburban living untenable for many of Rio's very poor, who lived on odd jobs that could be had only in the city's most prosperous regions.[70] Given this reality, laws banning unhealthy or unsightly housing were notoriously futile. Officials might eliminate some *cortiços*, only to see them replaced by equally unsanitary *casas de cômodos*, or rooming houses. Other *cortiços* would be conveniently ignored or could earn tolerance simply by renaming themselves *casinhas* (little houses) or *avenidas* (avenues).[71]

In a sense, though, this apparent futility was at the very center of the laws' real potency. Unable to achieve their stated purpose, they became instead selectively enforced instruments that effectively granted city officials the power to allocate the tolerance of illegality. Considerably less tangible than pavement or sewer pipes, legal tolerance nevertheless became a public good intensely coveted by the poor, who without it could claim no place in the newly "civilized" city.

LAW AND THE PUBLIC GOOD: LEGACIES OF THE *BOTA-ABAIXO*

After the turn of the century, a series of urban renewal and public health campaigns would both echo and amplify the anti-*cortiço* measures. Most famous was the celebrated (and vilified) transformation of Rio's central districts between 1902 and 1906.[72] Under President Francisco de

Paula Rodrigues Alves and Prefect Francisco Pereira Passos, engineers and urban planners renovated Rio's ports and razed broad swaths of the cramped downtown to make room for wide avenues and sumptuous belle époque architecture, including such landmarks as the Avenida Rio Branco, the Avenida Beira-Mar, the National Library, and the Municipal Theater (meant to evoke the Paris Opera).[73] At the same time, Oswaldo Cruz—physician, scientist, and director of the newly consolidated Diretoria Geral de Saúde Pública—spearheaded massive campaigns against smallpox, yellow fever, and plague, using new legal mechanisms to force vaccination, eliminate mosquitoes and rats, and demolish residences deemed insalubrious.[74]

The Pereira Passos–era reforms could claim some stunning successes. Rio's once shallow and antiquated ports became viable; dread diseases diminished; and myriad observers praised a newly graceful downtown district, more easily navigable and full of light and air. Like advances made under the anti-*cortiço* campaigns, however, this progress came at a high cost for poor residents. The historian Lilian Fessler Vaz has estimated that 2,240 central tenements, home to some 37,000 people, were destroyed as a direct result of the Pereira Passos reforms.[75] Countless other inhabitants lost their lodgings to the logic of the market, as owners themselves tore down buildings located on newly valorized central lots. Tenement owners received cash for their demolished properties, and construction companies and real-estate developers reaped a profit bonanza, but poor residents received neither compensation nor alternate housing.[76] Anger over the lopsided social equations of the demolitions arguably combined with resentment of forced vaccination to fuel the so-called *revolta da vacina*, one of the largest urban protests in Rio's modern history.[77]

The legal legacy of the Pereira Passos period reached even further than the reforms' immediate effects. The demolitions themselves had found relatively straightforward legal grounding in the 1824 and 1891 constitutions, which guaranteed the right to private property but allowed public authorities to expropriate it "for the public good" or "for reasons of public utility and necessity." More specific legislation, in 1855 and 1903, regulated application of this principle to the Federal District.[78] The definition of "public" welfare was, of course, highly subjective; arguably, Pereira Passos–era technocrats prioritized "civilizing" the population, honing Rio's international image, and lining the pockets of exporters and real-estate developers above representing the needs and desires of most Cariocas.[79] Be that as it may, the legal expropriation of properties standing in the projects' way was relatively straightforward, if also expensive and sometimes corrupt.[80]

Murkier, and ultimately as significant, were two new measures that justified sanitary condemnations and other demolitions outside the reforms' direct scope: the municipal building code of 1903 and the sanitary code of 1904.[81] The building code, the most comprehensive to that date, compiled and updated laws governing the licensing, site preparation, construction, and maintenance of all of Rio's structures. Building on nineteenth-century precedents, it outlawed many property and residential arrangements that were common among Rio's poor. It stipulated that no construction could be legally licensed without proof of property ownership, a seemingly elemental requirement made burdensome by the contested and ill-defined nature of turn-of-the-century Carioca property relations.[82] Every building site now had to be properly drained and graded, an especially tough standard for the sorts of marginal lands commonly available to the very poor. Every new or reconstructed edifice now had to meet strict new standards for piped water, drainage, ventilation, and building dimensions. The code also banned all wooden and "rural" structures from the central areas and wealthier southern suburbs, though *barracões toscos* (flimsy shacks, or baracoons) could remain on uninhabited hills (*morros*), an exception that might well have encouraged the favelas' early growth. It similarly outlawed new *cortiços* and *estalagens* as well as repairs on old ones, and it promised that health inspectors would rigorously target *casas de cômodos*. In short, the building code outlawed or restricted virtually all of the arrangements through which poor people clung to the right to live in central Rio, restricting their options to hillside favelas, backyard shacks, and the gradually crumbling, irreparable tenements.

The 1904 sanitary code's sweeping provisions threatened even these refuges. Part of a national bill regulating the entire federal public health system, the rules governing Rio's sanitary service mandated inspection of every dwelling within the city limits.[83] Every residence had to maintain an inspection record, and the legislation mandated new certification every time a rental tenant moved, even in rooming houses with highly itinerant populations. Inspectors were given a wide berth, but were to target especially any practices that facilitated mosquito breeding; they subjected water and waste arrangements to special vigilance and banned many common practices, including the washing of clothes in individual washtubs, a major source of income for many tenement women.[84] Tenements generally received disproportionate attention in the code; among other things, it banned wooden and cloth subdivisions in *casas de cômodos* and prohibited residents from cooking in corridors or individual rooms.[85] Even more significant than these specific provisions was the broad latitude granted to inspectors, who could summarily condemn and demolish any houses that "presented grave and irreparable hygienic defects and were thus considered uninhabitable."[86] Such slippery language could and did place poor inhabitants at the inspectors' mercy, even when their dwellings did not violate any technical specifications.

Like the nineteenth-century anti-*cortiço* measures, the building and sanitary codes were not enforceable. Officials did manage to eradicate "insalubrious collective dwellings" from the areas immediately surrounding the chic central avenues and shopping districts, and the overall percentage of residential buildings classified as "collective" did diminish between 1890 and 1920.[87] Yet the number of communal residences in the central districts actually increased between 1906 and 1920, and official reports complained that many of these dwellings violated both the building and sanitary codes, especially in the lower-class neighborhoods located in the port areas of Saúde and Gamboa, the southwestern regions of Santo Antônio and Lapa, and the extensive lowlands of the Cidade Nova. In an influential and relatively sympathetic 1906 report to the Minister of Justice on the reform-induced housing crisis, the civil engineer Everardo Backheuser minutely described the ever more crowded *casas de cômodos* in these areas, noting with horror their dilapidated wooden and burlap subdivisions (which allowed a "promiscuous common life") and the fire hazards posed by omnipresent coal cookstoves ("their coals glowing like cat-eyes"). He described additional anti-hygienic aspects of daily rooming-house life, in racially and socially derogatory language that echoed the nineteenth-century anti-*cortiço* crusaders:

Italian vagabonds waste days at a stretch in these nauseating atmospheres; black women, their kinky hair full of oil, sing little ditties, washing clothes right there in the alcoves and hanging it out to dry in their own rooms, which, because of this habitual practice, acquire a hot and humid atmosphere, entirely impossible to breathe; naked children scratch and scrub themselves on the filthy floor, dirtying it still more; and in the middle of all of this, women of low extraction, generally blacks, in scandalous outfits, all mix up in the same beehive with more modest poor girls who do heavy sewing for the military, who keep their little rooms almost luxuriously clean, and cover their walls with dearly loved pictures—theirs are islands of cleanliness in that ocean of filth.[88]

Similar facts (and sentiments) emerged in a 1910 tuberculosis report cited by historian Teresa Meade, and reports of health code violations in suburban regions were legion.[89] There is little doubt, moreover, that the shacks that proliferated between 1900 and 1930 on the flanks of such hills as Castelo, Santo Antônio, São Carlos, Providência, Catumbi, Salgueiro, Mangueira, Babilônia, Cabritos, Pasmado, and Rocinha "presented grave hygienic defects" that could have justified their removal.[90]

Yet, although strategically located tenements were sometimes torn down and favela communities experienced periodic raids, public officials just as often ignored, sanctioned, and even encouraged poor people's ex-tralegal dwellings. Pereira Passos himself may have approved some new *cortiço* construction, and most shantytowns, despite periodic violent evictions, received occasional water spigots, electric posts, and other such tokens of tacit recognition from municipal authorities, who sometimes even collaborated in the settlements' formation.[91] By the mid-1920s, the *morros* may have housed as many as 100,000 Cariocas.[92]

Rio's urbanists had thus created a legal and social paradox that would shape the city for decades to come. The Pereira Passos reforms had wors-ened Rio's nineteenth-century housing crisis, and the much discussed "workers' habitations" that were to replace the tenements mostly failed to materialize. Draconian expulsion of all tenement and shacktown resi-dents would have been both politically difficult and economically un-desirable; the potential evictees were, after all, the people who cleaned the city's mess and waste, carried its freight, stocked its shelves, fought in its military, manned its police forces, worked in its factories, and sold its goods. Rather than remold the law to reflect this reality, officials left most poor residents in a haze of tolerated illegality, allowing them to remain in their homes on the often fickle sufferance of sanitary officials and politicians.[93] The sanitary and building codes facilitated the piece-meal construction of an idealized city that reformers could not just create from whole cloth. But they also made illegality—and all the insecurity and dependence it entailed—a constituent feature of Carioca poverty.

URBANISM, AGACHE, AND THE MARVELOUS CITY'S "MASTER PLAN"

In the decades following Pereira Passos's prefecture, a number of laws and public works projects extended his legacies, most notably Prefect Carlos Sampaio's leveling of the Morro de Castelo in the early 1920s and the updating of the sanitary code in 1924–26.[94] But it was only in the late 1920s, when Prefect Antônio Prado Jr. contracted the French urbanist Alfred Agache to formulate Rio's first "master plan," that such relatively haphazard lawmaking and renovation began to take a more coherent form as part of a holistic vision for the city's "remodeling and beautifica-tion." Though revolution and outsized ambition rendered Agache's final plan unviable, it nevertheless retained enormous significance. Its underly-ing ideology and rationale would infuse 30 years of city planning; many of its specific measures would serve as blueprints for major public works; and its zoning and construction standards were the basis for the 1937 building code, the most important Carioca urban legislation of its era.

Agache's plan thus laid the groundwork for deep continuities between the early and middle twentieth centuries, both in terms of the inequitable distribution of public resources and in terms of the yawning gap between the legal and inhabited cities.

Agache was one of the founders and principal proponents of an innovative international school of urban design that he dubbed "the science of urbanism."[95] His arrival in Rio, during the summer of 1927, sparked vociferous debate among engineers, architects, politicians, city planners, and literate citizens of all stripes. Most of these people believed that some sort of centralized plan was necessary in order to contain Rio's accelerated and chaotic expansion. But many feared that Agache was not the man for the job; foreign-born, Eurocentric, and a novice in Rio, they thought that he not only would displace native professionals but also might reconceive the city in ways antithetical to its inhabitants' cultural and practical needs. His first public "diagnosis" of Rio's problems, given in the Teatro Municipal in July of 1927, most likely inflamed their doubts. He began with an evaluation that surely bit the pride of city officials who had presided over previous decades of urban renewal:

> The city of Rio de Janeiro, with her unparalleled surroundings, her flowing hair of jungle vegetation, her necklace of electric pearls, the mirror of water in which she sees herself reflected, is nevertheless in the midst of a process of certain debilitation; having developed too rapidly, she shows all of the morbid signs of a growth that was neither guided nor foreseen. One senses that only noble blood should circulate in this organism, and yet, behind an opulent facade, she seems, at least at present, and despite her growth in the periphery, like nothing more than a secondary provincial city.

He went on to laud his own presence as the antidote to the city's crisis, in language that at once feminized and infantilized the city, belittling its native efforts at improvement:

> Why this stark contrast between her vast territory and her slow and disappointing evolution? The problem is that the city was not shaped and guided by a plan in harmony with the promising future that awaits her. You all have done well to concern yourselves with the new science of urbanism. The sick patient must be the first to seek her own cure. I want you to see in me a sort of doctor, who was consulted by you and is happy to bring his knowledge to you and apply it to the pathological case that has been submitted to receive his evaluation. I say "pathological case" because Mademoiselle Carioca, whom I have just visited, is certainly very sick; never fear, though, because her disease is not congenital: it is of the sort that is curable because her disease is essentially a crisis of growth.
>
> You all know what happens when a child grows too suddenly. This sickness hides behind the child's apparently robust countenance, and, despite her beautiful features, one can see in her movement and in her entire being a certain indisposition. Any observer would conclude that if the necessary precautions are not adopted soon, the future of the child will be jeopardized.[96]

These "necessary precautions" would be prescribed with reference to an urban vision that Agache called "a science, an art . . . and above all a social philosophy."[97] For him, the city was at once civilization's apex and its potential undoing. Without the guiding hand of a professional "urbanist"—a hybrid of engineer, architect, and sociologist—any city risked not only its physical and economic functionality but also its inhabitants' social and moral health. Agache did not advocate any single, universal panacea for urban ills—geography, history, and social context mattered deeply to him—but he did believe in a set of universal goals toward which every metropolis should strive. Cities had, first, to perfect the functioning of their "circulatory, respiratory, and digestive systems"—to better their transportation and communication networks, to preserve and expand their parks and natural reserves, and to dispose efficiently of urban waste. But for Agache, always ready to extend the bodily metaphor, this was not enough. In his own words:

> Even if a person has strong muscles, and his or her organism functions as it should, we still must desire beauty. To assure that person complete enjoyment of life, we must add to the virtue of health that of equilibrium, everything that makes up beauty, that is, harmony and proportion. We must possess an urban aesthetic, just as we must have a human aesthetic.[98]

This "urban aesthetic," more than just an architectural vision of the layout and design of buildings, parks, and boulevards, entailed the apprehension of the "beauty" of a certain social order, in which each individual pertained to a clearly defined sociological group, and each group carried on its own social and economic life in a distinct, hierarchically delineated region of the city.[99] Through the legal mechanism of zoning, such social engineering would become an integral part of any "master plan" for urban development.

Opposition to the French doctor's diagnoses and bedside manner surfaced even before Agache and his team of engineers and architects occupied their offices behind the Teatro Municipal in 1928. Carioca elites opposed Agache's presence on the grounds of nationalism, practicality, and competence. Speaking against the authorization that eventually funded Agache's project, maverick city councilman Maurício de Lacerda mocked Agache's scientific pretensions ("If urbanism is a science, what should we call soccer?") and declared it "absurd" that "in Rio, with so many engineers and technicians capable of practicing urbanism," authorities were "willing to underwrite these 'celebrities' in order to attain these studies that they want to impose upon us."[100]

Later, as rumors of Agache's plans began to emerge, other opponents chimed in. Some accused Agache of plagiarism when it became apparent that portions of his plan closely resembled one that had been put together in 1921 by the Carioca engineering firm Cortez and Bruhns. Carlos Sampaio, the engineer and prefect responsible for major Carioca public works in the early 1920s, undertook an active campaign to highlight what he saw as Agache's insufficient engineering skills and patchy knowledge of Rio's geographic peculiarities. Others, with fewer nationalist compunctions, simply preferred other leading figures in the world of urban planning; this became especially evident when Agache's countryman Le Corbusier visited Rio in 1929 and promptly produced a widely circulated, if futuristic and utopian, city plan.[101] As Agache's stay in Rio stretched on toward 1930 with few palpable results, even those who had favored his appointment began to wonder if his entire tenure had been a phenomenal waste.[102]

Skepticism extended well beyond elite circles. As early as 1927, suburban residents were writing to the city dailies, concerned that Agache would repeat the perceived errors of his predecessors by ignoring the needs of suburban regions and giving only lip service to housing construction and service provision in poor neighborhoods.[103] The worries of favela residents ran even deeper, and justifiably so. Agache's main informant in matters related to the favelas was probably João Augusto de Mattos Pimenta, a journalist and Rotarian who led the first in a long line of anti-favela campaigns in the Carioca press between 1926 and 1928.[104] Mattos Pimenta expressed his views in a 1926 Rotary Club speech:

> Whatever form the plans for the city might take, and even before their adoption, we must put an immediate end to, raise a prophylactic barrier against, the devastating infiltration of Rio de Janeiro's beautiful mountains by the plague of the favelas—that aesthetic leprosy, which began over in the hill between the Central do Brasil railroad and the Avenida do Cáes do Porto and has gone disseminating itself everywhere, choosing the newest neighborhoods, most blessed with natural beauty, to fill with filth and miserable poverty: the hills of Leme, Copacabana, and Ipanema . . . and even the new lands next to the Centennial exposition! . . . They are not purely an impudent crime against aesthetics but are, especially, a grave and permanent menace to the tranquility and health of the public.[105]

As early as his third official address, in 1927, Agache echoed these views, referring to favelas as places "made up of a semi-nomadic population and completely lacking the basic rudiments of hygiene."[106] In the wake of such declarations, and of Agache's much touted visit to the Morro da Favela in the company of the renowned photographer Augusto Malta, rumors flew. One held that Agache had slated the Morro da Favela itself—already widely held to be the primordial shacktown— for extinction. It was in this context that the *sambista* Sinhô composed the wildly popular "A favela vai abaixo," using the song to successfully lobby against the hill's destruction. In the absence of direct testimonials from favela residents, the samba's romantic critique at least suggests their resistance to the notion that a city, made up of neighborhoods and communities bonded by ties of history, race, and culture, could simply be redrawn to fit a sterile, utopian vision. So, too, did a mocking carnival *marchinha* from 1927:

Já chegou o seu Agache	Mr. Agache has already arrived
Quem quiser que fale mal	No matter who criticizes him
Vai fazer dessa cidade	he's going to make of this city
Uma linda capital	a gorgeous capital
Seu Agache	Mr. Agache
Seu Agache anda solto e preparado	Mr. Agache is wandering free and well prepared
Quem for feio fuja dele	Anybody who is ugly had better run from him
Pra não ser remodelado	to keep from being remodeled
A cidade está mudando	The city is changing
Mais mudada vai ficar	and it's going to change further still
O prefeito que é de fato	The prefect is for real
Vai o povo embasbacar	and he is going to blow the people away[107]

Agache's plan was finally published in late 1930. Gorgeously illustrated, and nearly 400 pages long, the volume began with a detailed analysis of Rio's history, geography, economy, and climate. Agache showed an impressive grasp of Rio's delicate and contradictory position as both national capital and burgeoning industrial and commercial metropolis, and he evaluated at length the city's technical challenges in transportation, municipal service provision, sanitation, and drainage. On the basis of these observations, he proposed a drastic overhaul of everything from the functional role of Rio's neighborhoods to the structure of its transportation systems to the layout and design of its public spaces. The municipal government would level hills, destroy favelas, fill in wetlands, re-channel rivers, and uproot homes, factories, and businesses. In their place, Agache envisioned a series of neatly bounded, hierarchically organized neighborhoods, each serving a clearly defined economic or sociological purpose, all tied together by a new, highly efficient system of roads and public transportation, and crowned by beautifully designed public gardens and recreational spaces. All of this would be implemented through strict zoning laws and the amplification of municipal authority to expropriate and demolish any structures that countered the city's "general interest."

Agache analyzed some of Rio's troubles with great subtlety. He recognized, for example, that the favelas were the product of inadequate public transportation and high housing costs, and would thus reappear if those root problems remained unresolved. His proposed solutions to problems of drainage, water supply, and transportation would serve as models for decades of subsequent planning. And he understood the central place that Rio's stunning natural beauty held in shaping the city's destiny.

But Agache's insights were clouded by misapprehensions, especially with regard to Rio's popular classes and their place in the city. As was to be expected, given his generation and origins, social and racial prejudice tainted Agache's plan throughout. He referred to the favelas, for example, as "plagues" and "leprosies" and argued that "ethnological factors" were responsible for Rio having lagged behind São Paulo's industrial development.[108] Such disdain was symptomatic of a larger sense of Eurocentric distance from Rio's social realities. Agache understood social division in terms of social class, defined by European parameters. Thus, for Agache, Rio's poor were by definition members of the "working class," with housing and recreational needs that centered on proximity to ports and factories. This assumption was based partly on the 1920 census, which overestimated the role of industry in Rio's labor market by making it possible for informal or part-time laborers, small-time artisans and craftspeople, and the unemployed to label themselves as "industrial" workers.[109] Whatever the source of his error, Agache ignored the important roles of domestic service, informal piecework or odd jobs, and construction as sources of employment for the very poor.[110] The sorts of workers' housing that Agache suggested—located in factory districts far removed from the central and wealthier areas of the city—would have isolated these less formal laborers from their places of employment, imposing an enormous cost in time, transportation, and opportunity.

Agache also ignored important aspects of Rio's political and legal culture. To his credit, the plan called for new social legislation that would raise wages and provide public housing assistance to low-income residents. Before 1930, however, social legislation of any kind was in its infancy in Brazil, and Agache's ideas were vague and implausible; his plans to eliminate favelas and tenements, by contrast, were clear and immediate.[111] Agache's vision of public transportation went far beyond Rio's fiscal and administrative means, even though the functionality of his entire imagined city depended on them.[112] And the legal mechanisms of the plan (zoning and codification) presupposed an efficient and relatively transparent legal system in which property ownership was well established and laws were mostly applied as written. A deeper analysis of Rio's legal culture would have revealed that property rights were often precariously defined even in central areas of the city, and that the written law was more a baseline for negotiation than an enforceable mandate.[113]

Agache's plan also underestimated the significance of Rio's long history of uneasy social proximity. He seemed blind to the strong sense of community that bound together many of Rio's supposedly "nomadic" poor, connecting them to their *morros* and tenement homes and to the neighborhoods and public spaces that sustained popular music and traditions. He proposed, for example, the destruction of the Praça Onze, long a center of Afro-Brazilian cultural life, and the razing of all of Rio's favelas. Photos from official visits to the Morro da Favela and other embryonic shantytowns provide ample evidence of community life; the most poignant of them, reproduced at the beginning of this chapter, depicts a small interracial group, dressed to their ramshackle nines, playing music. "A favela vai abaixo" also suggested that many residents were deeply attached to the *morros*. But Agache continued to see them as "ulcers," unsanitary refuges of last resort whose residents could be relocated according to his own aesthetic and economic calculations.

In the end, Agache's misapprehensions proved largely irrelevant, at least in the short term. His plan was published in 1930, the same year that brought Getúlio Vargas to the presidency and disrupted the networks of power broking and accommodation that had pushed political projects forward in the Old Republic.[114] Agache lost his strongest advocate when Prefect Antônio Prado Jr. left office in November 1930, and Agache's elitist language and European pretensions struck a dissonant chord with Vargas's populist rhetoric. Earlier critics reaffirmed their reservations, but the plan's scope proved its final downfall. After initial approval by a commission organized by Prefect Adolfo Bergamini (1930–31), it was archived by Prefect Pedro Ernesto, former doctor and pioneering populist, who declared that "these plans could not be executed if we had 50 years!"[115]

AGACHE'S ECHOES: THE BUILDING CODE OF 1937

Still, Agache's plan was no mere relic of Old Republic–era Rio's Europhile longings. At an ideological level, the plan was as much a prelude as a swan song. It helped to inaugurate an age in which the social engineering of Brazilian cities would be conceived on a grand scale, shaped less by individual politicians and their pet projects than by larger visions of urban design and social order.[116] Subsequent legislation would echo the Agache plan's faith in technical solutions to complex social and economic tangles, its schematic social categorization of large populations, its hierarchical and functionalist understanding of poor people's place in the city, and its disdain for popular participation in the planning process. In all of these ways, despite vast ideological gulfs, Agache's plan foreshadowed not only several decades of Carioca urban planning but also the construction of Brasília in the late 1950s.[117]

More concretely, though it was never fully realized, Agache's plan served as a blueprint for some of the most important legislative and public works initiatives in mid-century Rio. The final flattening of the Morro de Santo Antônio, carried out in the 1950s, was part of the plan. So, too, was the construction of the Avenida Presidente Vargas, which demolished centers of popular culture such as the Praça Onze and part of the Campo de Santana, along with some 550 structures, many housing what was left of the central city's poor population.[118] These and other initiatives were written into the so-called Plano Geral de Melhoramentos, Prefect Henrique Dodsworth's Estado Novo updating of the Agache blueprint.[119]

The most authentic instrument of Agache's social vision was the 1937 building code, the first law to impose comprehensive rules of zoning, construction, and sanitary practices on Rio's entire municipal territory.[120] Following Agache's lead—and international trends—the code divided the city into five zones (commercial, maritime, industrial, residential, and rural).[121] Each zone contained numerous subzones, each with its own regulations specifying the sorts of residential, commercial, and industrial establishments that would be allowed there, and the degree to which their intermixture would be permitted. Like the 1903 code, the 1937 law also contained a long and detailed series of regulations concerning everything from construction standards to aesthetic requirements. Significantly, building standards varied by geographical region, revealing both the imprint of historical inequalities and Agache's vision of social order. Prosperous suburbs to the north and south had more exacting requirements than the older working-class neighborhoods and suburbs, and the loosest regulations of all governed the vast, poor, distant suburban regions.

Even at its loosest, though, the 1937 building code imposed onerous standards. Before a construction or remodeling project could begin, builders had to follow a number of expensive and time-consuming steps: a licensed architect, engineer, or contractor had to be hired to present a formal plan to the city; the plan had to receive official approval; and residents could move in only after a final city inspection.[122] The subdivision of old agricultural or empty land had to follow a similar procedure. In addition, the code required building lots to be large and fully drained, prohibited the use of wood and metal roofs except on selected hills and in agricultural zones, and required all houses either to connect to municipal water and sewer lines or to construct an officially approved alternative.[123]

There were only two exceptions to these rules, and both were bureaucratically burdensome and socially segregationist.[124] "Proletarian habitations of an economic sort" were meant to be small, modest homes for steadily employed laborers. Building standards for these structures

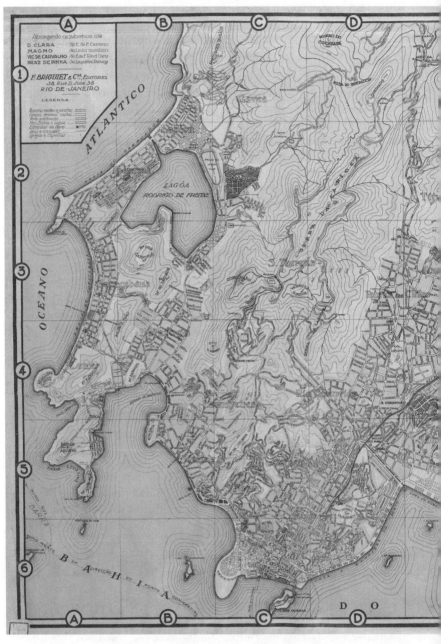

Rio de Janeiro city map, 1929. Courtesy of the Acervo da Fundação Biblioteca Nacional.

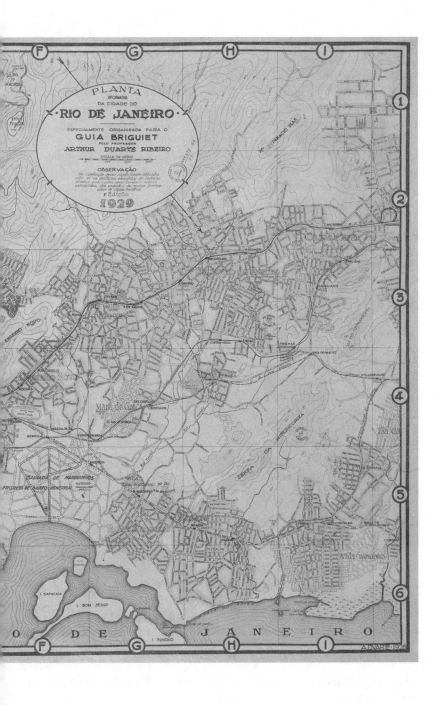

PLANTA
INFORMATIVA
DA CIDADE DO
·RIO DE JANEIRO·
ESPECIALMENTE ORGANISADA PARA O
GUIA BRIGUIET
PELO PROFESSOR
ARTHUR DUARTE RIBEIRO
ESCALA EM METROS

OBSERVAÇÃO

2ª Edição
1929

were still relatively strict, and they could be constructed only in distant and undesirable areas, mostly in relatively desolate regions in the railway suburbs and points further north and west.[125] "Minimum sorts of habitations" were substitutes for favela shacks and could be constructed only by the municipal government, on lands expropriated for that purpose. These residences could be sold only to those who were "certifiably poor"—certification was generally carried out in police stations—and they could not be resold to third parties. Residents also had to conform to standards of conduct that were to be set down by the municipal government.

The code made no other allowances for poor people's housing. Significantly, and for the first time, it entirely prohibited new favelas, defined as "conglomerations of two or more shacks, distributed in an orderly way or not, constructed with improvised materials that did not meet the dispositions of this decree"; it also proscribed repair or new construction within existing shacktowns.[126] Had they been enforced, these regulations would effectively have removed the very poor from Rio's prosperous and central quarters.

As it was, many of the building code's provisions proved sterile. Like the anti-*cortiço* measures and the building and sanitary codes of 1903 and 1904, the law outreached its grasp. Wealthier residents, industrialists, and entrepreneurs found numerous ways to carve exceptions into its stringent requirements, and popular outcry about its bureaucratic burdens led to important modifications (in 1942, 1946, and 1948) as well as to several attempted amnesties for non-licensed structures.[127] By the late 1940s, municipal councilmen regularly referred to the code as obsolete and useless, lamenting both its capricious enforcement and the impact of widespread illegality on municipal tax revenues.[128] Tito Lívio, a councilman from the conservative UDN party who showed particular disdain for the code, noted repeatedly that the city's own affordable housing developments violated the law's provisions. Others noted that the water spigots, schools, and roads that the municipal council sporadically funded in the *morros* were also technically illegal.[129]

Broad-based condemnations of the code sometimes blossomed into criticisms of law's wider role in shaping Rio's social geography. In 1947, as part of a justification for an amnesty law, councilman João Luis Carvalho noted that the code's failures could "not be attributed to a lack of enforcement," but showed rather "the inefficiency of laws that do not sanction local customs or that, as in this case, run contrary to the life circumstances of a parcel of the society in which these laws are supposed to be applied."[130] In 1948, while considering a broad amnesty bill, a city council subcommission wrote that the building code, like its 1925 predecessor, had caused the growth of "two cities, one legal and one

illegal, both growing remarkably, one beautiful, healthful, and seduc-
tive—the 'marvelous city' itself—and the other ugly, sickly, unsanitary
and horrible, the favelas, the *cortiços*, the tenements [*estalagens*], and the
populous suburban and rural nuclei, completely abandoned by public
officials."[131] A blunter condemnation came in the midst of debate over a
group of shacks knocked down by the municipal police in 1948. When
one councilman defended the police by noting that they were only doing their job as specified in the code, his fellow councilman, Joaquim
Antônio Leite de Castro, burst out with an incredulity that underlined
the law's absurdity: "So if a house doesn't have a license, we are going
to knock it down? What theory of destruction and savagery is that?"[132]
All in all, despite the code's prohibitions, favelas and semi-legal subdivisions grew as never before in the 1930s and 1940s, the result of massive
in-migration, scarce housing alternatives, residents' stubborn activism,
and the political and legal maneuverings of small-time speculators and
politicians who stood to benefit from the settlements' growth.[133]

And yet the code remained the legal framework of Rio's expansion for
over three decades, and as such it mattered profoundly. Enforced or not,
it rendered much of Rio's housing stock illegal. For wealthy builders who
could not be bothered to follow the regulations, there were always bribes
and favors; for middle- and lower-middle-class suburban residents who
could not quite afford to conform, there were periodic amnesties that
allowed them to legalize their dwellings. But for shack and shantytown
residents, whose numbers grew exponentially during the code's vigilance,
there was no legal recourse. At any moment, with little more than 24
hours' warning, entire extralegal communities could be flattened, and
anyone whose home violated the rules could be fined or evicted. For these
people, the price of permanence was mobilization, dependence, and insecurity; this triad would demarcate their place in the city from the 1930s
through the 1960s.

CHAPTER TWO

Rio and Brazil's Postwar Republic

Rio's rapid transformation during the middle decades of the twentieth century did not begin with Getúlio Vargas's 1930 revolution. Industrialization, rural-to-urban migration, and the cultural and practical influence of technological modernity had already begun to change Rio's profile by the late nineteenth century, and populist politics had already made significant inroads into the cozy political networks of the First Republic by the 1920s. But Vargas's fifteen-year rule catalyzed all of these phenomena. By the 1940s, they had reached critical mass; they were now the dominant trends of Carioca life, transforming the city in a manner and at a pace that neither Alfred Agache nor the drafters of the 1937 building code could have foreseen. By the 1960s, Rio was a sprawling metropolis, already pushing well past city limits that had run through rural lands 40 years earlier. Cars and buses transported most people, and commerce, the public bureaucracy, and informal activities surpassed industry as major sources of employment. Despite the continued disenfranchisement of illiterates, Rio's popular classes were now front and center in the urban political game; virtually no Carioca politician could get ahead without appealing to vital popular concerns regarding housing, transportation, and urban services. Yet scarce city resources, a conservative administrative structure, and equivocal political will made it impossible to meet these demands in ways consistent with Rio's legal and urbanistic blueprints. Instead, politicians' main currency was often informal toleration of a city whose social realities lay increasingly in the realm of legal ambiguity.

DEMOGRAPHIC SHIFTS

The most astounding transformation in mid-century Rio was demographic. Between 1920 and 1960, the city's official population nearly tripled, to 3,281,908. Between 1940 and 1960, it grew at over 3 percent per year. If poor areas adjacent to the city limits are taken into account—satellite cities such as Duque de Caxias, Nilópolis, Nova Iguaçu, São João de Meriti, and São Gonçalo, which were as much a part of Rio's metropolitan area in 1960 as the suburban regions had been in 1920—then the 1960 metropolitan population surged to 4,653,011, and Rio's annual growth rate rose to a remarkable 3.54 percent between 1920 and 1960 (see table 3).[134]

Rio had seen similar expansion before; as recently as 1872–1890, the population had grown at an average of 3.6 percent per year. But twentieth-century growth was more sustained than this earlier spurt, and its composition differed substantially. In the late nineteenth and early twentieth centuries, immigration from Portugal, Spain, and Italy had swelled the city's foreign-born population; in 1920, 20.7 percent of Rio's population had been born abroad, and foreigners made up 37 percent of the city's male labor force.[135] While slaves and freedpersons had fueled substantial rural-to-urban migration in the years surrounding abolition, they came mostly from Rio de Janeiro state and never overwhelmed native Cariocas; in 1920, 66 percent of Rio's Brazilian population was native to the city.[136]

In the years after World War I, these trends stagnated. European immigration to Rio slowed to a trickle during the war and never fully recovered, and rural-to-urban migration probably even reversed itself in the initial slump of the Great Depression.[137] In the late 1930s, a new wave of internal migrants arrived, pushed from the countryside by drought, landlessness, and agricultural crises and drawn to Rio by interlocking and widely publicized Vargas-era promises of industrial employment, bureaucratic expansion, and social welfare. These migrants came first from the neighboring states of Rio de Janeiro, Espírito Santo, and Minas Gerais. Later, especially after the construction of the Rio–Bahia highway

TABLE 3

Average Rates of Population Growth in Rio de Janeiro, 1799–1970

Avg. growth periods	Avg. percent growth per year	Avg. growth periods	Avg. percent growth per year
1799–1808	2.52	1890–1906	2.74
1808–1821	5.78	1906–1920	2.56
1821–1838	1.16	1920–1940	2.16
1838–1849	3.77	1940–1950	3.05
1849–1872	1.27	1950–1960	3.34
1872–1890	3.63	1960–1970	2.57

SOURCES: Recenseamentos Gerais do Brasil; Mary Karasch, *Slave Life in Rio de Janeiro, 1808–1850* (Princeton, N.J.: Princeton University Press, 1987).

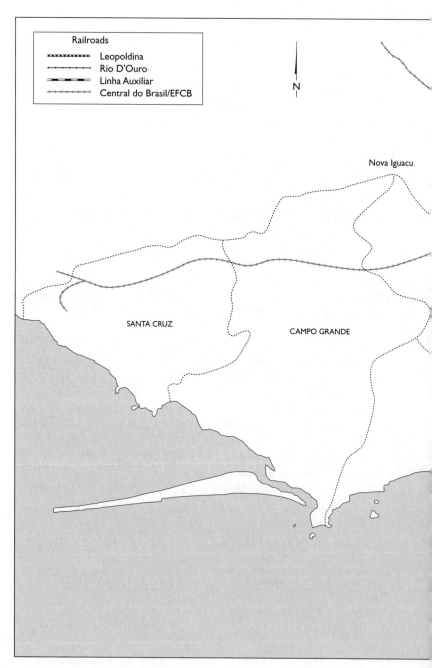

Rio de Janeiro in 1960

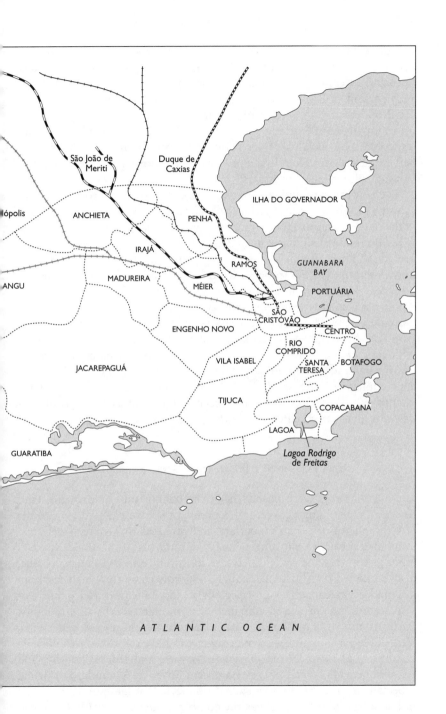

in the 1940s, they came just as often from the drought-stricken and desperately poor northeast, often traveling for days in infamously rickety open lorries called *pau-de-araras*.[138] By 1960, northeasterners made up 12.5 percent of Rio's Brazilian-born population; all in all, native Cariocas dropped to 55.4 percent of the city's Brazilians, and migrants made up 50.4 percent of working-age residents.[139] The city's old ethnic dynamics, colored by social divisions between Europeans and Brazilians, were being quickly overtaken by more intricate relations among Brazilians of varying cultural backgrounds.[140]

The new migrants did little to alter Rio's official racial profile. In 1960, as in 1940, about 71 percent of Rio's population was classified as white in the national census; the proportion classified as black (*preto*) or brown (*pardo*) remained similarly unchanged, at 11 percent and 18 percent, respectively. These numbers, however, may mask a quiet expansion in Rio's nonwhite population. To begin with, Rio's satellite cities were substantially less white than the area within the city limits; these areas' inclusion would have substantially impacted citywide figures.[141] The 1960 statistics, moreover, were based on self-classification, while the 1940 ones had been based on the judgments of census agents; this may have had a significant whitening effect.[142] And, even setting aside the long-debated inexactness of Brazilian racial terminology,[143] the massive migration of northeasterners complicated the task of racial classification enormously; many, while phenotypically white, would have been stereotyped as *paraíbas* or *nordestinos*, derogatory categories with considerable social import.[144]

EMPLOYMENT, HOUSING, AND SCARCITY

Rio's migrants were pushed from the countryside by drought, land loss, and a changing agricultural economy; they were also drawn to the city by images of urban modernity and progress that were widely disseminated through radio and cinema.[145] For the better-informed, Vargas's labor guarantees and social safety net, most fully effective in urban areas, also beckoned.[146] Above all, though, migrants came to Rio to work, in any and every capacity, but especially in the industrial and public service sectors that promised a chance of economic security and mobility. Such promise was quite real; particularly during the 1940s and 1950s, Vargas's labor guarantees seem genuinely to have improved the working conditions of formally recognized employees, and federal housing and pension benefits helped to create a decent lower-class standard of living, especially for those who were skilled, connected, or lucky enough to gain public sector jobs.[147] Moreover, the number of such choice jobs expanded remarkably rapidly during the mid-century decades. Between 1920 and 1960, the percentage of the Carioca workforce engaged in public service increased somewhere between 3 percent and 5 percent, and the absolute numbers grew a remarkable 300 percent.[148] The most reliable information on industrial employment also shows impressive gains; according to the declarations of industrial establishments, the number of industrial workers increased 314 percent between 1920 and 1960, and the number of establishments and the energy consumed by them increased by 350 percent and 520 percent, respectively.[149]

Even such rapid growth, however, was not enough to fulfill migrants' hopes. According to individual census declarations (which tended to exaggerate formal employment), no more than 13.1 percent of all laborers worked for governmental agencies, the police, or the military in 1960, and no more than 20.2 percent worked in industry; of these, somewhere around a quarter were probably employed off the books.[150] Commerce absorbed another 13.4 percent of workers, and transportation another 9.3 percent; many of these also probably worked informally. The largest single occupational category was "service" (23.7 percent), which in practice meant mostly informal, poorly compensated work; this sector absorbed the overwhelming majority of working women. Despite the growth in industry and the public sector, Rio's labor market could never provide nearly enough formal, stable, decently paid jobs to absorb the enormous influx of working-age people from the countryside.[151] The majority of these migrants ended up, for at least some portion of their working lives, finding occupations in the informal market—as cooks, maids, nannies, street vendors, construction workers, errand boys, or even informal industrial or service workers. A few informal laborers received decent pay, but none had the rights and benefits that had beckoned so many to Rio in the first place.

By the first decades of the twentieth century, short supply and rampant land speculation had already created a dramatically tight housing market in Rio. Beginning in the late 1930s, the enormous influx of poor, informally employed migrants—along with high rates of inflation, shortages of such critical materials as cement, and a paucity of public housing initiatives—helped to transform the housing crunch into a crisis. Between 1940 and 1960, according to census figures, there were 417,069 new households in Rio—and yet the city's Anuário Estatístico recorded a mere 192,387 new licenses for single-family residences. At the same time, the number of Carioca dwellings that could be classified as shacks grew from 51,625 in 1933 to some 220,000 in 1960.[152] Though many migrants continued to build their shacks in the backyards and vacant lots of formal neighborhoods, the vast majority chose instead to live in favelas and suburban subdivisions, where residential informality was less the exception than the rule. In 1933, only about 11,770 (or 23 percent) of the city's 51,625 shacks were located in groups of 50 or more, a criterion that would come officially to define the term "favela." In 1960, 69,690 (or 32 percent) of 220,000 total shacks were grouped in similarly large numbers, and the vast majority of the rest could be found in the distant suburbs. The number of officially recognized favelas in Rio grew from 59 in 1950 to 147 in 1960, and their population increased from 169,305 to 335,063.[153] In the face of such overwhelming numbers, the 1937 shack ban appeared futile indeed, and the moral and practical issues surrounding the favela "problem" took center stage in the Carioca political scene.

THE POLITICS OF LEGAL TOLERANCE

The politicians charged with managing the issues generated by rapid population growth, industrial expansion, underemployment, and inadequate housing navigated extraordinarily tumultuous waters. Until the 1920s, official politics in Rio had been mostly tightly controlled and clientelistic. Working- and middle-class protests were common throughout the First Republic, as were maverick politicians, especially on the left of the political spectrum.[154] But they rarely had much influence on the formal political process. The municipal prefects, who ran the city's executive branch and exercised veto power over all city council legislation, were appointed by the federal president; the electorate was tiny; and city councilmen and federal deputies and senators mostly reached office through a machine that was kept well oiled with patronage and cash.[155]

By the 1920s, the machine began to show signs of strain. Population growth made old ties of neighborhood and patronage unwieldy; a growing professional class took an interest in new political ideas; and dissident politicians, new political parties, and labor unions began to demand political transformation and social reform.[156] By the time Vargas triumphed, in 1930, reformers such as Maurício de Lacerda and Adolfo Bergamini were important figures in the Carioca political scene, and demands for labor legislation and improvements in public education, health, and housing were surging from increasingly heterogeneous and independent political camps.[157]

The new Vargas government, with its promises of electoral and social reform, both accelerated and rechanneled such currents. Fulfilling pledges made in the presidential campaign of 1929–30, Vargas's administration spearheaded a 1932 electoral reform law that expanded the franchise to women, lowered the voting age to 18, guaranteed the secret ballot, simplified procedures for voter registration, and established an independent judicial structure to supervise elections.[158] The law also explicitly sought to create a political base for the government among civil servants, and it allowed public agencies to register their employees automatically. Largely because of this law and the spurt of political energy it inspired, voter turnout in Rio's elections grew from 64,000 in the 1930 presidential election to 110,000 in 1934.[159] Though Rio's prefects continued to be federal appointees, Vargas's early choices—Adolfo Bergamini, Pedro Ernesto, and Padre Olympio de Melo—were Carioca reformers determined to transform the city's politics and social dynamics. Ernesto in particular pushed forward critical initiatives in housing, healthcare, education, and culture. He was also a pioneer in forging links between the city government and favela residents, subsidizing samba competitions and registering shacktown voters in unprecedented numbers.[160]

None of this eliminated some of the fundamental features of the old system. Clientelism and patronage retained their importance, and much of the supposedly new political structure had simply been grafted onto the organizational skeleton of the old one, adapting it to an age of mass politics, new social ideologies, and increased public resources. The old clientelist hierarchy, for example, was not eliminated from Pedro Ernesto's new Autonomist Party of the Federal District (PADF), the most dynamic party of 1930s Rio. Instead, the neighborhood and regional bosses who had pulled in the votes during the First Republic were simply subordinated to more media-savvy, centrally accountable political "managers."[161] Likewise, the political strategy of building popular support by distributing public resources as personal largesse remained fundamental; one of Vargas's own crowning achievements was the modernization of such relationships through agile use of radio, the print media, and an enormously expanded labor and public welfare bureaucracy.[162]

Political repression also continued, intensifying even before the Estado Novo dictatorship began in 1937. Independent activists, especially leftists, were persecuted even as many of their ideas were sold to the public as examples of the Vargas government's enlightenment. From 1937 to 1945, formal politics in Rio, as elsewhere, were simply shut down; the city council did not meet, elections were not held, and Vargas's new appointee to the prefecture, Henrique Dodsworth, closely resembled such elitist and authoritarian predecessors as Carlos Sampaio and Francisco Pereira Passos.[163]

The political changes heralded in 1930 were thus complex and contradictory, at once increasing the popular classes' centrality and restricting their autonomy, upsetting old political networks and appropriating their political scaffolding. While the municipal and federal governments offered greatly expanded public goods to poor and middle-class Cariocas during these years, the question of whether such benefits were to be claimed as rights or accepted as part of a personalistic political bargain remained cloudy.

The political ferment that followed Vargas's 1945 fall from power launched a competitive and democratic era characterized by mass participation, fierce political rivalry, and fundamental ideological divisions. While illiterates remained disenfranchised, the Carioca electorate as a whole expanded remarkably; in 1945, 496,771 people voted, nearly four times the 1934 turnout; by the 1962 congressional elections, the number was over 1 million, nearly a third of the city's total population.[164] Political parties from widely divergent political perspectives proliferated during these years; in Rio, such left-wing entities as the Brazilian Communist Party (PCB) and the Brazilian Socialist Party (PSB) fought for prominence with such centrist groups as Vargas's Trabalhista Party (PTB), the Social Democratic Party (PSD), and the center-right-wing National Democratic Union (UDN).[165] Local issues, such as migration, employment, inflation, urban planning, service provision, and the fate of the favelas, were hotly debated everywhere, from the federal chamber of deputies to the municipal council to the pages of Rio's many newspapers. No one active in Carioca politics during these years could succeed without engaging all sectors of the population; on the face of it, Carioca mass politics had reached their zenith.

Yet widespread political participation did not guarantee either grass-roots democracy or fundamental institutional or legal transformation. In part, the inherent conservatism of Rio's administrative structure impeded such changes. Until 1960, when the federal government moved to Brasília, Rio's prefects continued to be appointed by the president and thus were not directly accountable to Carioca citizens. The elected municipal council—which did frequently address critical issues such as land grabbing, public service provision, and favela growth—was often ineffectual, since the prefect's veto of council legislation could only be overcome by a vote in the federal senate.[166] In addition, even Rio's prefect could exercise very little control over the development of broad swaths of city territory, which were owned by the federal ministries, the Social Security Institutes, or the military. Because the federal government was housed in Rio, Brazil's leaders often viewed urban affairs as nationally critical, and they frequently intervened in issues such as public health and housing. In all of these ways, vital decision-making power rested in the hands of politicians and bureaucrats who were not directly answerable to the Carioca population, a fact that greatly limited the transformative possibilities of popular democracy.

More critically still, the deep currents of elitism and repression that had, in different ways, characterized both the First Republic and the Vargas regime were not entirely reversed during the postwar democracy. Limits on formal suffrage remained despite the 1932 law; illiterates could not vote, and procedural and documentary requirements made it very difficult for migrants to register.[167] Political expression, too, was restricted. The Brazilian Communist Party, which attracted more votes than any other in Rio's 1947 elections and was especially active in recruiting and representing workers and shantytown residents, was banned that same year, and in 1948 its members were purged from local and national office.[168] Finally, informal or private use of police violence remained an important part of the Carioca political scene, especially in relation to land issues and favela policies. Community leaders in shantytowns resisting elimination were often harassed, and the police frequently burned or tore down shacks in open defiance of court decisions or legal decrees.[169] Politics were baldly at the center of one 1949 incident, in which the headquarters of Vargas's PTB were partially destroyed during a police invasion of the south-zone favela of Cantagalo, where PTB councilman Frota Aguiar had long been active.[170] Restricted suffrage, bans on leftist politics, and the possibility of extralegal violence all limited the degree to which popular or radical views could influence the political process.

The upshot was a contradictory political landscape. On the one hand, conservatism and repression tended to muffle changes in Rio's fundamental legal and administrative structures. The restrictive building code of 1937 remained law until the 1960s, despite constant demands for reform. The public health service continued to exercise summary powers of eviction. The Agache Plan guided urban reform for decades, despite radical changes in Rio's size, residential structure, and transportation networks. And, though numerous commissions and agencies sought to ease the housing crunch and to curb the favelas' growth, no reform of the basic housing stock or the structures of property ownership took shape.

On the other hand, voters demanded more equitable distribution of city resources, vehemently enough that no ambitious politician could make a career without at least seeming to advocate the causes of poor residents. Suburban populations wanted drainage, water, and electric service; favela dwellers and purchasers of illegal subdivisions demanded tenure security and the full gamut of urban services; all poor neighborhoods needed schools, hospitals, and transportation. Though communists in particular were often accused of political demagoguery—and many left-wing politicians did indeed begin their careers as legal and political advocates for favela residents—politicians from across the political spectrum felt compelled to jump on the political bandwagon. Council debates on favela issues frequently descended into laughable arguments among politicians claiming organic knowledge, and thus political ownership, of the *mor-ros*.[171] In mockery of her paternalistic "representation" of the favelas, Councilwoman Sagramor di Scuvero—a former journalist and radio announcer representing the Partido Republicano—was sarcastically dubbed "Irmã-Paula da Nossa Praça" by fellow journalist and UDN councilman Carlos Lacerda. In turn, and for similar reasons, both Lacerda and his fellow UDN councilman Tito Lívio were bestowed with the moniker "Favela dos meus Amores," after a 1935 film of the same name.

Lacerda's own turbulent relationship with Rio's favelas encapsulates their centrality to Carioca politics. Lacerda, the son of 1920s reformer Maurício de Lacerda, began his career as a fiery and controversial journalist. He had a brief stint in Rio's municipal council in the late 1940s, became a lightning rod for opposition to Getúlio Vargas in the 1950s, and was elected Guanabara's first governor in 1960.[172] Lacerda had been a communist as a young man but by the late 1940s he had become fiercely anti-communist and anti-populist.

Lacerda engaged the favela issue from the very beginning of his political career. In 1947, he proposed some of the earliest and most comprehensive municipal favela bills, and in 1948 he launched a famous press campaign, called the Batalha do Rio de Janeiro, which sought to force city officials to abandon politics and demagoguery and find a definitive solution to the favela problem. By 1960, his opposition to what he considered to be demagogic favela politics had earned him few friends in Rio's *morros*, and his tenure as governor would witness some of the largest and most brutal favela razings in Rio's history.

Yet despite all of this, even Lacerda felt obliged to launch his 1960 gubernatorial campaign in the south-zone shantytowns of Pavão/Pavãozinho and Cantagalo. The *Tribuna da Imprensa*, Lacerda's own former newspaper, reported that he had spent the day in truly populist style: "He climbed the hill empty-handed. He drank coffee with Tolentino and Zaferina [a community leader and his wife]; ate *cuscus* in the shack of Idalice the seamstress; and visited Father Romualdo's chapel, the Assembléia de Deus [an evangelical church], the construction sites of the Fundação Leão XIII [a social service organization], various shacks, and the local chapter of the UDN."[173] This capitulation to the populist script underscores the extent to which such visits, accompanied by promises both extravagant and mundane, were the bread and butter of most Rio politicians between 1945 and 1964.

For the most part, politicians' actions in the favelas, as in other poor neighborhoods, were a matter of old-fashioned populism, often referred to as "water-spigot politics." Local bosses registered voters and brought out supporters, and politicians, usually through an elaborate structure of intermediaries, reciprocated by granting small concessions—a water tap, a soccer field, building materials for a shack, pavement for a street, a place in a public housing project for an especially favored local operator—that could be presented both as symbols of a politician's personal generosity and evidence of a local boss's influence.[174] Such services were often inadequate—in one instance, an elaborate system of water spigots and laundry sinks that had been installed at the top of the Cantagalo favela on the personal order of President Eurico Dutra never actually enjoyed running water—and services in poor areas were more often distributed on the basis of political loyalty than on that of need or right.[175] Lacerda again provides a typical example, this time from his term as Guanabara's governor (1960–64). In 1960, Gilson de Oliveira, a resident of the vast suburb of Campo Grande, wrote to ask Lacerda for various public services: a civil identification office, a justice of the peace, the eviction of illegal street vendors from local plazas and bus stops, extra policing next to the cinema he owned and outside a local school, pavement on various streets, and an electrical post. Lacerda, in justifying his unusual order to fulfill these requests, did not write about the importance of the proposed works or about their practicality; instead, he wrote simply, "Gilson is a real comrade."[176]

Letters from Henrique Dodsworth's personal archives and the municipal council records indicate similar interactions throughout the period. It is clear, moreover, that services were not the only public goods doled out as favors. Illegality itself also became a potent source of political currency. If the widespread violation of unrealistic codes governing property, building, and sanitation was a common feature of Carioca poverty, the defense of poor and vulnerable constituents against these laws' enforcement was one of the cheapest sources of political support.[177] When favela residents faced eviction, when agricultural squatters in rapidly suburbanizing rural areas found their land rights under siege, when residents with illegally pirated electricity were threatened with a blackout, their chief recourse was to local politicians willing to use the mechanisms of personal influence and legislative morass to block the laws' enforcement.[178]

Some politicians viewed such strategies as temporary measures taken in the absence of a more genuinely democratic municipal policy. Talk abounded of land expropriation, urbanization, and public housing construction, and successive administrations named a series of commissions and agencies to deal more definitively with the problems of favelas and informal settlements.[179] None of these measures prospered, however, and many politicians seem to have concluded that it was easier, cheaper, and more politically profitable to undermine unjust laws than it was to change them. Favela residents themselves clearly realized this; for them, the procuring of individual "favors" was often only one part of a more complex struggle to demand their version of justice.[180] But the fact remains that vulnerability, illegality, and lack of services became an essential part of Rio's political system, a pattern that partially explains the Carioca government's lack of decisive action on issues of urban social policy during the Postwar Republic.

THE SOCIAL GEOGRAPHY OF RIGHTS TO THE MARVELOUS CITY

Rio's inequalities changed in nature between the 1930s and the 1960s, reflecting the turbulent crosscurrents of overwhelming growth, administrative conservatism, and populist politics. In some ways, the cityscape reflected responses to popular demands; major public works projects made Rio's northern and western reaches more habitable and accessible, the reach of city services was extended, and significant public funds were poured into improving the lives of favela residents. Yet such improvements were limited by sparse resources, competing elite demands, and a political game in which favors were essential building blocks of power. In 1964, when the military coup voided the populist pact, most poor people's communities were still underserved, and many were still quite literally blanks on Rio's legal map. Even where they existed, populist payoffs—usually in the form of electricity, schools, medical posts, paved streets, water pipes, or sewer lines—did not translate into rights of participation or permanence, and illegality exacerbated the miserable living conditions of most poor Cariocas.

Rio's mid-century growth was stunning in its sheer scale. The city added nearly 2,000 streets to its legal grid in the years between 1933 and 1960; favelas, illegal subdivisions, and satellite cities outside Rio's official limits added thousands more.[181] Rio's industrial establishments increased from 1,541 in 1920 to 5,328 in 1960, and their physical and environmental footprints grew apace.[182] The city's densely populated areas burst from their early-twentieth-century limits, quickly filling in rural regions between the suburban railway tracks and pushing the metropolis into what had once been sleepy agricultural communities outside Rio's formal limits. At the same time, a feverous construction boom fueled the verticalization of Rio's central and southern neighborhoods; old mansions gave way to skyscrapers, belle époque ornamentation to clean modernist lines. Rio retained its patchy social geography. In the center and the south, favelas and dilapidated colonial two-stories jostled for space with sleek highrises; in the suburbs, modern factories and apartment buildings interrupted the overwhelming expanses of modest developments and auto-constructed favelas and subdivisions. But vaster distances and higher densities quickly transformed the shapes and meanings of those juxtapositions.

Although these changes often escaped direct regulation, governmental initiatives still set the broad parameters for urban growth. Monumental projects transformed Rio's central and southern regions. Feats of engineering such as road building, tunnel blasting, and swamp drainage radically altered the city's physical landscape. City planners, pressured by a steady stream of populist bargains, haphazardly expanded the city's web of public services. And poor people's place in the city was largely defined by social policies that sought alternately to eradicate and urbanize Rio's favela landscapes. By turns impressive, contradictory, and frankly incoherent, these public policies nonetheless laid the foundations for the democratic period's twin legacies of expanded services and restricted rights.

Some urban projects undertaken after 1930 continued to bear a decidedly elitist stamp, none so much as the construction of the Avenida Presidente Vargas, in the late 1930s. The new avenue, a grandiose swath cut westward from the Avenida Rio Branco, had been proposed by Agache and was executed in a style reminiscent of Pereira Passos. Inaugurated in the early 1940s, the Avenida came into being at the cost of thousands of low-cost residences, hundreds of petty commercial establishments, and two sites critical to Carioca popular culture: the Praça Onze and a good part of the Campo de Santana.[183] Emblematically, Dodsworth's own account of the project, published in the mid-1950s, contained no acknowledgment of its cultural and human cost and dismissed its many critics as enemies of "progress."[184]

The Avenida never lived up to its monumental blueprints. Once completed, it remained semi-deserted, barren of both the stately buildings Dodsworth had envisioned and of the popular activity common on neighboring lower-class commercial streets; it ultimately served mainly as a throughway to Rio's northern and northwestern districts.[185] Criticized and ridiculed by Dodsworth's political opponents, the Avenue became by the late 1940s a political symbol of expensive and misplaced urbanism.[186] Nonetheless, its very execution indicated that the grandiose urban restructuring characteristic of the early twentieth century had survived the Estado Novo. In the populist era, that tradition was again revitalized by such projects as the construction of the Maracanã soccer stadium for the 1950 World Cup and the leveling of the Morro de Santo Antônio.[187]

Other projects of the Vargas and populist eras broke the monumentalist mold, reflecting the period's demographic and political transformations and bringing considerable public resources to bear on problems of industrialization, transportation, suburban integration, and poverty. The largest single public works project undertaken anywhere in Rio in the 1930s was the so-called sanitation of the vast, swampy suburban regions known as the Baixada Fluminense.[188] Initiated by President Vargas in 1933, the project culminated centuries of haphazard drainage and land-fill that had gradually reclaimed Rio's central territories from the rivers and swamplands that passed through them; its ultimate goal was to cre-ate a continuous landscape from the tentacular smattering of elevated, permanently dry lands where Rio's suburbs had first entrenched them-selves. The problem was enormous and complex, not easily remedied by simple drainage or landfill. Water levels in many of the rivers that riddled the Baixada varied with the tides; many riverbeds were so shallow that their waters easily and frequently overflowed, creating vast, permanent, uninhabitable marshes along their banks, and the region's shallow lakes often flooded their surrounding territories. Although some of these lands could be "rescued" through a simple process of river dredging, others required more severe measures, such as the construction of permanent canals, dikes, artificial riverbeds, and underground drainage channels. Because of the sheer size and intricacy of the undertaking, it was not anywhere near completed in the years before 1964.[189] Nonetheless, the combined efforts of state and federal agencies did manage to extend the continuous limits of Rio's inhabitable urban frontier almost to the city's legal boundaries—an accomplishment that facilitated the vertiginous de-mographic and industrial growth of the Carioca suburbs.[190]

Also critical to that growth was a flurry of tunnel drilling and road building that spun an ever-expanding web of viaducts, expressways, tun-nels, bridges, and secondary thoroughfares over Rio's every region. The highest-profile projects benefited the central and southern zones; tun-nels such as Rebouças and Santa Bárbara, both completed in the 1960s, greatly improved mobility from the south to the center and the north; the construction of the Avenida Perimetral eased congestion in the center; and many of the south zone's internationally famous parks, avenues, and beachside playgrounds date from this era. But numerous expressways and tunnels were also built to benefit previously ignored outlying regions, connecting isolated railway suburbs to one another and facilitating com-munication between Rio and the Brazilian interior.

Key among these was the Avenida Brasil, a modern freeway inaugu-rated in 1946, which eventually extended northwest from Rio's port re-gions almost to the municipal border and then ran southwest, connecting along the way with the Rio–Petrópolis Highway and the Dutra Freeway to São Paulo (inaugurated in 1951). The Avenida Brasil project, initi-ated under Henrique Dodsworth in the 1930s, was meant to facilitate the transportation of industrial and commercial goods between Rio and the rest of the country, to make the newly drained lands of the Baixada Fluminense viable areas for industrial development, and also—rather incidentally—to link the railway suburbs along the Rio D'Ouro line to those of the Leopoldina, the Central do Brasil, and the Linha Auxiliar. The Avenida also—predictably but less deliberately—became the site of the city's most rapid favela expansion, and integrated the northwestern satellite cities into Rio's metropolitan area.[191] Other important suburban highways were built or improved, with similar effects. These included the Avenida Automóvel Clube, the Avenida Suburbana, the Avenida das Bandeiras, and the Avenida Radial Oeste.

Paradoxically, these very improvements in suburban roads—along with such measures as the electrification of train lines and the imposition of a unified fare system on public transportation throughout the Federal District—set the stage for a still larger challenge. How would the city extend public services to such far-flung and rapidly growing settlements? Rio's suburban population grew by 458 percent between 1920 and 1960, when it stood at well over 2 million people, or 63.3 percent of all Cariocas.[192] As early as the 1940s, this growth was no longer concentrated in the traditional suburbs of the Zona Norte and Central do Brasil railway, or even in more distant suburbs, such as Irajá, Madureira, and Penha. Instead, migrants streamed into Jacarepaguá, Pavuna, Campo Grande, and Santa Cruz, distant regions where the small-scale cultivation of bananas, oranges, common vegetables, and subsistence crops continued alongside poor, desolate, but unmistakably urban subdivisions.[193] Still more spectacular population increases occurred beyond Rio's formal borders; the satellite cities of Niterói, Duque de Caxias, Nilópolis, Nova Iguaçu, São João de Meriti, and São Gonçalo grew by an astounding 368 percent between 1940 and 1960.[194] Factories, too, followed the roads and drainage projects, especially along the Avenida Brasil, in search of cheaper land and readier access to São Paulo and the Brazilian interior.[195] By the mid-1950s, commerce and culture had followed settlement and industry, making major urban hubs of once sleepy suburbs such as Méier and Madureira.[196]

URBAN SERVICES

Power, sewer lines, water pipes, electricity, schools, hospitals, roads, security, public transportation, legal housing— suburban demands were countless and relentless, more overwhelming still when combined with the unmet needs of many more central areas. Given these realities, public authorities could nevertheless claim some notable advances. In 1933, only about 34 percent of Rio's streets had been paved, and only 44 percent had been connected to the city's electrical grid. By 1960, 45 percent of all streets had been paved, and more than 88 percent had electricity—an astounding increase, given that nearly 2,000 additional streets had been built. In 1933, 57.5 percent of all streets had access to public water, and 31.7 percent to public sewers; by 1960, 76.7 percent of all Carioca residences had been given access to city water, and 47.8 percent had been connected to public sewers. Schools and hospitals also expanded, though never rapidly enough to prevent overcrowding. In 1933, approximately 102,814 students frequented the city's primary schools; by 1964, that number had reached 393,238, and some 93 percent of Carioca children between the ages of 7 and 14 attended school.[197] In 1934, Rio had 133 medical establishments; by 1964, there were 173, and at least some poor communities were served by small medical posts.[198]

Unsurprisingly, though, these broad advances were patchy, and they tended to have the least reach in the neediest areas. Despite the surge in road building, 55 percent of Carioca streets were still unpaved in 1960, and the majority of these dirt roads and paths wound through the northern and western suburbs.[199] Almost by definition, pavement hardly existed in favelas and clandestine subdivisions; emblematically, favela slang appropriated "the asphalt" to describe the city's legalized neighborhoods. Even where roads were paved, moreover, they could do only so much to help people without cars. As late as 1970, no suburb could claim that more than 20 percent of its households had the use of an automobile, and in most suburbs the figure was well under 15 percent.[200] Woefully inadequate suburban bus service was the subject of countless pleas to local politicians.

The social implications of public investment in a car culture did not go entirely unnoticed. In 1947, opposition councilman Tito Lívio used the issue to attack former and current administrations, and to argue that highway and tunnel projects should be replaced by a metro.[201] But such pleas had little impact on public investment. The trains that still transported many suburban residents were poorly maintained and often enormously overcrowded; the electrified buses meant to substitute for the tramlines were never adequate in number or reach; and the metro, planned since Agache's time, would be inaugurated only in 1980 and would not reach suburban regions until well into the 1990s. By 1964, the Carioca suburbs had become bedroom communities for Rio's poor and working classes, just as Alfred Agache had envisioned. Yet the efficient transportation system that might have made such spatial segregation workable remained absent.

Despite constant appeals to city officials, suburban and favela residents also had scarce access to other urban public services. Most did receive electric power. 93.5 percent of all Carioca households had connections in 1960, as did about 80 percent in the distant suburbs and favelas; the situation in the satellite cities was, typically, somewhat worse.[202] In the distant suburbs and favelas, however, much electric power was probably pirated; as late as 1980, when the census distinguished for the first time between legal and self-service electricity, only 76.5 percent of suburban households had official connections.[203] Piracy was widely tolerated and frequently discussed. Already in 1947, Agildo Barata, a city councilman, described precisely how a resident of an officially electrified house on the borders of the Cantagalo favela extended a web of loose wires to his neighbors, charging a fortune and becoming his own little electric company. Though Barata labeled the man an exploiter, he also pointed out that this was the only real solution so long as public officials failed to extend the grid.[204] In most favelas, extralegal grid connections not only built personal fortunes but also became bargaining chips in local politics, giving authority both to local demagogues and to more democratic neighborhood associations.

Considerably fewer suburban and favela households had access to other public services. In 1960, while over 80 percent of Rio's central and near suburban households had public water, it reached only 56 percent of far suburban and 22 percent of favela households. In the satellite cities, the figure was well under 50 percent. Sewer connections reached fewer residences still: 80 percent in the central districts, 36 percent in the immediate suburbs, and only 8 percent in the distant ones. In the favelas, only 56 percent of homes even had a rudimentary septic system, and virtually none were hooked to city sewers. None of the satellite cities provided sewers to more than 16 percent of households.[205] Newer services, such as gas and telephone lines, followed similar patterns, an indication that the suburbs and favelas continued to have lower priority in service planning.[206]

Inequalities in service provision no longer paralleled race or literacy as closely as they had in the 1930s, but illiterates and Afro-Brazilians still suffered significantly scant access. While electricity did not correlate especially strongly with race or education in 1960, water service still correlated fairly highly with both, and sewer service sustained a strong link with whiteness, though not with literacy.[207] Newer services, such as gas, demonstrated a strong relationship with race, and all of the correlations strengthened when favelas were disaggregated from their surrounding neighborhoods.[208] Even these small improvements did not survive the military period; though racial statistics were not included in the 1970 census, correlations between services and literacy had returned to their previous high levels.[209]

Suburban and favela residents complained constantly about these inequities. The image of women and children lugging heavy water jugs up the *morros'* steep and muddy pathways became a staple of popular politics; the back-breaking task was blamed for everything from washerwomen's inability to work to children's lack of schooling to a litany of health problems.[210] Although residents' appeals were sometimes couched in a language of pleading or charity, they were also formulated as demands for rights, especially in the turbulent early years of postwar democracy. In 1947, for example, 359 residents of the downtown favela of Santo Antônio complained vehemently to communist councilmen about the "complete negligence of the public authorities" in relation to their water problem, and residents of Francisco de Sousa Street, in suburban Bento Ribeiro, demanded a law that would honor their "rights" to public schools, policing, pavement, and sewers.[211] Despite this incipient language of citizenship, official response usually came in the form of highly symbolic and personalized "favors," in part because city services could not officially be extended to settlements where streets were unrecognized and property rights were uncertain, but probably also because favors better suited the populist political game.

ILLEGAL CITIES AND THE POVERTIES OF RIGHTS

Clamor for a public solution to Rio's housing crisis had begun in the early twentieth century, with the widespread displacements brought on by the Pereira Passos reforms.[212] By the 1940s, as migrants streamed to the city and favelas grew in size and visibility, local papers teemed with demands for a governmental cure for the "social plague" that afflicted the city's hills and swamps.[213] For more than 20 years, favela commissions were formed, housing bureaucracies grew, and battles raged over funding, morality, and agency. Still, by the 1960s, Rio's housing policies remained contradictory and ineffectual, caught in the pendulum swing between insufficient aid and politically untenable repression.[214] Favelas, illegal subdivisions, and tenements mushroomed, but the building and sanitary codes that outlawed them remained. The result was an illegal city that increasingly interrupted and defined the legal one; home to close to 1 million people, too large to eliminate or ignore but mostly bereft of formal rights to exist, Rio's archipelago of shacks and tenements etched the reality of poor people's limited urban citizenship onto the city's physical map.

The large favelas that attracted the lion's share of public attention in the populist period were only the most visible portion of Rio's rights-poor city. The vast majority of the very poor lived elsewhere—in suburban *loteamentos* where rustic construction and lack of services were the rule rather than the exception, in backyard shanties scattered throughout the city's best neighborhoods, or in central tenements where conditions had improved little since the nineteenth century anti-*cortiço* campaigns.[215] Like the favelas, these places offered poor living conditions that violated various sanitary, building, and property laws. Also like the favelas, they were the product not only of extreme poverty, rapid migration, and rampant inflation but also of unbridled speculation and political opportunism. Viewed from this wide angle, Rio's housing crisis was a complex problem involving everything from local land and labor markets to transportation networks to questions of corruption and law enforcement. It was also an intensely individual problem that could not respond well to blanket solutions. Each shack or tenement room, while perceived as a problem by outsiders, was also a solution to a highly particular set of needs involving economics, family, work, schooling, and community, one that could not easily be replicated by overarching bureaucratic plans.[216]

While many observers noted this scope and complexity, only a few governmental initiatives even attempted to solve Rio's housing problem beyond the favelas' borders.[217] The earliest of these broader measures involved rent control, which first entered Carioca lawbooks in the 1920s; national legislation followed in August of 1942.[218] Intended to slow a sharp rise in rents triggered by scarcity and speculation, these laws may well also have slowed the construction of affordable rental housing and worsened the already poor maintenance of existing units.[219] Rent control may also unintentionally have served to keep the very poor in Rio's black market for rental housing. Even as much of the Carioca housing market moved toward formalization in the 1930s and 1940s—rental contracts helped to enforce rent control for tenants and protected landlords against squatting—many slumlords preferred to assume the risks of informal agreements in exchange for charging market rents, correctly assuming that most of their poor clients would never mount an effective protest.[220] If rent control benefited anyone, it was a narrow swath of working- and lower-middle-class tenants who had the knowledge and legal means to enforce their rights.

Broad-based governmental public housing initiatives served a similarly restricted clientele. During the Vargas years, policymakers—especially in the Ministério do Trabalho, Indústria e Comércio (Ministry of Work, Industry, and Commerce)—were clearly aware of the housing crisis. In the Ministry's monthly bulletin, numerous articles focused on housing.

In one typical example, architect and engineer Rubens Porto linked poor people's living environments to questions of family morality (and, implicitly, national character): "Man is man only through his home. The workplace is the means, but family is the end. (Man) earns a living operating a machine, but he lives in a house, amongst his loved ones, educating his children."[221]

Partially as a result of such concerns, the government's new Social Security Institutes undertook a series of housing and mortgage initiatives. Between the early 1930s and the 1970s, the institutes constructed 68 housing projects and, by the most generous accounts, provided housing for some 120,000 families.[222] The Fundação da Casa Popular—a federal initiative implemented in 1951, during Vargas's second administration—added another several hundred housing units a year to the mix during the 1950s, as did numerous smaller programs.[223]

Without these public projects, Rio's housing crises would surely have been worse. But such projects tended to benefit the working class far more than the very poor. Much of the problem had to do with location: the housing developments were mostly built on public lands in distant suburbs, far from the jobs in construction, petty commerce, and domestic service that occupied most of Rio's very poor. In addition, the subsidized mortgage payments required by the institutes were much higher than what a typical family might pay to construct its own home in a favela. Just as importantly, the public housing and mortgages provided by the pension institutes, like many other Vargas-era social welfare initiatives, went almost exclusively to the institutes' members, who were all formally employed, legally recognized workers a step or two above Rio's poorest classes.[224] Beyond this, the institutes were frequently accused of corruption and of neglecting their duty to provide for their poorest members, instead using their resources to build "sumptuous palaces" for a few privileged people.[225] The institutes did construct some housing aimed at favela residents during the Estado Novo, and the Fundação da Casa Popular aimed its projects at a broader population; perhaps inspired by these slim hopes, numerous people with no connection to the institutes wrote to politicians as varied as President Vargas, Prefect Dodsworth, and Governor Lacerda to request housing assistance. But the vast majority of institute housing units were only rarely available to the very poor, and then mostly as a populist favor.

This reality was already evident to one man who wrote to President Vargas in 1938. Francisco Gonçalves Martins was a poor elderly resident of a crumbling building (called, ironically, the Palacete Rio de Janeiro) located in one of Rio's most decadent central neighborhoods. Apologizing for taking Vargas's "precious time," but insisting that Vargas "must know the miseries we are experiencing, being the true Brazilians that we are," Martins described "an old tenement in a terrible state of ruin." The walls were full of holes, many of the floors had caved in, and leaks were everywhere. Rent was expensive for rooms that didn't "even have enough space in them to fit a table and bed." To save on electricity, the building manager had removed the weak bulbs that had once illuminated the halls and veranda; he had also plugged the water pipe that had filled the residents' laundry tubs, and he had restricted water use to the point that residents could barely wash themselves. "Juvenile delinquents" gambled and played soccer all day long, and at night the place was "an absolute scandal." In the face of all of this, municipal authorities would do nothing; Martins was thus appealing to Vargas, "the father of the forsaken," "the only one who can ease the troubles of all of us who live in these tenements":

> I am appealing to Your Excellency as our beloved leader, we can't live in any other place, we are not public employees, and we can't pay very much money . . . many of us are old and can't possibly buy houses. It is only because of Your Excellency's generous heart that we may have some hope, if you were to order the construction of some tiny houses where forsaken, poor people like us could live and pay affordable rents. I've heard that Your Excellency is thinking of benefiting favela dwellers with your valuable protection, and we here also hope to be graced with your charity, please have pity on us miserable Brazilians, victims of the greedy speculators of our beloved country.

Martins's hopes were dashed; he received in response only a short note explaining that nothing could be done for him because he did not belong to a social security institute—a curt encapsulation of the limits of broad-based public housing in the Vargas era.[226]

THE FAVELAS

As Francisco Gonçalves Martins correctly perceived, residents of the high-profile favelas in Rio's residential and industrial neighborhoods faced a somewhat different situation. Despite the fact that they comprised only a portion of Rio's illegal city, the favelas dominated Carioca housing debates during the populist era. Their irregular and sometimes brightly colored shacks, tin roofs glinting in the sun, were visible from nearly any vantage point—from Copacabana's high-rise apartment buildings or beaches, from the sinuous curves of beachfront highways, from the monotonous length of the Avenida Brasil.[227] To outsiders, favela residents seemed as ubiquitous as the favelas themselves; they were the laborers who saw to the toiling details of every middle- and upper-class family's daily life, the workers who constructed the chic apartment buildings that increasingly defined Carioca modernism, the dancers and musicians who brought Rio's carnival alive to international renown. This constant presence made the shacktown a symbol of Rio's social divide; it also made the favela a battleground over deeper issues of equity, domination, and political power. The result was contradiction and confusion, a slew of policies that sought simultaneously to eliminate and develop the shacktowns, leading to a stalemate of insecure permanence.

From the beginning, outsiders approached the favela issue from radically different standpoints.[228] At one extreme, initially the most influential, stood those who pointed to the favelas not only as aesthetic blights but also as nests of crime, vice, ignorance, and barbarism. In the favelas' early decades, this association was most often made by journalists eager to pique readers' curiosity about the rustic settlements arising in the center of "civilized" Rio. Among these was Benjamim Costallat, who described the "favela that [he] saw" in the early 1920s as "o morro do crime," a place outside the law, the site of mysterious and enticingly brutal violence. It was, Costallat noted, a lawless place where "the land belongs to no one and to everyone," "a city within a city" where no one married, no one paid taxes, and where bloodshed was the remedy for all offenses and conflicts.[229] The *morro* was also, according to Costallat, a site of terrible, chaotic poverty, of exotic, African-tinged culture, and, above all, of samba—which, more than a musical form, was a transcendent, stubborn happiness in the face of unspeakable privation. Costallat and others saw in samba an admirable *alegria*, a "marvelous example for those who have everything and still aren't satisfied"; in such fascination lay the roots of the process that brought samba to the forefront of Brazilian culture.[230] But the favela itself was little more than a barbarous curiosity, and only the sambas themselves defended such communities' rights to permanence.

In subsequent years, these views hardened, often consequentially. Agache (echoing the anti-favela crusader and Rotarian João Augusto Mattos Pimenta) dubbed the shantytowns "aesthetic leprosies" and slated them for destruction, a suggestion given legal force by the building code of 1937. Public health officials also fixed their gaze on the favelas, clearly reacting as much to the risk of moral contagion as to any menace to public health. One official, justifying to President Vargas a violent eradication of the Santo Antônio shantytown in the early 1920s, described it as having previously been "a nucleus of horrendous habitations, which cast all sorts of filthiness down onto the center of the city and was the home base of vagabonds, thieves, and disorderly characters of the worst sort, a place where not even the police could safely penetrate."[231] In the early

1940s, even Victor Tavares de Moura—supervisor of Rio's first comprehensive favela commission, and among the first to study the favela with sympathy and depth—saw migration control, forced eviction, and supervised readjustment as the only real solutions to the "pernicious" favelas, "stains" on the city where good, honest workers were corrupted by violence, alcoholism, laziness, and promiscuity.[232]

Moura's pioneering favela commission departed in many ways from the harsh recommendations of its contemporaries. Its report emphasized the need to study the favelas and to replace them with housing units located nearby so as not to disrupt work and family relationships. The censuses the commission carried out were the first to show that favela residents mostly belonged to working families. But Moura's own views on these matters were contradictory, and it was their draconian and paternalistic streak that dominated his commission's recommendations, which included border vigilance to slow rural-to-urban migration, the forced resettlement of rural migrants to other areas of Brazil, heightened supervision of migrants who took refuge in charitable shelters, and strict enforcement of the 1937 building code's anti-favela provisions. Though none of these policies was ever implemented, a final suggestion—the substitution, in the early 1940s, of several Carioca shacktowns with two ill-fated public housing projects called "proletarian parks"—became Rio's first concrete anti-favela policy.

The forced removal of favela residents to the new public housing projects began in 1942 with a spectacular burning. Prefect Henrique Dodsworth himself set fire to the first shack in the Largo da Memória, part of an enormous, rambling lakeside shantytown straddling the booming south-side neighborhoods of Leblon and Gávea.[233] When the fire subsided, little remained but charcoal skeletons. Residents of the Largo—and a few others who slipped in through the populist cracks—were transferred to the nearby Parque Proletário no. 1, a hastily built "provisional" settlement that replaced Gávea's Favela do Capinzal. Shortly thereafter, refugees from a dynamite explosion that had partially destroyed the north-zone favela of Livramento arrived at Parque Proletário no. 2, in Cajú, just north of central Rio; a third project was built in Leblon in 1943, and a final one in 1947, to house residents evicted from the south-zone Joquei Clube favela.[234]

Vargas himself visited the Gávea project—receiving, with great ceremony, the keys to a provisional house for his personal use—and the plan was hailed by Prefect Henrique Dodsworth and his supporters in the press as "exceeding the optimistic expectation with which it was conceived" and as "one of the happy realities that the Getúlio Vargas government is happy to present as the ripe fruit of its administration."[235]

In the long run, though, these quickly constructed, highly paternalistic projects never housed more than 7,500 people; public employees or people with politically powerful protectors occupied their better units, and the strict rules governing both admission to the projects and the daily rhythms within them probably excluded many prospective residents.[236] By the 1950s, these neglected public housing projects had become barely distinguishable from the surrounding favelas, a fact that opposition politicians across the political spectrum continually hammered home during municipal debates about the favelas' fate.[237] In one typical debate, iconoclastic UDN councilman Breno da Silveira called the Gávea project an "officialized favela" and "an affront to our claim to be a civilized city." Da Silveira went on to describe backed-up septic systems, broken pipes, "nauseating" odors, and broken-down houses—in sum, "an atmosphere of misery and abandonment." He described the Leblon project as a "concentration camp."[238]

Though the Parques Proletários failed to solve the favela "problem," they did signal the beginning of a period in which favela-related discourse and policy became more complex and contradictory. In the 1940s and 1950s, social service workers, religious organizations, politicians, academics, and even some urban planners and public health officials began to voice what favela residents themselves had been arguing for decades: namely, that favelas were home mainly to hardworking people whose economic circumstances left them few other residential choices; that ties of work, family, and community could not be broken without profound disruption of residents' lives; and that resolving the favela dilemma was an enormous and complex task that could not be carried out by a police order and a few strategically lighted matches.

Favela residents themselves forced some of this change; through letters to politicians, demonstrations, and press interviews, they made their views impossible to ignore. But the motivations for new elite views could also be more practical. In a particularly insightful 1953 article, Alberto Passos Guimarães pointed out that it would take 605 million bricks, 180,000 doors, and 90,000 windows to replace just a third of Rio's 90,000 shacks; in the face of that reality, he suggested that observers begin to look at the favelas less as a problem and more as an emergency solution to an extremely complex dilemma.[239] His arithmetic echoed that of municipal politicians, who made similar calculations from the municipal council floor throughout the late 1940s. In other cases, ideology or political opportunism drove changing policies—communists saw revolution in the *morros*, and populists saw votes. Religion, too, played its role, as Catholics from both the left and the anti-communist right increasingly understood advocacy for the poor as part of their mission. Throughout this period, reams of detailed censuses and studies made it harder for a thoughtful public to sustain a stereotype of the favelas as nests of vice, laziness, and immorality.

In the short term, all of this brought some departures in policy. Even during the Vargas era, politicians had regularly struck bargains with favela residents, granting small favors such as water spigots and electrical wires, brokering the settlement of publicly owned lands, and even guaranteeing permanence to the Mangueira favela, already famed as a birthplace of samba.[240] With the dawn of the populist republic, this haphazard service provision accelerated to the point where there was hardly a favela without a tiny bit of public infrastructure; the personal "protection" of one or several favelas became a critical part of any politician's local strategy.

At the same time, more systematic policies came into play. In the 1940s, the Fundação Leão XIII—a joint venture of the Catholic Church and the federal and municipal governments—began a broad-based social service program meant at once to combat communism, to provide health and educational services, and to ideologically "prepare" favela residents for the literal and figurative "urbanization" of their neighborhoods.[241] The Fundação was paternalistic, and many of its actions were rooted in the belief that the physical atmosphere of the *morros* somehow "dehumanized" their residents, making them vulnerable to all sorts of moral and political vice; among its solutions to the favela "problem" was the old suggestion of forced relocation to agricultural colonies.[242] At the same time, by recognizing the humanity of the residents and emphasizing knowledge, education, and urbanization over repression and eviction, the Fundação represented a new attitude. In the end, before its decline in the mid-1950s, the Fundação came to operate in some 34 favelas—including nearly all of the high-profile settlements—and played a vital role in bettering their infrastructure, in providing educational, medical, and juridical aid to their residents, and even in defending a few families against eviction.[243]

In 1955, another Catholic organization, the Cruzada São Sebastião, was founded by Bishop Hélder Câmara to "collaborate in the humane and Christian solution of this city's favela problem . . . through an educational action of community humanization and Christianization, beginning with 'urbanization' as the minimum condition necessary for human existence and moral, intellectual, social, and economic elevation."[244] Early on, the Cruzada accepted a large chunk of federal funding to "urbanize" the Praia do Pinto favela in Leblon; this was the first large-scale, permanent public housing project that did not attempt to "remove" residents from their favela site. By the time the organization's activities died down, in 1960—due largely to political conflicts with the incoming mayor, Carlos Lacerda—it had also presided over the "urbanization" of two other favelas, Morro Azul and Parque da Alegria; the latter transformation was carried out mainly by its residents. The Cruzada negotiated electrical services in some 51 favelas, brought water pipes to 10 more, and negotiated the installation of a dozen public telephones. More critically, especially toward the end of the 1950s, the Cruzada collaborated with residents in organizing neighborhood associations and resistance to court-ordered evictions, especially in the favelas of Borel and Santa Marta.[245] Like the Fundação Leão XIII, the Cruzada São Sebastião was moralistic and paternalistic, especially in its early years, and many of its activities were aimed specifically at undermining communist influence; for these reasons, more radical favela leaders often greeted it with cynicism. But the Cruzada's vision of the favelas' permanence, and of their residents' right to organize, represented a significant step toward giving communities a voice in the governmental programs that were meant to determine their fates.[246]

In the 1960s, two organizations pushed the notions of humanity, self-development, and permanence still further. The Serviço Especial de Recuperação das Favelas e Habitações Anti-Higiênicas (SERFHA), founded in 1956 by the municipal government, meant, as its name suggests, to deal not only with the favelas but also with the full range of extralegal housing within Rio's borders.[247] Initially starved of funds, the organization emerged in 1960, under the direction of José Artur Rios, with the clear philosophy of providing resources to strengthen residents' own organizational and practical capacities; the effort was dubbed Operação Mutirão."[248] SERFHA was a catalyst in building a network of mostly independent neighborhood associations in 75 of Rio's favelas, and in providing critical legal and organizational assistance in the struggle to promote on-site urbanization.[249] Carlos Lacerda abruptly fired Rios and shut down SERFHA's actions in 1962. But efforts to encourage urbanization and service provision were revitalized by Governor Negrão de Lima in 1968, in part as a bid for autonomy from the military government. The resulting Companhia de Desenvolvimento Comunitário (CODES-CO) was largely responsible for the urbanization of the long-embattled Brás de Pina favela in the north zone, and was one of the few institutional advocates of community permanence during the military years.

Through all of these organizations, some of Rio's favelas gained some incremental signals of urban belonging—light, pavement, water, schools, clinics, and soccer fields. But, with very few exceptions, the legacy of the organizations' actions was neither security nor permanence; few of the improvements were so extensive or expensive that they could not be swept away from one day to the next, and the fundamental building, health, and property statutes that outlawed the favelas remained in place. Even organizations as comparatively progressive as SERFHA were simply brokers that negotiated sufferance; none was a social agency that guaranteed rights.

None of this would have mattered much had the liberalization of attitudes toward favelas been generalized. But older ideas about degeneracy and social danger did not die out in the 1940s. Indeed, even as the Fundação Leão XIII began its work in 1947, a municipal commission charged with the favelas' "extinction" elaborated the city's first comprehensive favela census. Its widely read introduction, published in 1949, highlighted fears of racial degeneracy and social marginality, stating: "It is not surprising that *pretos* and *pardos* predominate in the favelas. Backward by virtue of heredity, without ambition, and badly adjusted to the social necessities of modern life, they form the largest contingent among the lowest classes in all of our urban nuclei."[250] In the municipal council during the same period, though such overt racism was rare, debates raged about the degree to which favelas resulted from necessity or from dereliction. Though politicians were usually careful to point out that some *favelados* were hardworking and honest, most argued simultaneously that the favelas facilitated "the formation of *malandros, metidos e valentes* (rascals, meddlers, and bullies)"; that their atmosphere "damaged the development of families"; and that they were the source "of the dispersion of criminals." Most often, the favelas' elimination was justified by the supposed ability of these bad elements to exploit the communities' emotionally and intellectually vulnerable populations.[251] In 1947, councilman Luís Paes Leme indicated the degree to which shame also drove some favela policies, noting that the favela problem constituted "a case of public calamity" that had to be solved "or we will be considered a barbarous people, because in a city like Rio de Janeiro, 20 meters from a skyscraper, we find uninhabitable flea dens, men living in the Stone Age."[252]

In the 1950s, the authors of an influential favela study blended racism with new currents of developmentalism and marginality theory, lamenting the supposed inability of "Neolithic" rural migrants and ex-slaves to overcome their backwardness and join a productive proletariat.[253] In the 1960s, trepidation increased in the wake of updated psychosocial theories connecting favela residence with social pathology and the disintegration of the family.[254] Throughout the period, fear of communist infiltration of the *morros* shaped outsiders' opinions of them; their supposedly ignorant and manipulable populations, their proximity to sites of wealth and political power, and the ways in which they symbolized the failure of

Brazilian capitalism all contributed to the settlements' perceived political perniciousness.

These attitudes served as the backdrop for a series of repressive measures, formal and informal, that worked at precise cross-purposes with the urbanization plans developed by the Fundação Leão XIII, the Cruzada de São Sebastião, and SERFHA. For most of the Vargas era and the Postwar Republic, these measures were generally small in scale; demands for mass deportations to the countryside never materialized, and, as chapter 8 will detail, favela residents themselves ensured the political impossibility of a general *bota-abaixo* (razing) such as the one that had been carried out by Pereira Passos. But smaller threats loomed constantly. Self-proclaimed property owners often received help from police in expelling residents of even the largest favelas, with or without judicial orders.[255] The health service, too, regularly "removed" small favelas and bits of larger ones, sometimes in response to neighbors' complaints, and often with little notice.[256] In 1941, for example, 44 residents of a small dockside shanty settlement described their imminent eviction in a letter sent to President Vargas:

> Your Excellency, we . . . residents of the São Cristóvão Beach, on the border of the Mineiro docks, approach you very respectfully in order to communicate . . . that we have been served with a notice from the General Secretary of Aviation, the Municipal Prefecture, and the Department of Health Inspection ordering us to evacuate this land within 15 days. . . . If we do not fulfill this order, we will be summarily evicted as stipulated by the law. We know very well that this land is not ours, but we are here because we cannot pay rent on a house, and our salaries are low, and the owners of houses will not allow us to rent there, because we have many children. We also have our children enrolled in nearby schools, and all are learning skills. If this terrible thing happens, it will cause us great harm and enormous difficulty. We are many families living here, hoping that Your Excellency and your Worthy administration will take the necessary steps.[257]

Neither Vargas nor Prefect Henrique Dodsworth did much to assist these or other petitioners, who wrote repeatedly with similar dilemmas over the course of the 1930s and 1940s; at most, the municipal government would resettle residents in another shantytown or on abandoned public lands far from Rio's center. This pattern continued in the Postwar Republic. In the late 1940s, for example, future favela leader Lúcio de Paula Bispo recalled being forced abruptly from an ephemeral shantytown near the south side of the Botafogo beach. By his account, municipal workers simply herded residents aboard trucks and dumped them (and what they had been able to preserve of their building materials and meager possessions) in the midst of a swampy, muddy plain near the Avenida Brasil.[258] Throughout the 1950s, municipal councilmen made an issue of the small evictions that were threatened within their jurisdictions, and references to such expulsions appeared frequently in newspapers and police records. The archives of Guanabara Governor Carlos Lacerda contain almost no appeals for clemency, but they do contain frequent eviction requests, most of which seem to have been honored.[259]

With Lacerda's ascension to the governorship, in 1960—and, later, with the 1964 coup—these incremental policies hardened into large-scale expulsions, or *remoções*. Lacerda's engagement with the favela issue had its roots in the 1940s, when he launched the Batalha do Rio de Janeiro, a spectacular but ultimately ineffectual journalistic campaign that sought an energetic collective solution to the favela crisis, but ended instead in a morass of political one-upmanship and demagoguery.[260] In those early writings, and in his service as a city council member, Lacerda voiced a firm but still somewhat sympathetic opposition to the favelas. As governor, Lacerda still sometimes demonstrated a measured populism in his favela policies, especially in communities with a strong symbolic presence, such as the samba archetype Mangueira; his archives also demonstrate numerous small projects concerned with bettering specific favelas.

But Lacerda's presidential ambitions, and his alliances with conservative Catholic and business interests (which included civil construction), tempered such initiatives.[261] After 1962, as a centerpiece of his administration, Lacerda pursued a bold policy of eviction and resettlement, coordinated by the Companhia de Habitação Popular do Estado de Guanabara (COHAB), with substantial funding from US-AID. Marshaling the on-site infrastructure of a revitalized Fundação Leão XIII (now officially a state agency), COHAB eliminated parts of 29 favelas in the years between 1961 and 1965; all in all, some 6,290 families, or more than 31,000 people, were evicted.[262] Nearly all of the affected favelas were located on potentially valuable public lands in the south zone or along the Avenida Brasil. Most of the residents, after passing through an evaluation of their suitability, were sent to one of several grandiosely named housing projects that were constructed in the far north and west of the city: the "Vilas" Kennedy, Aliança (Alliance), Esperança (Hope) and eventually Cidade de Deus (City of God). Ironically, Lacerda, as a city council representative in the late 1940s, had spoken out repeatedly against these sorts of resettlements, arguing that it made little sense to rip residents from their communities and workplaces.[263]

After the military coup, these municipal evictions were amplified by a number of federal programs spearheaded by the National Habitation Bank (BNH) and the Coordenação de Habitação de Interesse Social (CHISAM). The result was the complete or partial "removal" of between 50 and 60 favelas, home to around 100,000 people; residents were mostly sent to distant housing complexes, and the communities' lands were quickly filled by hotels and luxury highrises.[264] According to Lacerda and his allies, the *remoções* of the early 1960s were a bold break with more than 20 years of equivocation and corruption, a long-overdue confrontation with the "demagogues" and "communists" who had "profited from other people's misery" throughout the Postwar Republic, condemning the *favelados* to lives of misery. Lacerda's chief deputy, Sandra Cavalcanti, outlined the policies' benefits with reference to voguish notions about the influence of environment on personality:

> *Remoção* would take favela residents from their *context* [sic]. The favela, their habits, their customs, their upbringing—all of this represented the *favelado*'s conditioning. It would be great to free him of that. Change his previous attitude. Change his behavior. Create, for him, new customs, new ways of being, new atmospheres.[265]

Sympathetic newspapers portrayed the *remoções* as fairy-tale endings for the *favelados*. In December of 1964, for example, the *Globo* described the controversial partial razing of the north-zone community of Brás de Pina as an escape from the favela's "putridness and promiscuity." The paper celebrated the "happiness that rose from the mud" with a photo essay contrasting the filthy, unpaved streets of the favela with the wide, clean expanses of the housing project.[266] In the sanitized reports of *remoções* submitted by COHAB and other agencies, any dissent was said to be the work of demagogues and of those pitiful enough to be fooled by them; for every rare *favelado* who did not wish to leave the favela, they claimed, there were dozens who were aching for a spot in the sparkling new developments.[267]

Some residents did welcome the removals, and demand for COHAB's shiny new apartments seems to have been high, especially among people who already lived in the distant suburbs, and in much worse conditions.[268] But among those whose livelihood and community was centered in the regions around their favela homes, the reaction was mostly fierce resistance. They viewed the new houses and apartments as too small, distant, and expensive, and they resented the dismantling of their family and community networks. They also pointed out, correctly, that the programs only aimed to resettle "qualified" residents, leaving the rest to a nightmarish maze of temporary lodgings.[269] During the relatively open years before 1968, residents brought these complaints to the center of the public stage—camping out in front of the governor's palace, demanding audiences with Lacerda and President Castello Branco, and physically resisting the dismantling of their homes. The confrontations were frequently violent. In a particularly showy 1964 episode, Lacerda himself came to blows with a community religious leader who sought to block the Brás de Pina removal.[270] It took police shock battalions and fire to help the task of *remoção* in the north-zone Esqueleto favela, as well as in Leblon's Praia do Pinto. After the military crackdown of 1968, such public protests died out, but more subtle forms of resistance remained. Some residents simply slipped into neighboring favelas rather than moving to the suburbs; others quietly "passed on" their new homes and returned to favela life after discovering the new projects' shoddy construction, ever-escalating monthly costs, and great distance from most workplaces.[271]

As chapter 8 will detail, residents' protests—themselves the culmination of decades of activism—may well have frustrated elite dreams of freeing Rio from the scourge of its favelas. Indeed, given the prevalence of anti-favela prejudice, the fortunes to be made by redeveloping favela land, and the draconian atmosphere of military Brazil, the survival of dozens of Carioca favelas on prime industrial and residential land is far more remarkable than the *remoções* themselves. All the same, the evictions highlighted the fragility of *favelados'* gains during the Postwar Republic. Favelas had survived, becoming the de facto "solution" to an overwhelming housing crisis; as such, they had gained hard-won bits and pieces of urban comfort. But, like the clandestine suburban subdivisions that received much less attention, favelas remained illegal. That simple fact deprived favela residents of any claim to permanent urban rights and made vulnerability and dependence chronic features of Carioca poverty. Legal, permanent housing—like electricity, water, sewage, and transportation—remained a scarce resource in the marvelous city.

The Morro of Santo Antônio

No single community could encapsulate the mixture of scarcity, fragility, political entanglement, and political activism that characterized life in Rio's illegal cities at mid-century. The settlements ranged from fly-by-night jumbles to long-standing neighborhoods, rooted on their lands for half a century or more. Some were official favelas, others were simply poor; some were populated by tens of thousands, others by only a few hundred. Many were virtual fiefdoms long controlled by speculators, politicians, or both combined; a few were relatively autonomous political communities. The working class dominated numerous *morros*, but most residents in others were informal or even rural workers. Some community leaders proved skilled at the political game, but others failed at it miserably.

All the same, certain commonalities remained. In all of these places, poverty implied not only a lack of material goods but also a lack of rights to the legal city, the literal and figurative bedrock of full national citizenship. Lack of rights reinforced material poverty in the sense that residents received few public goods, and could not profit as non-squatters might have done from investments in "their" property.[272] Evictions destroyed housing materials and household goods and disrupted jobs and educations, often terminally. But as important as rights poverty was in reinforcing material lack, it also exposed deep linkages between class, race, and subcitizenship. The legal vulnerability of Rio's poorest residents helped to sustain a political system in which daily life was only sometimes governed by democratic and legally bounded relationships, and where formally constituted leaders rarely met political demands with officially sanctioned and openly debated policies. For the rights-poor, unofficial networks of power and influence were often critically important, allowing them to remain in the city despite a legal system that pushed them to the margins of urban life. For most poor Cariocas, the most effective politician was not one who worked within the legal system, but one who subverted it. This strategy often ensured survival; its details, and its triumphs, will be explored in Part IV. But it also ingrained extra-legality into the city's power structure, and left residents enormously vulnerable to shifts in ideology and political power.

No place was more emblematic of this vulnerability, and of residents' best efforts to combat it, than the Morro of Santo Antônio, one of the two "hamlets of affliction and destitution" long ensconced in the city's colonial heart.[273] In the name of opening Rio's central districts to light and air, urban planners had slated Santo Antônio for leveling since the late 1800s, sparing it mainly because of a long-running property dispute between the municipality and a private company.[274] Arguably home to the first of Rio's modern favelas—geographer Maurício de Almeida Abreu traces its origins to the aftermath of the Revolta da Armada, in 1893–94—Santo Antônio held nearly 400 shacks by 1901.[275] When sanitary police destroyed the favela that year, settlers quickly rebuilt, only to fall victim to fire, which Prefect Pereira Passos called his "best helper in reforming the city."[276] Regenerated and then ignored for some years, Santo Antônio again faced destruction in 1910, when municipal officials deliberately directed its expelled residents to build their homes on the then distant Morro do Telégrafo, next to what would become the Mangueira favela.[277] Huts had reappeared on Santo Antônio by the mid-1910s, by which point the hill's residents had organized themselves well enough to gain a judicial stay on a new eviction order. The stay proved useless in the wake of another fire, almost surely criminal, that was set in 1916; refugees from that blaze again took refuge in Mangueira and other embryonic favelas. Reborn from the ashes once more, Santo Antônio's shacks generated more bad press in 1919; in 1922, officials again demolished the settlement as part of the general urban spiff-up that preceded the city's centennial celebration.[278] By the early 1930s, Santo Antônio's favela had returned once more, and its residents were mobilizing to prevent another eviction; this time, they wrote to President Vargas himself and pointedly declared their willingness to remain "mute" "in this century of social demands" because of their trust in his "benevolence."[279] Vargas didn't help them, but the hill persevered. By the late 1940s, a former resident of the favela was on the city council, and the *morro*'s inhabitants wrote regularly to politicians, demanding water, services, and protection. In 1950, a city census estimated the *morro*'s population at 2,840.[280]

In the 1950s, however, the city's longtime judicial dispute over the *morro* ended, the urbanistic imperative to "develop" an area long considered a stain on the cityscape grew stronger, and all of the favela's vulnerabilities lay exposed. In the city council, whose members endlessly debated the financial and urbanistic dimensions of the *morro*'s razing, only a few councilmen even mentioned the project's human dimensions.[281] Santo Antônio's residents were far from quiescent—they went to the press, organized themselves along lines set out by communist politicians, and joined the quickly expanding União de Trabalhadores Favelados, the city's first favela federation. The *morro* even found a musical patron in the renowned composer and *sambista* Herivelto Martins. His samba "Morro de Santo Antônio" captured in simple terms the frustration of residents facing another, final, eviction from the hill:

Seu dotô não bote abaixo	Mr. Doctor, don't tear it down
Tem pena do meu barracão	Have pity on my shack
Quem é rico se atrapalha	If rich people have a hard time
Prá arranjar onde morar	finding a place to live
Quanto mais eu que sou pobre	I who am poor even more
Como vou me arrumar	How am I going to get it together
Prá me mudar?	to move away?
Seu dotô não bote abaixo	Mr. Doctor, don't tear it down
Tem pena do meu barracão	Have pity on my little shack
Seu dotô me compreenda	Mr. Doctor, understand me
O progresso é necessário	Progress is necessary
Mas seu dotô	But Mr. Doctor
Pense um pouco no operário	think a little about the worker
Meu barracão é todo meu patrimônio	My shack is my only patrimony
Por favor não bote abaixo	Please don't tear down
O Morro de Santo Antônio	the Morro of Santo Antônio[282]

This time, the samba and all of the residents' activism were no match for the political, urbanistic, and development interests pushing the *morro*'s elimination. In the winter of 1954, bulldozers began to eat away at the hill in earnest. Politicians and the press, preoccupied with the upcoming elections and the disintegration of Vargas's presidency, paid little mind to the residents or their fates. On 4 August 1927, a lone account in the left-leaning *Imprensa Popular* noted that 150 cubic meters of sandy soil had already been hauled away, and that the residents whose homes were next in the shovels' path had been offered nothing but a vague injunction to leave the city and become agriculturalists in the Brazilian interior.[283] Maria do Carmo Cabral, an immigrant from Paraíba do Norte with five children and another on the way, faced the loss of the small store that provided her family's only livelihood. When the reporter asked where she would go when the bulldozers approached, she threw up her hands: "Son, I don't even like to think about it. Who knows? To wherever God wishes." Another woman reportedly hummed a tune current in the *morro*: "Destroy the *morro* / not that! / to sacrifice the people / is heartless." A few weeks later, some 900 heads of families took more

A man observes digging on the Morro do Santo Antônio, where shacks in the background await razing. Courtesy of the Arquivo Geral da Cidade do Rio de Janeiro.

affirmative action, appealing to a leftist municipal councilman, Antenor Marques, to intervene.[284] He encouraged them to organize and force Vargas's government to respect "the sacred right to a home," but to little avail.

By the late 1950s, the Morro de Santo Antônio was gone, its shanty-town destroyed, and its earth appropriated to create the Aterro do Flamengo, a seaside park and expressway stretching from the city center south to Botafogo.[285] With the soil that had grounded their homes now transformed into a middle-class playground, Santo Antônio's residents dispersed to various city favelas; many settled in Leblon's Praia do Pinto or in the northern settlement of Esqueleto, both of which would themselves face violent destruction in the following decades.

PART II

Work, Law, and *Justiça Social* in Vargas's Rio

On the Borders of Social Class

During the first days of 1943, a mother named Ermelinda Soledade Campos wrote to President Getúlio Vargas from her shack in a Carioca favela called Babilônia, just north of Copacabana Beach. The letter's handwriting, spelling, and grammar were uncertain, but there was no mistaking its point:

> The present letter's purpose is only to implore an aid [*auxílio*] for me to rais [sic] my kids. Well I have 13 kids, seven boys and 6 girls, so, seeing myself brok [sic] and unable to give them comfort I send you this appeal to see if I might be happy. Besides this I am a poor invalid. Everyone [*todo povo*] tells me that, going to your prezence (sic), you will give me aid, because of this, knowing that Your Excellency is so generous, I am here to ask you for help I wanted Your Incelency [sic] to favor me at least with a little house to live in because my husband works every day but its not enough even to eat. So, knowing of your benevolence [*bondade*] I come to implore to see if I am happy.

Noting that she trusted "in God and in Your Incelency," and terming herself Vargas's "humblest servant" ("menor criada"), Campos signed off.[1]

It was no small matter for a destitute mother of so many to write such a letter. The composition itself was clearly a struggle, one that carried with it a great risk of humiliation. If Campos was like many others of her era, she probably brought her missive to the presidential palace herself, descending her *morro*'s treacherous paths to the asphalt below and traveling several miles across the city, in hopes of a personal audience with Vargas or his wife. Already by the early 1940s, Babilônia had been repeatedly threatened with eviction, and Campos likely felt in that journey the fear and disdain with which the Carioca population at large viewed the poor of the *morros*.[2] Writing and delivering this letter was a public and political act, and the word of "todo povo" must have been convincing indeed to inspire it.

Campos's saga was not unusual; thousands of equally poor Brazilians wrote to Vargas with similar hopes, and the Brazilian tradition of humble missives to the powerful stretched at least to the reign of the nine-teenth-century emperor Pedro II.[3] But the letter demands attention any-way because it confronted the president with the realities of a growing population of poor Cariocas whose voices were often muted during the Vargas era. These people were urban, but they or their parents had often migrated from desperately poor rural areas, and many were descended from slaves. They were not homeless, for the most part, but their homes were often legally precarious, rarely meeting municipal construction and health standards and most often perched on illegally occupied land. They typically worked hard, but they were rarely employed in the kinds of steady industrial, commercial, and bureaucratic occupations that had been exalted in Vargas's rhetoric since the early 1930s. Many had fami-lies, but the church or state only sometimes sanctified them.

Poorly educated and worse paid, these struggling poor people could hardly be said to constitute a distinct social class. They did not usually identify themselves that way; their occupations varied widely and some-times changed frequently, they rarely coalesced politically around their shared travails, and their lives intersected in countless ways with those of their working-class neighbors, friends, and relatives.[4] But poor people's experience of the Vargas years in some ways forced them to become a group apart. In an era when many working-class Brazilians came for the first time to define their social struggles in terms of rights guaranteed by law and the constitution, this group, alone among urban populations, could not.[5] The very qualities that relegated them to extreme poverty—their difficulty in finding steady, formal employment, their lack of legally constituted family ties, and their relatively weak access to networks of power and influence—also distanced them from Vargas's version of so-cial citizenship. Impoverished by law as well as by economic station, the rights-poor thus lived through the Vargas years with an intense mixture of hope and disillusion. For them, the Vargas era's legacy was the cre-ation of a realm of social and economic rights that was never quite theirs to inhabit. The next two chapters chronicle this ambiguous history, ex-ploring both the bases for poor Cariocas' optimism and the reasons why their faith received such incomplete reward.

CHAPTER THREE

Vargas and the *Voz do Povo*

⌐

Of all Brazil's presidents, none has left so extensive a trove of popular correspondence as Getúlio Vargas. Brazil's archives have preserved thousands of letters written to Vargas from Brazilians from every corner of the country, the first sent shortly after the 1930 revolution and the last at the very end of the Estado Novo. The vast majority came from people who self-identified as "poor workers" or just plain "poor." Some are typed and formal, most likely boilerplate documents composed by informal local scribes for their illiterate neighbors; others are scratched out on scraps of paper, in barely literate prose, and were more probably written by their signatories or those closest to them. The letters are full of antiquated formalities and obsequious phrasing, much of it taken directly from Vargas's speeches or his government's weekly radio addresses. The people who wrote to Vargas nearly always wanted something, and it would thus be a mistake to read their correspondence as a transparent window into the popular political imagination. And yet the letters do reveal a great deal about the ways in which Brazil's poor sought to apply Vargas's words to their own life experiences, tapping into his populist rhetoric in order to better their own concrete circumstances, and feeding with their hope Vargas's reputation as a uniquely generous benefactor. Neither Vargas nor his poorest correspondents may have been entirely sincere in their overtures, but together they created one of Brazil's most enduring political bonds.

One of the most striking qualities of these letters is their intensely personal tone. Among the letters sent from Rio, nearly all begin with the assumption—and the expectation—that Vargas might take a personal interest in the smallest and most private of troubles. "Everyone tells me that, going to your prezence (sic), you will give me aid," wrote Ermelinda Soledade Campos in 1943. A year earlier, José Patricio Barroso—a northern migrant who sold lottery tickets to sustain his family and referred to himself as Vargas's "Servant and Respector" ("Criado e Respeitador" (sic))—explained that he had the "audacity" to write because he knew "from the voice of the people" ("voz do povo") that Vargas "attends to everyone" ("a todos atende").[6] Another "Servant and Ademirer" ("Criado e Ademirador" [sic]) named Francisco Alipio de Menezes wrote in October of 1940, appealing for help in part because he knew "from the voice of the people that your Exclency [sic] is very Humanitarian" ("por voz do povo que vc. Exclia. é muito Umanitario" [sic]).[7] Jaime Figueira da Silva, a "desperate father" from Paraná, explained as a postscript that his letter had been written for him out of pity by a "cidadão" who assured him that "his appeal would not be in vain, as he knows many identical episodes that the illustrious president's great heart had resolved."[8] In 1939, Candido Francisco Egsindola, a low-level public health inspector, sent a letter that included a newspaper clipping of Vargas (one of five treasured in his home, all of them "totems of comfort" for him) and a tattered bit of Brazil's yellow-and-green flag. Outlining his family's desperate straits, he explained that he was writing because Vargas was "humanitarian president number one" who "would not let a child of the country go hungry."[9]

Sincere, strategic, or both, these appeals left little doubt that a broad spectrum of the Carioca popular classes viewed Vargas as a president who was—or who at least liked to be portrayed as—generous, humanitarian, and kind. This reputation has endured well after Vargas's 1954 suicide. Speaking in 2003, Odilia dos Santos Gama—an 82-year-old woman who had lived in the Babilônia favela community since 1938—recalled Vargas as a president who "liked the poor" ("gostava dos pobre" [sic]), noting that she used to listen to him on the radio and cried on the day he died.[10] Abdias José dos Santos—a 67-year-old northeastern migrant who came to Rio in 1952, went on to work in shipbuilding and industry, and emerged as a prominent favela leader in the early 1960s—recalled attending Vargas's independence and labor day rallies in 1950s Rio. He remembered the president's personal affection for the poor, and stated that with Vargas (implicitly in contrast to other politicians) "credibility existed" ("existia credibilidade").[11]

O PAI DOS POBRES

The entirely unmysterious origins of this reputation were a deliberate alchemy of propaganda, rhetoric, legislative deed, and orchestrated charity. Vargas was not a charismatic political personality.[12] But he was one of the first in Brazil to make the plight of the working poor central to his politics, emphasizing above all the concept of "social equality," whereby all laboring Brazilians had a right to basic dignity and subsistence in exchange for their contributions to Brazil's national greatness.[13] As president and dictator (1930–1945), Vargas offered Brazilian "workers" considerable material benefits—at least on paper—in the form of reams of legislation, eventually brought together in the Consolidação das Leis do Trabalho (Consolidation of Labor Laws, or CLT) in 1943.[14] He also took great pains to laud poor workers and their labors as fundamentally valuable and dignified, the cornerstones of Brazil's national greatness.[15] Though both of these gestures incorporated themes culled from decades of working-class activism,[16] they were most often presented as acts of personal generosity, aimed at elevating "the great mass of workers to the full dignity of their human condition" and eliminating "the divisive inequalities that separate societies into two distinct groups, people and subpeople."[17] Government propaganda also lauded Vargas's more limited initiatives to expand charity and "social service," claiming that they were created by Vargas himself "spontaneously," "to diminish or eliminate the deficiencies and sufferings caused by poverty and economic misery."[18]

Vargas's actions took on personal immediacy after 1937, when government speeches and propaganda broadcast the president's desire "to receive from the *povo*, directly, their complaints, hear them and examine them. . . ."[19] He made good on this promise throughout his administration, not only reading a good number of the letters that were sent to him but also acting on a great many.[20] Such actions were selective and often carefully publicized. On 20 March 1942, for instance, Labor Minister Alexandre Marcondes Filho devoted an entire radio address on the "Hora do Brasil" to Vargas's response to "a grievous story" contained in a letter written by an unnamed mutilation victim ("mutilado") who had lost both his arms in a 1909 railroad accident.[21] In Marcondes Filho's careful reconstruction, the man's woes illustrated the injustices of Brazil's First Republic; incapacitated for work, he received no recompense, because the law guaranteed him none. Luckily for the man, however, the Catete Palace now "was inhabited by a will of steel, at the service of a velvet heart"; at Getúlio Vargas's personal order, a solution was found, based, not accidentally, on the railroad company's "voluntary" acquiescence to the president's moral imperative.[22] Marcondes Filho concluded his address by calling the case "a jewel of public administration in which the president of the republic once more reveals his exceptional qualities as a protector of Brazil's workers."

The people who wrote to Vargas professed faith in such constructions, whether or not they actually believed them; given that they wrote with hopes of material help, and in an atmosphere, especially after 1937, of severe political repression, their flattering words cannot be taken entirely at face value.[23] But they do at least reveal the widespread dissemination of Vargas's carefully honed image. Governmental propaganda was not all-encompassing: the sycophantic books and speeches published by the Department of Press and Propaganda (DIP) had limited circulation; charitable requests were more often denied than granted; the administration's much lauded daily radio programs probably had less appeal than was once assumed; and newspaper transcripts of radio broadcasts, speeches, and rallies reached only literate individuals who had the money to buy newspapers and the leisure time to read them.[24] Nonetheless, these letters indicate that the word on Rio's streets was that, at the very least, Vargas wanted to be regarded as paternalistic and generous and was prepared to back up this image with concrete help. Carioca letter writers seemed to believe that if only they could weave their own life stories into the larger tapestry of national perdition and redemption that was the very fabric of the Vargas government's public statements, they just might gain a foothold in the still unfamiliar and mystified terrain of "social equality."

Accordingly, their letters integrated familiar themes into strikingly patterned narratives. Correspondents asked for all sorts of help: ship's passage to return to distant families and birthplaces; places for their children in schools and orphanages; houses and land; public sector jobs and promotions; and, above all, the benefits of specific social and labor laws. They also came from all walks of life; while most described themselves, generically, as "poor," occupationally they filled the spectrum, from public employees and petty businessmen to factory and transportation workers to washerwomen, street vendors, and day laborers. Some were rural migrants, some were foreign immigrants, and some were native Cariocas. But the stories of the poorest among them converged in a familiar autobiographical chorus: these were people who worked hard, struggling against myriad difficulties, and who sought valiantly and sometimes desperately to feed, protect, and educate their families, often explicitly for Brazil's greater good.[25]

Typical was a letter sent by Maria da Gloria Silva Varela, a mother of two who wrote from a downtown rooming house in June 1940.[26] Although Varela wrote seeking places in a public boarding school for her two boys, her letter did not open with a direct request.[27] Instead, she began by recounting her hardships and lining up her credentials as a mother, a worker, and a Brazilian. Ill enough to have had two operations in public emergency rooms, "with a tendency toward more," Varela wrote that she "had worked a lot" all the same, "in order to sustain [her] family." Her husband, Domingo Caetano da Silva, "also hardworking, like me" was a "common worker" ("operário comum") who labored when he could despite being "very, very sick" ("muitissimo doente" [sic]). The couple had two sons, 10 and 11 years of age, who, for lack of money, had never gone to school—though they did, Varela noted with some pride, know how to read and write. Might a place be found for them in a federal or municipal boarding school? They were "intelligent, perhaps two future servants of the great Brazilian nation," and they were also "sons of two workers; a class that is generally known to ADORE V.Ex." because of the "improvements" and "social laws" Vargas had "dispensed." Varela signed off by metaphorically kissing Vargas's hands.

Anyone who read the papers or listened to the radio in the 1930s and 1940s would have found parts of Varela's story very familiar, especially her emphasis on work, family, and patriotism, and the sense in which social laws and benefits were "dispensed" by an "adored" Vargas. The valorization of labor overwhelmingly dominated Vargas's appeals to the poor, urban and rural alike. Previous governments had placed a negative emphasis on work, enforcing vagrancy laws and blaming the worst sorts of urban poverty on laziness and improvidence.[28] But Vargas's appeals were different. They incorporated themes of dignity and masculinity that had long been present in the rhetoric of Brazil's radical working-class movements,[29] and they rejected the degradation that had been associated with work since the slave era.[30] Along these lines, Paulo de Madeyros, in a hagiographic account of Vargas's social reforms, wrote:

> The new social policy has only one objective: to make the divisive inequalities between the human and the subhuman disappear. In conclusion, it intends to elevate the great mass of workers "to the full dignity of their human condition." This is the only relevant role of the Modern State, with its policies aimed at protecting the worker. This is what President Getúlio Vargas is realizing; he is creating an honorable role in society for the worker, through a system of laws and institutions that serve to maintain the equilibrium of society. The government gives itself entirely to this goal of social justice.[31]

For Vargas's government, however, work was not only an individual attribute; it was also a fundamental element of patriotism, the action that made a man worthy of citizenship, the gesture that lifted him above his individual egoism and placed him in the service of society, the step that locked him into Brazil's march toward greatness.[32] Vargas stated in a 1940 May Day speech:

> Despite Brazil's vastness, the abundance of its natural resources, and the variety of its ways of life, the future of the country lies entirely in our capacity for accomplishment. Every *trabalhador,* whatever his occupation, is in this respect a patriot who adds his individual effort to the collective action in favor of the economic independence of our nation. Our progress cannot be only the work of the government; rather, it is the work of the Nation, of all the classes, of all the men and women who ennoble themselves through work, valorizing the land in which they were born.[33]

The Estado Novo's 1937 constitution formalized this melding of work and nationalism, defining work as a "social obligation" that deserved "the protection and solicitude of the State," and guaranteeing every Brazilian the right "to subsist by means of honest work."[34] The 1946 constitution, too, reified work as a component and a right of citizenship, stating: "Everyone is assured work that allows a dignified existence. Work is a social obligation."[35] The 1943 CLT, Brazil's most important twentieth-century compilation of labor laws, also explicitly connected the social and economic rights of citizenship to an individual's willingness and ability to work for a living.[36] But the emphasis on work as a civic duty, a nation-building activity, could extend also to lesser realms of policy, and especially to schools, worker-training institutes, and social service agencies. In this spirit, for example, the municipal government taught the following ode to the children of the *Parques Proletários*, the failed public housing projects that were intended to replace Rio's favelas in the early 1940s:

Oração ao Trabalho	Prayer to Work
Nas minhas mãos a ferramenta canta	In my hands, the tool sings
Canta minha alma um hino varonil	My soul sings a manly hymn
quando o sol na alvorada se levanta	when the sun rises in the dawn
dourando os céus e terras do Brasil	making gold the skies and lands of Brazil
Minha Pátria brasileira	My Brazilian homeland
dou-te quanto valho:	I give you what I'm worth
—coragem, sangue e suor!	—courage, blood, and sweat!
Por isso, canto e trabalho	This is why I sing and work
para ver nossa Bandeira	to see our Flag
sempre mais bela e maior!	always greater and more beautiful!
Nesta Oração de Fé, que enche a oficina	In this ode of Faith, which fills the workshop
E sobe a Deus, num preito juvenil,	and rises to God, in a juvenile homage
Celebramos a Pátria, ampla e divina	we celebrate the Homeland, great and divine
Trabalhando com amor, pelo Brasil!	working with love for Brazil![37]

The government might inspire such sentiments, but the family would inculcate them. Thus the home, too, figured prominently in Vargas's regime, and especially in his legislative initiatives and social assistance policies. Vargas's government articulated a clear, conservative, and largely catholic vision of the family's social role, in which the home would be the cradle and laboratory of Brazilian virtues, patriotism and the work ethic chief among them. As one official put it, "The family is the foundation, the elemental and organic base of the State. . . . The perfection and civilization of the State depends fundamentally on the moral and legal conditions of each of the families that constitute it."[38] Labor Minister Marcondes Filho highlighted the carefully delineated role of women in creating this idealized family, emphasizing the need to "protect" the *operária* from any function that might interfere with her natural role as "the devoted companion of the worker, the *senhora* of the proletarian home," and stressing her auxiliary function in the masculine world of work and politics.[39] In the spirit of such rhetoric, the 1934, 1937, and 1946 constitutions all declared the family to be under the specific protection of the state. A number of initiatives also aimed to restrict women's work and improve the physical and moral well-being of the Brazilian family, "in order," in the words of one observer, "to ensure the country new generations, healthy and strong in their patriotism as builders of the New Brazil."[40]

Rooming-house resident Maria da Gloria Silva Varela echoed this vision when she noted that she worked in order to sustain her family, when she made sure Vargas knew that she had taught her children to read and write, and when she asked that they be put in school so as to serve "the great Brazilian nation." Dozens of other missivists used similar language, none so precisely as a sparsely employed glass-factory named Evaristo de Muniz Coelho, who wrote in 1940 because he did not have the "resources necessary for the education and adequate nutrition that might satisfy the needs of [his] children's physical development, in order to make them future men and women useful as particles of our great and prosperous Brazil, which V. Excia. directs so well and with such reasoning and patriotism."[41]

This last phrase highlights a final way in which Vargas's rhetoric shaped the requests of Coelho, Varela, and others like them. When Varela wrote of social laws as being "dispensed" by Vargas, when she appealed to him personally, when she spoke of workers who "adored" him, she was tapping into a carefully cultivated story line. Before Vargas, according to this narrative, workers had lived victimized and helpless, prey to vicious capitalists and landlords, vulnerable to inappropriate "foreign" ideologies, and entirely unable to claim their own dignity. Urban workers lived

> fatigued, sordid, ragged, exhausted by work and malnutrition, entirely distant from the ministers of the State, living in dark attics, lacking the most elemental resources of individual and collective hygiene, oppressed by their deficient salaries, anguished by their unstable employment, tormented by the uncertainty of the future—their own and their offspring's—crippled by accidents suffered without compensation, beaten down by illness without aid, tortured in the desperation of disability and old age without bread, without shelter, and without hope.[42]

Rural workers were worse off still; speaking of Brazil's countryside after the abolition of slavery, Vargas stated in a 1932 speech:

> Flourishing zones, tamed by the force of the submissive Negro, were transformed into scrub-forests [*catingas*], where impoverished rural populations vegetate uprooted, at the mercy of the climate's inconstancies and of their own lack of re-

sources, sometimes almost nomads, living day to day, yoked to the voracity of the new masters [*senhores*] who exploit their crude labor, as if they were latter-day serfs of the soil.[43]

Vargas's ascent, seen in this light, marked a watershed in Brazil's history; his generosity and paternalism allowed the laboring classes to awaken from their monotonous and brutalized existence and become worker-citizens.[44] In 1940, even before the CLT had assumed its final form, Vargas declared victory, listing all of the measures the government had already enacted for the urban working classes and proclaiming: "The working man in Brazil can now consider himself an element perfectly integrated into social life. He has grown in political dignity and has come to see his effort stabilized, with his present and his children's futures now secure.[45]

In most of the letters written to Vargas, some version of this story appears; supplicants, buoyed by perceptions of Vargas's "humanitarian" nature and "just" laws, expressed the hope that he would perform in their own lives the miracles he claimed to have brought to the Brazilian worker.

WORK AND SOCIAL VALUE

The poor Cariocas who wrote to Vargas often tapped into his language and framed their lives with his story lines, responding to widely publicized images of Vargas as a humanitarian "father of the poor." But their letters did not simply parrot back concepts and stories spoon-fed to them through rumors and propaganda. Indeed, the special appeal of work, family, and patriotism as unifying concepts lay in their deep resonance with long-standing popular values and habits. In appropriating these capacious notions and filling them with meanings that made sense in the context of their personal life stories, correspondents presented Vargas not with fawning appeals but rather (or also) with challenges and rebukes. By their own definitions, they were workers who gave sustenance to family and nation. If Vargas meant what he said, then they, too, should find in his redemptive story line the path to social equality, or at least to a life less miserably hard. Thus interpreted, the letters reveal a powerful collective vision of what Vargas's rhetoric ought to have meant, from the point of view of Rio's poorest populations. In the distance between that interpretation and the one written into Vargas-era legislation lay the institutional bases of unequal citizenship in modern Brazil.

Not surprisingly, Vargas's correspondents took great pains to describe their dedication to hard work. It is easy to imagine that the Carioca poor adopted such language for strictly strategic purposes. Elite culture offered abundant motivation to disdain manual labor, which had been considered a stain of dishonor in the Iberian world for centuries, and was a brand of servile status in colonial and imperial Brazil.[46] But poor people would hardly have needed elite indoctrination to hate work that was often forced, by slavery and necessity before 1888 and by need and police coercion thereafter.[47] In the 1930s and 1940s, many among the Carioca poor were the children and grandchildren of slaves; in some modern oral accounts of this era, it is striking how often work is described in terms of its similarity to bondage. Speaking in 1995, Maria da Conceição Ferreira Pinto—an elderly community activist and ex–domestic servant from the south-zone favela Chapeu Mangueira, who was known as "Dona Filinha"—described an abusive domestic employer as a woman who "queria a gente como escravo" ("wanted us to be like slaves").[48] Dona Filinha finally walked out when the woman attempted to hit her because a pair of pants had come back stained from the cleaners. She recalled her reaction: "I said to her, not with me you don't, slavery is finished, I am not a slave, if you want to do that [hit someone], you do it with your daughter. You look here, your daughter is white, and I am black, really black. And I'm not staying here for a single minute more."[49] Dona Filinha's grandmother had been a slave in Minas Gerais, and she recalled vividly stories about the older woman's experience. Another Minas migrant and long-time Chapeu Mangueira resident, Lúcio de Paula Bispo, used similar language to describe his own early working experiences in Minas and Rio.[50]

Similarities to bondage were often marked in the types of work that the Carioca poor were able to obtain, especially if they were of African descent. The pay barely allowed subsistence; hours were long or, in the case of domestic service, unspecified; and job stability was virtually nonexistent. Some of these jobs gave poor people access to important networks of personal influence and patronage, but others did not, and even the strongest bonds of patronage were easily abused.[51] Work injuries were frequent and uncompensated, and social mobility over a lifetime was limited.[52] While workers often developed considerable skill over the years, their expertise was rarely recognized or compensated. For mature women, these issues were intensified by the fact that the need to work could itself be viewed as a failure, a signal of a man's inability to provide for his family or a woman's inability to hold on to a man. For all women, work outside the home also implied a threatening degree of independence and physical mobility.[53]

Little wonder, in this context, that work was hardly glorified in poor people's public cultural expressions, especially before the Estado Novo. The Carioca *malandro* (vagabond) of popular legend was emblematic, if mostly fantastic. Debonair, witty, and elegant, he lived in the shadows of all that was legal and bourgeois, always able to escape from poverty through his wits rather than giving in to the punishing routine of the *otário*, the beast of burden who barely survived through the harsh drudgery of wage work.[54] As many have pointed out, the *malandro* was the carnivalesque inversion of everything slavish in a poor man's life, a figure who used all the cracks and crevices in the system of cultural and class oppression to escape the injustices inherent, not necessarily in work itself, but in labor as practiced in an unequal and exploitative economy.[55]

By the 1920s, the *malandro* had become a standard reference in everything from literature to police discourse, but his figurative home was the samba, where he reigned supreme both as a producer of the music and as the protagonist of its playful but often dead-on critiques of official ideals of work, recreation, love, and community. Oliveira Dias's 1928 "Vagabundo (samba da Gamboa)" was typically lighthearted in its celebration of *malandro* life, but its comic tone was darkened by a bitter evaluation of work's role in the typical poor man's life:

Não sou amigo do trabalho	I am no friend of work
Viver só quero na orgia	I only want to live in revelry
Trabalho não dá futuro	Work doesn't lead to a future
Tira a força e alegria	It just sucks out vigor and joy
Oh! Que folia	Oh! What frolic
Gosto da vida do malandro	I like *malandro* life
Tenho paixão pelo baralho	I have a passion for cards
Frequento tascas e tendinhas	I go to low-class taverns and shops
Morro de fome, meu bem	I die of hunger, my dear
Mas não trabalho	but I don't work
Oh! Que gente séria	Oh! What serious people
Que gente pachola	What vain people
Mata para roubar	They kill in order to rob
Mas não pede esmola	but they don't ask for charity
Quem inventou o trabalho	Whoever invented work
Não foi cabra batisado	was not a baptized ruffian
Se o trabalho é honra	If work is honor
O burro é o mais honrado	then the jackass is the most honored creature of all
Oh! Que pecado	Oh! What a sin
Tive um parente no mundo	I had a relative in this world
Que viveu sempre acochado	who was always living under pressure
No fim de noventa anos	At the end of 90 years
Morreu pobre, meu bem	he died poor, my dear
E desgraçado!	and wretched![56]

Samba women most often expressed *malandragem* through promiscuity or manipulations of the heart, frequently rejecting *otários* in favor of the *orgia*, a betrayal that served to highlight the futility of poor men's labor. In other ways, too, women of the samba universe lamented work; the melancholy drudgery of the washerwoman's labor haunted many lyrics.[57] Women who cracked the norms of hard work, motherhood, and spousal fidelity were rarely glorified or celebrated as the male *malandros* were, but *sambistas* did paint their experience of work from a melancholy palette.

Samba, though, was a complex expression of popular sentiment, as much about possible social orders as about real ones. Apparent critiques of work itself could also be read, more subtly, as damnations of a system where work was not adequately or justly valued. Indeed, in other settings, while poor people often bemoaned exploitative working conditions, they just as frequently voiced work's necessity and even its virtue, both as a key to navigating the formal and informal systems that governed Brazilian public life and as an indicator of responsibility to family and community. Work was certainly a daily drudgery imposed by ideology, economics, and public force. Yet it was also the ubiquitous reality of most poor people's daily lives, not just an imposed duty but also the central activity in a nexus of personal and material relationships. In practical terms, paid work meant the difference between bearable poverty and desperate misery; by working, a man—or even a woman—signaled energy, vitality, and the ability to care for dependents and contribute to community well-being. Whatever the *sambistas* might have sung, these qualities were intensely valued among poor people whose very survival often hung in their balance.[58]

Nevertheless, during the Estado Novo—a time when the repressive political climate forced even samba composers to abandon glorification of the *malandro* in favor of odes to labor—it is tempting to dismiss poor people's praise of work as derivative of official political ideologies.[59] Vargas's equation of work with virtue among the poor was widespread among the Brazilian elite by the 1930s, and it derived from deep historical currents. Already in the nineteenth century, Brazil was heir to centuries of Western Christian social thought that separated the deserving poor from the deviant on the basis of their ability and willingness to work.[60] These ideas were coercively reinforced after abolition, when elite fears about the "natural" indolence and deviance of Afro-Brazilians led to the enactment of invigorated vagrancy laws (meant at once to be a method of labor procurement and an instrument of social control) and helped make affirmations of diligence a fundamental ingredient in the public defense of any poor man's character.[61] With entirely different motives, turn-of-the-century labor activists also encouraged poor people to value work culturally and politically, equating labor with dignity, honesty, and masculinity.[62] This tied in easily with centuries of Mediterranean thought that equated a man's honor with his ability to provide for and protect his family, but it also served the specific goals of labor politics.[63]

Without doubt, this barrage of outside incitements to praise and practice work shaped the ways that the Carioca poor thought and spoke, especially in public settings; only the ignorant or foolish would have failed to understand that professions of hard work were key to poor people's public credibility and even their physical freedom.[64] Accordingly, especially when such statements meshed seamlessly with official ideologies, they must be read cautiously, less as indications of private values than as strategic words chosen to advance people's interests in the public realm. Carioca correspondence with Vargas should obviously be analyzed with this in mind, as should criminal cases, which are so often a rich source of popular social history.[65] When a defendant in a vagrancy case pleaded his innocence with attestations that he had done his best to work despite adversity, his words hardly constituted proof that work was an important internal value, no matter how compelling the circumstances.[66] Similarly, when a young man accused of deflowering a young woman made character arguments based on his work ethic and professional reputation, or slandered his accuser with reference to the sullying freedom she had assumed because her mother worked outside of the home, his words did not necessarily express genuine work values or gender norms; they are more effectively read as a part of a tale engineered to seem plausible to policemen, prosecutors, and judges.[67] The same logic applies to the innumerable criminal cases in which references to a hardworking character constituted a core defense strategy.

The fact that common people frequently echoed official ideas about work thus does not indicate that these ideas were hegemonic, at least not in the sense that elite advocates may have intended. Poor people may or may not have seen work as a social responsibility, or viewed submission to work's discipline as the most important signal of their peers' honesty and moral worth. Certainly, few poor people spent their breath on "odes to work." But public language does show that many among the poor viewed the ability to credibly assume the role of devoted worker as crucial to the successful navigation of most public and private systems of punishment, reward, and patronage. The man (especially) who could not play that role failed his family, not only because he did not provide income, but also because he endangered his own liberty and failed to tap into the multiple non-monetary sources of social sustenance—relationships with patrons and, increasingly, the state—that made survival possible. The ability to talk the talk was prized, regardless of what might have been believed beneath the surface; to that extent, at least, elite discourse had sunk in.

But when poor people praised work, their words were not always derivative or utilitarian. At times, even in the official documentary sources, poor Cariocas voiced views of work's meaning that have a ring of authenticity, sometimes because these views served no obvious strategic purpose, and sometimes because they surfaced in descriptions of poor people's private lives that were voiced from numerous strategic points of view. Again, criminal cases serve as an example, especially those that involved fights or arguments in homes, workplaces, and public spaces. In these cases—and especially in those leading to insult, or *injúria*, charges—the court transcript usually includes descriptions of the fights given by people partial to both parties.[68] While witnesses frequently disagreed on the details of who said what, they were remarkably unified in identifying the kinds of words that constituted insults, and in interpreting the meaning of such words in familial and community settings.

Many of the damnations they described would have been familiar virtually anywhere ("son of a bitch," "cuckold"). But other, less common invectives shed light on Brazilian popular understandings of honest work, emphasizing either a man's inability to support his family or his tendency toward dishonesty and thievery.[69] In one 1927 case involving insults between a Portuguese landlady and a Portuguese tenant in a downtown rooming house, several witnesses reported that the landlady had injured her tenant not only by calling her a pig (*porca*) and a slut (*cadella* [sic]) but also by stating that she should find another man (or even turn to prostitution) because her husband was "tubercular" and thus useless as a provider.[70] In a 1929 *injúria* case, also between two Portuguese immigrants, a female shantytown resident, angry with a local landlord for digging a ditch below her shack, called him a bandit (*bandido*) and a thief (*ladrão*), and, in one version, "o português mais bandido que havia no Morro da Formiga" ("the biggest Portuguese bandit in the Morro da Formiga").[71] In yet another *injúria* case (1930), this time between a Brazilian couple and a Portuguese man, two defense witnesses claimed that the Brazilian woman in question had called the defendant a *coscamano*, a *bandido*, a *ladrão*, and a *vagabundo*, all words that imply laziness, dishonesty, or both.[72]

In all of these cases, witnesses may simply have been pandering to officials' perceived sympathy for men whose honesty and work ethic had been insulted. But such insults, in order to seem plausible to experienced policemen, prosecutors, and judges, had to involve words commonly spoken among the very poor; otherwise, one of the parties would surely have called foul. It is thus likely either that these were the actual words spoken or that they plausibly could have been; in either case, such insults, voiced by a range of poor Cariocas, demonstrate that a man's status as a capable and honest provider was among the most important components of his public honor.

Myriad scattered indications buttress this impression. In a wide variety of criminal cases, witnesses who seemed to have no special stake in the outcome made a point of evaluating defendants' and victims' proclivities for work. While this may have been the result of police questioning, it could also reflect the issue's importance for the witnesses themselves.[73] Sueann Caulfield has found that poor young women's families seemed to pursue forced marriage through criminal defloration suits mainly when the social status of the young men in question was equal to or slightly higher than the young women's own; of 303 defloration cases for which Caulfield has information, none involved an unemployed defendant, and only 12 of the accused were undifferentiated "manual laborers," among the lowest categories of worker.[74] This is hardly surprising; husbands were breadwinners, and poor Cariocas lived too close to the margin of survival to ignore a man's ability to support a family. In addition, historians of the Carioca working class have found that pride in professional skill and in the ability to sustain a family were critical components of working-class politics and of working-class identity; there were enough ties between the working class and the very poor that such views can probably be generalized.[75] And finally, scattered oral accounts indicate that the well-known modern distinction between workers and *marginais* in favela communities has roots that reach back to the communities' origins; then as now, residents affirmed that they were not the *malandros* and *marginais* of popular lore, but rather hard-working people whose deepest respect was reserved for fellow laborers.[76]

None of these indications is unequivocal, and none can be separated entirely from increasingly consequential elite and official expectations. But they all suggest that poor Cariocas valued a work ethic, not only as a strategic cloak but also as a quality that was essential to familial survival and personal self-esteem. The resentment broadcast in the sambas with regard to exploitative work relationships did not preclude the valorization of work as an act of familial or community responsibility.

Even if poor Cariocas sometimes converged with Vargas in valuing work, however, they had their own ideas about what labor was, and about who merited "worker" status. In Vargas's rhetoric, the term *trabalhador* was sometimes applied broadly, referring to women as well as to men, to rural as well as to urban laborers, even to professionals and capitalists. But while Vargas and his ministers frequently glorified the factory worker or the rural frontier laborer as sources of national pride and progress, they rarely—if ever—so dignified the occupations of the poorest urban Brazilians, especially the women among them. "Brazilians" could be, as Vargas put it in an Independence Day speech in 1934, "rubber tappers of the Amazon forests, rafters [*jangadeiros*] of the north, fishermen from the coast, miners of the central massif, sugar processors from Pernambuco or Rio de Janeiro, owners of agricultural estates (*fazendeiros*) from São Paulo, ranchers [*pastores*] of the Southern Prairies, industrialists and workers." All of these were male occupations, and all were either associated with "progress" or integral to a glorified national identity. Young women might occasionally come into the picture as factory or office workers, though always with the implication that such activities were temporary and auxiliary to women's natural and most important roles as mothers and household managers.[77] But "workers" and "Brazilians" were never washerwomen or odd-jobbers, servants or itinerant construction workers, landless rural peons or subsistence farmers. When such people did enter Vargas's rhetoric, it was mainly to serve as an example of the dire social consequences of negligent rural policies or rural-to-urban migration run amok.[78]

For many poor Cariocas, though, work had a different meaning, one distilled from the act and attitude of working, and from the worker's attempt to fulfill family and community needs, rather than from work's role in promoting economic progress and national identity. Typically, the Babilônia shantytown resident Ermelinda da Soledade Campos, in justifying her request for housing from President Vargas, thought it important to mention that her husband labored "every day," but she did not describe his line of work. Maria da Gloria Silva Varela, the mother who wrote in 1940 seeking a boarding school for her two sons, was careful to seize the title of "worker" for herself and her husband, but her occupation was unspecified, and her husband's was described as that of an occasionally employed "operário comum"—not a category exalted by Vargas.[79] Others—destitute barbers, street salesmen, itinerant lottery vendors, washerwomen, subsistence farmers—wrote to Vargas with a degree of long-suffering pride about their backbreaking labor, linking work to merit not only because of its contribution to Brazil's national destiny, but also because of what it demonstrated about the correspondents' good-faith efforts to fulfill their obligations in the face of bitterly tough circumstances. Although the women who wrote these letters followed Vargas's lead in generally subordinating their status as workers to their roles as mothers, they also asserted their independence by treating compensated work as a central component of female identity.

In criminal cases, the same kinds of values emerged in the transcribed language of working-class and poor witnesses, who often argued that even those whose occupations were highly precarious or of low status had merit as workers. Witnesses described defendants in all sorts of occupations as "hardworking" and "honest"; a motorist's assistant, an itinerant fruit vendor, a part-time stevedore, a poultry vendor, a mother-daughter team who served meals to rooming-house residents, or a generic *operário* could all qualify, so long as they worked regularly and seemed to contribute to their families' support.[80] Defendants claimed the title of "worker" for a similar range of occupations.[81] In a particularly striking instance from 1932, Octávio da Silva—a young, illiterate rural migrant who sold beverages on a street corner—was accused of physical assault for hitting a shoeshiner over the head when the latter refused to pay for a drink. In his defense, clearly composed with aid but without formal legal assistance, da Silva defended his status as a worker, stating that he knew that street-corner selling was illegal, but that his was an honest occupation and his only alternative to starvation or crime.[82] Participants in these cases also frequently presented women's labor in a slightly different light than did the Vargas government; in several instances, poor women were praised by neighbors and friends for their work outside the home, and a relative openly criticized one poor female migrant because she did not have the "habit of work."[83]

Surely many of the same poor people who voiced respect for hardworking friends and neighbors longed in other settings to follow samba *malandros*, to reject work's drudgery and exploitation and live the unrespectable but free life of the trickster. Surely, too, many would have laughed to hear their neighbors' and drinking buddies' pious assumptions of the work ethic in police stations, government offices, and written appeals—even as they also slipped into such roles in search of work, public assistance, or protection from bureaucratic abuse. For these people, work seems to have been both an imposed obligation and an indication of internal worth, both an assumed role and a deeply felt duty, both their lives' central occupation and that which least defined their humanity. In the end, Vargas's rhetorical gestures must have resonated deeply with the strain of popular thought that viewed work with pride and respect. But the gulf between popular and governmental visions of what work was, and of who legitimately practiced it, must also have fueled cynicism about the extent to which hard work was truly to be rewarded in Brazilian public life. As Vargas funneled his expansive rhetoric into narrowly targeted legislation over the course of the 1930s and 1940s, that cynicism would prove to be largely justified.

FAMILY AND *PÁTRIA*

Superficial convergences between governmental and popular conceptions of work thus masked deep rifts about work's nature and the reasons for its importance. Similarly, surface agreements about the importance of family and nation masked gulfs of definition and moral logic. Everywhere from samba to court testimony to popular correspondence, poor Cariocas' appreciation of family and country emerged, in ways both derivative and organic. But the external characteristics and behaviors that embodied family virtue and patriotic loyalty for the poor often differed radically from those that mattered to politicians, or to elite thinkers more generally. Once more, the patterns of exclusion that would characterize Vargas's legislative action were rooted not only in divergent values but also in differing conceptions of how those values might best be incarnated.

The early twentieth century was a period of intense transformation for the Brazilian family, particularly with regard to gender relations.[84] As Susan Besse has pointed out, this was partially the result of conscious efforts on the part of elite and middle class women—inspired both by international trends and by local economic and social conditions—to curb perceived male tyrannies at home and to assume more important roles in public and professional life.[85] Commercial culture challenged the traditional family as well, all across the socio-economic spectrum. As music, movies, and magazines touted new and more liberated patterns of dress, recreation, and sexual comportment, young Carioca women—an increasing proportion of whom were commuting workers only loosely supervised by families and patrons—soaked in these trends, often flouting patriarchal boundaries and gender norms in the process.[86] In addition, migration brought to the cities increasing numbers of young, relatively unsupervised people of both sexes;[87] industrialization created more formal opportunities for poor women outside the domestic setting;[88] and improvements in transportation increased women's physical mobility, removing them from the vigilance of family and neighbors.[89]

Together, these trends convinced many public commentators that the traditional Brazilian family—anchored by patriarchal control and economic sustenance, and sealed by women's sexual modesty, loyalty, and willing supervision of the domestic sphere—was endangered, and with it the moral health of the nation. For elite women, such fears had few practical ramifications, though they did discourage them from devoting their lives to the public sphere and encourage conservative views of wifely and motherly obligations.[90] But for working-class and poor families, more direct forms of suasion could be brought to bear. Judges could grant the benefits of laws meant to protect sexual honor only to young women whose comportment, in their view, justified the privilege.[91] Private and public charities could grant assistance and vocational training only to women willing to live within specified moral bounds.[92] Factories and public agencies could grant low-income housing only to those who fit their mold of proper family form and function.[93] Labor legislation could discourage females from working in occupations thought to endanger their biological and social roles as mothers.[94] Governmental social welfare legislation could easily be tied to conformity with specific familial models.[95] And, finally, men who committed adultery or refused to support their families could theoretically be punished by law.[96] Through all of these avenues, throughout the 1930s and 1940s, poor and working-class Cariocas found themselves pressured to conform to broadly conservative ideals of gender and family.

Given the scope and intensity of these influences, it is tempting, just as in the case of work, to dismiss popular expressions of conservative familial ideals as assumed or derivative. Certainly, when correspondents with Vargas and other public officials claimed virtue as good wives, mothers, and providers, their words reflected strategic choices, and were rarely windows into popular mores. The same goes for defloration defendants' declarations about the importance of women's sexual purity as a prerequisite for marriage, or even trial witnesses' assurances that victims and defendants were worthy wives and providers and thus incapable of the most heinous crimes. All of these people may or may not have been sincere in their appreciation of restrictive, gendered models of familial life. Given the contexts of their declarations, the only certainty is that poor people viewed the ability to assume the role of a good husband, wife, or child as a critical tool in navigating public life, and they were apparently willing to uphold conservative ideals in the service of their individual goals.

In other contexts, though, popular affirmations of conservative views of family, and especially of gender roles therein, could ring truer. Even in the relatively liberal realm of samba, most songs romanticize a gendered and traditional model of love, and it is rare to find a woman glorified for defying norms such as sexual loyalty and maternal duty.[97] In modern oral accounts, favela residents often take great pride in their ability to fulfill gendered family roles—the stay-at-home mother, the working father—and their stories about other residents frequently emphasize the importance of family membership in establishing local identities.[98] Sueann Caulfield's work provides further indications: the very fact that so many families would pursue defloration cases, and some young men's obvious care in establishing that the women they were sleeping with were not virgins, suggest that at least a large segment of Rio's poor and working-class populations valued female sexual purity and loyalty and viewed monogamous matrimony as every woman's ideal goal.[99] Though young women sometimes flouted those ideals, engaging in sex before marriage, their transgressions mostly rejected morality's form rather than its content; most of the rebellious girls in Caulfield's study seem ultimately to have accepted gendered family and sexual values even as they questioned the behavioral restrictions that had commonly embodied them.[100]

Well away from the public eye, poor Cariocas also demonstrated that they cared a great deal about gendered family roles. Insult cases, again, illustrate the point. Witnesses to slanderous arguments often highlighted words that implied women's sexual impurity and men's inability to control them; terms such as *puta, vaca, cadela, cabrão,* and *corno.* Insults could be subtler as well, and the events surrounding them could speak as forcefully as the words themselves. In one 1927 case, for example, a nasty conflict broke out among tenants in a rooming house near the city center. The fight had begun when two married neighbors had called Italian-born Maria José Cherre's honor into question by accusing her of answering telephones for a brothel. The accusation hit hard; her common-law husband was worried enough to spend days investigating it, and he took the trouble to file the *injúria* suit when he found the claims false. The evidence that quieted the husband's worries was as gendered as the accusation itself: several friends, coming to the woman's defense, pointed to her compassion in caring for other people's children, and to her model behavior as a wife, as signs that she was a moral and decent woman.[101] None of the participants in this or other domestic dramas lived in isolation from external ideals of family and gender. But, even when they were far removed from the public spotlight, most participants seemed to see female purity, maternal devotion, male control and responsibility, and gendered divisions of labor as central to their social worlds.[102]

Many poor people undermined Vargas's ideals of family and gender, contradicting with their actions norms and values that they may never have vocally, or even consciously, opposed. Many women clearly had sex before marriage; many men either refused to marry or abandoned their wives; many wives exercised both economic and moral control of their families. In other contexts, however, Vargas's ideals of family and gender probably made good sense; many poor people would not have perceived them as foreign ideologies, imposed entirely from the outside, but rather as an aggrandized version of their own daily moral logic.

But if politicians and *populares* converged at the level of abstraction, they frequently diverged, and radically, at the level of practice. Most poor Cariocas, for example, seemed to believe that stable relationships between men and women were an important ideal. They could never agree, though, on the connection between formal marriage—civil or religious—

and morality. Informal unions had a long history in Rio, especially among the poor, for a long series of practical reasons. For most slaves, and for many of the rural poor, legal marriage was often not a viable option, given its cost, the opposition of owners or employers, and the enslaved people's common isolation from the bureaucratic infrastructure.[103] Even for free urban people, marriage was expensive, and it presented many bureaucratic hurdles. It was also permanent: divorce was illegal in Brazil until 1977, and legal separation—*desquite*—was bureaucratically complicated and still precluded remarriage.[104] This meant not only that single people—and especially young men—thought twice before marrying, but also that Rio was a city full of legally married but functionally single adults; migrants long separated from rural or foreign families, women (and sometimes men) abandoned by unfaithful spouses, couples whose mutual differences made common life unbearable. Any new union that such people might seek would necessarily be extralegal. Such practicalities often became major roadblocks, even when potential mates were not discouraged from formal marriage by the legal subordination it implied for women before 1962, the legal obligations it imposed on men after 1940, or the belief that virginity was a necessary prerequisite for formal marriage.[105] Little wonder, then, that in 1960 well over a third of Rio's favela population lived in extralegal unions.[106]

Given the prevalence of informal marriage, most poor people had little choice but to accept it as a fact of life among their friends and neighbors. The question of moral equivalency, though, is more complex. Certainly, for some, legal marriage was still the gold standard, however unattainable. Striking examples included mothers, themselves single, who sought marriage for their deflowered daughters in Rio's police stations, or men in the same cases who refused to marry non-virgin partners, but proved willing enough to live with them and start a family.[107] Such sentiments emerged in nastier ways through some insult cases. In one 1932 example, a Portuguese immigrant woman by the name of Alcira Fernandes railed against her informally married Brazilian neighbor, Aurora Villela, whose children were making noise. Fernandes said that she herself was "a married woman" and didn't "want anything to do with a tramp," and that Villela was a "nigger" who was "not even married."[108] While some of what went on that day might be chalked up to long-standing cultural and economic rifts between poor European immigrants and their Brazilian-born neighbors, this case and others suggest that some poor Cariocas viewed formal marriage as a seal of moral worth, at least to the extent that it could be lorded over a despised neighbor.[109]

Fernandes's views, however, were often in the minority. Villela's neighbors indicated that they saw allusions to race and marital status as entirely beyond the pale. When Maria José Cherre was accused of answering telephone calls for a brothel, the informal nature of their union did not stop her common-law husband from investigating the slight to his companion's honor. In many other insult cases, informally married women made strong claims to female honor.[110] In the defloration suits investigated by Caulfield, some women seemed content to live in consensual unions, only complaining to police when those promises were broken.[111] And among the women who wrote to Vargas, informal marriage did not impede claims to honorable femininity. Many women simply never mentioned the nature of their marriages, although elements of their stories—extreme poverty, rural origins, shantytown residence, last names that differed from those of their partners—suggested that their unions might not have been formal. Others did indicate that they were single mothers or informal wives, while at the same time appealing to Vargas in the language of female honor and duty.

Maria Cabral de Freitas, who wrote to Vargas in 1941 asking for a monthly stipend to support her eleven children, was a case in point. Though Freitas claimed to have been a widow for ten years, only five of her children were old enough to work at the time she wrote. Unless several of those children were twins or triplets or began working at an unusually advanced age—most poor Cariocas seem to have begun to earn income by their mid-teens, if not before—simple arithmetic would suggest that some of them had been born of a more recent, informal union. This impression is heightened by the fact that Freitas claimed that several were "pequenos" ("small") and that a pension would allow her to raise them in her own home, a precaution that would have been less urgent with older children. All the same, Freitas freely used the language of patriotic maternity, saying that she had "given" the children to the "pátria," and speaking proudly of her struggles to raise them well.[112] Similar incongruities arise in other letters from "widows"; taken together, they suggest that these women were aware of the importance of appearing married, but in fact saw no incompatibility between Vargas's projections of female virtue and the reality of single motherhood or informal partnership.

In other ways, too, poor Carioca correspondents seem to have lived family values in ways that pushed at the limits of Vargas's moral universe. Women's work, for example, emerged from these letters as a lifelong necessity, not as a single woman's passing occupation. Most women claimed hard work as a virtue, just as men did; they generally subordinated their own labors to those of their male partners, but they seemed to see wage work as a fulfillment of their maternal and familial duties, not as an activity that took them away from their rightful place in the home. In one appeal, Clotilde da Silva, who lived in a shantytown settlement in the industrial port neighborhood of Cajú, made no bones about her backbreaking labor. Although her whole family had been finding employment in a local factory for a decade and a half, and although she and her family "never waste[d] a cent on foolishness" and didn't "spend money on entertainment, swets [sic] or clothes," their funds "just plain [fell] short." To compensate, da Silva—a mother of nine, whose newborn twins temporarily kept her out of factory work—washed clothes at night, work that caused her to arrive home so late that dinner was never on the table until half of her family was asleep. Many middle-class reformers probably would have understood da Silva's long hours as an example of the kind of motherly inattention that corrupted children and tore poor families apart. Here, though, it is presented as part of what made her application for help worth considering.[113] It is notable that da Silva and others seem rarely to have considered their underemployed, underpaid, or crippled husbands failures for not fulfilling the manly role of father and provider; what seemed to matter, in their narratives, was that these men did their best, and that it was the entire family's natural role to fill the gaps when the principal providers could not. Men, in narrating their own family struggles and failures, generally took a similar tack, rarely projecting a sense that their inability to provide adequately for their families constituted a failure that would make them less worthy of belonging to Vargas's imagined moral universe.

As in the case of work, then, poor Cariocas who spoke publicly about the family generally agreed with Vargas about its importance but diverged when it came to its constitution. In the case of patriotism, scant existing evidence suggests a similar pattern. In the Brazil of the 1930s, love of nation does not seem to have been as deeply rooted a sentiment as love of work or family. Relations between immigrants (especially Portuguese immigrants) and native Brazilians had long been strained, and it is certainly possible to find examples from the 1930s and 1940s of the sorts of rivalries and alignments that led Sidney Chalhoub to see this fissure as central to working-class life in belle époque Rio.[114] But, half a century later, poor Cariocas did not generally use their status as Brazilians to bolster their positions in police stations and courts, and nativist insults do not seem to have been common in daily conversations and arguments. If patriotism contributed to a poor Carioca's standing within his or her family or community, it did so without leaving much trace.

Patriotism's public-use value, though, was never in question, especially during the Estado Novo. The letters that poor and working-class people wrote to Vargas brimmed over with professed love of country. These sources tell us virtually nothing about the sincerity of poor people's patriotism, but they do indicate that Rio's poor, like their compatriots elsewhere, had their own distinctive take on the flesh-and-blood characteristics and actions qualified them as deserving Brazilians. While most echoed Vargas's notion that poor people's service to country was embodied through men's work and women's domestic dedication, their generous definitions of family and work colored their conceptions of national belonging. In this vision, single mothers could raise future contributors to national progress, and unemployed men could claim social citizenship by virtue of their fervent (if futile) efforts to work.

Correspondents also questioned less central tenets of Vargas's nationalism, like his nativist streak, or his ministers' tendency to view shantytowns as a parasitical anathema to national progress. In December 1941, Adolpho Cohen, a Syrian immigrant, wrote to request aid for his large family.[115] Although he was a foreigner and a street peddler, who admittedly lacked the documents that would prove his legal marriage and his children's birth, Cohen nonetheless claimed help as a Brazilian. He may have been foreign, but he was married to a Brazilian woman and raising Brazilian children. His employment may have been tenuous and his income "totally insufficient" to sustain his "numerous family," but he was a man who had been "dedicated to work" for his "whole life," laboring from "dawn to dusk." His children may have been forced to withdraw from school on occasion because they lacked shoes or school supplies, but he had "tried, in the best way possible, to give physical, moral, and religious education" to them. Membership in the Brazilian nation, in this vision, was earned through intention and internal values, by making do in the best possible way when, as every poor person understood, circumstances made it impossible to fulfill official expectations.

Maria José Francisco, a widow who wrote to Vargas in 1941, voiced a similar sentiment.[116] An "operária e viuva" ("worker and widow"), Francisco narrated four years of fruitless struggle to place her child in school; in spite of appeals to the children's courts, her son had not yet set foot inside a classroom, and she still lacked "sufficient resources to educate him and make him a Brazilian." Moreover, she saw herself "obligated to live in a *morro* [shantytown] because she could not buy a house in a civilized place," and she greatly feared that her son was "only learning bad habits" and would end up jailed as a "vagabond" or a "thief." Would Vargas, as a "father," and as one who knew her sacrifice, find a school for her son? Though Francisco's external characteristics—she was a single mother and a shantytown resident who had never sent her child to school—would have placed her outside Vargas's carefully constructed national family, to her those signs were artificial, imposed by circumstance and not by intention. What mattered was her desire to fulfill nationalist ideals, and that desire in itself justified her national belonging.

In this sense, Francisco's letter could have been the model for a 1941 carnival samba, "Recenseamento" ("Census"), popularized by Carmen

Miranda. The samba was inspired by the 1940 census, the first to try to count the populations of the city's shacks and hills, and it captured the feelings of vulnerability and inadequacy that must have overwhelmed some favela residents when the first census takers showed up to quantify and categorize their lives. At the same time, the samba cleverly demanded that its readers look beyond external signs of family, work, and nation to see what true patriotism really was:

Em 1940	In 1940
lá no morro começaram o recenseamento	Over in the *morro* they began to take the census
E o agente recenseador	and the census agent
esmiuçou a minha vida	minutely examined my life
que foi um horror	which was a horror
E quando viu a minha mão sem aliança	and when he saw my hand without a wedding ring
encarou para a criança	he looked at my child
que no chão dormia	sleeping on the floor
E perguntou se meu moreno era decente	and asked if my [dark-skinned] man was decent
se era do batente ou se era da folia	if he was a worker or a carouser
Obediente como a tudo que é da lei	Obedient as I am to everything to do with the law
fiquei logo sossegada e falei então:	I quickly relaxed and then I said:
O meu moreno é brasileiro, é fuzileiro,	My man is Brazilian and a navy gunner
é o que sai com a bandeira do seu batalhão!	He is the one who carries his battalion's flag!
A nossa casa não tem nada de grandeza	Our house has no grandeur
nós vivemos na fartura sem dever tostão	We live well without owing a penny
Tem um pandeiro, um cavaquinho, um tamborim	We have a *pandeiro*, a *cuíca*, and a *tamborim*
um reco-reco, uma cuíca e um violão	a *reco-reco*, a *cavaquinho*, and a guitar
Fiquei pensando e comecei a descrever	I thought a little and began to describe
tudo, tudo de valor	everything, every valuable thing
que meu Brasil me deu	that my Brazil has given me
Um céu azul, um Pão de Açúcar sem farelo	A blue sky, a Sugarloaf without charging a trifle
um pano verde e amarelo	a cloth of green and yellow
Tudo isso é meu!	All of this is mine
Tem feriado que pra mim vale fortuna	There are holidays worth a fortune to me
a Retirada da Laguna vale um cabedal!	The "Retirada da Laguna" is worth even more
Tem Pernambuco, tem São Paulo, tem Bahia	There's Pernambuco, there's São Paulo, and there's Bahia
um conjunto de harmonia que não tem rival	A harmonious whole without rival[117]

No matter that this woman was unmarried, or that her man was unable to give her more than a shack to live in; these people were grateful Brazilians nonetheless. Even when they could not attain externally imposed signs of civilization and belonging, they embodied their patriotism through service, culture, and values, and deserved social citizenship as expressed in Vargas's generous labor laws. Though it was doubtless carefully worded to conform to Estado Novo censorship, "Recenseamento"—like many of the letters to Vargas—can easily be read as a sharp critique and challenge. As the Vargas government's rhetoric was filtered into legislative existence, which vision of national belonging would prevail? Would the new laws only recognize rigidly defined, often unattainable embodiments of work, family, and love of country? Or would they recognize instead the inherent moral value of the struggle to live those values, even when circumstances made their full realization impossible?

CHAPTER FOUR

Word into Law: Work and Family
in Vargas-Era Legislation

⋐

Vargas's rhetoric would have had little power without the force of law. While his acknowledgment of poor people's dignity and humanity might in itself have been compelling, his proclamations gained dynamic urgency precisely because they were not merely words.[118] As part of a larger legal revolution that laid the foundations for more than half a century of governance in every realm of public life, Vargas's labor, social security, and social welfare laws were new, radical, and wide-ranging. Yet, like other Vargas-era reforms, their technical details belied their inclusive goals. Social and economic citizenship, as these laws defined them, were not birthrights or even rewards for patriotism, hard work, or familial duty. Rather, they were privileges won through narrowly circumscribed forms of labor, morality, loyalty, and bureaucratic agility; in many ways, they were more akin to patronage than to rights.

The vision of social and economic citizenship laid out in the constitutions of 1934, 1937, and 1946 was frankly utopian, the legal expression of Vargas's most expansive rhetoric. Despite clear differences among them, all three constitutions proclaimed the equality of all Brazilians, regardless of status at birth and of sex, race, class, profession, religion, or political creed. All three documents also rejected the laissez-faire liberalism of their 1891 counterpart, giving the state an active role in regulating the nation's social and economic life. The national government would morally and academically educate all Brazilians and promote the physical and economic well-being of all families. It would guarantee Brazilians the constitutional right to provide for their families through honest work. It would give assistance to those who could not provide for themselves. And it would become the intermediary between capital and labor, eliminating wrenching conflict and guaranteeing workers a remarkable package of benefits, including an eight-hour day, yearly vacations, a minimum wage, limitations on child labor, maternity leaves, and protection against summary firing. Moreover, all three constitutions enshrined the notion of social property, whereby "the use of property" would be "conditioned by the interests of social well-being," thus making the government a more active mediator between private property holders and the interests of society at large.[119]

The constitutions' utopian nature was entirely within the tradition of Brazilian lawmaking, as well as that of the civil law world; law, here, was meant to be a beacon rather than a reflection of reality.[120] But in the drafting of a set of practical laws and guidelines to fulfill these expectations, two circumstances limited the Vargas government's actions. At the helm of a relatively fragile national state, with a weakened, hardly industrialized economy and a scanty tax base, Vargas's government could not possibly have granted so much to so many all at once; it did not possess the bureaucracy, the money, or the political clout.[121] At the same time, for political as well as ideological reasons, many members of the Vargas government clearly viewed some Brazilians as much more politically, economically, and culturally prepared for equality than others. Brazilians were born, but citizens had to be made.[122] The reams of revolutionary measures pushed into law under the Estado Novo reflected these practical limitations, social biases, and political priorities. The rights they offered were generous but also conditional, available in practice only to those (mostly urban) workers whose occupations and family structures fit the narrow definitions sanctified by Vargas's labor and social welfare decrees.

INEQUITIES OF PRACTICE

Many of the restrictions that plagued Vargas's laws stemmed from Brazil's rapid, frequently chaotic, and sometimes wrenching transition toward a modernized bureaucratic state. Social and economic rights had to be administered. Beneficiaries had to be counted, their claims validated, their benefits apportioned and accounted for—and all of this in a nation that, in 1930, had no national identification system, no current census figures, unreliable registration of births and marriages, limited formalization of work relations, and virtually no bureaucratic or judicial experience in the areas of labor law and social welfare.[123]

Given the enormity of these challenges, it is little wonder that Vargas's government scrambled rather chaotically to respond to them throughout the 1930s and 1940s. Some initiatives were foundational. The Instituto Brasileiro de Geografia e Estatística (IBGE, later the Fundação IBGE) was created in 1936 to augment and coordinate Brazilian statistical studies at the municipal, state, and federal levels. The fruits of the institute's efforts, in the form of regular decennial censuses and more extensive yearly statistical compilations, made possible a relatively accurate assessment of the Brazilian population's size, distribution, occupational structure, and living conditions.[124] Numerous ministerial and local agencies pursued more targeted research as well.

At the same time, Brazil's public bureaucracy expanded swiftly. Vargas created the Ministério do Trabalho, Indústria e Comércio in 1930, and the labor courts and official unions that would be the backbone of his work legislation came into being during the 1930s and 1940s. Social security grew, too, spawning an enormous web of company- and occupation-based agencies.[125] Other preexisting entities, such as the ministries of education and health, took new forms, and governmental agencies and employment mushroomed. In Rio alone, the number of public employees jumped from approximately 81,431 in 1920 to 200,802 in 1950, and the proportion of public employees in the workforce jumped from 15.7 percent to 20.9 percent.[126] All of this augmented greatly the administration's ability to study, draft, and implement the concrete policies that would make a reality of constitutional promise.

The thoroughness and the geographical reach of these new bureaucracies were inevitably patchy. Statistics were shaped both by the questions statisticians asked and by practical limitations to their full and accurate compilation. Many scholars have emphasized the degree to which race was naturalized and reified as a significant category through its inclusion in censuses and other statistical surveys from the 1920s through the 1940s.[127] In other ways, too, governmental statistics at once reflected and reinforced the social views of their architects. Categories of work, for example, were quite broad and generally incapable of distinguishing well among workers at the bottom of the social spectrum. This limitation reflected bureaucratic assumptions about the homogeneity of this group, but it also perpetuated them; for example, if statistics did not differentiate between shoemakers employed in tiny, flailing itinerant business and shoemakers in well-established factories, it was impossible to fine-tune labor legislation to the very different needs of these two kinds of workers.[128] And if statistics on housing did not include information on land ownership or access to city services, or if they did not distinguish among favelas, illegal subdivisions, and legalized neighborhoods, it was impossible to solve rationally the problems of residential insecurity and hygiene that plagued the lives of most poor Cariocas.[129]

The questions present in the surveys, moreover, could not be asked of everyone in the degree of detail that would have been needed to craft fine-tuned local policy. Even in Rio, whose inhabitants were researched more thoroughly than most, statisticians struggled mightily throughout the 1930s and 1940s to accurately collect data on the city's residential and employment situation, especially among the very poor. This effort was especially evident in national and municipal attempts to study people who lived in the city's shantytowns. Such settlements changed constantly, as a result of migration (rural to urban and sometimes back again) and eviction (private and public, massive and individual). Residents of illegal settlements did not always wish to divulge details about family composition, work status, and residential circumstances. Officials, moreover, could never even agree about which favelas were worth counting. Municipal studies focused only on the larger and more central favelas—situated, not coincidentally, in prosperous residential and booming industrial neighborhoods—and all surveys set arbitrary floors on the number of shacks that qualified a community for shantytown status, thus excluding many of the poorest and most isolated settlements.[130] Symptomatically, only a handful of relatively high-profile favelas were studied at all until 1948; the federal census of 1950 counted over 30,000 more residents than the municipal survey of 1948 (an unlikely 22 percent growth in two years), and many of the settlements counted in the 1948 favela census did not appear in 1950.[131] Even this degree of statistical detail was available in only a few other locations (especially São Paulo and Recife, where a late-1930s campaign against *mocambos* yielded significant data). Outside the major urban areas, problems of staffing, transportation, and knowledge made it difficult if not impossible to assess the life circumstances of most Brazilians.

Similar problems plagued the expansion of federal bureaucracies meant to respond to the needs of Brazil's citizenry. Entities such as the ministries of work and health, though theoretically national, grew slowly and unevenly, and their ability to respond to popular demands and to enforce social, labor, and health laws was proportional to their organizational density. The labor courts established by Vargas's *trabalhista* laws clearly reflected this. In 1947–49, the cities of Rio and São Paulo were responsible for 20–26 percent and 34–37 percent, respectively, of all of the cases brought to the courts. Rio Grande do Sul was responsible for around 10 percent; Pernambuco, Bahia, Minas Gerais, and Rio state each brought in another 5–7 percent; and the rest of Brazil's states had insignificant activity.[132] The issuance of work ID documents and the establishment of unions followed similar patterns.[133] Even in Rio, where federal entities were very much present, their geographical centralization often precluded or delayed effective access, a fact often lamented by social workers in the 1940s and 1950s.

Even when governmental agencies were available and their policies were statistically well informed, fundamental technical problems remained. The process of extending economic and social rights necessarily involved registration and documentation; without procedures capable of authenticating individual claims, no entitlement bureaucracy could work. Yet the challenge of equitably introducing such a system was enormous in a country with an undocumented, dispersed, and illiterate population. Even in a best-case scenario—one in which statistical knowledge of the population's needs was complete and registration campaigns were energetic, well-organized, extensive, and well funded—it would have been difficult for state officials to document quickly every Brazilian family and worker to whom the constitutions had promised new rights, not least because many Brazilians actively resisted such official meddling.[134] As it was, the scenario was far from ideal. Both work and social welfare legislation made documents essential passports to the realm of rights, and yet the Vargas government did little to speed or ease their acquisition. As a result, bureaucratic agility became a source of entitlement, and documents became the chief intermediaries and obstacles between ordinary Brazilians and full social and economic rights.

An enormous array of papers became markers of citizenship during the Vargas years, everything from proof of military service to voter registration documents, national identification cards, and work papers. None of these was strictly required of all Brazilians; only accused criminals, soldiers, policemen, registered voters, domestic servants, chauffeurs, and certain public employees were forced to have official identification.[135] But each of these documents was a passport to a specific realm of rights; each dimension of Brazilian citizenship had its paper signifier, and without it, none could enter, thus making the question of coercion somewhat mute.

The process of attaining these documents always began with the humble birth certificate, in itself a significant stumbling block. The registration of births, deaths, and marriages had become common in most urban areas of Brazil by the early twentieth century and had in fact been formally required of all citizens since 1889. Yet the process was still notoriously incomplete by the early 1930s.[136] With Vargas's 1939 civil registry law (Decreto 4857), the government gestured toward transforming this situation, criminalizing non-registration of births and establishing detailed procedural rules. Yet the law spelled out no specific penalties for non-compliance and set up few new mechanisms to make its own mandate effective. These shortcomings were significant in view of the enormous registration gap officials faced during these years; a comparison of the civil registry with the national census of 1940 revealed that even in São Paulo (which had the highest rate of registration for births), 35.7 percent of all children under 1 year of age were not registered. In Rio, the figure was 36.9 percent, and in the north and northeast of the country rates of noncompliance ranged between 87.5 percent and 98.7 percent.[137]

According to the 1939 law, the procedures for registration should have been straightforward enough. Within the first 15 days after a birth, the child's father—or, in his absence, the mother, a relative, or a legal guardian—was to register him or her with the local notary. Mothers registering their children received a 45-day extension. Anyone who lived more than 30 kilometers from a registration office could take 90 days. After this period, registration required judicial approval and a fine of 10 *cruzeiros*; those who had been born before civil registration was declared mandatory (presumably before 1889), or young adults between the ages of 18 and 21, could request registration without payment, though the process still required judicial approval. Late male registrants between the ages of 18 and 30 would be reported to local military officials. The duly certified poor paid nothing for timely registration.[138]

But complaints sent to Vargas in the early 1940s indicated the decree's flaws. It made no provisions for poor adults who had been born after registration was mandated in 1889, and it did nothing to expand the number of registry offices. Distance, ignorance, bureaucratic inefficiency, and outright corruption frequently made the registration of newborns difficult. Most importantly, the fine of 10 *cruzeiros*, which may have seemed insignificant to bureaucrats, was equivalent to a Carioca's daily minimum wage in 1940 and was worth much more in rural areas. For large families, the cumulative burden would have been enormous.[139]

Many of Vargas's correspondents lamented these costs and made clear the wide range of opportunities that depended on a valid birth certificate. In 1941, Armindo Ribeiro Pinto Filho—a resident of suburban Madureira who described himself as Vargas's "humble and thankful servant"—explained that he needed the president's assistance because the aunts who had raised him had never registered him, and he now wanted "to enter military service" and "had no money" to pay registration fees and fines.[140] In 1942, Leonor Tostes Pires, an orphan and a "born Brazilian" who had recently passed a civil service exam, found that she could not attain a permanent post without proof of age, which would require civil registration. Pires wrote that she was over 21 and "absolutely unable to pay the required penalty," which she was "innocent of incurring" because of her "modest economic situation" and because she was "already in debt because of the expenses related to [her] preparation for the civil service exam." She appealed to Vargas's "magnanimous and proverbial concern for the difficulties and necessities of the Brazilian people" so that her fine "might be waived." Pires requested further that all of this might be done while taking into account her "urgent need for a birth certificate" so that she might "be placed in a job that would guarantee" her "daily bread," a "prize" that she had "earned with tremendous effort," which she had "spent in hopes of gaining placement in a productive and rewarding enterprise" that would "guarantee" her future and make her as "confident and happy" as she could be, given that she was "a lonely orphan."[141] In 1942, 12-year-old Lucy Cabral de Lacerda wrote to Vargas because she had heard that he was "very good for poor people," and she asked for his help in obtaining a birth certificate. After finishing primary school, she had "a great desire to continue studying" and wanted to take the entrance exam to study commerce. There was one thing holding her back, however: "I am not registered, and this makes me sad, because without a birth certificate I am nobody." Her father did not have the money to pay the requisite fines, and she appealed to Vargas to waive them "for the love of God" because she wanted to study "in order to be useful to [her] country."[142]

Many other correspondents complained that missing birth certificates blocked their access to social security, labor, and other benefits. In 1943, Leopoldo Maciel, an official of the Legião Brasileira de Assistência (LBA), a quasi-governmental charitable organization established under Vargas, confirmed their concerns.[143] "Given the rapid development of the country over the last several years," Maciel first noted, "the civil registration of native Brazilians . . . has become absolutely essential to individuals of every social condition." Nevertheless, he claimed, "the registration of poor people—and especially of the miserably poor, who, because of overwhelming difficulties, negligence, or malice, are not registered within the established time limits," was an intractable problem, despite the efforts of numerous charitable institutions, the LBA included. As an example of the overwhelming demand for aid with registration, Maciel claimed that the district attorney's office, "assisted by an entire body of substitute prosecutors and administrators," had attempted to set up a civil registration service "with great enthusiasm and much publicity." After just a few days, however, "in the face of an avalanche of candidates that inundated the courthouse," the service had been shut down, "leaving the judicial offices choked with requests and half-finished paperwork."

The main problem, according to Maciel, was the burdensome, bureaucratic nature of the late-registration process, which entailed "a court procedure requiring witness testimony before a judge as well as . . . documents such as marriage certificates, when the birth was legitimate, baptismal certificates, and certification that no other registration has been made." If these requirements were tough for "any normal candidate," they were "much more so for the poor or miserably poor person who often, besides being ignorant of the basic facts," lacked transportation and bureaucratic savvy. "Illiterate, unknown, and with no documents," most poor people had to procure not only someone to sign in their stead but also two witnesses to their birth. Again, this was hard enough for a "normal" candidate but proved a nearly insurmountable obstacle for "some unlucky being who drifts like a pilgrim from one part of the country to another" and is asked to provide witnesses long "after the memories of his birthplace and family have . . . faded." The result was corruption and frustration, which left the poor unable to deal legally with questions of custody, matrimony, separation, pension, and insurance settlements. Some action, according to Maciel, was urgent.

In subsequent years, Vargas's government and its successors attempted to ease such burdens. A 1943 law waived late fees for certifiably poor families registering children under the age of 12; with a judge's approval, the fine was also waived for children between the ages of 12 and 18. The same law left the presentation of witnesses and documents up to the judge's discretion.[144] Separate laws passed in 1945 and 1949 exempted everyone over 18 from penalties during designated voter registration periods and eliminated fines altogether for anyone over 17 who was required to register for military service. In all of these cases, candidates had to present two documented witnesses but were dispensed from all other requirements.[145] The LBA and other charitable organizations, such as the Serviço de Obras Sociais (SOS), the Albergue da Boa Vontade, the Cruzado São Sebastião, and the Fundação Leão XIII, did receive state support to establish registration services for the very poor. Still, even within Rio, intractable problems remained. Poor information, bureaucratic inefficiency, and a lack of corroborating witnesses continued to plague poor Cariocas, an increasing proportion of whom were migrants from distant rural areas. Corruption, too, complicated the process. In a 1942 letter, Otávio Pereira de Oliveira wrote to Vargas to complain that scribes and judges were charging (illegally) as much as 50–70 *mil-reis* for a single registration; he claimed that the situation was "out of control in the Capital of the Republic, and in the states it is worse," the result being widespread dishonesty and nonregistration.[146] No comprehensive legal measures were taken to combat such practices.

Evidence of registration rates becomes sketchy in the decades after 1940, but what exists indicates that Brazil's most basic document of citizenship remained far from universal. An admittedly rough estimate suggests that around 90 percent of children born in Rio were registered in the early 1950s; a comparison of Carioca births registered for the years 1951–55 with the number of native Carioca children between the ages of 5 and 9 reported in the 1960 census yields roughly comparable numbers.[147] But for the large numbers of very poor people who were not native Cariocas, the story was different. The favela census of 1948—the only statistical study to publish such figures—estimated that 23.4 percent of favela residents had never possessed a birth certificate.[148] Well into the 1950s, social service organizations such as the SOS (a local agency that provided medical, nutritional, economic, and educational assistance to poor residents throughout Rio) continued to lament that many of their clients did not possess proper birth certificates.[149] In 1959, the renowned statistician Giorgio Mortara claimed that Brazil's civil registries were still neither complete nor reliable enough to use for demographic research; agents from the IBGE, who always used census data rather than notarial records in calculating birth rates, confirmed this opinion.[150] More than one modern witness testifies that parents in the 1950s and 1960s commonly altered their children's ages so as not to incur fines for late registration.[151]

Like so many Vargas-era laws, the 1939 civil registration decree was more declaratory than constructive; its legacy was one of ambiguous precedent rather than altered practice. By reiterating that civil registration was mandatory, and by gesturing toward streamlined registration procedures, the law allowed documentary proof of birth to become the legal norm. Responsibility for its lack thus shifted from an inept state to an irresponsible populace. Because every Brazilian was now expected to have a birth certificate, the document could now be required, without legal contest, as the first bureaucratic stepping-stone to the realm of social and economic rights. And from there, rights seekers entered multiple bureaucratic gauntlets, each leading to a precious piece of paper—the reservist's card, the state ID card, the work ID card, the union card, the social security institute membership—which would serve as a key to one more realm of rights.

The requirements for the civil ID card exemplify the ways in which each bureaucratic process built on the others, amplifying and adding to their complications. Generalized civil identification began in Rio as an offshoot of the police identification service, which was itself part of a larger project of universal registration that was meant to greatly facilitate the apprehension of criminals and the "correction" of potential infractors.[152] According to the foundational 1923 law, applicants for civil identification were required to present a "certification of personal identity" from their local police delegate as well as documents attesting to their parents' identities, place and date of birth, nationality, educational level, occupation, and civil status.[153] Though special ID cards could be furnished to those without such papers (though not to those unable to attain police certification), they would not contain any civil information and would thus be virtually useless in the myriad arenas where civil IDs facilitated relationships with public authorities and the acquisition of other public documents, such as voter registration cards.

The most determined and agile among poor Cariocas managed to become documented, despite the legal hurdles; the task was not Sisyphean, just hard. But even in the best of cases, these bureaucratic hurdles to documentation caused months or years of delay and missed opportunities—jobs lost, school registrations abandoned, benefits denied. They also often encouraged the very poor either to depend heavily on patrons and shady intermediaries or to act extra-legally—presenting false witnesses and papers, lying about birth dates, bribing notaries—in order to secure their legal rights. This string of actions undermined both the credibility of the system and the individual relationship with the state that the law theoretically intended to bolster. This was a best-case scenario; at the other end of the spectrum, many among the poor simply failed to attain documents, resigning themselves, in the words of Lucy Cabral de Lacerda, to an existence as civic "nobodies." Such situations could last a lifetime. Speaking in 1996, long-time shantytown resident Maria da Conceião Ferreira Pinto (or "Dona Filinha") told the story of a woman in her 80s who had only recently attained papers; finally, Dona Filinha recounted, the woman was able to "feel like a person."[154]

EXCLUSIONS OF KIND: WORK AND CITIZENSHIP IN VARGAS'S RIO

The merger of citizenship rights with the documents that signified them generated a subtle and gradated form of social exclusion, one that operated less through legally explicit interdictions than through procedural myopia, a refusal to recognize that the burdens of establishing formal, documentary identities would weigh especially heavily on the shoulders of poor or rural people. Other exclusions operated more categorically. Both Vargas's labor laws and his limited social welfare provisions applied only to the fully documented; here, as elsewhere, papers mediated access to benefits, with all the requisite hassles and inequities. Yet papers alone did not guarantee citizenship. According to these laws, only those who lived out the values of work, family, and patriotism in narrowly prescribed ways merited state protection and largesse. Work was urban and formal, and family was traditional, large, and legally constituted; patriotism involved loyalty to Vargas and to his notions of morality and economic productivity. Clearly, these definitions fit uncomfortably with the habits, choices, and capacities of many poor Brazilians, a fact that Vargas tacitly recognized through his expansive rhetoric and responsiveness to popular correspondence. But alternate incarnations of Vargas's core values did not generate rights, only vague claims to charity. Social and economic citizenship was a privilege, not an entitlement; thus, oddly, it often came to reinforce, not ameliorate, long-entrenched inequities of power and opportunity.

For Vargas, work was the currency of poor people's citizenship. In his imagined social compact, the citizen-worker would, through his labor, at once ensure Brazil's economic advancement and enhance the nation's social well-being; in exchange, a grateful state would "dignify" his moral and material existence.[155] The constitutions of 1934 and 1937 formalized such rhetorical flourishes, but only specific labor laws could make them concrete. This legislation—published gradually over the course of the 1930s and early 1940s, and brought together in the 1943 CLT—bestowed great (if incomplete) benefits on most formalized urban workers. At the same time, it entrenched a narrow and formalistic definition of work that effectively devalued most of the labor performed by the very poor, urban and rural alike. "Work," here, did not denote any productive or paid labor; the term instead referred to a narrow range of occupations recognized as work by the national state.[156]

This legislation could give hope even to those it excluded. Civic advancement had been virtually inconceivable for the very poor. Now, through the lens of the CLT, it at least beckoned, attainable through the tough but fully imaginable transition from a rural to an urban livelihood, or from informal to formal labor. Benefits and protections that were extended to one family or community member often helped many more. Nevertheless, the law's exclusiveness fundamentally changed the nature of what was hoped for. This was not a form of citizenship rooted in natural rights or even moral logic, as was implied by Vargas's rhetorical and constitutional declarations. It was, rather, a form of patronage, a reward for membership in a system that hierarchically bound employees to their employers and to the national state.

The CLT, incorporating elements found in both the Italian Labor Charter of 1927 and Franklin D. Roosevelt's New Deal legislation, formalized a four-tier structure governing relations between capital and labor in Brazil.[157] First the CLT laid down legal definitions of the terms "workers" and "employers." It also ratified the constitutional provisions and earlier laws that had guaranteed the proportional dominance of Brazilians in most workplaces, and granted all legally established workers limited work hours, a minimum wage, yearly holidays, basic standards of labor safety and hygiene, restrictions on the extent and nature of female and child labor, and maternity leaves. Second, the CLT laid out the procedures through which workers could formalize work contracts, limited the employer's power to rescind or alter such contracts without prior notice, and established tenure guarantees for workers who stayed in their places of employment for ten years or more. Third, the CLT outlined a complex system regulating the procedural rules, rights, and obligations of official unions, which were limited in number and could function only with state sanction. The CLT uniquely empowered these unions to negotiate collective work contracts, collect union taxes, and serve as the workers' voice in the political arena. Fourth, the CLT established a new branch of the Brazilian judicial system, the Justiça do Trabalho, dedicated to the mediation and resolution of workplace conflicts. The Justiça do Trabalho functioned entirely independently of the civil and criminal legal systems, with its own judges, prosecutors, and courts, which received absolute power to adjudicate work-related disputes. Although they were not officially part of the CLT, later laws insuring workers against workplace accidents and systematizing the operation of the Brazilian social security system filled out the spectrum of Vargas's labor legislation.[158]

Many of the CLT's limitations appeared in its nooks and crannies, more a matter of omission and procedural detail than of open and outright exclusion. The first obstacle was documentary: no worker could claim the law's protection without obtaining and correctly using the so-called *carteira profissional* (work card). The document, instituted in 1932, functioned as a sort of worker's passport; political scientist Wanderley Guilherme dos Santos has called it "a civic birth certificate."[159] Any adult could obtain a *carteira* in the offices of the Departamento Nacional do Trabalho by providing comprehensive personal information—date and place of birth, both parents' names, civil status, occupation, address, educational level—along with a photograph, fingerprints, and a signature.[160] Applicants also had to provide the names, primary activities, and locations of their present and previous workplaces, describe their responsibilities within those establishments, and give their salaries and dates of employment. In addition, workers listed the names, ages, and civil status of all of their economic dependents and the names of any unions of which they were members. Men had to prove that they had met the requirements for military service, and naturalized Brazilians had to give the dates when they had arrived in Brazil and received their naturalization certificates. Official documentation or the testimony of two witnesses who already possessed the *carteira* had to substantiate all declarations;

foreigners faced additional requirements. Illiterate applicants had to have three witnesses, one of whom was willing to sign in their place, and all applicants had to certify their occupations through diplomas, letters from previous employers, or the testimony of two *carteira*-bearing witnesses. Each *carteira* cost 5 *cruzeiros*, which could be waived for unemployed workers or for those who earned less than the minimum wage. Neither domestic employees nor rural workers were eligible for the *carteira* or for most of the benefits it entailed.[161]

Once a *carteira* was obtained, the worker presented it to his or her employer, who then had 48 hours to inscribe it with the individual's date of hire, employment type, employee number, and wage. Employers could not officially note any negative observations about a worker's character or conduct unless the comments involved convictions in a civil, criminal, or labor court. Once signed by an employer, the *carteira* served both as general identification and as a legal labor contract, valid in all disputes brought before the labor court as well as in cases relating to social security and workplace accidents. Without a signed *carteira*, a worker's employment did not exist in the eyes of the law, and most of the CLT's protections or guarantees did not apply.

For those who were able to obtain the *carteira* and the requisite signatures, the document served as both a curriculum vitae and a contract, legal proof of a life dedicated to gainful employment and a legal guarantee that certain basic rights ought not to be violated. For those who could not or did not acquire and use the *carteira*, however, its absence became a liability, a burden that they would not have carried had Vargas's labor laws never existed at all. Established factories or commercial establishments almost always required a *carteira* of any prospective worker; men and women without one were usually relegated to shady, casual, or informal work where conditions remained as bad as or worse than they had been before 1930. The *carteira* also became a powerful symbol of righteous citizenship—and especially of male citizenship—outside of the workplace. Police authorities habitually demanded one from any individual suspected of vagrancy, and the document also proved a virtual guarantee that authorities would grant bail to a defendant in most criminal cases.[162] The *carteira* thus evolved into a sort of distinguishing mark—more surely reliable even than color, dress, address, or style of speech—that allowed employers and judicial authorities alike to separate those they regarded as citizens from those they saw as *marginais*.

There were many reasons why a Carioca worker might not have wanted to have or utilize the *carteira profissional* in the 1930s and 1940s. Anyone with a spotty job history or criminal record may not have wanted to expose such things to potential employers; some might have been able to make more money off the books; others may have opposed in principle the governmental supervision the *carteira* entailed.[163] But, especially in the 1940s and early 1950s—before inflation had permanently eroded some of the CLT's material advantages, and when its unfulfilled provisions could still be chalked up to novelty—most poor Cariocas probably preferred the advantages of having a signed *carteira* over the uncertainties of going without one.

Still, many did not have much of a choice; obtaining the card was complicated, and convincing employers to sign it was more difficult still. Social workers, academics, and statisticians frequently lamented that many workers, especially rural migrants, could not find decent work because they lacked the proper documentation. A typical complaint appeared in the *Boletim* of the SOS in February 1947:

> The *carteira profissional* is absolutely indispensable, but many of our applicants do not have one because the regulations governing its acquisition are too burdensome; they require applicants to have a birth certificate, which many do not possess—many do not even know if they were ever registered, and those who do, when they come from other states, often do not know enough details for the SOS to help them order a certificate through the mail, making it very difficult indeed to satisfy this requirement.[164]

It is hard to know how generalized these problems were, because statistical surveys on the question were never carried out. The Ministério do Trabalho did keep records on the number of *carteiras* issued in Rio; these figures, along with general Carioca death rates and estimates of the population eligible for work cards between 1940 and 1960, suggest that around 50 percent of the adult population held work cards in 1940, and around 75 percent possessed them in 1960 (fig. 1). Given that access to cards was likely more difficult among the very poor than among the population at large, and that most poor people, including women, had to work outside the home at least sometimes, such figures probably underestimate the gravity of the situation among Rio's poorest. These estimates are also rough for other reasons; among other things, they don't separate the economically active from the inactive, and they do not account for workers who retired, migrated from Rio, or left the formal workforce because of marriage, disability, incarceration, or unemployment.[165] Nevertheless, they do roughly confirm social workers' complaints from the 1940s, which were echoed in scattered sources well into the 1960s and 1970s. In 1967, the only favela survey from these decades to provide precise statistics on *carteiras* noted that about 79 percent of the economically active population of the north-zone industrial favela of Brás de Pina

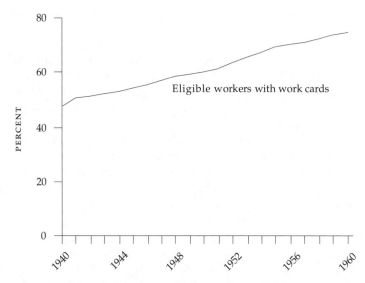

FIG. 1. Percentage of eligible workers with work cards.

possessed work cards, and that this percentage was probably consider-ably higher than that found in other shantytowns, where more adults worked in construction, odd jobs, and domestic service.[166]

Anthropologist Janice E. Perlman reported similar difficulties among the favela residents she worked with in the late 1960s:

> Favela workers are for the most part denied benefits and guarantees won by other workers in the labor legislation passed under Vargas in the 1930s and 1940s. . . . One reason *favelados* cannot claim these benefits or qualify for better jobs is that they do not have a work card (*carteira de trabalho*). To receive a *carteira*, Brazil-ians must have a birth certificate to prove they are recognized citizens. In most of the countryside, births are performed by midwives, and birth certificates are not available. Even for those whose *documentos* are in order . . . there is an incredible mass of red tape requiring visits to bureau after bureau. Thus many migrants are defeated before they start. The final blow, described to me by a 60-year-old man who persevered for six months to obtain his *carteira*, is to be told by a manager that a job is available only on condition that the work card *not* be signed, so that the firm will not have to pay social security benefits, pensions, sick leave, and overtime rates. Since he received his card, this man has been working a 12-hour shift for half the minimum wage, without any worker protection. To his firm he is non-registered, a nonentity.[167]

Perlman's text highlights another bleak reality: simple possession of a *carteira* did nothing to guarantee that it would be signed, and without an employer's signature, the card meant nothing. In certain cases, like that noted by Perlman, the problem was employer recalcitrance; some workers, caught in the unfavorable currents of an urban labor market flooded by a constant stream of new migrants, found themselves forced to accept jobs off the books. In other cases, coercion could be subtler or even a matter of choice. Abdias José dos Santos, an ex–construction worker and longtime resident and community leader in the central favela of São Carlos, recalled that highly skilled construction workers such as himself were often given a choice of working legally, with lower wages, or informally, with higher wages. For a poor man with a young family to support, the choice was obvious. Occasionally, moreover, even when workers believed they were working formally, companies would cheat, failing to pay the requisite taxes and appropriating workers' social security contributions as their own.[168]

It is difficult to estimate how many people working in recognized professions did so without a signed *carteira*; their labor was, by definition, illegal, and they were hardly likely to say as much to government census agents or social workers. Nonetheless, we can gain some notion of their prevalence in two of Rio's three largest employment sectors—industry and commerce—by comparing the number of people who claimed these two professions in the demographic censuses with the number of workers who were actually declared as such by companies in the economic censuses.[169] In industry—which, according to individual declarations, employed 23.3 percent of the economically active population in 1940, 26.1 percent in 1950, and 20.2 percent in 1960—between 15 percent and 27 percent of self-defined workers were not claimed by companies (table 4). In commerce—which was the declared profession of 16.3 percent of the economically active population in 1940, of 12.9 percent in 1950, and of 13.4 percent in 1960—the figures are somewhat more erratic; although employers claimed most workers in 1950, nearly 29 percent were left out in 1940, and over 12 percent were omitted in 1960 (table 5).

Unfortunately, the censuses do not provide enough information to estimate informality in other categories. In at least one sector—services,

TABLE 4

Percentage of Informal Workers in Industry, 1940–1960

Year	Industry—workers' declarations	Industry—company declarations	Percent informal workers
1940	145,677	123,459	15.25
1950	233,079	171,463	26.44
1960	161,981	137,212	15.29

SOURCES: Recenseamentos Gerais do Brasil, 1940, 1950, 1960 (demographic and economic data).

TABLE 5

Percentage of Informal Workers in Commerce, 1940–1960

Year	Commerce—workers' declarations	Commerce—company declarations	Percent informal workers
1940	73,221	52,139	28.79
1950	81,524	80,986	.66
1960	109,230	96,008	12.10

SOURCES: Recenseamentos Gerais do Brasil, 1940, 1950, 1960 (demographic and economic data).

which by 1960 had surpassed industry as Rio's largest—the percentages were likely quite high. In others, such as the liberal professions, they were probably minimal.[170] In any case, it seems clear that a very large portion—between 10 percent and 30 percent—of Rio's population active in CLT-recognized sectors worked informally in the years between 1940 and 1960; this percentage was doubtless higher among the poorest of the poor.

In some other lines of work, virtually all labor occurred, by definition, off the books. Here, procedural ambiguity gave way to categorical exclusion. According to its seventh article, most of the CLT simply did not apply to domestic and "autonomous" workers, regardless of their work-card status.[171] Rural laborers were also mainly excluded, though they could theoretically claim rights to the minimum wage, vacation time, layoff notice, and individual contracts.[172] According to census figures, these three categories of workers composed anywhere from 20 to 26 percent of Rio's economically active population between 1942 and 1960.[173] Among the poor, and especially among women, the problem was much worse. According to the 1950 favela census, nearly 65 percent of economically active women worked in the service sector, which was often shorthand for domestic service; by 1960, services accounted for nearly 70 percent of female favela workers.[174] Valdecir Lopes's 1953 survey of the Cantagalo favela, on the border between Copacabana and Ipanema, indicated that of 344 women heads of household, 42 percent worked in domestic services, 14.5 percent as washerwomen, and 9.9 percent at odd jobs; another 42 percent were in the category of unspecified or miscellaneous work.[175] Lopes's analysis of the near-north-zone favela of Bareira do Vasco yielded similar figures: of 242 female heads of household, 34 percent were domestic employees, 16 percent were washerwomen, 8 percent worked in commerce (which could include street vending), and 41 percent did not specify a line of work.[176] Nonwhites were also disproportionately concentrated in excluded occupational categories.[177] The fact

TABLE 6

*Agricultural, Domestic, and "Autonomous" Workers
in Rio de Janeiro, 1940–1960*

Year	Agricultural workers	Domestic workers	Autonomous workers	Total not covered by CLT	Percent total workforce not covered by CLT
1940	18,023	74,315	78,948	171,286	25.46
1950	15,997	102,604	76,315	194,916	20.33
1960	15,081	126,105	109,880	251,066	21.35

SOURCES: Recenseamentos Gerais do Brasil, 1940, 1950, 1960.

that many formally inactive individuals in fact worked off the books to help support their families meant that such statistics likely understated the problem. All in all, the most general provisions of the CLT applied inconstantly or not at all to most poor Carioca workers.

Workers with signed *carteiras* gained access only to the first level of benefits and guarantees set out in the CLT.[178] In order to profit from collective bargaining and social security, individuals had to pass through two entirely separate bureaucratic gauntlets, a process that winnowed still further the number of working people able to take full advantage of Vargas's labor legislation. Collective bargaining—virtually the only tool available to low-level workers in search of additional wages and benefits—could be carried out only by recognized unions, which by the 1960s had become extremely hierarchical and notoriously corrupt.[179] Due to this, and also to numerous procedural obstacles, union membership among Rio's economically active population remained quite low despite the exhortations of Vargas and his political heirs. In 1940, only about 20.7 percent of working Cariocas were union members, and of these almost 80 percent were male; percentages within individual economic sectors range from 14.7 percent in services to 37 percent in transport and communications. By 1960, about 28 percent of all workers belonged to unions—an increase, to be sure, but certainly not enough to indicate that collective bargaining was a tool widely available to the Carioca working population.[180]

The social security system was similarly restricted.[181] It had its origins in 1923, in the form of company-specific *Caixas de Aposentadoria e Pensões* (CAPs), which were financed through contributions from workers, employers, and the state.[182] Between 1930 and 1960, the CAPs gradually faded in favor of sector wide *Institutos de Aposentadoria e Pensões* (IAPs), managed publicly and often subordinated to union bosses.[183] In

1960, the government standardized the procedures and benefits of all IAPs—a project that had been in the works since the 1940s—and in 1966 the Instituto Nacional de Previdência Social brought them all under a single administrative umbrella.[184] In all of their incarnations, the CAPs and IAPs provided workers with accident insurance, retirement and disability income, medical insurance, and unemployment benefits. They were also an extremely important source of low-to-moderate-income housing. Nonetheless, membership lagged far behind employment, even in Rio. According to the 1940 census, only 39.5 percent of the economically active Carioca population belonged to IAPs or CAPs; 85 percent of members were men, and participation by employment sector ranged from 23.4 percent for services to 64 percent for public administration. Later censuses do not provide comprehensive information, but the global number would have stood at about 48 percent of Rio's economically active population if membership there grew at a rate similar to that elsewhere in the country.[185]

Here, too, women were especially likely to be excluded, and percentages among low-income workers were also lower because autonomous, domestic, and rural workers were not eligible for membership until the early 1970s.[186] Favela studies provide more proximate figures for Rio's poor population in the 1950s and 1960s. According to Lopes's 1953 study of family heads in Cantagalo, 76 percent of all men and 14 percent of all women heads of household belonged to IAPs and CAPs; the global figure was around 59 percent of all family heads. A 1953 study of the city's first Parque Proletário found that 39 percent of residents did not belong to any CAP or IAP, a fact especially surprising because these residents tended to be better employed and more thoroughly documented than the average favela resident.[187] A 1965 study of another municipal public housing project indicated that little had changed: only 59 percent of the complex's heads of household were affiliated with social security institutes.[188]

The guarantees of the CLT and the social security laws were initially little more than ink on paper; even for workers who should legally have qualified for full benefits, the struggle for effective rights was bitter. Even before the CLT's publication, letters to Vargas exposed wide-ranging dysfunctions in the individual laws that the code would bring together. In 1937, an unemployed ship's steward complained that he could not afford the exorbitant (and extralegal) fees charged for union membership; yet if he did not join, he would find no work at all.[189] In June 1941, a longshoreman lamented that, after more than 18 years of service, no one would hire him because he was over the age of 35 and thus ineligible for union membership.[190] In 1939 and 1940, a widowed mother of seven wrote repeatedly to Vargas and his labor minister to complain that she had spent two fruitless years in pursuit of death benefits she believed she was due from the maritime workers' IAP after her husband's workplace death. Despite a court decision in her favor, and despite weekly visits to the IAP's offices (each of which implied leaving her children and losing a day of laundering work), she was still penniless, in the midst of a seemingly endless cycle of court appeals.[191] In July 1940, another worker wrote from a semi-rural part of western Rio to "expose" the fact that many employers were firing employees just short of the ten-year mark that would have guaranteed them job stability.[192] In 1941, 318 workers from the Companhia de Carrís, Luz e Força do Rio de Janeiro wrote to complain that the company was deliberately contracting labor on a day-to-day basis rather than accepting workers as permanent employees, in order to avoid its legal obligations; this policy put the workers in the position of "slaves," ineligible for paid rest and other benefits, and forced to show up every day without sure work ("a useless daily pilgrimage").[193] These letters—respectful, and always conferring on Vargas his projected role of the workers' "father" and "protector"—foreshadowed decades of more combative workers' struggles in workplaces, courtrooms, and city streets.[194] Seen through the letters' lens, Vargas's laws were less a gift that headed off social struggle than an ideal that guided and shaped it.[195]

Still, all of these complaints were written in the language of rights wronged. These writers may have been tripped up by a mass of red tape, corruption, and inefficiency; but they wrote as citizen-workers, with the assurance of claims founded in law, rather than as poor supplicants. This placed them at the more privileged end of a spectrum that began with workers categorically excluded from social and economic citizenship; continued with those theoretically eligible but unable to attain work cards or get them signed; went on to those legally employed but unable to unionize, join social security institutes, or otherwise qualify for full protections and benefits; and ended with legally employed, fully unionized and entitled workers, who nonetheless often struggled to transform all of their paper rights into concrete benefits. Rights, here, were a privilege, and the kind of labor that paved the path to them was narrowly and bureaucratically defined, a fact that tore at the seams of Vargas's rhetorical fusion of work, virtue, and citizenship.

At least one Carioca laborer did not let the poor fit between law and rhetoric stand unnoticed. In an unusually explicit 1939 letter, a rural worker named Rosário Patané respectfully confronted Vargas with the gap between his promises to working people and his legislative exclusion of the rural poor.[196] Brazilian-born, 63 years old, and a reservist in the army, Patané had made his home in the Morro de São Carlos, in central

Rio. His work had always been in the country, though, most recently on a small plot off of the E. F. Rio D'Ouro train line, purchased on monthly installments and planted with "national plants." He wrote because, after 35 years of labor, disaster had struck suddenly, leaving him hospitalized with a "fatal" lung infection. His family was alone "in the most desolate misery," and his lands were abandoned; he wrote to Vargas for help, sure that the president would receive his request "with the affection and consideration for justice and charity with which you were endowed by God as the Supreme Leader of a Nationality on this earth." Patané went on to praise Vargas's "c[l]ear-sightedness and extreme generosity," qualities that had led him to concede "salvation" to the public, giving all Brazilians "a certain and patriotic moral and educational path" as well as "a sure and secure guarantee with respect to their economic and individual lives." With his "intelligent social organization," Vargas had made it so that "every and any working stratum of the country enjoys such a guaranthy [sic] that there is now no human being in Brazil who is left at luck's whim if he becomes unfit to work." Workers, organized in unions and making regular contributions, were now insured against "final indigence after working so much"; there was "nothing . . . more Saintly and just."

Here, though, the praise stopped. The legislation was not complete: there was "a class of workers left at the margins of the law, without any guarantee," laborers who were "working the land, in the rain and the sun, feed[ing] the rest and cooperat[ing] with their parcel of work for Brazil's greatness." Rural workers were as worthy, in moral terms, as any laborer who received the benefits of Vargas's legislation; why were they excluded?

Vargas's government provided no answer, though it did investigate the complaint thoroughly and invite Patané to Catete Palace to receive unspecified charity. Emblematically, Patané had virtually acknowledged that this would be the best that he could hope for, signing his letter with the emblematic request that Vargas grant him "the benefit, or the charity, of giving me a pension." Patané's letter, with its hope for rights, its criticism of citizenship's limitations, and its ultimate resignation to supplication, could have been written in the name of many other poor Cariocas.

BOUNDING THE REALM OF RIGHTS: WELFARE AND CHARITY UNDER VARGAS

Certified work kept the gates not only to labor benefits but also to many of the measures intended to fulfill Vargas's constitutional promises to help the poor. Almost every national program that defined social welfare as an individual right—from aid to the elderly to medical care to housing to disability and death benefits—entitled only officially recognized workers and their dependents.[197] The one major exception was the *abono familiar,* or family allowance, a federal program that provided cash payments to large families throughout Brazil for more than 30 years.[198] Anticipated in the 1937 constitution and widely publicized, the measure generated enormous popular response and was probably critical to Vargas's image as the "father of the poor."[199] In its final form, however, the law operated in ways quite parallel to the CLT. Even though it targeted a rural rather than an urban public, the law still defined families narrowly and bureaucratically, prejudiced the undocumented, favored those with close state ties, and entirely excluded people whose families did not fit state-sanctioned molds. Though the law inspired enormous public optimism in Rio, it transformed only a select few into entitled citizens.

The *abono* came into being as part of the 1941 Lei de Família, or Family Law, a broad measure that aimed to fulfill constitutional promises of governmental "protection" for large families through a wide range of provisions, most of which converged on the triple goals of aiding poor families, molding familial behavior, and extending state regulation.[200] The *abono* was a small salary supplement for all working parents, conceived as a reward for their dual social function. Ideologically, the notion had roots in Catholic social doctrine, and especially in the *Rerum Novarum;* practically, its models were French and Belgian.[201] As published, the measure provided cash entitlements to public employees and "heads of large families . . . whose compensation [was] by no means sufficient to provide minimal sustenance for their children."[202]

The law tempered such promises with a long list of caveats and restrictions. Public employees automatically received a higher *abono* than any other class of workers.[203] In order to claim any benefit, the law required couples to provide legal proof of marriage and birth certificates for all of their children, who had to be "legitimate"; the law also mandated a vaguely defined yearly certification (provided by local police and school officials) that a parent had "provided education" for the children, "not only physical and intellectual but also moral."[204] In the end, only public employees with steady jobs and stable marriages, who were successfully providing eight or more biological children with "education" while requiring none to contribute to the family income, could claim the full range of entitlements.[205] The original legislation's expansive populist appeal dissipated quickly with its implementation, leaving at its core a set of benefits that constituted individual privilege rather than public entitlement.

The *abono*'s mention in the 1937 constitution generated popular correspondence even before the law took effect; the national archives retain some 95 letters written to Vargas by Rio residents who hoped to receive the benefit. Written by a wide spectrum of the Carioca poor, they suggest that most people knew that distinctions between deserving and undeserving need belied the generosity of Vargas's rhetoric. Only a few supplicants, though—all men, all apparently stably employed, and some perhaps speaking through professional scribes—had mastered the technical and moral minutiae that would eventually make them eligible for benefits, and able to claim them in the language of entitlement. Otávio Almada, who wrote to Vargas shortly after the Family Law passed, presented his case in concise legalistic terms:

> Otávio Almada, carrier of identity card no. 504,208, Brazilian, 43 years of age, married to Julieta Cartriola Almada, resident in Bangú, on Rangel Pestana Street, no. 66, in this federal district, established with a small shoe-repair workshop, father of eight (8) minors, finding himself with serious difficulties in maintaining and educating them, comes very respectfully to ask Your Excellency if you might order the concession to me of the aid foreseen in Decreto-Lei no. 3200, published in the *Diario Oficial* on 19 April 1941 and signed by Your Excellency, in which Decreto-Lei I find myself qualified for the benefits of article 29, for which purpose I am attaching to this letter all of the necessary documents required by article 39, and I am not sealing this request with an official stamp in accord with the provisions of article 40.[206]

Respectful but exigent, Almada's letter was that of a citizen who knew how the law defined the core values of family and work, and who had taken great pains to fulfill its requirements by marrying legally, working steadily, procuring documents, and seeking to maintain and educate his children. Most other Carioca letters lacked both Almada's technical assiduity and his confident use of the language of rights.[207] Frequently, Carioca families simply did not fit the targeted profile. Most often, like urban residents throughout Brazil, they had too few children, or too few children under the age of 18; other times, families lacked documents or did not understand the law's basic procedures. Letters from these families rarely mentioned rights. Rather, they called on older notions of patriarchal responsibility to the poor or weak and emphasized Vargas's rhetorical inclusiveness, claiming charity by virtue of their hard work and daily struggles to raise families that would contribute to Brazil's greater glory. Typical was an ultrapatriotic letter sent by Cantídio Francisco Egsindola, the same federal plague-eradication employee who had included a bit of the Brazilian flag with his 1939 letter:

> Your Excellency has no idea, this passionate friend of Your Excellency, this public employee, feels so much friendship for Your Excellency, that the portrait that I

have in my tiny house is an *imamm* [sic] of comfort, I have had this portrait close to me for a long time as proof of my eternal friendship. . . . . This humble public servant, knowing that Your Excellency is humanitarian President number one who doesn't let the child of the Country suffer miserable poverty, for this reason I come very respectfully to ask Your Excellency to end this need. It's the following Senhor President, I, Cantídio Francisco Egsindola Sanitary guard, class D am Suffering the greatest necessity. With four children there are Days that they Go without lunch and without dinner Senhor President my train fare alone costs 1$800 *reis* per day. . . . . This friend of Your Excellency Goes entire days without eating I'm already weak. Senhor President I need some help from Your Excellency in order to feed my beloved children Senhor President. . . . Nothing more to say, your servant and loyal friend, Cantídio Francisco Egsindola.208

Another letter, of less certainly Carioca origins, made an even more dramatic plea. After detailing the "great necessity" that she and her nine dependents had suffered since her husband's 1942 death, and making it clear that she and her children worked hard but still couldn't afford food or the clothes and books they would need to attend school, a rural worker named Petronilha Silva dos Anjos, appealed to Vargas "for the love of the Milk that Fed you at the breast of your esteemed mother" to help her out. Her historical allusion was especially illuminating: "Dom Pedor [sic] 2 Freed our Nation from that terrible strain [of slavery] and helped many Poor people. In this way our governor might also relieve a Poor person like me, I am asking for Charity."209

In the end, numbers narrate most eloquently the destiny of most such hopes. By 1944, only 311 Carioca families (and 2,640 individuals) had benefited from the *abono*; by 1953, the total had climbed to only 745 families and 6,194 individuals, and throughout the 1950s the annual number of *abonos* paid to Cariocas annually did not rise above 500.210 The subsidies Cariocas did receive, moreover, would not have gotten them very far. In April 1943, when the law finally went into effect, the *abono* for nonpublic employees was only 100 *cruzeiros* for a family with eight children and 20 *cruzeiros* for each additional child. The base amount was enough to meet the basic monthly nutritional needs of one adult or two children, one-third of the monthly minimum salary set in May of that year.211 In 1953, the average Carioca beneficiary family received about 1,490 *cruzeiros* for the entire year, only equivalent to about one month's minimum wage. By 1957, the yearly payment was only equivalent to about one-third of one month's minimum wage.212 Relatively small to start with, and quickly eroded by inflation, the *abono* barely qualified as social welfare by the late 1950s.

What, then, remained of Vargas's promises to Rio's rights-poor? His government could claim, with some reason, to have greatly expanded public support of private charity in the years after 1930. In accordance with article 30 of the Family Law, the government subsidized a number of social service agencies, and both Rio's municipal administration and the private sector followed suit. The number of nongovernmental charitable organizations registered in Rio grew from about 10 in 1930 to 67 in 1945; it diminished to 39 in 1952 and again expanded to 65 by 1962, though these shifts may simply reflect varying accuracy in reporting. The Vargas years also saw the birth of large quasi-public establishments such as the LBA (1942) and the SOS; governmental partnerships with churches would further blur the public/private line as the struggle over favela policy heated up in the 1940s, 1950s, and 1960s.[213]

The scope of even the largest of these organizations remained narrow. Between 1932 and 1945, the average private charity served somewhere between 113 and 184 people per day.[214] The municipal Albergue da Boa Vontade, one of Rio's largest public shelters for the desperately poor, served an average of between 214 and 225 people at each of its three simple meals in the early 1940s, and gave additional daily rations to some 160 especially sick or needy individuals; a 1945 report puts the daily average served at 382.[215] The SOS—which, along with the LBA, probably provided more direct assistance than any other Carioca organization—distributed an average of 230 snacks and 170 kilograms of foodstuffs per day between 1934 and 1962, and these programs were the organization's largest.[216] Its other, more forward-looking projects—which included support for civil registration and work documents as well as literacy classes, job training, and employment services—had a drastically more limited scope. Patterns in other agencies were probably similar: in 1952, Rio's 39 establishments claimed to have helped 343,397 people. These numbers represent single instances of small-scale help—meals given, documents procured, food handed out.[217]

Even these limited forms of charity came with strings attached. Given the context of the day, within and outside of Brazil, it is not surprising that most charities had religious or moralizing intentions.[218] If Barbara Weinstein's work on later decades in São Paulo is any indication, moreover, poor and working-class people were not always entirely opposed to the sort of educational and moral programs that many charities provided, often as a condition of aid.[219] But the drive to push the dependent poor into better conformity with the charities' own definitions of work, family, and morality must sometimes have grated. Most charitable groups, like Vargas himself, divided the very poor into distinct categories. The virtuous poor were those who could not be expected to help themselves—children, the aged, the infirm. Unemployed men, single mothers, and others who found themselves unaccountably destitute fell into another category; their dilemma was material but also social and moral, and it demanded didactic as well as practical assistance. For men, the remedy was straightforward: vocational training and, often, aid that was given only in exchange for low-wage labor brokered through aid organizations.[220] For women, vocational training was important, but their special role as mothers urged a strong dose of moral education as well.

Victor Tavares de Moura, who served for many years as head of the municipal Department for Social Assistance, offered insight into the reasons why social workers believed such educational efforts were necessary for women. In the late 1940s, he wrote a letter proposing that the Albergue da Boa Vontade be expanded to include a "maternal house" whose principal aims would be to "reeducate through work" the women who frequented the shelter. This was necessary, he wrote, because "it is well known what a grave problem the sheltered woman represents. Without wanting to work, used to life on the street, indolent and lacking morality, [these women] go on acquiring new children, whose paternity is difficult to determine, and these children serve as an excuse to receive aid from the shelter, that sometimes goes on indefinitely."[221] There was little room here for poor women's dignity, much less for their independent moral codes. Along the same lines, the SOS closely supervised poor mothers, teaching them basic eugenic precepts and training them for appropriately female labors; part of the organization's stated task was to teach young women to accept "in their spirit the conviction that all work is ennobling, even the most lowly," with the implication that they were not capable of arriving independently at that conclusion. The Casa do Pobre da Nossa Senhora de Copacabana—a neighborhood charity that provided child care, medical and dental clinics, some foodstuffs, and an employment agency for domestic servants—implicitly dismissed the parenting skills of poor mothers in a 1936 proposal for a primary and vocational school for indigent children:

> The Casa do Pobre intends in this way to begin working with children when they are still in preschool and, giving them the proper treatments, according to the prescriptions of modern science, to hand them over to Society able to efficiently integrate themselves as useful elements, not only materially but also morally.[222]

A similar philosophy underlay an otherwise progressive proposal for the Casa do Doméstico, an organization that aimed to provide medical, legal, and educational assistance and child care to Carioca domestic servants, an urgent necessity in a society where, "so many years after the abolition of slavery . . . domestic servants are still denied the least bit of access to rights, protection, or help." At the same time that the proposal's author decried such exclusion, however, she reinforced some of its assumptions, specifying that the organization would thoroughly investigate applicants' personal and criminal backgrounds and would require all servants to take courses aimed at "morally perfecting" them because "the domestic servant has generally paid little attention to anything related to intellectual or moral education, either because of lack of free time . . . or because of a simple question of mentality."[223]

Charity, in short, was quite literally a poor alternative to rights. Although many were surely grateful for what help the charities provided, it was often scanty, moralistic, and dependent on strict adherence to the charities' idealized conceptions of poor people's social role. In this sense, it fit neatly with the Vargas government's general conception of social and economic citizenship as a restricted and meritocratic sphere; rights for the poor were really privileges, earned through model social behavior and agile bureaucratic navigation. In this light, the charities' main roles were to alleviate poverty's most disturbing manifestations—public homelessness, infant mortality, starvation—and incrementally prepare the poor to earn citizenship status. But for those who believed that Vargas's ideals of work, family, and patriotism could intersect with their own, relegation to such a sparse and narrow realm of charity must have been a rude awakening.

Work, Welfare, and Citizenship, 1945–64

The blueprint for social and economic citizenship set out in the CLT, the Family Law, and adjacent legislation proved durable. At the end of the Estado Novo, in 1945, Vargas's labor and social welfare laws were still mostly paper; their effective meaning would be worked out over more than half a century of social struggle, individual and collective, judicial and extralegal. But the basic principles of what Wanderley Guilherme dos Santos famously dubbed "regulated citizenship" would remain for decades. Legally recognized work would be the link between personhood and citizenship; work would be recognized as such only through the signed *carteira de trabalho*; official unions would be the only legitimate expression of collective demands; and certain categories of workers—rural, domestic, and autonomous—would be excluded entirely from the labor and social security systems until the 1960s and 1970s.[224] Without worker status, state aid would be sparse and charity was often the only alternative.

Pressures for change certainly surfaced. Rural laborers especially battled vociferously for inclusion in the labor law system, challenging restrictions in labor courts, organizing rural syndicates, and attracting support from numerous luminaries, including, from early on, Vargas himself.[225] Factory workers in Rio, São Paulo, and elsewhere struggled, often publicly, for a more autonomous collective voice.[226] And small challenges to bureaucratic restrictions on active citizenship—individual attempts to evade bureaucratic roadblocks on the road to rights—surely continued long after Vargas's correspondence ceased to be preserved.[227] Some small victories resulted; rural laborers eventually won their statute, though not, for the most part, its enforcement; some bureaucratic procedures were eased; and the government instituted a few measures, such as price controls on consumer goods, which skirted entirely the issue of employment.[228] All the same, the formal structure of economic and social citizenship remained in the early 1960s much as it had been laid out 20 years before.

What did change, and drastically, were the laws' effective meanings—the degree and manner of their enforcement, and the external circumstances that conditioned their significance. The institutions laid out in the CLT and the various social security laws grew and deepened during these years. The number of *carteiras* issued in Rio more than kept up with population growth; it is likely that some 75 percent of the working-age Carioca population possessed one by 1960.[229] Cases tried annually by the Carioca Justiça do Trabalho expanded similarly, as did the number of cases won by workers.[230] More and more Cariocas became union members—the total number of *sindicatos* in Rio jumped from 61 in 1942 to 93 in 1963, and the numbers of workers per union increased from 3,725 to 4,834 in the same period.[231] Social Security Institutes grew, and some offered increasingly significant benefits, especially in the area of housing.[232] At the same time, the *carteira de trabalho*'s importance quickly extended beyond the realm of work; by the 1950s, it was an irreplaceable badge of respectability in most public arenas, especially those involving the justice system.[233] In all of these ways, institutions and emblems of social and economic citizenship—and struggles for them—came to mark the lives of many poor Cariocas, shaping the circumstances in which they lived, worked, and thought about themselves as citizens.

Even as *trabalhista* institutions grew, though, their power to transform both individual lives and Brazil's culture of citizenship expanded only erratically. In part, as in other areas of Brazilian (and other) law, practice simply eroded legally consecrated ideals. Clogged courts, employers' intransigence, inadequate regulation, and collusion between judicial officials and employers all constrained the battle for legal rights.[234] Some employers flouted the laws secretly, or corruptly; others found ways around the law (*jeitinhos*), offering workers higher wages to work off the books, or changing their employment practices to avoid hiring full-time workers at all.[235] Economic and demographic developments spurred such practices. In Rio as elsewhere, the number of jobs of the sort that would be recognized by the CLT only barely kept pace with population growth through 1960, as Brazil's economy grew unevenly, industrial expansion concentrated ever more heavily in São Paulo, and bureaucratic resources shifted abruptly to Brasília.[236] Many poor Cariocas remember work as being abundant during these years, especially in comparison to the disastrous decades of the 1980s and 1990s.[237] But there were never enough jobs for unorganized, low-skilled workers to force formal recognition of their work. At the same time, inflation—accelerating in fits and starts from the mid-1940s through the mid-1960s, and peaking at nearly 87 percent in 1964—eroded the value of the minimum wage, the *abono familiar*, the *salário família*, and benefits paid out by the Social Security

Institutes, making the most accessible of Vargas-era privileges seem less worth fighting for in the first place.[238]

For workers whose skills, experience, and job tenure immunized them somewhat from such tumultuous circumstances, the CLT and adjacent laws could still mean a great deal—stable work, retirement, housing, the not unimportant prestige of belonging solidly within the realm of economic citizenship. But for poor people whose livelihoods hung in a more precarious balance, the CLT and social welfare legislation did not transform the nature of citizenship by irrevocably "dignifying" work and family through state protection and recognition, as Vargas repeatedly claimed. Instead, the legislation became simply another tool—unreliable and unwieldy, but a tool nonetheless—to be deployed whenever luck, struggle, and circumstances made it possible and desirable, rendering advantages little different from those sporadically conferred by networks of family or patronage.

Such circumstances perhaps explain why Vargas-era legislation seems to have done so little to alter poor people's understanding of work and its meanings. Vargas's emblems of worker-citizenship did carry great weight in many poor communities. Abdias Nascimento dos Santos, a worker and favela leader recalling the 1950s and 1960s with half a century's hindsight, spoke wistfully and with sly humor about the prestige that young men gained from participating in vocational training programs such as the Serviço Nacional de Aprendizagem Industrial (SENAI) during the Vargas and Kubitschek years ("My God! The SENAI was something!"), and about the pride and hope that workers felt during those years.[239] In his words: "We believed that through work we would realize our dreams." Both dos Santos and his old colleague in favela struggles, Lúcio de Paula Bispo, remembered that stable, formal work was admired and respected in favela communities during these years; while workers might occasionally choose *biscate*, or odd-jobbing, a job with *trabalhista* benefits (vacations, hospital care, social security) was seen as the real incarnation of work.[240] Odília dos Santos Gama—the longtime Babilônia favela resident who washed clothes to make ends meet, even as she raised ten children—saw as a major transformation her husband's promotion from undocumented work laying the "Portuguese stones" that paved Rio's south-zone sidewalks to formal employment as a chauffeur for the municipal government.[241] Luiz Antônio Machado da Silva, writing in 1969 about favela *botequins* in Rio and Fortaleza, observed that social groups within the bars were largely based on social status, and that one of the principal symbols of that status was a work card, which implied job stability, creditworthiness, and immunity from police persecution.[242]

Yet this sort of prestige did not imply that poor Cariocas had adopted the Vargas legislation's definition of valuable work. Appreciation of the signed *carteira* and the formal job was at root utilitarian, based not on moral criteria but rather on the clearheaded recognition that formal employment brought material advantages and some immunity to the indignities of poverty and favela residence. When asked about the distinctions between formal and informal workers, both Abdias and Lúcio emphasized the thinness of the line between the two; the fact that a signed *carteira* or social security institute membership conferred a certain prestige did not mean that odd-jobbers or those laboring off the books were not placed in the category of "workers" or recognized as valuable members of the community. In Bispo's estimation, these people were workers as well, performing important services. In dos Santos's view, informal work was a rational choice, exercised whenever the worker "perceived that the product of his work was benefiting the person you were working for more than you." And for women such as Chapeu Mangueira resident Maria da Conceição Ferreira Pinto and others who lived in favelas, domestic work, washing clothes, or selling petty goods on street corners simply *was* work, the only employment available, the difference between making a living and destitution.[243]

Favela residents testifying in criminal trials from the 1960s defined the term "worker" in similarly undiscriminating ways. Manoel Salvador de Moraes, an illiterate 78-year-old migrant from Minas Gerais who lived in the Morro Macedo Sobrinho (also called Morro da Guarda), did not distinguish between formal and informal labor in defining the categories of worker and *desordeiro*. When asked about Haroldo da Silva, a 27-year-old domestic employee accused of pushing an alcoholic neighbor named Orlando to his death, de Moraes said that the fall was an accident and unequivocally assigned Haroldo the label *trabalhador*, despite the informal nature of his work; Orlando, by contrast, fell clearly into a more dangerous category—that of the coward, aggressive posturer, and drunk.[244] Witnesses in the 1960 murder trial of Eugenio dos Santos, a white 32-year-old manual laborer and father of two who lived in the favela Cordovil, made clear that work and family were defined through actions, not legal status. Though dos Santos was described as single by police officials and possessed no work documents, his neighbor José Moises, a 34-year-old northeastern migrant and also a manual laborer, did not hesitate to declare dos Santos "married" and "the one who supported the household" with his work. Manoel Gomes da Silva, a 27-year-old northeastern migrant who worked as a mechanic, said that dos Santos was "a hard-working guy" (*um rapaz trabalhador*), "upright" (*direito*), "with a wife and two kids, a good head of family." Pedro Miguel da Silva, 32, a manual laborer also from the northeast, described him as "a hardworking man" and "married," adding that he fully supported his family.[245] In these and other cases, favela residents from throughout the city validated the moral distinction between workers and *marginais*, family men and *desordeiros*.[246] But they also argued forcefully that formal definitions had nothing to do with their moral categories; workers were defined as such because they labored, not because they sported papers with the right stamps; family men became such because they supported their wives and children, not because they had been married by a judge or a priest.

The kinds of work poor that Cariocas valued did not coincide with those rewarded in *trabalhista* legislation; thus, the moral logic that Vargas had seemed to share with so many poor Cariocas unraveled. In rhetoric, social and economic citizenship had been a right universally offered in exchange for hard labor and responsible, patriotic parenthood. In fact, Vargas's social and economic benefits became less a variant of citizenship than a sophisticated form of patronage, an uncertain basket of perks distributed to the skilled, the lucky, the well connected, and the bureaucratically agile. Poor people's citizenship remained a partial and uncertain enterprise, defined by scarcity rather than security of rights. And work endured as a fraught endeavor, respected because of what it said about a person's commitment to family and community, but degraded by its ongoing futility in a society that, 70 years after slavery's abolition, still did not reward or respect work as the concept was understood by most poor Cariocas. This, perhaps, explains the *malandro*'s continued popular appeal, and the near-immediate extinction of odes to work upon the Estado Novo's demise. A 1962 *choro* captures well the ultimate disillusionment of Rio's rights-poor:

Quem foi que disse	Who was it that said
que trabalho dá futuro	that work can lead to a future?
eu não trabalho	I don't work
e ando sempre com dinheiro	and I always have money
quero viver sempre socegado	I want to live the peaceful life
meu pai trabalhou tanto	My father worked so much
que eu nasci cansado	that I was born tired
meu pai quando morreu	When my father died
não deixou nada	he left nothing
quazi não foi sepultado	He was almost not buried
porque não havia grana	because there was no cash
foi porque não fazia	All of this because he didn't do
como eu faço	what I do
que descanço	I take it easy
os sete dias da semana	seven days a week
Certa vez	One time
fui trabalhar numa pedreira	I went to work in a quarry
tive uma tremedeira	I started trembling so much

desta vez quase que eu morro	I nearly died
fui quebrar pedra	I went to break up rock
e quase fiz um estrago	and almost made havoc
fiquei preto fiquei branco	I turned black, I turned white
fiquei surdo, fiquei gago	I went deaf, I went mute
sou inimigo do trabalho	I am an enemy of work
com razão	for good reason
pois eu vejo quem trabalha	I see people who work
andar pronto sem tostão	go around ready and penniless
trabalhar prá que	Work, for what?
se a vida assim é bem melhor	If life is so much better this way
tenho casa e comida	I have a house and I have food
tenho calça e palitó!	I have slacks and I have a jacket![247]

PART III

Rights Poverty in the Criminal Courts

Judicial Honor in the *Morro*

Urban planning may have delimited poor Cariocas' physical and legal horizons, and social welfare and labor laws may have transformed or dashed their hopes for citizenship. But in the nitty-gritty of poor people's daily lives, "the law" most often meant the police, the jails, and the criminal courts. Although lore would have it that even the police feared some favelas, in fact there were few areas of Rio where policemen did not appear from time to time, breaking up local disputes, investigating criminal complaints, and enforcing court decisions, municipal decrees, or sanitary regulations. These interactions were often predictably repressive. Yet many of them—and especially those involving criminal complaints—were initiated by poor residents, who often had little other contact with the government or the legal system. Criminal investigations often had enormously complex economic and social impact in poor communities, and it is little wonder that many poor people effectively understood their connection with the law through such experiences.

Unsurprisingly, the relationship between the poor and the criminal justice system changed greatly during the Vargas years. Police, judges, jurists, and common citizens grappled to reconcile competing notions of citizenship, social hierarchy, and civil rights through revolutionary changes in legal codes and practices, a process that was complicated considerably by urban growth and diversification. The end result was again paradoxical. New criminal legal codes published in the early 1940s sought to render individual criminal law more transparent, and especially to clarify critical questions regarding the extent to which individual personality or circumstance should influence judicial outcomes. Yet the new codes contained a series of assumptions—some sociological, some practical—that would combine with judicial backlog and inefficiency to fortify a system that effectively deprived most poor people of full civil rights.

By the 1960s, poor people's lives were often intimately connected with the criminal justice system; they had family members who were police officers, they paid police rent or bribes to live in favelas located on public lands, they called on the police in emergencies or out of revenge, they were asked to show their documents in police raids, and they were defendants or witnesses in judicial trials. But the notion that criminal justice could serve as a fair and consistent mediator or protector for Rio's poor was more distant than ever. With scant access to civil rights protections and little chance of seeing their problems fairly resolved, poor Cariocas opted out of the criminal justice system as often as chance allowed, preferring the inconstancies of local dispute resolution to the hazards, delays, and abuses of formal law. The following two chapters chronicle that evolution, highlighting the ways in which criminal law—like law and practice in the areas of labor regulation, social welfare, and urban planning—helped to make scarcity of rights a critical component of modern Carioca poverty.

CHAPTER FIVE

The Poor in Classical Criminal Law

⤳

HONOR IN THE MORRO DA FORMIGA

The many tensions that had accumulated in Rio's criminal justice system by 1930 emerge most clearly through an extended example. On 26 June 1929, a heated discussion broke out in a tiny community known as the Morro da Formiga. The place was more a settlement than a full-fledged favela, a haphazard collection of zinc-roofed shacks scattered on the northwestern flanks of the Serra da Carioca, a lush prominence marking the geographical boundary of Tijuca, a middle-class neighborhood in Rio's north zone. The settlement was relatively new and mostly illicit, the product of extralegal speculation involving vacant *terras devolutas* (abandoned lands), hastily erected *barracões* (shacks), and poor tenants who could no longer afford housing in Rio's more central districts. The *morro*'s main access road boasted rough stone pavement, electricity, water, and sewer service—all symbols of municipal recognition—but most of the area's shacks had been erected far from such luxuries, on the borders of rough paths and alleyways crisscrossed by crude drainage ditches that made navigation on foot treacherous, even in the dry season. The *barracões* were not structurally illegal prior to the 1937 building code, but neither their "owners" nor their "tenants" could make more than a tenuous claim to legal dominion, and custom rather than law governed neighborhood property relations.[1]

Custom was a murky business, though, especially when it regulated waste disposal, drainage, and soil erosion, all sticky matters that pitted private against collective interests. The June 26 dispute arose from just such a conflict. At around 8 A.M., Antônio Mendes Coelho—Portuguese, married, a self-described "businessman and property owner" who rented

out many of the *morro's* shacks—assembled a few men to clean and ex-
cavate a drainage ditch that ran across the backyard of one of "his" *barracões*.[2] The ditch's waste came mainly from the property of Maximina
de Souza, an illiterate Portuguese cook who had lived in the *morro* with
her husband for about five years, and who rented out a small shack of her
own.[3] When Maximina saw the excavation, she told the workers to stop,
afraid they would destabilize the soil supporting her shack, which sat a
few meters above the ditch. Antônio told the men to keep digging.

The result was a nasty exchange. According to some witnesses, Maximina hurled at Antônio every verbal insult she could think of, calling
him a "bandido" (bandit), a "corno" (cuckold), a "filho da puta" (son of
a bitch), a "ladrão" (thief), a "feiticeiro" (black magician), and a "pat-
ife" (scoundrel) and saying that he was "ordinário" (common, immoral),
"semvergonha" (shameless), and "o resto dos portugueses do Morro da
Formiga" (the refuse of the Portuguese who live in the Morro da Formiga). Antônio's repertoire was apparently more limited; according to
some witnesses, he called Maximina a "vaca" (cow, whore), "ordinária"
(common), and "a rainha das putas," "the queen of whores." In any
case, the argument was loud and violent—so much so that one observer
suffered a nervous attack and another marked it on her calendar of "notable days"—and it ended only when both parties traipsed down the hill,
witnesses in tow, each vowing to demand the other's arrest.

It was not unusual for such cases to wind up before local police delegates in the late 1920s and early 1930s. Although Rio's police forces had
gradually lost many of their nineteenth-century judicial functions, they
often still arbitrated local or familial disputes, especially when those lay
outside the boundaries of formal law.[4] Usually, the simple threat of police
intervention forced resolution. Most poor Cariocas—and especially those
living or working extra-legally—dreaded interference by a reputedly corrupt and abusive police force; being identified as a suspect in a crime
could permanently prejudice an individual's civil rights and civic reputation. Ironically, this fear of the police's extralegal activities may well have
been what made recourse to legal authority an effective coercive tool.[5]
When mere menace could not force a concession, police authorities often
mediated more directly, using the threat of further police action to force
compliance. By Maximina's lawyer's account, the local police delegate
attempted to do precisely this in 1929, telling Antônio—who was "well-
known for disturbing the order of the *morro*, where he . . . exploited the
residents' poverty"—that the police would imprison him and open an
official investigation if he continued to endanger Maximina's home and
menace her family's well-being.

This was no idle threat. Formal law probably did not regulate Antônio's actions on that day. But the 1890 criminal code had declared illegal so many common practices—adultery, physical fights, use of insulting language, abortion, certain sexual practices, spiritism, gambling, vagrancy, and *capoeira*—that the police could nearly always cook up charges against someone accused of violating the unwritten rules of neighborhood morality and conduct. As elsewhere, informal power was rooted in an ability to enforce the law selectively within large spheres of tolerated illegality. Many such scurrilous cases would be dropped before trial (because they were baseless, or because the parties had reached an informal agreement), but their very existence could mean jail time, physical abuse, and significant legal expense.

Yet Antônio refused to be intimidated, and instead moved independently to escalate the dispute over a drainage ditch to a full-fledged criminal proceeding. Antônio claimed that Maximina's heated words constituted criminal *injúria,* defined as "the imputation of vices or defects, with or without specific details, that might expose a person to hatred or public disdain; the imputation of facts offensive to an individual's reputation, decorum, and honor; or a word, gesture, or signal considered by public opinion to be insulting."[6] He also accused her of *calúmnia,* "the false imputation . . . of an act that the law defines as a crime," on the basis of the fact that thievery and black magic were illegal.[7] Because *calúmnia* and *injúria* were "private" offenses—prosecuted only at the victim's initiative and expense—Antônio's complaint went directly to a lower-circuit judge, and neither police authorities nor the district attorney's office could obstruct it.[8] If convicted, Maximina faced up to fifteen months in prison and a considerable fine.

Given elite perceptions of favela life in the late 1920s, Antônio's recourse to the courts for the protection of his honor may seem peculiar. This was, after all, the period when the *morros* first came to be characterized as an urbanistic and social problem, an era when favela residents were regularly portrayed as ignorant, backward criminals, content to live in nests of filth and immorality.[9] The favela "problem" appeared only infrequently in legal discourse or police training manuals; Brazilian criminologists still privileged the purported biological, racial, and psychological roots of crime over its social origins, and favelas still had not become distinct enough in the popular imagination to be separated from the tenements and prostitution zones that authorities had traditionally associated with social danger.[10] Still, crime and the *morros* were already inextricably linked in the elite imagination. Benjamim Costallat, writing in the 1920s, considered the Morro da Favela an obligatory stop on his tour of the Carioca underworld, transcribing with easy assurance his police associate's description of the favela's criminal tendencies:

Almost everyone who lives on the Rua da América is a thief or a swindler. . . .
Along with the favela, this zone sends the largest number of boarders to the prisons. Up there on the *morro*, it's all about violent crime, stabbings, violence, vengeance, and bravado; down here on the Rua da América, the deal is robbery, it's
cunning, it's the professional picklock who knows how to use a file and a crowbar.
. . . Crime has its specialists and its own perfect order. On the Morro do Pinto,
everyone is a con man. There's never any confusion. Every professional criminal
has his pet neighborhood.[11]

Nominally, however, formal Brazilian law left no room for such preconceptions; and that, apparently, is what Antônio was counting on. According to the 1890 penal code and its interpreters, honor was a serious
business, protected with the same vigor as property or physical integrity.
The code reserved its most vigilant protection for female sexual honor—
defined, significantly, as an offense not against the women themselves but
"against the security, honor, and honesty of families and public modesty
and decency."[12] But the code also criminalized most verbal offenses and
instructed judges to accept all but the most serious physical attacks as
"legitimate defense" of wounded honor, although judges rarely accepted
verbal attacks as a legitimate defense of other rights.[13]

More significantly still, Brazilian law formally adhered to the so-called
classical school of criminology, which left little room for jurists to consider social standing or moral worth in *injúria* cases, despite nearly half a
century of attacks from the opposing "positivist" school. Positivist criminal jurists—who had risen to prominence in Europe, and especially in
Italy, in the late nineteenth century—saw crime not as a problem in and
of itself but rather as the symptom of a deeper biological, psychological, or social disorder. In this view, the purpose of criminal justice was
not to punish individual acts, but rather to defend society through social
diagnosis, control, and rehabilitation.[14] In contrast, the classical school
conceived of criminal justice solely as an arena for punishing specific
illegal acts, duly defined in the written law. In this view, all individuals were formally equal, and perfectly capable of exercising free will in
choosing either to respect the law or to violate it. At least in theory, social
class, psychology, and milieu could neither justify a criminal act nor ex-
acerbate its seriousness. The judicial system, in this view, should punish
specific crimes, not protect society at large from acts that individuals
might potentially commit. According to the classical school, no one who
stayed within the boundaries of the law could lose his or her liberty, and a
criminal act was considered such regardless of who carried it out against
whom.[15]

These crisp doctrines of classical legal thought always became somewhat soiled in their practical application, not least because, by the early
twentieth century, many in the Brazilian legal community adhered to the

positivist school. Their views gradually infused the law's interpretation, and occasionally even its letter. Judges rarely based their decisions explicitly on social status or moral stature, but they virtually never barred such evidence from trials.[16] Police officials, prosecutors, and defense lawyers accordingly often spent far more energy arguing the relative moral and social merits of a trial's participants than they did discussing the facts of the case, especially in *injúria* cases, where no physical or written evidence existed, and where the very definition of the crime depended on such ambiguous notions as good name, reputation, self-worth, and dignity. The result was something of a paradox. Analyses of character and circumstance often dominated honor cases, a practice that suggested that such arguments influenced trial verdicts. But judges, bound by the dictates of the penal code, rarely allowed such considerations into their public legal reasoning. It is thus difficult to distinguish between those judges who adhered to the classical tradition and those who used classical language to defend conclusions reached through positivist logic. On the basis of trial transcripts, however, it seems that lawyers and prosecutors in the 1920s and 1930s banked a great deal on the existence of the latter.

Antônio's and Maximina's lawyers proved to be no exception. From the outset, Maximina's counsel emphasized deficiencies in Antônio's character. He contended that harsh words had been spoken on both sides, and that Maximina's anger had been provoked by the unjust threat that Antônio had posed to her home. Both arguments had a solid base in Brazilian law and jurisprudence.[17] But he also traipsed into more subjective territory, accusing Antônio of economic exploitation and community disruption, and arguing that Maximina's insults could not be taken seriously because of the social level of the parties involved. The lawyer's final argument read, in part:

> The evidence in this case has proven that there was a harsh discussion between the two parties, provoked because the plaintiff attempted to dig a drainage ditch on land that could be claimed by the defendant, his enemy, with the intention of demolishing her little abode in the Morro da Formiga. This naturally provoked an exchange of coarse words between them, words that included profanities, which is also natural, given the upbringing of the two parties, both immigrants—Portuguese—he the owner of numerous zinc shacks in the *morro* and an exploiter of poverty, she a simple cook.

Antônio's prolific lawyer initially focused more exclusively on the facts. He highlighted the testimony of five prosecution witnesses who claimed to have heard Maximina's tirade (and swore vehemently that Antônio had not responded with a single offensive word); he asserted the legitimacy of the ditch digging that had provoked Maximina's anger; he pointed to supposed inconsistencies in the testimony of Maximina's defense witnesses (two of whom claimed that Antônio had responded with insults of his own); and he called the judge's attention to minutiae in the letter of the law that prohibited violent and injurious words.[18] For good measure, however, he also used scattered paragraphs in his final argument to mount a vigorous defense of his client's good character, exalting Antônio as an honorable, exemplary citizen, deeply wounded by Maximina's vulgarity and fully deserving of the court's protection. Antônio was, he said,

> a well-mannered man, hardworking and honorable, married with children, who could boast an impeccable life history; when humiliated and injured in such an unjust fashion, he knocked on the doors of justice rather than responding with words or violence, certain of the reparation established by law. His act is not one of vengeance but rather one taken with the intention of vindicating his wounded rights. . . .
> We also see from the evidence that the victim is an upright man, honorable and hardworking. The fact that he is a businessman and a property owner, but of humble stature in society, does not deprive him of his right to esteem, consideration, and honor on the part of his co-citizens, his wife, and his children.

Such rhetoric may have been initially superfluous. The lower-court judge, Eurico Rodolfo Paixão, rarely acknowledged subjective considerations in his decisions, and he based his solid condemnation of Maximina purely on eyewitness testimony and the letter of the law.[19] In these terms, Antônio clearly held the advantage; even though one of his five witnesses worked for him, and two were his tenants, they were mostly consistent in their indictment of Maximina. Two of Maximina's five witnesses—one of whom was her tenant—failed even to appear, and the other three proved vague and equivocal. According to Brazilian law, Maximina, as a defendant, carried the burden of proof.[20] Little wonder that Judge Paixão convicted Maximina and sentenced her to one month's prison time and a fine of 150 mil-reis.[21]

Maximina's lawyer immediately appealed, and, in doing so, attempted to move the court's attention from the case's content to its context. The crux of his argument lay in Antônio's character and in the favela's social norms. Antônio was the favela's evil landlord, exploiting the poverty and misery of its inhabitants. Maximina, a humble cook, had made great sacrifices in order to construct her small wood-and-zinc shack. Since her arrival on the *morro*, she had been persecuted by Antônio and his "lover" (whom Antônio referred to as his wife); the disputes had led Maximina to call for police intervention several times. The *injúria* case, the lawyer argued, was a ruse intended to intensify Maximina's suffering. The supposed *injúrias* had come in the midst of an argument; thus, especially "among people of a low social sphere," they lacked criminal intent. The words were "vulgar expressions, often used even by the well bred," and it was "no surprise . . . that they were heard coming out of the mouth of a cook." What happened was "an exchange of swear words, certainly nothing to be surprised at among humble people who are both from a low social class." The court had no responsibility to protect an avaricious, grasping slumlord from words that escaped as easily as breath from the mouths of the poor.

Antônio's lawyer responded in kind. "Penal law," he wrote, "neither inquires into nor differentiates on the basis of the intellectual or educational conditions of those who carry out crimes. It matters little that the appellant has neither culture nor education . . . whether she is a doctor or cook, the law cannot differentiate." Bristling at Maximina's lawyer's insinuations about Antônio's character, the lawyer continued: "He is a man of humble social condition, a small-time businessman and property owner, but he is not of a *low social sphere.* It is exactly because he is an upright and well-bred citizen, useful to his family and to the social milieu where he lives, that he has come to ask the justice system—in which he has entire confidence—for reparation for the damage he has suffered." The injurious words constituted a crime; their meaning could not change according to who had spoken them, where, or to whom—and, in any case, Antônio was precisely the sort of person whose honor the courts should most protect.

The struggle over the standards that should be used to judge the case continued among officials of the district attorney's office. The prosecutor agreed with Maximina's lawyer; "dirty language" was nothing among these people; it was "the patois, the argot, the usual slang among them, and cannot be taken to have an injurious intention." It was surprising, he implied, that the case had not ended in a physical fight. The district attorney himself took the opposite tack, claiming that the words were injurious regardless of social milieu, and that the sensibilities of the favela residents were sharp enough that Maximina's words had wounded Antônio and deeply impressed the witnesses. The case of Maximina and Antônio—begun as a dispute over a drainage ditch and originally tried as an offense to personal honor—had thus become a legal argument over the legitimacy of differential enforcement in Brazilian criminal law. Were some offenses considered crimes only when committed against "honorable" citizens? And, if so, what were the legitimate symbols of worthy citizenship?

The higher-court justices did not openly discuss such weighty matters. Their dry final brief granted Maximina's appeal solely on the grounds of testimony that the *injúrias* had been reciprocal. But this silence did not rob the lawyers' earlier discussions of their significance. Throughout Rio in the late 1920s and early 1930s, similarly odd juxtapositions of strict judicial legalism and passionate ideological argument abounded as positivist lawyers, judges, and jurists struggled to find space within the 1890 penal code for new notions of criminal law. Legal professionals rarely argued over the values that the penal code purported to protect—national security, public order, individual liberty, administrative honesty, personal and familial honor, physical integrity, and property—but they frequently clashed over how well these values were protected by the criminalization of specific symbolic acts. In a hierarchical, vastly unequal society, could, and should, certain actions constitute crimes regardless of status or circumstance? Or should rights, and the definition of the acts that violated them, depend on individual worthiness?

No other question would so perturb Brazilian legal professionals in the first decades of the twentieth century. By the 1930s, the clash between the text of the 1890 code and the norms of judicial practice had become unsustainable. Like most civil law systems, Brazil's was built on the notion that legislation, not precedent, created law. When practice diverged from written doctrine, only a legislative change could reestablish legitimacy. The major task that confronted Vargas's Ministry of Justice was thus to construct new codes of penal law and criminal procedure that would reconcile classical and positivist views, at once protecting citizens' individual rights and shielding society from biological, psychological, and social depravity. The resulting codes formally incorporated Vargas-era notions of civic worthiness into the letter of criminal law, sanctioning differential access to citizenship rights in this most basic of legal arenas and further fraying the fragile ties that bound Rio's poor to the realm of rights.

PERSONALITY AND CIRCUMSTANCE IN REPUBLICAN LAW

It is an enormously knotty task to gauge the signs and symbols of worthy citizenship that most impacted Carioca trials in the late 1920s and early 1930s. Most criminal cases were complex, and their written records represent actual events only schematically. Considerations of circumstance, character, and moral value could creep into criminal trials in a variety of ways, some explicit, some unspoken, and it is often impossible to determine which most influenced the final verdict. Yet by juxtaposing written law and juridical discourse with trial transcripts, one can begin to glimpse an inconsistent and heterogeneous legal culture, one in which nearly everyone acknowledged the importance of individual circumstance, character, and moral worth in determining guilt, innocence, and access to basic procedural protections, but in which few could agree on what constituted legitimate representations of civic worthiness. The challenge of authenticating such representations—of creating "rights of institution" that would definitively link certain personal characteristics and circumstances to judicial leniency—would eventually fall to the authors of the 1940 criminal code.[22]

Until 1940, Brazilian criminal law adhered roughly to the classical school.[23] In broad terms, both the 1890 penal code and the 1924 code of criminal procedure aimed to punish specific acts, not criminal potential, and generally rejected the "individualization" of criminal procedure or sanctions.[24] Both codes, however, also contained numerous exceptions. Some represented conscious concessions to the positivist school; others emerged from the uneasy coexistence of social hierarchy and liberal doctrine that characterized Brazilian public life during the First Republic; many more were legacies from the Brazilian criminal code of 1830 and the Napoleonic codes that had inspired it. Together, such exceptions opened an ambiguous space that allowed lawyers, judges, and jurists to determine an act's criminality by gauging the social and moral worth of its perpetrators and victims.

Most transparently, both the criminal and procedural codes guaranteed differential treatment for some clearly defined groups. In the 1890 penal code, a few classes of individuals regarded as incapable of exercising free will—children, deaf-mutes, and the insane—were entirely exempt from criminal responsibility.[25] The 1924 procedural code echoed this concern, requiring the courts to provide special legal assistance to minors between the ages of 18 and 21 and to the insane.[26] Provisions prohibiting married women from bringing criminal complaints without their husbands' permission reflected a similar preoccupation with dependency.[27]

Several other directives openly legitimized disparate treatment on the basis of social or economic status. The procedural code held that military personnel, public employees, and anyone with an advanced degree had the right to be imprisoned in special facilities, apart from common criminals.[28] Anyone who possessed a civil identification card—a population that was, at the time, essentially confined to public employees, professionals, and members of the military—could refuse to undergo the humiliating and highly prejudicial identification procedure normally required of everyone accused of a crime.[29] Finally, several provisions mandated more stringent treatment for "vagrants," ambiguously defined as people who lacked a fixed job, home, or income.[30] Judges could imprison vagrants before trial, and people so branded were uniquely ineligible for release on their own recognizance, for the right to post bail, and for early release, privileges that even accused murderers usually enjoyed. In a system where long pretrial delays were the rule, such procedural details could significantly impact a defendant's punishment. In the interest of protecting society from the rootless poor, and of recognizing the special status of the educated or well connected, the laws of criminal procedure thus frequently undermined the classical school's dictum that action trumped personality in determining guilt and punishment.

Other measures allowed judicial leniency based on circumstance. In the 1890 criminal code, some situations exculpated a defendant entirely from even the most heinous of crimes. Articles 26 and 32 stipulated that those who had acted "while completely deprived of their senses and their intelligence," "under coercion," "in order to avoid a greater evil," or in "legitimate self-defense" could, like children, deaf-mutes, and the insane, be relieved of criminal responsibility. Such mandates pushed beyond the confines of classical law, since their enforcement implied a case-by-case evaluation of circumstance, character, motivation, and moral judgment. "Legitimate self-defense," for example, could be exercised not only in cases of mortal peril but also whenever any legitimate right was endangered. Since the code did not define the term "right," lawyers, judges, and juries were left with considerable space for legal maneuvering.[31] The concept of avoiding a greater evil proved similarly unsettling, since lawyers could define that greater evil as anything from hunger to treason.[32]

The phrase "completely deprived of their senses and their intelligence" raised equally vexing issues. These emerged especially in the arguments about the criminally mitigating effects of alcohol and of temporary insanity rooted in "uncontrollable passion." Brazilian jurists generally agreed that intoxication could render a defendant inculpable. But positivists— aided by the code's ambiguous wording—argued that, in the interest of social defense, such exemptions should be granted only when intoxication had been either incidental to the crime or accidental. Such determinations of intention would force judges and juries into an individualized enforcement of the law.[33] Similarly, the code's vague wording allowed positivists to argue that complete deprivation of senses and intelligence could result from uncontrollable passion. While some jurists denied the ameliorating power of extreme emotion, holding that all crimes resulted from some excess of passion, others advocated the legally intangible notion that certain "morally grounded" passions could annul criminal responsibility. Still others argued that any extreme passion was akin to insanity.[34] Because precedent could not strictly define Brazilian law, these conflicts remained unresolved, injecting considerable plasticity into the criminal legal process.

Other provisions in the 1890 code allowed circumstance to attenuate rather than annul responsibility and punishment. Some of the aggravating and attenuating circumstances defined in the 1890 code literally reproduced similar clauses from its 1830 predecessor.[35] Most concerned the concrete factual circumstances of the crime—whether or not it had been committed through fraud, or in a dark place, or against someone who was physically frailer than the defendant. Other stipulations concerned intangibles like the mental state and psychological motivations of the defendant; in this vein, a crime grew in seriousness when its motivations were "frivolous" or "reproachable," or when it had been committed out of vengeance; it diminished if the criminal had not intended to commit the crime, or had done so when provoked by the victim, when partially drunk, when attempting to defend himself, or when seeking to avoid a greater evil. Another series of measures explicitly evaluated a crime's seriousness according to the social status of its victims and perpetrators. Criminality intensified if an act had been committed against public employees, the elderly, the infirm, or relatives; the code likewise judged more harshly crimes committed between teachers and students, masters and servants, or any parties tied by similar bonds. Criminality diminished if the perpetrator had a clean record, "exemplary previous behavior," or had in any way performed "good services for society." If both aggravating and attenuating circumstances existed, the final verdict would depend on the defendant's perceived "perversity" and dangerousness.

Attenuating and aggravating circumstances determined the severity of judicial sentences, but procedural rules often had a greater impact on actual punishment. Until 1924, the penal and procedural codes left little room for subjectivity. In the penal code, only good behavior during incarceration (as defined by prison officials) could ease punishment. The code's statute of limitations also left some room for maneuver, since police and court officials could easily delay proceedings to the point where a crime was no longer punishable, but such manipulations occurred strictly under the table.

In 1924, with the publication of the Federal District's procedural code and a national law governing suspended sentences and early release, both the police and judicial authorities gained leeway. In the procedural code, the most important articles involved pretrial imprisonment. In theory, everyone who was caught red-handed in a criminal action—or against whom police authorities held compelling evidence—could be imprisoned, with bail dependent on the crime and the defendant's vagrancy status. According to the code, however, judges could withhold arrest warrants even in the most serious crimes, "either because of circumstance contained in the trial records or because the profession, social conditions, or interests of the defendant indicate that he or she will not flee or . . . disturb the progress of the investigation or destroy evidence." Social station thus explicitly shaped pretrial punishment.

The 1924 laws governing suspended sentences and early release—open concessions to the positivist camp—allowed similarly broad discretion.[36] Judges (in conjunction with the Penitentiary Council, and with the advice of prison authorities) could halve the prison time of anyone sentenced to more than four years, on the condition of good behavior "indicative of regeneration" and willingness to work and perform "services useful to the community." Those thus released agreed to meet certain requirements, set by a judge, which could include "submission to a patron, the observance of certain rules of comportment, prohibitions against living in certain places, requirements to abstain from alcohol, and the adoption of honest and useful ways of life." The Penitentiary Council, at least in theory, would inform every beneficiary of early release about these conditions in a special ceremony, where the convict would also be presented with a small identification booklet, which was to be carried at all times.[37]

A suspended sentence, or *sursis,* allowed judges still further leeway. *Sursis* had been conceived by positivist criminologists as a species of "conditional condemnation," more a warning than a punishment. It was given only to first-time offenders who had been sentenced to one year or less in prison and had not "revealed a perverse or corrupt character." In allotting it, judges were to keep in mind the defendant's "individual conditions" and "the motivations that determined and the circumstances that surrounded the criminal infraction." If the *sursis* beneficiary managed to maintain a clean record throughout the suspension period, authorities would expunge his or her conviction. Taken together, *sursis* and early release allowed judges and prison officials to give almost as much weight to individual personality, social station, and circumstance as they did to the criminal act.

Thus circumstance, group membership, and social status could help to shape criminal responsibility and punishment. A final set of dispositions went further still, allowing the social and moral characteristics of victims and perpetrators to determine the very criminality of certain acts. Such distinctions affected nearly every law's practical application, but some statutes explicitly highlighted their importance. The insertion of moral or social criteria could be relatively subtle, and was sometimes written into the definition of the criminal act. The crime of defloration, for example, resulted from sexual intercourse with a virgin "through the employment of seduction, deception, or fraud." In practice, as Sueann Caulfield has shown, lawyers tended to argue—and judges tended to accept—that only well-behaved, modest girls who engaged in none of the techniques of modern female sexual provocation could suffer defloration. Coincidentally or not, many of the practices that jurists defined as antithetical to the sexual innocence that the defloration statutes sought to protect—physical mobility around the city, scanty parental supervision, the frequenting of dance halls—were also important elements of daily life and culture for poor and working-class girls.[38] As Antônio's and Maximina's case makes clear, laws against *injúria* and *calúmnia* contained similar ambiguities; words or accusations could be considered injurious, or not, depending on the social level and moral habits of the person whose honor was to be protected. While neither defloration nor *injúria* statutes explicitly excluded any social class, these crimes' legal definitions left ample room for lawyers and jurists to use victims' social and moral status as criteria for determining criminality.

Other statutes were less subtle, especially those governing sexual assaults and public customs. In defining the crime of rape, for example, the code explicitly distinguished between "honest" women and "public women or prostitutes"; an attack on the latter carried a significantly lighter punishment. Similarly, the code criminalized *rapto* (abduction for sexual purposes) only if the girl involved was "honest." The definition of vagrancy—a notion already central to a number of procedural distinctions—went even further. Criminal vagrants were "adults of either sex who, without means of subsistence either from a private fortune or from a profession, artisanal skill, or legal and honest occupation, . . . loiter around the city in a state of idleness." The open, class-based discrimination implied by such a definition moved even normally circumspect jurists to take note. Afrânio Peixoto, whose 1933 work *Criminologia* was considered by many to be the last word on the study of modern criminal justice, wrote about the law with some irony:

> It would be unjust not to include among these poor vagabonds those moderately well-off and rich individuals who, equally lazy and indolent, live, lounging around, from handout to handout, on the beaches, in the mountain retreats, in lakeshore cities, crossing the ocean in transatlantic vessels, gambling in casinos and at racetracks, moving from one oceanfront resort to another, spending prodigiously, and occupied only in serving cocktails, flirting, committing adultery, gambling, and patronizing prostitutes . . . individuals who, in sum, reproduce all the vices and idleness of their poor counterparts, distinguished from them only by their higher incomes. The law, however, does not apply to rich vagabonds, on the basis of a logic that is almost humorous: a poor vagrant is a vagrant; a rich vagrant is rich.[39]

Such critiques notwithstanding, the vagrancy statutes remained—Brazilian criminal law's clearest manifestation of social discrimination.

The 1890 criminal code and the 1924 procedural code could thus be elastic, pliable instruments. Although classical legal precepts undergirded the codes, their eclectic construction, exacerbated by numerous reforms, allowed numerous gestures toward positivist criminology. In defining crimes, in allotting punishment, and in determining criminal responsibility, the codes allowed victims, defendants, witnesses, lawyers, and judges to insert considerations of individual circumstance and character into their narrations and judgments of criminal acts.

DOCUMENTING THE LAW IN ACTION

In the written law, such openings were mere possibilities. Their significance surfaced only in practice, when the actors in thousands of legal dramas faced off in Rio's police stations and criminal courts. Here, underlying all of the arguments about guilt and innocence, damage inflicted and reparations required, debates raged about the appropriate utilization of Brazilian law's plasticities. Which individual traits justified greater or lesser judicial leniency? What symbolized virtue and honesty in women, hard work and virtuous citizenship in men? How great a role could such symbols play in the criminal justice system without eroding its classical core? Such questions received only hesitant and contradictory resolution in the daily practice of Carioca criminal justice in the years surrounding 1930. The result was a system in which any number of social and moral circumstances potentially affected a final verdict, but in which none was sure to; while the potential for social discrimination was always present, its bases remained largely undetermined. The great innovation of the 1940 criminal code and the 1942 procedural code would be the explicit linkage of specific signs of virtuous citizenship with legally sanctioned forms of judicial bias.

The written records of Carioca criminal trials and police investigations are rich documents. Lawyers, judges, and jurists often repeated the dictum that what was not in the records was not in the world; in the eyes of Brazilian law, a criminal case grew not from oral testimony and confrontational questioning but rather from the written record of interrogations and investigations.[40] That record began with the civil police, effectively the court's investigative branch, who interrogated suspects, witnesses, and victims; evaluated a crime's physical evidence; and determined a suspect's criminal background. From that point, if the prosecutor decided to go forward with a case, it would move to one of three court systems: the *pretorias*, or misdemeanor courts; the *varas*, or first-instance criminal courts; and the *tribunais do júri*, or jury courts, reserved for the most serious of crimes.[41] From there, the trial might be reviewed by one or several appellate courts. The judges for each lower court would conduct interrogations of all participants, which would also be transcribed or summarized for the record, and they might also ask for supplementary investigative work.[42] Over the course of any trial, the judges, lawyers, and police chiefs frequently rotated, and their replacements had only the trial's written records to go on. What was actually said or discovered thus mattered less than its representation, its reduction into a few pages of scribbled notes, undertaken by rushed and harried scribes.

These records present a wealth of information. Each page of written testimony hints at the daily social world of witnesses, victims, and defendants. The documents identify them by name, age, race, civil status, parentage, place of birth, occupation, and address. Their transcribed testimony describes intimate details of daily life—conjugal arguments, sexual practices, workplace conflicts, neighborhood disputes, anonymous urban encounters, acts of insanity and desperation. The transcriptions depart from standard judicial jargon just often enough to insinuate that here, between the lines, these records speak in the voices of the people whose names grace their pages.

Much recent Western social and cultural history has been written on the basis of such critical readings; in Latin America, where judicial records are often the least fragmented portion of overwhelmed and underfunded public archives, their beacon is stronger still. At their best, historians of Brazil have kept this hope at arm's length, reading transcripts with the same suspicious rigor with which they would greet any other filtered representation of popular life, seeking to describe "thickly" not only the documents' contents but also their omissions and silences.[43] Some have found meaning not in individual testimony but rather in the spaces where multiple accounts come together or tear apart. Some have regarded trial testimony as a representation of what was possible and credible in the social universe, regardless of literal truth. Others have found insights in the legally irrelevant—in snatches of description that seemingly had no bearing on the outcome of a case, fragments that neither witnesses nor their scribes would have had any imaginable reason to misrepresent.[44] Thus, largely, have scholars begun to write their tales of Brazilians "without histories," those who left their only tenuous traces in the historical record through the flawed transcriptions of court testimony.

But there is another story in these transcripts as well. If much of the trial participants' social and cultural world can only be inferred between the lines, a great deal about their legal and civic universe can be read rather more directly. Each case is a highly formalized account of an encounter between ordinary Brazilians and the legal system. In each of its prescribed rituals, participants made use of what must have been a relatively familiar set of legal and cultural representations in order to advance their own interests. By choosing to mold their experiences to fit some moral arguments and archetypes, while ignoring others, trial participants effectively contributed to public debates about the appropriate interpretation of abstract legal concepts; in this way, sea changes in the broader public domains of popular culture could and did mold the legal arena.[45] Yet the menu of representations from which trial participants chose was shaped by experience with the judicial system and its values as well as by popular morality. Thus what appeared in trial testimony is best seen as a strained compromise between judicial norms and public expectations of the legal system.

Read in this way, court cases seem a rather thick lens through which to view popular culture and social life, and they surely also distort common people's "genuine" beliefs about the proper function of legal authority. But as windows into the tug-of-war between popular and professional notions of judicial legitimacy, the Carioca trial transcripts are illuminating indeed. Almost every criminal trial dealt at some fundamental level with the appropriate symbolization of civic worthiness and the extent to which judicial leniency should reward such merit. It may be impossible to separate the views of individual citizens from those of the scribes and lawyers who crafted their legal representation, but it is possible to view in these formalized accounts the spectrum of representations that trial participants regarded as potentially legitimate. Such analysis, paired with more concrete statistical evaluation of judicial verdicts and procedural practices, reveals as much as anything is likely to about the contested allocation of judicial leniency in Rio de Janeiro in the late 1920s and early 1930s.

Police investigations and courtroom trials produced thick documents, replete with years' worth of overlapping scribbles, official stamps, and signatures. All in all, the scribes in Rio's thirty regular police stations, six special *delegacias*, and eighteen criminal courts probably produced some 8,000 such records annually in the 1920s and 1930s; they now sit in Rio's national and judicial archives, crudely bound, dirty, organized only by the defendants' last names.[46] For the purposes of quantitative analysis, I chose a sample of 251 cases for the years 1928 through 1940, a minimal proportion of all those produced during the period.[47] Of this sample, 30 percent consisted of police inquiries, and the rest were full judicial cases. Among the court cases, 48 percent of defendants were found at least partially guilty.[48] The cases represent Rio de Janeiro's most common crimes and misdemeanors, including physical assault, theft, breaking and entering, arms possession, vagrancy, sexual crimes, and honor crimes.[49] I excluded two other common crimes—traffic accidents and gambling violations—the former because records rarely include more than a factual physical description of the offense, the latter because such trials tended to be largely formulaic and probably involved higher than the usual levels of police corruption.[50] Within these crime categories, I selected records at random, with an eye only to obtaining a reasonable geographical distribution within the city.

ELASTICITIES IN PRACTICE

It is not difficult, in these dusty pages, to find conflicting opinions about the juridical value of various signifiers of social status and moral worth. Judges and police *delegados*—likely wary of the classical restrictions of the 1890 penal code—were usually circumspect about circumstance, social station, and personality. But most other trial participants were not. Lawyers, defendants, victims, and witnesses tried to exercise Brazilian law's every space for flexibility; indeed, as the case of Antônio and Maximina exemplifies, subjective or circumstantial arguments often overshadowed the cases' factual and legal aspects. Most often, trial participants—echoing the criminal and procedural codes—asserted the legal relevance of personality and circumstance.[51] In relation to personality, they argued that both the criminality of an act and the need for punishment depended on the juridical identities of the perpetrators and victims, constructed over the course of the trials from moral, social, and, occasionally, civic components. Regarding circumstance, participants argued that apparently criminal acts should not be punishable when committed under certain conditions: material need; defense of honor, property, or physical well-being; drunkenness; or understandable emotional distress. Going considerably further than the written codes, participants also frequently questioned the legitimacy of legal interference itself; this argument appeared most frequently with reference to physical fights, sexual offenses, vagrancy, and arms possession.

Few participants emphasized identity more categorically than those who believed that social class was its defining feature. And, among these, very few defined the symbols of class as rigidly as Eugenie Juliette Carneiro Leão de Barros de Icarahy, the widowed, French-born "Baroness of Icarahy." In February 1930, Eugenie's lawyer, touting her inherited (and by then rather decrepit) noble title, filed an *injúria* complaint with Rio de Janeiro's Third Criminal Pretoria. Eugenie claimed that a lawyer named José Santos Camara Lima had intentionally slandered her by stating—on the steps of a police *delegacia*, no less—that she had stolen furniture and was in the habit of "maintaining" a young man; in later testimony, he was referred to as a *cáften*, or pimp. According to the lawyer, these accusations—inherently "highly slanderous and spoken with the intent to denigrate"—were especially vicious because they had been spoken in a very public setting, and Eugenie was "a person of fortune and social position, with business transactions in the neighborhood of the police station."

The complaint was only slightly unusual. Honor crimes were among the few that regularly involved people from across Rio's class spectrum, and women participated in them with unusual frequency. As in most *injúria* cases, the complaint culminated a long-simmering conflict. Eugenie and José had become friends and business associates while her husband was still alive. After the baron's death, the association had begun to unravel when a rancorous dispute arose between José and a young Belgian man whom Eugenie referred to as her nephew, and who José described as her lover (and a thief). A few months before the alleged *injúria,* the two men had come to blows, and Eugenie had tried unsuccessfully to prosecute José for physical assault. Finally, in what Eugenie characterized as a desperate attempt to escape José's persecutions, she had fled to the summer resort of Petrópolis. When her moving men returned to Rio, José had them hauled into the local police station for questioning, accusing them of transporting stolen goods and demanding to know Eugenie's whereabouts. The moving men kept silent, at which point José convinced the police to send them to the fearsome 4th Delegacia Auxiliar for further questioning. En route, Eugenie claimed, José spoke the injurious words.

The *injúria* complaint may have been a genuine response to wounded honor. More probably it was Eugenie's latest attempt to settle an old vendetta, a tit-for-tat response to José's legal manipulations. In either case, it came to naught; after a trial fraught with mutual character assassination and legal maneuvers, Judge Leonardo Smith e Lima found José not guilty. But the verdict, in this case, mattered less than the arguments put forth. According to Eugenie's lawyer, José's crime was not defined by the words he had spoken so much as by whom they referred to and who had heard them. In his final argument, after noting that accusations of thievery and insinuations about being the protectress of a pimp would be at least mildly offensive to anyone, her lawyer came to the crux of his point:

> It is important to note that high society, of which the victim is a part, does not tolerate or pardon people who act in these ways; this is obviously not true of the lower social classes, where such acts are forgivable. It is also important to note that the accused, when he proffered the insults, did so in front of people from inferior social classes, who have no notion of secrecy or decorum, and who . . . might easily spread these insults as rumors. . . . Evidently, the defendant . . . sought to stain and denigrate the reputation of the victim, seeking to expose her to public scorn, imputing to her facts that were offensive to her station, her honor, and her decorum,

attempting to vilify her by comparing her to a prostitute, a thief, and a concubine, all in an obvious attempt to place her in an unsustainable and unbearable position in the society she frequented.

Like Maximina's counsel in the case that opened this chapter, Eugenie's lawyer argued essentially for the differential application of *injúria* laws. Discrete sectors of Carioca society possessed such varying levels of culture and decorum that the juridical significance of any action should depend on the participants' social station.

If these two cases converged in the belief that social class should matter in court, they also suggest that its symbolization was highly controversial. For Eugenie, social standing existed in a tattered paper title. For Maximina's lawyer, it depended on place of residence. For Maximina's archrival Antônio, it was symbolized by property ownership, however humble and legally tenuous. For Paulo Ferreira Alves Junqueira, another defendant who protested a suspicious arrest for vagrancy in 1930, the criteria were family connections and social milieu; when brought before a judge, Junqueira defended himself by stating that his family members were "property owners, highly involved with the best of Brazilian society, with the elements who best represent the high commerce of this capital and of São Paulo, in whose milieu" he lived and worked as a broker, as he was willing to "prove . . . in writing."[52] In contrast, for dozens of less illustrious participants in other trials, social class was defined by a highly gendered and contested conception of work: even poor men could distinguish themselves from the dishonorable poor if they worked steadily to sustain their families, but women's labor was often (but not always) considered class degradation. Lawyers, prosecutors, judicial experts, witnesses, defendants, and victims may have mostly agreed that social status should have juridical significance, but its symbolization varied according to its observers' own perspective.

Nowhere was this as apparent as in discussions surrounding residential circumstances. The issue arose in countless cases where class appeared as a justification for differential legal treatment, especially when participants lived in favelas or in seedy, crowded rooming houses. Some parties—usually lawyers, prosecutors, mental health experts, or those of similarly high status—saw living in such places as proof that a person was less reliable as a witness, less worthy of protection as a victim, and more menacing to society as a defendant. Favela observers were *testemunhas de viveiro*, "barnyard witnesses," incapable of independent discernment. Girls who had grown up sleeping in crowded tenement rooms with parents and coupled siblings could hardly claim purity. And it only stood to reason that the inhabitants of *morros*, ostensibly infested with *arruaceiros* (hooligans), *malfeitores* (gangsters), and *desordeiros* (disorderly characters), were most likely to commit crimes.[53] Other observers—usually witnesses, defendants, and victims—disagreed, lending less significance to a person's place of residence than to the character of the resident. In their eyes, respectable poverty—symbolized by steady, stable tenure in a single community, regardless of its location or physical amenities—did not imply judicial degradation. For them, the dishonorable poor were itinerant individuals with no established community ties, whose habitations combined economic misery with rootlessness and moral laxity.

Participants in Rio's criminal trials frequently pointed to class as the single most important determinant of someone's juridical identity. But numerous other components stood out as well: moral character, adherence to gender norms, nationality, race, personal connections, and even civil status. In every one of these categories, with the exception of race, a similar pattern emerges: participants most often agreed on such factors' importance, and even about their relevance to judicial proceedings, but their symbolization proved problematic. Was formal civil marriage critical, or was an informal but stable union equally virtuous? Who was high enough on the social scale to certify that someone else was a hard worker, a good neighbor, or a good citizen? Could a foreign-born naturalized Brazilian be patriotic? Was a man worthy of state protection if he called for the courts to protect his honor rather than defending it with his fists? Was he more likely to be a criminal if he lived off a woman, if he had no patron willing to speak for him, if he was dishonest, or exploitative in business? Could a girl deserve legal protection of her virtue if she had been born illegitimate, if she worked outside the home, if her parents left her unsupervised, if she moved freely around the city, if she went to dances and celebrated *carnaval*? Did a woman reveal an unsavory character if she gossiped, if she was avaricious or aggressive, if she took lovers, if she left home without her husband's permission? Was good moral character best certified by police authorities, employers, and patrons, or did it reside in such qualities as neighborliness and generosity, to which anyone could bear witness?

Nearly always, those sitting on the upper end of the scale articulated the most rigid, blunt, and immutable social divisions, while the lower-class victims of their blanket condemnations sought subtler distinctions within broader social and moral categories. The only issue that assumed a markedly different pattern was race, which participants in the Carioca trials only very rarely linked directly to juridical identity, despite the fact that it appeared frequently as a component of police identification and was often discussed as an essential personality trait by positivist criminologists.[54] Those few who did speak overtly about race were invariably either foreigners or legal professionals, whose offhand comments about Afro-Brazilian sexuality, personality, and criminal tendencies crassly echoed the antiquated racist jargon of late-nineteenth- and early-twentieth-century European criminologists and anthropologists. Judge Mario Antônio da Costa penned a typical example in 1932 when, upon finding a young black man not guilty of deflowering a *parda* girl, he noted that the whole affair "only reflected the animal sexual instinct, uncontrolled and impetuous as it tends always to be among the Negro race."[55] The statement, tacked on to the end of his verdict, served as a general comment on the case rather than as an integral part of the judge's judicial reasoning; it thus mostly serves to give a flicker of insight into the racial prejudices underlying many decisions that were more explicitly based on class, adherence to gender norms, and moral standing. On the whole, arguments to the effect that racial characteristics should be taken explicitly into account in determining juridical identity were rare.

If prosecutors, lawyers, and judges wrote only rarely about race, defendants, victims, and witnesses mostly avoided the subject altogether. Indeed, in 251 cases, I found only two openly racial comments. In 1930, the Brazilian-born plaintiff in one *injúria* case complained that her neighbor, an Italian journal vendor, had woken her up yelling, "You, my shameless nigger, are a huge whore, an extremely common trollop" ("tu minha negra sem vergonha, és uma grandecissima puta, uma cadella muito ordinária" [sic]).[56] In a 1932 case, another witness claimed that the Portuguese plaintiff in an *injúria* trial had in fact herself insulted the Brazilian-born defendant, calling her a "negro" ("negra") who "wasn't even married." It is significant that both speakers were European-born, and the racial epithets in both cases were spoken as sexually tinged insults, not as character descriptions meant to have legal weight.[57] And, aside from these instances, silence reigned; at most, it was slightly more common for witnesses to mention racial identity with reference to darker-skinned individuals and to omit it for whites. This does not indicate that racial prejudice or discrimination was absent either from popular culture or from criminal trials. On the contrary, as we will see below, race seems to have been one of several factors that heavily influenced patterns of arrest, judicial abuses, and criminal condemnations. But the general silence in my sample indicates that race, unlike class, operated mainly as an unspoken subtext in Carioca police stations and courtrooms.[58]

Juridical identity thus proved an important but highly contested component of discussions involving criminality and punishment. While participants could mostly agree on which factors should be relevant to an individual's juridical identity—social class, adherence to gender norms, moral fortitude—they disagreed about the signifiers of these qualities, with participants of higher status generally advocating the most categorical symbolizations. Identity, however, proved to be only one of several individualizing elements used to manipulate Brazilian criminal law's plasticities. Circumstance, too, mattered deeply, in ways that revealed similarly subtle divisions within Carioca society. Everyone could agree on the categories of circumstance that eliminated or attenuated criminal responsibility, but countless fractures emerged when it came time to identify those categories' specific features.

From the perspective of trial participants, the circumstances that eliminated or attenuated criminal responsibility generally conformed to the criminal codes' authorized categories: complete or partial deprivation of senses and intelligence, the need to avoid a greater evil, and legitimate self-defense. Sometimes all participants could also agree about which circumstances merited inclusion in these categories. Self-defense was always legitimate in the face of an actual or imminent attack against person or property (although, as we will see below, participants often disagreed as to what signaled imminence). Most people also recognized a right to defense against certain widely recognized, gender-specific assaults on personal or family honor: imputations involving the sexual purity and monogamy of a woman, or slurs questioning a man's honesty in business and public life, his ability to control women and other dependents, and his willingness to actively defend himself and his family against attacks and insults.[59] Participants also generally exempted from prosecution anyone who acted in order to prevent a more serious crime. Likewise, legal professionals and common citizens concurred in considering drunkenness, extreme mental perturbation, emotional distress, or insanity to be relevant mitigating factors.

Yet elsewhere, trial participants disagreed sharply. Sometimes these conflicts centered on the relative weight of aggravating and attenuating factors. Judges and prosecutors, following the criminal code, tended to consider a physical offense much more serious when a man attacked a woman (aside from his wife or lover), or when an employee or dependent assaulted an employer or patron. In the eyes of many defendants and witnesses, though, there were situations in which such an attack might be justified as a legitimate defense of honor. In 1929, for example, José Libânio dos Santos, a day laborer from Rio's port district, was arrested for physically assaulting his tenement landlady. Dos Santos claimed that she had provoked the attack by bombarding him with "threats and vulgarities," threatening to evict him, and—a final indignity—grabbing him by the testicles, all while her husband looked on. In José's testimony, whatever respect he might have owed the purported victim, as a woman and as an authority figure in the tenement, was eroded by her aggressive, offensive, crude attack on his honor and physical dignity, the right to which was his by judicial law and practice.[60]

Defendants and witnesses in other cases involving physical assault resorted to similar logic, especially in relation to issues of authority, status, and gender. Some implied that bosses or patrons lost their due consideration when they humiliated or offended their employees. In 1932, a white Portuguese-born dry-goods salesman justified his physical assault of a neighboring store owner, explaining that the victim had unfairly told the defendant's boss that the defendant was a *moleque* (juvenile rascal) and had stolen some cloth.[61] Similarly, Jovilo Candido, a resident of the central São Carlos favela who was accused of attacking his boss with a razor in 1930, claimed that his actions were justified because the boss had demeaned him, fired him, and hit him in the face.[62]

Others argued that women who violated gender norms by demonstrating aggression, avarice, promiscuity, or disobedience to their husbands or lovers lost any special judicial protection. In one particularly brutal 1930 case, Elvira Costa Carmo complained to police that her husband of a few months had "beaten and kicked" her while his mother and stepfather "cheered him on," simply because she had visited a neighbor against the husband's wishes. At the forensic medical exam, which revealed extensive battering, she added that he had also hit her with a leather strap and that she had bled from the mouth after being brutally kicked in the abdomen. While her husband denied the beating, claiming that she had fallen against a sewing machine, he did admit to admonishing her because of the visit, claiming that the right to do so was his by marriage. In this case, as in many others involving domestic abuse, the police chief found himself in the paradoxical position of being the woman's only defender in the face of community and family indifference. Even after several eyewitnesses refused to testify against the husband, the chief pursued the case, claiming that a fall could not possibly have caused such extensive bruising. But neither the public prosecutor nor the judge shared his zeal, and the case was closed. Here, clearly, Elvira lost her feminine right to special protection; in light of her supposed disobedience to gender norms—in this case, the duty to obey her husband—her neighbors would not support her, and the judicial system ultimately failed her.[63]

In cases such as these, trial participants could agree in the abstract about which situations constituted mitigating and aggravating circumstances, but they might disagree sharply about their significance in the context of any particular trial. In other cases, witnesses and defendants diverged more radically from judges and prosecutors, arguing that circumstances not generally recognized by Brazilian law and jurisprudence should shape criminal culpability. Such was often the case, for example, when a defendant claimed to have committed a crime in order to stop unneighborly or otherwise unacceptable behavior that was not regulated by law. Maximina's excuse for arguing with Antônio over the drainage ditch fit this pattern, as did a 1931 physical assault case in which a man attacked his neighbor for disturbing his brother-in-law's wake with an argument over a cockfight.[64] A similar situation ensued when offenders claimed to have been defending "rights" that were not legally theirs. In 1932, for example, an itinerant soft-drink vendor—writing from prison with some assistance but no lawyer, and addressing the judge as "Santo Julgador"—explained that he had physically assaulted his "victim" because the latter had tried to steal a drink, and that he, the defendant, had a right to protect his livelihood even if municipal statutes did not sanction its legality.[65]

Judges and prosecutors tended to view such claims dimly. They also rarely favored lower-class offenders claiming to defend controversial or class-specific signs and symbols of personal honor. One man, for example, unsuccessfully justified his aggression against police officers who had attempted to search him by saying that he had to defend his *prestígio* on the street—a form of masculine honor that was generally not upheld in Carioca police stations.[66] Officials and common citizens also clashed when defendants claimed to have been protecting themselves from police abuse. In a 1930 breaking-and-entering case, for instance, authorities were not convinced when Alfredo Silva not only stated that he had sneaked into a private garden solely in order to escape police harassment but also claimed that he had achieved his goal, since the presence of the garden's owner had prevented the police from beating him upon his arrest.[67] Although lawyers did acknowledge Carioca police abuses from time to time, judges and prosecutors never went so far as to consider contact with police a "greater evil," the avoidance of which could justify criminal action.[68]

Of all the divergences between poor citizens and judicial officials, however, none was weightier than that centered on the attenuating value of economic need. For most poor witnesses and defendants, its relevance was both obvious and multifaceted. In some cases, their logic was simply beyond judicial officials' range of tolerance. In 1933, for example, police arrested a resident of the Mangueira favela for urinating in a downtown tunnel; neither they nor the judge proved sympathetic when the defendant pleaded that he had no other choice, since bar proprietors would not allow poor people to use their restrooms.[69] In defloration suits, need-based arguments routinely gained better traction. Because defense lawyers often flagged both working girls' independence and their mothers' absence from the home as signs of moral laxity, women often made a point of noting that they worked out of necessity, not choice, and were nonetheless as zealous of sexual honor as anyone else.[70] Arguments about need also surfaced frequently in physical assault cases. Tenants, for example, often justified assaults on landlords by saying that the latter had inhumanely threatened them with eviction when they were sick, unemployed, or in otherwise desperate economic straits;[71] in the face of such greedy and inconsiderate threats, their violent physical reactions were only just and natural. Finally, need often justified theft: defendants cited hungry families and unemployment, and one man even said that he had broken into the kitchen of a restaurant adjoining his tenement because its owner had refused his just request for a bit of bread and cheese to relieve his hunger.[72] Such reasoning was not limited to criminal trials; as chapters 7 and 8 will discuss, a similar moral logic underlay favela residents' defense of illegal settlements throughout the 1930s, 1940s, and 1950s. There, as here, many poor Cariocas believed that the requirements of need trumped the mandates of law. Nonetheless, although some jurists allowed extreme poverty as an attenuating factor in theft cases (considering hunger and suffering a "greater evil"), the judges and police officers in my sample never acknowledged economic necessity as a judicially relevant circumstance.[73]

For the most part, judicial authorities greeted with similar silence arguments that questioned the legitimacy of legal interference. They would occasionally agree with defendants and witnesses as to the public irrelevance of private conflicts—mutual insults, physical fights, family arguments. By the late 1920s, jurists and judges also began occasionally to credit arguments asserting the private nature of young women's decisions about their own sexuality. Male defendants had long claimed that the courts had no business policing sexual acts practiced with "impure" women. Increasingly, though, young women whose parents brought defloration suits on their behalf also refused to cooperate, throwing aside timeworn platitudes about marriage promises and painful, bloody sexual initiations and unashamedly claiming a right to sexual enjoyment and free will. When faced with such recalcitrant virtue, judicial authorities tended simply to throw up their hands.[74]

But lawyers and poor citizens put forth other pleas that met with less official sympathy. They contended, for example, that police officials used vagrancy laws as a form of sanctioned harassment, or that such laws were grossly unfair in the face of widespread underemployment; they criticized laws against arms possession because some poor people used knives for work or needed weapons in order to defend themselves in neighborhoods that lacked police protection.[75] Police officials in my sample never dropped charges of vagrancy or arms possession after a case opened, and they generally framed accusations in a formulaic language that signaled their discriminatory or aleatory nature.[76] Judges showed a bit more flexibility, often absolving a defendant when a clean criminal record and a few upstanding citizens attested to his or her good character. When defendants had previous arrests, though, or lacked the wherewithal to produce higher-status witnesses, judges applied a stricter legalism, releasing only those who positively disproved the accusations. In cases where defendants questioned not the truth of the allegations but rather the legitimacy of their criminalization, judges turned a deaf ear.

Such uneven enforcement may have been the laws' unstated intention. In a city where a good portion of the population was chronically underemployed, and where official protection tended to stop at the frontiers of urban formality, laws pertaining to vagrancy and arms possession did more to sanction police surveillance of the poor than to prohibit dangerous behavior. Those who fit the highly formalized profile of poor offenders could hardly defend themselves when they were charged simply with displaying the external symbols of poverty. It is little wonder that their only recourse was to question the law itself. In 1930, such challenges to the very legitimacy of criminal statutes were still rare. By the 1950s and 1960s, as socially discriminatory judgments about personal character gained an ever more pervasive role in the criminal justice process, they would become commonplace.

Quantifying Judicial Bias

Rio's criminal trial transcripts reveal much about the signs and symbols of character and circumstance to which lawyers, witnesses, defendants, and victims attached juridical significance. Judges and police chiefs tended to be more circumspect, however, restricting their comments to each case's finer factual and technical details. Even when police reports and final verdicts expressed character judgments, they did so mainly with reference to factors deemed legally significant in Brazilian jurisprudence (work status, criminal arrest records, and a sexually offended woman's sexual purity). Observations about circumstance tended to be similarly narrow. Judges, especially, gave few hints as to which subtle factors swayed their allocations of leniency. At most, they would list aggravating and attenuating factors in the legal codes' dry, vague language, usually without reference to alternate arguments offered by defendants, victims, and lawyers. Accordingly, it is difficult to unpack through textual scrutiny the extralegal influences on judges' decisions. Often, especially in cases where circumstance and character are not mentioned at all, the only way to discern the relationship between verdicts and juridical identities is through statistical analysis. While statistical work with this kind of sample is in itself problematic, it does strongly indicate that authorities from the 1920s to the 1940s allowed personality and circumstance to influence their verdicts in predictably patterned ways.

Several scholars of Rio de Janeiro's criminal justice system have studied statistical patterns of judicial bias, most notably with attention to race. Martha Abreu, writing about belle époque defloration cases, found that judges and juries tended to find defendants guilty more frequently when the offended girls were white and lived with their families.[77] Sueann Caulfield, writing about the same kinds of cases from the 1920s and 1930s, highlighted different results. Although white defendants were far less likely than their black and *pardo* counterparts to see their cases reach trial, there was little difference in trial outcomes. Caulfield also found, however, that defendants in defloration cases involving interracial couples faced lower rates of punishment than did those in cases where victims and defendants had similar skin tones.[78] Sam Adamo, studying published statistics and prison records, found that darker-skinned, illiterate, poor individuals in the first four decades of the twentieth century were far more likely to be convicted of crimes than their white counterparts, and that such disparities increased over time. Carlos Antônio Costa Ribeiro, analyzing jury cases that came to trial between 1900 and 1930, found that verdicts showed a clear racial bias with reference both to victims and to defendants.[79] Olívia Gomes da Cunha, writing about vagrancy, reached similar qualitative conclusions with regard to arrests and police treatment of defendants in the 1920s and 1930s.[80]

Important as all of these findings are, several lacunae remain. First, race undoubtedly influenced Carioca trials' progressions and outcomes, but class, literacy, civil status, and residential circumstances also had important—and intertwining—impacts. Although most analyses of Carioca criminal trials have acknowledged this complexity, only Costa Ribeiro has analyzed it statistically, and then only with reference to occupation and civil status. Second, as noted above, procedure shaped the punishment meted out within the Carioca judicial system at least as much as did formal outcomes; police and judicial authorities routinely bent the rules of the procedural code, inordinately imprisoning some defendants and allowing other cases to drift until the statute of limitations proscribed prosecution. Any full analysis of the Carioca criminal justice system must make some reference to these patterns of informal justice. And, third, each crime had both different constituencies and different patterns of progression; the system as a whole cannot be understood without analyzing multiple crimes.

The following analysis of the relationship between individual defendants and the progression and outcomes of Carioca criminal trials between 1927 and 1942, undertaken with these imperatives in mind, makes no claim to infallibility. My sample of 251 cases is relatively small, my information is not always complete, and I analyze it with the simplistic assumption that the defendants' personal characteristics influenced the trials' course more heavily than the traits of their victims. Nonetheless, my analysis suggests that judges, prosecutors, and police authorities demonstrated the same combination of abundant bias and weak consensus that characterized trial participants as a whole. Judicial authorities—like lawyers, witnesses, defendants, and victims—all seemed to recognize that there was a place within the criminal justice process for personality and circumstance, but they did not yet agree as to which specific characteristics should mold the law's plasticities.

In considering my sample, I sought to associate various of the defendants' personal characteristics with four separate dimensions of judicial procedure and outcome: (1) whether a case was dismissed before trial; (2) whether a defendant was found guilty; (3) whether a defendant spent time in prison; and (4) whether civil rights guaranteed in the procedural codes were respected or violated.[81] The first and second dimensions often reflect the facts of the case (some defendants were in fact more guilty than others), and they are also good measures of the defendant's success in navigating the Brazilian criminal justice system. The third dimension essentially gauges punishment, and the fourth indicates procedural harshness or leniency.

In studying these relationships, I began with a simple cross-tabulation, determining the percentage of defendants with each of eleven characteristics who received determined types of treatment, and comparing these percentages with the statistical average for all defendants. For the cross-tabulations, the personal characteristics evaluated included occupational level; work status; race; housing type (shack, rooming house, apartment, and so on); neighborhood type (formal, informal, or mixed); place of birth; educational background; civil status; possession of civil identification cards; arrest record; and access to legal counsel.[82] I went on to run a series of logistic regressions, which illuminated the independent influence of each variable, but which produced few statistically significant results because of the large number of variables and the relatively small sample size.[83] Here, the personal characteristics evaluated were fewer and varied slightly in each regression, to maximize predictive power. Neither analysis should be considered statistically definitive, but both point toward the strong influence of social status on judicial outcomes.[84]

Before delving into the statistical results, a brief note about the impor-

TABLE 7

Variance from Average Judicial Treatment by Type of Crime, 1928–1942

(Figures indicate the numbers by which the average percentages for each group
of crimes vary from the average percentages for all defendants)

	Ends with inquerito	Spends no jail time	Civil rights respected	Found innocent
Calumnia, injúria, induc. suicide, etc.	−11.7	24.9	20.9	28.8
Sexual crimes	19.1	26.1	11.6	23.3
Physical violence, resisting arrest	11.1	9.8	5.9	3.6
Vagrancy/arms possession	−22.9	−54.7	−36.1	−8.1
Larceny, breaking and entering	−14.7	−17.8	−25.5	−22.4

tance of the crimes themselves is in order. The simplest cross-tabulation indicates that police delegates and judges treated defendants differently according to the sorts of crimes they were accused of committing. In general, crimes fell into two categories. Defendants in cases involving physical assault, sexual crimes, and *injúria* received better than average treatment; they were less likely to go to trial (except, for procedural reasons, in slander cases), to spend time in jail, to have their rights violated, or, ultimately, to be found guilty (unless they were accused of physical violence). At the other end of the scale, defendants in cases involving vagrancy and/or arms possession, breaking and entering, and theft nearly always lost out, and by significant margins (see table 7).

If all criminal cases had involved defendants and victims who had similar profiles, these findings would seem to reflect a simple and routine set of informal procedures, intended to allot gentler treatment to offenders in what legal officials considered the least pernicious crimes. But my data suggest that the situation was more complex. If each crime revealed a certain pattern of treatment, each also tended to attract a specific class of criminal. In general, as numerous other researchers have noted, the statistical profile of the population that passed through the criminal justice system differed from that of the Carioca population as a whole; people accused of crimes were darker-skinned, poorer, less educated, and over-whelmingly single and male. My sample certainly conforms to this pattern; 90 percent of its defendants were male, and the percentage of whites among them was relatively low. But each type of crime also tended to cluster its own kind of defendant. In general, people accused of physical assault conformed most closely to the profile of Rio's general population. Defendants in slander crimes were likely to be white and had unusu-ally high marriage rates. Defendants in sexual crimes, predictably, were more often single. Defendants in cases of theft tended to be the darkest-

TABLE 8

*Comparison of Sampled Defendants with Rio de Janeiro's 1940
Population by Race, Marital Status, and Education*

(percent)

	White	Parda	Preta	Married	Single	Illiterate
In overall population	70	17	11	40	51	22
In overall sample	54	25	21	36	59	26
Physical assault	59	15	28	37	55	20
Sexual crimes	54	31	15	23	70	21
Theft/robbery	39	26	35	39	59	35
Vagrancy/arms possession	48	32	20	24	76	43
Injúria, calumnia, etc.	60	40	0	76	18	24

skinned, and defendants in vagrancy cases were most frequently identified as illiterate. Though the table does not separate the categories, cases
of vagrancy and arms possession—both "crimes" that were prosecuted
entirely on police discretion—presented surprisingly different racial profiles, as well as slightly varying literacy rates; in both cases, those accused
of arms possession tended to be of slightly higher status.

If defendants in various types of criminal cases received markedly divergent treatment, and if they also demonstrated noticeably different racial, social, and educational profiles, we are still left with something of
a quandary. On the one hand, it could still be the case that legal officials
found some crimes more worthy of punishment than others, and that
members of some racial, social, and educational groups simply committed certain types of crimes more frequently. The highly debatable corol-
lary of this assumption, of course, would be that the overall divergences
between the Carioca population and the sample population only reflected
differences in each group's tendencies toward criminality. On the other
hand, it is entirely possible that the divergences in treatment, including
rates of arrest and accusation, reflected more about the defendants themselves than about the crimes they may have committed.

In this case—as in many others involving questions of race, class, and
social status in Brazil—the truth probably lies somewhere in between.
But the data presented in statistical appendices I and II indicate that individual identity played an extraordinarily prominent role in determining
both the progression and the outcome of Rio's criminal trials. This in
itself is not particularly shocking; other researchers have reached similar
conclusions, and positivist legal philosophies popular among the era's
jurists prescribed precisely such a focus on individual personality and circumstance. What is surprising, however, is the number of traits that have

some relationship with trial progression and outcome, and the degree to which their relative importance diverges from the predictions of studies that have privileged race as the preeminent vector of judicial discrimination.

In relation to case dismissal, the cross-tabulations in statistical appendix I indicate that professionals, occupants of supervised or formal housing, rural residents, and whites tended to see their cases dismissed significantly more frequently than average (a divergence of at least 10 percent was considered significant). Factory laborers or unskilled workers, people previously accused or convicted of crimes, some immigrants, illiterates, the unemployed, and residents of shacks and informal neighborhoods experienced significantly lower dismissal rates. The logistic regressions in statistical appendix II show similar results: whites, literates, professionals, and residents of formal, private housing had higher probabilities of seeing their cases dismissed, while shantytown or tenement residents, factory workers or skilled laborers, and unskilled workers all had very high odds of facing trial. All in all, treatment generally mirrored status, in predictable ways.

Trial verdicts also tended to match social indicators (with the exception of race) though here bureaucratic factors, such as access to counsel, criminal history, and document possession, had a stronger influence still. The cross-tabulations indicate that professionals and factory workers, people with access to private counsel, literates, and occupants of formal housing all received innocent verdicts significantly more often than average. Residents of shacks or supervised housing; defendants with no lawyer, public counsel, or a criminal record; and the unemployed all received significantly higher percentages of guilty verdicts. In the regressions, statistically significant results suggest that whites were considerably more likely to be convicted than blacks, defendants with public counsel were more likely to be condemned than those with private lawyers, and defendants with clean criminal records and civil identity cards faced slim odds of conviction. The surprising racial dynamics may, paradoxically, be the flip side of a tendency for nonwhite defendants to be sent to trial on the basis of flimsy evidence.

Imprisonment patterns—a measure of punishment rather than of guilt—also link social and bureaucratic status to judicial treatment, though race, again, confounds. In the cross-tabulations, homemakers, professionals, factory workers, literates, policemen or military recruits, and residents of formal housing all had low average imprisonment rates; while illiterates, skilled laborers, residents of supervised housing or rural neighborhoods, those with criminal records, and the unemployed had high ones. The regression analysis yields somewhat clearer results: here, defendants who worked in factories or had criminal records faced increased odds of prison time, while those with civil identification, foreign birth, or residence in formal housing or in the wealthy Zona Sul faced low odds of imprisonment. The racial results here were truly unexpected; the probability of prison time for *pretos* was less than half that of *brancos*. This finding, along with the negative results for factory workers, may be explained by a tendency for crimes committed against higher-status victims to be punished more harshly than those against victims perceived as lowly by police and judicial officials.

In general, then, judges bestowed guilt, innocence, and punishment in largely predictable ways, and numerous characteristics—especially those related to bureaucratic status, residence, and work—seemed to influence their judgments. One sticky issue remains, however: it is possible, if distasteful, to imagine that poor, uneducated, unemployed, undocumented defendants with criminal histories were simply more often guilty and dangerous than were their more prosperous, educated, employed, documented, criminally virgin counterparts. A close analysis of the ways in which judges and police officers violated procedural rules, especially those involving legal counsel, trial delays, and pretrial imprisonment, invalidates this hypothesis.[85] Inasmuch as informal justice was dispensed through selective respect for civil rights, judges and police officials distributed it with the same social biases that colored verdicts and imprisonment. In the cross-tabulations, defendants who worked as professionals, police, military recruits, or white-collar employees tended to enjoy more than an average level of respect for their civil rights. People who were literate, foreign, or holders of civil identification documents also did well, as did residents of supervised housing. Defendants who were illiterate, unskilled, or unemployed fared worse all around, as did those with criminal records and those who lived in shacks or informal neighborhoods. In the regression analysis, *pretos'* rights have a relatively high chance of being respected, as do those of people living in formal housing, people living in the Zona Sul, professionals, and holders of civil identification. Defendants with high odds of rights violations included shack and tenement dwellers; residents of Rio's center, north, and west; workers; unskilled laborers; and defendants with criminal records. While race, again, operated unpredictably, the other results are roughly in line with what we know about Carioca social prejudice.

These statistical patterns should be read with skepticism. Yet they tend to echo the trials' qualitative evidence in suggestive ways. In particular, biases demonstrated in the actions of judges and police officials reflected those openly expressed by lawyers and other well-to-do participants, mostly favoring high status over low, with status defined by broad, superficial criteria. The significant exception is race, where only police chiefs and public prosecutors—those responsible for determining whether or not a case went to trial—gave people of African descent harsher treatment than whites. The explanation may be that defendants who victimized nonwhites were treated more leniently.[86] It also may lie in an odd quirk of the process itself: perhaps so many nonwhite defendants were sent unjustly to trial that their cases were generally weaker than those of whites. Most likely, it also represents the influence of formal law in creating informal bias; the written law itself opened space for "social" prejudice, while its silence effectively delegitimized open racial discrimination. Whatever the case, the results give pause, for they indicate that race should not be thought of as the single or most important source of bias in the criminal justice system; most likely, racial prejudice represented one string in a tangle of social biases that molded defendants' judicial fates.

Quantitatively as well as qualitatively, it seems apparent that Rio's criminal courts adhered only inconsistently to the classical school of criminal law. Even the letter of Brazil's criminal and procedural codes allowed personal circumstance and personality to creep in; in practice, nearly every trial participant brought such factors to bear. What none of these actors could agree upon, however, was the definition of social and civic worth that should be at the basis of such subjective criteria. The result was an aleatory and conflictual system, decried by observers from every angle. Untangling its knotty contradictions would become the principal charge of Vargas-era judicial reformers, and the success of their work would hinge on the police and judicial officials who attempted to apply a new generation of laws to Rio's enormously heterogeneous mid-century population.

CHAPTER SIX

Positivist Criminology and Paper Poverty

In the decades following 1940, conflict about identity's weight in determining rights endured. But Vargas-era changes in the criminal and procedural codes—together with the rising civic importance of identity documents, marriage certificates, and legalized property rights—began to winnow the plethora of signs and symbols that signified juridical worthiness for Carioca trial participants in the 1930s. Witnesses, defendants, lawyers, and victims still emphasized honor, need, and adherence to gender norms; policemen, prosecutors, and judges still associated individual worthiness with color, civil status, birthplace, family origins, living conditions, and habitual employment. But the decades between 1940 and 1970 saw a subtle shift in language and emphasis. For judges, lawyers, and prosecutors, bureaucratic status—as symbolized by identity cards, work cards, criminal records, and police assessments of personality—assumed a central role in signifying juridical identity. For witnesses, defendants, and victims, however, the use of such symbols signaled an incipient but significant division. For some, documentation entailed liberty: by simply presenting a piece of paper, they could escape from the categories of class, race, and family origin that once would have consigned them to legal marginality. For the rights-poor, though, who lacked such legal credentials, demands for documentation only reinforced their status as subcitizens, adding a new and often virtually insurmountable barrier to whatever frayed hopes they may have held for justice in the Carioca criminal courts. This chapter chronicles these divergent experiences and their degrading impact on Rio's criminal justice system as a whole.

Criminology for the New State

The 1940 criminal code was widely anticipated as a legislative tonic for the Brazilian criminal justice system's many ambiguities and contradictions. Legal professionals of all stripes had criticized the 1890 penal code almost from its inception, complaining that it was a muddled and antiquated document, maladapted to "modern" theories of criminal law and entirely inadequate as a beacon of legal precision and clarity.[87] Already in 1893, Federal Deputy Vieira de Araujo presented an unsuccessful proposal for a new code. In 1911, jurist Galdino de Siqueira authored another barren project, and a 1928 initiative, authored by civil law jurist Sá Pereira, might have become law had it not been for the 1930 revolution. In the years following Vargas's ascent, discontent with the existing criminal code only increased. Many of Vargas's ideological companions sympathized with the leanings of positivist criminologists, and their critiques were fueled further by the publication of several new interpretations of the 1890 law.[88]

Criminal code reform thus became a central preoccupation of the Vargas government. In the wake of a 1936 conference on criminology, which was devoted to debating the Sá Pereira proposal, Vargas appointed the *paulista* jurist Alcântara Machado to pen yet another criminal code. Following a volley of criticism of the project, perceived by some as erring too far toward positivism, Justice Minister Francisco Campos appointed a commission to revise it. The 1940 criminal code was the fruit of their efforts. The 1941 misdemeanor law and the 1942 procedural code responded to similarly longstanding complaints and were generally seen as equally vital to effective criminal justice reform.

Given the elastic interpretations that many judges, prosecutors, lawyers, and jurists had given to previous codes, the 1940 criminal code, the 1941 misdemeanor law, and the 1942 procedural code did not signify the radical revolution in judicial practice that their most ardent advocates had hoped for. All three were eclectic documents, at once advocating authoritarian ideals of collective social advancement and constituting a written truce in the ongoing battle between the positivist and classical schools of criminal justice.[89] From the classical school, the authors retained the notions of free will and individual moral responsibility, mostly rejecting the idea that criminal sanction should be applied as social therapy for "dangerous" individuals rather than as punishment for consummated criminal acts. The notion of criminal justice as social defense was not entirely absent, however, especially from the misdemeanor and procedural codes—an unsurprising fact, given the Estado Novo's more authoritarian currents. All three codes thus incorporated the positivist notion that punishment, if not guilt, should be determined by individual personality and circumstance, and that certain restricted situations warranted a kind of "therapeutic" sanction for "dangerous" individuals who had not committed any specific crimes. Although this latter provision—the *medida de segurança*, or security measure—was entirely new to Brazilian law, the individualization of punishment only gave legal sanction and structure to a practice that had already become commonplace in Carioca criminal courtrooms by the 1920s.

The new codes did clarify somewhat the criteria according to which punishment might be "individualized," formally endorsing some of the signs and symbols of worthy citizenship that had long justified differential sanctions. The 1940 criminal code, like its 1890 predecessor, ameliorated both responsibility and punishment on the basis of a spectrum of standards, some relatively clear-cut and others quite ambiguous. Certain specific groups were again relieved entirely of criminal responsibility: minors 18 years of age or younger, or those who, because of "mental illness or incomplete or retarded mental development," could not understand the criminality of their actions. The criminality of certain acts also continued to depend largely on the identities of their perpetrators and victims; despite protests from left-leaning jurists such as Roberto Lyra, the rich still could not be vagrants, and protection against sexual crimes remained largely limited to "honest" women and girls. The codes granted other clearly defined groups differential punishment. Government officials, police chiefs, citizens inscribed in the national "book of merit," military personnel, firemen, judges, those possessing university diplomas, and anyone who had ever served on a jury had a right to be imprisoned in separate facilities. A civil ID card still exempted its holder from police identification procedures, and "vagrants," still considered inherently dangerous, received automatic pretrial imprisonment with no right to post bail. The codes also flagged vagrants, the insane, and those who had committed a crime while drunk as prime candidates for the *medida de segurança*.

With regard to the more elastic criteria for exemption from criminal responsibility and punishment, the criminal code in particular presented a few significant changes. Complete circumstantial acquittal, in the new code, occurred when a crime had been undertaken either under orders from a superior or "in a state of necessity, in legitimate self-defense, or in strict obedience to a legal duty or in the regular exercise of a legal right." Although these provisions resembled those of the 1890 code, the specific emphasis on "a state of necessity" broadened the admissibility of arguments involving economic need as well as "avoidance of a greater evil." The new law explicitly excluded "passion" as a mitigator of criminal responsibility, though it could attenuate punishment; and drunkenness justified leniency only when prosecutors could demonstrate no previous criminal intent. The code also significantly altered the impact of attenuating and aggravating circumstances on punishment; most significantly, a crime no longer automatically increased in seriousness when committed against a woman or an authority figure, although crimes committed with abuse of power, or against family or household members, still merited tougher sanction. As before, anyone with a criminal record automatically received harsher treatment, a provision that lent great significance to essentially aleatory arrests for arms possession or vagrancy, which not only implied immediate sanctions but also established a criminal history that would affect the purported "vagrants" for the rest of their lives.

Perhaps the greatest changes with respect to the symbolization of worthy citizenship were more a matter of procedure than of substance. Modern scholars and contemporary observers have made much of the *medida de segurança*; as a sanction meted out on the basis of personality rather than criminal responsibility, it certainly represented an innovation in the letter of Brazilian criminal law. In practice, however, patterns of punishment in the late 1920s and 1930s had already demonstrated a marked link with the personal identities of defendants. In fact, if not in law, judges had long exercised a sort of informal *medida de segurança* under the 1890 criminal code. They lacked only formal sanction and, more importantly, formal criteria upon which to base differential treatment.

Both the misdemeanor law and the criminal code made gestures toward defining such criteria, not only by formally linking *medidas de segurança* to the supposed "dangerousness" of any individual, but also by pinpointing several specific indicators of such menace. Vagrancy, beggary, habitual drunkenness, insanity, gang violence, and repeated offenses would all now theoretically oblige a judge to impose a *medida de segurança* on a defendant, regardless of guilt in any particular crime.[90]

But judges also received a much more open-ended authority. An individual who did not fit into any of the legally articulated categories could still be subject to the *medida de segurança* if his "personality and antecedents, as well as the motives and circumstances of the crime, authorized the supposition that he might commit a criminal act, either again or for the first time."[91] Similarly broad dispositions guided judges in the application of *sursis* and early release. Given that the new procedural code also considerably expanded judges' authority and flexibility—authorizing them not only to participate in the production of proof, either for or against the defendant, but also to evaluate the relative importance of evidence, circumstance, and personality entirely according to their *livre convencimento* (free conviction)—such open-ended mandates seemed to muddle further the already murky process through which individual personality traits and circumstances became judicial symbols of worthy citizenship.[92]

In practice, though, the criteria by which legal professionals judged worthiness or juridical personality became considerably clearer in the wake of the new codes. This was thanks both to a rarely discussed procedural innovation called the *vida pregressa* and to the growing importance of official documents as components of juridical identity. The *vida pregressa* effectively extended the identification system that had become universal in Carioca police stations by the early 1930s. Dactyloscopic identification had concerned itself only with basic information that might help to distinguish an accused criminal from all others—fingerprints, name, parents' names, a place of birth, literacy, and, usually, "color" or racial identification. The *vida pregressa,* as its name implies, included anything that might help a judge or prosecutor to measure what jurist Francisco Campos called the "character or personality of the defendant—meaning . . . his curriculum vitae, his individual, family, and social conditions, and his conduct both before and immediately after the crime."[93]

The *vida pregressa* was hardly the extensive psychological profile that some Carioca criminologists had dreamed of establishing for every Brazilian in the early 1930s. Yet it still represented a concession to modern currents of criminal sociology, which, discarding nineteenth-century notions about the biological or racial origins of criminality and deviance, pointed instead to psychiatric anomalies and to the psychologically degenerative effects of poverty, ignorance, and social inequality.[94] The *vida pregressa* would be a brief life history that would serve as a judge's main recourse in determining any defendant's worthiness before the law. The characteristics noted in the *vida pregressa* thus became, by definition, those that would most influence judges' decisions. Police officials, as the documents' authors, obtained radically broader powers to influence a case's final outcome. Although the shapers of the procedural code took great pride in extending broader rights to defendants in the form of mandatory legal representation, they inserted no checks and balances to ensure that the *vida pregressa* accurately represented an individual's personal and social identity.

In fact, though defendants' "new rights" under the new code were celebrated widely, such optimism was largely misplaced. The mere presence of public defenders certainly did not guarantee effective legal representation. In my 1927–42 sample, for instance, defendants with public counsel actually fared considerably worse than those without it. As judges alone bore responsibility for monitoring the defense's quality, defendants had virtually no recourse in cases where a judge failed to do his duty. This happened frequently, sometimes because a judge was too busy to fully evaluate the defense counsel's effectiveness, sometimes because a judge was convinced of a defendant's guilt and thus indifferent to the issue of adequate defense, and sometimes because a judge was himself part of a procedural problem that a competent counsel should have raised.

Moreover, if guaranteed defense counsel and other concessions (such as discretionary bail reduction for the indigent) aimed to broaden defendants' rights, many more measures sought explicitly to restrict them, on the grounds that the old system had, in the words of Francisco Campos, "assured defendants, even when they were caught in the act or wholly implicated by the evidence, such an extensive catalogue of guarantees and favors that their repression necessarily became defective and retarded, thus stimulating the expansion of criminality"[95] Given widespread abuses in the Carioca justice system during the 1930s, Campos's words seem misplaced, even bizarre, as does his conclusion: "The unjustifiable primacy of individual interests over those of society at large must end. We cannot continue to temporize individuals with pseudo-rights while prejudicing our common well-being." Notwithstanding, the code followed Campos's directives, restricting doctrine that had granted defendants the benefit of the doubt in unclear cases, lengthening the time limits on police investigations and trials, reducing guarantees against illegal arrest, and generally entrusting judges with the right to determine the importance of any procedural violations that might occur. In view of such restrictions on defendants' rights, one cannot help but doubt assertions by jurists such as the left-leaning Roberto Lyra, who claimed in his 1956 *Novíssimas escolas penais* that "the procedural code consummated an irresistible ideal of juridical unity and equality before the law for all Brazilians, benefited by common rights and guarantees."

Considering its importance, the *vida pregressa* received surprisingly perfunctory attention in the procedural code, which simply instructed police officials to "verify the suspect's *vida pregressa* from an individual, family, and social point of view, also taking into account his economic condition, his attitude and mood before, during and after the crime, and whatever other elements might contribute to the appreciation of his temperament and character."[96] Such instructions indicated that punishment should be individualized on the basis of social and psychological factors rather than biological or scientifically psychiatric ones, but they also left police officials remarkable flexibility in shaping a suspect's juridical identity.

In the years immediately following the new procedural code's publication, numerous police manuals provided more specific directions. One such manual, published in 1945, specified that investigations for the *vida pregressa* should involve conversations not only with the suspect himself but also with colleagues and neighbors.[97] The manual instructed police investigators to ask the suspect about his educational level, the social atmosphere in which he had grown up, his financial resources, his work history, the reason he had left any past places of employment, how well he fit into the social atmosphere in which he lived, the degree to which he demonstrated proper bonds of affection with his family members, his criminal history, the reasons he had committed the crime, his attitude upon apprehension, and his family history of mental illness, epilepsy, alcoholism, and criminality. The guide suggested that investigators query neighbors and co-workers about a suspect's reputation in his neighborhood and workplace; the way he treated his family and his neighbors; the extent to which he seemed to meet his familial economic obligations; his gambling, drinking, and smoking habits; the moral character of his friends and companions; and his morality, temperament, and tendencies.[98]

These instructions stand out not so much for their meticulous detail—like most police procedures, they were rarely carried out in full—but rather for the extent to which they endorsed policemen as the official interpreters of witnesses' opinions regarding character and behavior. The official criteria for judgment of character corresponded remarkably to those utilized by most witnesses in my 1927–42 sample; the *vida pregressa*, following the participants' lead, was meant to incorporate what had previously been judicially elusive expectations, such as courtesy to neighbors, adherence to gender roles, and financial responsibility. Yet it is also striking that the *vida pregressa*, while recognizing such standards' value, still allowed policeman to serve as their official filter. As a legal document, with a formally preeminent role in the evaluation of character and the individualization of punishment, the *vida pregressa* would carry far more weight than the individual observations of witnesses, defendants, or even lawyers. It became not only a repository for the signs and symbols of judicial worthiness deemed most important by trial participants but also in itself a signifier of merit.

In my second sample, involving 263 criminal defendants tried from the early 1950s through the early 1960s, 225 records included *vidas pregressas*.[99] In some cases, the documents were strictly pro forma, little more than detailed versions of the standard criminal identification form; defendants themselves seem to have provided most of their information, which included such details as nationality, occupation, place of birth, place of work, age, civil status, educational level, address, religion, a brief summary of the defendant's mood at the time of arrest, and information about any property the defendant may have owned. In other cases, the *vida pregressa* was even more formulaic, and probably less faithful to the truth. Particularly in vagrancy investigations, it frequently became simply another repetition of the original arrest report's often-spurious allegations. One 1950 *vida pregressa* was typical, describing Oscar Silva, a young *pardo* mechanic accused of vagrancy in 1950, as a "customary vagrant, with every possible vice, possessing a violent temperament and a record of various arrests, with no honest occupation or way of support-ing himself, who is constantly found wandering lazily through the streets in the company of thieves, vagrants, and disorderly characters."[100] Before the judge, Silva fruitlessly contradicted this characterization, claiming that he had work and identification documents, and even giving the ad-dress of his supposed employer. The judge found him guilty without even attempting to verify his claims, and Silva spent 39 days in prison. Such, apparently, could be the power of even the most formulaic of character-izations.

Most *vidas pregressas* in my sample provided more detailed informa-tion. Many police officials echoed Vargas's notions of citizenship, noting carefully whether or not suspects were patriotic, hardworking, respon-sible to their families, living in a stable residence, and committed to per-sonal and familial advancement. Others reflected modern criminological trends. In one case, a man's supposed tendency toward criminality was explained by his social ambience: he lived in a favela, his mother did not care about education, his family was unstable, he kept derelict company, and his father was a communist.[101]

Less predictably, police officers also frequently voiced perspectives that had been more typical of witnesses, victims, and defendants in my earlier sample. Officials often granted informal marriage the same respect as formal union, so long as the couples constituted stable families; and they did not necessarily frown on a faulty education, scarce economic re-sources, or even lack of documents or officially sanctioned residential or work circumstances, so long as a suspect could be described as honestly struggling to overcome his or her difficulties in life. Conversely, although police investigators often paid homage to the external symbols of higher social status—property ownership, dress, higher education—they did not necessarily base the tenor of the *vida pregressa* on such factors. They fre-quently described wealthy or well-educated defendants as slick or dishon-est, and one investigator even wrote that a high-ranking military official, who had been accused of attempted murder, bore more responsibility for his actions than the average citizen, because he should have known bet-ter.[102] In a case involving a wealthy doctor accused of performing abor-tions, a police official lauded the suspect, not because of his status, but rather because he did not flaunt his social position and treated police officers with courtesy and respect.[103] In general, the *vida pregressa* tended to be more positive if a defendant upheld popularly held values such as generosity, familial sacrifice, and mainstream gender norms, and it was generally negative for a defendant who violated these norms or routinely incited neighborhood disturbances.

Despite such occasional and apparent coincidences in spirit between *populares* and police investigators, there was one aspect of the *vida pregressa* that many witnesses, defendants, and even victims refused to accept as legitimate. The original procedural code had made no mention of the official documents (identity cards, work cards, property titles) that became general symbols of worthy citizenship in the years between 1930 and 1964. Yet many police officers in the 1950s and 1960s came to see the possession of such documents as a kind of shorthand for good character. Too lazy or pressed for time to properly investigate a suspect's *vida pregressa*, numerous investigators based their impressions largely on the bits of paper in a suspect's possession. Although some officers demonstrated sympathy for the undocumented, most considered possession of a signed work card, a voter registration card, a civil identity card, or proof of property ownership to be an unambiguous sign of civic honor. Thus these papers, quite aside from their inherent significance, also became the foundation for the juridical identity established in the *vida pregressa*.

The documents' importance was especially marked in vagrancy cases, as was their illegitimacy in the eyes of many poor Cariocas. Vagrancy had long been a sort of catch-all charge, more an excuse for repressing and harassing people considered "dangerous by nature" than a true criminal act. Yet in the late 1920s and early 1930s, vagrancy verdicts were often at least vaguely related to work status. Defendants characterized by the police as vagrants, "roaming the streets without purpose," were frequently acquitted when judges verified that they did indeed work for the employers they had named, at the addresses they had provided. With the advent of *trabalhista* labor laws, however, the legal concept of vagrancy underwent a gradual and subtle mutation, becoming a sanction against the undocumented as well as the unemployed. By the mid-1950s, most judges no longer even took the trouble to verify a defendant's work address and employer's name, relying almost exclusively on the defendant's ability to produce a signed work card. The defendant's protests to the effect that he was temporarily unemployed, or worked informally, or was unable to procure proper documentation because he had not served in the military or did not have a birth certificate, fell on deaf ears.[104] Although some jurists did acknowledge such problems' existence, few judges paid them effective heed.[105]

A 1950 vagrancy case highlighted the quandary presented by a law that recognized only legally sanctioned work and yet was enforced in an economy with an extensive informal employment market. In 1950, a *pardo* favela resident named Luis Alves dos Santos told a judge that he had been arrested not because he was unemployed but rather because he did not have documents, and that his restaurant job could not earn him legal sanction because he was still waiting to take care of his military service requirement. Even though Santos explained that he was not a legal worker, police officers investigated his work claims by looking at the official employee list of the restaurant where he claimed to work; naturally, his name did not appear, and he was convicted to 30 days in prison.[106]

Significantly, by the late 1950s even defendants arrested for other types of crimes began regularly to highlight the connection between documents and decent treatment. In one case involving a charge of physical assault, a defendant summarized before a judge the problems created for a worker without a signed *carteira*: "Colonel Cavalcante, for whom the deponent works, makes no declaration in his *carteira de trabalho*, and this affected the deponent's situation because in the police station they thought they were dealing with a vagrant."[107] In a 1960 case, a defendant was arrested for attempted murder because he shot at policemen who were conducting a random document check, believing that the officers were thieves. Several of the witnesses in the case stated that they had been arrested and detained that night for simple lack of documents.[108]

CIVIL RIGHTS AND THE NEW CRIMINOLOGY

The outcomes of vagrancy cases thus showed an especially strong relationship both with the defendants' possession of Vargas-era citizenship papers and with their portrayal in the *vida pregressa*. This was not, however, a singular trend; a statistical analysis of court processes and outcomes in the 1950s and 1960s demonstrates that such documents assumed increasing importance in nearly every arena of criminal law.

In considering the important question of how the transformations wrought by the new procedural and criminal codes of the early 1940s affected legal professionals' practice of criminal law, statistics are, once again, the only real recourse, since judges rarely wrote extralegal biases into their decisions. The statistics for the decades following the codified transformation of the criminal justice system are at once more abundant and more elusive than those from the late 1920s and early 1930s. Their abundance is due to a detailed, if not entirely accurate, compilation of citywide figures on judicial outcomes and defendants' identifying information, which began in 1942 and ran continuously until 1964. The statistics' elusiveness is due both to the fact that broad figures failed to disaggregate judicial outcomes by defendants' demographic or social subgroups, and to the fact that the rich archive of criminal cases I consulted for my earlier sample was partially destroyed for this later period.[109] All the same, I have tried to make use of both statistics and archives, using each to balance the other. My analysis of a new case sample allows me to disaggregate case processes and outcomes and explore the importance of individual social traits, while my analysis of larger statistical trends helps both to place the sample in context and to fill in some of the archival gaps.

This later case sample includes information regarding 263 accusations from the 1950s and 1960s, 168 of which reached the trial phase. The types of cases included differ somewhat from their earlier counterparts because, after the early 1950s, archives have preserved cases with non-guilty verdicts only for crimes with jury trials—murder, attempted murder, abortion, and suicide.[110] Given this difficulty, cases from the early 1950s are similar to those from 1927–42, but those after 1955 include several new crimes—attempted murder, murder, instigation of suicide, and abortion. All in all, the crimes included were sexual offenses (6.8 percent), physical violence (27.8 percent), vagrancy and arms possession (12.2 percent), attempted murder (11.8 percent), larceny and breaking and entering (12.2 percent), and murder (17.1 percent); the remainder involved *injúria/calúmnia*, inducement to suicide, and other miscellaneous crimes. Of these 263 cases, 34.6 percent ended in guilty verdicts, 29.3 percent ended with a finding of innocence, and 29.7 percent ended as *inquéritos*. One defloration case ended in marriage, and slightly more than 6 percent of the cases ended with a murder defendant's violent death. The defendants in these cases were, again, overwhelmingly male (86.3 percent), less white than in the earlier sample (39.3 percent), and largely single (43.7 percent) or informally married (23.8 percent). Defendants' educational levels were low (17.7 percent illiterate, 35.4 percent with only rudimentary education), but such rates were in proportion to citywide figures.[111] I analyzed these cases in the same way I analyzed the earlier sample, but added two personal variables, the nature of the *vida pregressa* and the possession of a work card, both of which had already become important building blocks of juridical identity.

According to citywide data, the categories of crime included in my sample accounted for roughly half the spectrum of cases in the criminal justice system between 1942 and 1959, and variations in the rate of reported crime within these categories generally shadowed those for Rio at large.[112] Given the differential treatment allotted to defendants accused of disparate crimes, I have restricted my analysis of the citywide statistics to the sample crimes. My most significant omissions are arrests for traffic accidents, for the *jogo do bicho* (numbers game), and for so-called

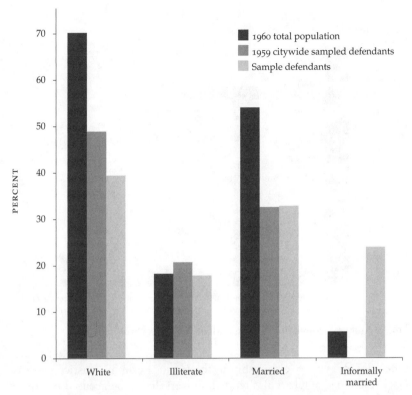

FIG. 2. Proportion of white, illiterate, and married individuals in Rio de Janeiro at large, in citywide statistics for sample crimes, and case sample, 1959–1960.

crimes against the popular economy, all of which, while worthy of study, would have disrupted the balance of my analysis because they involved either a distinct "clientele" or unusual levels of corruption.[113] As Figure 2 demonstrates, the case categories included in my sample involved defendants who were darker-skinned and less frequently married than Rio's overall population; my sample exaggerated these trends and involved an unusually large proportion of informally married individuals. Literacy rates were roughly the same across all crimes, and my sample included the smallest proportion of illiterates.[114] As Figure 3 makes apparent, trial outcomes tended to be more negative in my sample than in the citywide statistics for sample crimes; fewer of my cases were archived, a larger proportion ended in guilty verdicts, and a greater number, though still surprisingly few, involved the imposition of a *medida de segurança*.[115]

The citywide statistics provide some general insights into the sym-

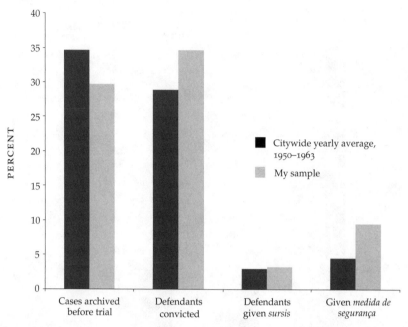

FIG. 3. Archival, conviction, *sursis*, and *medida de segurança* rates.

bolization of worthy citizenship in the Carioca criminal justice process. Darker-skinned single males tended, universally, to be accused of crimes more frequently than their lighter-skinned married counterparts, and a statistical analysis of tables over the entire 1942–1959 period reveals a suggestive correlation between white skin, higher rates of archived cases, greater rates of *sursis*, and lower incidence of the *medida de segurança*.[116] Yet while the information in the citywide statistics is important, it suggests more about patterns of arrest than about actual treatment within the criminal justice system. And, as in 1927–42, race, literacy, and marriage could still have been only some of a wide array of symbols that influenced Carioca criminal trials' processes and outcomes.

The patterns of symbolization that can be qualitatively observed in both the letter and the practice of post-1941 criminal law emerge more clearly from a statistical analysis of the sample cases, presented in statistical appendixes I and III. A few observations deserve particular mention. Many of the factors that were important in the 1930 sample had at least some degree of significance in the 1950s and 1960s. Yet all except the possession of documents showed more variable patterns than before. In the cross-tabulations, averages for subgroups of defendants veered further from the overall mean than they had in the earlier sample.

In general, factors related to work and residence continued to correlate with judicial treatment. Race showed more predictable patterns than earlier—an especially interesting development, given the contemporaneous rise of the Brazilian ideology of racial democracy—but skin color remained relatively insignificant when compared to work and residential status. The regression analysis yielded few statistically significant results, probably because of the great number of crimes considered, and what results did emerge were somewhat contradictory. Four kinds of defendants—residents of informal housing, unskilled laborers, illiterates, and, oddly, white-collar workers—emerged with statistically significant prejudice. This last category may be an anomaly, since professional criminals often declared their occupation as "commercial employee." Race, as in the earlier regressions, influenced trials only unpredictably.

Both in the correlations and in the regressions, the most striking results pointed to the increasing importance of documents as predictors of judicial outcomes. No factors showed stronger and more consistent relationships with trial processes and outcomes than the work card, the criminal record, and the *vida pregressa*. The work card seemed most important as a positive symbol, a kind of talisman against abuse, while a negative *vida pregressa* or criminal record virtually ensured poorer treatment and a higher likelihood of conviction. Possession of a work card helped a defendant more than the mere fact of working, and the *vida pregressa* was a better predictor of judicial outcomes than were most of the personal characteristics that supposedly contributed to it. Thus, apparently, the Vargas-era formalization of civil status translated quite effectively into the practice of criminal law.

CIVIL RIGHTS AND THE PUBLIC TRUST

Criminal trial participants from the 1950s and 1960s reacted in a variety of ways to the increasingly formal judicial symbolization of worthy citizenship. Most witnesses, defendants, and victims seemed to know what legal officials cared about in determining punishment, and this awareness often translated into testimony that reinforced official views. By the 1950s, any defendant who possessed documents lost no time in showing them. Only the most legally ignorant of character witnesses failed to mention a defendant's or victim's devotion to work and family. And many witnesses, victims, and defendants adeptly manipulated stock rhetorical representations of honorable poverty or dangerous marginality. Some trial participants still pointed to indicators of character that prosecutors, judges, and jurists did not recognize as legally relevant. A lawyer in one case argued that the fact that a man had obtained water and light for his illegal *barracão* signified civic virtue; at the other end of the social spectrum, a defendant claimed that a judge could not believe charges brought by people the defendant considered his *protegidos,* because, in leveling such accusations, they had shown themselves to be disloyal, ungrateful traitors.[117] But such exceptions became increasingly scarce, and they rarely were unaccompanied by references to more standard moral signposts.

As in the years surrounding 1930, however, trial participants' ideas about what constituted virtuous work and family life often clashed with those of legal officials, and many participants also questioned the legitimacy of individual laws and of the procedures through which juridical identity had come to be established. Conflicts about the symbolization of legitimate work, family, and residential circumstances recalled those from the 1930 sample, but also highlighted a growing dissonance with regard to the proper role of Vargas-era paper signifiers. On one end of the spectrum, most legal officials, many police officers, and even many common citizens—who often viewed work cards, identity cards, voter registration cards, and property ownership as effective passports from legal marginality to the realm of standard citizenship rights—advocated and legitimized the increasing formalization of standards for civic virtue. Many of those same people became adept at manipulating newer symbols of citizenship and degeneracy, which derived from standard sociological theories of the 1950s and 1960s and blamed the anomie of the great metropolis and the degenerative effects of favela life for everything from social marginality to rising criminality and underemployment. Even lawyers representing the poorest of favela residents often legitimized such language, arguing not that their clients were citizens worthy of standard legal respect but rather that they were victims of society and deserved compassion and tutelage rather than punishment. The lawyer in a 1950 theft case put it thus:

> The accused, your honor, is yet another of these fungi produced by society in the thousands; it ferments them in the favelas but remains passive in the face of their destinies, criminally abandoning them in the harsh struggle for life, at the mercy of the most basic human instincts—the search for food—only in order to bury them at the bottom of a prison at the least violation of a formal legal precept, and, what's more, all of this in the name of justice!
>
> Your honor, Jorge Barros is a young man, 20 years of age, of good will, calm, with a friendly temperament, a first offender who, being illiterate and having no profession, has long suffered all of the hardships of a poor and ignorant young man in a large metropolis, where even the lowliest jobs require the ability to read and write.

The lawyer ended his argument by eulogizing the 1940 penal code for allowing judges to grant judicial leniency to young men such as Jorge, affording them a second chance. The judge, however, either ignored the argument or saw Jorge's low social origins—the degenerative meaning of which Jorge's lawyer had confirmed rather than contested—as all the more incentive to detain him. In the end, the trial greatly exceeded legal time limits, and Jorge spent three months behind bars—although, as a first offender, he should have been immediately eligible for *sursis*. Lawyers usually presented such arguments in the name of social justice. Yet by choosing to argue that Rio's poor were guileless victims of society rather than full and independent citizens, they indirectly reinforced patterns of differential treatment by strengthening the idea that poor migrants and favela residents needed special tutelage from the state before they could become worthy of receiving full rights.[118]

At the other end of the spectrum, those witnesses, victims, and defendants in my sample who lacked paper symbols, or who themselves fit the profile of urban "marginality," contested in a variety of ways the validity of sociological and documentary criteria for civic worthiness. Some of their challenges, as in 1930, remained implicit. Witnesses, victims, defendants, and even many police officers spoke of the upstanding character, good work habits, and moral family life of people who lived in favelas, worked at informal jobs, and were either single parents or only informally married, thus quietly asserting the judicial validity of their own standards for good citizenship. In one case, the mother of a young black man murdered by a Portuguese bar owner went to great lengths to contest characterizations of her son as "marginal," hiring a lawyer and calling in numerous witnesses to attest that her son, a well known cyclist, had been an upstanding and hardworking young man.[119] In other instances, defendants and victims substantiated similar claims by presenting their own versions of paper legitimacy, in the form of extensive petitions from neighbors, employers, and co-workers who praised or condemned individuals on the basis of decidedly informal criteria.[120] Two typical documents emerged from a 1957 murder case involving an undocumented 45-year-old married black man who had killed his neighbor and extralegal tenant over a rent dispute in Santa Teresa's Morro do Escondidinho.[121] In one petition, 70 individuals affirmed:

> We, residents of the Favela do Escondidinho, sign below in order to declare that we know Pedro Baptista Filho (the defendant) as a law-abiding, hardworking, and honest person whom we have never seen involved in any sort of brawl. We knew Sebastião Ernesto Pacífico (the victim) and know that he was an individual detested in the *morro* because he constantly assaulted others, exploited women, drank, and failed to pay people to whom he owed money.

The other petition, signed by 75 people, declared, in a similar vein:

> We, residents at the Rua Barão de Petrópolis 780, known as the Favela do Escondidinho, want to say, regarding the death of Sebastião Ernesto Pacífico, that we know that, if this indeed happened, it can only be the result of a fight provoked by Sebastião, because Pedro, who has lived in the *morro* for many years, is not one to be involved in fights and has never had any problem, but Sebastião was a dangerous element, so much so that, among other cases, he stabbed Miguel, the brother of Marcello, he beat up Edgard, and he even tried to rape a minor by the name of Conceição, the daughter of Senhor Manuel do Centro. Sebastião's death was even received with happiness by the honest residents of the *morro*, whom he constantly perturbed.

These petitions do not seem to have had any direct effect on Pedro's pretrial treatment; he was imprisoned for nearly a year while waiting for his case to come to trial, and his legal counsel was entirely inadequate. Yet the documents did convince the judge to give Pedro a minimum sentence and may have had some influence on his subsequent early release. Whatever their effect on this particular case, such petitions were a bold attempt by undocumented, mostly poor favela residents to assert their own standards of worthy citizenship in the form of papers constructed without state aid or tutelage.[122]

Other defendants, facing more obvious and dramatic violations of their citizenship rights, challenged official criteria more explicitly. One man, arrested for arms possession during a 1949 police raid of a party in the "Boogie-Woogie" favela, protested to no avail that his arrest was simply an example of police harassment of favela residents.[123] Defendants in other cases voiced similar protests against arms possession and vagrancy laws that essentially sanctioned police harassment. When a young man named Aristeu Esteves da Silva was arrested while playing an evening game of soccer, and was then held incommunicado for three days before being falsely charged with vagrancy, members of his athletic club hired a lawyer and submitted a petition denouncing the police abuse. The petition convinced the judge of da Silva's innocence and sparked a criminal prosecution of the police delegate and several of his detectives, who were accused of many other instances of falsification, torture, and even murder.[124] This sort of police abuse was so common in Carioca favelas by the 1950s that it became the subject of a formal complaint by favela activists.

Civil rights violations were part of a broader deterioration in relations between the Carioca police forces and the poor neighborhoods they lived in and patrolled. Much of this breakdown was rooted in police threats—perceived and real—to the very existence of poor communities. The Carioca police had been eyed with suspicion and fear in poor neighborhoods ever since the anti-*cortiço* campaigns of the late 1880s and early 1890s; from that point right into the twentieth century, sanitary police and *guardas municipais* were frequently sent to demolish illegal tenements, shacks, or shantytowns, and their violence was notorious.[125] In the late 1940s, however, these kinds of assaults intensified.[126] As disputes over increasingly valuable urban properties escalated, the police operated both as enforcers of unpopular eviction decrees and as privately paid thugs for parties intent on controlling disputed lands; in both roles, they appeared on the *morros* with increasing frequency, often armed to the teeth. In 1956, left-leaning Congressman Bruzzi Mendonça highlighted one such abuse. In early January, as was widely reported in the press, ten *policiais municipais* had gone up the flanks of the disputed Morro da Cachoeirinha, along with several thugs paid by one of the hill's claimants. Once there, they had threatened to kill the rebellious residents, and one policeman had shot two female bystanders.[127] The local civil police chief, perhaps in solidarity with his officers, had refused on technical grounds to register the residents' complaint about the incident, even in the face of the two women's serious wounds.

While the details are particular to this case, the general picture—of police officers assisting private thugs and violently intimidating favela residents into giving up their land claims—repeated itself hundreds of times in the 1940s and 1950s. The political disputes that erupted around favela property cases, many of which were led by communists, brought the political police into the picture as well, and they staged numerous violent raids aimed at ridding the hills of so-called agitators.[128] Police officers from various divisions, well aware of these events, grabbed the opportunity to begin extorting "protection" fees from worried shantytown residents, adding yet another layer of corruption and violence to favela affairs. The *guardas municipais*, the military police, and the political police were more frequently on the front lines of these disputes than were the civil forces. Yet it was not unheard of for the latter to become involved as they apparently had in Cachoeira, refusing to respond to complaints of official abuse, threatening community leaders with arrest, and otherwise aiding the causes of private property owners who had reputedly paid them off.[129]

Police abuses were not limited to property issues. Throughout the 1940s and 1950s, press reports of generalized police violence and brutality became steadily more commonplace. Many such reports focused on police beatings and torture. Already in 1948, the National Congress instituted a commission of parliamentary investigation to look into reported police abuses in Rio's civil police stations; in a series of "surprise" visits, the commission reported numerous outrages, among them prisoners held in unhygienic and overcrowded "cages," beaten by investigative officers, and held illegally without charges.[130] Perhaps more startling than the abuses themselves were the officers' offhand explanations of them; on one occasion, a low-ranking policeman simply explained to the deputies that in the "combat against pilferers," the use of beatings was "to a certain point justifiable."

By the 1950s, abuse allegations regularly found their way into defendants' testimony before judges and were seldom seriously questioned by lawyers. In a particularly revealing 1958 vagrancy case, the judge let loose against Ary Leão, then chief in the 21st police Delegacia, laying out a long series of examples of his abusive practices. In one instance, Leão's district had been found to be full of torture instruments. In another, Leão had forced the 54 occupants of a single four-by-five meter cell to strip down to their underwear, as punishment for a simple fight that had broken out between two of them. In yet another case, Leão had allegedly allowed his detectives to murder a suspect who was wanted for killing a police officer. In frustration, the judge declared, "It is not possible to police the city by fooling judges and defaming police investigations. . . ."[131]

By the 1960s, such routine abuses had begun to assume more sinister proportions. With considerable backing from local authorities, police were told to use deadly force against suspects who resisted arrest. In 1963, in the midst of an unnerving crime wave, Governor Carlos Lacerda himself instructed Rio's local forces to instill in "criminals" "the certainty that they will be killed if they resist the police" and also called for increased legal protection for officers who killed on the job.[132] Perhaps as a result of such official tolerance, it became relatively common practice for police officers, both civil and military, to assassinate accused cop killers in cold blood.[133] Emblematically, in a widely publicized 1963 case, civilians and civil police uncovered a series of brutal police murders of suspected beggars. Over the course of two years, officers in the civil police's Secção de Repressão à Mendicância—several of whom had once been part of Vargas's presidential guard—had routinely stolen money from detained suspects. Any who complained or resisted were beaten, "deported" to abandoned suburban outposts, and, in the very worst cases, thrown—alive or dead—into a suburban river. All in all, thirteen people were killed, and the civil police's reputation for brutal abuse of poor populations was all the more deeply engraved.[134]

Complaints of police abuse also abounded outside of police stations, especially in favelas, where military police officers staged frequent large-scale raids, known as blitzes. In 1956, Congressman Bruzzi Mendonça recounted the story of one Coronel Côrtes, who had been reputed to lead nocturnal incursions into the favelas, "in which he sowed terror, practiced violence, and committed crimes and even robberies, which he later confessed to in the papers." When one of his agents was accused of some of the thefts, Côrtes denied the charges, saying that the only items taken had been radios and musical instruments, which were in any case (in a neat inversion of the burden of proof) only being held in the police station until residents could prove that they owned them.[135]

It may have been this particular series of raids that placed the police issue front and center for the favela residents' first formal organization, the União de Trabalhadores Favelados (UTF).[136] Shortly after the UTF's founding, in 1954, the group's lawyer, Antoine Magarinos Torres, asked for formal intervention by Seabra Fagundes, then Minister of Justice. The UTF lawyer charged that the police had mounted a harassment campaign in the *morros*, illegally searching private homes, detaining anyone without documents, and illegally seizing anything alleged to be a weapon.[137] In the end, however, the Ministry—apparently sharing the perception that the *morros* often harbored criminals—ruled the searches legal, and the practice continued. Symptomatically, in a 1963 meeting, Governor Carlos Lacerda encouraged police to respond to a recent crime wave by following Côrtes's example, staging police raids (*batidas policiais*) in the favelas, complete with search dogs and as many as 500 military policemen, a "massive, spectacular concentration of force."[138]

A sense of what such raids might have meant in the communities that experienced them emerged from a lost 1961 account of favela life, published by José de Almeida Neto, a longtime resident of the Praia do Pinto favela in Leblon.[139] In one press interview, Almeida Neto, known as Zezinho, elaborated on the police blitzes and the negative impact they had on relations between favela residents and the police.[140] In most blitzes, he recounted, "200 people are detained and 195 are let loose. . . . Even beyond this ineffectiveness, the blitzes have caused true terror among the *favelados*." Most of the real criminals, he claimed, left before the raids, leaving only "the unemployed and those who are leaving for work." In the end, "the *favelado* is usually imprisoned because he doesn't have a signed *carteira*, or even for lack of documents." That kind of imprisonment, Zezinho suggested, generated disgust (*revolta*) both in the individual and within the community: "It is with enormous sadness and disillusionment that we see a child or an adult imprisoned and handcuffed in the favela or the street, only to return without charges half an hour later. This really discredits the police among the *favelados*. Violence breeds violence."

Even in the context of these sorts of abuses, relationships between police and poor communities could vary enormously. Police did sometimes defend as well as attack favelas, refusing on at least one occasion to carry out a mass eviction ordered by the courts.[141] Policemen and their officers usually lived in poor communities themselves, and in several cases—most notably, that of São Carlos, in downtown Rio—they even regulated and encouraged informal settlement on the hills.[142] Even more importantly, poor people were not only the police forces' chief victims, they were also frequently their chief clients. In court cases from the 1950s and 1960s, favela residents often went to the police over relatively minor insults or threats, and police logbooks for the 1940s, 1950s, and 1960s still report daily criminal complaints by poor people, sometimes even regarding police abuse.[143] The explanation may be that individuals found the police functional as a deterrent, even—or especially—in the face of such known abuses; or, perhaps, that they did not necessarily blame the whole police force for widely publicized individual crimes. Abdias José dos Santos, a longtime São Carlos resident who was himself a political prisoner in the 1960s, was careful in a 2003 interview to distinguish between the police he knew in the 1950s and 1960s and their counterparts at the turn of the twenty-first century. In the earlier period, he recounted, police abuses certainly existed, but officers also worked with the neighborhood association and knew how to distinguish "workers" from *malandros*. In his neighborhood, at least, "it would have been tough to find a policeman stopping a worker, really tough."[144]

Notwithstanding such subtleties, deteriorating relations between the police and poor neighborhoods drew a notable, if mostly quiet, reaction. Over the course of the 1950s and 1960s, many poor communities began effectively to remove themselves from police jurisdiction for all but the most serious crimes. In some cases, other local authorities simply took over policing responsibilities; such was the case, for example, in Babilônia, in south-zone Leme, where army officials controlled the territory and most of what went on within it.[145] Elsewhere, residents or "landlords" assumed informal judicial functions, sometimes with backing from organizations outside of the communities. In Santa Marta, for instance, a "commission" with the support of local religious authorities assumed a mediating role in all but the most serious of personal disputes by the early 1950s.[146] In the central São Carlos favela, where the police actually regulated most of the territory, a neighborhood association also mediated most conflicts, though residents did still call on the police for some forms of negotiation, or in any case that required coercion or punishment.[147] Longtime Chapeu Mangueira resident Lúcio dos Santos Bispo described a similar procedure for that *morro* as early as the 1950s. It is important not to idealize such "informal" channels of justice; much of it was dispensed by corrupt local bosses, and there was no guarantee that even the more respected neighborhood associations represented all of the neighborhood's constituencies.[148] But it does seem that many residents preferred this sort of mediation to any interaction with a police force widely acknowledged to be corrupt and abusive.

Just as important as these semi-formalized alternatives was an increasingly distinctive pattern of police use by poor residents, and especially by those living in favelas. As already noted, it was not at all uncommon for favela residents and other poor Cariocas to call on the police in the 1950s, a fact that may seem surprising, given widespread vilification. And yet those calls did not always signify faith in the justice system; indeed, they could sometimes indicate precisely the opposite. In complaining about an alleged crime—anything from neighborhood insults to domestic abuse, sexual assault, or even murder—a resident of a poor community guaranteed the accused person an immediate punishment, which had nothing to do with the official deliberations of Carioca justice; involvement with the police and the courts was a sentence in and of itself. A poor person accused of a crime would at a bare minimum have to spend a good deal of time and money disproving the charges, and would probably suffer a damaged reputation among his or her neighbors. If the accusation was serious, and if the accused person was undocumented, he or she would quite likely be detained and maltreated; lose his or her job; and perhaps even lose important claims to shantytown land and services. The very threat of police involvement was thus an effective coercive tool—one that police themselves sometimes used in order to force a settlement before a formal investigation was opened—and any complaint was likely to put an effective and immediate end to whatever offense was being suffered.[149] This dynamic may explain one of the most puzzling aspects of many poor people's complaints in the 1950s and 1960s; though individuals and even small communities might come into a case with great determination—calling the police, volunteering to go to the station as witnesses, helping agents to find an accused criminal—that interest most often turned to recalcitrance by the case's end, a shift that frequently made formal conviction impossible.

Poor people who were not actively involved in a complaint often greeted police requests for aid and testimony with such silence from the start. The majority of detectives assigned to investigate crimes in favelas and similar communities complained about a lack of cooperation. Neighbors would claim not to know witnesses or defendants, and would refuse to provide directions to unnumbered houses on twisting, unnamed streets; residents would not admit to having heard or witnessed dramatic crimes committed in public, or in shacks whose windows were mere feet from their own.[150] This early "law of silence" was probably partially grounded in fear: bandits often threatened anyone known to have cooperated with the police, who did not offer witnesses any real protection. The silence also probably had something to do with local sensibilities about being a "good neighbor" who didn't get involved in other people's business. But such reticence also may have been rooted in a sense of the police as fundamentally disconnected from poor communities, and from the pursuit of justice as local residents understood it.

Perhaps the most eloquent witness to this is, again, the São Carlos community leader Abdias José dos Santos. In a 2003 interview, he recalled an event that had taken place on Christmas Eve sometime in the early 1960s. As he sat alone in the local neighborhood association building, a young man appeared on the doorstep; dos Santos recognized him as being from the community, a fugitive wanted for having killed a police officer. São Carlos was a place especially dependent on the Carioca police—much of it was located on police lands, and many residents belonged to the force. Giving refuge to this young man entailed enormous risk for the association, not to mention for dos Santos personally. And yet, surely aware of the common fate of suspected police killers, he offered sanctuary. In explaining that action, and the general tendency for his neighbors to stonewall police investigations, dos Santos noted that bandits, while clearly different from workers, could not be entirely disconnected from what was still a relatively close-knit community: "They were considered sons of the *morro*. And they were sons of workers. They were not sons of *malandros*." Bandits or not, they could not be lightly abandoned to the violence and abuse of the criminal justice system.

Most generalizations about poor people's interactions with the Carioca criminal justice system in the 1940s and 1950s can be quickly contradicted. Police forces, divisions, and detectives varied enormously, and the police were too linked to too many aspects of poor people's lives to conform to any single description. The same civil police that systematically deprived the undocumented of their civil rights could also be poor people's only recourse in the case of violence or emergency; the same military police force that helped to burn down favela shacks might in the same week help rid a neighborhood of a violent band of extortionists; the same police that might hunt down and kill a suspected cop killer might save a local sex offender from a popular lynching.

And yet in criminal law, as in other areas, at least one clearly defined pattern did emerge from the Vargas-era transformations. Poor Cariocas' scarce access to legal housing and legal work translated directly into a poverty of rights in the criminal justice system. People whose poverty and lack of bureaucratic knowledge had already left them more likely to be undocumented, illegally housed, and unstably employed also found themselves much more likely to be arrested, abused, and convicted in criminal courts, events that in turn deepened their material and legal poverty. Poor people might have gained some benefit from the police or the criminal courts—an abusive spouse might have been arrested, a meddlesome neighbor put in her place, a sexual predator imprisoned and abused. But when poor people asked for police intervention in the 1950s and 1960s, they were as likely to see their version of justice produced by police abuse as by the system's capacity to reach a fair legal outcome; and the police seem mostly to have been appreciated for their ability to coerce informal settlements of neighborhood problems. Here, as in other legal arenas, poor Cariocas often found ways of making a biased and corrupt system work, albeit poorly, for their own purposes. But such uncertain functionality was not equivalent to rights. In criminal law as elsewhere, material poverty often translated into legal destitution.

PART IV

Owning the Illegal City

Urban Ground

On 17 December 1930, fresh on the heels of Getúlio Vargas's triumphant revolution, 30 agricultural laborers appeared in the offices of the *Diário da Noite,* a new and stridently pro-revolutionary daily newspaper.[1] The committee had come from Guaratiba, a mostly rural region well within Rio's municipal borders. It bore a petition addressed to the head of Vargas's newly minted Ministry of Labor, demanding protection from a cycle of violence, lawlessness, and land grabbing that threatened to leave the region's informal smallholders homeless and destitute. The petition began:

> The petitioners, representatives of the residents of Guaratiba, come to implore for the Government of the Republic's valuable aid in putting an end to the unheard of acts of violence with which the laboring and unhappy people of that region are periodically embittered.[2]

It went on to describe the aggressive actions of a bankrupt mortgage company called the Banco de Crédito Móvel (BCM), whose shareholders had since the late 1920s laid claim to hundreds of rural properties in Guaratiba and the neighboring district of Jacarepaguá. The petitioners annexed documents to support their contention that Rio's civil courts had denied the BCM's claims. Despite these decisions, the bank's shareholders had continued violently to harass local laborers, deploying a "band of hooligans" to intimidate them into signing false "rental" agreements that would recognize the bank's ownership of lands that had been held by many of the laborers' families since their ancestors worked them as slaves. Most recently, on 13 December, "a dozen or more residents and their families [had been] thrown out onto the highway, and their huts burnt, in the midst of all sorts of improper jokes and vulgarities, without so much as a vestige of human sympathy for the affliction and weeping of women and children." The 2,500 laborers the committee claimed to represent were "poor people" who could not have afforded to defend their rights in court even before the forced evictions. Now that they were

homeless, such legal recourse was impossible. Thus, the petition continued,

> the signatories, humble workers, invoke the aid of the Ministry of Work so that the
> law's efficiency can extinguish the force of arbitrariness, administratively restoring
> them to the situation that was despoiled by the crime, in a place where the major-
> ity have possessed their lands from time immemorial, conserving them from one
> generation to the next. This is a gesture of desperation, a roar of protest raised by
> a humiliated, duped, and persecuted population.

The petition was remarkable on many counts, not least for its high degree of political consciousness and rhetorical savvy. It was probably not
the pure expression of local sentiment, if such a thing existed; Communist
Party activists and reformist politicians such as Maurício de Lacerda had
been active in mediating these conflicts since the late 1920s, and a young
lawyer by the name of Vicente Carino had passionately taken up the occupants' causes, including those of several of the petition's signatories.[3]
All the same, its authors were precociously aware of Vargas's rhetorical
and administrative emphasis on work as the avenue toward social inclusion, and they also savvily elided their cause with notions of protection
and masculine honor that would be central to the Vargas regime. Their
emphasis on "immemorial possession" showed awareness of the place of
such claims in the Brazilian legal tradition, and their appeal to the law in
the face of uncontrolled private violence presaged Vargas's own attempts
to transform the law's meaning and significance. These particular rural
workers, in short, had lost no time in seeking to use the revolution's opportunities to further an already long-fought cause.

Even more remarkable than the petitioners' actions, though, was the
context in which the Guaratiba drama played itself out. In the rural
areas of Brazil's southeast, land conflict erupted frequently in the late
nineteenth and early twentieth centuries, the product of ill-defined property rights, changing agricultural economies, widespread bankruptcies,
and endemic speculation.[4] Throughout the Brazilian interior, moreover,
the sort of violence described in the petition was iconic. Ever since the
late-nineteenth-century Canudos War, the formerly rather romantic geographic term for these regions—*sertão*—had for city dwellers come also
to denote mysticism, lawlessness, brutality, and enormous vulnerability to the cruelties and contradictions of "civilization" itself.[5] A steady
stream of news about the spectacular feats of northeastern *cangaceiros,*
or bandits, often working in the employ of large landowners, had kept
this association alive through the early decades of the twentieth century.
Given these larger patterns of conflict over rural land and power, their
outbreak in Guaratiba—part of a region of Rio already known as the
sertão carioca, or the Carioca backlands—was hardly surprising.

And yet the very term *sertão carioca* was an odd one, juxtaposing as it did Brazil's most "supercivilized" city with what was perceived as its raw hinterland.[6] For some, largely drawing on a nineteenth-century romantic tradition, Rio's *sertão* invoked an Edenic and nostalgic world of spectacular natural beauty, small-scale agriculture, and pastoral rhythms, a kind of nationalist antidote to the corruptions of cosmopolitan civilization.[7] But for others, the *sertão carioca*'s contradictions were more foreboding, invoking the still very fragile reach of liberal European institutions and customs into the "vast hospital"—the immense expanse of sickness, pathology, and backwardness—that was said to constitute the Brazilian interior.[8] To describe Rio's semi-rural environs as the *sertão carioca* was to reaffirm Afrânio Peixoto's well-known dictum that the *sertão* began at the borders of Rio's Avenida Central.[9]

Guaratiba's conflicts, which would extend well into the 1950s, highlighted this uncomfortable reality by pointing out how metropolitan expansion, rather than civilizing the backlands, had exacerbated tensions born of chronically insecure property rights and the weak reach of public law. As a December 1931 article in the radical daily *A Batalha* put it:

> No one could imagine that the Federal District would be transformed into a true "far west." But the revolting scene [in Guaratiba] is the sad proof that, in the Capital of the Republic, under the complacent gaze of the police, "Lampião" operates, cloaked in the gentlemanly mantle of a banking establishment.[10]

If such claims of shock and outrage were to be believed, the intrusion of quintessentially rural banditry into the Federal District was an absurd aberration. And yet the Guaratiba events were important not because they were unusual, but rather because they were not. Beginning in the 1920s, and continuing into at least the 1970s, Rio de Janeiro was the site of hundreds of violent land conflicts, most of which would echo the complex interplay of legal action, private brutality, and intense politicking that had characterized Guaratiba. Some of these confrontations occurred in quickly suburbanizing rural areas, pitting longtime agricultural occupants against speculators and land developers. Many more took place in well-established parts of the city, in the swamplands, hills, and backyards that had over several decades become home to a good proportion of Rio's poor. In many of these areas, property rights had never been clearly defined. In other places, both public and private, owners had long seen fit to permit and profit from informal occupation. Either way, beginning in the early 1900s and accelerating in the 1920s, rising land values incited landowners and shysters to make and enforce legal claims to such lands, in the process evicting hundreds, thousands, and even tens of thousands of residents.

These legal claims, taken together, attempted to transform the relationship between law and property in Rio. They aimed not only to formalize property relations but also to undermine the logic of long-term possession and need that had undergirded many poor people's hold on Rio's soil, replacing such claims with the notion that contracts and capitalist transactions were the only legitimate routes to urban landholding. As in other legal fields that underwent drastic transformation in these years, this shift would have simultaneously expanded the arena of legal regulation and limited poor people's access to it, in essence denying legal sanction to relationships that poor people believed to be both necessary and legitimate.

The threat from changing property relations, however, was both more basic and more tangible than that resulting from other legal transformations. It was more tangible because these were dramatic and specific struggles, waged against a clearly defined opponent; it was much easier to mobilize a community against an eviction decree than it was to marshal opposition to an abstract building or sanitary code. It was more basic because a hold on a patch of urban land was arguably the foundation of the entire corpus of rights constructed during the Vargas era. Without proof of legal property rights, the city would not normally certify a home as complying with building and sanitary codes, and access to city services or even recognition on an official city grid was out of the question. And without a hold on urban soil, few could hope to take advantage of the social and economic citizenship so touted by Vargas and his successors. The right to occupy urban property was, almost literally, the foundation of Brazilian citizenship.

The struggle for property rights in Rio was thus more direct and intense than that in any other legal arena, and the result was a remarkable constraint of the law's grasp. Undoubtedly, Rio's poor were at a distinct disadvantage in formal property and eviction suits; even when they had potentially legitimate land claims—and frequently they did—they most often lacked the money, records, legal knowledge, and bureaucratic know-how that it took to prevail. Yet unfavorable verdicts were rarely the last word; the civil courts' decisions about legal ownership failed ultimately to determine who would occupy most disputed lands. Residents and their various allies greeted the verdicts with intense collective activism. Informal communities wrote letters to the full gamut of local and national politicians, courted the press, demonstrated publicly, and openly confronted police and judicial officials sent to enforce court decrees. As in Guaratiba, such activism was only sometimes autonomous; favela residents' interests intersected constantly with those of the politicians, speculators, and intermediaries who built careers on the communities' insecurities, and all of those parties had a part in the movements against eviction. Whatever the means, though, the result was significant. In numerous cases, poor communities that were settled on valuable land in Rio's commercial and residential heart managed to render unenforceable decisions that would have deprived them of their homes. They held on de facto to what they could not obtain de jure, thus preserving their ability to remain within the urban arena.

The two chapters that follow tell the story of these struggles, in much of their considerable complexity. Despite the communities' tenacity, the history of their property battles is not simply a litany of popular triumph. By the early 1960s, when this story ends, officials had failed to wipe most informal occupation by Rio's poorest people from the city's face. But informality had become more concentrated, mostly bounded within a few hundred relatively well-defined favelas and suburban regions. Elsewhere, including in Guaratiba, court evictions and sanitary sweeps had wiped away countless rural settlements, backyard shacks, and smaller favelas, leaving little memory of a Rio de Janeiro where informal and formal settlement had once mingled more intimately. Even where favelas and informal subdivisions continued, moreover, they remained communities with few rights, their survival ensured by political sufferance rather than positive claim. *Favelados* and other informal residents were surely better off than they might have been had their communities been eliminated. But even as they stood proudly in Rio de Janeiro's very heart, their homes remained part of the legal *sertão*.

CHAPTER SEVEN

Informality in Law and Custom

≈⟩

There is a deeply rooted popular belief, in Brazil and throughout most of the world where shantytowns proliferate, that they are the inevitable and chaotic result of poverty, political marginality, and social disorganization. Shantytowns and other extralegal settlements, this commonsense storyline would hold, are created by desperately impoverished people, setting up house wherever and however they can. Disdained by most cities' "civilized" elites, and opposed by anyone in a position of economic or political authority, they persist as a living symbol of a society's unresolved inequalities. From the left, their residents are alternately understood as victims or heroes; from the right, they might be portrayed as parasites or repressed capitalists. But in either case, it is understood that shantytowns are formed on their residents' initiative, with physical structures separate from, and in opposition to, the cities that house them.

Yet in Rio de Janeiro, as elsewhere, the story is not nearly so simple. Rio's favelas have always been part of the city's urban fabric, not only because their residents have long been economically, politically, and culturally integrated into the larger city, but also because people from outside their borders have long built wealth and power from them.[11] The shantytowns' development was conditioned by the not entirely accidental ambiguity of Brazilian property law. Their persistence—despite very significant challenges—is explained only by the vested interest in their continued existence that developed among speculators, politicians, local political operators, and petty entrepreneurs. Extra-legality, in this form, was not a marginal offshoot of urbanization and modernization, but rather a fundamental component of both processes as they played themselves out in a sharply unequal society. For the wealthy, the poor, and everyone in between, the existence of urban areas that did not play by officially constituted rules offered an escape from the contradictions wrought by laws that conformed only patchily to the ambitions, material capacities, and social practices of Brazilian society. In tracing the favelas' early entrench-

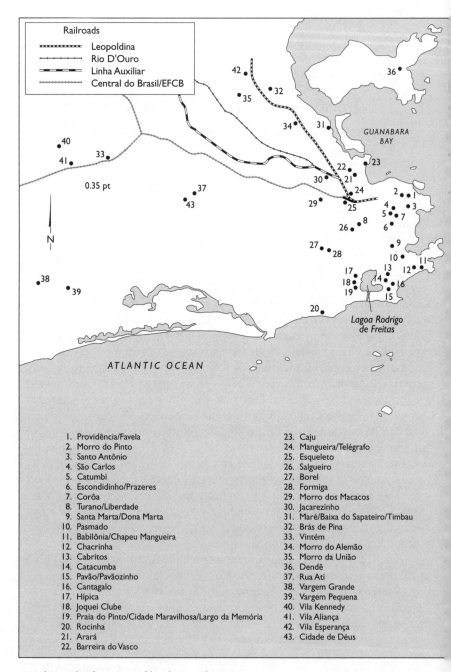

Favelas and other sites of land struggles.

ment, this chapter thus suggests that Rio's territorial history is largely unintelligible without serious attention to the deeply functional role of extra-legality within it.

PROPERTY IN LAW AND FACT

The tangle surrounding Rio's property relations was deeply rooted in both legal doctrine and political and social practice.[12] Historically, as elsewhere in Brazil, all land rights in Rio had originated with the Portuguese Crown, which distributed them to colonists in the form of *sesmarias,* or inheritable land-use grants, from the mid-sixteenth through the early nineteenth centuries.[13] Under this regime, most of Rio's downtown lands had been awarded as corporate *sesmarias* to the church or to the municipality, which had divvied them up among the city's prominent citizens in perpetual emphyteusis, or leasehold agreements. Much of what would become suburban land was given in *sesmaria* form to prominent colonizers, or to religious orders, most notably the Jesuits and the Benedictines. *Sesmarias* that remained unused, or those whose owners died without an heir, theoretically reverted to the Crown, as did the extensive holdings of the Jesuits when the order was expelled from Brazil in 1759.

The *sesmaria* system was, on the face of it, straightforward and even surprisingly egalitarian, given its periodically reiterated linkage of landholding and land use.[14] Yet it also laid the groundwork for centuries of confusion and conflict. Among the most persistent problems was that of demarcation: the Portuguese state lacked the power to enforce the bounding of *sesmaria* grants, and landowners often saw it in their interest to leave such limits vague.[15] Rio was no exception: even in the city center, the demarcation process took nearly 100 years after the lands were donated in 1567, and the boundaries thus set were still so vague that religious orders and private colonists would argue over them for generations to come.[16] In addition, despite theoretical limits on *sesmaria* size, the grants tended to be much larger than their owners could effectively use, even within the municipal boundaries. "Surplus" *sesmaria* lands—distributed but empty—ought to have reverted to the Crown, but in fact they were often gradually occupied by informal settlers, some clandestine and others willing participants in a complex network of rural power in which informal land rights were traded for labor and loyalty.[17] A similar patchwork of occupation spread out in lands whose *sesmaria* holders had died heirless, or had long since allowed their claims to lapse; though these were theoretically *terras devolutas* (literally, returned lands) ripe for redistribution, in practice many became the de facto property of squatters—poor, wealthy, and middling alike. When the *sesmaria* system formally ended with Brazilian Independence in 1822, it left a legacy of unclear boundaries, contested claims, and extensive extralegal settlement.

Underlying the *sesmaria* regime was an important tension over the degree to which productive occupation of land ought to establish a legal basis for ownership.[18] Though the *sesmaria* system had no formal place for rights grounded in *posse,* or simple possession, the fact that grants theoretically hinged on effective land use gave the notion some legitimacy, and rights earned through *posse* also had some grounding in the Philippine Code that governed civil law in colonial Brazil.[19] *Posse* also found some legal backing in the so-called Lei da Boa Razão of 1769, which opened the possibility that long-held custom might acquire the force of law.[20] The reality of extensive informal occupation gave the notion of *posse* additional practical weight. In many areas, as historian Hebe Mattos has argued for Rio de Janeiro state in the nineteenth century, "even when legal titles existed, the consensual and customary recognition of someone's possession rights depended ultimately on their effective power over those lands."[21]

After 1822, these tensions were reflected in a bewildering succession of land measures that alternately favored possession and legal purchase as sources of land rights. From 1822 through 1850, old *sesmaria* grants retained their validity, but all new land claims were made on the basis of simple *posse.* In 1850, the system changed yet again: whereas all lands previously acquired through *sesmarias* and *posse* would be recognized so long as they were promptly registered, subsequent transfers of national lands would come only through public auctions.[22] In the eyes of many historians, the 1850 law effectively shut the door on the sort of "homesteading rights" that might have rendered land ownership in Brazil more egalitarian.[23]

This vanquishing of possession as a source of rights to public lands theoretically governed land distribution into the twentieth century. Yet the specter of *posse* survived. Article 8 of the 1850 act itself opened the door by declaring that *posseiros* who failed to register their holdings would lose their rights but maintain their possession, a provision that would give rise to any number of conflicting interpretations, especially because lack of registration was endemic in many parts of Brazil.[24] Possession as a source of rights also made its way into the 1916 Brazilian civil code in the form of *usucapião,* which granted ownership to any individual able to prove long-term peaceful land occupation.[25] In 1934, the new constitution sanctified the notion that the right of property could "not be exercised against the social or collective interest"; this further complicated the picture by giving legal articulation to social necessity as yet another source of property rights, a precedent that all subsequent constitutions would follow.[26] In the end, commercial transaction, possession, and social need constituted a conflicting triad of principles from which Brazilian property rights could spring, setting the stage for extensive juridical and political battles over which notion would prevail.

Rio's legal and geographical peculiarities added unique dimensions to these ambiguities. In downtown Rio, the emphyteusis leaseholds granted to early settlers by the municipality were as loosely regulated as the *sesmarias* themselves; in theory, lands held in emphyteusis were inheritable but not otherwise transferable, and would lapse without payment of a yearly *fôro* to the city. In reality, however, the leaseholds were frequently bought and sold as if they were private property, and in many cases leaseholders simply stopped paying *fôros* altogether. Over time, such extralegal situations gained the force of custom, complicating any attempt to reassert the legal norm. The confusion over emphyteusis, taken in combination with the tangle of conflicts that surrounded Rio's imprecise *sesmaria* boundaries and disputed *terras devolutas*, helped to create a situation in which many properties were so tangled in claims and counterclaims that it was virtually impossible to determine legal ownership with any certainty.[27]

Rio's topography and the nature of its physical expansion complicated legal regulation still further. Enormous areas of the city rested on homemade landfill. Often the swamps and coastal areas where the landfill occurred had never been given in *sesmaria*, but the people who had rendered land from water claimed it, logically, as property. Other swamplands and hills had been part of *sesmarias*, but *sesmeiros* rarely occupied them, thus leaving the way clear for squatters. Rural lands within the municipality had the same fate if they were too distant from roads or commercial centers. Much of Rio's territory was also held in reserve by the church, the military, or the local or national governments; many of these properties were scarcely policed, and over time they became the object of numerous and overlapping private land claims. Altogether, the Federal District was riddled with lands of questionable legal status, from its hilly heart to its most distant suburbs. This situation set the stage for conflicts as complex as any fought out in Brazil's most distant rural regions.

LAYING CLAIMS

It was by no means inevitable that Rio's legacy of patchy and uncertain property rights would translate into a series of mid-twentieth-century standoffs between poor squatters and wealthy titleholders. As in the rest of Brazil, squatting in Rio was never the exclusive realm of the destitute: in the colony and the empire, rich and poor alike had sought to gain land from legal uncertainty, and in the twentieth century some of Rio's grandest land occupations were in fact engineered by wealthy and well-connected entrepreneurs. Poor people's informal claims grew up in the context of these elite appropriations, not separately from them; indeed, the only way to make sense of the fact that so much of Rio's land ended up under the feet of its poorest people is to delve into the complex network of cross-class interests that developed around poor people's extralegal settlements in the late nineteenth and early twentieth centuries. It was clearly in poor people's direct interest to squat on vacant lands in hopes of claiming them as their own, though they often did so in unexpected ways. But illegal settlement could take countless other forms and serve myriad interests; speculators, old landed families, local entrepreneurs, politicians, lawyers, and intermediaries all believed they had something to gain from claiming doubtful dominion and promoting extralegal settlement. It was the convergence of their interests with those of poor residents that made the problem of the land such an intractable one by the mid-twentieth century.

MYTHS AND ORIGINS

According to a version of history sanctified in countless court records, press interviews, and oral histories, poor squatters created Rio's modern favelas from virtual wilderness. A lyrical early recounting of this story appeared in a 1907 *Correio da Manhã* article about poor people's exodus to the city's newly visible favelas:

> The exodus never ceases. Daily, carts pass by, carrying mismatched dishes, tin cans, earthenware vessels, cages, archaic trunks, and they take the suburban highways to the foothills of the mountains. The alpine [sic] woods and those of the plains open themselves in welcome, and among the trees the outcasts lodge themselves; they sit on the rocks or the thick roots, hang their bundles from the trees, and, while the men hurriedly go about building their huts, the women install their kitchen in the open air . . . the mountain becomes populated. It is the charity of the Earth. . . . Thus poverty goes receding to any elevated ground, taking shelter in the hills, repelled by Greatness, by the cheerful destruction of humble houses, by Progress, which will not allow a single dilapidated structure to remain in the city's heart. The mountain opens her green mantle and takes in the poor little folk like the saints in the gentle times of the hermits.[28]

For this author, the genesis of favelas in the wilderness implied a naive primitivism, a deep and timeless connection between the poor and wild nature. But outsiders were not the only ones to invoke the favelas' sylvan origins. In 1934, a shacktown resident named Antônia Maria da Conceição offered a similar articulation in initiating a *usucapião* suit in Rio's Third Civil Court.[29] As stipulated in the 1916 civil code, *usucapião* could be claimed after 30 years of uninterrupted possession.[30] Accordingly, da Conceição began to justify her claim to land in Salgueiro—one of Rio's oldest north-zone favelas—by portraying the place as having been empty and untamed at the time of her arrival:

> It was in 1902 that the supplicant went to live in the Morro do Salgueiro, in a little area of land of which she took possession because its owner was not known, and it was said around there that the lands of that *morro* were abandoned, which showed itself to be true, seeing as how that land was a true jungle when the supplicant arrived.

Da Conceição went on to describe her painstaking struggle to pull the bases of a decent urban community from the jaws of the jungle. Similar heroic narratives would infuse subsequent accounts. In the early 1950s, a press rendering of mass evictions in the south-zone favela of Catacumba began by describing the community's early years in the 1920s:

> In those times, the jungle covered the *morro*, dense, almost impenetrable. . . . Horténcio Pinheiro was one of the first to tame the wilderness of Catacumba. He felled the first trees 30 years ago and staked out his shack of wood and zinc at the base of the hill, right in front of the Lagoa Rodrigo de Freitas. Afterward, more, and many more, would come.[31]

Thirty years later, Guida Nunes began a journalistic compilation of favela leaders' oral testimonies with an account of her protagonist's arrival in Borel, a north-zone favela that was the site of some of Rio's most intense land struggles in the 1950s. After describing a rural migrant's bewildering streetcar journey to the place where another settler had told him he might construct a shack, Nunes described the act of occupation in simple and romantic terms:

> When he arrived at the place where they had told him he could live, Elias thought that he was back in the interior of Rio state, with its cities full of wilderness. . . . He got off the tram and walked a bit until he reached the foot of a hill full of trees, waterfalls, a river of clean water at the entrance, and a few wooden houses. He liked the place, left his suitcase under a tree, and tried to arrange for some wood. The construction didn't take more than a day. . . . In a little while everyone was friends with Elias, and the Chácara do Borel seemed like one family.[32]

These characterizations of favela lands as abandoned or untamed, ripe for occupation, surface also in modern oral histories.[33] Describing in 2005 her long life as "one of the first residents" of the Mangueira favela, 104-year-old Lucíola de Jesus remembered that when she arrived there, "at the age of only 1 year," there were "just two other houses" aside from hers, and "an immense jungle."[34] In 2003, 80-year-old Salomão Pereira da Silva recalled that when he arrived among the first residents of the south-zone community of Pavão-Pavãozinho in 1945, the place was "virgin jungle" and "the houses were made of the planks of wooden crates and covered with pieces of tin that served as roof tiles."[35] Nilo Gomes dos Santos recalled in 2003 that when he arrived fifty years before in what would become the north-zone Nova Brasília favela, "it was all jungle, all pasture. My two daughters were raised with milk from here; the cows belonged to a Portuguese who also lived right nearby." In a 2005 interview, 70-year-old Marina da Silva described the neighboring Morro do Alemão in 1959 as "pretty much just jungle . . . there were mango trees, a pine, but only a few houses."[36]

There are many reasons why residents may have recounted their experiences in these ways. In part, they were simply telling history as they had seen it. Places like Mangueira and Salgueiro were relatively empty at the beginning of the century; literally carved out from rural *fazendas*, or summer estates, they were covered with jungle and devoid of pavement and urban services (see photo of the Babilônia Favela, p. 245). Residents in swampy north-zone favelas literally created the land under their homes from trash and bucketfuls of landfill (see photo of Esqueleto, p. 239). For rural migrants or refugees from Rio's center-city urban reforms, the issue of whom such territories belonged to probably mattered less than the fact that they were empty and free enough of vigilance for newcomers to stake out their shacks; their initial claims were usually not to ownership but rather to shelter. Moreover, vestiges of rural life were abundant in Rio's hills and suburbs; well into the twentieth century, residents of many informal communities raised chickens, pigs, or even cows and goats, and kept gardens and fruit trees to supplement their cash income.[37] Some mid-twentieth-century sociologists would point to such "rural" lifestyles as atavistic holdovers, indicative of migrants' supposed maladjustment to urban life.[38] But for residents, rural elements probably reinforced the sense that these lands were exceptions to the urban landscape, ignored by developers and city officials and therefore open for the taking. In the moral logic underlying these stories, these places became communities because their residents made them so, literally creating city from wilderness; that history itself became the source of rights, regardless of who held paper title.

At the same time, there have always also been strong political and legal reasons for favela residents to reinforce a narrative in which shack-town lands were peacefully claimed from sea and jungle. Principal among these reasons was the definition of *usucapião*, the only legal mechanism in the Brazilian Civil Code that allowed ownership grounded in possession. Simply put, if favela lands had been anything but empty at the time of settlement, no *usucapião* claim could be made. This was obviously most relevant when the city-from-wilderness narrative appeared in a court case; at the time of Antônia Maria da Conceição's 1934 petition, for example, Salgueiro's lands were already hotly disputed, and their ownership hinged directly on the notion of residents' "occupation without interruption or opposition."[39] A similar logic applied in virtually every other favela where *usucapião* was contemplated as a source of rights. Even when it was not, moreover, residents and their advocates sometimes appealed to constitutional provisions linking property to "collective or social need," and that case, too, was stronger when made for a community that residents had created on land with no previous use or claim.[40] This may partially explain why the myth of primordial origins appears even in places, such as Borel and the Morro do Alemão, where settlement was already relatively dense during years for which witnesses describe only forest and wilderness.[41] Whatever the particulars, much informal settlement in Rio seems to have originated from more complex and deeply rooted relationships than the primordial story would suggest.

RURAL CONVERGENCES

The question of why and how legally uncertain property relations became so dominant in Rio is most difficult to unravel for the *sertão carioca* and other distant suburbs, areas that were essentially rural well into the twentieth century, where modern landholding was shaped by the often violent collision of urban speculation with long-standing rural settlement patterns. In these places, even in the early 1900s, legal ownership patterns only thinly represented the complex networks of history, work, family, and dependence that really determined property use and possession. In some cases, these relationships had originated in slavery, and in the complex negotiations that surrounded emancipation. In 1931, for example, a rural laborer named José de Lima Soares wrote to Getúlio Vargas from Jacarepaguá, then a rural district of Rio that was caught up in the same wave of violent property usurpation that was devastating Guaratiba. Explaining the context for the Banco de Crédito Móvel's violent evictions in his region, and making a desperate appeal for Vargas's aid in stopping them, Lima Soares offered a rare explicit insight into the origins of his and his neighbors' settlement there:

> I am going to esplain [sic] to Your Excellency why [sic] has motivated these questions, these lands in other times belong to the Monastery of São Bento, yet, the monastery populated the Soil with its slaves since 1864 in that time there were no documents, and later the monastery mortgage to the Banco Credito Movel [sic],

this bank went bankrupt in 1891 and never bothered anyone, no *situante* has a
rental contract with the Banco Credito Movel.[42]

Few other written records draw as direct a link between manumis-
sion and rural property relations, or reveal so clearly the ways in which
these sorts of poor rural workers understood their claims to land. It was
not literally accurate that in the mid-nineteenth century there were "no
documents"; at least one modern account traces a paper trail from the
Mosteiro de São Bento to the bank's heirs, who would eventually gain
recognized title to most of the disputed lands.[43] But Lima Soares's perception that there were none indicates that papers had little practical function for poor people living in these regions during the late nineteenth and
early twentieth centuries. His insistence that the bank never established
rental contracts or "bothered anyone" is also significant because it indicates a popular understanding that property ownership was nullified by
abandonment, an idea formalized in the civil code's *usucapião* provision
and repeatedly reaffirmed by Brazil's highest courts. By Lima Soares's
logic, occupants of these lands had earned them through a long history
of undisturbed occupation and cultivation; their emancipation as slaves
had not been greeted by any official recompense but had left them room
to build lives for themselves and their children on a bit of open land.

Lima Soares's words were echoed in many other land conflicts, where
claims to undisturbed occupation for various generations, or "from time
immemorial," frequently cropped up.[44] In some critical eviction cases,
such arguments would prove the key to residents' permanence, since failure to collect rents on occupied land was widely taken to imply abandonment.[45] But in many other cases, informal occupation in rural areas took
a more complex form, and the rights that poor people understood to
derive from it were considerably more ambiguous. Unlike the Mosteiro
de São Bento or the BCM, many owners were quite careful to enforce
full ownership rights of rural lands that were occupied by others, most
often by charging yearly rents; in some cases, these arrangements also included the promise of agricultural labor from the tenants, usually called
arrendatários.[46] This did not mean, however, that such occupations were
entirely formal. Even when small-time rental agreements assumed written form—and they rarely did before the first decades of the twentieth
century—the borders of lands were almost never demarcated with care,
and the rentiers themselves sometimes lacked written proof of ownership. The establishment of rental arrangements was, in fact, quite a common strategy for land grabbing, because courts would sometimes accept
even verbal rental contracts as confirmation of the rentier's ownership.[47]
In Brazilian property law, moreover, it was both legal and customary for
ownership of improvements on land—houses, orchards, fences, fields—to

be separate from ownership of the land itself.[48] These improvements were frequently sold, formally and informally, as were the rights to long-term rental contracts.

The result was a landscape in which neither possession nor ownership rights were absolute or unambiguous, where many poor residents developed a strong sense of perpetual rights over lands they made no claim to owning. A 1936 land dispute among rural laborers in Guaratiba—this time quite separate from the actions of the BCM—illustrated these dynamics.[49] In June of that year, a barely literate rural worker named Alain Luiz de Souza went to court to reclaim a portion of "his" land that—he contended—had been violently usurped by his neighbors, recent arrivals in the region whom he knew only as Marcelino Martins and Dona Constanza. De Souza's family had occupied the lands in question for more than 20 years; in 1931, his mother had signed a formal lease agreement with the property's owner, an illiterate man by the name of Manoel Pinto de Faria, agreeing to pay an almost token yearly amount (100$000 *reis*) in exchange for continued occupation rights.[50] Since then, however, both de Souza's mother and the land's owner had died, and several of the owner's heirs had sold their inheritance rights, which had ultimately come to rest with Marcelo Martins and his wife, Constanza.[51] According to de Souza and several witnesses, the couple had first offered to buy the lease rights to the lands from him at a price that was much too low; when he refused, they proceeded to "exercise acts of disturbance" and, "accompanied by bullying individuals," to cut fences, topple trees, and generally take possession of a "large swath" of de Souza's little *sítio*. This done, they proceeded to declare aloud that they would "stay there forever, for better or for worse" and would "use every possible means to confront anyone who had the audacity to oppose" them.[52] De Souza appealed to the courts for "reintegração de posse," not only to restore his possession of the contested lands, but also to force Martins and Dona Constanza to repay him for the damages done to the property.[53]

De Souza's suit led to nearly two years of judicial arguments. The Martins vigorously contested the authenticity of de Souza's rental contract, his rights to possess land clearly owned by others, and the shape and size of the parcel he claimed; they backed their arguments with witnesses and with legal argumentation that was clearly more sophisticated than that employed by de Souza. The end result, however, favored the plaintiff. A lower court awarded de Souza full possession of the contested lands, pending final unraveling of the original owner's will; the appellate court mostly upheld that decision, and the whole case finally ended in March 1938.

In reaching this outcome, the civil courts—like others before and after them—implicitly recognized the ways in which legality and informality were interwoven in Rio's countryside, as well as the strong informal rights local people accorded to longtime tenants. The case hinged on de Souza's ability to prove not only his family's rights as tenants, but also their ownership of their simple houses and of the extensive orange groves they had cultivated for 20 years. And yet the formal evidence for this was thin. The rental contract had been drawn up in 1931, at least fifteen years into the family's occupation. It was never notarized or registered, though it did boast the official stamp that generally formalized such agreements, and it had been signed not by the owner but by his son.[54] Witnesses all recognized that the de Souza family had long cultivated the lands, but neighbors' estimations of the time of that occupation and the exact dimensions of the property varied. When asked about the parcel's boundaries, one elderly neighbor simply said that "everyone knew" where the *sítio* of Alain and his brothers ended because there was a "stand of wood in front of the highway there, and in the back a coconut palm."[55] Several other witnesses described the borders in similar terms, though noting that the *coqueiro* in question had been destroyed as part of the Martins' incursion.[56] The case for the de Souza family's occupational rights, in short, hinged not so much on objective evidence as on local people's informal understandings of their neighbors' rights and histories.

And yet judges, like witnesses, seemed generally to accept these at face value. No judge asked why no written agreement had existed before 1931; no one wondered why the rent paid was so low; no authority demanded concrete evidence that the de Souza family had built the lands' houses and planted its orange groves; and no one ever required any proof of the original owner's rights to the property. This silence implies that the justices found none of this unusual, and that they recognized—like the witnesses themselves—that property relations in these areas had been built mostly on informal local agreements that invested long-term renters with significant implicit rights. In a revealing comment, one witness, immediately after affirming that the de Souzas were simple tenants, expressed outrage that they had been "usurped of their property" ("esbulhados da sua propriedade") by the Martins' incursions; the legally precise phrase implied that the de Souzas were legal possessors of the land and had a right to its restoration.[57]

Unlike the conflicts surrounding the Banco de Crédito Móvel's Guaratiba land ventures, de Souza's case gained no publicity and probably had little lasting impact. Unless the family was eventually able to purchase the lands outright, this verdict probably did little more than delay the de Souzas' eventual dispossession as Guaratiba's lands gradually came into the orbit of metropolitan speculation and development. Yet, like the BCM cases, de Souza's suit exposed the fabric of social and property relations that would be torn apart by these transformations. Over many decades, property owners and cultivators in Rio's rural outskirts found mutual advantage—if not exactly harmony—in property arrangements that granted possession without ownership and left borders and contract terms vague. For owners with papers, such arrangements could bring local prestige, a small income, and use to land that otherwise might sit vacant. For "owners" whose legal status itself was unsure, informal rental also established effective dominion that could become the basis of firmer ownership further down the road. And for occupants, informal occupancy brought access to land—which would for the most part have been considerably more expensive to buy outright—as well as income, community, and independence.

FAVELAS, POLITICS, AND PROFIT

Similarly diverse interests drove informal settlement in Rio's center and immediate suburbs in the late nineteenth and early twentieth centuries. In these areas, however, informal property claims tended to be more shallowly rooted than they were in the *sertão carioca*, and they were also complicated considerably earlier by politics and speculation. Well before the beginning of the Vargas era, Rio's various forms of urban informality had already begun to concentrate in the form of favelas, and those settlements' growth had already come to depend on a fragile convergence of interests. Shacktowns at once provided housing for poor Cariocas unable to afford legal land, turned over quick and easy profits to property owners and speculators whose claims still lay outside Rio's urban frontiers, and became cheap sources of political capital for politicians and their operators. It was this coincidence of need, profit, and power that allowed favelas to lay their early roots.

Informal settlement was nothing new to downtown Rio. Although tenement dwellings have long been portrayed as the nineteenth century city's dominant form of cheap housing, this impression may spring as much from the drama of the nineteenth-century anti-*cortiço* campaigns as from the reality of most poor people's living arrangements. In 1888, for example, when Rio's total population stood close to the 1890 figure of 522,651, only 46,680 people lived in dwellings classified as *cortiços*, or slums.[58] Many others surely lived in smaller rooming houses or tenements; as Sidney Chalhoub has shown, use of the derogatory label *cortiço* had much to do with politics and social prejudice.[59] But there is also much evidence of alternate arrangements. From very early on, some poor people began to construct scattered homes on the flanks of Rio's central hillsides; runaway slave settlements appeared everywhere from Santa Teresa to Laranjeiras to the Corcovado to Tijuca, and settlements that could be called *quilombos* operated openly in areas such as Leblon in the years preceding abolition.[60] Scattered shacks were also a frequent early option for free Brazilians and immigrants in search of cheap shelter; some settled in hills or swamps, and many others seem to have rented shacks or tiny patches of land in backyards and vacant lots throughout the city, especially during the late nineteenth century, when waves of migrants streamed into Rio from Europe and the city's adjacent countryside. By 1933, shacks were present on nearly 42 percent of Rio's urban streets and over 81 percent of suburban ones, and only 23 percent of the city's 51,625 shacks were on streets with 50 or more such homes.[61] While we do not possess equivalent figures for earlier years, there is much reason to suppose that this kind of dispersed informality had roots deep in the nineteenth century.

Informality could also appear in more ambiguous forms. Servants and slaves frequently lived in the homes of their masters or employers, often in small rooms constructed some distance from family living quarters; many of these rooms approximated early favela shacks.[62] Tenements, too, were often the cradles of settlements resembling shantytowns; though many began with the subdivision of decadent mansions, they frequently grew through informal, even spontaneous, construction. In *O cortiço,* Aluísio de Azevedo's iconic fictional portrayal of tenement life, the avaristic Portuguese immigrant João Romão builds a housing empire from an alchemy of double dealing and relentless self-denial; over the space of just a few years, what began as "three tiny rooms with only a single door and window" became the giant *cortiço* of São Romão, a maze of rooms to rent that had been built from stolen and scavenged material on land gradually acquired from surrounding territories.[63] Though Azevedo does not enter into the details of Romão's land titles and building code compliance, it seems safe to assume that the real-life tenement entrepreneurs his character was based on rarely missed opportunities for profitably legal shortcuts.

The shacks and tenements that most of Rio's poor called home in the mid-nineteenth century thus shared key features with twentieth-century shantytowns. Yet it was only in the late nineteenth century that this spectrum of informal housing began to consolidate into the densely settled, more clearly bounded settlements that would come to be known as favelas. By most accounts, the main catalysts in this transition were military mobilizations and public health campaigns.[64] According to geographer Maurício de Almeida Abreu, the favela phenomenon officially began with a military order; in 1893–94, in the wake of the failed *Revolta da Armada*, commanders gave homeless soldiers leave to inhabit the convent of Santo Antônio, on the eponymous hill in central Rio. When there was no longer enough room in the convent, soldiers began to spill out into makeshift shacks, thus forming the embryo of Rio's first shantytown. During the same period, Rio's nineteenth-century anti-*cortiço* campaign culminated in the destruction of the enormous Cabeça de Porco *cortiço* near the Morro da Providência. According to historian Lilian Fessler Vaz, one of the *cortiço*'s owners, whose property nuzzled the hill's edge, began to rent bits of land on its slopes to displaced residents.[65] Five years later, troops returning from the Canudos War were given leave to join the expanding settlement; according to legend, it was they who dubbed the hill "favela," after a plant commonly found in Brazil's northeastern backlands, thus granting the phenomenon its name.[66]

After 1900, as chapter 1 recounts, public policies continued to favor the favelas' growth. Central-city *cortiços* were virtually eliminated with Pereira Passos's urban reforms, and former residents were left with a stark few choices. Some managed to hold on a bit longer to cheap lodgings in the remaining slums around the central periphery, in areas such as Gamboa, Santana, and the Cidade Nova, subsequently famous as the cradles of samba. More found shelter in the burgeoning railroad suburbs, where much cheap housing was both extralegal and rustic. And others made their way up the hills, the only centrally located patches where the 1903 building code still permitted the construction of the sorts of shacks and wooden houses they could afford to build or rent. By 1915, many of Rio's best-known favelas were already well established; besides Santo Antônio and Providência, these included Salguiero, Babilônia, Mangueira, Andaraí, São Carlos, Catumbi, Cabritos, Pasmado, and various settlements on the Lagoa Rodrigo de Freitas (see map, p. 220). By the time of the 1933 building census, clusters of shacks already existed on most of Rio's central hills, and a good many shacks were already located in groups of ten or more.

Given the coincidence of exclusive urban planning, quick population growth, capricious physical and legal geography, and widespread poverty, some form of shanty settlement may have been predetermined in early-twentieth-century Rio. But it was perhaps also inevitable that the favelas' growth rarely served the shacktown residents' interests alone. From the beginning, favelas were at the very center of larger political and economic strategies, involving a spectrum of outside actors that ranged from small-time shysters to self-made political operators to some of the city's wealthiest property owners and most powerful politicians. Bit by bit, Rio's shantytowns began to create not only crevices of affordable urbanity, but also building blocks of real wealth and influence; previously moribund hills and swamps began to generate rent and loyal political clients, the importance of which often quietly silenced critics of the favelas' illegality, shabbiness, and filth. In this sense, far from being marginal to Rio's development, as many mid-century critics would argue, the city's shantytowns were fundamentally integrated into many levels of Rio's social and economic life.[67]

POLITICS

Chapter 1 suggests many of the more obvious political dimensions of this early integration. Before the 1940s, Carioca politicians rarely devoted aboveboard legal or financial resources to ameliorating Rio's affordable housing shortage. But from the 1890s on, they willingly allowed favelas to dissipate the crisis. Prefect Barata Ribeiro probably authorized the first settlements on the Morro da Providência in the 1890s, and military commanders and police officials facilitated the settlement of Santo Antônio, Providência, São Carlos, Babilônia, and others. Scores of politicians averted their eyes in the 1900s as clearly illegal settlements mushroomed in such central areas as the Morro de Santo Antônio and Babilônia. When Santo Antônio was mysteriously burned down in 1916, municipal officials brokered its residents' resettlement in nearby Mangueira.[68] With the advent of more populist local politics in the 1920s, legions of political organizers swarmed up the slopes of the best-known *morros*.[69] By the 1930s, shantytown residents were regularly requesting eviction protection from prominent political figures such as Prefects Pedro Ernesto and Henrique Dodsworth, or even Getúlio Vargas himself.

In the case of big-time politicians, the payoff for favela tolerance was simple: without spending a cent on public housing, they could keep poor families off the street and cultivate their own images as charitable benefactors. Getúlio Vargas was repeatedly portrayed as a charitable protector of favela residents. In 1941, for example, a government publication entitled *Os morros cariocas no novo regime*—which at once celebrated a folkloric favela population and commemorated the planned elimination of the favela "plague"—encapsulated succinctly Vargas's projected image: "The man, woman, or child of the *morro* has a delicate esteem, a permanent and emotional remembrance, of Getúlio Vargas's name, founded in the certainty of the goodness, without artificiality, of 'their' president; it is only comparable to that of his gentle wife, who, for all of these people, is a tutelary figure."[70]

Petitioners to President Vargas showed awareness of this idealized relationship, but few seemed willing to buy into it blindly; in their missives, political support was understood more as a quid pro quo, in which the president would stave off threats from the health service and the civil courts in exchange for subservience and loyalty. In 1934, for example, petitioners from the Morro of Santo Antônio asked the president to call off an eviction by the health service, pointedly offering political tranquility in exchange for his help: "In the difficult era we are gaing [sic] through in this century of social reinvinculations (sic), our voise [sic] is mute, or better mild because we always trust completely in the goodness of Your Excellency."[71] Other petitioners were less radical, but nearly all made at least vague reference to their qualities as "workers" or members of the "national communion," thus implicitly claiming protection on the basis of their adherence to Vargas's national vision.[72] In a typical letter, Eulália Moreira Santos pleaded with the president in 1942 to do something to avoid the threatened razing of a shantytown in Santa Tereza by the Hospital Alemão, which claimed the lands as its own. Noting that the residents had paid rent for years, and that theirs was a "trancwil [sic] *morro*" full of "well-behaved families," Moreira Santos concluded that "beneath god we only count on your protection and as adevocate [sic] of the poor clas [sic] we already hope by God and your good heart that we will be taken care of to alleviate our afflictions."[73]

To such appeals, Vargas offered an oblique response. Officially, most were met with silence or noncommittal investigations. Though the Santa Tereza petitioners sent the president at least four separate letters, the only reply was a brief note to the effect that it was a judicial matter in which Vargas could not interfere.[74] In Santo Antônio, Vargas carried out an extensive investigation but sent no formal answer; ironically, the excuse given was the petitioners' lack of a formal address.[75]

Yet informally, Vargas seems to have been considerably more active, often directing supplicants to request personal protection from his wife, Darcy Vargas. There is some indication that the first lady herself resolved the Santa Tereza case; late-twentieth-century oral histories of two Santa Tereza favelas—the Morro do Escondidinho and the Morro dos Prazeres—cite threats to the *morros* from a "Banco Alemão" or a "grupo Alemão" during the World War II years. They also note that a committee from one of the shantytowns appealed for Vargas's help, and recount that Darcy Vargas visited one of the favelas and gave residents "a document donating the land" ("um documento de doação da terra.")[76] Darcy Vargas may also have come to the aid of Mangueira residents threatened with eviction in the early 1940s: in a 1947 article in *O Mundo*, reporter Rimus Prazeres claimed that Darcy Vargas had frequently visited the *morro*, and that a school there had been named in her honor.[77]

In Jacarezinho, a north-zone favela that would briefly become Rio's largest, Darcy Vargas seems to have taken a still more forceful role. In an interview with researcher Jane de Souto Oliveira during the early 1980s, a 63-year-old retired worker remembered the mid-1940s as a period of intense community struggle. As the settlement mushroomed from a scant few houses in the 1930s to hundreds in the early 1940s, and as various private owners laid claim to Jacarezinho's lands, property conflicts became intense and violent; police would come mounted on horses and destroy the *morro*'s adobe huts, which the residents would then rebuild by night. In the face of this situation, some 200 people crowded onto a streetcar and made their way to Catete Palace to appeal directly to the president, who happened to arrive just as the committee began to tell its story to one of his advisors. De Souto Oliveira's informant recounted:

> So Getúlio asked which favela it was, that he wasn't familiar with it. So Manoel Padeiro said: "President, it's Jacarezinho. This favela, it was the madam that gave it to us. It was Dona Darcy who gave it to us." "And what's going on?" "The police are mistreating [*judiando com*] the people. They go there, they knock down the house, bring the horses in on top of it." So he goes like this, "OK, I am going to take care of it. You all go away, come back on Thursday, and you are going to look for Darcy."

According to de Souto's informant, Manoel Padeiro's reference to Darcy Vargas had been baseless and purely opportunistic. But it worked. They returned to the Catete Palace as bid, and through Darcy Vargas and the Legião Brasileira de Assistência they succeeded in warding off the immediate threat, and even gained provisional permission to occupy their lots.[78] In 1949, municipal councilman Anésio Frota Aguiar indicated how those events had made their way into the political mythology of the Trabalhista Party (PTB), declaring that when "a rich man, a very rich man, the owner of those lands" had tried to seize control of Jacarezinho during the Estado Novo, the "Primeira Dama" herself had interceded, and "with her social aid, with her humanitarian spirit, she obligated the magnate to recoil from his inhuman intentions."[79]

While largely anecdotal, these accounts suggest that Vargas played a subtle hand with the favelas, one that mirrored in many ways his broader political strategy. Though the president rarely granted the poorest supplicants aboveboard rights to their properties, he did respond to them through the Legião Brasileira de Assistência and the feminine charity of his wife, thus preserving his image as protector of the poor while making no permanent commitment or investment.

Vargas also seemed to condone an activist approach on the part of his political subordinates. The first mayor he appointed for Rio, the famed physician Pedro Ernesto, began to build a political infrastructure in the *morros* in the early 1930s.[80] He made personal visits to several communities, including São Carlos, Mangueira, and the Morro do Pinto, and probably constructed the first public elementary school built within a favela.[81] He also accelerated the already established tradition of offering favela residents occasional water taps and paved roads, and was said to have mediated several disputes between shantytown residents and private landowners, most notably in Mangueira.[82] Ernesto also channeled public resources to the samba schools of the *morros*, a practice that at once promoted a folkloric image of Brazilian cultural fusion and gave the favelas a privileged position in the nationalist imagination.[83] Though the number of registered voters who lived in favelas continued to be relatively small, Ernesto's decision to engage directly with them had considerable symbolic value, adding to his image as a protector of the poor and opening the door to the brazenly populist politics that would follow Vargas's fall from power in 1945.[84]

Henrique Dodsworth, whom Vargas named to the prefecture between 1937 and 1945, seemed at first to veer sharply away from Ernesto's populist gestures. His public stance on the favelas was frankly and ambitiously negative. In a 1945 article, Dodsworth touted his administration's steps toward eliminating the favelas—which he associated with "malnutrition, promiscuity, lack of hygiene, and social disintegration"—and looked forward to their total elimination: "Of the absent favelas, only the romantic aspect of their songs will remain."[85] It was under Dodsworth's watch that the 1937 building code began to be enforced, and that many of Agache's more elitist ideas were integrated into a general plan for urban renewal. Dodsworth's most ambitious social project was the creation of a "favela commission" meant to study and eventually destroy all of the favelas in Rio's central areas.[86] Though the larger project sank in the ill-fated morass of the *Parque Proletário* experiment of the early 1940s, Dodsworth's most public action on the favela question was the literal setting alight of the Largo da Memória, an enormous settlement on the shores of the Lagoa Rodrigo de Freitas.[87]

Behind the scenes, however, even Dodsworth's administration seemed to accept the necessity and political utility of some shack settlements. Vitor Tavares de Moura (whom Dodsworth named to head his favela eradication commission and, later, Rio's entire social assistance department) approached the favela question with a pragmatic appreciation of its complexity, along with a well-grounded awareness that most favela residents were workers with few viable housing alternatives.[88] Even as he spearheaded the *Parque Proletário* project and publicly advocated some draconian favela eradication policies, Tavares de Moura also bargained realistically with favela residents, landowners, charities, and intermediaries, often quietly using municipal resources to create or expand shacktown settlements. It is perhaps symptomatic of this tolerance that the first Vargas era witnessed a singular expansion of shacks; while the 1933 building census had counted 51,625, in 1949 the Yellow Fever Service tallied some 89,635.[89]

Dodsworth's archives offer considerable insight into the ways in which this expansion came about, and into the webs of political power and influence that favela protection was already generating. In some cases, the administration seems tacitly to have condoned favelas by simply ignoring reports of their illegal expansion. In 1940, for example, Dodsworth received a letter from Dr. Thibeu Junior, head of the 8th sanitary district, lamenting the filthy and unsanitary state of lands surrounding the abandoned skeleton of a São Cristóvão building once intended to be a new hospital.[90] What was worse, he complained, "in the middle of all of this sordidness, taking advantage of part of the abandoned concrete scaffolding and also of improvised wooden structures, a favela has formed, where innumerable families live in the greatest destitution [*miséria*]." Because the lands were federal, the municipal sanitary service could do nothing about the favela, and the official wanted Dodsworth to intervene. Dodsworth, however, did not: in 1947, a census revealed some 1,400 shacks at the site, now referred to as the Favela do Esqueleto (see photo of Esqueleto, p. 239). Many of its residents had access to electricity (pirated by a military police sergeant), and most reportedly paid rent to federal ministries.[91] Residents interviewed for a 1947 article indicated that officials from the Ministry of Education and even Prefect Hildebrando de Goiás had given tacit permission for the land to be settled. The favela was not fully destroyed until 1964–65; though the precise negotiations that ensured its endurance remained undocumented, it is clear that Dodsworth, his successors, and their counterparts in the federal government chose to allow the Favela do Esqueleto's precipitous growth.[92]

Dodsworth's administration also sometimes chose to promote favela settlements more directly. One indication of this appeared in a 1944 letter in which representatives of the Serviço de Obras Sociais (SOS), one of the era's largest publicly subsidized charities, asked the prefect himself to provide wood for the construction of favela shacks for homeless Cariocas.[93] Though the request was refused, its very existence shows that there was nothing especially unusual about public participation in favela construction. The same awareness can be seen in another 1944 letter, written by an official of the EFCB, Brazil's most important railway company,

The Esqueleto favela at water's edge, no date. Courtesy of the Arquivo Geral da Cidade do Rio de Janeiro.

who sought municipal assistance in removing a small favela from EFCB lands in the port neighborhood of Cajú.[94] Apparently city authorities had convinced railroad officials to accept the favela's temporary location on EFCB land, with the understanding that its residents would soon be moved to the Praia do Pinto favela, on the Lagoa. This had not happened, and the official wrote to Dodsworth in hopes of a speedy solution. Vitor Tavares de Moura responded on Dodsworth's orders with a deal that would have simply moved favela shacks to municipal land in suburban Penha. Five years later, however, debates in the Municipal Council suggested that the prefecture did not or could not live up to its promise, and the favela still stood precariously on EFCB lands.[95] Like the SOS letter, this case reveals the degree to which municipal authorities were willing to actively coordinate favela construction in the absence of more permanent alternatives.

That willingness opened the door for any number of political opportunists. Typical in this regard was Atila dos Santos Couto, a mercurial figure who inserted himself into numerous negotiations between municipal authorities and favela residents throughout the 1940s. Couto first appears in the archival records in March 1945, when he wrote to Henrique Dodsworth in the name of a group of shantytown inhabitants from São Cristóvão, an industrial port neighborhood on Rio's near north side.[96] Sending his missive in the hands of a "committee" of residents, Couto wrote that the federal government had threatened to evict some 50 families in the Barreira do Vasco favela. Couto claimed to have personally intervened on their behalf, buying more time and placing several families in two nearby shantytowns. Some three dozen families remained under imminent threat, however, and Couto pointedly highlighted the municipal government's stake in resolving their problem:

> Seeing as how these residents find themselves in a desperate situation, and foreseeing the possibility that public authorities merely fulfilling their obligations might be faced with opposition to any energetic measures they might take, and also considering that it is not the right political moment for confrontations between authorities and poor populations, I solicit that Your Excellency find a bit of land where certifiably poor people might construct small hygienic houses of the sort that their means allow; far from forming favelas, these houses would become proletarian and worker parks, following the example of what's been done in the Barreira do Vasco already, where since October 500 families have been sheltered, among them dozens belonging to soldiers from our glorious Expeditionary Forces.

Couto was bold to suggest the possibility of physical resistance to the eviction order, and clever to echo the municipal government's practically meaningless distinction between shacks and "hygienic houses." In inserting himself in the midst of the fight, as a selfless defender of poor residents' interests, he showed a keen awareness of the political capital that this sort of intermediary might accumulate, especially on the eve of Brazil's redemocratization.

More fascinating still, though, was the underbelly of Couto's operations, revealed by Dodsworth's and Moura's full investigation of the case.[97] Couto, as it turns out, was not solely an advocate for residents' best interests. Along with a retired military police sergeant by the name of Rubens de Carvalho, he was also a sort of favela entrepreneur, a wheeler and dealer who posed as an administrator of public lands and charged residents steep rents for the privilege of constructing their shacks there. He and Carvalho had in fact encouraged the settlement of the lands that were being cleared, charging about 250–350 *cruzeiros* for the right to "put up a shack." What's more, Couto's operations extended well beyond Barreira de Vasco: he appeared also to be one of the driving forces behind the rapid expansion of Jacarezinho, the same favela in Rio's northern industrial zone that was the object of Darcy Vargas's charity in the early 1940s. Moura's informant wrote:

I had a big shock, because the favela that Your Excellency and I visited a few months ago has been transformed into a veritable city, all of this thanks to the "philanthropy" of Senhores Atila dos Santos Couto, Avelino Alves David, Manoel de Andrade, and Manoel Félix de Oliveira.

The informant complained that "professional *favelados*" and "favela builders" such as Couto had appropriated the rights to divide public land, grant residents construction permits, and even license commercial establishments, many of which were in fact "chains" with franchises in various shacktowns. Couto and others advertised shack sales with public placards, bought out early settlers in order to establish their own property boundaries, and even provided receipts properly sealed with federal stamps. Providing several examples of such receipts, the official recommended that Moura and Dodsworth take steps to control this growth by destroying empty shacks, banishing intermediaries such as Couto, prohibiting the sale of shacks, and eliminating all of the *biroscas* (small shops) that proliferated in favelas throughout the city.

In the face of such a damning report, Dodsworth's administration took no official action on Couto's request. Neither, however, did the government sanction Couto or take any of the steps the investigators recommended. Indeed, both Jacarezinho and Barreira do Vasco grew apace, and a few short years later Couto resurfaced, first presenting a 1947 request that the Municipal Council create a "relief service in the *morros* and favelas"[98] and then emerging as Jacarezinho's self-styled champion in the face of a 1947 civil land claim that threatened to evict some 30,000 people. Couto was named principal defendant in that suit and was instrumental in the political mobilization that eventually blocked the eviction's enforcement.[99] At least some local residents named the community's single public plaza after him, and the Municipal Council went so far as to officially hail Couto as a "worker and leader of the workers of Jacarezinho," though he was subsequently also denounced on the Council floor as an "exploiter" who had profited from the *morro*'s settlement.[100]

Hero or exploiter, Couto's material claims were undeniably reinforced by his political agility. He may have made his fortune by extracting usurious rents from people eager for a bit of shelter, but neither their claims nor his own might have survived without his self-interested political mediation. People like Couto were, in a sense, simply the pettiest players in a symbiotic political game. By the end of the Estado Novo, the relationship of mutual dependency was already well established. Poor Cariocas depended on illegal favelas for affordable housing, and politicians—from the president down to the pettiest wheeler and dealer—depended on that very illegality to create networks of political gratitude, loyalty, and power.

SPECULATION

The most obvious political payoff for favela tolerance came from residents, whose support would become especially critical after the return to elections and relatively freewheeling street politics in 1945. But Atila dos Santos Couto's case also demonstrates the degree to which the favelas' survival suited the interests of shantytown entrepreneurs, men and women whose economic fortunes depended on the settlements' continued existence. Such people could sometimes be quite humble, simple residents who had managed to stake out a bit of extra land and rent it out at a small profit. Others were big-time land grabbers who built small fortunes on the practice, or scions of wealthy families who turned a considerable profit illegally renting out otherwise fallow land. So long as favela terrain remained marginal to Rio's urban expansion—too swampy or steep for legal construction, too distant from commercial centers or public transportation to fetch much value on the open market, and too undervalued for serious legal ownership claims to be made—this whole range of actors stood to benefit from its extralegal exploitation.

In any number of cases, favelas began as informal real estate investments on the part of some of Rio's most prominent families and businesses.[101] An intermediary for the Associação do Hospital Alemão, for example, long provided rental receipts for shanty residents on its Santa Teresa properties. Textile factories such as Bangú, Confiança, and Aliança charged workers for the privilege of erecting shacks in "workers' villas," which were often just embryonic favelas.[102] The Morro do Turano began as an extension of a small *cortiço* on the Rua Barão de Itapegipe, owned by the heirs of Manoel Ferreira da Costa e Souza, the Barão de Famalição. Part of the Morro dos Prazeres, in central Santa Teresa, was said to be owned by "Senhor Moniz de Aragão, ambassador in the munificent court of His Majesty George VI, King of England."[103] A good part of the Mangueira favela began as the personal claim of Alberto Negreiros Saião Lobato, the Visconde of Niterói, who collected rents on the favela shacks by way of a Portuguese intermediary by the name of Tomás Martins; after his death, his widow continued the practice, as did the company to which she later sold her by then doubtful claim to the property.[104] None of these elite figures dirtied their hands with day-to-day management—all of that was left to intermediaries, many of whom became powerful figures in their own right—but they were clearly aware of the use to which their properties were being put.

Among all of these elite figures whose fortunes were tied to the early favelas, none left so transparent a paper trail as Eduardo Duvivier; his story provides unique insight into the intersection of big-time real estate development, politics, and the settlements' early growth. Duvivier was a wealthy lawyer and politician who in the early decades of the twentieth century laid claim to a good part of the Morro da Babilônia, in the tony south-zone neighborhood of Leme. He was born in 1890 to a wealthy Rio de Janeiro family, which by that point had already begun investing heavily in urban development in what was then the remote south zone. His father, Theodoro Duvivier, and his uncle, Otto Simon, were important early promoters of the tramways that allowed the south zone to expand, and his grandfather, a German immigrant named Alexander Wagner, was a pioneering real estate developer who by the early 1870s had accumulated title to much of Copacabana and Leme.[105] Duvivier himself was many things; a *fazendeiro*, the president of a milk marketing cooperative, an active associate in banking and construction firms, a federal deputy both in the mid-1930s and in the late 1940s, and a signatory to Brazil's 1946 constitution.[106] A Copacabana street is named after his father, and Duvivier was a pioneering investor in the genre of elegant apartment buildings that would define the neighborhood's easy opulence in the mid-twentieth century.[107]

Less well known, however, was the degree to which the Duvivier family's formal real estate enterprises melded seamlessly with the origins of Copacabana's favelas. As early as the 1910s, Eduardo Duvivier, by then a young lawyer, began to show up in civil court cases representing the Empresa de Construções Civis (ECC), an important real estate company that had been partially founded by Theodoro Duvivier and Otto Simon in order to divide and sell a good part of Copacabana and Leme.[108] In the late nineteenth century, the company worked closely with Jardim Botânico Railways, the tram company that facilitated Copacabana's development, and had a number of extraordinarily powerful board members, among them the future prefect Carlos Sampaio, the renowned physician Hilário de Gouveia, and the acclaimed engineer Antônio de Paula Freitas.[109]

By the time Eduardo Duvivier began to play a role, the company had already sold off many of its best lands and was in a state of "amicable liquidation." Nonetheless, it still claimed most of the Babilônia and São João hills, which straddled the borders of Copacabana, Leme, and Botafogo and were already becoming the sites of several favelas, including Babilônia, Chacrinha, and Chapeu Mangueira.[110] As early as 1916, Eduardo Duvivier began to represent the ECC in eviction cases that involved shacks and wattle-and-daub houses built on the hills.

Eduardo Duvivier did occasionally advocate the destruction of these shanties, especially when their occupants challenged the ECC's ownership claims. In 1916, he evicted four families who had erected shacks without permission in the backyard of a garage at the foot of the Morro da Babilônia, and in 1917 he brought suit against 22 residents of *casinhas* or *barracões* on the same *morro*, alleging that the city health service had ordered their removal and that they had long since stopped paying rent.[111] But, for the most part, the company tolerated and profited from the hills' rustic structures. In 1926, for example, Duvivier represented the ECC in a heated judicial dispute over who had the right to collect rents from 22 tenants of shacks on the Ladeira do Leme, in the area that would become the Chacrinha favela.[112] In 1927–28, the company rented out several wattle-and-daub houses on the Morro de Babilônia, many of which had the same numbers as the houses that had been condemned by the sanitation department ten years before.[113] While these structures were a step up from the most primitive of shacks, with some whitewash and rustic tile roofs, they still lacked plumbing and adherence to basic urban construction norms, and most seem to have been classified as shacks in the 1933 building census.[114] When Duvivier himself bought much of Babilônia Hill, in 1928, the sale contract indicated that the land held any number of "casinhas and barracões," from which he continued to collect rents into the early 1930s. Clearly, and over several generations, the growth of shacks on Cobacabana's hillsides was condoned and even promoted by the very same illustrious developers who engineered the neighborhood's evolution into a seaside paradise (see photo on p. 245).

The story of Duvivier's involvement in the formation of the Babilônia and Chapeu Mangueira favelas ended in the early 1930s with an oddly fitting twist. In 1934, when Duvivier was on the verge of becoming a federal deputy, a federal law was passed specifically to deny the validity of his family's claims to the *morros* of Babilônia and São João.[115] According to the decree, the hills, which occupied a uniquely protective position at the opening of Guanabara Bay, were and always had been military lands, geographically critical to national security. In the law's careful historical rendering, the 1873 sale that had placed the lands in the hands of Duvivier's maternal grandfather, Alexander Wagner, had been based on false premises, and was clearly limited by an 1867 judicial embargo. According to the law's text, Wagner, aware of the lands' doubtful status, had apparently gone about his business nonetheless, holding on to the lands for nearly 20 years and then selling them in 1891 to Theodoro Duvivier and Otto Simon's ECC. The ECC demarcated and sold much of the land, but the judicial dispute over its hilly portions continued, and when Eduardo Duvivier bought the property from his father's company, in 1928, the federal courts were already in the process of reclaiming it for the army.

A 1931 Supreme Court decision sealed that fate. Duvivier may have

Hut and residents of Babilônia, 1912. Courtesy of the Arquivo Geral da Cidade do Rio de Janeiro.

managed to divest himself of the lands before the 1934 decree that final-ized it—his long string of eviction lawsuits ended in 1931, and a 1942 law that granted compensation to a number of innocent third-party buy-ers included several chunks of land that Duvivier and the ECC had rented out in the 1910s and 1920s.[116] Whatever Duvivier's precise exit strat-egy, however, the memory of his role as an early favela developer faded quickly. As a federal deputy in the turbulent 1940s, he played no part in the intense debates about the fate of Rio's shantytowns, though he did gain some notoriety for his strong belief in the unconstitutionality of rent control.[117] Duvivier also seems to hold little place in local memory. In various oral histories of Babilônia and Chapeu Mangueira, there is no mention of him; even Odília dos Santos Gama, who was born in 1920 in the very area then claimed by the ECC, could not remember anything before the army's subsequent tight regulation of the hill.[118]

It is no mystery that a family of the Duviviers' stature might have be-come involved in the business of the *morros*. Hillside lands were a tricky prospect for traditional real estate development; their steep, rocky sur-faces made sturdy construction almost impossible well into the twentieth century, and also made it costly to open streets and install public services. When property rights also proved judicially doubtful—as in Babilônia and countless other *morros*, most notoriously Santo Antônio—above-board sales were made quite difficult. In those circumstances, informal development beckoned. Favelas also soon proved to be an enormously profitable business. In the early 1930s, Duvivier charged anywhere from 80–120 *mil-reis* per month for each of his small houses (the gardens of which tenants often then sublet to still poorer residents). That amount was small change for a wealthy person, though it was roughly equal to the monthly wages of the poorest day laborers.[119] But when such rent was multiplied, as Duvivier's was, even by a modest 20, a landlord's annual income could rise to 19,200–28,800 *mil-reis*—enough to buy an elegant Copacabana apartment in cash.[120] Duvivier's rents represented the high end of the market, probably because many of his tenants sublet their small plots of land for further shack construction. Others charged less and rented only the right to construct rustic wood-and-zinc shacks, and some chose simply to sign their entire properties over to an intermediary for a relatively low flat fee.[121] But even those smaller rates of return were remarkable for what otherwise might have been a moribund investment. Vitor Tavares de Moura, considering the puzzle of elite collusion with favela growth in the early 1940s, neatly summed up the well-heeled landowner's logic:

> It is curious to note that favelas often emerge on private lands, without so much as a protest from the owners; on the contrary, they even help to construct the shacks and attract new residents. It is an easy way to pay no taxes and reap enormous income. In the meanwhile, the land values continue to appreciate, with no need for help from anything but time.[122]

LOCAL PROFITEERING

Property owners' assent was fundamental to the favelas' early growth, not least because their clout probably brought with it immunity to health service persecution. But wealthy Cariocas were hardly the only ones to notice the settlements' lucrative potential, or to become heavily invested in their continued existence. Regardless of whether the lands they stood on were public or private, claimed or abandoned, favelas also became, from their earliest origins, the sites of intricate networks of appropriation and profiteering by middling and even humble Cariocas. These men and women, while less obviously influential than figures such as Duvivier, were critical catalysts in the favelas' early growth and survival. To an even greater degree than elite property holders, small-time favela entrepreneurs occupied themselves with the details of creating sturdy physical and political infrastructures on the *morros*; they recruited residents, subdivided abandoned lands, built shacks, acquired materials for more, settled local disputes, negotiated service provision, haggled with property owners and politicians, and mobilized communities threatened with eviction. For these small players, favelas were their main chance; the settlements' very extra-legality transformed them into a bargain-basement investment, an otherwise impossibly expensive ticket to social mobility, be it from desperate to respectable poverty or from small-time commerce to the bigger leagues of wealth and influence. Thus driven, these small players were as critical as their wealthier counterparts in ensuring the favelas' continued extralegal survival.

Residents themselves often spurred the transformation of settlement into a business. Many began quite humbly, arriving in the hills and swamps with little or nothing, and using any extra bit of soil to generate a little extra income. Despite the inherent invisibility of such small-scale (and illegal) transactions, glimpses of them appear periodically. In the early 1900s, for example, the poor soldiers who first inhabited Santo Antônio and Providência had already begun to sell their shacks and lease their lots.[123] In many of the eviction suits brought by Duvivier and the ECC in the 1910s, there was evidence of petty entrepreneurs who were renting out a handful of shacks. And in the early 1930s, Maximina de Souza—the illiterate Portuguese immigrant involved in the insult case on the Morro da Formiga—supplemented her meager earnings as a cook by renting out a single small shack on her precarious lands.[124]

In a 1947 article about the Esqueleto favela (the community that had grown up inside the enormous "skeleton" of an unfinished hospital), an unidentified resident explained the commonsense logic of this process. According to him, the settlement inside the structure had begun with the tacit consent of the minister of education, and its development as a business had proceeded chaotically and organically:

> When that engineer gave his consent for people to go live in the big *barracão*, it was a crazy rush. Everyone tried to grab his little corner, and the subdivision of the big building began. Each person used whatever materials they could lay their hands on and did the work as they saw fit. . . . Everyone was already settled into their little corners when some, perhaps driven by necessity, began to make a business of it [*fazer negócio*]. . . . In order to get a little money, they "sold" a little of the space they controlled, and, in this way, the population of the *barracão* grew bit by bit.[125]

A 1934 *usucapião* case from the Salgueiro favela, in the northern neighborhood of Tijuca, suggests that not all resident entrepreneurs kept their ambitions so humble. Salgueiro was one of Rio's first favelas, named after a Portuguese real estate investor by the name of Domingos Alves Salgueiro, who already owned several Carioca properties by the 1880s and was renting out shacks on the *morro* as late as the 1910s.[126] It seems, though, that Salgueiro's hold on the *morro* was both fragile and partial. In the 1930s, a number of residents began to file *usucapião* suits, claiming that they had lived in the area undisturbed since the early 1900s and had now acquired legal rights to it.[127] One such suit came from Dona Antônia Maria da Conceição. As recounted above, da Conceição's is one of the earliest recorded arguments for the favelas' primordial origins; she claimed to have arrived in 1902, when the lands were "abandoned," with no known owner, "a real jungle." Widowed early on, she managed to construct a small shack, later finding ways to connect it to water lines and a primitive septic system. From those beginnings, she eventually laid claim to over 8,000 square meters, bounded on all sides with plots that also seem to have been informally claimed. On that land, Conceição began to build other small shacks, which she then sold to some 24 other families. In filing her *usucapião* suit, she hoped not only to gain legal title to her own home, but also to legitimize all of those sales, presumably at considerable personal profit.

There is no known record of the outcome of da Conceição's suit, though at least some Salgueiro claimants eventually received *usucapião* rights.[128] It is clear, though, that residents everywhere followed her example, accumulating, renting, and selling as many as several dozen shacks. Nearly all of Vitor Tavares de Moura's 1940s censuses mention the presence of people he termed "exploradores" (exploiters) and "grileiros" (land grabbers), most with only a handful of shacks. In the Hípica favela, on the Lagoa, census agents pointed to one rentier, a woman named Aurea Gonçalves who ran a small store from her shack and also "made shacks to rent and sell."[129] In the south-zone favela of Catacumba, the census pointed to three men controlling between five and eight shacks, each of whom presented documents meant to constitute proof of ownership—tax receipts, water receipts, maps, even a sale contract.[130] While such documents were often accumulated by land grabbers in order to establish "ownership" of favela lands, it is possible that these were at least partially valid: a 1945 law had decreed that the public lands that Catacumba sat on were to be sold off to the area's residents, though the sales seem never to have been finalized, and the government recognized none of them when it destroyed the favela entirely in 1970.[131]

By the 1940s, newspaper reports regularly highlighted the roles of resident "exploiters," whose profiteering was often used to negate the argument that favelas grew as a result of pure need. In Esqueleto, where settlement quickly spread outside of the initial unfinished building, one report claimed that various *expertelhões* (shysters) quickly built shacks that sold at anywhere from 5,000 to 20,000 *cruzeiros* or rented from 50–200 *cruzeiros* per month.[132] In a generally sympathetic 1947 interview published in the daily *O Globo*, Jacarezinho resident Wilson da Silva—who lived on a street named for Darcy Vargas—carefully maintained that most people on the hill owned their shacks. When pressed, though, he noted that there was "a lot of exploitation in that matter up there on the top of the hill. Certain individuals are taking advantage and building four or five shacks, and renting them for high prices or even requiring bribes." He went on to describe a certain José Vidal who already owned a *botequim* and several shacks on the *morro*, and who walked around with "two leather bags, full of wooden stakes and a roll of twine," in order to claim and demarcate any empty lots he came across.[133]

José Vidal was nothing compared to Zé Vagalume, a resident of the Morro dos Macacos, near the old Zoo in Villa Isabel. When he was described in a 1948 *Globo* article, this "preto retinto, moço ainda" ("coal-black man, still young") had arrived on the *morro* only one month previously. Strategically situating his house at the *morro*'s entrance, he began to charge new residents for cleared lots; but eventually, "seeing that everyone was willing to obey him," he began to charge simply for granting new residents his personal brand of building permit. Thus, according to the article, Zé Vagalume "began to become the rainmaker of the *morro*" ("o manda-chuvas do morro"), making his fortune from a void of legal control.[134]

Resident entrepreneurs often moved quickly beyond simply renting space. In every community, residents with the skill or resources to bring electric lines to their homes sold pirated electricity to other households in the favelas' interiors, often combining the practice with shack rentals.[135] In most favelas surveyed by Vitor Tavares de Moura's commission in the 1940s, there were also small stores, called *biroscas,* that operated out of favela shacks. Most of these were simple family businesses, operated by residents who supplied their neighbors with tiny quantities of food and basic household supplies. In the Botafogo favela of Santa Marta, for example, resident and local authority Antônio José Lopes pointedly told a *Globo* reporter in 1948 that the hill's *biroscas* sold only "basic necessities" at "prices lower than those on the outside." Items sold, he claimed, ranged "from matches to ham" but did not include "alcoholic beverages," which were prohibited by neighborhood authorities.[136]

In other cases, though, *biroscas* were owned by outsiders or sold less wholesome wares. The worst among them were pilloried in the press and the Municipal Council, which used them as examples of the supposed moral rot of favela life. In a particularly incendiary 1947 article, for example, the radical newspaper *Vanguarda* profiled "Pernambuco Come Gordo," a resident of the Barreira do Vasco favela, whom the paper accused not only of renting out *barracões*, monopolizing the scrap wood business, and stocking his "store of perdition" with little but "bananas and *cachaça* [cane liquor]," but also of running a brothel where "young people of both sexes" were "being led to the road of perdition." Avoiding crackdowns by cultivating "special" relationships with politicians and police officials, Pernambuco Come Gordo had become "the strong man with iron fists who commands everything, doing whatever he wishes, without being persecuted by anyone, for he is the king of the shacks."[137]

Small-time entrepreneurship didn't usually generate real wealth. The novelist Lúcio Cardoso may have put it best in describing the semi-fictional Thomaz de Aquino, the fat and demanding owner of a "tendinha" (little informal store) and "the better portion of the shacks" on the Salgueiro *morro*, for which Cardoso's 1935 novel was named. "It was already murmured," Cardoso writes of Aquino, "that he had become rich on the sweat of the poor." This, however, was not entirely true: "Thomaz de Aquino was not rich, because money from Salgueiro wasn't going to make anyone rich."[138] Favelas were poor places, and while men such as Aquino looked like millionaires in the midst of such destitution, there was only so much money to be made on wooden shacks, small bundles of matches, and tiny rations of beans, rice, sugar, or cooking oil.

In more than a few exceptional cases, however, favela entrepreneurship did result in real fortunes, and resident entrepreneurs entered another category, thoroughly despised in public discourse: that of the nonresident land grabber, or *grileiro*, said to be rolling in riches ill gained from "exploiting destitution." For municipal Saúde e Assistência official Vitor Tavares de Moura, these figures deserved to be policed as "a separate social type" because they sucked "exorbitant profits" from the favelas.[139] In a 1957 speech recalling his tenure in the municipal government during the 1940s, Tavares de Moura recalled:

> On the Cantagalo *morro*, the Modesto brothers are the ones—and I call them by name because they are *marginais*—they have a luxury apartment in Copacabana and yet live in the *morro*. They own 190 shacks rented at 400 a month, 52 *biroscas* and an electrical grid on which they charge 35 cruzeiros for every shack with fifteen light bulbs. Just think about all of the profit these Modestos took in. They were not one bit modest.[140]

Though the word *grileiro* was used to describe everyone from the lowliest resident rentier to the most exalted baron, its special bile was reserved for those, many of foreign origin, who made their fortunes almost exclusively from the favela business. In both the press and the Municipal Council, these became constant whipping boys for politicians eager to raise public hackles about the favela problem. Typical was the verbal beating given to the "ex-German and current Pole Leonardo Kacsmarklwig, owner of the Terezinha de Jesus *morro*, better known as the Morro do Alemão," whom councilman Tito Lívio denounced for his "keen spirit of iniquity and greed."[141]

The ascent of some of these figures could be truly spectacular. Emilio Turano, whose story will be explored in greater detail below, began as an immigrant shoe salesman, made a fortune from the management of a noble patrimony, and ended up using a few street addresses to claim the two enormous favelas that rose behind them, one of which came to be known as the Morro do Turano.[142] In a similar operation, a Portuguese immigrant, Daniel Gonçalves, began his career as the manager of a tenement on Conde de Bomfim Street, which bordered what would become the Borel favela.[143] By 1931, most of Borel's hill was already controlled by other *grileiros*, but Gonçalves seems to have begun to join the business, renting out bits of the land behind the tenements for shack construction, thus gradually extending their de facto property lines.[144] By the 1940s, he and a partner had bought out the *grileiros* and controlled the hill entirely.[145] Gonçalves, like Turano, seems to have successfully applied the *cortiço* business model to the favela, using an initial precarious foothold to build a fortune from abandoned lands, poor people, and legal uncertainty.

Turano, Gonçalves, and Leonardo Kacsmarklwig all became well known for their supposed exploits, their names public shorthand for everything that was rotten about the business of the favelas. But for pure tawdriness and drama, none of them could compare with Jorge Chediac, a Middle Eastern immigrant who came to be known as Jorge Turco. Chediac, who described himself in judicial documents only as "Arab," began as a small-time slum manager in central Rio. In the late 1920s, he seems to have hit hard times: in default on the rent on at least one of "his" tenements, he sank low enough to allow the goods of his illiterate subletters to be seized for his debt.[146] A year later, one court opponent accused Chediac not only of falsifying signatures on debt receipts but also of being a well-known "lady-killer among cheap prostitutes or seducer of easy married women" and "a repeated, perverse, unrehabilitable criminal."[147] None of this, however, impeded his quick rise in the favela business: by the early 1950s, when he was brutally murdered, Chediac was the acknowledged "owner" of the Morro da União in suburban Coelho Neto, nicknamed the Morro do Jorge Turco in his honor.

Men such as Chediac, Turano, and Gonçalves might easily be thought of as a distinct social type, just as Tavares de Moura had argued. So, for that matter, might each of the other loosely defined "favela constituencies" described above—the wealthy landowners, the small-time land grabbers, the simple squatters, the poor renters, the local political operators, the big-time politicians. Though Chediac, Turano, and Gonçalves were rumored to be *riquíssimos*, they hardly belonged to high society, as Duvivier did. And though politicians undoubtedly struck frequent covert deals with both *grileiros* and moneyed landlords, in public they showered them with derision as *tubarões* (sharks) and exploiters, and did their best to keep a safe distance. Neither big-time *grileiros* nor moneyed society men nor prominent politicians had much to do with entrepreneurial squatters like Salgueiro's Antônia da Conceição, and their publicized relationships with the favela shacks' penniless occupants were stubbornly asymmetrical. The political intermediaries and corrupt judicial, sanitary, and police officials who made the whole extralegal process possible certainly sought as much public distance as possible from the favela morass. In press reports and political speeches, all of these groups were placed in constant opposition; supposedly rapacious favela entrepreneurs, corrupt officials, and vote-grabbing politicians were juxtaposed with their allegedly innocent, ignorant favela "victims."

Yet such distinctions disintegrated quickly as all of these groups' lives and fortunes intersected in the favelas. From the late nineteenth century to the early decades of the twentieth, all of them were locked in a sort of perverse dependence, each relying on intricate and fragile relationships with the others in order to achieve separate and mostly contradictory goals. Capitalists hoped to collect income for rents, or to hold on to lands long enough for them to attain real value; but to do this they needed tenants, managers, and political protectors. Land grabbers tried to use the recognition of favela "tenants" to establish ownership of questionable lands, but their initial foothold often depended on the indulgence or employment of wealthy landholders, their fortunes were built on rents and fees, and their authority often depended on their ability to extract protections and small favors from politicians. Politicians sought to build a political infrastructure in the favelas on the basis of unending "protection" from the law of the land, and yet that political infrastructure depended both on the personal loyalty of residents and the coercive and organizational capacity of local bosses. Residents usually just wanted a patch of soil, but to establish a stable foothold they usually depended not only on their families and neighbors but also on politicians, landlords, and local political operators. Rio's favelas came to exist because they were the places where all of these fragile interdependencies uneasily functioned. Neither marginal nor even covert, the settlements may in fact have been one of the main arenas in which Cariocas of such varying social positions united in common interest.

CHAPTER EIGHT

The Land Wars of Rio de Janeiro

Shared interests and grudging interdependency never made favelas peaceful places. Many of the relationships that sustained them were deeply exploitative or competitive, and stubborn disputes abounded over everything from rent, ownership, and borders to issues of public order and political loyalty. Longtime settlers sought *usucapião* rights that threatened the ownership and authority of *grileiros* and landlords; property owners or *grileiros* sold out to developers whose plans included neither favela residents nor the politicians who protected them; local political bosses sometimes worked arm in arm with the larger favela entrepreneurs, often to the detriment of small-time squatters; and politicians frequently wavered between protecting favelas and meeting the demands of wealthier constituents who found the settlements dangerous, unsanitary, and deeply embarrassing. The conflicts thus generated could turn nasty and violent. Fights broke out between neighbors; individuals and families were beaten and intimidated by both police and hired guns; and homes and even whole settlements were destroyed. There was, of course, much more to favela life than these constant tensions, but they were always in the background of day-to-day life during these communities' formative years.

At the same time, these early troubles differed in frequency, intensity, and scale from the sort of favela conflicts that would arise during the Vargas period and beyond. The reasons were twofold. On the one hand, open space was running out in Rio's center and immediate suburbs by the early 1930s, even as both industry and population began a quick rise.[148] The resulting wave of subdivision and development in the city's less traditional recesses—distant rural suburbs, previously ignored hillsides, swamps newly crisscrossed by modern roads—drove soaring prices and intense speculation, and both encouraged landowners and *grileiros* to cash in on their favela claims, expelling longtime residents along the way. On the other hand, political currents ran in precisely the opposite direction. The favelas matured both as communities and political organizations during the Vargas era, and they found an ever more receptive political audience for claims to real permanence, first among the deepening leftist parties in the 1920s and 1930s, then from Vargas's paternalistic bureaucracy, and then from virtually everywhere in the frantic political scramble of the post-1945 republic. As a result, residents and politicians quickly became as adamant about gaining defensible land rights as landlords were about demanding eviction.

By the end of the first Vargas regime, these two opposing trends had come to a head, and the circumstantial coalition that had sustained the favelas' early growth had splintered into bitter and constant conflict. With the survival of dozens of communities hanging in the balance, residents and land claimants squared off in a series of high-profile court cases; their conflicts quickly spilled out onto the streets and into the halls of government, providing ample fodder for the local press. The fact that so many of Rio's favelas survived was an almost incredible triumph for the communities' residents. But, as the following pages will recount, the manner of that victory rendered it bittersweet. Residents sought real permanence, justified by logics of history, need, and rights; what they mostly received was indefinite tolerance, forged from political convenience, logistical incapacity, and societal impasse. Here, as in so many other areas, poor people's salvation lay in protection from, rather than inclusion in, a society of laws.

RUMBLINGS IN THE URBAN *SERTÃO*

One of Rio's earliest widely publicized land disputes took place in the *sertão carioca*, near Rio's outermost boundaries. As chapter 7 partially recounted, in the 1920s a bankrupt mortgage company called the Banco de Crédito Móvel (BCM) began a series of large-scale and violent expulsions, in a largely successful attempt to subdivide and sell off enormous tracts of agricultural land in Guaratiba and Jacarepaguá. The bank's attempted displacement of rural *posseiros* was hardly unique. Speculators had been grabbing, buying up, and developing Rio's rural land on a massive scale since at least the 1870s; given the indefinite nature of property relations in so many rural districts, it would be surprising if these developments had not come at the cost of widespread and possibly violent eviction.[149] What was distinctive, and modern, about the BCM cases was that they were so bitterly and publicly contested; residents organized themselves and fought back, using every conceivable political, legal, and rhetorical strategy to avoid eviction. Though they did not always, or ultimately, succeed, these rural workers' struggle was a direct and early template for the urban land wars that would follow.[150]

The Guaratiba and Jacarepaguá conflicts began in the early 1920s. In 1891, the BCM had acquired the *fazendas* of Vargem Grande, Vargem Pequena, and Camorim from Benedictine monks whose sugar plantations had hit hard times. The bank soon went into bankruptcy, and for 30 years its holders mostly ignored the already well-settled lands, many cultivated by slave descendants. In the early 1920s, the situation abruptly changed. According to some, heirs of the BCM's shareholders merely attempted to raise rents on their longtime rural tenants, who reacted with fierce protest. According to others, no tenancy agreement had ever existed, and the conflict stemmed from the heirs' illegitimate and violent attempts to reclaim lands their fathers had long since abandoned.[151] Some of the rural workers organized themselves and, assisted by the early populist politician Maurício de Lacerda, sought to buy the contested territories.[152] Others refused to pay for lands that they felt were theirs by right of possession. By the end of the decade, with no compromise in sight, things began to turn uglier. The bank sought widespread evictions on ever-expanding territories, and used violence and intimidation against residents who resisted them; occupants refused to give in and hired an ambitious young lawyer named Vicente Carino to fight for their cause. By the early 1930s, the conflict was already a morass of claims and counterclaims, fated to drag on for the next three decades.

The bank, for its part, marshaled a number of tactics that would become familiar in Rio's twentieth-century land wars. Initially, the BCM worked mostly through the courts, trying to evict residents by means of simple *despejo,* or eviction based on rent default. The legally tricky part of such a case was proving that a rental agreement had ever existed in the first place.[153] Here, the BCM's job was made easier by the fact that most small-scale rural rental agreements were oral during that period; because of this, the bank could establish the existence of tenancy simply by presenting a few witnesses (many with ties to the company) and certifying that they had paid the requisite land tax (a procedure that did not require a property title).

In the lower courts, this strategy often worked. In multiple appeals, however, residents pressed the issue, calling into question the existence of rental agreements and presenting their own multiple witnesses to document long-term occupancy. In the face of such arguments, the higher courts began to balk; in at least five cases in the early 1930s, appellate judges vacated *despejo* orders, citing both the BCM's lack of documentary ownership in Guaratiba and the occupants' multigenerational claims.[154] There was also, in many of these decisions, a note of commonsense logic that deemphasized technical legal criteria. In one case, the judge summarized his decision as follows:

> It is not possible to allow that the owner of certain supposedly leased-out lands can go dozens of years without charging, or at least without showing proof of having charged, any lease fee, and can then, after a long time has passed, without the slightest verbal or written proof of the lease, come and use a notification in hopes of creating the right to evict . . . the occupants of those same lands.[155]

These court battles were accompanied, and surely shaped by, a number of extrajudicial strategies on both sides. The BCM seems often to have resorted to the dirtiest possible tactics, co-opting entire police delegations, buying off notaries, and sending its thugs to beat and assault intransigent occupants. Occupants, for their part, made it their business to give the widest possible publicity to these kinds of abuses. In 1930, barely months after Vargas's revolution, the Guaratiba committee described at the beginning of this section had already traveled to the news offices of the *Diário da Noite*—petition to the Ministério de Trabalho in hand—to tell the world about the bank's burnings, beatings, and lootings. By no accident, three of the five squatters who won appeals against the BCM were members of that committee. In 1931 and 1932, the press campaign continued: both the mainstream daily *O Globo* and the leftist *A Batalha* published multiple articles detailing alleged BCM abuses, and the majority of these profiled residents who either had been members of the 1930 Guaratiba committee or were represented in judicial land battles by Vicente Carino.

These articles often followed similar formulas, telling individual residents' stories in order both to showcase the BCM's alleged brutality and to build a moral case for links between history, virtue, and land rights. In December 1931, for example, *A Batalha* related to its readers the moving saga of Quintino Francisco Guedes, whose cousin Antônio had been a member of the *A Noite* committee the previous year. A semi-paralytic widower, Guedes had been violently expelled from his home of 44 years by Napoleão de Castro and Caetano de Camorim, notorious BCM thugs whose supposedly ferocious barbarity earned them frequent comparisons to the famed bandit Lampião.[156] In describing Francisco Guedes' life, the article clearly meant to tug at readers' sentimental notions of rural virtue:

> This rural worker, 44 years ago, acquired lot #969, on the Estrada de Guaratiba, from Joaquim José de Lacerda. Young and strong, Quintino dedicated himself to the rude work of the countryside. And, little by little, he went about constructing a small house where he and his could take shelter. And, always working the soil, which prodigiously rewarded his efforts, the rural worker became old, surrounded by his family.

The article's author used such evocations to argue strongly that history should hold sway in the allocation of land rights: now that Guedes was widowed, old, and unable to work, it was an outrage that a bunch of opportunistic land grabbers could throw him violently from the home he had taken a lifetime to build.

Residents took pains to bring similar arguments to the highest ranks of government. As noted earlier, the 1930 Guaratiba committee wanted *O Diário da Noite* to publicize their cause, but their memorial was addressed to the Ministry of Labor, and showed keen political sensibility. In 1931, a still more remarkable missive was directed to Vargas himself by José de Lima Soares, the barely literate rural worker whose lands in Jacarepaguá were targeted as part of the same land grab that threatened Guaratiba. Lima Soares accused the BCM, in collusion with the local police, of sending Caetano de Camorim (nicknamed the Lampião de Jacarepaguá) to commit the worst possible abuses "at any time of the day and night." He and his thugs arrested heads of family, burned houses, and even "deflowered maidens," undertaking "the worst barbarities in the middle of the civilized capital." In one particularly awful recent case, Lima Soares claimed, Caetano de Camorim and his thugs "assaulted Domingo Rodrigues Sotellos's property, beat his family, broke his furniture," and "robbed and took over the house." Sotellos was in the hospital with a broken leg, and his family ended up "hiding out in the bush."[157]

Harrowing though the scenes he described were, Lima Soares did not seek to convince the president through shock value alone. In the second half of the letter, he turned directly to the question of rights. The lands' current occupants, he recounted, were the descendants of slaves of the São Bento monastery, who had been allowed by the monks to settle the lands after they were freed in 1864. Though not the lands' legal owners (a fact Lima Soares explained simply by saying that "at that time there were no documents"), the occupants had never been disturbed until the BCM's recent incursions. The BCM and its henchmen, ignoring this history, and seeking to take advantage of the occupants' ignorance ("knowing that the people were all illiterate"), had bought off notaries, police officials, and even a judge's aide, seeking to gain the land through dirty tricks because "they couldn't run anyone out judicially, since they have no title that prove that they are the land's legitimate owners." Lima Soares called on Vargas, both as a man and as the president of a nation of laws, to stop the outrage:

> Senhor Presidente, is it possible that we, men who wear trousers, can stand by and watch such an act of vandalism, such a stupid crime against individual liberty and movement? It is not possible, Senhor Presidente, we demand of Your Excellency an

energetic and immediate remedy and the restoration of the civil and penal codes [because] the revolution only revoked the political portion of the Constitution.

The letter ended with a list of possible witnesses to the outrages, many of whom had been part of the *Diário da Noite* committee: Lima Soares urged haste and noted that "the people have a horrible fear of that [Napoleão] Castro."

Like the favela residents who would later appeal to Vargas in similar terms, Lima Soares received no immediate satisfaction. But his letter made enough of an impression on Vargas and his ministers that they ordered a full investigation. This report, while contesting the involvement of police chiefs and laying the blame for the situation on the prerevolutionary government, documented the BCM's violence and some police collusion with it.[158] It also revealed that the occupants—not satisfied with civil appeals, publicity, and political missives—had on at least one occasion taken the law into their own hands: led by a local tough nicknamed the Preto Bibiano, a "numerous group" of rural workers had performed a citizens' arrest of a BCM employee named Libanio dos Santos and brought him to the 2nd auxiliary district. At other times, they had made more conventional use of the criminal justice system, bringing criminal complaints against the BCM's henchmen, including Caetano de Camorim and at least two police officers. Throughout, residents consistently avoided the police district whose chief they believed to be involved, relying instead on other authorities who were less directly implicated.[159] Years later, when former police chief Frota Aguiar became a municipal councilman, he would still recall these cases, calling the BCM an "assailant of the small cultivators' properties."[160]

The multilayered resistance to the BCM's claims involved any number of actors external to the rural communities of Guaratiba and Jacarepaguá—reporters, sympathetic or ambitious police chiefs, judges willing to give credence to the stories of poor, uneducated occupants with few documents to prove their claims. The young lawyer Vicente Carino resurfaced everywhere, officially representing some 300 evicted families but also acting as a mediator and representative in ways that went far beyond the strict requirements of legal service.

Yet, important as all of these outsiders were, a core group of highly committed residents seems to have been at the movement's heart. Surviving records indicate more than 50 occupants who took part in the group's varied strategies, telling their stories to the press, forming part of the 1930 Guaratiba committee, writing to the president, taking part in citizens' arrests and criminal complaints, and contesting eviction decrees in the civil courts. If their names are any indication, many of these people were related by blood or marriage, and nearly all were engaged in multiple ways. Leopoldino Luiz dos Santos, for example, was a father of six who had been expelled from a small *sítio* called Portão, where his family had lived "for dozens and dozens of years."[161] An original member of the 1930 *Diário da Noite* committee, dos Santos also participated in the citizens' arrest of BCM employee Libânio dos Santos. Luiz dos Santos testified to the 2nd auxiliary district in that case, told his eviction story to at least one reporter, and was also among the first to win a civil appeal. On 16 March 1932, he and a large group of officials and neighbors formed a "caravan" to officially repossess his lands and those of two other victorious families; the group also included lawyer Vicente Carino and one of the local police chiefs. The highly partisan communist daily, *A Batalha*, reported the caravan's day-long sojourn in triumphal and romantic terms: "For more than three hours, mounted on horseback, everyone climbed a steep mountain. . . . Once the [BCM's] eviction was finished, all those who accompanied the caravan, and who had also been victimized, gave themselves over to manifestations of joy, shouting 'vivas' and setting off fireworks." Even a "formidable downpour" didn't "dampen the group's happiness" about the "bank's notorious defeat."[162]

The BCM story did not, in the end, have such a celebratory outcome for most of the rural claimants. By 1932, the bank was already back in court with new and equally questionable strategies, this time calling not for eviction but rather for *reintegração de posse*. In two nearly identical cases, the bank claimed that two illiterate rural workers had bought its lands and then defaulted on their payments. The BCM presented the purchase and sale contracts and also called on local witnesses. In both cases, however, other occupants—Turíbio and Manoel Luiz dos Santos, quite likely brothers of Leopoldo—asked the courts to stay the case. According to them, it was all an elaborate ruse; the bank and the supposed evictees had colluded on a fake sale agreement meant to trick the courts into accepting the BCM's ownership. In reality, they said, these lands were theirs, and the witnesses who had testified were just the bank's *capangas*. This claim seems to have held water: one of the bank's witnesses was Napoleão de Castro, a defendant in several of the occupants' criminal complaints, and another was none other than Caetano Francisco de Assis, also known as Caetano de Camorim—the famed and feared "Lampião de Jacarepaguá."

Despite Vicente Carino's impassioned arguments, neither of these complaints was of any avail; the BCM emerged victorious. While these particular cases may have gone on to be won on appeal—we have no further record of them—the region's long-term history also seems to have evolved in favor of the BCM and other, similar outfits.[163] Over the course of the 1940s and 1950s, rural *grileiros* continually resurfaced in Municipal Council debates and press reports, their violence and exploits assuming legendary proportions. Breno da Silveira, a *vereador* and congressman who was unusually outspoken on favela land issues, became something of a champion for the rural workers' cause, hailing their virtue as pastoral laborers who supplied the Federal District's tables, and attacking the BCM and a number of other legendary *grileiros* for mounting a frontal assault on the rural districts' peoples and ways of life.[164] Occupants could still occasionally block *grileiro* actions,[165] often with the help of an engineer named Pedro Coutinho Filho. The Municipal Council came forward in favor of rural workers as well, even passing legislation meant to regularize the situation of rural regions, where, councilmen asserted, as many as 90 percent of occupants had no formal claim to their lands.[166] But the legislation seems to have been enforced only patchily, and few who occupied territory coveted by the BCM could secure the *usucapião* rights that would have precluded future eviction. Over the long term, the speculators' incessant litigation and continued violence chipped away at the smallholders, and the *grileiros* became the legal owners of the territory, part of which would eventually become one of the hottest land markets in the city.[167] Councilman Breno da Silveira summed up the case in 1948, making reference to a colleague who had successfully defended his own family's properties against the BCM's pretensions:

> The ones who triumph in the much talked-about *usu-capião* [sic] cases are those who have resources, like councilman Caldeira de Alvarengo, . . . a prestigious politician who had the means to pay good lawyers to struggle against the BCM, one of the big landowners' greatest guides in the Federal District. Even so, the councilman . . . took ten years to triumph. Imagine . . . a small-time squatter, ignorant and without any means whatsoever. He is forced to give up in the middle of the struggle, and what happens is what we are now seeing.[168]

What they were seeing was the last throes of a battle that would end with the surrender of these rural places to real estate development. It is revealing of the extent of this dispossession that the most complete modern account of the territorial history of Vargem Grande, Vargem Pequena, and Camorim does not even mention the BCM conflict, noting only the bank's continuous ownership from 1891 until the lands were subdivided and developed as summer homes in the 1940s and 1950s.[169]

URBAN OUTBREAKS

The sheer drama of the BCM conflicts gave them a higher profile than that of many others in the 1930s. But during the same period, urban settlements also began to witness breakdowns in the informal truces that had allowed their early growth, and the result was a similarly volatile mix of litigation, resistance, and violence. Conflict and eviction were nothing new in central Rio; small-scale private expulsions were quotidian occurrences, and massive public health eradications had a history that ran from the *cortiço* demolitions of the 1880s and 1890s right through the Santo Antônio evictions of the early twentieth century. But several of the disputes that emerged in the 1930s were qualitatively different than these, and they recalled the BCM conflicts in critical ways. They mostly began on the initiative of private owners or *grileiros* eager to cash in on their investments. Yet they involved lands that by that point had grown into substantial, and significantly coherent, communities, whose members followed the rural squatters' lead in using sophisticated and multifaceted strategies to resist eviction.[170] Like the BCM struggles, these marked the beginning of the all-out property wars that would wrack the city through the 1970s. Unlike the struggles of the countryside, however, the favela conflicts often ended in substantial victories for their occupants.

Because of the centralized and often repressive nature of the Vargas government, many of Rio's urban land conflicts were negotiated away from public view before 1945. Yet, even so, archival traces of eviction threats and citizens' reactions remain. In the early 1930s, as recounted above, threatened residents of Santo Antônio, Mangueira, and Jacarezinho were already writing letters to the president, sending personal committees to Catete Palace and other halls of government, seeking the aid of well-connected political intermediaries, and even sometimes prevailing in court.[171] According to geographer Maria Lais Pereira da Silva, residents of the São Carlos favela in central Rio employed a similar array of tactics when they were threatened with eviction by a private "owner" in 1932.[172] They wrote to Vargas, hired a lawyer, and sent committees to the press; in 1937, long before most analysts recognize the existence of organized resistance among *favelados*, they even established the "Sociedade dos Trabalhadores Humildes do Morro de São Carlos."[173] In many of their public communications, São Carlos's occupants echoed the rural workers of the *sertão carioca*, emphasizing critical arguments about law and rights. In a neat inversion, they alleged that the supposed owner had obtained his court order through dirty tricks, effectively using the law's technical processes for illegitimate means; at the same time, residents argued that their protests were questioning the court's orders in order to defend their "rights," effectively using extralegal means to fulfill the law's intentions. In the end, Vargas stayed the São Carlos eviction ruling, and residents eventually overturned it on appeal.

In the Salgueiro favela, also threatened by a private owner in the early 1930s, occupants used still more varied strategies and arguments.

As indicated above, Salgueiro—with one of the longest histories of any favela—in many ways exemplified the early strategic alliance of squatters', owners', and *grileiros'* interests. In the early 1930s, however, all of that began to change when several residents went to court demanding *usucapião* rights to their hillside properties.[174] Most likely spurred by the *usucapião* cases, the hill's supposed owner (Dona Maria Joanna Miranda de Araujo, Condêssa de Mantebrial) sold the land she claimed in July of 1933. The purchaser was none other than Emilio Turano, the Italian shoe salesman and tenement manager who was at that point already a decade into the tenement and favela business. Remarkably, just three days after the sale—and long before Turano officially notified the occupants of it—three residents had already whipped out an intriguingly worded telegram to Getúlio Vargas himself:

> Undersigned live [on] Salgueiro hill . . . many years' residence, having grown children born there. Now a gentleman has appeared who invites their evacuation in name [of] false rights never claimed. Cannot obey this order because have the *usocapião* [sic] of these lands cultivated and improved by undersigned, disposed to defend domain to last breath. Are poor people living life of suffering and ask of Yr. Exc. government protection, even to avoid disagreeable incidents as there are families wanting heated action that signatories have tried to contain. Will send memorandum explaining but ask Yr. Exc. for immediate orders to police in order to avoid violence.

In that short space, Aquino, de Sá, and Gonçalves both echoed the arguments marshaled by victims of the Banco de Crédito Móvel and added to them an urban urgency and tension. Some of their claims were moral—as poor, long-suffering people whose children had been born on the hill, they were asking for the traditional "protection" owed to the powerless by a Brazilian ruler. Elsewhere, though, the petitioners demanded far more than paternalistic charity, asserting *usucapião* rights in a language that showed a strong connection with rural life: not only had these lands long been occupied (as *usucapião* would require), they had also been "improved and cultivated" by the shantytown residents, a fact with considerable weight in rural land claims.[175] What's more, these residents were not willing simply to sit back and wait for the president's grace; they would fight for their rights, and the signatories could not prevent violence if something was not done.

There is no sign that Vargas intervened directly in the case. But the residents forged ahead. Reportedly led by the famed *sambista* Antenor Gargalhada, they mobilized Salgueiro's samba school to struggle against the eviction, and they urged their lawyer (João Luis Regada) to argue for *usucapião* in the name of Basileu Xavier Valentim and other longtime residents.[176] On 9 January 1934, the future juridical luminary Nelson

Hungria ruled in the occupants' favor, reportedly noting that although Valentim had "not proved the trinteniary precept on all of the disputed territories," he nonetheless surely had "docile and peaceful possession" of his house and those he had built for third parties, and that in any case "the inhabitants of the *morros*, because of their humble station, cannot but deserve Justice's aid."

The case ran into some roadblocks after that early triumph, but it would eventually become an emblem of the potential power of Salgueiro's multifaceted strategy. Initially, Turano's successful appeal restricted Hungria's verdict to Valentim's own lands, leaving all of the other residents open to eviction.[177] In response, Salgueiro's lawyer, João Luis Regada, took on at least five new *usucapião* clients (including Antônia Maria da Conceição, whose claim was discussed above) and continued to fight in court.[178] The whole affair reached its startling conclusion some ten years later, when Judge Heráclito de Quieroz, in a stridently worded decision, rejected Turano's final eviction claim. Noting that Turano had paid no taxes on the shacks he claimed, and also that rent law would prevent the residents' eviction even if Turano could prove they were tenants, Quieroz went on to attack the very practice of speculation:

> [These] lands, held for long years diuternally and uninterruptedly, occupied in good faith by proletarians sheltered in humble huts, were long ago relegated to oblivion by their supposed possessors, who only remember them now because of the valorization that has resulted from the city's development, to which they contribute nothing. These are abandoned areas, on the *morro*'s slope, never placed in the public register, where Tijuca's population formed their favela more than 50 years ago, and they remained there until the *grileiro*, by means of artifice, came to perpetuate his usurpation.[179]

With those words, Quieroz asserted a combination of moral and legal reasoning that would be echoed often by lawyers and politicians in the tumultuous land wars of the 1940s and 1950s: *grileiros* were parasites, the lands had been abandoned, and no paper trick would justify expelling the hardworking "proletarians" who had made their homes on the hill. Quieroz also seems to have guaranteed Salgueiro residents their long-sought peace of mind: occupants and politicians alike would later point to the 1944 decision as the hill's liberation from Turano's claims. Though other threats would surface when Turano's heirs attempted to auction the hill off in 1958, none dislodged the settlement as a whole.[180] In the relatively small world of Rio's favelas in the 1940s, this kind of permanence was everything, and it would not be long before activists from dozens of other threatened *morros* would marshal equally heterogeneous strategies in defense of their own perceived rights.

The Battles of Rio de Janeiro

The most intense phase of Rio's twentieth-century property wars broke out after the end of the Estado Novo in 1945, as land values and immigration accelerated, the favela issue moved to the center of a rowdy political stage, and the federal government lost much of its ability to enforce behind-the-scenes compromises. During the Estado Novo, the Carioca courts had often allowed considerations of legislation's social effects to trump the law's strict application. After Vargas's fall, the courts unleashed a flood of eviction decrees, which together threatened tens of thousands of homes.[181] At the same time, Rio's Communist Party, which won a majority in Rio's 1947 Municipal Council elections, placed the issue of court-ordered evictions at the center of its political strategy, framing the issue in terms of rights rather than charity, and forcing members of any other party that hoped to gain the favela vote to follow suit. This politicization, which endured even after the Communist Party was banned in 1948, would prove central to the favelas' survival.

In the late 1940s, the issue of property ownership at first appeared to be only one of many swirling around the favela phenomenon, and the courts were only one of several public entities jockeying for a say in the settlements' destinies. Prefects, city councilmen, national legislators, cabinet ministers, and President Eurico Dutra himself all had something to say on the issue, as did journalists, social service workers, and church officials. Legislative commissions and governmental agencies began to proliferate; their proposals included shacktown eradication and the deportation of rural migrants; the construction of suburban public housing; and even the on-site urbanization and civic/social "education" of favela communities. To complicate the picture still further, the favelas' full potential as political bases became apparent with the return of legal elections, and every Carioca political party jumped into the fray, setting up elaborate networks of local political operators (*cabos eleitorais*) and promising the moon and the stars to residents willing to pledge their votes.

In this heady atmosphere, it was not initially obvious that favela permanence would be viewed as a viable public policy option, or that private court battles—rather than urban planning and health policy—would be the main arena of struggle. Following the basic ideological lines that had been drawn by Prefect Henrique Dodsworth and by Saúde e Assistência head Vitor Tavares de Moura in the early 1940s, the municipal government initially focused its public debates not on whether to eliminate the favelas but rather on how and when to do so. While more tolerant politicians and officials might grant the favelas a temporary reprieve or offer charitable help and "education," such aid was never meant to grant rights or facilitate permanence. Several bills introduced during those first legislative sessions advocated the deportation of many favela residents to the rural hinterland, and demanded the immediate enforcement of the 1937 building code's ban on favela expansion or repair. Even the Fundação Leão XIII—the joint Catholic-municipal venture that would be critical between 1947 and 1954 in building up the favelas' infrastructure and preventing mass evictions—had as part of its initial mission the favelas' eventual eradication.

Relatively quickly, however, residents and left-leaning members of the Municipal Council—especially socialists and communists—began to frame the favela question in terms of residents' rights to occupy their lands permanently. The catalysts were a stream of eviction threats, both private and public; in 1947 and 1948 alone, sixteen large-scale expulsion threats were widely reported.[182] Though several came from the civil courts, most of these private suits were instantly bogged down in appeals. Thus the most consequential evictions during these years were from public lands, and were carried out because of public health and building code violations, often on the personal order of Prefect Mendes de Morais. Publicly ordered expulsions intensified especially during the so-called Battle of Rio de Janeiro in 1948, which started as the councilman and journalist Carlos Lacerda's attempt to focus municipal attention on the complexity of the favela problem, and which ended as a widely publicized municipal crackdown.[183]

Many of these public evictions were quite violent, and the majority brought municipal police (and especially *guardas municipais*) into direct conflict with resistant occupants. In 1947, for example, municipal police armed with "machine guns and automatic pistols" destroyed some 60 shacks behind a cemetery in the central neighborhood of Catumbi; each dwelling, the residents claimed, represented some 500–600 *cruzeiros* of investment, and many people had lived there for more than 30 years.[184] During a 1948 eviction in the Morro dos Macacos—built on the public grounds of an old zoo in the north-zone neighborhood of Vila Isabel—*O Globo* described the arrival in June 1948 of a "a great bellicose apparatus": municipal policemen, "armed with portable machine guns and automatic pistols," who went up and surrounded the hill while workers from the city's Limpeza Pública destroyed more than 100 shacks with "axes, picks, and other 'arms' of destruction."[185] In the tumult, a local boss was badly beaten, and various residents lost everything they had; because of such abuses, the *Correio da Manhã* called the police the "SS."[186] In 1948, the *Diário de Notícias* summed up the sensationalist view of such expulsions, noting that, in a typical case, "the residents, dumbfounded, are expelled from their huts and improvised homes, and the flame of the law (a mixture of officious stupidity with gasoline and matches) transforms everything into a mountain of ashes."[187]

Awful though it was, this sort of violence also served to place favelas and their residents squarely at the center of public attention, a position that activists and their allies used to great effect. Many of their strategies were familiar. Like Guaratiba's *posseiros*, the threatened communities sent frequent committees to a wide array of local newspapers, which generally complied by printing sympathetic stories and photographs highlighting the favelas' plight.[188] Activists also continued to send letters and delegations to meet with the president, his ministers, and the prefect, and they tried to establish critical relationships with lower-ranking governmental officials more directly responsible for their fate.[189] The organizing of neighborhood committees also continued, now sometimes impelled by religious agencies like the Fundação Leão XIII or carried out in cooperation with local politicians.[190] In the Rio Municipal Council's very first post-dictatorship session, for example, the communist Octávio Brandão Rego proudly announced the formation of the Lakeshore Resident's Association, meant "to defend the [residential] rights established in the Constitution, among Brazilians' most fundamental rights." The communist press continued to agitate for such organization in subsequent years.[191] Not to be outdone, and recognizing the political potential of such organizations, by 1948 more mainstream politicians, such as Lígia Maria Lessa Bastos (UDN), Anésio Frota Aguiar (PTB), and José Osório de Morais Borbosa (ED), were actively collaborating with residents' associations from Catacumba and elsewhere.[192]

The new political context also allowed for significant strategic innovations. With the reopening of the city council and the national legislatures, local residents became constituents of particular representatives or senators, and a host of local party bosses set up shop to court favela residents' votes. Municipal Council representatives in particular dove headlong into favela politics; communist Council members, such as Octávio Brandão, Arcelina Mochel, and Amarílio Vasconcelos, seemed to have the strongest initial presence; but others, such as Breno da Silveira, Frota Aguiar, Sagramor di Scuvero, Lígia Bastos, and Geraldo Moreira, rapidly caught up. While many politicians quickly became famous for appearing in the favelas only around election time, others became consistent advocates for everything from infrastructural improvements to urban permanence. In a constant stream of letters, delegations, and requests, residents placed particular emphasis on infrastructure, not only because of its intrinsic value but also because even the smallest urban convenience was seen as a small entrenchment, a movement toward urbanity that would make any future expulsion less viable. In making such requests, some occupants hedged their bets by contacting representatives from across the political spectrum. Jacarezinho, for example, eventually found its self-proclaimed champion in PTB politician Geraldo Moreira, but its residents were careful in the midst of a 1947 eviction threat to send a long appeal to politicians from the archrival UDN party —including samba singer Ari Barroso, who read the letter aloud to the Municipal Council.[193]

Residents sought also to entrench their communities by establishing links with other, intermediate players, both inside and outside the government. The Santa Marta favela, in the south-zone neighborhood of Botafogo, was exemplary.[194] Already in 1948, the community had a neighborhood committee of five "longtime residents," which took it upon itself to regulate "the area of hygiene and cleanliness, maintaining order and respect among the inhabitants." That committee, and the community as a whole, had established close ties with Padre Veloso, the rector of Rio's Catholic University, and Dona Laura do Rego Monteiro of the Nossa Senhora Auxiliadora parish, which also offered the community material support.[195] After 1946, Nossa Senhora Auxiliadora combined its efforts with those of the Fundação Leão XIII, the joint city government–Catholic Church venture that was the first to promote a limited form of urbanization in a number of Carioca favelas.[196] This kind of alliance with Catholic Church leaders extended to numerous favelas, where nuns and priests sympathetic to the line of thought that would develop into liberation theology often stood at the front lines of community organization and defense.[197]

Residents' outreach efforts also extended to the police, both in Santa Marta and elsewhere. According to *birosca* owner and longtime resident Antônio José Lopes, Odilar José Lopes, another of Santa Marta's "longtime residents," was "the element linking the *morro* and the police. If there's any abnormality in the area, Senhor Odilar is called and can serve as lawyer, prosecutor, or defense."[198] Presumably, this kind of mediation prevented the police from interfering in *morro* affairs except in the most extreme cases, and the threat of police intervention lent Odilar and other local authorities the clout they needed to keep order in the area. With order came respectability, as well as a lower risk that police intervention might escalate into calls for the hill's eradication. Similar arrangements were common early on in São Carlos and Chapeu Mangueira, where community leaders recall the active intervention of the neighborhood committee in all sorts of internal disputes.

When this whole range of pacific tactics failed, residents often chose to exert public pressure more directly, through marches, mass visits to the chambers of government, and open resistance. Already in 1947, residents threatened with eviction had marched en masse to the *prefeitura* and were occupying the municipal chambers from time to time, often at the urging of local politicians.[199] A good part of the Catumbi favela's population, threatened in late 1947, reacted in dramatic fashion, descending "to demonstrate on the city streets at various times, bringing their appeal to the people, and demanding in front of the Catete and Guanabara Palaces that the demolition be suspended."[200] When police surrounded the hill with armed men in an attempt to stop those marches, 88-year-old grandmother Josefa Teixeira da Silva took the lead, allegedly crying "Let them kill me!" as she charged ahead.[201] Paper leaflets urging similar resistance rained down on some south-zone favelas in 1948;[202] during that same year, residents in places like the Morro dos Macacos and Cantagalo turned words into action, physically resisting demolition. As rumors swirled about the scope and scale of the prefect's eradication campaign, one south-zone resident, described as an "old African who helped Brazil to grow," exclaimed to a reporter, "They will only pull me from this shack dead!"[203]

In all of these actions, residents and their allies justified their stances in enormously varied ways. At the simplest extreme, pity was the hook; newspapers, especially, highlighted the violence and brutality of the evictions, printing tragic profiles and abundant pictures—mainly of broken homes, tearful women, wide-eyed children, and the elderly, but also of the suited and serious men who led the communities' public appeals, quite the opposite of the derelicts and thieves said to inhabit the favelas.[204] Need, morality, and common sense were also prime arguments. Mass eviction was an "inhuman measure" that threatened to "throw to the street hundreds and hundreds of people, whose only crime is poverty."[205] The places where residents were being sent to build new shacks were far away—many were assigned to public lands in suburban Penha—and the time spent constructing new homes would take breadwinners away from their work.[206] Most importantly, as one south-zone residents' committee wrote to councilman Breno da Silveira, the removals threatened residents' ability to contribute to society through honest labor: "The residents have organized their lives in Leblon and nearby. They are workers, domestics, washerwomen, cooks; many work in civil construction. How can they be brutally removed from there?"[207]

All of these arguments echoed Vargas's Estado Novo rhetoric with their emphasis on pity, virtuous poverty, and work as a source of entitlement; by the 1940s, such themes were so deeply embedded in Carioca political culture that few dared publicly to argue with them. Other strains of the debate pushed the envelope further, stepping firmly over the line between supplication and demand and articulating a rights-based argu-

The Praia do Pinto favela, 1941. Courtesy of the Arquivo Geral da Cidade do Rio de Janeiro.

ment rooted in favela residents' intrinsic connection to the city that attempted to eject them. One such view was forwarded in 1948 by Praia do Pinto resident Timoteo Barbosa, a moustached "sexagenarian" who reminded a journalist of "those virile figures" from their "grandfathers' times" with the "composure of a poor but honorable man." Barbosa said that the struggle for permanence was one in which residents were "trying to save our very existence, our past and our future." The people who lived in the Praia do Pinto had earned their place in the city by helping to construct it, and any attempt to take them from their homes violated a fundamental right:

> How can carpenters, masons, joiners, etc., all of the people who live in those *morros* and help to construct buildings in Leblon, in Copacabana, in the center of the city, move to infested lands, far from the city? And who will guarantee our permanence there? I have lived with my family for eight years in this little favela. I myself constructed this little shack, which is the only thing that I possess, with these hands that God gave me."[208]

Barbosa clearly understood the projected move to Penha as an expulsion from the city, which he and his neighbors had helped to build, and of which his favela settlement was very much a part. Many of his fellow shanty residents took this argument still further, not only linking favela permanence with rights to the city but also claiming both as entitlements rooted in their long service in a rural world still closely linked to Brazil's slaveholding past. As rumors flew in 1947 and 1948 of proposed expulsions and mass deportations of favela residents to the countryside, elderly occupants minced no words in linking favelas, urban life, and freedom. In a 1948 interview, Santo Antônio resident Joaquim Lopes recounted, "In Minas, I worked like a mule for others. Stuck to the handle of the hoe day and night. I came here to not die from hunger. And from here I am not going back to that wretchedness. Only if they kill me." One of his neighbors chimed in, adding that she was not about to "fall into the folly of going back to the fields to live as the slave of the *senhor do engenho*, without a bit of land."[209] The next month, Josefa Teixeira da Silva, the 88-year-old grandmother who had taken the lead in Catumbi's public demonstrations, exclaimed to a reporter, "Josefa is not the one who is going to be anyone's slave in the fields. Josefa is poor, but she has shame and dignity, son."[210] That same year, an article in the nationalist daily *O Mundo* fleshed out the argument in its portrait of Fernando Rosa da Silva, a 68-year-old rural migrant and Praia do Pinto resident whose "close ancestors came from faraway Africa and helped to construct this magnificent Brazil." According to the paper, da Silva, "tired of exploitation, fled to Rio," where "his purely African type" made it impossible for him to find housing anywhere but in a favela. When asked about the potential mass eviction, da Silva objected forcefully, simultaneously evoking a version of Vargas's social contract and rights born of thankless rural servitude:

> They want to beautify the city at our expense. So our lives and work mean nothing. And the children that I gave the fatherland. And the right to live in peace? We helped to make this great city. We constructed the skyscrapers, the *palacetes*, and they don't even want to allow us to live in the wretched cardboard shacks we live in. But, Mr. Reporter, you can write in your paper: I will only leave my home dead. I couldn't continue living after being expelled from my own house, I wouldn't even have anyplace to go. I am 68 well-lived years old. I worked like a slave. I came from the countryside fed up with exploitation, and I am not going back there as an old man.[211]

Ten days later, da Silva's neighbors adopted his words as their mantra, sending a letter to councilman Breno da Silveira that bracingly concluded, "We are not animals, *senhores vereadores*, nor slaves. We are not anyone's property, we are free citizens with the right to seek our own betterment. And the government's responsibility is to help those who want to work and produce."[212]

There is no telling the extent to which outsiders collaborated in writing these words, nor the degree to which the letter represented the views of most favela residents. But the entire array of arguments and strategies marshaled by the residents and their political and journalistic allies was often enough to stop the *prefeitura* in its tracks. Definitive legal solutions were not forthcoming. A radical Municipal Council bill, which would have prevented all expulsions until new housing was built, faded quickly after the Communist Party was banned in 1948; the municipal government, citing the 1937 building code, frequently refused to allow favela residents to make even the smallest repairs on their shacks; and small-scale demolitions and threats continued to surface throughout the 1950s. But the Municipal Council did pass a resolution against the 1948 Cantagalo eviction, and informal political pressures slowed or stopped most other expulsions. As late as 1960, virtually all of the threatened communities located on public lands remained in place, never enjoying real security, but at least anchored to the city by the combined weight of community resistance, populist politics, and scarcely viable alternatives.[213]

PRIVATE WARS: JACAREZINHO AND THE SHIFTING TERRAIN OF THE FAVELA DEBATE

Expulsions from privately owned lands were a different story, and it was for this reason that property eventually emerged as the most explosive issue in the favela debates of the post-1946 republic. Although many of the eviction decisions that appeared in 1947 were bogged down in appeal, they resurfaced in full force by 1949. Some courts did eventually deny private land claims, but the vast majority did not; the result was stalemate. On one side stood the courts and the police forces, charged with putting civil rulings into effect, as well as a number of political allies who advocated the shacktowns' eradication. On the other stood residents and the politicians who linked their careers to the communities' defense, all of whom harnessed every resource to argue their vision that right, and rights, lay on the other side of the courts' ruling. The critical question at the center of the standoff was whether or not the same balance of forces that had temporarily blocked most expulsions from public lands would be strong enough to overrule property rights duly confirmed by Brazil's highest courts.

One of the first fronts in these new legal land wars was the north-zone community of Jacarezinho. The settlement—the same one that had fallen under Darcy Vargas's protection in the early 1940s—had unusually strong and multifaceted political connections, as well as an extraordinarily coherent internal organization; in many ways it embodied the coincidence of interests that had sustained the favelas' early growth. Jacarezinho had originated on lands claimed by one Mário de Almeida. Although he was perceived as a "benfeitor" by some residents,[214] Almeida seems to have followed the path of many other landowners before him, first renting settlers small plots carved from abandoned territory—much of it swamp—and then attempting to evict them as land values rose in the booming industrial neighborhood that grew around the shacktown. Court threats were initially held off by residents' wily recourse to Darcy Vargas, but neither the first lady nor her husband nor the Legião Brasileira de Assistência—which sanctioned the settlement in the mid-1940s—did anything to ensure residents permanent land rights after the dictatorship's end.[215] In October 1947, Almeida, now acting through a company called Concordia Sociedade Imobiliária, secured an order confirming his ownership from Rio's Fifth Civil Court.[216]

The residents' response reflected their long political experience. Within a few days, they had sent committees to Prefect Mendes de Morais, the municipal secretary of finance, and to President Dutra himself, appealing for help and asking that the hill be expropriated by the city along outlines already drafted by Atila dos Santos Couto, the politically agile *grileiro* and intermediary who had been named as one of the defendants in the suit.[217] The letters were printed in various newspapers, which received their basic message sympathetically; though residents recognized Almeida's property rights, they had nowhere else to go, the lands had long stood empty, and the Vargas regime (though admittedly "the last government, from the dictatorial era") had made them promises that ought to be kept.[218] Residents also pointed to the significant urbanization that had already gone on in Jacarezinho—"streets, water, electricity, and even schools"—implying that such investment had made their shacktown a true neighborhood, which could not simply be wiped from the city's face.[219]

Initially, the case was suspended on appeal. While waiting for the appeal to play itself out, residents and allies worked in various and innovative ways to strengthen Jacarezinho's standing. Municipal Council members, led principally by the UDN's iconoclastic Breno da Silveira, introduced several measures that would have fortified the community's infrastructure: bringing it a post office, officially recognizing its streets, and appropriating a million *cruzeiros* for the community's "urbanization."[220] The Fundação Leão XIII worked in a similar fashion, simultaneously promoting urbanization, social work, and its own particular brand of community organization.[221] At the same time, politicians from across the political spectrum began to echo the residents' own argument that Jacarezinho was different from most favelas. Many of its homes were made of brick, and it contained numerous well-capitalized small businesses; it was, in short, one of relatively few "decent" communities whose residents were workers rather than *malandros*, and whose lands and homes could reasonably be reformed on-site to create a true neighborhood. In August 1948, the efficacy of these multiple lines of action and argument seemed confirmed when President Eurico Dutra and Prefect Mendes de Morais made a widely publicized visit to the hill, promising that none of its residents would ever be evicted until fully urbanized housing was available.[222]

Less than a week after the president's visit, however, the fourth Câmara of the Tribunal de Justiça showed itself unswayed by his pronouncements, upholding the Fifth Civil Court's eviction ruling. On 30 November 1948, Judge Augusto Moura—rumored by some papers to be a vehement opponent of Getúlio Vargas—informed residents of the *reintegração de posse*, and on 16 May the court issued a *despejo* order for somewhere between 10,000 and 20,000 people, to be enforced by the military police on 20 May, with the especially harsh stipulation that residents would not receive compensation for the "imprestável" (useless, junky) material with which they had constructed their homes.[223]

By the next day, a residents' committee had contacted the press, the president, and the prefect to demand intervention. The popular Rádio Tupi aired the issue as well, and various dailies ran scathing (and, in some cases, disingenuous) exposés of Almeida and his machinations. For example, Venerando da Graça, a future councilman, published an article in *O Radical* on 17 May that seemed designed to exploit every conceivable sympathetic cliché in service of the residents' cause.[224] He described Mário de Almeida as "a rich man" with "mountains of *terras devolutas*" that he neither used nor needed nor cultivated. The lands' first residents had arrived hungry, thirsty, cold, and desperate, "without clothes, without beds, without money, without any protection whatsoever," left to their own devices "when the right to live in a house definitively abandoned the poor." Almeida had pretended to accept them, allowing Jacarezinho's spectacular growth, only to sell the settlement off the moment he realized its potential worth. Da Graça proclaimed Almeida "a feudal lord of 30,000 tatters, of 30,000 tortures." After tugging at his readers' heartstrings with the laments of a destitute mother of four, he ended the article by evoking fear of a general revolt, quoting a passerby whom he described as possessing "they eyes of a rebel" and "the air of someone who would know how to defend his own to the death:"[225]

Who will give a house to me and mine? No one. . . . We are going to be thrown on the street like stray dogs. . . . We are going to be driven out of here with kicks or bullets. But I swear, for my children's happiness, for the love I have for my wife, I will only leave here as a cadaver on its way to the morgue.[226]

Politicians evidently read the papers, and it was immediately clear that the furor over Jacarezinho had transformed the terms of the favela debate. The day after the ruling, nearly a dozen PTB city councilmen proposed a bill authorizing the prefect to expropriate the hill and sell or rent its lands to the current occupants. A similar bill proposed by the communists for the Turano hill in 1947 had gone nowhere, and the Council had virtually ignored a nearly identical one suggested a year later by the UDN's Tito Lívio.[227] This time, however, the atmosphere was charged, not only by the size of the potential expulsion and the proximity of the 1950 elections, but also by the number and variety of political ties binding councilmen to Jacarezinho's residents. In Council debates, Breno da Silveira took his habitual advocacy of rural *posseiros* and urban favela dwellers a step beyond the usual paternalism, urging "the Morro do Jacarezinho's residents" to organize independently "because, organized, they will be a force capable of defending their own interests." Essentially advocating civil disobedience, he said that occupants should not "give ground, in any way, on that spot that belongs to them," because "they have lived there for many years and deserve to continue there in peace, for the Morro de Jacarezinho's residents' laborious spirit is outstanding."[228]

Frota Aguiar, a PTB councilman and former police chief, took similar ideas in a different direction, elaborating this rebellious language into an embryonic legal doctrine that recalled in many ways the Estado Novo's hybrid paternalism. Claiming to know from his experience as a "city police authority" that "there are certain orders that one does not follow,"[229] he went on to criticize the judge's sentence for not heeding "a social necessity," privileging a rigid formalism over a sociological approach that would "study the environment," "measure and weight the interests in play," and always let the needs of the "collectivity" outweigh "individual ambition."[230] As if on cue, a delegation from Jacarezinho entered the Council galleries just as Frota Aguiar finished his speech. His words must have struck a chord with other councilmen, because the notion of law's social and sociological purpose would be at the heart of much political action on favela issues over the subsequent few decades.

Even as Frota Aguiar spoke, the head of the military police, General Lima Câmara, was getting ready to declare his unwillingness to command his troops to carry out the eviction.[231] Geraldo Moreira, the PTB councilman who had already served as Jacarezinho's lawyer and subsequently became its self-declared champion, suggested that time was too short for a formal bill, and that the Council should simply send a delegation of party heads to tell the prefect that they would support any expropriation he decreed. After intense negotiations, which included Fundação Leão XIII officials, Cardinal Jaime Câmara, General Lima Câmara, and even the interim president, Nereu Ramos, Prefect Mendes de Morais proclaimed the community's expropriation on 24 May 1949. For the first time in Carioca history, public authorities had intervened legally to preserve a *morro*'s existence as a poor community.

The Jacarezinho expropriation decree was a critical benchmark. The fact that Mendes de Morais, well known for his desire to eradicate the favelas, felt compelled even symbolically to protect and preserve one such settlement signaled a political and urbanistic sea change—one that was earlier than standard policy-oriented accounts have always suggested, and rooted much more deeply in the communities themselves.[232] Yet the prefect's decree by no means spelled the end of Jacarezinho's story. Mendes de Morais proved more willing to promise expropriation than to deliver it, and the prefecture dragged on for years without making the full payment or land exchange that would have put private claims permanently to rest.

In July of 1951, the Cia. Administradora São Paulo (also apparently connected to Mário de Almeida) surfaced with a Ninth Civil Court ruling that threatened to raze a different part of the hill, unleashing another enormous furor. By that time, Jacarezinho had grown so quickly that some politicians began to fear that it would become "an immense 'Canudos,'" ready to explode in "just and uncontrollable popular revolution."[233] In the face of such worries—and of renewed mobilization among the hill's occupants—the Council passed another expropriation bill, this time substituting a land swap for a cash payment. That bill, too, was enacted, but its enforcement was slow and incomplete; it was only in the mid-1950s that Jacarezinho's lands finally became public.[234]

Thanks to that final expropriation, Jacarezinho quickly became one of Rio's most urbanized favelas. Through the Fundação Leão XIII and the personalistic protection of Geraldo Moreira, the community eventually acquired streets, electric lines, water, health clinics, and schools. In the early 1960s, during Carlos de Lacerda's tumultuous municipal administration, Jacarezinho was one of the few favelas to be graced with a full urbanization project. Throughout these years, residents—perhaps fully aware that the more their settlement looked like a city, the harder it would be to destroy it—worked as quickly as their budgets would allow to transform wood-and-zinc shacks into brick houses, and to build up a volume and complexity of commerce that would prove a magnet for north-zone residents of all stripes.[235]

Yet even with such unusually strong evidence of urban belonging, Jacarezinho's residents still could not claim their lands fully as their own. In October 1949, Mendes de Morais had vetoed a Council bill that would have forced him to guarantee residents' permanence, effectively blocking the Council's attempt to turn a paternalistic salvation into a vehicle for real urban rights.[236] Subsequent legislation made no deeper promises, and politicians, most notably from the PTB, quickly made political loyalty an explicit condition of urbanization.[237] In the end, Jacarezinho won its expropriation because the old coincidence of landowners' and residents' interests had been replaced by an ultimately more resilient convergence. Small-time *grileiros* and entrepreneurs, community organizers, local political operators like Atila dos Santos Couto, politically ambitious lawyers like Geraldo Moreira, communist revolutionaries, Catholic anti-communists, Catholic progressives, and mainstream politicians with even the slightest interest in playing at populist electioneering—all of these groups now depended on each of the others to maintain Jacarezinho's many networks of community, commerce, and power. Yet the fragile coalition that was willing to protect tolerance divided quickly when the envelope was pushed to rights; as a result, residents were still left with something short of the urban citizenship that property ownership might have helped to confer. Jacarezinho had in essence been won because politics trumped rights, not because its residents had themselves become enfranchised. Unentitled permanence thus proved the ultimate legacy of the community's legal battles.

PUSHING THE ENVELOPE

The Jacarezinho expropriation unmistakably raised the stakes in Rio's turf battles. For residents, it proved the value of organization, resistance, and carefully cultivated relationships with politicians and the Carioca press; in many cases, it also led activists to hope for a further radicalization of the movement. For landowners, ironically, expropriation could become an incentive to attempt unfeasible evictions, holding as it did the promise of voluptuous public compensation for otherwise useless land. At the same time, though, "owners" faced increasingly rebellious "tenants," many of whom began to use the Jacarezinho example as a justification for ending rent payments, and the promise of public expropriation often remained unfulfilled. This frequently led owners to follow the model of the BCM in Guaratiba and Jacarepaguá, resorting to violence and corruption to extract income and force evictions.

In the face of such heightened tensions, politicians found themselves at the very heart of a rapidly shifting debate. The Jacarezinho expropriation—in conjunction with other trends, most notably Getúlio Vargas's post-1950 electoral populism and the entrenchment of the Fundação Leão XIII's community development work—had decreased the political feasibility of advocating mass favela eradication. Once expropriation was on the table, the whole range of possible responses to eviction threats shifted to the left. More subtly, residents, politicians, and even some jurists began to develop a number of arguments about the nature of property and the need to fulfill the constitution's injunction that property rights always be limited by "social necessity." For members of the PTB, this generally entailed a need for judges and governors to mediate the needs of the collectivity, or a Catholic duty to temper individual egoism with a sense of common purpose and obligation. For socialists and communists, it could mean something far more transformative: an injunction for poor residents to demand property for themselves on the basis of collective need, constitutional protections, and historical rights. In many ways, the political battles in the first half of the 1950s centered more on the terms upon which the favelas would continue to exist than on the question of their eradication.

These debates played themselves out through a number of dramatic eviction showdowns. The first of these surfaced in the Morro do Turano, a long-embattled north-zone favela whose struggle quickly took on a much more radical and violent cast than had Jacarezinho's. Turano was named for the same Italian shoe salesman–turned–slumlord who had made a failed bid for the ownership of the neighboring Salgueiro favela in the 1930s and early 1940s. Turano's claims to his namesake hill began in the early 1920s, when he left the shoe business and won a contract to sublet an old tenement house at Rua Barão de Itapagipe 393, near the hill's border.[238] From there, he acquired paper title to that and several other buildings on the same street, including numbers 443, 447, and 319. Turano appears also to have established himself as the hill's owner, building a house at its top and also setting up a lucrative business extending illegal electric wires from his asphalt properties to the hill's many shacks.[239]

Some residents have recalled the hill's early years as ones of relative harmony, but things seem to have broken down by the early 1940s. According to then-councilman Breno da Silveira—pinpointed by some residents as the hill's chief political patron in those years—the worst troubles began after 1944, when Turano, frustrated by the final futility of his claims to the neighboring Salgueiro hill, intensified his rent demands from several of Turano's longtime residents.[240] They then "revolted against their exploitation," perhaps inspired by the Salgueiro example, and almost certainly in collaboration with a few outside lawyers and communist activists.[241] They rechristened their hill the Morro da Liberdade, refused to pay further rent, and contracted a young labor lawyer named Benedito Calheiros Bomfim (a communist sympathizer who would go on to become one of Brazil's premier labor law jurists and president of the Instituto dos Advogados Brasileiros).[242] Already in 1946, the residents were politically organized enough to assemble 300 of the hill's families for a large rally in the nearby Praça Saenz Peña, which was addressed by federal congressmen ranging from the Communist Party's Maurício Grabois to the PRP's Café Filho to the UDN's Euclides Figueiredo.[243]

In July 1947, Turano attempted violently to evict some 70 families for nonpayment of rent, and the event was widely reported in the press. Two days later, in response to a memorial from Liberdade's residents, fifteen communist Municipal Council members introduced a revolutionary bill to expropriate the *morro*.[244] This bill, predating Jacarezinho's expropriation by two years, was in many ways much more radical. It justified the expropriation, not with paternalistic appeals to social harmony, but rather with reference to two constitutional articles, one of which stipulated that property rights could be limited by "social interest," and the other of which guaranteed rural *posseiros* title to lands that they had lived on and made productive for ten years or more.[245] What's more, the bill in its original form promised to "regularize" the situation of Liberdade's occupants, guaranteeing them a permanent home there. Like other communist measures introduced that year—including one that would have banned all favela evictions for a year—the Turano bill stalled and then disappeared when the communists were banned from political office in 1948.[246]

Without Council action, and in the face of a series of judicial decisions striking down Turano's claims, the situation turned nasty.[247] In December 1947, according to Breno da Silveira, Turano's lawyer and son-in-law took advantage of "friends and relatives on the police force" and "decided to drive everyone to submission with brute force." He and his police henchmen began to climb the hill, demanding rents; things quickly turned violent, and two residents were killed.[248] Though a large group of Liberdade's prominent neighbors, many of them communists, formed a committee to defend the *morro*, and though residents filed a criminal case against Turano's son-in-law, sporadic violence continued throughout 1948.[249] Much of it seems to have been justified by the community's supposed communist connections.

Perhaps because of these radical political links, and perhaps because Turano/Liberdade lacked Jacarezinho's strong ties with the Catholic church and the Fundação Leão XIII, the community's violence remained mostly under the political radar until the summer of 1949.[250] In the wake of the Jacarezinho expropriation, however, Breno da Silveira began to pressure the Municipal Council to act. Dramatically brandishing in the Council chambers a spent bullet that he claimed had been fired by a police rent collector on the hill, Silveira introduced a new expropriation bill; he also personally arranged a negotiation to halt all rent raids. On 10 October 1949, Silveira's bill—which granted land rights only to the municipality, not to the residents themselves—became the second expropriation measure to be voted into Carioca law.[251]

To an even greater extent than in Jacarezinho, Turano/Liberdade's fate was more stalemate than victory. Precisely because neither Turano nor his heirs never managed to prove their claims to the hill, neither the prefect nor the Câmara was ultimately willing to allocate the 9 million *cruzeiros* it would have taken to make the hill public property; when the Câmara debated one such expropriation bill, in 1950, it was pilloried in the press for catering to the corruption of *grileiros*.[252] Though reports of scattered violence continued to crop up over the years, and though many residents remained politically mobilized and active, the property situation in Turano/Liberdade was never entirely resolved. For the most part, the hill's residents never gained full rights to the homes they had managed to defend, a situation that left them open both to political coercion and to small-scale extortion by local *grileiros*.

On a spectrum of communities that wrung expropriation decrees from Rio's municipal government in the late 1940s and early 1950s, Jacarezinho and Turano stood at the two extremes. Jacarezinho—with its storied history, largely working-class population, deep and multitiered political connections, strong ties with the Fundação Leão XIII, and judicially certified land claimant—was the only private favela to achieve full expropriation during the 1950s. Turano/Liberdade—with its communist ties, violent rent disputes, relative lack of institutional connections, and contentious property status—achieved mainly an informal end to the Turano family's violent attempts to usurp residents' homes. Yet, in functional terms, the two hills had both arrived at a similar impasse. When their communities were energetically mobilized in the face of imminent mass eviction, they could galvanize public sympathy, political ambition, and some degree of genuine idealism in order to retain their homes. But that was as far as it went; once the urgent danger had passed, most residents went back to their more immediate daily worries, and the press backed off except for an occasional exposé or sympathy piece. Some politicians—most notably councilman and undeclared communist Amarílio de Vasconcellos and UDN member–turned–socialist Breno da Silveira—argued consistently for favela occupants' rights to full urban citizenship. But most either saw favela tolerance as a temporarily necessary evil or continued to believe, in relative silence, that the settlements should be eliminated at all costs.

In the half decade after 1949, a number of other contests pushed the limits of Turano's and Jacarezinho's achievements. In the preelectoral climate of 1949–50, public authorities attempted many evictions, most notably in Ipanema's Morro dos Cabritos, where the city's Departamento de Viação e Obras was reportedly acting on the request of a local *grileiro*.[253] The residents organized a mass demonstration at the Câmara Municipal; in the face of these protests and the press's outrage, the eviction was called off.[254]

But the major political focus of the favela debate continued to be issues of private property and judicial evictions. Conflicts broke out on the Rua Ati (in an urbanized section of Jacarepaguá); in the Marechal Mallet favela, in far-suburban Magalhães Bastos; in Lagoa's long-embattled Catacumba favela; and on the Morro da Coroa, in downtown Santa Tereza. Of these, the Coroa conflict—stemming from a judicial ruling that had been handed down in early July—received the most intense public attention. Coroa's judicial claimant, married to the consul of Panama, was a noted medium and the daughter of one of Brazil's most influential nineteenth-century spiritists; that—in combination with the *morro*'s proximity to central Rio, the brutality of the military police who were sent to enforce the eviction, and a violent assault on a reporter trying to cover the story—led to abundant press exposure of residents' outraged protests.[255] On 11 July, Breno da Silveira, along with the UDN's Lígia Bastos, the PTB's João Luis Carvalho, and João Machado, introduced a bill to expropriate the hill, arguing for its passage with reference to constitutional provisions guaranteeing the inviolability of the home, and decrying the expulsion's suddenness and violence.[256] Less than a month later, on 7 August, Breno da Silveira introduced two more expropriation bills, these for the Marechal Mallet and Catacumba favelas.[257]

The 1950 elections significantly changed Rio's political climate. Throughout Brazil, Vargas's turbulent tenure from 1951 to 1954 would be marked by expansive promises, rampant inflation, violent political intrigues, and mass strikes and protests against climbing prices. At the local level, the former statistician and longtime Vargas ally João Carlos Vital became prefect from 1951 to 1952. He was replaced in 1952–54 by Dulcídio Cardoso, a military man and former head of the political police (DOPS), who had also long supported Vargas.[258] While neither man made the favelas' elimination a centerpiece of his administration, both took a relatively tough public stance on the settlements, seeking to restrict their growth and to use the Fundação Leão XIII to "educate" their residents and root out all signs of political radicalism.[259] At the same time, Breno Silveira, Frota Aguiar, and several other Municipal Council members who had been steady advocates of the favelas' urban permanence moved on to the National Congress. The new Municipal Council was dominated by Vargas's PTB and the opposition UDN and PSD, but the communists—who had lost all direct influence on the municipal government with their official expulsion in 1948—also elected several of their sympathizers to the Câmara, this time under the basically empty shell of the PRT.[260] They, in combination with the lone representative from the Brazilian Socialist Party, would catalyze the gradual radicalization of the favela property debate throughout the early 1950s.[261]

In this context, eviction threats continued to pour in. In 1951, the Municipal Council discussed major public expulsions from the Morro da Capela, the "Boogie-Woogie" favela, Favela Frei José, and the Morro do Rádio Nacional. In April of that year, Rio's 5th Vara Cível ordered a mass eviction from the relatively small Morro do Simão, in north-zone Vila Isabel. Residents staged effective public protests, including a mass visit to the Câmara Municipal, and the press eagerly chimed in to condemn the man supposedly behind the court case, dubbed "Seu Zica da Praça Mauá." The Council's new members—led by the unofficial communist Antenor Marques, but with broad cross-party consensus—passed an expropriation decree, which was voted into law on 9 May and later signed by Prefect Vital.[262] Upon its passage, communist sympathizer Aristides Saldanha made a speech that demonstrated the continuing influence of the rights-based argument for favela permanence, stating that: ". . . favela populations can no longer be thought of as illegal, clandestine, or a plague; they are a reality in our capital . . . we must . . . think of *favelados* as Carioca citizens."[263]

A similar tone marked discussions of a number of violent expulsions carried out in 1952–53. In 1952, Colonel Oswaldo Melchiades de Almeida—head of the Municipal Polícia de Vigilância and of the prefect's Comissão de Favelas, and nicknamed by residents the Nero of the favelas—led a new, fiery expulsion near the Lagoa, this time in the Hípica favela.[264] The neighboring settlement of Sacopan was also destroyed that year, with most of its residents sent to nearby Catacumba.[265] In 1953 there were renewed confrontations in Arará—the patch of EFCB land originally settled under Vargas's tutelage in the 1930s—as well as another violent judicial expulsion on the Rua Ati in Jacarepaguá.[266] Though none of these provoked expropriation bills, they did mobilize residents to protest in all of the now customary ways: marching en masse to the Municipal Council or the National Congress, sending committees to meet with the president and the prefect, hiring activist lawyers, pushing for infrastructural improvements that would make mass eviction more difficult to justify, working closely with sympathetic church and neighborhood committees, and negotiating behind the scenes with local police, sanitary officials, and *cabos eleitorais*. Partially as a result, the Municipal Council did actively pursue two rights-based initiatives during these years—one of which would have legalized structures that violated the 1937 building code, and another of which concentrated on the issue of rural property—and also discussed any number of more palliative and paternalistic measures.[267]

It was in the chaotic early months of 1954, however, that a remarkable series of mass *despejo* orders once more forced the property issue front and center. The run began in early February, with an eviction threat on the Morro do Borel that seemed at first much like all of the others. As noted above, Borel was a north-zone community with roots that stretched back at least to the 1910s; since that time, the hill had been controlled by a long line of "managers" claiming to represent its supposedly absentee owners.[268] By the early 1940s, that claim had fallen into the hands of the Portuguese Daniel Gonçalves and a partner named Manuel Pacheco, who lived on the hill, collected rents, and had most direct contact with residents.[269] By one occupant's account, in the mid-1940s the residents—again, possibly inspired by neighboring Salgueiro—began to doubt the authenticity of Gonçalves's claims and refused to pay rent.[270] From there, the breakdown of relations between the "owners" and the residents followed a familiar path. Gonçalves first tried to coerce recalcitrant renters, and then stopped charging rent altogether, a common strategy used by owners who wanted to strip favela tenants of rent-control protections in anticipation of a mass eviction. Gonçalves also prohibited any new construction and seems finally to have decided to sell his "rights" to the hill to a company called Borel, Meuron Imóveis, a subsidiary of the textile firm Seda Moderna, which had purchased a number of buildings on neighboring Conde de Bomfim Street.[271] The company then brought a *despejo* and rescission-of-contract case against Gonçalves, who was listed as the hill's sublessor.[272] According to residents, Gonçalves was in cahoots with the suit and only "pretended to mount a defense"; by early 1954, a mass eviction seemed imminent.[273]

In the early days of February, municipal policemen began to appear on the hill, worrying the uneasy residents. On 1 February, four armed guards told them that the prefect had given them four days to move to a prearranged site in distant suburban Engenho de Dentro; if they did not leave, the punishment would be "prison for the recalcitrant, and the burning and demolition of their little houses." In the face of the threat, residents mobilized quickly. Many gave interviews to the press, often highlighting the human angle of their plight.[274] On 5 February, for example, the communist daily *Imprensa Popular*—the only newspaper to cover the 1954 property disputes from beginning to end—ran a story announcing that 15,000 people were to be evicted from Borel. The story was no journalistic masterpiece—it was published the day after residents were to be evicted, and its population numbers were wrong—but it did serve as an effective tearjerker, featuring pictures of women and children and profiles of longtime occupants.[275] The article stated that one of them, a veteran factory worker named Noémia Ramos, had lived on the hill since 1913 and had constructed her *barracão* "with great sacrifice"; now, "worn down by age, she sees herself about to be thrown in the street." Other prospective evictees included a man partially paralyzed by polio and a 76-year-old woman with no family or help who had lived on the hill for 27 years. To drive the point home, the story ended with a malevolent threat from an anonymous *guarda municipal*, who claimed that the force would return soon to "incinerate all of this."

Sympathy, however, was far from the residents' only recourse; a group of them—"the most radical," according to Manoel Gomes's eyewitness account—also acted quickly in the judicial and political arenas. One of their first moves was to seek out a lawyer. Their choice—which turned out to be fateful both for Borel and for the favela movement more broadly—was Antoine Magarinos Torres, a left-leaning litigator who lived in neighboring Tijuca and had clear sympathies and ambitions for the favela cause.[276] On 2 February, Magarinos Torres and "representatives of 548 families" from Borel filed a criminal complaint against the policemen and the authorities who had sent them to Borel, alleging "coercion in the course of a trial" and "arbitrary use or abuse of power."[277] Though police denied the accusations, stating that they had gone to the *morro* merely to help anyone who might choose voluntarily to move, the complaint received wide press attention. Shortly thereafter, as many as 1,000 Borel residents marched with Magarinos Torres to the nearby home of high-court judge (*desembargador*) Sady de Gusmão. Gusmão could find no actual court order for the *despejo*, and even Melchiades, the Guarda Municipal's chief, denied having given an order for his agents to evict residents.[278] At that, the threat seemed to dissipate, with the official *despejo* put off until late February.[279]

The respite proved uneasy. On 11 February, police from the 17th district responded to a call from Magarinos Torres, who complained that agents were once again climbing the hill to evict residents.[280] The police again pled innocence, alleging that they had come only to aid a resident named José Oliveira Arruda, who had chosen to move, and that destroying his *barracão* upon his departure was part of the agreement.[281] But another Borel resident, José Joaquim Barbosa indignantly objected to "his" shack's destruction, claiming that Arruda had only been his tenant; he filed another official complaint with the 17th district, along with 86 of his neighbors.[282] In the complaint, written by Magarinos Torres, a radical slant was manifest in a description of Barbosa's home as a "humble abode of a worker, as respectable as, or more respectable than, the palaces of the potentates, erected as it was with the sweat of his brow, with no stain of the dishonesty that tends to lurk beneath the foundations of great riches."

On 12 February, "hundreds" of Barbosa's neighbors, in association with Magarinos Torres and the unofficial communist councilman Aristides Saldanha, marched to the National Congress to speak against the eviction and police abuse, protesting indignantly when Congressman Lútero Vargas (Getúlio's son) suggested that Melchiades would never have ordered violence against *morro* occupants.[283] Though no such public displays followed in the following weeks (which coincided with *Carnaval* and the height of summer), one of the movement's leaders—described in the *Imprensa Popular* as "the venerable Casemiro, longtime resident of the *morro* and one of the central figures in the struggle against the pillagers"—recalled "countless meetings" during these months, "including assemblies" with Magarinos Torres and Congressman Roberto Morena, one of Brazil's most important twentieth-century communist politicians.[284]

By April 1954, this groundwork appeared to have paid off. On 26 March, Magarinos Torres and many of the hill's residents filed a new criminal complaint, claiming that ten armed policemen had come to the hill on the previous day and destroyed the shacks of three people, one a fully documented "worker," another an illiterate 102-year-old "watchman," and the last a single mother.[285] According to Manoel Gomes's memoir of these events, Borel, Meuron Imóveis had ordered the demolitions—despite the fact that the hill's fate was still being fought out in the civil courts—in order to clear a road to the hill's peak that would facilitate subdivision and development.[286] In response, on 2 April some 500 people—many of them women and children—marched through downtown Rio to the Câmara Municipal and the Câmara Federal, calling for guarantees against the eviction and also for Colonel Melchiades's resignation as head of the Guarda Municipal.[287] They were met by Breno da Silveira—now a federal deputy and socialist—and his colleague Roberto Morena. In interviews with an *Imprensa Popular* reporter, some protesters dug in their heels; Senhora Teresa Gonçalves, for example, seemed to speak straight to the heart of middle-class fears of revolution descending from the *morros* when she declared:

> Our right to live in Borel is something we will not even discuss. I, for example, will only leave the *morro* under gunfire. That is what we came to tell the councilmen. And if they can't resolve the issue, they can leave it to us.[288]

Days later, on 5 April, residents proved true to Gonçalves' word; when workmen appeared on the *morro* to begin to lay the projected road, they were met with what Manoel Gomes later described as "a tremendous civil war, unplanned and commanded by no one," in which residents attacked the "invaders" with "sticks, rocks, stones, knives, broken daggers, pocketknives, and broom handles" and even "some sticks of dynamite" taken from a local quarry.[289] According to the *Imprensa Popular,* which did not mention the violence in such detail, "the prompt and courageous reaction of the workers put an end to the pillage attempt."[290] That very night, residents also marched to the Câmara Federal, and a meeting was held at Magarino Torres' Tijuca home, where the lawyer urged residents to call a massive assembly in Borel itself in order to strengthen and amplify their cause.[291]

That massive assembly would prove a turning point in Rio's property struggles. Most of the Borel residents' actions through those early April days were notable but not unprecedented. Many favelas had boasted relatively organized neighborhood leadership since the 1930s, and there are numerous examples of cross-favela communication and collaboration.[292] Marches to the halls of government were established practice by the 1950s, as were recourse to the press and physical resistance to police troops. The residents' fiery rights-based rhetoric echoed language common among communists since the end of the Vargas dictatorship; more moderate politicians, such as Breno da Silveira, voiced similar reasoning. Even Magarinos Torres was simply the latest in a long line of lawyer-activists that had begun in Guaratiba with Vicente Carino and included such mainstream politicians as the PTB's Geraldo Moreira. On 21 April, however, it became clear that the Borel movement, led by Magarinos Torres, would push the envelope. In a Borel assembly attended by some 1,000 residents—as well as by a wide spectrum of prominent politicians, union representatives, and occupants from various other threatened hills—community activists announced the formation of the União Geral dos Trabalhadores de Favela, later simply called the União de Trabalhadores Favelados, or UTF. For the first time, activists sought systematically to create a unified political coalition of all of the city's favela residents; in the hopeful words of Magarinos Torres, "Not a single favela in Rio will go without its own union."[293]

Despite such aspirations, no favela outside of Borel might have joined the União Geral dos Trabalhadores de Favela if its founding had not coincided with a remarkable concentration of threats to other *morros*, all occurring in one of the most turbulent election years in Brazil's twentieth-century history. As Borel's story was unfolding, several other favelas were already under intense threat. In early April, Judge Hugo Auler of the 3d Vara Cível sent military police to enforce a high-court eviction ruling on the Rua Ati in Jacarepaguá.[294] The favela had been the site of intense conflict at least since the 1930s, when its residents had written to Getúlio Vargas for aid, and smaller violent incursions had occurred throughout the early 1950s; according to one politician, the area had been claimed by no fewer than eight separate *grileiros*. Largely thanks to Breno da Silveira, the settlement's strongest political ally, the April eviction made headlines throughout the city and drew protest in the Câmara Municipal and in the National Congress.[295]

Other threats came quickly after that. On 14 April, socialist council-man Urbano Lóes proposed the disappropriation of Morro da União, the north-zone hill once known as the Morro do Jorge Turco because of its shady local *grileiro*, the Middle Eastern immigrant Jorge Chediac. Here, threats had been building ever since Chediac's late-1953 assassination, which had left his heirs struggling with those of his ex-partner for control of the hill.[296] On 22 April—the day after the foundation of the UTF—another expulsion loomed in Botafogo's Santa Marta favela: UDN council-man Cotrim Neto announced that the hill's lands had been awarded to an outside claimant in mid-February, and that a mass eviction of some 2,000 people was soon to begin.[297] The next day, the news made head-lines throughout the city.[298] In mid-May, yet another community came under threat when the 16th Vara Cível awarded possession of the Morro do Dendê, on the Ilha do Governador, to one Rómulo de Avelar, thus threatening some 2,000 people, many of whom had been expelled from the neighboring Querosene favela only a few years before.[299] And finally, in mid-June, the military ordered the destruction of Timbau, a favela on army lands in north suburban Bonsuccesso from which officials had col-lected rents for several years.[300]

Although the protests related to Ati and Timbau intensified the UTF's sense of urgency, neither ultimately joined the organization. The Rua Ati settlement was the only 1954 case in which neither the residents' protests nor its political allies' negotiations succeeded; there, the *despejo* seems to have been effective and final. In Timbau, the only community in which the lands were public, negotiations fell into a well-worn groove. On 15 June, city papers reported that the army had "assaulted" the favela and destroyed a dozen shacks; residents organized a neighborhood associa-tion, told their stories to the press, and sent a committee to the Câmara Municipal.[301] Councilmen and congressmen decried the army's actions and attempted to negotiate a solution, highlighting the fact that Timbau's rent-paying inhabitants should have been entitled to rent-law protections. councilman Couto de Souza, in a classic populist gesture, offered personally to help a woman whose shack had been destroyed while she was still inside, and the entire settlement was preserved, thanks to back-room negotiations among politicians and army officials. In 1960, the federal census listed the population of Timbau at 3,136.[302]

Santa Marta, União, and Dendê were a different story. In the months following the creation of the UTF, these communities, along with Borel, conducted a tumultuous public campaign for expropriation. At stake were not only the interests of residents and property claimants—fiercely defended, on both sides—but also those struggles' political meaning. For the UTF, and for socialist and communist politicians and sympathizers, the land wars presented an enormous opportunity to mobilize and radicalize the favela masses, and they also set the stage for potentially powerful election-year theatrics. For other members of the opposition—the UDN above all—the explosion of the favela problem exposed the failures of Getúlio Vargas's populism, as well as the revolutionary threats those failures were generating. And for the governing PTB, resolving the land issue was a chance to show the government's willingness—and, critically, its ability—to act as "father of the poor," protecting the country's humblest from certain calamity. As conflicts escalated in each community, tensions among these distinct factions heightened, negotiations stalled, and residents took matters into their own hands on an unprecedented scale.

Santa Marta's struggle, which erupted publicly in late April, showcased the spectrum of political and religious actors who could come together in support of favela expropriations on the eve of an important election. The first person to bring the mass eviction to the Municipal Council's attention was Alberto Bittencourt Cotrim Neto, the legalistic lone representative of the nearly defunct Partido Rebublicano Progressista; his brief speech highlighted the social consciousness that the 9th Vara Cível judge had shown in delaying the eviction from February to April, and it issued a blistering critique of Prefect Dulcídio Cardoso's inaction on the issue.[303] The communist press was also quick to criticize the prefect, publishing an article on 23 April titled "Dulcídio Plots Another Monstrous Eviction" and publicizing a planned protest by residents.[304] On 26 April, hundreds of men, women, and children marched first to the home of Judge Ney Palmeira Cidade of the 9th Vara Cível and to the Câmara Municipal; though the *Imprensa Popular* attributed leadership to the UTF and the communists, the marchers were also (or perhaps even principally) led by Padre Belisário Veloso, the rector of Rio's Catholic University, who had a long-standing involvement in the *morro*'s affairs. On that same day, Aristides Saldanha introduced a bill to expropriate the hill, but its 30 signatories also included everyone from the PTB councilman and journalist José Venerando da Graça to the UDN's Gladstone Chaves de Mello. In a long discourse, Chaves de Mello linked Santa Marta's struggle to the humanitarian impulses of the Catholic Church, highlighting the long-running work of Padre Veloso and the Pequena Obra da Nossa Senhora Auxiliadora, and claiming that he himself had founded a "Conferência Vincentina" with fieldwork on the hill while still a student at Catholic University.[305]

These competing claims for leadership seemed to help rather than hurt Santa Marta's cause. The bill passed in record time, as residents were still crowding the galleries. On 5 May—as several thousand people demonstrated outside nearby Guanabara Palace, brandishing signs that read "We want the hill's expropriation," "Long live the UTF," and "We want the right to live"—Dulcídio Cardoso signed the bill into law.[306] But competing claims remained even in victory. While the staid *Correio da Manhã* reported only that "a project signed by all the party leaders was approved," the *Imprensa Popular* ran a long series of articles emphasizing the UTF's role and the continued vigilance and increasing radicalism of Santa Marta's residents. In one story, the paper quoted councilman Aristides Saldanha, who declared that "only organization and unity will give victory to the *favelados*." In another, it profiled Maria Luiza Silva, a woman with three small children who had demonstrated from 4 A.M. to nightfall on 26 April in favor of the expropriation. And in still another, the paper interviewed several residents who viewed the battle as ongoing: Claudelino Freitas, a six-year Santa Marta resident, declared that the approval of the project by the Câmara only "added up to half a victory," and another man anonymously urged his neighbors to stick with the UTF.

On 2 May, days before the prefect signed the Santa Marta bill into law, the UTF showed its determination to build on the Santa Marta movement. The organization sponsored a large victory party in Borel, publicized by the communist newspaper, which promised the presence of "well-known cinema and radio artists."[307] Several thousand residents attended, including some from União, Santa Marta, and Jacarezinho. During the party, the UTF inaugurated its new headquarters, and the singer Stella Egg animated the crowd. Other luminaries attended as well, including General Edgar Buxbawm (one of the founders and early leaders of the intensely nationalist Liga de Emancipação Nacional); the communist deputy Roberto Morena; the journalist and Carioca congressman Heitor Beltrão; and both Padre Veloso and Aristides Saldanha, in whose honor the party had been given. The celebration was in some sense a great show of unity between Catholic and communist activists, but their differences remained apparent. For Magarinos Torres Filho, the party was "a sign of the total organization of all of the Federal District's *favelados*," and for Saldanha it was a moment to celebrate the UTF, which had "already shown its combativeness, its strength, and its energy in the struggle for the most elemental of rights, the right to live." But Veloso, decidedly more restrained, simply led the Côro do Apostolado da Oração in a performance of "Beneditus" and blessed the *favelados'* cause.[308]

In the following months, Rio's prefect did nothing to enforce the Santa Marta law, the Borel struggle dragged on through the judiciary, and both the UTF and leftist politicians did their best to build on these continued uncertainties. Just days after the prefect signed the Santa Marta bill into law, the *Imprensa Popular* was touting the *morro's* alleged support for Aristides Saldanha's reelection, which marked the beginning of a longer campaign heightening consciousness of favela threats and linking leftist candidates to the *favelados'* security and prosperity.[309] On 7 June, Saldanha himself met with Santa Marta residents, who were unhappy with the continued uncertainty; he then proclaimed to the Câmara Municipal that: "The law we passed is not worth anything, nor is the fact that the prefect sanctioned it and allocated the funds." Without action, he declared, the favela residents would "not rest" or "disarm their vigilance"; on the contrary, he said, they would "reinforce their unity" until city government effectively enforced the law.[310] A day later, the UTF sponsored an "assembly" on Santa Marta, complete with a "succulent *feijoada*" where Saldanha, Roberto Morena, and Câmara Municipal candidate Henrique Miranda all addressed a small crowd that also included residents from Borel, Dendê, and São Carlos. Miranda, who had been involved in Turano/Liberdade's early struggles, reinforced the rights-based line of argument that had been sustained by the communists since the late 1940s: "We all . . . pay the same taxes and thus have equal rights. We should all unite so that our rights will be respected."[311]

In mid-June, Aristides Saldanha accused Police Chief Melchiades of authorizing the destruction of more Borel shacks—including a school that the *moradores* had constructed themselves—and also of brutally beating a man who had resisted them.[312] Women and children reportedly had blocked the incursion and sent for the police, and neighbors quickly reconstructed the destroyed shacks, deciding in the process to rechristen the hill "Independência" (a name that never stuck).[313] Residents also sent committees to various newspapers, and the demolitions stopped. But two days later, the UTF and communist activists led a demonstration of *moradores* from Santa Marta and Borel to the steps of the Câmara Municipal. According to the *Imprensa Popular*, the 800 demonstrators—carrying signs that read "Down with Colonel Melchiades, enemy of the poor" and "You can't get rid of the favelas by knocking down shacks and beating *favelados*"—demanded punishment for the police officer involved in the Borel beating, and they also insisted that the prefect act on the still moribund Santa Marta law. Aristides Saldanha heightened the demonstration's political tension by attacking the PTB's Geraldo Moreira for supposed corruption and false populism in Jacarezinho.[314]

The demonstration provoked a vehement reaction from Melchiades. On 23 June, he held a press conference in which he set out a blistering attack on Magarinos Torres and the UTF. According to the *Correio da Manhã,* which published Melchiades's remarks under the headline "Communist Agitation on the Morro of Borel," he claimed that "no violence, no arbitrary act" had ever been carried out by him or his agents "against humble and honorable workers who inhabit the Morro do Borel or any other Carioca favela." His actions on the *morro,* he said, had been limited to taking a census of Borel's inhabitants and transmitting to them a proposal that they move to lands that Borel, Meuron Imóveis had arranged for them in north suburban Engenho Dentro. On that basis alone, Melchiades claimed, Magarinos Torres had moved in to bring suit against his agents and to found the UTF, putting in practice "the Marxist methods of agitation, insult to authority, and defamation." Given this history, he said, the public could "easily make up its own mind" about who was "really against the *favelados*: the communists, who try to abuse their good faith, not permitting them to accept a human, Christian, and patriotic proposal . . . or the authorities, who have done everything to ensure the well-being and tranquility of this working mass."[315]

In this contentious atmosphere, the 1954 land struggles crested, catalyzed by the imminent demolitions of Dendê and the Morro da União. Dendê's rather sordid story attracted especially avid public attention. In mid-May, Judge Gouveia Coelho awarded the hill's lands to an outside claimant. Following, he said, the mandate of "l'adoucissement du droit," the judge allowed residents to keep their shacks' materials and refused to fine them for destroying the hill's vegetation. But he did not question the plaintiff's claim that the residents had been on the hill for less than a year, and he accepted part and parcel the claimant's version of the residents' supposedly "violent" and "clandestine" "invasion" of the hill; both of these conditions had significant legal implications for the residents, whose scant defense was rejected out of hand.[316] To make things worse, the claimant, Rómulo de Avelar, nicknamed "Coca-Cola," had originally bought the lands with money garnered to build housing for "victims of the integralist attack" of 1937. Though he incorporated a company with the sunny name "A Home for Everyone," Avelar never laid a brick for housing—a fraud for which he was criminally prosecuted, and which made his intended expulsion of some 2,000 to 4,000 residents all the more scandalous.[317] In the face of this ruling, its publicity, and a subsequent eviction order, Roberto Morena and Magarinos Torres went quickly to the *morro* to offer their services, and councilman Joaquim de Couto Souza of the PSD began to push for expropriation.

That expropriation would eventually become law, thanks mainly to the eruption of another, still more urgent case in the Morro da União. Socialist councilman Urbano Lóes had proposed União's expropriation in mid-April, and even before then Henrique Miranda had been working there for some time. But it was only in late May that the 14th Vara Cível gave definitive ownership of the hill to one of the families that had disputed the lands since Jorge Chediac's 1953 murder.[318] By mid-June, the residents' legal recourses were exhausted, and Congressman Breno da Silveira warned that the looming *despejo* would "lead to new interminable lines" of residents who would begin to flood the National Congress, the Municipal Council, and Catete Palace. Perhaps conscious of the explosive conflicts surrounding communist and socialist involvement in the favela issue, he appealed for action in the most moderate of terms, asking his colleagues to pass a measure "consonant with our human qualities, with our Christian qualities, giving the less favored classes, the poor classes, at least an opportunity to live and a place to inhabit, even if it be in humble shacks."[319]

By the very next day, residents and councilmen made it clear that União's expropriation would not proceed along such conciliatory lines. As councilmen announced that the demolitions were about to begin, hundreds of União's residents crowded into the Câmara's galleries. The Council leadership, citing vaguely worded rules that all visitors had to be "decently dressed," tried to restrict anyone without a tie and hat to one side of the chambers. The socialist Raimundo Magalhães Júnior railed against the ruling, saying, "This is a house of the people, and as long as a citizen is not offending public morality, he has the right to enter here to defend his threatened rights."[320] But the leadership held firm and also refused to debate the expropriation bill.

The frustrated residents returned to the Council on Monday, 28 June, but leaders still refused to discuss the appropriation bill, insisting that the Câmara first vote on a concession for a municipal gas station. As the cycle repeated itself over the following days, members of the majority repeatedly walked out of the chambers so as to deny proponents a quorum and keep União's *despejo* from the top of the agenda. In the meantime, the crowds from União swelled, organized mainly by the UTF, and Magalhães Júnior and Aristides Saldanha incited them to press the issue still more vigorously. The real content of the political dispute became clear in a blistering speech by majority leader Salomão Filho, who railed against the communists and framed expropriation as something that could only be "given" by the political mainstream:

All of the *favelados* from all of the *morros* need to know that neither the communists nor the socialists will ever resolve a single case in this house. The only thing
they do is berate, and beraters achieve nothing. If *favelados* have had their lands
expropriated by the government, or if they intend it to happen, the people who will
provide this are the men of the government, not the communists, who give them
nothing and only exploit their misery. Those who give them everything are the
councilors of all parties who make up the Câmara of the Federal District.[321]

The demonstrators, however, showed themselves to be in no mood
for deference. Frustrated by a fourth day of delays, "women and children cried . . . men protested, yelling, stamping their feet on the ground
and banging on the double doors . . . some recounted out loud that the
shacks were being torn down."[322] According to the *Correio da Manhã*,
the communists were to blame: "Taking advantage of the reigning spirit,
they called an assembly in the foyer, inciting the *favelados* to disorder," to
the extent that there were "threats that the building would be stoned."[323]
Finally, in an unprecedented gesture, the residents resolved to occupy the
Câmara overnight, declaring, in the *Imprensa Popular*'s summary, that
"the Câmara is the people's house, so let it shelter us until our project
is approved."[324] Though majority councilman Levi Neves urged them
to go home and promised the vote would come, the *Correio da Manha*
claimed that "spirits remained exalted . . . to cries of 'From here I won't
go, from here nobody will take me,' men, women, and children invaded
the building's inner reaches, resolved to spend the night and stay until the
project was voted upon."[325]

Not surprisingly, descriptions of the occupation varied enormously.
The *Correio da Manhã* downplayed the movement's radicalism, reporting that Levi Neves had decided early on that it would not be "desirable"
to forcibly extract the demonstrators and had agreed to make things easier on them, opening up back rooms and even arranging food. From there,
the paper seemed to argue, the main story became one of cheap populism
catering to the hungry masses, as other politicians quickly piled onto the
food-donation wagon. When all was said and done, the paper reported
with odd precision, the demonstrators had consumed 600 liters of milk, 5
boxes of apples, 50 kilos of cookies and crackers, 300 kilos of bread, and
20 boxes of banana paste, "all of this given by the Council members."

The *Imprensa Popular* was more interested in political radicalism than
in gluttonous detail; by its rendering, the occupation was an "indignant
protest against the sabotage of the bill that would expropriate the Morro
da União." Protesters, that paper claimed, were joined by UTF members
from Santa Marta, Dendê, Borel, Liberdade, and Catacumba and were
accompanied by the radical politicians Saldanha, Henrique Miranda,

Alves, and others. The paper also noted that the demonstrators were well fed. But the paper gave credit for the food to the Feminine Association of the Federal District, an organization led by Eline Mochel, a favela physician and communist congressional candidate whose sister, Arcelina, had led the communist bloc of the Câmara before its 1948 expulsion.[326]

Whatever the occupation's tone, it worked, and the demonstrators seem to have given much of the credit to the UTF and leftist politicians. On 3 July, the Câmara unanimously approved a bill that expropriated both União and Dendê, and on 5 July the prefect signed it into law.[327] The day following the Câmara's vote, even the *Correio da Manhã* published pictures of demonstrators—most of them women raising their right fists in victory—and described a celebration in which "the multitude intoned the national anthem and gave way to their joy with embraces, smiles, and even tears." The *Imprensa Popular* exuded jubilance, publishing pictures of communist and socialist leaders being lifted into the air by an ecstatic crowd, and giving celebratory accounts of the political consciousness that the Câmara events supposedly had awoken among the demonstrators. For all the contention and controversy the UTF had provoked, its election-year protests had succeeded in pushing the favela residents' struggle for property rights to the threshold of legality.

THE LAW OF THE FAVELA

Neither União's story nor the saga of Rio's property wars ended with the municipal Council occupation. After the tumultuous events of late 1954—Getúlio Vargas's suicide in August, the national elections of 5 October—the UTF, Borel, and União soon returned to public controversy. The very day after the elections, two or three squadrons of police, armed with machine guns and tear gas, arrived without warning to expel Borel's residents, only to be repulsed by the hill's women. Some 200 families occupied the court that had issued the order, ending their protest only when the eviction stopped and the Minister of Justice himself promised to ensure Borel's permanence.[328] On 10 October, Interim President Café Filho himself confirmed the minister's promise.[329] At this seeming final victory, the activists rechristened Borel "Cidade Independência," and the *Imprensa Popular* ran a series of articles celebrating the new peace and prosperity that had supposedly been born of the Dendê, União, Borel, and Santa Marta movements. In late October, the paper reported on an enormous UTF celebration that had included delegations from a dozen favelas, including one group of "composers and singers" from Salgueiro as well as the usual radical politicians and even Minister of Justice Seabra

Fagundes.[330] The organization seized the moment to announce a planned congress of all favela leaders and to give publicity to a radical proposal that would have required the prefect to expropriate and urbanize any favela that could organize 100 or more residents in its favor.[331]

Yet, despite all the drama and high ambitions, the 1954 expropriation victories never moved beyond the realm of promise. In Borel, where an expropriation decree had never even been formally proposed, new threats surfaced in March 1955.[332] When thousands of residents again came to the city center to protest, the new Minister of Justice, Marcondes Filho, not only downplayed his predecessor's promises but also notoriously rejected the protestor's claims that police had violated their homes, stating that a shack was not, "strictly speaking, a home."[333] In the tumultuous month that followed, União also came under threat from owners frustrated with the prefect's failure to act on the July law.[334] Mass protests ensued, spurred on by Magarinos Torres and a new slate of leftist congressmen and Council members, and scenes turned ugly both in downtown Rio and on the hills themselves: two demonstrators were shot by police on the steps of the Câmara Municipal, Magarinos Torres scuffled with officers who wanted to prevent him from participating in political negotiations, military police in full riot gear staged early-morning raids on both hills, and hundreds of União residents slept on the steps of the governor's palace to protest the violence.[335] It was only at the end of the month that a tentative agreement was reached in both cases; the prefect finally agreed to expropriate União, and the residents and "owners" of Borel agreed to a plan by which residents would pay 200 *cruzeiros* per month per family for five years, in exchange for eventual title to their lots.[336]

These plans, like others before them, remained just that, never actually leading to legal residential certainty. Both communities settled into the same uneasy permanence as Turano, Coroa, and Santa Marta had before them; residents knew that the political process had temporarily annulled the judicial evictions, but they were still subject to periodic threats and unable to claim full rights to their property, their neighborhood, or their city.[337] And as they waited, other conflicts surfaced. In 1955, eviction threats arose in the suburban communities of Vila Vintém, Vigário Geral (Maloca), Juramento, and Mata Machado as well as in Mangueira, various Leme favelas, and the Maré complex, a swampy area off the Avenida Brasil.[338] All of these generated extensive protests, which involved the UTF, Magarinos Torres, the newly elected unofficial communist councilman Waldemiro Vianna, and, most prominently of all, a newly radicalized PTB councilman, Geraldo Moreira. Under Moreira's leadership, a bill expropriating the Maré properties passed the Câmara in September

1955; during that same year, the prefecture undertook a never-enforced expropriation in Vintém.[339] In 1956, attention shifted to the rural *fazenda* Piai, to a church-ordered eviction in suburban Penha, and to the "Boogie-Woogie" favela on the Ilha do Governador.[340]

In the wake of such constant threat and turmoil, the politics surrounding the favela issue continued their unsteady veer to the left. The change was perhaps best incarnated in the PTB's Geraldo Moreira, whose legal and political advocacy for favela communities such as Jacarezinho had carried a heavy charge of paternalistic populism in the late 1940s and early 1950s.[341] Moreira's stance seemed to change, however, after the heightened activism of 1954 and under the pressure exerted by the UTF's militant, rights-based demands. Though he had been Maré's legal counsel since the early 1950s, Moreira began after 1954 to talk of the favela's situation in a language that strongly echoed the words of Breno da Silveira, Magarinos Torres, and Aristides Saldanha. At one point, while calling for Council action before a full house of favela residents from Maré, Moreira incited them to physically resist the judicial eviction order, stating bluntly that they were Brazilian and had "the right to live in some part of Brazil," and that they were "living in that mud hole and wish[ed] to continue there."[342]

Some branded Moreira a communist for his pains, and his words were indicative of two important trends. First and foremost, they reflected the opening of a period in which a wide range of Carioca policymakers acknowledged that favela eradication would never be feasible; now, the political watchword became favela "urbanization," carried out with considerable participation by the residents themselves.[343] Second, Moreira's words indicated a critical approximation between the PTB and the UTF, which would reach full fruition in the late 1950s.[344]

Symptomatically, in mid-July 1955, Moreira introduced a bill that echoed the UTF's own very similar initiative.[345] The bill would have required the prefecture to ascertain the juridical status of every favela property, to expropriate any that lay in private hands, to provide those areas with significant urban services, and to give residents permanent claim to lots where they themselves would build structurally sound homes. Moreira justified the bill by claiming that the favelas were a symptom of wider structural inequalities and transformations, a problem that would "never be resolved through charity . . . or punitive expeditions or mass expulsion of *favelados* and incineration of their shacks." What was needed, Moreira argued, was "the *favelados'* own participation in solving their material and social problems"—and that, apparently, would come only when they had permanent and undeniable claim to their lands.[346]

Moreira's bill did not pass the Câmara for several years, and other measures that would have ended judicial evictions also stalled.[347] But the cycle of judicial threats, popular protests, and unfulfilled expropriation promises had reached fever pitch by 1955, and a wide array of politicians, lawyers, and jurists began to demand some type of solution. For some, the problem lay in the fact that expropriations were promised and never carried out, the result being a process of "mystification" that was little more than demagoguery. Though Geraldo Moreira argued—probably accurately—that even the promise of expropriation had a "psychological power" that had helped to preserve the favelas, the fact remained that expropriation decrees had no legal power unless they were funded.[348] At the same time, many others saw problems in the promise and possibility of expropriation itself. Not only did it incite residents to radicalism, it also spurred landowners to bad behavior: speculators, some argued, were driven by the possibility of a huge public payoff and were buying land and expelling residents with the sole aim of having their properties expropriated. Municipal Counsel Manuel de Carvalho Barroso highlighted this perception in an important 1956 legal brief about the União expropriation:

> The scheme is well known: the owner allows the favela to invade his property. Once (the community) is established, he decides to reclaim the land or benefit from it—for which purpose he demands the requisite possessory order. This results without fail in the sale of the land to the city, which the owner obliges to comply with the purchase by using the pressure of the dislodged, and exploiting the emotional atmosphere that surrounds the case. From the beginning, one can point to one sure beneficiary—the owner, who rids himself cleanly of the property, which he surely would never use, since he formulated the use proposal only to ensure expropriation.[349]

Such considerations, along with a growing acknowledgment that there were no realistic alternatives to Rio's favelas, led to a series of national initiatives that would have been unthinkable ten years before. In 1955, the National Congress, following the UTF's initiative, constituted a Comissão Parlamentar de Inquérito (Parliamentary Investigative Commission, or CPI) to ascertain the ownership of all Carioca favelas. Though the CPI never actually completed its work, it did seem to have a chilling effect on the *despejo* cycle. According to Congressman Cardoso de Menezes, favela rent payments stopped during the CPI's authorized term, and between 1955 and 1956 "there was never a single collective eviction in any favela in the Federal District."[350] Cardoso de Menezes's support for the CPI—and also for the expropriation of the Vintém favela—was in itself a strong indicator of the changing terrain of the favela debate among Carioca politicians; a religious conservative and ex-Integralist who would later staunchly support the military government, Menezes was hardly a likely bedfellow for the UTF rabble-rousers or even the PTB populists.[351]

Even as the CPI stretched on, two other initiatives appeared that would more definitively suspend Rio's cycle of judicial evictions. In 1955, Interim President Café Filho called on the National Congress to appropriate 50 million *cruzeiros* to Helder Câmara's newly created Cruzada de São Sebastião, a Catholic entity that aimed, among other things, to urbanize on-site Rio's most notorious favelas. The National Congress began a fiery debate on the proposal in late 1955; though the lone communist deputy, Bruzzi Mendonça, was among its strong supporters, he was joined by a broad coalition that included virtually all of the Carioca representatives.[352]

During those same months, in the Senate, an interim PSD senator, Moura Brasil, proposed the suspension of all judicial evictions of the Carioca favelas—a near-exact replica of a 1947 communist initiative that, ironically, had been soundly defeated by councilmen from the UDN and the PSD.[353] The new bill's justification reflected the growing conventional wisdom about the settlements. The favelas were "a real, concrete problem of public interest," and the national state was "uniquely capable of resolving it, given its proportions." Favela residents were too poor to pay almost any rent, and because they constructed their shacks in an "evident state of need," their occupation of empty lands could not be taken as "clandestine or violent possession," as many judges had argued in stripping them of their possessory rights.[354] Thus it was natural that the *favelados* would cling to their lands "as a castaway clings to a life raft," and the state "would betray its purpose if it remained indifferent and contemplative before such a dramatic reality." The situation called for a comprehensive and definitive state solution, and this could not be found so long as the *favelados* themselves were in a constant state of politicized emergency; given these circumstances, the bill mandated a "respite"—a year-long ban on all private evictions—that would allow officials to "to face, objectively, the favela problem."[355]

Moura Brasil's bill stalled in the senate. But on 23 January, the unofficial communist congressman Bruzzi Mendonça proposed an important amendment to the Cruzada de São Sebastião bill, according to which all *despejos* in Rio would be suspended for two years, and all of the favelas' residents would be guaranteed permanence in their homes until better housing could be built.[356] Mendonça, justifying these amendments, emphasized the enormous number of favelas that were under threat of *despejo* (fourteen or fifteen in that year alone, he claimed), and also the utter insufficiency of even 50 million *cruzeiros* in the face of a problem so enormous.[357] In September 1956, he would amplify those arguments in language clearly drawn from the 1954 campaigns: "The *favelados*, at the very least, need to have a minimum of tranquility, at least the assurance that, the next day, they will still have that humble shelter, often dirty, but at least a shelter that for them is a home, as . . . a mansion or an apartment might be for others."[358]

Despite strenuous objections from some senators and many rural congressmen, the bill became law in September 1956, complete with funding both for the Cruzada São Sebastião and for Mendonça's two amendments blocking evictions and ensuring permanence. The law also included moneys for favela initiatives in São Paulo, Recife, and Vitória.[359] Though this so-called Lei das Favelas (law of the favelas) technically banned evictions for only two years, in fact it marked the end of the era in which property conflicts would be the shacktowns' most significant threat. It tacitly accepted—as favela advocates had argued for years—that housing was the sort of public need that the civil code obliged judges to take into account when applying the law, and that the broader "social well-being" demanded that private property rights be restricted to protect the settlements.[360] More concretely, as many of the law's framers had intended, it effectively took the wind out of the *grileiros*' sails.[361] Not only did the eviction ban cut off the expropriation cycle, it also convinced many residents to stop paying rents, since no legal threat could now be made against them.

A number of other policies, laws, and interpretive practices deepened the impact of the Lei das Favelas. The two most important public agencies dealing with the favelas between 1956 and 1962 were the Cruzada de São Sebastião and the Serviço Especial de Recuperação das Favelas e Habitações Anti-Higiênicas (SERFHA), each of which promoted, in its own way, the sort of self-organization and auto-urbanization that served to further entrench the *morros*.[362] At SERFHA's urging, a 1961 municipal law reinforced the Lei das Favelas by indefinitely prohibiting all rents charged for *barracões*—a provision that, if enforced, would have had an enormous impact on modest favela entrepreneurs as well as on *grileiros*—and strictly regulating rents charged for favela lands.[363] What's more, some critical policymakers—following a labyrinthine legal logic, which endured even after the 1964 military coup—argued that the Lei das Favelas was self-renewing in the absence of contrary legislation.[364] Some jurists eventually claimed that the permanence guarantee of the Lei das Favelas did not apply to private lands. But Rio's local government continued in the 1960s the unofficial practice begun under pressure from the favela residents in the 1940s. Whenever a large judicial eviction surfaced, the government would issue an expropriation decree, which it never intended to enforce with payment; such decrees, renewed periodically, effectively froze the eviction cycle.[365]

All of these policies, legal measures, and practices effectively marked the end of an era. From the Lei das Favelas forward, private landowners' legal ambitions were mostly neutralized in Rio's largest favelas. Though large-scale evictions would continue over the following decades, private owners and civil courts would no longer be their principal instigators. The question of community permanence came to reside with the local and national governments, now an issue of politics rather than law.

"É uma cidade, no duro"

The property wars of the 1940s and 1950s barely surface in oral histories and academic accounts of Rio's twentieth-century favela struggles. At most, the 1954 events in Borel and perhaps União are acknowledged as the beginning of a more significant era: the point at which favela residents began to organize across neighborhood lines and interact in a meaningful way with the local and national governments, which were taken for granted as the most critical arbiters of the settlements' fates.[366] The real story, for many activists whose testimonies have become central to favela histories, began in the early 1960s, when Guanabara Governor Carlos Lacerda initiated an era of mass public evictions that would run through the early 1970s and permanently transform the face of Rio's south zone.[367] In the early 1960s, activists—by then often linked to radical Catholics, independent unions, and a left wing of the PTB—organized the FAFEG, a legendary pan-favela organization, and attempted with increasing radicalism to resist the so-called removals.[368] With the military coup of 1964, however, and especially with the crackdown on political expression that intensified in 1968, many settlements lost their struggles. All told, more than 41,447 families—or some 207,235 people—were forced by the government to leave their homes between 1962 and 1973, and many favela activists were stripped of their political rights and forced into exile and hiding.[369] Residents whose oral histories have become the core of the *morros'* own memory banks—people like Dona Filinha, Seu Lúcio, and Seu Abdias, all cited throughout this book—forged their early political identities during these years. So did many of the most prominent favela scholars, people like Luciano Parisse, Anthony and Elizabeth Leeds, Lícia Prado Valladares, Janice Perlman, and Luiz Antônio Machado da Silva. Little wonder that images from that later period—burning shacks, broken furniture, bedraggled settlers disembarking in the distant suburbs—have largely eclipsed those earlier memories.

Even if these vagaries of memory and intellectual production are set aside, the property wars of the 1940s and 1950s remain more difficult to analyze than those of the 1960s. The protests against judicial evictions fit only with great difficulty into either classic or postmodern narratives of popular resistance. Like the favelas themselves, these movements were built by a broad range of actors, some more sincere and more savory than others. Most residents probably mobilized solely to defend their homes, but many small-time entrepreneurs sought also to defend their rights to profit from their still poorer neighbors. Some politicians and lawyers probably acted out of charity or ideology, some were sheer opportunists, and surely most were moved by a messy mixed bag of motives.

In ideological terms, these movements were also strikingly heterogeneous. Though many of the activists' tactics were radical and innovative—the press campaigns, the marches and occupations, the placement of women on the front lines, the physical struggles with municipal police—they still often had a deferential and conciliatory quality. For the most part, residents allowed the lawyers and politicians to negotiate settlements without their direct participation; in the 1955 Borel conflicts, for example, residents were left on the steps of the National Congress while federal deputies tried to hammer out an acceptable agreement with the minister of justice.[370] In newspaper photographs, the people who marched seemed to be wearing their Sunday best, and they generally mixed a truly radical demand for rights with a more conciliatory and moral language that demanded only charity and social responsibility. Even the UTF, with its strong communist support, took pains to include a wide spectrum of politicians and religious figures in its activities, seeking to avoid an openly partisan stance.[371] The women on the front lines generally used traditional gender roles as a political weapon rather than contradicting them, and the protests—like urban popular movements throughout Latin America highlighted by Manuel Castells and others—generally died down once the immediate eviction threat had passed.

All of which, it might be argued, begins to explain the movements' ultimate limitations. Diluted by their actors' cross-purposes, and lacking in radicalism and full ideological coherence, they ultimately compromised their most radical goal—that of full urban rights—in favor of dependent clientelism, against which later generations would be left to fight. Following this logic, the obvious conclusion would be that the land wars of the 1940s and 1950s were a mostly aborted social movement, and it is little wonder that they have faded into memory.

Yet this line of reasoning holds only if full rights are the sole measure of success, and only if recognizable revolutionary radicalism is the lone yardstick of meaningful political consciousness. Rio's anti-eviction struggles fit only uncomfortably into a heroic narrative of popular resistance.

Their signal achievement—the shift of land struggles from the legal to the political arena—may seem at best semantic and at worst a demagogic concession. But without those struggles and their politicization, most of Rio's centrally located favelas would probably have been wiped from the city's face, literally burned to the ground by legions of municipal police. Those communities that survived would not have gained the political experience and social infrastructure capable of protecting their residents from the later eviction wave; significantly, of the favelas eliminated entirely in the 1960s and 1970s, only one—Catacumba—had organized in the private eviction struggles of the 1940s and 1950s. Those messy battles laid the groundwork for subsequent permanence; thanks to them, property ripe for profitable speculation and development was effectively removed from the open land market; communities won vital time to root themselves physically and politically; and valuable lands were preserved, however tenuously, for the use of very poor people. Just as important, an abstract set of legal guarantees that limited the exercise of private property for the sake of the public good moved from parchment to daily judicial and legislative practice, and residents' assertions of historically and morally grounded rights to urban property and permanence migrated from the informal fringes to the very center of political debate.

In a context where many favela residents were the direct descendants of slaves, or were migrants from rural areas where legal strictures had only minimal practical impact, the very fact that poor communities had claimed and won a space from which to demand urban rights was enormously significant. Favelas stayed in the city; what existed within their borders was, in the words of one Jacarezinho resident, "uma cidade, no duro" ("a city, damn straight"). It may also have been a city on the cheap—dependent, inadequately serviced, forever under the axe of eviction, begging for the tiniest share of public resources. Yet if Mário de Almeida and his fellow developers had gotten their way, even this would have been out of reach. The "cidade, no duro," had not been given, but won, through a fight that was as hardscrabble and multifaceted as the settlements themselves. The battle for urban tolerance did not always fit a heroic mold, but without the critical foothold in the city that it rendered, poor Cariocas would have been hard pressed to struggle for any rights at all.

Poverty and Citizenship

É o pensamento de todos aqueles que à Lei das Favelas são fiéis
A revolta te consome da cabeça aos pés

This is what everyone loyal to the law of the favelas knows
Revolt consumes you from your head to your toes

—MV Bill, "Cidadão Comum Refém"

In chronicling Rio's poverties of rights, this book has clung closely to Brazil's mid-twentieth century. Many of the histories recounted here began long before Vargas's 1930 revolution, and most continued well after Brazil's 1964 military coup. Yet the 34 years between those events marked a sea change in the nature of Brazilian citizenship, a transformation not only in the content of Brazilians' rights and obligations but also in the very role that rights, laws, and legal institutions would play in governing Brazilian society. It is only by viewing these developments in their own time and context that we can understand the impossibly paradoxical historical relationship between Rio de Janeiro's poor and the rule of law—the degree to which hope has coexisted with cynicism, the use of laws and rights has expanded in lockstep with vital informalities, and poverties of rights have become integral to the city's ability to incorporate its poorest inhabitants.

And yet, grounded as this book may be in the mid-twentieth century, it was inevitably shaped by its own era, in which questions of citizenship, democracy, and inclusion once more monopolized Brazilian politics and culture. In the 1990s and early 2000s, it was tough to escape talk of citizenship in Brazil. Especially when the subject was poverty or racism, the word was everywhere, from the mission statements of nongovernmental organizations to the manifestos of popular demonstrations, from book titles to political speeches. One 1996 *samba-enredo* from Rio imagined a utopian future in which the world would see "real citizenship"; one 2006 rap ironically blasted the emptiness of the whole concept by describing a dead drug dealer as "um cidadão que nunca teve nada / que encontrou a sociedade de porta fechada" ("a citizen who never had a thing / who found society's door slammed shut").[1] Brazil's deepest problems may have been rooted in economic stagnation, inequality, corruption, and racism. But citizenship was thought to open a path toward resolving such troubles, and Brazilians used the concept to lay claim to everything from the traditional triad of civil, political, and social rights to racial equality, land redistribution, environmental sustainability, and cultural autonomy. In the aftermath of more than two decades of military rule, citizenship became a vessel for every imaginable hope, and its lack became the explanation for every ill, the "capitalist exploitation" of the post-Marxist age.

Much of citizenship's ubiquity was born of optimism. During the years that this book has chronicled, certain dimensions of Brazilian citizenship expanded steadily in depth and significance: the electorate grew, labor and social welfare rights came into existence, and the rule of law displaced webs of personal power and influence in new geographical areas and spheres of social life. Much of this expansion continued right through the military dictatorship, during which illiterates were given the vote and domestic employees were finally entitled to *trabalhista* protections; ironically, the poorest of Brazilians were in some ways considerably more entitled as citizens in 1986 than they had been in 1964.[2] With the end of military rule, in the mid-1980s, this expanded political enfranchisement became meaningful, and Brazilians from every corner of the country embraced the right to demand rights and thought deeply about how citizenship might be a catalyst for social transformation. The 1988 constitution was a testament to this optimism. Each of its most wildly idealistic provisions was both an expression of a social demand and the legal foundation for those demands' fulfillment, a promise that Brazilians could utilize to create new dimensions of citizenship through the mechanisms of popular democracy.

And yet citizenship's conceptual magnetism also sprang from its ambiguities and failures, both historical and actual. As was true during the years covered in this book, many Brazilians used the notion of citizenship at the turn of the twenty-first century, not because it was powerful, but rather because it was a tool of unproven utility, its efficacy as a mediator of social and political life still in dispute, its promises still unfulfilled. The right to vote finally became universal in the 1980s, but political democracy was still stained by bribery, patronage, skewed media coverage, and networks of private interests. The right to decent work at a living wage, enshrined in every constitution since 1934, had became a mockery in the face of an economy that veered from crisis to stagnation. Economic rights expanded, but they also lost much of their original value; by the 1980s, the minimum wage was far too low to decently support anyone, the most meaningful benefits of social security accrued to people who were already better off than most other Brazilians, and the tax and wage benefits of informal work could far outweigh the economic benefits of working with a *carteira assinada*. Laws and courts may have been more involved than ever before in mediating social life, but that involvement was as likely to lead to permanent uncertainly and abuse as to just resolution.[3]

Just as significantly, underlying all of these caveats to the promises of citizenship was a brutal reality that economic and legal inequalities together had wrought. Even when Brazilians could claim meaningful rights, protections, and guarantees, the Brazilian state was mostly incapable of protecting them from the lawless violence that had become ubiquitous throughout the nation since the 1980s. In rural areas, thugs killed rural workers and activists who defended their land rights; in urban areas, drug gangs assassinated many who seemed to stand in their way; everywhere, many soldiers and police, rather than containing the violence, brutally and corruptly perpetuated it. In the face of this reality, every Brazilian was forced to ask what it meant to be a citizen of a state that could neither enforce its laws nor protect its residents' lives, and the frequent cynicism of their responses was hardly surprising.

Rio de Janeiro is often touted as Brazil's *cartão-postal*, or picture postcard; the city is equally emblematic when it comes to questions of citizenship and violence. As in so many other parts of Brazil, the end of the dictatorship awakened enormous optimism in Rio. Many Cariocas set aside their customary irony to embrace the democratization movement, and they flocked to a throng of NGOs that were created with the hope that a strengthened civil society would lend depth and substance to electoral democracy. Rio elected Brazil's first black woman senator, NGOs denounced racism and social marginalization, and Rio joined other cities in unprecedented campaigns to urbanize and regularize favelas and other extralegal settlements.[4] And yet nothing those movements contained was enough to counter Rio's disastrous economic stagnation, the government's persistent inability to turn its lofty promises into even the most prosaic of realities, and a consequential sense of hopelessness and revolt, especially among young people born and raised in the slums.

The drug trade grew easily in such terrain, as did many other extralegal economies, both criminal and benign. In the 1980s, residents across the social spectrum were shocked by the first violent struggles for control of the favela drug trade and frightened by a seemingly sudden wave of common crime. By the 1990s, neither phenomenon was remarkable, nor was the brutality of the police and death squads who fed on public panic about drugs and theft. The headlines blurred together, each shocking in its time, and each quickly overshadowed by news that was worse still. Street children were massacred on the steps of the Candelária Cathedral; residents were mowed down in the Vigário Geral favela; a boy who had survived Candelária was brutally killed after hijacking a city bus; and off-duty police officers massacred 29 randomly chosen bystanders in the Baixada Fluminense.[5] Through all of this, military police so regularly killed civilians in drug shakedowns that many communities openly expressed their preference for the drug thugs. At the same time, drug organizations wove increasingly complex webs of connections and influence in the city; drug sales were ever more closely linked to international networks of drugs, arms, and money; and drug wars became steadily more brutal and violent. At various points, traffickers imposed their own brand of brutal martial law on some favela communities, shut down commerce at will in formal neighborhoods, burned buses in the middle of major thoroughfares, and attacked police posts in broad daylight.

What did it mean to talk of citizenship in the midst of such troubles, especially for the poor people whose lives were most closely touched? For those who had struggled for urban citizenship since the Vargas era, the contradictions of Brazil's new democratic age frequently evoked nostalgia for its first one. Many of these people had been among the streams of migrants who had come to Rio in the 1940s and 1950s, drawn not only by the promise of better work or the glamour of the city, but also by the idea that Rio was the city where citizenship could be made most consequential. Others had been born in the city, but they and their parents had nonetheless witnessed a remarkable transformation, one that placed poor workers at the center of discussions about national rights and obligations and made the laws and legal institutions newly relevant to their lives. As this book has documented, nothing about this transformation was smooth, simple, or unidirectional; but by the 1960s, laws and citizenship rights came to mean something serious to Rio's poor, in ways that their parents and grandparents could scarcely have imagined. Little wonder that the vast majority of older favela residents, when interviewed about Vargas, still respond with elegies: he was "fantastic," "the best president we ever had"; "Brazil's great president" who "did a lot for us"; "the best president of the country, the only one worth anything."[6]

Many intellectual observers have doubted, justifiably, the depth of citizenship's mid-century transformation, questioning especially the degree to which any form of citizenship and democracy can exist without strong civil rights protections. In formulating this argument, most hark back to

T. H. Marshall's classic division of citizenship rights into civil, political, and social components. In Marshall's often cited conception, based on the historical experience of Great Britain, the most foundational of this triad are civil rights, which he defined as "the rights necessary for individual freedom—liberty of the person, freedom of speech, thought and faith, the right to own property and to conclude valid contracts, and the right to justice."[7] In Britain, by the early nineteenth century, "civil rights had come to man's estate and bore, in most essentials, the appearance that they have today," and it was on the basis of those guarantees that British citizens were able to consolidate political rights in the nineteenth century and finally struggle for social rights in the twentieth.

Marshall's positivistic notions of progress have often raised hackles, but the basic logic of his formulation has persisted. James Holston, among citizenship's most thoughtful interrogators, rejects the singularity of Brazil's experience but argues nevertheless for the "disjunctive" nature of a Brazilian democracy in which social rights were guaranteed before political ones, and where civil rights have never been fully guaranteed by the state.[8] José Murilo de Carvalho, citizenship's most prominent Brazilian historian, roots a similar argument in the *longue durée*, arguing for a direct connection between historically weak civil and political rights and what he views as a passive and powerless citizenry. In his words, in the nineteenth century "there was no justice, there was no true public power, there were no civil citizens. In those circumstances, there could be no political citizens."[9] Because social rights were subsequently "given" by Vargas's government in a period of "low or nonexistent political participation,"[10] they were understood as "favors" rather than rights, and the "citizenship that thus resulted was passive and receptive rather than active and demanding."[11]

Weak civil rights are without doubt at the center of Brazil's current democratic paradox. By the 1990s, in the face of police violence, clogged and biased courts, and unenforceable laws, no one was arguing that Brazilians, and especially poor Brazilians, could count on a legal infrastructure to enforce and respect their basic freedoms under the rule of law. Yet it is in many respects problematic to view this situation as only the culmination of a timeless weakness in civil rights, the result of an "original sin" that granted social rights prematurely, thus corrupting an otherwise inevitable progression of citizenship.[12] As this book has shown, social rights in mid-century Brazil were neither universal among urban workers nor simply given to a passive and compliant populace. Conversely, the optimism that many poor people felt about the government and "the law" in mid-century Brazil did not spring only from the expansion of social rights. In important and durable respects, those years also witnessed a strengthening of certain civil and political rights. That strengthening was not universal, or uniform, and the military government undermined key aspects of it. But the key historical question, in attempting to understand the historical context of the current citizenship impasse, is not why civil and political rights have always been weak or nonexistent in Brazil. It is, rather, how it is that an era that witnessed the strengthening of so many dimensions of citizenship has given way to one in which fury over citizenship's limitations could snuff out hope that Brazil will ever be a republic of laws.

That question has haunted this book from its inception, for its answer seems to lie in this story's central and paradoxical theme: the degree to which poverties of rights were woven fundamentally into Brazilian law's twentieth-century expansion. By all sorts of measures, Brazilian law and politics opened up to poor and working-class Brazilians between the 1920s and the 1960s. Humble Cariocas had long made some use of Brazilian civil courts—the nineteenth-century freedom suits of slaves are perhaps the most powerful example—but the sorts of legal claims they made to property, labor, and welfare rights in the mid-twentieth century were unprecedented in their scale and efficacy.[13] While some of Rio's poor communities had a long history of political awareness and activism, their participation had never been as widespread, vigorous, or multifaceted as it was between the 1940s and the 1960s. The language of rights with which suburban communities claimed schools, clinics, and city services at mid-century had only a weak counterpart in earlier years. And even in the realm of criminal law, the documented working class did in fact gain something with the code reforms of the early 1940s; even as police systematically violated the rights of the poorest Cariocas, those with stable addresses and work documents could count on a good degree of civil rights protection, and all defendants could for the first time demand free legal defense, in itself no small advance. In this context, the notion that Vargas "colocou a lei" ("placed the law") in Brazil has real truth to it.

And yet, if Rio's experience can be taken as typical, nearly every advance in the rule of law was accompanied by—and often depended to some degree upon—the persistence of extralegal realms. In relation to urban planning, work, crime, and property—arguably, along with family law, the dimensions of legal practice that touched most directly on the poor—Brazilian law was rife with ill-fitting socioeconomic assumptions, bureaucratic hurdles, and outright exclusions, which together ensured that the vast majority of Rio's poor would live a significant portion of their lives outside the sphere of citizenship. The creation or toleration of these informal spheres was an ad hoc process, perhaps the product of patterned thinking about citizenship and social inequality but never an explicit or ultimate aim. And yet, as informality persisted and grew, it also became entrenched, both as a source of wealth and power and as a mechanism that served to ease potentially overwhelming social and political tensions. Virtually no one wanted informality outright, but over time it became clear that Carioca society could not function without it.

The notion that the elites or the middle class had something to gain from poor people's informality is somewhat counterintuitive. Politicians, jurists, and people even a few steps higher on the economic ladder frequently cited extra-legality as a menace. Favelas were said to blight the cityscape, fomenting crime, disease, and social disintegration. Migrants with no place in the formal economy were considered backward and rural, a marginal mass of surplus laborers who threatened to stymie both civilization and economic progress. Yet, just under this veneer of rebuke, informality served countless purposes. Favelas generated wealth. Informal settlements saved the city from devoting scanty resources to the poor. Informal work cut labor and tax bills for employers and saved government from investing scarce economic and political resources in the poorest and least organized workers. The vulnerability of the extralegal poor became a source of power for bureaucrats and politicians and allowed the police to continue exercising virtually aleatory repressive power among the undocumented. The toleration of informality allowed formal legal codes to reflect international ideals that were often wildly at odds with the material, cultural, and political realities of Brazilian life, serving in the process as both a codified aspiration and as window-dressing, "pra inglês ver." Whatever informality's aesthetic or human costs, it also consistently mediated between the contradictory mandates of entrenched inequality and social democracy, allowing for an uneasy and fragmented coexistence.

For Rio's poor, informality had similarly contradictory implications. Importantly, informality was more a matter of continuity than of exclusion for many poor people in mid-century Rio. Rural migrants, shantytown residents, and informal laborers had never had all that many rights to claim before 1930, and the fact that their jobs, homes, or families had no sanction or protection under the law was nothing new. On the contrary, the novelty was the notion that laws, courts, and social rights might be used routinely by working people to counter Brazil's deeply entrenched inequalities, most of which had long been reinforced by the limited scope of public law. Whether they were migrants partially drawn to the city by the possibility of citizenship or longtime residents witnessing an augmentation of the law's scope and grasp, many Cariocas saw a rapid increase in their ability to gain something from laws and rights during the middle decades of the twentieth century. But this was a process, not an abrupt shift, and during its course constant trespass of the line between law and informality was both common and necessary. Rights and citizenship, in this context, were not a birthright conferred whole but rather a set of possibilities to be made gradually incarnate.

The paradox in this process was the degree to which informality was so often critical to the pursuit of rights. As in so many other parts of the world, Brazilian citizenship began in the city itself; without an urban home or income, few poor people could expect, then or now, ever to reap its full advantages. And so long as good jobs were scarce and cheap housing scarcer, informality was frequently the only path to those crucial urban footholds. Most favela residents who left some record of their thoughts in the 1940s and 1950s wanted permanent land rights and homes that met city codes; all things being equal, most informal workers would probably have chosen to labor with the rights and guarantees of the CLT. But if, or while, they could not achieve legality and rights, either through social mobility or through legislative change, they made their way without them, and fought vigorously to preserve their ability to do so. Urban informality may have been the antithesis of citizenship, but it was also often its prerequisite.

Informality among the poor thus emerged in mid-century Brazil as a terrain of compromise, a legal no-man's land that allowed Rio's urban society to continue to function without ever resolving explosive disputes over issues as fundamental as the moral basis of legality, the proper social composition of the city, the relationship between citizenship and social station, the balance between public and private power, and the causes and consequences of social inequality. The compromise functioned, to the extent that it did, largely because virtually no one conceived of it as permanent—not the wealthy, who initially imagined that industrialization, development, and education would eliminate the worst social contradictions, and not the poor, who imagined themselves and their children acquiring progressively more trappings of citizenship and legality. Few foresaw how tightly woven legality and illegality would become, or how much the poverty of rights would burden both Rio's poor and the city they helped to create.

And yet, in the early twenty-first century, the paradoxes of rights poverty seem poised to erode most of what poor people have managed to gain over lifetimes of work, negotiation, and struggle. Informality has allowed poor people to stay in the city, and to claim its geography, culture, economy, and politics as their own in unprecedented ways. But it has also contributed to the fact that the poor have never been able to enjoy anything close to equal opportunity. Rio's poor, in accordance with a definition forged since the beginning of the Estado Novo, are only partial citizens. They rarely have a clear legal hold on their homes, they often have no legal protections in their work, they almost never enjoy equal access to civil rights, and the combination of all of these things corrupts and depreciates their political power, forcing them to request as political favors the sorts of basic public goods they might otherwise claim as rights.

All of these things have a clear economic cost: rights to property, urban services, social security, and collective bargaining translate into real assets, and lack of basic civil guarantees can mean economic calamity for poor families forced to do without an unjustly imprisoned breadwinner. Just as significant, however, is the cost that poverties of rights have extracted in hope. Young people whose grandparents spent most of their lives struggling for social mobility and fuller citizenship look around and see continued inequality and stagnation. The schools and health clinics their communities negotiated and fought to build are overcrowded, poorly staffed, and badly supplied. The brick houses that have now mostly replaced the mid-century favelas' wood-and-zinc shacks are still cramped and plain, and every year many collapse in mudslides or floods. The electricity, drainage, sewage, and transportation networks in favela neighborhoods are scanty and prone to failure, and many of the favelas' streets are still unpaved mud paths. Many poor people now work with signed work cards, but *trabalhista* rights for people without skills have become close to worthless outside the public sector, and formal work for the young, unskilled, and poor often seems to equate with futility and humiliation. Police harassment is so common as to be taken for granted, and blatant racism often compounds its effects. Three-quarters of a century after Vargas claimed to have begun to extend rights to the poor, it is little wonder that all of the modern talk of citizenship rings hollow.

The drug trade has taken a stranglehold on Rio for many reasons quite separate from these failures of law and citizenship. Rio became a strategic point in the international drug trade in the 1980s and is also critical in national distribution networks. Local demand is rich, and much of the trade's financing and money laundering are carried out by a network of silent collaborators from the Carioca mainstream.[14] The development of Rio's first drug cartels was helped along by the juxtaposition of common and political criminals in Rio's prisons during the 1970s; from the "politicals," Rio's first drug lords learned enough about organization, revolutionary Marxism, and community activism to lend a Robin Hood dimension to their first inroads into the favelas.[15] And the drug trade certainly would never have prospered as it has without the successive economic crises that substantially lowered poor people's real standard of living in the 1980s and early 1990s, closing opportunities for legal social mobility and leaving many young people—and especially young men—embittered, humiliated, and hopeless.[16]

Yet the drug business has also built directly on the poverties of rights: without them, it arguably would never have brought Rio to the brink of chaos. Lack of meaningful labor rights and social welfare guarantees have colluded with a weak labor market to make formal work seem worthless for some young men. Consistent police abuse and judicial inequities have eroded poor communities' already scant faith in the justice system, making law enforcement even less possible than it might have been, given police corruption and the drug lords' violent intimidations. Above all, it was the weakness of rights in favelas and other extralegal settlements that made it possible for incipient drug gangs to establish the territorial domination that has been their distinctive linchpin. Following in the footsteps of so many other extralegal operators—from the local land grabbers and political bosses this book has chronicled to the kingpins of the *jogo do bicho*—drug entrepreneurs understood early on that they could turn such communities' weak rights to their advantage. At first they offered some communities much that the state could not; they policed petty crime, they paid for school supplies and soccer uniforms, they stocked medical clinics, they helped to adjudicate local disputes, they provided emergency aid, and they even sometimes served as political intermediaries and helped to bring in public services. Once the trade was entrenched, it became as important to the favelas' local economies as it now undoubtedly is to Rio as a whole, bringing jobs—however dangerous and unsavory—and commercial traffic to communities hard hit by unemployment and stagnation. Even as the drug trade has become more violent and has abandoned whatever communitarian roots it initially had, many uninvolved residents prefer the traffickers to the corrupt police who alternately extort and pursue them.

The early drug trade thus fit easily into a pattern that had been ingrained in poor communities since the favelas' inception. It became a form of essential illegality, just like the illegal activities of the land grabbers, the electricity pirates, and the informal shopkeepers of the early twentieth century. Some community members accepted it both as a bridge between needs and rights and as a source of much-needed income. Key outsiders—police, investors, money launderers, politicians—allowed it to continue out of sheer self-interest. By the time the drug traffic's unique destructiveness became apparent—in its alchemy of violence, quick money, disregard for community needs, and nihilism—the trade was already deeply ingrained. The irony was bitter. For generations of poor Cariocas, extra-legality had been the price of urban permanence and survival. But the poverties of rights that it ingrained over generations had opened the door to this new lawlessness, which served not to create a terrain of compromise between law and possibility, but rather to corrode both.

Rio's contemporary crises constitute a moment, not an ending, and the violent events that grab headlines and dominate movie screens represent only one small facet of poor Cariocas' lives. Even in the midst of the traffickers' wars, the vast majority of favela and suburban residents manage to get by, working and studying and raising their families with the urgent and probably quixotic hope that the extralegal drug economy, like so many before it, will eventually stabilize its internal structure and somehow find accommodation alongside the legal order. The assumption that drugs, crime, and violence now entirely define most poor people's lives is as wrong, and as dangerous, as the multifaceted myths of marginalization that shaped outsiders' views of favelas in the mid-twentieth century.

Yet the surge of drugs, arms, crime, and violence is still different from anything that has come before it, and it highlights the corrosive consequences of poor Cariocas' weak access to rights and legality. Neither hope in the transformative power of democracy, nor faith in the mediating authority of laws and legal institutions can flourish in a context where extra-legality serves as such a ubiquitous compromise between law and everyday life, and where legal status serves to justify the unequal distribution of public benefits. Brazil's democracy still seems to stand a real chance of failing—not, as in the past, because of coup threats from the military and conservative interest groups, but rather through a subtle process of internal disintegration.

Brazil is in no way alone in facing these questions. Legality and extra-legality coexist everywhere, as does the tendency for poverties of rights to accompany and reinforce economic lack. In the United States, both undocumented immigrants and disenfranchised poor people commonly live and work extra-legally, and many sectors of the broader society have come to depend on the economic and political benefits that such people's vulnerabilities produce. In countries with more fully acknowledged histories of poverty and extreme inequality than the United States, poor people almost always have a weak hold on citizenship and legality, to the point that it would often seem absurd to view the law as anything but an instrument of power and privilege. What is remarkable about Brazil since the 1930s is, paradoxically, the degree to which hope in the progressive power of law and citizenship has served as a counterweight to the inequality, anger, and cynicism fueled by successive economic crises and consistently unequal rights. The critical question, in the face of drug wars, rising crime rates, and growing paranoia, is whether that balance can hold—whether the national debate on citizenship will convince Rio's poor that democracy and the rule of law will ever grant them more than a poverty of rights.

Reference Matter

Statistical Appendixes

The appendixes that follow represent bi- and multivariate analysis of two separate samples of criminal cases tried in Rio de Janeiro's criminal courts, the first involving 251 accusations from the late 1920s through the early 1940s, and the second involving 263 accusations from the 1950s and early 1960s. The cases were held in the Brazilian National Archives, Rio's state judicial archives, and the archives of Rio's sentencing court.[1] Both samples included a variety of crime types, with roughly equal proportions of guilty verdicts. They had a fairly even geographical distribution throughout Rio de Janeiro but were otherwise chosen at random.

In analyzing these cases, I sought to study the connections between race, social status, and the workings of Rio's criminal justice system by measuring the relationship between various personal characteristics of defendants and four distinct questions of judicial procedure and outcome: (1) whether or not the defendant's case was dismissed before trial; (2) whether or not a defendant was found guilty; (3) whether or not a defendant spent any time in prison; and (4) the degree to which the civil rights guaranteed to each defendant in the codes of criminal procedure were respected or violated. In analyzing these factors, I used two techniques: a simple cross-tabulation (merely determining the percentage of defendants with each characteristic that received determined types of treatment, and comparing these percentages with the statistical average for all defendants), and a series of logistic regressions (which allowed me to look at the independent influence of each variable, but which have the disadvantage of being somewhat speculative because of the number of variables I considered and the relatively small size of my two samples).

THE CROSS-TABULATIONS
(Statistical Appendix I, Tables I.1–I.4)

In the 1930 sample cross-tabulations, I compared these questions of procedure and outcome with eleven categories classifying defendants' personal characteristics, as detailed in chapter 5. For the cross-tabulations calculated for the post-1950 sample, I analyzed two additional factors: (1) whether or not a defendant possessed a *carteira profissional*, and (2) how each defendant was personally characterized by the *vida pregressa* mandated by Brazil's 1942 code of criminal procedure. In the tables for both periods, I have indicated with italics when the number of defendants with the said characteristic was fewer than fifteen; in these cases, the results should be seen as highly speculative.

THE LOGISTIC REGRESSIONS
(Statistical Appendixes II and III, Tables II.1 and III.1)

Cross-tabulations and qualitative analysis both strongly suggest that a number of factors influenced the course of Carioca criminal trials in both periods, with documents assuming ever-greater importance among them. Only a multivariate statistical method, however, can test this hypothesis with some degree of precision, measuring the influence of individual variables while holding all others steady. Because of the qualitative nature of the data involved, logistic regression proved to be the most appropriate multivariate technique. Using it, I constructed models for both samples predicting the four types of outcome explored in my cross-tabulations. I analyzed separately the pre- and post-1945 samples, running eight separate regressions.[2] The results for each sample are presented in table II.1 and table III.1. For both samples, model 1 predicts the likelihood that a defendant will go to trial, model 2 predicts the likelihood that a defendant will be found guilty at trial, model 3 predicts the likelihood that he or she will spend any time in prison, and model 4 predicts the likelihood that his or her civil rights will be violated. The models were able to predict correct outcomes between 71 and 86 percent of the time, and in all cases they were significantly better predictors than random guesses.

The individual characteristics considered in all of these models differ in a few ways from those used in the cross-tabulations. In the interest of maximizing the statistical significance of the findings, I reduced the number of categories considered, added a few new types of information, and also greatly simplified the sub-classifications within each category. In all cases, I did this with the objective of increasing the predictive power of the model as a whole. While this led to some loss of precision, it allowed me to build models that often yielded significant results and were relatively accurate in predicting outcomes. Nonetheless, given the small sample numbers and the large number of variables considered, many of the numbers here do not have true statistical significance.[3]

The results tables show three variables: *B*, *Exp (B)*, and *Exp (B)/Exp (B) + 1*. *B* represents the natural log of the odds that an individual with a specific characteristic will spend time in prison, be found guilty, and have his or her civil rights violated. To a layperson, *B* simply indicates the scale and direction of the relationship with the so-called omitted category (marked in the tables); a negative number here means that an individual in this category is less likely to face a negative outcome as compared to the omitted category, and a positive number means the opposite. The total natural log of the odds that any individual will face a given outcome, *B(ind)*, is equal to the constant plus the *B* corresponding to each individual characteristic that the individual possesses. Thus, for Manuel Francisco dos Santos—a *preto* dump guard with a primary education who was accused of murder, lived in a formal neighborhood, was employed as a security guard, had a civil ID and a work ID, had no criminal record, had a positive *vida pregressa* (VP), and hired a private lawyer—the equation predicting the likelihood that he would face trial would be: *B(ind) = 1.248 (constant) − 2.617 (murder) + 2.150* (preto*) + .056 (formal neighborhood) − .032 (labor) − .293 (primary education) + .605 (positive VP) − .659 (no criminal record)*. The equation works out to .458. In order for this number to mean something to the uninitiated, however, it must first be transformed into *Exp (B)* (equivalent to the odds) and then to *Exp B/(Exp B + 1)* (equivalent to the probability). For Manuel, these numbers are, respectively, 1.581 and .613; the latter number indicates that a person with Manuel's characteristic has, according to the model, a 61 percent probability of facing trial. The general odds and probabilities for each category are presented in the tables as *Exp (B)* and *Exp (B)/Exp (B) + 1*.

As a whole, these statistics are better read as suggestions regarding the direction and strength of relationships than as definitive conclusions. But they are valuable nonetheless because this is the largest historical sample of criminal cases ever to consider questions of procedure, and to include many of the variables considered (possession of documents and representation by police being the most important among them).

TABLE I.1

*Deviation from Average Percentage of Cases Dismissed Before
Trial Stage, by Characteristics of Defendants*

Pre-1945		Post-1945	
Individual characteristics	Deviation (%)	Individual characteristics	Deviation (%)
Professional occupation	26.3	Domestic occupation (nonpaid)	36.4
Supervised housing	14.8	Other Brazil birth	23.6
Rural neighborhood	11.5	*Factory occupation*	18
Formal housing	10.1	*Rural neighborhood*	14.2
Branco	10	Police/military occupation	11.8
High literacy	7.7	Formal housing	10
Primary literacy	7.7	Professional occupation	9.2
White-collar occupation	6.2	Formal neighborhood	8.5
Mixed neighborhood	5	High literacy	7
Skilled labor occupation	3.3	Primary literacy	5.8
Foreign birth	3	Married or widowed	5.8
Police/military occupation	1.6	Informal union	4.7
Southeast birth	1.4	Has work ID	3.8
Birth in Distrito Federal	1.2	Has civil ID	3.5
Married or widowed	0.8	Pardo	2.8
Informal union	0.5	Positive VP[a]	2.7
Defendant works	0.5	Defendant works	2.3
Has civil ID	0.4	Birth in Distrito Federal	2.2
Pardo	0.2	Branco	1.7
Domestic occupation (nonpaid)	0.1	No criminal record	0.6
Rudimentary literacy	0	Northeast birth	0.4
Formal neighborhood	−0.2	Mixed neighborhood	−0.5
Single	−0.3	Neutral VP[a]	−0.7
No criminal record	−1.6	No work ID	−1.4
No civil ID	−1.9	*Foreign birth*	−2
Northeast birth	−4.2	No civil ID	−2.1
Preto	−6.6	Collective housing	−2.6
Collective housing	−9.6	Shack housing	−3.3
Factory occupation	−10.2	*Supervised housing*	−3.4
Inquérito record	−10.2	Inquérito record	−4.4
General Brazil birth	−10.2	Unskilled labor occupation	−4.9
Unskilled labor occupation	−12	Southeast birth	−5.6
Criminal record	−12.5	Illiterate	−7.7
Illiterate	−13.7	Preto	−8.2
Shack housing	−14.6	Skilled labor occupation	−8.6
Informal neighborhood	−19.2	Single	−8.7
Defendant doesn't work	−21.7	White-collar occupation	−10.8
		Informal neighborhood	−11
		Rudimentary literacy	−11.9
		Defendant doesn't work	−13.8
		Criminal record	−22.8
		Negative VP[a]	−23.8

NOTE: Italics indicate 15 or fewer defendants in category.

[a] VP = *vida pregressa*.

TABLE I.2

*Deviation from Average Percentage of Innocent Verdicts,
by Characteristics of Defendants*

Pre-1945	Deviation (%)	Post-1945	Deviation (%)
Factory occupation	18.6	*High literacy*	46.8
Private lawyer	17.7	Professional occupation	44.2
Formal housing	12.9	Domestic occupation (nonpaid)	37.5
Professional occupation	11.9	Police/military occupation	32
High literacy	10.2	Has work ID	26.3
Rudimentary literacy	9.5	*Foreign birth*	25.6
Has civil ID	8.2	Private lawyer	23.2
Defendant works	8.1	Has civil ID	15.9
Married or widowed	8	*Supervised housing*	14.2
Foreign birth	7.8	Positive VP[a]	11.6
Informal union	7.5	Primary literacy	9.5
Birth in Distrito Federal	6.7	Informal union	9.5
Domestic occupation (nonpaid)	6.4	Birth in Distrito Federal	8
Preto	5.2	Formal housing	7.4
Mixed neighborhood	5	Married or widowed	7.1
White-collar occupation	4.8	No criminal record	5.4
Formal neighborhood	4.5	Defendant works	5
Police/military occupation	1.9	Shack housing	4.9
Collective housing	1.9	Branco	3.7
No criminal record	1.3	Formal neighborhood	3.1
Pardo	0.3	Pardo	3
Informal neighborhood	−0.5	Neutral VP[a]	2.7
Inquérito record	−2.3	Informal neighborhood	2.6
Skilled labor occupation	−3.1	White-collar occupation	0.4
No civil ID	−3.4	Skilled labor occupation	0
Southeast birth	−3.7	*Factory occupation*	−2.9
Branco	−4.2	*Rural neighborhood*	−2.9
Unskilled labor occupation	−4.7	Southeast birth	−3.5
Primary literacy	−5.6	Preto	−4.8
Single	−6	Illiterate	−4.9
Northeast birth	−6.7	Mixed neighborhood	−5.8
Illiterate	−8.9	Inquérito record	−8.3
Shack housing	−11.1	*Other Brazil birth*	−8.3
No lawyer	−12.8	No civil ID	−8.8
Criminal record	−12.8	No work ID	−9
Supervised housing	−14.8	Single	−9.1
General Brazil birth	−14.8	Criminal record	−10.5
Public defender	−16.5	Northeast birth	−11
Defendant doesn't work	−22.1	Public defender	−11.5
Rural neighborhood	−48.1	Rudimentary literacy	−16.2
		Collective housing	−16.6
		Negative VP[a]	−16.9
		Unskilled labor occupation	−18.3
		Defendant doesn't work	−23.6

NOTE: Italics indicate 15 or fewer defendants in category.

[a] VP = *vida pregressa*.

TABLE I.3

*Deviation from Average Percentage of Cases with No
Prison Time, by Characteristics of Defendants*

Pre-1945	Deviation (%)	Post-1945	Deviation (%)
Domestic occupation (nonpaid)	24.9	Domestic occupation (nonpaid)	30.2
High literacy	17.7	Professional occupation	23.1
Police/military occupation	15.6	Police/military occupation	18.5
Professional occupation	*13.6*	Has work ID	16
Formal housing	12.7	Other Brazil birth	14.6
Factory occupation	*11.7*	*Factory occupation*	*14*
Foreign birth	9.4	*Rural neighborhood*	*14*
Has civil ID	8.9	Positive VP[a]	13.3
Defendant works	8.6	Has civil ID	12.1
Informal union	*8.1*	Married or widowed	10.1
White-collar occupation	7.9	Formal housing	8.1
Married or widowed	7.5	High literacy	7.5
Primary literacy	7.1	No criminal record	7.1
Mixed neighborhood	6.2	Defendant works	4.9
Birth in Distrito Federal	5.4	Primary literacy	4.2
No criminal record	4.8	DF birth	3.5
Informal neighborhood	4.7	Mixed neighborhood	3.4
Preto	3.4	Neutral VP[a]	2.7
Branco	2.1	Branco	2.1
Formal neighborhood	0.3	Formal neighborhood	−0.3
Collective housing	0.3	Pardo	−0.4
Southeast birth	−1.3	Shack housing	−1
Rudimentary literacy	−4	Informal union	−1.2
No civil ID	−4	*Supervised housing*	*−2.2*
Shack housing	−4.5	Preto	−2.7
Single	−4.8	Southeast birth	−3.3
Pardo	−5	Unskilled labor occupation	−4
Unskilled labor occupation	−8.2	Northeast birth	−5
Northeast birth	−8.5	Informal neighborhood	−5.4
Illiterate	−9.5	No work ID	−6.1
Skilled labor occupation	−12.5	No civil ID	−7.2
Supervised housing	*−13.3*	Single	−7.5
Rural neighborhood	*−16.6*	Collective housing	−7.9
Inquérito record	−19.5	Illiterate	−8
General Brazil birth	−25.8	*Foreign birth*	*−9.3*
Criminal record	−29.2	Inquérito record	−10.4
Defendant doesn't work	−40.9	White-collar occupation	−10.7
		Skilled labor occupation	−11.2
		Rudimentary literacy	−11.5
		Defendant doesn't work	−20.8
		Criminal record	−34.9
		Negative VP[a]	−38.1

NOTE: Italics indicate 15 or fewer defendants in category.

[a] VP = *vida pregressa*.

TABLE I.4

*Deviation from Average Percentage of Cases with No Civil Rights
Violations, by Characteristics of Defendants*

Pre-1945	Deviation (%)	Post-1945	Deviation (%)
Police/military occupation	21.5	Domestic occupation (nonpaid)	30.4
Professional occupation	*19.1*	Police/military occupation	29.8
High literacy	17.3	Professional occupation	23.2
Factory occupation	*14.3*	Has work ID	22.7
Foreign birth	12.3	*Factory occupation*	*21.4*
Formal housing	12.1	High literacy	21.2
Has civil ID	11.6	Has civil ID	17.8
White-collar occupation	11.3	*Rural neighborhood*	*15.7*
Primary literacy	11.1	Positive VP[a]	15.2
Supervised housing	*10.1*	Formal housing	13.7
Domestic occupation (nonpaid)	9.2	No criminal record	10.4
Married or widowed	7.7	Married or widowed	8.5
Mixed neighborhood	7.3	Defendant works	7.9
No criminal record	6.7	Primary literacy	7.4
Defendant works	5.8	Branco	7.3
Branco	5.6	*Supervised housing*	*7.1*
Informal union	*5.4*	Formal neighborhood	6.6
Birth in Distrito Federal	4.1	*Foreign birth*	*5.7*
Formal neighborhood	0.3	Neutral VP[a]	5.4
Northeast birth	−1.8	Mixed neighborhood	5.1
Rudimentary literacy	−2.9	Other Brazil birth	4.5
Collective housing	−3.4	Birth in Distrito Federal	4.4
Preto	−4.2	White-collar occupation	−0.7
Single	−4.7	Southeast birth	−2
No civil ID	−5.4	Informal union	−2.2
Skilled labor occupation	−5.5	Pardo	−2.5
Southeast birth	−5.6	Illiterate	−2.6
Pardo	−6.5	Collective housing	−3.7
Rural neighborhood	*−6.5*	Shack housing	−5.1
Shack housing	−11.4	Single	−6
Informal neighborhood	−13.2	Preto	−8
Illiterate	−14.7	Northeast birth	−8.4
Unskilled labor occupation	−16.7	No work ID	−8.7
Inquérito record	−17	Skilled labor occupation	−9.8
Criminal record	−27.8	Inquérito record	−10.1
General Brazil birth	−29.4	No civil ID	−11.1
Defendant doesn't work	−37.1	Unskilled labor occupation	−12.9
		Rudimentary literacy	−13.3
		Informal neighborhood	−13.7
		Defendant doesn't work	−33.9
		Criminal record	−35.3
		Negative VP[a]	−37.4

NOTE: Italics indicate 15 or fewer defendants in category.
[a] VP = *vida pregressa*.

TABLE II.1

Regressions on Pre-1945 Sample for Chapter 5

Exp B=odds	Model 1	Trial likelihood		Model 2	Guilt likelihood	
Exp B/(Exp B+1)=probability	B	Odds	Probability	B	Odds	Probability
Variables describing crime type						
Sexual crimes	−2.714	0.066	0.06	*−1.003*	*0.367*	*0.27*
Physical violence	−2.233	0.107	0.10	−0.09	0.914	0.48
Vagrancy/arms possession	7.2	1339.59	1.00	0.184	1.202	0.55
Theft/robbery	−1.367	3.469	0.78	0.736	2.087	0.68
Calumnia/injuria (omitted)						
Variables describing region of birth						
Foreign	*0.487*	*1.628*	*0.62*	−0.445	0.641	0.39
Rio de Janeiro (DF)	0.115	1.122	0.53	−0.245	0.783	0.44
Migrants (born in SE or NE)	−0.22	0.803	0.45	0.302	1.352	0.57
Migrants (born elsewhere in Brazil) (omitted)						
Variables describing color						
Branco	*−0.862*	*0.422*	*0.30*	0.833	2.3	0.70
Pardo	0.112	1.119	0.53	0.012	0.977	0.49
Preto	0.291	1.337	0.57	−0.754	0.097	0.09
Unknown (omitted)						
Variables describing housing type						
Formal/supervised	−0.555	*0.574*	0.36	*0.661*	*0.40*	
Shacks/collective/rural	0.803	2.233	0.69	0.367	1.443	0.59
Unknown (omitted)						
Variables describing address region						
Zona Sul	−0.495	*0.61*	*0.38*	−0.479	0.619	0.38
Centro or elsewhere in Rio	0.376	*1.456*	*0.59*	−0.426	0.653	0.40
Rural (omitted)						
Variables describing occupation						
Professional	−1.818	*0.162*	*0.14*	1.1294	3.646	0.78
White-collar occupation	0.433	1.541	0.61	−0.403	0.668	0.40
Worker	*0.848*	*2.336*	*0.70*	−0.509	0.601	0.38
Unskilled labor occupation	0.792	2.207	0.69	−0.617	*0.539*	*0.35*
Domestic occupation, unpaid (omitted)						
Variables describing literacy						
Primary literacy	−0.563	*0.569*	*0.36*	−0.252	0.777	0.44
Illiterate	−0.418	0.658	0.40	0.202	1.224	0.55
Highly literate (omitted)						
Other variables						
Has a civil ID	−0.168	0.845	0.46	−0.488	0.614	0.38
Has a work card				−1.292	*0.275*	*0.22*
Has a criminal record				0.562	1.754	0.64
Does not have a criminal record				0.716	*2.046*	*0.67*
Unknown criminal record (omitted)						
Has a private lawyer				−0.925	*0.397*	*0.28*
Has a public defender				0.559	1.749	0.64
Has no lawyer (omitted)						
Constant	2.393			0.569		

	Model 3	Prison-time likelihood		Model 4	Rights-violation likelihood	
	B	Odds	Probability	B	Odds	Probability
Variables describing crime type						
Sexual crimes	−2.333	0.097	0.09	−0.689	0.502	0.33
Physical violence	−0.699	0.497	0.33	−1.082	0.339	0.25
Vagrancy/arms possession	2.877	17.756	0.95	1.645	5.179	0.84
Theft/robbery	0.183	1.201	0.55	0.985	2.679	0.73
Calumnia/injuria (omitted)						
Variables describing region of birth						
Foreign	−0.736	0.479	0.32	−1.217	0.296	0.23
Rio de Janeiro (DF)	−0.448	0.639	0.39	−0.303	0.738	0.42
Migrants (born in SE or NE)	0.424	1.528	0.60	0.444	1.56	0.61
Migrants (born elsewhere in Brazil) (omitted)						
Variables describing color						
Branco	0.647	1.909	0.66	0.318	1.374	0.58
Pardo	0.352	1.422	0.59	0.323	1.381	0.58
Preto	−0.938	0.391	0.28	−0.779	0.459	0.31
Unknown (omitted)						
Variables describing housing type						
Formal/supervised	−0.429	0.651	0.39	−0.53	0.589	0.37
Shacks/collective/rural	0.301	1.352	0.57	0.553	1.738	0.63
Unknown (omitted)						
Variables describing address region						
Zona Sul	−0.837	0.433	0.30	−0.881	0.414	0.29
Centro or elsewhere in Rio	0.061	1.062	0.52	0.745	2.107	0.68
Rural (omitted)						
Variables describing occupation						
Professional	0.34	1.406	0.58	−1.826	0.161	0.14
White-collar occupation	0.437	1.549	0.61	0.184	1.202	0.55
Worker	0.858	2.359	0.70	0.579	1.785	0.64
Unskilled labor occupation	0.251	1.285	0.56	1.099	3.001	0.75
Domestic occupation, unpaid (omitted)						
Variables describing literacy						
Primary literacy	−0.229	0.795	0.44	−0.233	0.792	0.44
Illiterate	0.418	1.519	0.60	0.392	1.481	0.60
Highly literate (omitted)						
Other variables						
Has a civil ID	−0.957	0.384	0.28	−1.008	0.365	0.27
Has a work card						
Has a criminal record	1.306	3.693	0.79	0.841	2.319	0.70
Does not have a criminal record	0.563	1.756	0.64	0.319	1.375	0.58
Unknown criminal record (omitted)						
Has a private lawyer						
Has a public defender						
Has no lawyer (omitted)						
Constant	−1.006			−2.233		

NOTE: Italics and bold = significance at 0 –.054; bold = significance at .055–.149; italics = significance at .15–.249.

TABLE III.1
Regressions on Post-1945 Data for Chapter 6

Exp B=odds	Model 1	Trial likelihood		Model 2	Guilt likelihood	
Exp B/(Exp B+1)=probability	B	Odds	Probability	B	Odds	Probabil
Variables describing crime type						
Sexual crimes	−1.935	0.144	0.13	−0.083	0.92	0.48
Physical violence	−3.055	0.047	0.04	0.459	1.582	0.61
Vagrancy/arms possession	10.556	38425.603	1.00	17.915	60300884	1.00
Theft/robbery	−0.633	0.531	0.35	0.167	1.181	0.54
Attempted murder	0.657	1.93	0.66	−3.699	0.025	0.02
Murder	−2.617	0.073	0.07	−1.742	0.175	0.15
Calumnia/injuria (omitted)						
Variables describing color						
Branco	1.935	6.925	0.87	3.021	20.519	0.95
Pardo	1.328	3.774	0.79	1.744	5.719	0.85
Preto	2.15	8.582	0.90	1.614	5.023	0.83
Unknown (omitted)						
Variables describing neighborhood type						
Formal	0.056	1.058	0.51	0.263	1.3	0.57
Mixed	0.333	1.395	0.58	0.214	1.238	0.55
Informal	*0.871*	*2.389*	*0.70*	*0.542*	*1.719*	*0.63*
Rural (omitted)						
Variables describing occupation						
Professional	*1.007*	*2.737*	*0.73*	*−1.641*	*0.194*	*0.16*
White-collar occupation	*1.078*	*2.938*	*0.75*	1.195	3.302	0.77
Worker	−0.032	0.968	0.49	0.167	1.182	0.54
Unskilled labor occupation	−0.65	0.522	0.34	*1.515*	*4.55*	*0.82*
Domestic, women (omitted)						
Variables describing literacy						
Primary literacy	−0.293	0.746	0.43	3.586	36.092	0.97
Illiterate	0.5	1.649	0.62	3.727	41.569	0.98
Highly literate (omitted)						
Other variables						
Has a civil ID				1.153	3.167	0.76
Has a work card				**−2.646**	*0.071*	*0.07*
Has a criminal record	0.992	2.698	0.73	−0.745	0.475	0.32
Does not have a criminal record	−0.659	0.517	0.34	−0.902	0.406	0.29
Has a positive VP[a]	0.605	0.136	0.12	−0.288	0.75	0.43
Has a negative VP[a]	*1.056*	*2.876*	*0.74*	0.391	1.478	0.60
Has a private lawyer				−2.64	0.071	0.07
Has a public defender				−2.775	0.062	0.06
Constant	1.248			−2.146		

	Model 3	Prison-time likelihood		Model 4	Rights-violation likelihood	
	B	Odds	Probability	B	Odds	Probability
riables describing crime type						
Sexual crimes	0.651	1.918	0.66	0.412	1.509	0.60
Physical violence	−0.126	0.881	0.47	−0.801	0.449	0.31
Vagrancy/arms possession	2.182	8.864	0.90	2.286	9.833	0.91
Theft/robbery	2.032	7.627	0.88	2.008	7.45	0.88
Attempted murder	1.341	3.823	0.79	1.425	4.16	0.81
Murder	1.473	4.362	0.81	1.417	4.125	0.80
Calumnia/injuria (omitted)						
riables describing color						
Branco	−0.4	0.67	0.40	−0.326	0.721	0.42
Pardo	**−0.915**	**0.4**	**0.29**	−0.183	0.833	0.45
Preto	**−0.822**	**0.44**	**0.31**	0.038	1.039	0.51
Unknown (omitted)						
riables describing neighborhood type						
Formal	**0.723**	**2.06**	**0.67**	*0.633*	*0.161*	*0.14*
Mixed	0.245	1.277	0.56	−0.067	0.936	0.48
Informal	**0.513**	**1.67**	**0.63**	*1.005*	*2.731*	*0.73*
Rural (omitted)						
riables describing occupation						
Professional	−0.329	0.72	0.42	0.477	1.611	0.62
White-collar occupation	**0.79**	**2.204**	**0.69**	0.524	1.689	0.63
Worker	0.366	1.442	0.59	−0.214	0.807	0.45
Unskilled labor occupation	−0.299	0.742	0.43	0.279	1.321	0.57
Domestic, women (omitted)						
riables describing literacy						
Primary literacy	*−0.441*	*0.643*	*0.39*	0.2	1.222	0.55
Illiterate	0.397	1.488	0.60	0.299	1.348	0.57
Highly literate (omitted)						
her variables						
Has a civil ID	−0.219	0.803	0.45	−0.585	0.557	0.36
Has a work card	−0.642	0.526	0.34	−0.97	0.379	0.27
Has a criminal record	*0.946*	*2.576*	*0.72*	*1.122*	*3.072*	*0.75*
Does not have criminal record	0.331	1.392	0.58	0.264	1.303	0.57
Has a positive VP[a]	−0.648	0.523	0.34	−0.42	0.657	0.40
Has a negative VP[a]	*1.146*	*3.147*	*0.76*	*1.209*	*3.351*	*0.77*
Has a private lawyer						
Has a public defender						
nstant	−.483			−1.856		

[a] VP = *vida pregressa*.

Notes

All translations, here and in the body of the text, are the author's unless otherwise noted. All quotations in Portuguese retain the original spelling and grammar. All works cited here are listed in the bibliography alphabetically by the author's final surname. The following abbreviations are used in the notes:

ACDF *Anais da Câmara do Distrito Federal*
AJ   Arquivo Judiciário
AN   Arquivo Nacional, Rio de Janeiro
IBGE Instituto Brasileiro de Geografia e Estatística
TJ   Tribunal de Júri
PC   Pretoria Cível
PCr   Pretoria Criminal
VC   Vara Cível
VCr   Vara Criminal

INTRODUCTION

1. See, most notably, Parisse, *Favelas*; Leeds and Leeds, *A sociologia*; Machado da Silva, "O significado"; Tavares de Moura, "Favelas"; Tavares de Moura, *Relatório*; Perlman, *The Myth*; Conn, *The Squatters' Rights*; Sociedade de Análises Gráficas e Mecanográficas Aplicadas aos Complexos Sociais, "Aspectos humanos"; Souza Santos, "The Law"; and Valladares, *Passa-se*.

2. On the law's uses and exclusions during slavery and abolition, see, among many others, Grinberg, *Liberata*; Grinberg, *O fiador*; Mattos de Castro, *Das cores*; Motta, *Nas fronteiras*; Chalhoub, *Visões*; Chalhoub, "The Politics of Silence"; Naro, "Customary Rightholders"; and Holloway, *Policing Rio*. On the First Republic, see Chalhoub, *Trabalho*; Fausto, *Crime e cotidiano*; Kowarick, *Trabalho e vadiagem*; Abreu Esteves, *Meninas*; Caulfield, *In Defense*; Bretas, *A guerra*; and Bretas, "You Can't." For both periods, see essays collected in Lara and Mendonça, eds., *Direitos e justiças*; and dos Santos Gomes and Gomes da Cunha, *Quase cidadão*.

3. On labor and criminal law after Vargas, see especially works by Wanderley Guilherme dos Santos, John French, Alexandre Fontes, Maria Célia Paoli, Olívia Maria Gomes da Cunha, Carlos Antônio Costa Ribeiro, Sueann Caulfield, Cliff Welch, and Barbara Weinstein. On the 1980s and beyond, see especially the writings of Elizabeth Leeds, Alba Zaluar, Paulo Sérgio Pinheiro, James Holston, and Teresa Caldeira.

4. Merryman, *Civil Law Tradition*.

PART I: RIGHTS TO THE MARVELOUS CITY

1. On samba, see Vianna, *O mistério*; McCann, *Hello*; Shaw, *Social History*; and Matos, *Acertei*. On Alves, see Marcondes, *Enciclopédia*.

2. On the early history of popular culture in these regions, see Pereira Cunha, *Ecos*; and Vianna, *Geografia*.

3. Moura, *Tia Ciata*.

4. Matos, *Acertei*.

5. See McCann, *Hello*; and Vianna, *O mistério*.

6. On the long history of representations of favelas in samba, see Oliveira and Marcier, "A palavra." For a lesser-known musical reaction to Agache, see Conniff, *Urban Politics*, 33–34.

7. On Agache's visit to Rio, see Stuckenbruck, *O Rio*; Bruant, "Donat Alfred Agache"; M. da Silva Pereira, "Pensando a metrópole"; and L. Silva, "A trajetória." Agache's "master plan" was published in 1930 as *Rio de Janeiro, extensão, remodelação, embellezamento*.

8. On discourses surrounding Rio's favelas, see Valladares, "A gênese"; and Valladares, *A invenção*. Mattos Pimenta, who coined the term "leprosy" to describe the favelas, was one of Agache's guides in Rio and would later become president of Rio's Bolsa de Valores. See Almeida Abreu, "Reconstruindo."

9. See Zylberberg, *Morro*. Lilian Fessler Vaz suggests an alternate history in "Contribuição."

10. On Rio's early history, see Bernardes, "Evolução." See also Roxo and Ferreira, "O saneamento"; Novaes Pinto, "A cidade"; Backheuser, "A geologia"; and Antunes, "Transformações."

11. Geographer and engineer Everardo Backheuser described this process as follows: "The city clearly went surging forth from the marshlands. So great was the need for a dry space for urban expansion in the first centuries that, even without any technical knowledge of sanitation, the plains began to be dried out. No attempt was made to be done with the quagmire with drainage; earth was simply placed on top of it, as is still done today. . . ." Backheuser, "A faixa litorânea," cited in Novaes Pinto, "A cidade."

12. See Bicalho, *A cidade*, chap. 7.

13. Karasch, *Slave Life*, 15.

14. Ibid., 61. See also Almeida Abreu, *Evolução*.

15. Cruls, *Aparência*.

16. On Rio's nineteenth-century geographical evolution, see Almeida Abreu, *Evolução*.

17. On life among Rio's urban poor in the nineteenth century, see Karasch, *Slave Life*; Lauderdale Graham, *House and Street*; Chalhoub, *Visões*; Campos Abreu, *O Império*; E. da Silva, *Prince*; and Líbano Soares, *A capoeira*.

18. See especially Chalhoub, *Visões*; and E. da Silva, *Prince*.

19. Diretoria Geral de Estatística, *Recenseamento Geral da República dos Estados Unidos do Brasil em 31 de Dezembro de 1890*. The percentage of foreign residents in Rio was actually higher in 1872, though the absolute number was greater in 1890.

20. Chalhoub, *Visões*, 199.

21. Diretoria Geral de Estatística, *Recenseamento Geral da República dos Estados Unidos do Brasil em 31 de Dezembro de 1890*.

22. Almeida Abreu, *Evolução*.

23. See Needell, *A Tropical Belle Epoque*; Chalhoub, *Cidade febril*; Murilo de Carvalho, *Os bestializados*; Meade, *"Civilizing" Rio*; Benchimol, *Pereira Passos*; Benchimol, *Dos micróbios*; and Hochman, *A era*.

24. Ruy Maurício de Lima e Silva, "Iluminação."

25. Roxo and Ferreira, "O saneamento." On "tigers," see Karasch, *Slave Life*, 266.

26. Rosauro Mariano da Silva, "A luta."

27. On elite public space, see Needell, *A Tropical Belle Epoque*. On cinema and popular uses of public space, see Caulfield, *In Defense*; and Sevcenko, "A capital."

28. See Benchimol, *Pereira Passos*; Needell, *A Tropical Belle Epoque*; Lauderdale Graham, *House and Street*; and Sevcenko, "A capital." For a journalistic memorial, see Edmundo, *O Rio*. On similar processes in Latin America, see Piccato, *City*; Scobie, *Buenos Aires*; and Moya, *Cousins*.

29. Edmundo, *O Rio*, 121.

30. Ibid., chap. 7.

31. Ibid., 147.

32. Ibid., 151.

33. Ibid., 154.

34. Ibid., chap. 8.

35. Nonato and Santos, *Era uma vez*.

36. The 1933 building census notes that there were services but no pavement on the hill (Ministério do Trabalho, Indústria, e Comércio, Departamento de Estatística e Publicidade, *Estatística Predial*, 195), whereas other evidence suggests that this was at most partially true; see, for example, Edmundo, *O Rio*. See also a report from the 1920s attached to a letter from the residents of Santo Antônio dated 7 August 1934, found in AN, records of the Secretaria da Presidência da República, Série 17.4, caixa 33, pasta 1934.

37. See Vaz, *Modernidade*; Vaz, "Contribuição"; Aquino Carvalho, *Habitações*; Almeida Abreu, "Reconstruindo"; Chalhoub, *Cidade febril*; Edmundo, *O Rio*; Backheuser, "Onde moram"; and Backheuser, *Habitações*.

38. The extension of transportation routes in Rio de Janeiro has been studied extensively; see especially N. Santos, *Meios*; Pereira da Silva, *Os transportes*; Rocha, *A era*; and Almeida Abreu, *Evolução*, chap. 3, sec. 3. For a study of the

interactions between transportation routes and urban expansion in São Paulo, see Morse, *From Community*. For a comparison with Buenos Aires, see Scobie, *Buenos Aires*. For a comparison with the United States, see Stilgoe, *Metropolitan Corridor*.

39. Almeida Abreu, *Evolução*.

40. See Rocha, *A era*; Almeida Abreu, *Evolução*; and Quieroz Ribeiro, *Dos cortiços*. See also chapter 7, this volume.

41. There were, of course, other neighborhoods with tram service besides these, which are mentioned only as examples of the most important new areas opened up by the tramways. The Botanical Garden Railway Company (originally conceived by none other than the famous Barão de Mauá but sold to an American company in 1868) was responsible for the construction and operation of lines from the city center to Glória and Catete (1868), to Botafogo and the Jardim Botânico at what is now the Praça Santos Dumont (1871), to Laranjeiras (1871), to Gávea (1872), to Copacabana (1892), to Ipanema (1901), and to Leblon (1914). Electrification of these lines began in 1892. Lines operated by the Rio de Janeiro Street Railway Company, later the Companhia São Cristóvão, extended routes to São Cristóvão, Tijuca, Saúde, Santo Cristo, Gamboa, Cajú, Catumbi, and Rio Comprido between 1870 and 1894. The Companhia Ferro-Carril da Vila Isabel opened service to Vila Isabel in 1873 and to Andaraí, Grajaú, and Maracanã in 1875. In 1878 and 1879, the Companhia Carris Urbanos consolidated several other companies and opened service within and between the Centro Commercial, port districts to the north, the central railway station, and several of the neighborhoods of Rio's central periphery. For a detailed account, see N. Santos, *Meios*, 257–395. All of these companies were later united, between 1904 and 1908, under the Canadian-owned Rio de Janeiro Tramway, Light, and Power Company. For more detail, see McDowall, *The Light*, 140–43.

42. An interesting exception to both of these patterns is São Cristóvão, which started out as an elite residential neighborhood and the site of the Imperial Palace and ended up a heavily industrial and working-class area; see Almeida Abreu, *Evolução*.

43. The neighborhood of Gávea, now an upper-middle-class enclave, housed many such experiments.

44. N. Santos, *Meios*, 489–91. On Madureira, see Segadas Soares, "Fisonomia"; and Geiger, "Esbôço."

45. N. Santos, *Meios*, 314. The full text reads: "By that time [after 1896], it was already a veritable martyrdom to ride on the suburban trains in the morning or in the evening. The population elbowed each other in the principal stations, struggling with one another in the rush hours, as if they were a band of gasping wrestlers, to get a place on a train, where people of all castes jammed up against one another." Santos's horror at the mixture of castes hints that elite aversion to the poor often had a racist subtext.

46. Barreto, *Triste fim de Policarpo Quaresma*, 103–4.

47. For popular memories of early stilt shantytowns, see Varella, Bertazzo, and Jacques, *Maré*.

48. One of the best accounts of the growth and development of Rio's suburbs in the late nineteenth century is Pechman, "A gênese."

49. Ministério do Trabalho, Indústria, e Comércio, Departamento de Estatística e Publicidade, *Estatística Predial do Distrito Federal, 1933*. There are no reliable earlier figures on service provision.

50. Citywide, the correlation coefficients describing the relationship between the percentage of Rio's 1940 population living in a given area and the percentage of total city streets served by electricity and piped water that were located in that same area in 1933 are, respectively, .82 and .73, indicating a relatively strong relationship between population and service provision in these areas. These findings add some nuance to the conclusions of other historians, notably Teresa Meade, who argues convincingly for a general imbalance in service provision between Rio's north and south zones in the early twentieth century; see Meade, *"Civilizing" Rio*. Service figures are taken from Ministério do Trabalho, Indústria, e Comércio, Departamento de Estatística e Publicidade, *Estatística Predial do Distrito Federal, 1933*; population figures, from IBGE, *Recenseamento Geral do Brasil, 1 de Setembro de 1940*.

51. The correlation coefficients describing these relationships were .27 for pavement, .28 for public transportation, and .25 for sewer lines.

52. The percentage of illiterates in each neighborhood correlated with the percentage of its streets served by sewers at –.75; by water, at –.81; by electricity, at –.83; by pavement, at –.72; and by transportation, at –.56.

53. The percentage of each neighborhood's population declared white in the census correlated with the percentage of its streets served by sewers at .82; by water, at .83; by electricity, at .88; by pavement, at .83; and by transportation, at .67. Whiteness and illiteracy were correlated at –.91.

54. The percentage of homes in each neighborhood that was constructed of wood or other provisional materials correlated with illiteracy at .96 and with whiteness at –.91. This percentage correlated with the percentage of streets served by sewers at –.72; by water, at –.77; by electricity, at –.82; by pavement, at –.74; and by transportation, at –.56.

55. The Cuban physician Carlos Finlay first suggested in the early 1880s that mosquitoes were the carriers of yellow-fever infection, but the theory was not universally accepted until the early 1900s. On yellow fever, see Benchimol, *Dos micróbios*; and Stepan, *Beginnings*. On yellow fever and other diseases in Rio, see Chalhoub, *Cidade febril*; and Vaz, "Contribuição."

56. *Cortiços* were loosely defined as tenements created either from subdividing larger structures or from the rough-and-tumble agglomeration of precariously built wooden rooms added on to existing buildings; *estalagens* were tenement rooms or shacks constructed around an open corridor or patio. Sidney Chalhoub has argued that these labels were notoriously slippery, since dwellings with similar physical forms were not always slapped with the same stigmatizing label. On links between disease, poverty, *cortiços*, and public housing policy in the nineteenth century, see Chalhoub, *Cidade febril*; Vaz, "Contribuição"; and Vaz, *Modernidade*.

57. Chalhoub, *Cidade febril*, 30–33.

58. For international attitudes toward poverty and the poor in the nineteenth century, see Geremek, *Poverty*; Jones, *Outcast London*; Patterson, *America's Struggle*; Iliffe, *The African Poor*; Skocpol, *Protecting Soldiers*; Chevalier, *Laboring Classes*; and Arrom, *Containing*.

59. José Pereira Rego, códice 44-2-7, "Habitações coletivas, estalagens, ou 'cortiços,'" Arquivo Geral da Cidade do Rio de Janeiro, quoted in Chalhoub, *Cidade febril*, 34.

60. See Vaz, "Contribuição," 207; Chalhoub, *Cidade febril*, 34; and Aquino Carvalho, *Habitações*.

61. The most famous of these were Francisco Pereira Passos and Carlos Sampaio.

62. Pereira Passos and Sampaio were actually present for the destruction; see Vaz, "Contribuição"; and Vaz, *Modernidade*.

63. On these events, see Chalhoub, *Cidade febril*, 15–20; and Vaz, "Contribuição."

64. Vaz, "Notas sobre o Cabeça de Porco."

65. Chalhoub, *Cidade febril*, 51.

66. Ibid., chap. 2.

67. Vaz, "Contribuição."

68. The usual comparison is to Haussmann's Paris, but reforms of cities such as Buenos Aires and New York are also relevant.

69. Vaz, "Contribuição."

70. Plans to facilitate the construction of "houses for workers" abounded after the mid-nineteenth century. Most early plans promoted private construction of workers' housing by giving development companies free title to municipal or federal lands, reducing import taxes on building materials, and exempting such developments from municipal taxes. These plans generally fell far short of expectations. Most of the successful projects were run by factories and were thus open only to their own workers, a relatively privileged group within the Carioca lower classes. The few projects constructed by building companies were expensive and nowhere near extensive enough to house poor residents who had been evicted during sanitary crackdowns on tenement houses and shacks in the city center. Materials exempted from import taxes for the purpose of constructing workers' residences were probably often sold on the black market. In the early twentieth century, both the municipal and the federal governments made feeble attempts to construct public housing, but neither of the two largest undertakings was ever completed; a series of federal and municipal tax exemptions and land grants meant to promote the construction of cheap housing in the first three decades of the twentieth century was equally ineffectual. Hard numbers are difficult to come by, but the few available are illuminating; historian Eulália Lahmeyer Lobo estimates that public incentives to private development companies and factories resulted in the construction of housing for about 8,420 workers in the late nineteenth century, but that 36,830 workers were turned out of their tenement homes by the public health services in 1887 alone. Similarly, while Pereira Passos's urban reforms and Oswaldo Cruz's sanitary campaigns of the early 1900s resulted in

the eviction of somewhere near 14,000 families, the prefect planned to construct only 90 worker homes. Two planned federal housing projects, Orsina da Fonseca and Marechal Hermes, never came anywhere near completion, even after they were transferred to the municipal government in the early 1920s, supposedly to provide shelter for some of the thousands of residents expelled when the Morro do Castello was destroyed. In general, while the public works that expelled the poor from Rio's center and prosperous neighborhoods were nearly all concluded, the projects meant to provide alternative housing rarely were, and the poor were left to fend for themselves in less privileged parts of the city. See Lobo, Carvalho, and Stanley, *Questão habitacional*, chaps. 3–5; Almeida Abreu, "Da habitação"; Benchimol, *Pereira Passos*; and Lobo, "Condições."

71. See Almeida Abreu, "Reconstruindo." Some later municipal rules explicitly addressed this slippery nomenclature, such as sec. VII, article 1 of an 1889 *postura municipal* cited by Aquino Carvalho, *Habitações*, 160, which prohibited "cortiços, casinhas, e outras edificações acanhadas para a habitação das classes menos favorecidas, e ainda mesmo nos quintais dos prédios."

72. See Meade, *"Civilizing" Rio*; Benchimol, *Pereira Passos*; Vaz, "Contribuição"; Rocha, *A era*; Aquino Carvalho, *Habitações*.

73. The port works were not completed until 1910.

74. See Benchimol, *Dos micróbios*. See also Needell, *A Tropical Belle Epoque*; and Murilo de Carvalho, *Os bestializados*.

75. Vaz, "Contribuição," 226, estimates that 1,040 buildings were destroyed because of the prefect's road-building and alignment projects, 450 because of port works, 700 because of work on the Avenida Central, and 670 because of the health service's enforcement of building and sanitary codes.

76. The ownership structure of *cortiços* and other tenements was often complex, with separate owners for the land and the structures built thereon; the properties' managers often owned neither. See Vaz, "Contribuição." This complexity would be reproduced in the early favelas; see chapter 7, this volume.

77. For variants of this view, see Meade, *"Civilizing" Rio*; Needell, *A Tropical Belle Epoque*; and Chalhoub, *Cidade febril*. For a counter-argument, see Murilo de Carvalho, *Os bestializados*.

78. The measure authorizing most of the expropriations was Lei 1021 (26 August 1903), which somewhat modified Decreto Legislativo 816 (10 July 1855), the imperial regulation.

79. Benchimol, *Pereira Passos*; Vaz, "Contribuição"; Meade, *"Civilizing" Rio*. On elite attitudes toward Rio's poor population during this period, see Murilo de Carvalho, *Os bestializados*.

80. Financial incentives and individual influence manifested themselves in the selection of which buildings would be demolished and which would be spared as well as in the awarding of contracts for carrying out the works and redeveloping the expropriated properties. See Rocha, *A era*; Benchimol, *Pereira Passos*.

81. Decreto Municipal 391 (10 February 1903); Decreto Federal 5156, Regulamento dos Serviços Sanitários a Cargo da União (8 March 1904).

82. See chapter 7, this volume.

83. Decreto Federal 5156 (8 March 1904), part 3, title 1, article 84.

84. Ibid., article 105.
85. Ibid., articles 104, 106.
86. Ibid., article 123.
87. According to figures from the censuses of 1890, 1906, and 1920, the percentage of residential buildings classified as collective residences in the "urban" areas of the city (all districts excluding Inhaúma, Irajá, Jacarepaguá, Campo Grande, Guaratiba, Santa Cruz, and the Ilhas) actually increased from 4.5 percent to 4.7 percent between 1890 and 1906 but then decreased to 3.5 percent in 1920. The suburban figures followed a similar pattern, rising from close to 0 to 1.1 percent between 1890 and 1906 but then decreasing to 0.3 percent by 1920. These numbers may be somewhat inaccurate because the 1890 figures were not for "collective dwellings" but rather for *estalagens,* though all indications are that this word was used to refer generally to collective residences rather than specifically to the type of common residence Backheuser classified as an *estalagem.* The figures also probably mask a rise in the number of collective habitations in the city between 1890 and the onset of the Pereira Passos reforms in 1902. Figures taken from Diretoria Geral de Estatística. *Recenseamento Geral da República dos Estados Unidos do Brasil em 31 de Dezembro de 1890;* from República dos Estados Unidos do Brasil, Officina de Estatística, *Recenseamento do Rio de Janeiro (Distrito Federal), 20 de Setembro de 1906,* 390–91; and from the Ministério da Agricultura, Indústria e Comércio, Directoria Geral de Estatística, *Recenseamento do Brasil, 1 de Setembro de 1920,* vol. 2, part 1 (População do Rio de Janeiro), xxxii.
88. Backheuser, "Onde moram." This published article was a compressed version of a *relatório* sent to the Ministry of Justice and Interior Affairs in 1906. Like many other engineers and urban planners, Backheuser was at once exemplary in his social prejudice and minute in his descriptions of poor people's lives; his less torrid descriptions of lower-class dwellings are, paradoxically, among the only surviving detailed accounts of day-to-day existence in Rio's turn-of-the-century tenements and favelas.
89. Meade, *"Civilizing" Rio,* 126, quoting an article originally published by Dr. Alfredo Leal de Sá Pereira in the *Jornal do Brasil.*
90. Geographer Maurício de Almeida Abreu has documented extensive complaints from suburban residents about the lack of public health enforcement in such regions, and his findings are echoed by those of historian Teresa Meade; such grievances also appeared in the late 1930s in repeated letters sent to President Vargas by members of the obscure suburban right-wing organization L.N.P.S.–Fundação da Imprensa Carioca to complain about sanitary conditions of the residences in the suburban neighborhood of Maria da Graça. See Almeida Abreu, "Da habitação"; Meade, *"Civilizing" Rio,* 90–91; and letters held at AN, records of the Secretaria da Presidência da República, série 17.4, caixa 192, pasta 1939. On favelas during this period, see Almeida Abreu, "Reconstruindo," and chapters 7 and 8, this volume.
91. On Pereira Passos and the *cortiços,* see Vaz, "Contribuição," 230.
92. Almeida Abreu, "Reconstruindo," 41.
93. A clue to the logic of this decision emerges in Backheuser's 1906 *relatório,*

where he wrote, in regard to poor people's homes, that "officials should actually be even more rigorous with these houses than with the rest" because the poor, lacking education, would not sanitize themselves; the government must, he believed, use the law "to introduce abundant light, air, water, and space, so that, even without wanting it or knowing it, the poor resident will enjoy the well-being that the State has already given to the rich through education."

94. On Castelo, see Nonato and Santos, *Era uma vez*; and Almeida Abreu, *Evolução.* The new sanitary codes were passed as Decreto 2021 (11 September 1924), Decreto 2087 (19 January 1925), and Decreto 2474 (9 November 1926).

95. On Agache, see note 7 to part I, above.

96. Agache, *Rio de Janeiro,* 5. For background and accounts of the controversies surrounding Agache's visit to Rio, see Stuckenbruck, *O Rio.*

97. Agache, *Rio de Janeiro,* 8.

98. Ibid., 7. Agache's fondness for medical and bodily metaphors echoed nineteenth-century social discourse, especially that influenced by early positivist thought. It is notable that such language was being used in the 1930s specifically to describe social bodies and the "cures" for their ills in Fascist Italy, Nazi Germany, and, eventually, in Vargas's Estado Novo. On this and other comparisons with Nazism and Fascism, see Lenharo, *Sacralização.*

99. See Bruant, "Donat Alfred Agache."

100. *Anais do Conselho Municipal,* Projeto 123 (November 1927).

101. For an interesting account of Le Corbusier's visits to Rio, and of the general involvement of Brazilian architects and engineers in the international urbanism and town planning movements, see M. da Silva Pereira, "Pensando a metrópole."

102. See Stuckenbruck, *O Rio.* See also Sampaio, *Idéias e impressões*; and L. Silva, "A trajetória."

103. See Stuckenbruck, *O Rio,* 85–100.

104. On Mattos Pimenta, see Valladares, "A gênese"; and Valladares, *A invenção.*

105. Speech given to the Rotary Club on 12 November 1926 and published in João Augusto de Mattos Pimenta, *Para a remodelação do Rio de Janeiro,* quoted in Stuckenbruck, *O Rio,* 86. The lands near the Centennial Exposition were those that had been cleared by the partial removal of Castelo Hill under the administration of Prefect Carlos Sampaio between 1920 and 1922.

106. Agache, *Rio de Janeiro,* 20.

107. Ari Kerner, "Seu Agache," 1927, cited in Alencar, *o Carnaval carioca,* 177. The *marchinha* was a popular musical form in Rio's carnivals before the samba eclipsed it in the 1920s and 1930s. In Portuguese, the verb *embasbacar,* translated here as the English slang term "to blow away," is most often used to denote wonder or amazement in the positive sense. But it can also serve as a synonym for *espantar,* generally translated into English with the verbs "to frighten," "to startle," or even "to chase away." Whether or not Kerner intended the last line of his song as an ironic double entendre, it was this latter sense of the word that proved most prophetic.

108. Agache, *Rio de Janeiro,* 90.

109. If the declarations of employers are compared with those of workers, it appears that as many as 59 percent of people who claimed industrial employment were probably in one of these other subcategories. This technique of calculating workers' and companies' declarations is used to estimate "informal" workers in Merrick and Graham, *Population*, 239–40.

110. See chapters 3 and 4, this volume.

111. On social legislation before 1930, see Castro Gomes, *Burguesia*.

112. It may have been beyond the city's political will as well—in 1920, a loan secured for the much needed electrification of the EFCB had instead been used for the showier project of destroying Castelo Hill, in Rio's city center; see Conniff, *Urban Politics*.

113. On property rights during this period, see chapter 7, this volume.

114. On the 1930 revolution, see Castro Gomes, *A invenção*; Ferreira and Delgado, eds., *O Brasil republicano*, vol. 2; Skidmore, *Politics*; and Levine, *Father*.

115. See L. Silva, "A trajetória"; and Stuckenbruck, *O Rio*. On Pedro Ernesto, see Conniff, *Urban Politics*.

116. On Carioca city plans, see Rezende, *Planejamento*; and Rezende, "Planos."

117. See Holston, *The Modernist City.*

118. On the Avenida Presidente Vargas, see Werneck Lima, *Avenida*. On the significance of the Campo de Santana for Carioca popular culture, see Campos Abreu, *O Império.*

119. This plan differed from Agache's more in emphasis than in style, prioritizing street and highway building over public transportation and aesthetic reorganization, and slightly loosening the rigid social segregation foreseen in the 1927 plan. For a brief but clear summary of the evolution of the plan, see Leal, "A construção."

120. *Código de Obras do Distrito Federal,* Decreto Municipal 6000 (1 July 1937).

121. Ibid., chap. 2.

122. Ibid, chaps. 3–6.

123. Ibid., chaps. 8–10, 13.

124. Ibid., chap. 14, titles 3–4.

125. In a particularly revealing complaint from the 1940s, a resident from the distant suburb of Vaz Lobo said that, though he had tried his mightiest to adhere to the code's standards, his attempts to build a "proletarian habitation" had finally been frustrated because the trucks that were to bring his building materials could not get through the region's narrow, muddy, poorly maintained roads; see letter from Antônio Machado to members of the PCB, published in the *ACDF,* 22 April 1947, 72.

126. *Código de Obras do Distrito Federal,* Decreto Municipal 6000 (1 July 1937), chap. 15, title 1.

127. See, for example, Projeto-Lei 18/1948, passed by the municipal council but later vetoed by Prefect Mendes de Moraes; see also Projeto-Lei 3/1948.

128. See, for example, speeches by João Machado, Paes Leme, and Tito Lívio, 15 June 1948, *ACDF,* 16 June 1948, 759, 783. See also speech by Tito Lívio, 12 June 1948, *ACDF,* 15 June 1948, 742; and speech by Tito Lívio, 21 June 1948, *ACDF,* 22 June 1948, 818.

129. Tito Lívio, speaking in the 77a Sessão Ordinária, 6 August 1948, *ACDF,* 7 August 1948, 1762. The 1942 modifications were contained in Decree 7363 (25 September 1942).

130. João Carvalho, speaking in the 68a Sessão Ordinária, 12 August 1947, *Diário da Câmara do Distrito Federal,* 13 August 1947.

131. Report of the Comissão de Viação, Obras e Urbanismo, given in the 74a Sessão Ordinária, 3 August 1948, *Diário da Câmara do Distrito Federal,* 4 August 1948, 1692. The 1925 law was Lei 2087/25.

132. Joaquim Antônio Leite de Castro, speaking in the 78a Sessão Ordinária, 9 August 1948, *Diário da Câmara do Distrito Federal,* 10 August 1948, 1826.

133. On the growth of favelas in these years, see Almeida Abreu, *Evolução;* Zaluar and Alvito, eds., *Um século;* Machado da Silva, "A continuidade"; and Pandolfi and Grynszpan, "Poder público." Among the few authors to deal with illegal subdivisions as well as favelas are Leeds and Leeds, *A sociologia;* and Quieroz Ribeiro, *Dos cortiços.*

134. Ministério da Agricultura, Indústria e Comércio, Directoria Geral de Estatística, *Recenseamento do Brasil, 1 de Setembro de 1920,* vol. 2, part 1 (População do Rio de Janeiro). See also IBGE, Departamento de Censos, *VII Recenseamento Geral do Brasil, 1960,* série regional, vol. 1, book 12, parts 1 and 2.

135. Merrick and Graham, *Population,* 106.

136. Ministério da Agricultura, Indústria e Comércio, Directoria Geral de Estatística, *Recenseamento do Brasil, 1 de Setembro de 1920.*

137. Conniff, *Urban Politics.*

138. On the highway, see Almeida Abreu, *Evolução,* 96.

139. Ministério da Agricultura, Indústria e Comércio, Directoria Geral de Estatística, *Recenseamento do Brasil, 1 de Setembro de 1920.*

140. On these older divisions, see Ribeiro, *A liberdade;* and Chalhoub, *Trabalho.*

141. IBGE, Departamento de Censos, *VII Recenseamento Geral do Brasil, 1960.*

142. The notion of the flexibility of Brazilian racial identification predates its famous formulation by Gilberto Freyre, and it was probably argued most subtly by Thales de Azevedo in the 1950s. See Freyre, *The Masters and the Slaves;* and Azevedo, *As elites.* See also Guimarães, "Côr, classe e *status.*" In recent decades, this line of analysis has shifted dramatically because of extensive quantitative and qualitative research, and in response to the ascendance of Afro-Brazilian political movements. See especially Telles, *Race;* Andrews, *Blacks and Whites;* Butler, *Freedoms Given;* Hasenbalg, *Discriminação;* Schwarcz and Quieroz, *Raça;* Fontaine, *Race;* Lovell, *Desigualidade;* Valle e Silva and Hasenbalg, eds., *Estrutura* and *Relações;* Reichmann, *Race;* Ribeiro, *Côr;* Sheriff, "Exposing Silence"; Sheriff, *Dreaming Equality;* Fry, "Color"; and Chor Maio and Ventura Santos, eds.,

Raça, ciência e sociedade. The most radical challenges to the idea that Brazil is either a racial democracy or a society divided more by class than by race are Hanchard, *Orpheus and Power*; Marx, *Making Race*; and Twine, *Racism*.

143. Valle e Silva, "Côr." See also Moema Pacheco, "A questão."

144. Cunha, *Os sertões*, imprinted on the elite imagination an image of northeasterners rooted in melancholy, bravery, stubbornness, violence, and messianism. Writers like Francisco José de Oliveira Vianna echoed these characterizations; see, for example, Oliveira Vianna, *Evolução do povo brasileiro*. In the 1920s, new concerns with health, nutrition, and culture and their influence on society and individual character added new layers to these stereotypes; northeasterners were no longer viewed as doomed by biology and heredity, but they were still a group apart, physically and psychologically debilitated by hunger and disease; see Josué de Castro, *Geografia da fome* (1946). On general links between public health policy and racial thought, see Trinidade Lima and Hochman, "Condenado pela raça." The use of *paraíba* and *nordestino* has interesting parallels with the category of "Irish" in the United States; see Ignatiev, *How the Irish*.

145. Rio was by no means the fastest-growing of Brazil's cities during these years. Between 1920 and 1970, the proportion of urban residents in Brazil's population expanded from 25 percent to 50 percent. In 1970, Belo Horizonte was thirteen times its 1920 size, São Paulo and Fortaleza sextupled, Curitiba more than quadrupled, and Porto Alegre nearly did so; see Burns, *A History*, 409–10. On migration, see Wood and Carvalho, *The Demography*, chap. 9; and Katzman, "Urbanization since 1945." On the cultural allure of urban modernity, see Bomeny, "Utopias."

146. See chapter 3, this volume.

147. See chapter 4, this volume; for a comparison with São Paulo, see French, *Drowning*.

148. There are two methods of calculating public employees. The first takes into account all employees, regardless of their employment sectors (it would include, for example, workers in publicly owned industrial establishments or transportation companies); by these calculations, the proportion of workers engaged in public service went up by 5.5 percent between 1920 and 1960, and the absolute numbers increased 306 percent, from 81,431 to 249,334. The second method counts only those directly affiliated with the security forces or with municipal, state, and federal government agencies; here, the percentage increase was only 3.4 percent, but the numerical increase was still around 300 percent. See Ministério da Agricultura, Indústria e Comércio, Directoria Geral de Estatística, *Recenseamento do Brasil, 1 de Setembro de 1920*; IBGE, *Recenseamento Geral do Brasil, 1 September 1940*; IBGE, Conselho Nacional de Estatística, Serviço Nacional de Recenseamento, *VI Recenseamento Geral do Brasil, 1950* (Rio de Janeiro, 1955); and IBGE, Departamento de Censos, *VII Recenseamento Geral do Brasil, 1960*.

149. Figures from the industrial censuses of 1920 and 1960. Civil construction, which in 1950 was Rio's largest "industry" in terms of employment, was excluded from these calculations because it was not included in the 1960 census;

with it, the increase would doubtless have been larger still. If calculations are made from workers' own declarations, then gains are much weaker; the percentage of workers who categorized themselves as industrial actually decreased, and absolute numbers grew by only 55 percent. These figures are suspect, however, because of the excessively broad definition of industry in the 1920 census and the exclusion of construction from the industrial category in 1960.

150. Informality is estimated here by comparing the number of workers who declared themselves industrial workers with the number claimed as such by industrial companies.

151. For more on Vargas's labor guarantees and Rio's labor market, see chapters 3 and 4, this volume.

152. Ministério do Trabalho, Indústria, e Comércio, Departamento de Estatística e Publicidade, *Estatística Predial do Distrito Federal, 1933*. For 1960, see Parisse, *Favelas*.

153. See IBGE, Conselho Nacional de Estatística, Serviço Nacional de Recenseamento, *VI Recenseamento Geral do Brasil, 1950*; and IBGE, Departamento de Censos, *VII Recenseamento Geral do Brasil, 1960*.

154. Among the best-known of these was Maurício de Lacerda, father of the controversial governor and journalist Carlos Lacerda. For a good summary of working-class protest in Rio during the First Republic, see Batalha, "Formação." See also Meade, *"Civilizing" Rio*; and Conniff, *Urban Politics*.

155. See Conniff, *Urban Politics*, especially chap. 3.

156. Ibid.

157. Ibid.

158. Decreto 21076 (24 February 1932).

159. Conniff, *Urban Politics*.

160. Ibid.

161. Ibid.

162. See chapter 3, this volume.

163. Dodsworth was the "nephew and protégé" of Senator Paulo de Frontin, the ex-prefect and a major figure in 1920s Carioca politics; see Conniff, *Urban Politics*, 70. Dodsworth's most important project, the building of the Avenida Presidente Vargas, resembled the construction of the Avenida Central in its elitist conception and its razing of centrally located popular housing. For a defense of the policy, see Dodsworth, *A Avenida*. For a more critical view, see Werneck Lima, *Avenida*.

164. W. G. dos Santos, *Votos e partidos*, 19, 24.

165. The PCB was banned in 1947 after receiving more votes in Rio's local elections than any other party. Subsequently, the PTB, the PSB, and the UDN were the dominant parties in Rio politics, though communists continued to work through a renegade umbrella party called the PRT. For election statistics, see W. G. dos Santos and Abreu, *Estatísticas*.

166. Lei 196 (18 January 1936) and Lei 217 (15 November 1948) are different incarnations of the Lei Orgânica that regulated the Federal District.

167. Decreto 21076 (24 February 1932); Decreto-Lei 7586 (28 May 1945).

168. On communist politics and ideology during these years, see Ferreira,

Prisioneiros. The best sources for communist politics in the city are the municipal council debates and the two major communist newspapers, the *Tribuna Popular* and the *Imprensa Popular.*

169. This harassment also extended to individual communist politicians. In July 1948, for example, city council members protested police harassment of Arcelina Mochel, a former councilperson impeached with the ban on communism; see *ACDF,* 14 July 1948, 1379.

170. See *ACDF,* 17 August 1949, 1327; and *ACDF,* 18 August 1949, 1341–42.

171. See, for example, a debate between communists and PTB members in May 1947, *ACDF,* 26 May 1947, 291–92. See also Frota Aguiar and Sagramor di Scuvero, *ACDF,* 17 July 1948, 1438. Such attitudes were sharply criticized by Ary Barroso, a samba musician turned politician, who knew the favelas somewhat more intimately than other city councilmen; see his speech of 24 May 1948, *ACDF,* 25 May 1948, 521.

172. The city of Rio de Janeiro became the state of Guanabara when it lost its status as Brazil's Federal District in 1960. Lacerda was also well known for his fierce opposition to Getúlio Vargas in the early 1950s, and for having been the intended victim of the assassination attempt that drove Vargas's government to ruin—and the president himself to suicide—in August 1954.

173. *Tribuna da Imprensa,* 19 May 1960, 1; bracketed explanations are mine.

174. On politics in the favela, see Leeds and Leeds, "Favelas." See also Parisse, *Favelas,* 86–87. Contemporary accounts often placed much of the blame for this on the shoulders of the favela residents themselves; see, for example, Medina, *A favela.*

175. See municipal council debates of 17 August 1948, *ACDF,* 19 August 1948, 1989–90. Similarly, see remarks by Ary Barroso, 20 August 1948, *ACDF,* 21 August 1948, 2045; according to Barroso, Dutra and Rio's Catholic cardinal jointly inaugurated a water spigot in São Carlos in 1947, but the water never functioned.

176. Carlos Lacerda archives, dossiê Gabinete/Correspondência, 1960, caixa 155.

177. See Parisse, *Favelas,* 86–87.

178. Though some parties did this more often, and more effectively, than others, none was immune; see *ACDF,* 1947–64.

179. Ibid. The best summaries are Parisse, *Favelas;* and Leeds and Leeds, *A sociologia.*

180. Such actions negate the argument, made most famously in Medina, *A favela,* that the supposed political "passivity" and "limited mental capacity" of the *favelados* were responsible for the prevalence of such politics. For a more detailed analysis of residents' fights agains eviction, see chapter 8, this volume.

181. See Ministério do Trabalho, Indústria, e Comércio, Departamento de Estatística e Publicidade, *Estatística Predial do Distrito Federal, 1933; Anuário Estatístico do Rio de Janeiro* (1959–60).

182. *Censos Industriais,* from the censuses of 1920 and 1960. The combined

energy consumption capacity of Carioca industries was 364,510 HP in 1960, as opposed to 69,703 in 1920; the energy expended per worker employed grew from 1.24 to 2.06.

183. On the Campo de Santana and nineteenth-century popular culture, see Campos Abreu, *O Império*. For an account of the significance of the Praça Onze as the center of popular carnival festivities, see Moura, *Tia Ciata*. On the Dodsworth administration, see Macedo, *Henrique Dodsworth*. For a more critical analysis of both the social and architectonic significance of the Avenida Presidente Vargas and its symbolic importance as the expression of state power under the Estado Novo, see Werneck Lima, *Avenida*.

184. Dodsworth, *A Avenida*.

185. In some ways, the Avenida anticipated the "death of the street" that characterized modernist Brasília; see Holston, *The Modernist City*.

186. See, for example, Tito Lívio's discourse on 16 August 1948, *ACDF,* 17 August 1948, 1938; see also the PTB/UDN discussion, *ACDF,* 20 March 1947, 200–210.

187. For a concise account of Rio's prefects and their achievements, see Reis, "As administrações"; and Reis, *O Rio*.

188. In popular use, Baixada Fluminense now refers mainly to the area of Rio state just outside Rio's municipal limits. Geographically, the Baixada Fluminense in fact consisted of four separate *baixadas,* or swampy valleys, where rivers from the Serra do Mar drained into the Bahia de Guanabara and the surrounding sea. The two that contained portions of Rio de Janeiro's municipal territory were the Baixada da Guanabara, which contained all of Rio's central districts and most of its northern and western suburbs, and the Baixada de Sepetiba, which contained the districts of Santa Cruz, Campo Grande, and Guaratiba. For a full account of the history of the drainage and landfill of these territories through 1964, see Roxo and Ferreira, "O saneamento."

189. The project was carried out first by the federal Departamento Nacional de Obras de Saneamento and then by an autonomous, municipally funded agency known as the Superintendência de Urbanização e Saneamento (SURSAN), created specifically to supervise public works in Rio de Janeiro. SURSAN had originally been proposed by Prefect João Carlos Vital (in office 1951–52) but was not brought into being until 1957, under Prefect Francisco Negrão de Lima.

190. On the climatic and environmental consequences of this and other alterations of Rio's natural environment, see Brandão, "As alterações climáticas."

191. See Almeida Abreu and Bronstein, "Políticas públicas," 172.

192. Ministério da Agricultura, Indústria e Comércio, Directoria Geral de Estatística, *Recenseamento do Brasil, 1 de Setembro de 1920* (Rio de Janeiro, 1924); IBGE, Departamento de Censos, *VII Recenseamento Geral do Brasil,* 1960.

193. For two interesting essays about Rio de Janeiro's "rural" areas in the early 1960s, see Galvão, "Aspectos"; and Bernardes, "Notas."

194. Almeida Abreu, *Evolução,* 110, 118.

195. Ibid.

196. See Segadas Soares, "Fisonomia"; and Geiger, "Esbôço." On cultural

hierarchies and social geography in the 1950s, see Pimenta Velloso, "A dupla face."

197. *Anuário Estatístico do Brasil* (1965); *Anuário Estatístico do Brasil* (1936).

198. W. G. dos Santos and Abreu, *Estatísticas.*

199. IBGE, Departamento de Censos, *VII Recenseamento Geral do Brasil*, 1960.

200. IBGE, *VIII Recenseamento Geral*, 1970.

201. Tito Lívio, 7 July 1947, *ACDF*, 8 July 1947, 1163.

202. IBGE, Departamento de Censos, *VII Recenseamento Geral do Brasil*, 1960.

203. IBGE, *IX Recenseamento do Brasil, 1980.*

204. Agildo Barata, speaking in the 18a Sessão Ordinária, *ACDF*, 30 May 1947, 510.

205. IBGE, Departamento de Censos, *VII Recenseamento Geral do Brasil*, 1960.

206. In 1980, when such statistics were collected for the first time, 72.6 percent of central households had access to gas, and 58.3 percent had telephones; in the suburbs, the figures were less than 30 percent and 20.9 percent. The satellite cities had virtually no gas lines, and fewer than 10 percent of their households had telephone service.

207. Whiteness correlated with water at .72; electricity, at .58; and sewer service, at .74. The equivalent correlations for literacy were .80, .68, and .59.

208. The correlation between gas stoves and whiteness was .79; the correlation with literacy was .90. With the favelas disaggregated, whiteness and water service correlated at .77; whiteness and electricity, at .59; literacy and water service, at .89; and literacy and electricity, at .72. Favela statistics for 1960 statistics did not include data on sewers, probably because their presence was negligible.

209. Water correlated with whiteness at .76; with electricity, at .85; and with sewers, at .82.

210. On washerwomen, see, for example, a note sent to communist council members by the União Feminina do Morro do Pinto, published in the *ACDF*, 30 April 1947, 347.

211. Letters published in the *ACDF*, 18 April 1947, 15–17.

212. See Backheuser, *Habitações.*

213. "A cidade e as favelas," *Observador econômico e financeiro*, July 1942, 116.

214. Many scholars have traced the history of favela policy in these years. See Parisse, *Favelas*; Leeds and Leeds, *A sociologia*; Perlman, *The Myth*; Valladares, *A invenção*; and Burgos, "Dos parques." On the evolution of paternalism and popular agency in these policies, see Valla, *Educação.*

215. There are no numerical estimates of tenement populations at mid-century. A comparison of figures from the Serviço Nacional da Febre Amarela and the official census (which defined favelas as illegal conglomerations of 50 or more shacks deprived of services) indicates that somewhere around half of all shacks were located in officially recognized favelas in 1940; in 1960, the figure was

around 32 percent (figures from the Serviço Nacional da Febre Amarela, quoted in Parisse, *Favelas*). Almeida Abreu and Bronstein ("Políticas públicas," 180) estimate that only about 12 percent of migrants to the city in the 1940s settled in favelas.

216. The first well-known source to coin this language of the favela as a "solution" was Alberto Passos Guimarães, "As favelas do Distrito Federal."

217. Vitor Tavares de Moura and, later, Anthony Leeds and Luciano Parisse are among the writers who noted this complexity; it was also taken for granted in the municipal council, in which criticisms of the 1937 building code regularly surfaced with reference to illegal subdivisions as well as to favelas. But the only real actions on this front at the municipal level were periodic building amnesties, which typically excluded the favelas themselves.

218. The 1942 federal law, Decreto-Lei 4598 (20 August 1942), was altered in 1943, 1944, 1946, and 1950. On the law and its effects, see Trinidade Lima, "O movimento," 66.

219. Almeida Abreu and Bronstein, "Políticas públicas," 198; Trinidade Lima, "O movimento," 66. This perspective was especially promoted by the center-right UDN party in Rio's city council debates in the late 1940s. According to politicians like Carlos Lacerda and Luiz Paes Leme, the favela problem was rooted in disincentives to private construction, including the rent law, wasted expenditures of the corrupt Social Security Institutes, and price and import controls that kept vital materials like cement in constant short supply. See *ACDF*, 30 May 1947, 499–500.

220. The best evidence is found in civil *despejo* cases: in a sample of several dozen examined from the 1940s and 1950s, only a few included formal contracts.

221. R. Porto, "O problema da habitação operária," 245.

222. Almeida Abreu and Bronstein, "Políticas públicas," 258. For the 1932–66 period, FINEP (Financiadora de Estudos e Projetos) arrives at a smaller total of 77,229.

223. See Almeida Abreu, *Evolução*.

224. See chapter 4, this volume.

225. See, for example, debates in the municipal council, 21 July 1947, *ACDF*, 22 July 1947, 1334.

226. AN, records of the Secretaria da Presidência da República, série 17.7, caixa 126.

227. The bright colors, though sometimes chosen by residents, also resulted from official policies meant to make the favela "stain" brighter and more picturesque. A bill meant to achieve this effect was debated in the 1959 city council; see *ACDF*, 8 October 1959, 2472; and *ACDF*, 15 October 1959, 2556–57. This project was also the subject of a well-known samba, "Favela Amarela," by Jota Jr. and O. Magalhães; its lyrics are, in part, "Favela amarela! / Ironia da vida! / Pintem a favela / Façam aquarela / Da miséria colorida / Favela Amarela" ("Yellow favela! / Irony of life! / Paint the favela / Make a watercolor / Of multicolored wretchedness / Yellow favela").

228. For analyses of the discourse related to favelas in the twentieth century,

see Parisse, *Favelas*; Perlman, *The Myth*; Valla, *Educação*; Leeds and Leeds, *A sociologia*; and Valladares, "A gênese."

229. Benjamim Costallat, "A favela que eu vi," 33–39.

230. See Vianna, *O mistério*.

231. This comment was a formal response to a letter of complaint sent by Santo Antônio residents to President Vargas in 1934; see AN, records of the Secretaria da Presidência da República, série 17.4, caixa 33, pasta 1934.

232. Undated report from Vitor Tavares de Moura to Jesuino de Albuquerque, municipal secretary of health and social welfare, Fundação Oswaldo Cruz archives, Vitor Tavares de Moura papers, série Parques Proletários e Favelas, caixa 1. A version of these observations was later published as Tavares de Moura, "Favelas."

233. Pictures of this burning are preserved in Vitor Tavares de Moura's private archive; the events are also chronicled by Parisse, *Favelas, 71*.

234. Most sources reference only the first three; the fourth park is discussed in Bezerra Pacheco, "Uma experiência," as having been located on the Avenida Suburbana and inaugurated in 1947. It is also mentioned in one of Vitor Tavares de Moura's *relatórios* dated 10 April 1947, found in Fundação Oswaldo Cruz archives, Vitor Tavares de Moura papers, série Parques Proletários e Favelas, caixa 1, with the location described as "Amorim," on the border of the Lagoa near the Hospital Miguel Couto. In city council debates, the name Amorim is given to a Parque Proletário built near the intersection of the Avenida dos Democráticos and the Avenida Suburbana, in the northern suburbs; see *ACDF*, August–September 1947, especially 1661–63, 2109, 2249.

235. "Tem uma casa proletária o próprio chefe do governo," *O Globo*, 4 November 1943; Henrique Dodsworth, "Favelas," *A Noite*, 17 October 1945; Deodato de Morais, quoted in Parisse, *Favelas, 73*.

236. The high estimate is from Parisse, *Favelas*; the lowest estimate is of around 5,000 people, repeated in Valla, *Educação*, and in Bezerra Pacheco, "Uma experiência." On politics, see Parisse, *Favelas, 86–87*. On the daily functioning of Gávea's Parque Proletário, see Tôrres, "Parque"; and Santos Oliveira, "Parque Proletário." For the strict paternalistic rules governing the projects, see Valla, *Educação*, as well as rule sheets and selection criteria preserved in Fundação Oswaldo Cruz archives, Vitor Tavares de Moura papers, série Parques Proletários e Favelas, caixa 1. For selection criteria, also see Santos Oliveira, "Parque Proletário."

237. On the parks, see Parisse, *Favelas*; Valla, *Educação*; and Leeds and Leeds, *A sociologia*. For a more detailed view of the Gávea project, see Tôrres, "Parque"; and Santos Oliveira, "Parque Proletário." On the Leblon project (which eventually blended into the Praia do Pinto favela), see Bezerra Pacheco, "Uma experiência."

238. Breno da Silveira, Lígia Bastos, Acioli Lins, *ACDF*, 22 July 1948, 1528. For other political attacks on the Parques Proletários as "official favelas," see communist councilmen Coelho Filho, Neiva Filho, and Carvalho Braga, *ACDF*, 6 September 1947, 1918; Paracer of the Comission of Roads, Public Works, and Transportation, *ACDF*, 20 September 1947; communist councilwoman Arcelina

Mochel, *ACDF,* 9 September 1947, 2249; and Breno da Silveira, *ACDF,* 26 May 1948, 539.

239. Passos Guimarães, "As favelas."

240. H. Dias da Cruz's propagandistic *Os morros cariocas no novo regime* is almost entirely devoted to the Vargas government's "social assistance" in the favelas, emphasizing the ways in which Vargas and his wife were "venerated" for their good will. On these dynamics, see chapter 7, this volume.

241. The Fundação Leão XIII was created by Decree 22498 (22 January 1947).

242. See Fundação Leão XIII, *Morros e favelas.* The relocation recommendation followed a model first put forth by Vitor Tavares de Moura for the Parques Proletários, in which favela residents would be classified according to their capacity for "recuperation"; the agricultural colonies would be repositories for those who could not adapt to "urban" life. That suggestion was echoed in numerous city council bills through the early 1950s.

243. See Valla, *Educação,* 46–55; Leeds and Leeds, *A sociologia*; Valladares, *A invenção*; and Parisse, *Favelas.*

244. Cruzada São Sebastião, "Duas experiências."

245. See especially Leeds and Leeds, *A sociologia*; and Valla, *Educação.* Frequent references to these activities also appear in the debates of the Câmara Municipal.

246. According to Machado Rios, "O desenvolvimentismo," the Cruzada São Sebastião, unlike the Fundação Leão XIII, adhered to the strategy of "community development," though the organization never called it by this name. Parisse, *Favelas,* also argues that the Cruzada São Sebastião moved noticeably toward promoting grassroots community action in these years.

247. See Leeds and Leeds, *A sociologia,* 211.

248. José Arthur Rios coined the phrase in an important 1960 study, published as a supplement to the *Estado de São Paulo* and widely circulated; see Sociedade de Análises Gráficas e Mecanográficas Aplicadas aos Complexos Sociais, "Aspectos humanos." For Rios's recollections of the favela politics of these years, see the interview from 2000 published in Freire and Lippi Oliveira, *Capítulos.*

249. Leeds and Leeds, *A sociologia,* offer a generally positive view of SERFHA's actions, as does Valla, *Educação.* Nísia Trinidade Lima, who conducted numerous interviews with favela leaders in the 1980s, gives a more nuanced evaluation, noting especially how SERFHA and the neighborhood associations fit into the political junctures of their time, and noting their limited achievements; see Trinidade Lima, "O movimento."

250. Prefeitura do Distrito Federal, Secretaria Geral do Interior e Segurança, Departamento de Geografia e Estatística, *Censo das Favelas.*

251. Paes Leme and Agildo Barata, *ACDF,* 30 May 1947, 507–8.

252. *ACDF,* 30 May 1947, 500.

253. See Instituto de Pesquisa e Estudos do Mercado, *Favelas*; and Instituto de Pesquisa e Estudos do Mercado, *A vida mental.*

254. See Parisse, *Favelas*; Leeds and Leeds, *A sociologia*; Valladares, *A invenção*; and Perlman, *The Myth.*

255. See chapters 7 and 8, this volume.

256. Several such complaints can be found in the Dodsworth and Vargas correspondence archives, and they were constantly brought to the attention of the municipal council in the late 1940s and 1950s.

257. Letter from March of 1941, AN, records of the Secretaria da Presidência da República, série 14.6, caixa 511.

258. Lúcio de Paula Bispo, personal interview with the author, 4 December 2003.

259. In April 1961, for example, Lacerda himself wrote a note to José Arthur Rios, then director of SERFHA, demanding that Rios take steps to eradicate a small favela growing near the Gávea Golf Club; see Carlos Lacerda archives, dossiê Gabinete/Correspondência, caixa 158. In July of the same year, Lacerda complained three times to Rios about a small favela being built behind a billboard on the Rua Alice, in Laranjeiras; see Carlos Lacerda archives, dossiê Gabinete/Correspondência, caixa 157. In 1960, a group calling itself the Fundação Líder dos Amigos de Mato Alto, in Campo Grande, requested that a growing favela be expelled from a hospital construction site on the Rua Jurari; see letter dated 26 December 1960, Carlos Lacerda archives, dossiê Gabinete/Correspondência, caixa 155. In late March 1963, Lacerda was similarly concerned by shacks being built over the Pasmado tunnel; he may have been alerted to the situation by the British Consulate. See Carlos Lacerda archives, dossiê Gabinete/Correspondência, caixa 165.

260. See *ACDF,* especially June–September, 1948. On the Batalha do Rio de Janeiro itself, see also Pereira da Silva, *Favelas Cariocas.*

261. See Leeds and Leeds, *A sociologia,* 214–27.

262. Ibid., 220.

263. See especially Lacerda's speech in the session of 14 August 1947, *ACDF,* 16 August 1947, 1662, where he noted that thus removing favela residents would simply replace the miserable working life of those who lived in favelas with a miserable state of unemployment in the distant suburbs.

264. Estimates vary for the exact number of favelas removed. Valladares estimates more than 53 favelas, and somewhat fewer than 100,000 residents *(Passa-se,* 39); Burgos estimates 60 favelas, and 100,000 residents ("Dos parques," 38).

265. S. Cavalcanti, *Rio,* 29. Cavalcanti had a long political career after her stint at the BNH, and in a 2000 interview her views about the favelas and their residents reflected continued thinking along the same lines; that interview was published in Freire and Lippi Oliveira, *Capítulos,* 78–102.

266. "Os favelados de Brás de Pina vendem alegria na Vila Aliança," *O Globo,* 26 December 1964.

267. Letters from COHAB reports, held in the Carlos Lacerda archives.

268. See letters from 1962–63 in the Carlos Lacerda archives.

269. Valladares, *Passa-se;* Perlman, *The Myth.*

270. Carlos Lacerda archives, Caixa 120, Pasta COHAB (2), 1964. For a general account of the Brás de Pina conflicts, see Ferreira dos Santos, *Movimentos.*

271. Valladares, *Passa-se.*

272. For a provocative (if ultimately frustrating) exploration of these costs in Lima, Peru, see de Soto, *The Other Path*.

273. Edmundo, *O Rio*.

274. See Companhia Industrial Santa Fé, *A questão*.

275. Almeida Abreu, "Reconstruindo," 37.

276. On the fire, see also Cruz, *Os morros*, 43–44.

277. Almeida Abreu, "Da habitação." The origins of another favela, Tiuiti, may also lie in this order (Benjamin Penglase, anthropologist, personal conversation with the author, 8 October 2004).

278. On the early history of Santo Antônio, see Almeida Abreu, "Reconstruindo," 41. On King Albert's visit, see Caulfield, *In Defense*.

279. Letter dated August 1934, AN, records of the Secretaria da Presidência da República, série 17.4, caixa 33, pasta 1934.

280. IBGE, Conselho Nacional de Estatística, Serviço Nacional de Recenseamento, *As Favelas do Distrito Federal e o Censo Demográfico de 1950*, 39.

281. Among them was councilman Manuel Blasquez, who had lived on the *morro* between the ages of 9 months and 9 years; see *ACDF*, v. 53/1952, 31.

282. The samba was cowritten by Benedito Lacerda and orchestrated by Pixinguinha; it was recorded in 1950 by Martins's famous Trio de Ouro.

283. "Para onde irão os moradores do Morro de Santo Antônio," *Imprensa Popular*, 4 August 1954.

284. "Ameaçados pelos escavaderos da PDF," *Imprensa Popular*, 18 August 1954.

285. Reis, "As administrações" and *O Rio*.

PART II: WORK, LAW, AND *JUSTIÇA SOCIAL* IN VARGAS'S RIO

1. AN, records of the Secretaria da Presidência da República, série 17.4, caixa 516, processo 1516/43. Campos probably meant *excelência*, the standard title for dignitaries, rather than "incelencia," not a word in Portuguese. In this letter, as in others, it is of course possible that someone else wrote on Campos's behalf—a common practice among Rio's poor. However, the handwriting and spelling are both extremely rudimentary, and the handwriting matches the signature, which would indicate that this was not the case here; even if it were, the writer would probably have been a semi-literate relative or neighbor rather than a professional.

2. For a more detailed history of property in Babilônia, see chapter 7, this volume; on public health and favelas in Rio, see chapters 1 and 2.

3. See Ferreira, *Trabalhadores*.

4. This rather strict definition of class follows the tradition of scholars of the English and European experience. See Thompson, *The Making*; Katznelson and Zolberg, *Working-Class Formation*; and Jones, *Languages*. On distinctions between the working class and the very poor in nineteenth-century London, see Jones, *Outcast London*.

5. Contrary to more traditional analysts, who see the Estado Novo either as the onset of complete co-optation of the working classes by a corporatist state or as the working classes' betrayal by a communist movement increasingly out

of touch with the rank and file, historian Alexandre Fortes (writing on metal-workers and bakers in Porto Alegre) argues that the Estado Novo saw instead a movement—partially forced, partially chosen—toward struggles that focused on the realization of rights put on the books over the course of Vargas's tenure; see Fortes, "Revendo." John French, writing mainly on São Paulo, makes a similar argument in *Drowning in Laws*.

6. 15 November 1941, AN, records of the Secretaria da Presidência da República, série 17.4, caixa 342, processo 33069/41.

7. 10 October 1940, AN, records of the Secretaria da Presidência da República, série 17.4, caixa 194, processo 24399/40.

8. 8 September 1941, AN, records of the Secretaria da Presidência da República, série 17.4, caixa 342, processo 25245/1941.

9. 10 July 1939, AN, records of the Secretaria da Presidência da República, série 17.4, caixa 193, processo 19625/39.

10. Odília dos Santos Gama, personal interview with the author, 2 December 2003. Her husband was relatively privileged for a favela resident: after spending many years as a manual laborer, he found formal work as a motorist for the municipal government and went on to become a community leader. Nevertheless, dos Santos Gama had worked most of her life, washing clothes for cash even as she raised her ten children, two of whom died young.

11. Dos Santos was especially impressed when, during a May Day rally in the Campo de São Cristóvão, Vargas put his hand on the shoulder of a poor woman who had lugged her heavy water container to the rally to emphasize her community's desperate need for running water (Abdias José Nascimento dos Santos, personal interview with the author, 27 November 2003). He had lived most of his life in São Carlos, a central Rio favela, and was imprisoned in the 1960s for his activism in Guanabara's Favela Federation. Dos Santos's views are not universally held: his friend and fellow favela leader Lúcio de Paula Bispo recalled that Vargas was "capricious," "full of bad will," and "very paternalistic," never quite making good on his promises (Lúcio de Paula Bispo, personal interview with the author, 4 December 2003). For views of Vargas from Rio and beyond, see Levine, *Father*. See also Jesús, *Bitita's Diary*.

12. On Vargas and the source of his political appeal, see Castro Gomes, *A invenção*; Ferreira, *Trabalhadores*; Levine, *Father*; and Skidmore, *Politics*.

13. According to Medeyros (*Getúlio Vargas*), Vargas explicitly opposed this ideal to that of "political equality," which he rejected as a myth of the oligarchical First Republic and "um absurdo gerado no cérebro de Rousseau" ("an absurdity generated in Rousseau's brain") as well as to "economic equality," which he defined as "outro absurdo gerado no cérebro de Marx" ("another absurdity generated in Marx's brain"). See also Castro Gomes, *A invenção*.

14. Decreto-Lei 5452 (1 May 1943). On the progression of labor laws in the 1930s, see Castro Gomes, *Burguesia*. On the CLT and labor legislation more broadly, see Castro Gomes, *A Invenção*; W. G. dos Santos, *Cidadania*; and French, *Drowning*.

15. See, for example, Vargas, *Unidade moral*, 5–6, where Vargas echoes constitutional language in calling work "the first social duty" and in pitting those who worked for Brazil's greatness against the *ociosos* and parasites who did noth-

ing for the country's greatness. For discussion of this theme, see Castro Gomes, *A invenção*; and Castro Gomes, "A construção."

16. See Castro Gomes, *A invenção*. For more immediate links between Vargas's legislative actions and working-class demands, see Fortes, "Revendo."

17. Medeyros, *Getúlio Vargas*, 21.

18. Lacombe, *A força nacionalizadora*, 211. The quotation's source is probably Vargas, though Lacombe does not attribute it to him.

19. "Problemas e realizações do Estado Novo," interviews granted to the national press in Petrópolis on 19 February 1938 and in São Lourenço on 22 April 1938; published in Vargas, *A nova política*, vol. 5, 167.

20. Vargas often indicated that he had seen the letters by writing a large V over their text.

21. Alexandre Marcondes Filho, "Uma história verdadeira contada aos operários do Brasil," 20 March 1942, Fundação Getúlio Vargas, Centro de Pesquisa e Documentação de História Contemporânea do Brasil, Alexandre Marcondes Filho papers, AMF 1942.01.22. On "A Hora do Brasil," see McCann, *Hello*.

22. This kind of solution was tailored to broadcast another of the Vargas regime's central tenets, that is, that social conflict between employers and workers should be resolved by compromises freely agreed to by both parties in the name of social peace. For an example of Vargas's own words, see Vargas, *Todos são necessários*; and Vargas, *Unidade moral*. See also Castro Gomes, *A invenção*; and French, *Drowning*. For a distinct angle, see Weinstein, *For Social Peace*.

23. Jorge Ferreira takes a slightly different tack, arguing that "the conjuncture of ideas, values, concepts, and images socially recognized and manifested by workers in the correspondence" can be read as "the expression of the era's popular political culture." (*Trabalhadores*, 23). On repression, see Cancelli, *O mundo*; Levine, *Father*; and Morais, *Olga*.

24. McCann, *Hello*, injects special doubt into the question of radio's propagandistic powers. Castro Gomes and Alcir Lenharo make the strongest cases for the government's effectiveness.

25. This pattern seems to have held for letters from Brazil as a whole. See Ferreira, *Trabalhadores*, chap. 1.

26. AN, records of the Secretaria da Presidência da República, série 14.6, caixa 511, processo 14827/40.

27. On schools and their social role in the Vargas era, see Dávila, *Diploma*.

28. On governmental attitudes toward work during Brazil's First Republic, see Chalhoub, *Trabalho*, especially 64–88. On vagrancy laws, see Gomes da Cunha, *Intenção*; Holloway, *Policing Rio*; Huggins, *From Slavery to Vagrancy*; Fausto, *Crime e cotidiano*; and Kowarick, *Trabalho e vadiagem*. Attitudes that evaluated the poor's virtues by their willingness to work were nothing new. For a general history of "honorable" poverty and European social policy toward the poor, see Geremek, *Poverty*. On the history of American poverty policy, see Patterson, *America's Struggle*.

29. On connections with working-class rhetoric, see Castro Gomes, *A invenção*.

30. This degradation was associated especially with dependent agricultural

work, heavy manual labor, and domestic service. It continued long after the slave era as workers in such occupations—many the descendants of slaves or freedpersons—found themselves locked into a vicious cycle. In the aftermath of abolition, it was a given in many elite circles that ex-slaves and their descendants were unfit for the most stable, best-paid jobs, both rural and urban. Many believed that ex-slaves were simply too demanding, too eager to distance themselves from the humiliation and suffering of slavery, to accept the kind of discipline necessary for efficient agriculture or manufacturing. Others were more blatantly racist, believing that only white European immigrants had the moral discipline and intellectual aptitude for "modern" modes of employment. Although these beliefs were repeatedly disproved in practice—even the flood of European immigrants who came to Brazil in the late nineteenth and early twentieth centuries was not sufficient to fill all of the choicest agricultural and urban jobs—they translated into measurable discrimination in most sectors. This funneled nonwhites into the least desirable work, and that in turn combined with racism to add further stigma both to such employment and to the people who undertook it. These problems were even more acute for unskilled female workers. For thoughtful accounts of the interplay between slavery, race, and work in the late nineteenth and early twentieth centuries, see Mattos de Castro, *Das cores*; Dean, *Rio Claro*; Chalhoub, *Trabalho*; and Andrews, *Blacks and Whites*. For twentieth-century statistical associations between race, gender, and urban occupations, see Instituto Brasileiro de Geografia e Estatística, "Atividades e posições"; Telles, "Industrialization"; and Telles, "Who Gets Formal Sector Jobs?"

31. Medeyros, *Getúlio Vargas*, 21–22.

32. The masculine is intentionally used here, since Vargas's speeches to worker-citizens usually targeted men, who were envisioned in much of Vargas's legislation as the proper breadwinners and protectors of women and children; see Caulfield, *In Defense*, epilogue.

33. Vargas, *A nova política*, vol. 8, 291. See also Vargas, *Unidade moral*; and Vargas, "A união sagrada dos brasileiros," 7 September 1934 (*A nova política*, vol. 3, 283), where "Brazilians" are defined by their occupations.

34. Article 137.

35. Title 5, article 145, single paragraph.

36. W. G. dos Santos, *Cidadania*.

37. "Offered to the children of the Proletarian Parks of the Municipal Government's General Secretariat of Health and Social Aid," 11 June 1943, Fundação Oswaldo Cruz archives, Vitor Tavares de Moura papers, série Parques Proletários e Favelas, caixa 1.

38. Baptista de Mello, "Política de família," *Arquivo Judiciário* (Supplemento) 56:3 (1940), 37–40, quoted in Besse, *Restructuring*. On gender and family values during the Vargas era, see again Besse, *Restructuring*; and Caulfield, *In Defense*.

39. Marcondes Filho, "Um apelo às mães, uma palavra às colaboradoras da grandeza no Brasil," 6 March 1942, Fundação Getúlio Vargas, Centro de Pesquisa e Documentação de História Contemporânea do Brasil, Alexandre Marcondes Filho papers, AMF 1942.01.22.

40. Medeyros, *Getúlio Vargas*, 127. Vargas's major legislative initiative involving the family was Decreto-Lei 3200 (19 April 1941), discussed further below.

41. Evaristo de Muniz Coêlho to Vargas, 8 July 1940, AN, records of the Secretaria da Presidência da República, série 17.4, caixa 194. Coêlho's linkage of nutrition, growth, and the ability to contribute to Brazil's greatness echoed articles and speeches written by Vargas's ministers and by the doctors, social workers, and intellectuals who worked with them in creating the blueprints for Brazilian nation-building. See, for example, Alexandre Moscoso's "A alimentação" (the article's subtitle read "Everything that can be done to favor the adequate nourishment of the National worker will be a contribution to the strengthening of the race and the enrichment of the country because every individual who produces is a worker, irrespective of his type of activity"). Moscoso published a number of other articles on the same theme, among them "O problema alimentar." Others who wrote on nutrition and its relation to nation-building included Leopoldo de Lima e Silva, who argued for the establishment of a national "health card" that would certify the health of every worker and "eliminate from the workplace anyone who is unfit to work there" ("Alimentação e trabalho"); Cleto Seabra Velloso, who lamented the lack of quality and quantity in the Brazilian diet ("A alimentação do povo"); Ladário de Carvalho, who argued that it would be in the best interests of Brazilian industrialists to contribute to the nourishment of their workers, who in turn would become more productive and benefit the industry ("A alimentação do operário"); and, most famously, Josué de Castro, whose numerous works on the subject of nutrition and its relation to the quality of the "Brazilian race" and prospects for nation-building included the well-known *Geografia da fome* and *O Problema da alimentação no Brasil*, as well as various articles published in the *Boletim do Ministério do Trabalho, Indústria, e Comércio* and other government periodicals. The question of nutrition was also an important part of the debate surrounding the establishment of the minimum wage in Brazil, as shown in Josué de Castro's *Salário mínimo*; see also Moscoso's "Alimentação e o salário mínimo."

42. Medeyros, *Getúlio Vargas*, 26, quoting the prominent intellectual (and frequent muse of the Vargas regime) Oliveira Vianna. On Oliveira Vianna and Vargas, see Lippi Oliveira, Pimenta Velloso, and Castro Gomes, eds., *Estado Novo*; and Lippi Oliveira, "O ambiente intelectual."

43. Vargas, *A nova política*, vol. 2, 115.

44. Until recently, Brazilian labor history tended to mirror this version darkly, viewing Vargas's ascent as an interruption of the "natural" process of proletarianization and class awakening incipient in Brazil during the twentieth century's early decades; according to this view, Brazilian industrial workers between 1930 and the 1970s were mostly subservient to corrupt state institutions, and their attempts at independent organization and activism were mostly crushed. Recently, however, numerous historians have begun to refute such views. See Jorge Ferreira, ed., *O populismo*, especially Silva and Costa, "Trabalhadores urbanos"; Castro Gomes, "O populismo"; and Ferreira, "O nome e a coisa." See also Fortes, "Revendo"; and French, *Drowning*.

45. Vargas, *Unidade moral*, 20–21.

46. On work and honor in colonial Latin America, see Johnson, "Dangerous Words," 129. On colonial Brazil, see Mello e Souza, *Desclassificados*. On nineteenth-century Brazil, see Mattos de Castro, *Das cores*; and Chalhoub, *Trabalho*.

47. See note 30 to part II, above.

48. Maria da Conceição Ferreira Pinto (Dona Filinha), personal interviews with the author, November and December 1995.

49. "Eu falei para ela que eu não, a escravidão já acabou, eu não sou escrava, você quiser fazer, você faz com sua filha, comigo não. Olha bem, a sua filha é branca, eu sou negra e bem negra. Eu não fico aqui mais, nem um minuto, está?" Slave descendants interviewed for Lugão Rios and Mattos's *Memórias* indicated that the absence of physical abuse was one of the most important markers of free labor (see especially 174).

50. Lúcio de Paula Bispo, personal interview with the author, 4 December 2003. These testimonies parallel many in Mattos de Castro, *Das cores*, and in Lugão Rios and Mattos, *Memórias*.

51. See Lauderdale Graham, *House and Street*.

52. On work conditions and industrialization in the First Republic, see Pinheiro, "O proletariado industrial." On legislation and the working class, see Castro Gomes, *Burguesia*; and Castro Gomes, *A invenção*.

53. Chalhoub gives a different interpretation, noting that, from the perspective of the poor, "paid work is an essential aspect in the construction of [a woman's] social identity"(*Trabalho*, 207). On employment as a component of the threatening image of the "modern woman," see Caulfield, *In Defense*, 80–81. Dona Filinha, cited above (see note 49 to part II), said that her family had not wanted her to work either in a factory or in a private home when she first arrived in Rio as a young woman, for fear of moral corruption.

54. On the *malandro* during the Estado Novo, see Matos, *Acertei,* especially 77–106.

55. See Matta, "Pedro Malasartes," especially 229–35.

56. Oliveira Dias, "Vagabundo," published in 1928 by Casa Bevilacqua.

57. Shaw, *Social History*. On women's rejection of *otários*, see Matos, *Acertei*, 95–96; she cites, in particular, Wilson Batista and Ataulfo Alves, "O Bonde São Januario" (1939) and Geraldo Pereira and J. Portela, "Até hoje não voltou" (1946). Examples of washerwomen's sambas and related genres are Monsueto Menezes, Nilo Chagas, and João Violão (João Vieira Filho), "O Lamento da Lavadeira" (1956); Obdúlio Morales and Merion Sunshine, "A lavadeira" ("Afromambo," 1954); and, most famously, a *lundu* by Cartola, "Ensaboa, Mulata" (undated).

58. Lugão Rios and Mattos, *Memórias,* highlights similar values in interviews with surviving slave descendants in rural Rio and Minas Gerais.

59. Cláudia Matos demonstrates how concessions to censorship were sometimes less than complete, highlighting the ways in which irony and subtlety often undermined apparent odes to work (*Acertei*, 90–97).

60. For international comparisons, see note 58 to part I, above. For Brazilian

attitudes toward poverty and the poor before the twentieth century, see especially Chalhoub, *Cidade febril*; and Mello e Souza, *Desclassificados.*

61. See Chalhoub, "Vadios e barões"; Chalhoub, *Trabalho*; Abreu Esteves, *Meninas*; Caulfield, *In Defense*; Gomes da Cunha, *Intenção*; Fausto, *Crime e cotidiano*; Huggins, *From Slavery to Vagrancy*; and Kowarick, *Trabalho e vadiagem.*

62. Castro Gomes, *A invenção.*

63. Pitt-Rivers, "Honor and Social Status." For Latin American comparisons, see Johnson and Lipsett-Rivera, eds., *The Faces of Honor.*

64. The able-bodied poor (men and women alike) were subject to arrest for vagrancy if they failed to work for a living. See Gomes da Cunha, *Intenção*; see also chapters 5 and 6, this volume.

65. These observations are based on a qualitative examination of some 800 criminal cases from the years 1927–64, drawn from Rio's Arquivo Nacional, Rio de Janeiro's now defunct state judicial archive, and the archives of the 20th Vara Criminal in Rio; see chapters 5 and 6, this volume.

66. Vagrancy defendants in the nineteen cases I examined for the years between 1928 and 1945 nearly always attested their innocence and dedication to work, and they often offered the names and addresses of employers in mostly vain attempts to avoid imprisonment and conviction. In one especially moving case, a 58-year-old Portuguese fruit vendor from Jacarepaguá named João Lourenço da Silva argued that he worked as hard as he could, despite the fact that the recent loss of his right arm had made it very difficult. Typically, da Silva spent 40 days in prison before being found not guilty and released. See AN, 5a PCr, CF 70.11702.

67. The reference to the mother's work is from AN, 7a VCr, caixa 10851/1931/55. For a more expansive reading of what might be culled from court testimony about lower-class sexual values, see Caulfield, *In Defense, 13.*

68. On *injúria* cases, see Fischer, "Slandering Citizens."

69. For international comparisons, see Gotkowitz, "Trading Insults"; Putnam, "Sex and Standing"; Garrioch, *Neighborhood*; Garrioch, "Verbal Insults"; Moogke, "'Thieving Buggers'"; and Norton, "Gender and Defamation."

70. AN, 5a PCr, CF 70.6948.

71. Ibid., CF 70.9476.

72. Ibid., CF 70.10839.

73. Exploring an earlier period, Chalhoub found that leading police questions about character often involved binary distinctions between *morigerados* and *trabalhadores* (*Trabalho*, 87).

74. Caulfield, *In Defense.* Of 45 defloration cases I examined for 1927–42, the same pattern applied; only a few involved unspecified manual laborers, and all claimed to be employed.

75. Castro Gomes, *A invenção.*

76. Zaluar, *A maquina*; Abdias José Nascimento dos Santos, personal interview with the author, 27 November 2003; and Lúcio de Paula Bispo, personal interview with the author, 4 December 2003. Research on favela residents from the 1940s through the 1960s indicates similar attitudes; see, for example, Nascimento Silva, "Impressões"; and Perlman, *The Myth.*

77. Marcondes Filho, "Um apelo às mães" (document cited above, Part II, note 39). For the extension of these themes into the 1940s and 1950s, see Weinstein, *For Social Peace.*

78. In a 1941 Labor Day speech, Vargas called for land reform, stating that without it Brazil would "run the risk of witnessing an exodus from the country and the overpopulation of the cities, a disequilibrium of unforeseeable consequences, capable of weakening or annulling the effects of the campaign for the integral valorization of the Brazilian man" (Vargas, *Todos são necessários*). Nearly ten years earlier, Vargas, describing the end of slavery and its effect on urban areas, had presented this danger as historical fact: "Making such disorganization worse, we saw the exodus of inhabitants of the interior, attracted by the illusory ease of abundant and well-paid work, for urban centers of intense life. The proletariat of these cities augmented disproportionately, originating pauperism and all of the ills springing from an excess of workers without fixed occupations." This sentiment was echoed often by Vargas and his ministers, including Vitor Tavares de Moura, who was responsible for favela policy in Rio during the Estado Novo. Such observations had some validity; and land reform, had it been enacted, might indeed have avoided many mid-century urban ills. But to the vast majority of Rio's very poor in the 1930s and 1940s, who were either rural migrants or the children of rural migrants, and who had not found industrial or other formal urban employment, such words were also a judgment that their very presence in the city was anomalous and dangerous, a problem to be remedied with expulsion, a solution repeatedly proposed at the time.

79. Varela to Vargas, AN, records of the Secretaria da Presidência da República, série 14.6, caixa 511, pastas 39–40.

80. See AN, 5a PCr, CF 70.10095, CF 70.10840, and CF 70.9291; 1a PCr, caixa 2390/123; 6a VCr, caixa 1846/307; and 8a VCr, caixa 2685/115.

81. Defendants in *vadiagem* cases, for example, claimed not to be vagrants because they worked as painters (AN, 5a PCr, CF 70.11263), coal stokers (AN, 5a PCr, CF 70.11648), itinerant construction workers (AN, 5a PCr, CF 70.11683 and AN, 3a PCr, caixa 3658/619), washerwomen (AN, 5a PCr, CF 70.12176), domestic servants (AN, 5a PCr, CF 70.11640 and AN, 1a PCr, caixa 2395/147), fruit vendors (AN, 5a PCr, CF 70.11702 and 9a VCr, Caixa 2570/793), café employees (AN, 5a PCr, CF 70.11670), and casually employed factory workers (AN, 9a VCr, caixa 2395/152). Given the circumstances, these may well have been false declarations, but they indicate the range of professions that these defendants imagined would qualify them as workers.

82. AN, 6a PCr, CF 71.0488, 1932. The lack of legal aid was clear from grammatical and spelling errors as well as from the language of the letter, which, for example, addressed the judge as "santo julgador" ("sainted judge").

83. Carminda Prudente Santana, a housewife and migrant whose husband worked as a low-level commercial employee; see AN, 6a VCr, caixa 1846/460.

84. See Borges, *The Family*; Caulfield, *In Defense*; and Besse, *Restructuring.*

85. See Besse, *Restructuring,* especially chaps. 1 and 2.

86. See Besse, *Restructuring*; and Caulfield, *In Defense.*

87. See chapters 1 and 2, this volume.

88. As early as 1920, São Paulo had already taken over as Brazil's industrial center; see Dean, *Industrialization of São Paulo*. Nevertheless, industrial employment in Rio climbed relatively quickly in the early twentieth century; see chapter 2, this volume.

89. See chapter 1, this volume.

90. Besse, *Restructuring*. Conservative fears were for the most part overblown. Despite pressure from some early-feminist quarters, divorce was not legalized in Brazil until 1977. Women were formally required to ask their husbands' permission to work until 1943; see Besse, *Restructuring*, 140. Moreover, it was only in 1962 that women ceased to be considered "incapable of personally exercising certain legal acts of civil life," which included accepting employment, litigating in a civil or commercial case, becoming a legal guardian, or having an equal say in the location of the family residence or the care and education of a couple's children. See Lei 4121; see also Brazilian Civil Code, articles 233 and 242. On women's legal inequality to men in the 1916 Civil Code, see articles 6, 233, 240, 242, 246, 248, 269, 273, 326, 380, 393, 1579, and 1611.

91. Caulfield, *In Defense*, especially 137–44, portrays these attempts as failures, since they did not, on the whole, seem to prevent young women from challenging sexual mores; indeed, by the early 1940s, the law itself had been altered to reflect changing sexual and gender norms.

92. One of the bureaus most relevant to Rio's very poor was the municipal Department of Social Assistance (DAS), within which the Serviço de Reeducação e Readaptação was responsible for everything from vocational education to medical care to moral "readaptation." In a 1946 report, officials took pride in the maternal regeneration of women under their instruction, claiming "women who before would have given thanks to God when they lost a child, because it freed them from the onus of caring for them [sic], are now reeducated and able to exercise the maternal mission." Responsible also for the "registration of the needy," the service required anyone it helped to subject his or her "personal habits" and customs of "family organization" to correction; see Vitor Tavares de Moura, report to Samuel Libânio, Secretário Geral de Saúde e Assistência, 7 March 1946, 10, in Fundação Oswaldo Cruz archives, Vitor Tavares de Moura papers, DAS, caixa 1. The Serviço de Obras Sociais (SOS) was another example. Founded in 1934 as a private Protestant charity, the SOS quickly forged strong links with Vargas-era governments and by the 1940s was among the most important providers of assistance to Rio's poor, working closely with the Legião Brasileira de Assistência. Among the SOS's goals was "to keep the institution of the family from decomposing because of miserable poverty"; this goal was to be achieved both through practical measures (provision of direct aid and help to men in search of work) and projects that mixed aid and moral instruction (including vocational training that steered women to "feminine" work, such as waitressing, cooking, and bed making) and medical and nutritional assistance doled out with moral instruction about proper mothering. See "Síntese do programa da 'SOS,'" published in every issue of the *Boletim da SOS*, 1934–62.

93. In Rio, such measures were common. For example, a 1940s municipal project meant to replace one of the city's largest shantytowns with government-

subsidized apartments specified that units would be rented only to those who had "a legally constituted family" in addition to "good social conduct"; see "Orientação para o emprego de capital para construção de casas populares," Fundação Oswaldo Cruz archives, Vitor Tavares de Moura papers, série Parques Proletários e Favelas, caixa 1. The rules for all of the Parques Proletários in the 1940s insisted that residents maintain harmony among family members and legally constitute their marriages; unmarried individuals were not to live together; see Prefeitura do Distrito Federal, Secretaria Geral de Saúde e Assistência, Serviço Social, "Parque Proletário no. ___," Fundação Oswaldo Cruz archives, Vitor Tavares de Moura papers, série Parques Proletários e Favelas, caixa 1. In a 1946 review of the activities of the Serviço de Vilas e Parques Proletários, which was the agency responsible for all public housing projects for the poor in the 1940s, favelas were portrayed as both a moral and a physical problem, and the Parques were seen as responsible for reeducating a population that, without aid, would naturally bring habits such as drunkenness, wife abuse, and child abuse into the new dwellings. Part of the agency's mission, therefore, was to regulate "conjugal situations" and change social "habits" of residents; see Vitor Tavares de Moura, report to Samuel Libânio, Secretário Geral de Saúde e Assistência, 7 March 1946, 10, in Fundação Oswaldo Cruz archives, Vitor Tavares de Moura papers, DAS, caixa 1. For factory housing policies in São Paulo, see Besse, *Restructuring*, 86–87.

94. For laws restricting nocturnal work and limiting work hours in the 1930s, see Besse, *Restructuring*, 140–41. The CLT brought these laws together in title II, chapter III, "Da proteção do trabalho da mulher," which, among other things, guaranteed paid maternity leave, prohibited most night work, banned labor in industries considered dangerous, mandated rest periods, and required medical attestations for employed women. While some such "protections" met the demands of working-class groups and some women, they also provided a disincentive for women's employment.

95. The case in point is Decreto-Lei 3200 (19 April 1941), the so-called Lei de Familia, discussed below in detail. Unlike some labor and social security legislation cited by Caulfield, *In Defense*, 194, this law required formal marriage for all beneficiaries.

96. Besse, *Restructuring*, 81, cites penalties for adultery and abandonment. Such sanctions seem to have existed mainly on paper, however; very few such cases were tried in Rio during these years.

97. Shaw, *Social History*.

98. Abdias José Nascimento dos Santos, a longtime resident and community leader in the central favela of São Carlos, made repeated reference to "good families" and to how membership in one could attenuate other sorts of faults, even criminality. He also spoke with great pride about his wife, who never worked for wages but never had help from a soul in running her household and raising seven children. He went on at length about the amount of work that represented ("21 meals a day") and about the respect he had for her (Abdias José Nascimento dos Santos, personal interview with the author, 27 November 2003). Lúcio de Paula Bispo made similar references, which are also frequent in other testimonies (personal interview with the author, 4 December 2003).

99. Caulfield, *In Defense*, 121–37.

100. Ibid.

101. AN, 3a PCr, caixa 3658/849. For more extensive analysis of this case, see Fischer, "Slandering Citizens."

102. Caulfield reaches similar conclusions with respect to sexual mores, which she portrays as differing from those of elites more in form than in content. On the contrary, Besse, *Restructuring*, sees gendered norms mainly as imposed from the outside, especially on poor women.

103. Drawing on recent research, Sandra Lauderdale Graham argues that opportunities for marriage among slaves were more extensive than previously thought; see *Caetana*.

104. Civil Code of 1916, Lei 6515 (26 December 1977).

105. On the importance of virginity to young men, see Caulfield, *In Defense*, 111–13.

106. IBGE, Departamento de Censos, *VII Recenseamento Geral do Brasil, 1960*.

107. Caulfield, *In Defense*.

108. AN, 8a PCr, 1932/524. For a more detailed exploration of this case, see Fischer, "Slandering Citizens."

109. On immigrant-native disputes among the Carioca poor, see Chalhoub, *Trabalho*.

110. AN, 8a PCr, 1932/524; AN, 3a PCr, caixa 3658/849.

111. Caulfield, *In Defense*.

112. AN, records of the Secretaria da Presidência da República, série 17.4, caixa 343, 1941/36216.

113. 4 October 1941, AN, records of the Secretaria da Presidência da República, série 17.4, caixa 277.

114. Chalhoub, *Trabalho*; on ethnic divisions, see also Ribeiro, *A liberdade*.

115. 13 December 1941, AN, records of the Secretaria da Presidência da República, série 17.4, caixa 277.

116. 1 September 1941, AN, records of the Secretaria da Presidência da República, série 14.6, caixa 511.

117. Assis Valente, "Recenseamento" (1940). Valente, Bahian by birth, lived a life divided between relatively protean work as a pharmacist and maker of dental prosthetics and impressive success as a composer of sambas, many of which commented indirectly on issues of class, race, and education. Carmen Miranda was his best-known interpreter. The reference to yearly vacations (a widely publicized feature of Vargas's labor legislation), as well as the stark contrast between the resentment apparent in the first stanza and the patriotic optimism of the last, suggest that this samba was influenced, directly or indirectly, by the Vargas government's censorship machine. On samba and censorship during the Vargas era, see Matos, *Acertei*. The instruments referred to in the second stanza are all fundamental to samba: the *pandeiro* is a kind of tambourine; the *cuíca* is a percussion instrument, said to have been brought originally to Brazil by African slaves of Bantu origin; the *tamborim* is a small drum covered on one end with animal skin; the *reco-reco* is another percussion instrument, usually made of a

serrated piece of bamboo that is rubbed with another piece of wood to produce a sound; and the *cavaquinho* is a stringed instrument similar to a ukulele.

118. The same would be true a decade later in Perón's Argentina; see James, *Resistance*.

119. 1946 constitution, article 147; 1937 constitution, article 122, no.14; 1934 constitution, article 113, no. 4.

120. See French, *Drowning*; and Merryman, *Civil Law Tradition*.

121. On the political context of the Vargas government, see Levine, *The Vargas Regime*; Levine, *Father*; Skidmore, *Politics*; and D'Araujo, ed., *As instituções*.

122. On the political front, Vargas's government made this evident during the Estado Novo, when it denied basic political rights to all Brazilians, justifying its actions with the argument that the Brazilian electorate would be ready for political democracy only after the government had instilled in them an enlightened sense of nationalism through basic moral, social, and economic reforms. Even during the more moderate periods before and after the Estado Novo, political rights were conditional rather than automatic. Most strikingly, illiterates—never less than 46 percent of the Brazilian population before 1964—were denied the vote until 1986. In 1920, 75.5 percent of the Brazilian population was illiterate. In 1940, the figure dipped to 61.2 percent; in 1950, to 57.2 percent; in 1960, to 46.7 percent; and in 1970, to 38.7 percent. See Ludwig, *Brazil*, 132.

123. Though Brazil had both a commitment to decennial censuses and a statistics bureau long before 1936 (the Diretoria Geral de Estatística was founded in 1872), there was no census in 1930, and the last year before 1920 when a relatively accurate count was produced had been 1890. Though statistics were kept sporadically on such matters as crime and population in Brazil's major urban centers, the same could not be said of smaller towns and rural areas, and comprehensive information was lacking. On the racial dimensions of census taking in Brazil and elsewhere, see Nobles, *Shades*, chap. 3.

124. On the history of the Instituto Brasileiro de Geografia e Estatística, see W. G. dos Santos and Abreu, *Estatísticas*. For a discussion of some aspects of the ideological environment behind the gathering of some statistics, see Dávila, *Diploma*.

125. On the history of social security in Brazil, see W. G. dos Santos, *Cidadania*; Coutinho and Salm, "Social Welfare"; and Hochman, "Previdência."

126. See Ministério da Agricultura, Indústria e Comércio, Directoria Geral de Estatística, *Recenseamento do Brasil, 1 de Setembro de 1920*; and IBGE, Conselho Nacional de Estatística, Serviço Nacional de Recenseamento, *VI Recenseamento Geral do Brasil, 1950*.

127. See Nobles, *Shades*; Dávila, *Diploma*; Gomes da Cunha, *Intenção*.

128. The 1920 census's use of the term "industry" provides a case in point: by allowing an expansive definition of the term, one that included many forms of production that were far from "industrial," the census made it impossible for policymakers (such as Alfred Agache) to understand the nature of the Carioca economy.

129. Rio's 1933 building census included street-by-street information on housing type and service provision, but the 1920 and 1940 national censuses did not. Until 1948, no census made a point of surveying favela settlements, and even the 1948 survey did not clarify questions of land ownership. Though scattered surveys in the 1940s did ask questions about whether land was owned or rented, they did not investigate whether "ownership" was legal or customary.

130. The 1950 favela census—part of the national census for the first time—counted settlements of 50 or more shacks as favelas, a definition that endured into the 1960s; see IBGE, Conselho Nacional de Estatística, Serviço Nacional de Recenseamento, *As Favelas do Distrito Federal e o Censo Demográfico de 1950*.

131. The 1940s favela surveys were never published. They are summarized in Parisse, *Favelas*; the originals are held in the Vitor Tavares de Moura archives.

132. See Moreira Cardoso, "Sindicalismo."

133. Ibid.

134. In rural areas especially, there had historically been considerable resistance to the idea of civil registration, let alone systems of national identification. On connections between civil registration, religion, tax collection, and one of Brazil's most celebrated nineteenth-century rebellions, see Levine, *Vale*.

135. See Paula, *Do direito*. Interestingly, although domestic servants were not eligible for official worker identification cards, which would have granted them access to the benefits spelled out in the federal labor laws, they were theoretically required to register their fingerprints and vital statistics with the police identification bureau in Rio; see Decreto-Lei 3078 (27 February 1941). See also the discussion of Brazilian labor law, below.

136. Attempts to register deaths in Rio de Janeiro began as early as 1814, and an 1861 law (Decreto 1144) had given the government the right to register the births, deaths, and marriages of all non-Catholics. But only in 1888 did the imperial government establish a civil registry to record the births, deaths, and marriages of all Brazilians. This registry was inaugurated on 1 January 1889, and the law declared that all citizens and foreign residents had the obligation to report to it. The civil code of 1916 repeated these provisions, and a 1928 law (Decreto 18542) established a set of rules governing the public registries and regulating the extension of their jurisdiction to the formal registration of juridical persons and titles and documents pertaining to literary, scientific, artistic, and material property. Despite all of these laws, however, a number of factors—including poverty, illiteracy, rural isolation, the prevalence of home births, lack of tangible consequences for noncooperation, and fear that registration would result in military conscription—impeded public compliance.

137. See Bracet, "O registro."

138. See Decreto 4857 (9 November 1939), especially articles 40, 55, 63, and 65.

139. The minimum wage was set out in Decreto-Lei 2162 (1 May 1940).

140. Undated letter received on 3 October 1941, AN, records of the Secretaria da Presidência da República, série 17.7, caixa 339.

141. Letter dated 19 October 1942, AN, records of the Secretaria da Presidência da República, série 17.7, caixa 473. Pires referred to herself in the third person throughout the letter.

142. Letter dated 9 November 1942, AN, records of the Secretaria da Presidência da República, série 17.7, caixa 473.

143. Memorandum written by Leopoldo Maciel, dated 11 February 1943. AN, records of the Secretaria da Presidência da República, série 17.7, caixa 340.

144. Decreto 13556 (30 September 1943).

145. Decreto-Lei 7845 (9 August 1945); Lei 765 (14 July 1949).

146. 4 October 1942, AN, records of the Secretaria da Presidência da República, série 17.7, caixa 473.

147. Registrations reported in the *Anuário Estatístico do Brasil* (volumes 15–18, 1954–57); for tables, see W. G. dos Santos and Abreu, *Estatísticas*. For census figures, see IBGE, Departamento de Censos, *VII Recenseamento Geral do Brasil, 1960*, vol. I, book XII, part 1, 10–11. Because registration figures were not provided for the year 1955 (the children who would have been 5 in 1960), I estimated registrations on the basis of their average rates of growth between 1951 and 1954, coming up with 69,310 live births. The total number of registered live births between 1951 and 1955, by this estimate, would have been 311,852, a number that exceeded the census statistic by 10,560. Other figures allow us to discount children who died before the age of 1 in these years; taking this into account, some 277,106 registered children would still have been alive by the 1960 census, or about 92 percent of the children reported in the census. Allowing for infant mortality after age 1 (approximately 5 percent per year in the early 1950s, the only years for which data are available) and emigration from the city (common both in the form of reverse migration and in the form of mobility to Rio suburbs officially outside the city limits), this number probably underestimates unreported births in 1950s Rio. For infant mortality statistics for children under the age of 1 year, see IBGE, *O Brasil em números*; and W. G. dos Santos and Abreu, *Estatísticas*. For mortality statistics for children between the ages of 1 and 4 years from 1949 to 1951, see IBGE, Laboratório de Estatística, Estudos Demográficos, no. 24, Rio de Janeiro; and *Anuário Estatístico do Brasil (1955)* (both in W. G. dos Santos and Abreu, *Estatísticas*).

148. Prefeitura do Distrito Federal, Secretaria Geral do Interior e Segurança, Departamento de Geografia e Estatística, *Censo das Favelas*, 10.

149. See the monthly publication of the organization, the *Boletim da SOS*, 1934–62.

150. See Mortara, "Os estudos," 6.

151. Abdias José Nascimento dos Santos, personal interview with the author, 27 November 2003; "Dieque," in O'Gorman and Mulheres de Rocinha e Santa Marta, *Morro mulher*, 25.

152. For an interesting reflection on the genesis of state identification in Brazil and its links to social control and citizenship, see Carrara, "A sciência." On the relationship between identification, police practice, and racial preconceptions, see Gomes da Cunha, "1933."

153. Decreto 16039 (14 May 1923), chap. XII, article 54.

154. Maria da Conceição Ferreira Pinto (Dona Filinha), personal interview with the author, November 1995.

155. Castro Gomes uses the term *homem novo* to describe this figure; see "A construção."

156. Wanderley Guilherme dos Santos first noted this narrowing, writing in 1979 that "citizenship rights arise from employment rights, and employment only exists through state regulation"; see W. G. dos Santos, *Cidadania*, 69.

157. On the CLT's origins, see Castro Gomes, *A invenção*. See also W. G. dos Santos, *Cidadania*; French, *Drowning*; Coutinho and Salm, "Social Welfare"; Lippi Oliveira, Pimenta Velloso, and Castro Gomes, eds., *Estado Novo*; Ferreira, *Trabalhadores*; and Ferreira, *O populismo*.

158. See especially Decreto-Lei 7036 (10 November 1944), which was the most comprehensive law on work accidents passed during the Vargas years. On the social security system, highly fragmented before 1960, see W. G. dos Santos, *Cidadania*, 21–32; see also Hochman, "Previdência." The CLT was published as Decreto-Lei 5452 (1 May 1943).

159. W. G. dos Santos, *Cidadania*.

160. The rules listed here are those published with the CLT. The original law instituting the *carteira* was Decreto 21175 (21 March 1932), altered slightly by Decreto 21580 (29 June 1932). Both closely resembled the CLT in this respect.

161. CLT, article 7. Rural workers could formally claim rights to the minimum wage, protection from dismissal without wages, the right to an individual contract, and rights to yearly vacation time, though these were less enforceable in rural areas. On the evolution of rural workers' formal rights, see Welch, *The Seed*, chap. 2. On rural workers' attitudes toward these laws, see Lugão Rios and Mattos, *Memórias*.

162. On the importance of the *carteira* in the universe of criminal justice, see chapter 6, this volume. On favela residents' understandings of the *carteira*'s importance, see Machado da Silva, "O significado."

163. Several articles published in the *Boletim do Ministério do Trabalho, Indústria, e Comércio* in the 1930s suggested that some workers, like many Europeans who had worked under similar arrangements, disliked and feared the work card system for both political and practical reasons. One such article, published in March 1935, began by reassuring workers that "professional identification is not an instrument of oppression; on the contrary, it is, according to Brazilian law, a respectful document that safeguards rights and guarantees the recognition of special professional abilities." The article reassured workers that it was illegal for any employer to write negative comments on the *carteira*, and that it was the necessary instrument of a government that sought to "prevent conflicts in the workplace so as not to interfere with the normal rhythm of production, always keeping in mind the social level of the worker who is faced with rising costs and diminished acquisitive powers in recent years."

164. Between 1934 and 1962, every one of the SOS's published yearly accounts of work with job seekers contains some version of this complaint, and

it was also a common feature of other social workers' accounts in Rio from the 1940s through the 1960s.

165. In my calculation, I used population estimates to arrive at the total number of adults who would have been eligible for a work card. I then compared this with a running total of the number of *carteiras* issued since 1933, discounting every year a percentage equal to the general death rate. It would have been impossible to compare *carteira* numbers with the economically active population, because many of those who obtained *carteiras* early on would have been part of the inactive population in later years, and thus the estimates would have been greatly distorted.

166. Brito, Bastos, and Alves, "Tres favelas." Because the 1960 favela census puts civil construction and industrial activity within a single grouping, it is difficult to make a comparison between zones in which factory production predominated and zones in which construction work was the norm. Nevertheless, according to that census, 24.05 percent of the economically active population worked in "industry" in the south-zone favelas (where the construction boom was most intense, and where domestic and other services were an important source of income), and 34.64 percent worked in such industries in Brás de Pina.

167. Perlman, *The Myth*, 158. The terms *carteira profissional* and *carteira de trabalho* were used interchangeably to refer to the work card, although the first term was always used in labor legislation.

168. Abdias José Nascimento dos Santos, personal interview with the author, 27 November 2003.

169. This method, while admittedly far from perfect, is probably the best available, given the paucity of statistical evidence on Rio's informal sector. The same technique was used by Merrick and Graham, *Population*, 239–40. For my own calculations, I omitted from individual declarations those workers who claimed to be employers, family members of owners, and "autonomous" workers, and I omitted from company declarations those employees whose occupations (mainly in sales and administration) were probably not classified as industrial by the employees themselves, counting only those whom the companies claimed as "workers."

170. Merrick and Graham, *Population*, do attempt to estimate the informal sector in personal services for Brazil as a whole; they calculate that in 1940, 82.5 percent of workers in this sector were employed informally; in 1950, the percentage fell to 76.8 percent; in 1960, it rose to 80.2 percent; and in 1970, it fell again to 75.6 percent. The percentages were probably lower for Rio.

171. "Autonomous" workers were defined as those who worked on their own account. Domestic employment was meant to be regulated by Decreto-Lei 3078 (27 February 1941); this law required all domestic employees to use a *carteira profissional*, which they could obtain only after providing proof of identity, a letter from the police authorities guaranteeing good past conduct, and a certificate proving that they had been vaccinated and were in good health (these certifications had to be renewed every two years). The *carteiras* were to be issued by the police rather than the Ministry of Labor. The law provided some minimal protections for domestic workers—after six months of steady work, for instance, they could not be dismissed without a week's notice, and the Ministry of Labor

could be informed if their salaries were not paid on time—but the law was generally much more an instrument of security and control for employers than of protection for workers. It seems never to have been enforced, however, and most domestic work remained strictly informal. Domestic employees and autonomous workers were finally incorporated into the labor law system in 1972 and 1973, respectively. Informal workers, by definition, were never protected by the CLT.

172. Vargas consistently indicated his desire to incorporate rural workers into the CLT, but this did not occur for decades, largely because of opposition from well-organized rural employers; see Welch, *The Seed*.

173. These figures are approximate, not only because of the inherent fallacies of any census but also because the census categories are not wholly consistent either with those utilized in table 4 or with one another across the decades. The most problematic category here is "autonomous workers." In all three censuses, each professional category has a subcategory labeled "workers on their own account," but the workers placed in this subcategory were in fact a haphazard mixture of individuals who officially worked for themselves, ranging from liberal professionals, with their own practices and no employees, to people who sold trinkets on street corners to casual laborers who contracted their work to different employers on a day-to-day or week-to-week basis. Although all of these people would have been ineligible for coverage under the CLT, the liberal professionals, as members of professional associations covered by private retirement and insurance plans, would most likely have received approximately equivalent benefits. Therefore, in calculating this category, I included only autonomous workers in employment sectors where individuals probably had little access to any guarantees or protections without the CLT. These sectors included "extractive industries," "industries," "commerce," "services," "transportation and communications," and "social activities." In considering "autonomous" workers, I did not try to calculate the entire so-called informal sector, which included many workers who were in fact, if not by law, employees of particular companies or individuals (those workers are considered below).

174. See *As favelas do Distrito Federal*, 34; 1960 favela census, 13.

175. Lopes, "Duas favelas," 287. Women were 28 percent of all heads of household in Cantagalo.

176. Ibid., 292. Women were about 25 percent of all heads of household in Barreira do Vasco.

177. For a summary of 1940 figures, see Costa Pinto, *O Negro*, 87–124.

178. Among other things, as mentioned above, these individuals were insured against workplace accidents; their contracts had to be formulated according to specific rules and regulations; their work hours were limited; they would be granted a measure of job security after ten years' employment; they could bring their complaints to the lowest level of the labor court system; and they were guaranteed a minimum wage, yearly vacations, and a series of other perquisites.

179. For a summary of debates surrounding labor, unions, and the state, see Batalha, "A historiografia." See also Castro Gomes, "O populismo."

180. See the *Anuário Estatístico do Distrito Federal*, 1960; see also IBGE, *Recenseamento Geral do Brasil, 1 September 1940*.

181. See W. G. dos Santos, _Cidadania,_ 21–34; Hochman, "Previdência"; and Coutinho and Salm, "Social Welfare."

182. The first CAP was created for railroad workers by Decreto 4682 (24 January 1923) and was called the Lei Elói Chaves.

183. The first IAP, for maritime workers, was created by Decreto 22872 (29 July 1933); other institutes followed on their own timelines. On institute administration, see Hochman, "Os cardeais."

184. See Lei 3807 (26 August 1960), known as the Lei Orgânica da Previdência Social; see also Decreto-Lei 72 (21 November 1966).

185. See Coutinho and Salm, "Social Welfare," 245.

186. These changes occurred in 1971 for rural workers, in 1972 for domestic workers, and in 1973 for autonomous workers; see W. G. dos Santos, _Cidadania,_ 33.

187. Tôrres, "Parque." On the Parques Proletários, see chapter 2, this volume.

188. Franco, "Vila Aliança."

189. Manoel Roberto da Silva, 3 December 1937, AN, records of the Secretaria da Presidência da República, série 17.10, caixa 124.

190. Manoel Faustino Demásio, June 1941, AN, records of the Secretaria da Presidência da República, série 17.10, caixa 345.

191. Maria Pereira de Souza, 11 November 1939, 14 November 1939, and 1 December 1939, AN, records of the Secretaria da Presidência da República, série 17.10, caixa 203.

192. J. P. Lima, 2 July 1940, AN, records of the Secretaria da Presidência da República, série 17.10, caixa 282.

193. João Baptista de Araujo et al., 3 April 1941, AN, records of the Secretaria da Presidência da República, série 17.10, caixa 206.

194. See French, _Drowning;_ and Fortes, "Revendo."

195. The Ministry of Labor has destroyed its holdings of cases that passed through the Justiça do Trabalho; without them, it is impossible to detail the ways in which workers tested the limits of the CLT in the years after 1943. Some appealed cases may have been preserved in the national archives through the mid-1950s, but they have not yet been unearthed.

196. 7 November 1939, AN, records of the Secretaria da Presidência da República, série 17.10, caixa 206.

197. This was not unique to Brazil; see Skocpol, _Protecting Soldiers;_ and Cohen, _Making._

198. Decreto-Lei 3200 (19 April 1941), put into effect by Decreto 12299 (22 April 1943). This program was strikingly similar to the _bolsa família_ program enacted by President Luiz Inácio Lula da Silva in the early 2000s.

199. On the image, see Levine, _Father,_ 199; on the Family Law, see Besse, _Restructuring._

200. Among other things, the law guaranteed that civil marriages could be performed and recorded free of charge; it simplified procedures for legally recognizing illegitimate children; it promised bonuses and housing assistance to legally recognized workers who married; it directly aided married couples who ad-

equately cared for and educated numerous children; it outlined procedural steps for guaranteeing child support to abandoned wives; it reduced the fees charged for secondary and professional education to families with more than one child; it promised that federal, state, and local governments would subsidize local charities that assisted "miserably poor" families; and it mandated that young people's recreational or sporting clubs were to admit a certain proportion of poor children free of charge.

201. Sá, "Abonos."

202. Decreto-Lei 3200 (19 April 1941), article 29.

203. Ibid., article 28. This provision was later replaced (1943) with the *salário-família*, which provided greater benefit but was not available to all workers until the early 1960s.

204. Ibid., article 39.

205. Public employees composed about 27 percent of Rio's workforce in 1940, 21 percent in 1950, and 21 percent in 1960. These numbers are rough estimates based on the censuses of 1940, 1950, and 1960. The 1950 census was the only one to provide a complete tally of public employees; I estimated the numbers for 1940 and 1960 by calculating the ratio, in 1950, between and the total number counted as public employees and the sum of the total number of workers classified as "public administrators, etc." and as policemen and members of the armed services; this ratio was 1.62 to 1. Since both the 1940 and the 1960 calculations included the latter two categories, I estimated the number of public employees for these years by adding together the public administrators and the policemen and members of the armed services and multiplying this number by 1.62. In doing this, I probably overestimated the number of public employees for 1940, since the category of "public administrators" included public school teachers in this year, while it did not in 1950 or 1960.

206. Letter dated 8 August 1941, AN, records of the Secretaria da Presidência da República, série 17.4, caixa 277. Article 29 guaranteed an *abono familiar* of 100 cruzeiros to every head of household, with eight or more children, who "working in any kind of job earns a salary that by no means covers the basic, minimum subsistence needs of his family." Article 39 required anyone who wanted to receive benefits from the *abono familiar* provision "to produce proof that he has done everything possible to provide his children with education, not only physical and intellectual but also moral, in accordance with the religious orientation of the parents, and adequate to his social condition, as much as circumstances permit. This proof will be renewed each year." In 1943, when the mechanisms of Decreto-Lei 3200 were finally laid down by Decreto 12299, article 3 specified that such proof could come from any judicial, police, or school authority. Article 40 of Decreto-Lei 3200 (19 April 1941) exempted applicants for the benefits of the *abono familiar* from purchasing the stamps and seals that usually had to accompany any official request.

207. Of 95 archived letters, only 17 used the language of rights; of these, all but three of the writers were employed in a clearly defined profession, all but two were male, and all but three claimed to have eight or more children.

208. 10 July 1939, AN, records of the Secretaria da Presidência da República,

série 17.4, caixa 193, processo 19625/39. This case is also mentioned above.

209. 20 January 1943, AN, records of the Secretaria da Presidência da República, série 17.4, caixa 516. It is not entirely clear from the letter where dos Anjos lived; her letter only reads "Estação do Retiro, Sítio do Grotão." There was no "Estação do Retiro" in Rio, though there was one off of the Leopoldinha Railway line in Minas Gerais, near the other places mentioned in this letter. This is the letter's most probable origin, though the fact that it was filed with letters from Rio may indicate that dos Anjos lived on the Estrada do Retiro, near the Estação de Bangú in still-rural Rio.

210. Hochman, "Previdência"; see tables drawn from the Anuários Estatísticos do Brasil. In Brazil as a whole, 2,640 families had begun to receive benefits by 1944, and well over 100,000 families per year (or over 1 million individuals) were receiving the benefit annually by the late 1950s.

211. The cost of fulfilling the "basic nutritional needs" of Carioca adults in the years between 1940 and 1945 was calculated by the Ministério do Trabalho, Indústria e Comércio; in 1941, it worked out to about 2.79 cruzeiros per day (*Levantamento, 1946*). An alternate calculation can be made with the daily nutritional intake recommended by Moscoso ("A alimentação," 115) and the yearly price averages published in the *Anuário Estatístico do Distrito Federal*. Using this method, I calculated the food costs for one adult male at about 2.90 cruzeiros per day. If a 1938 study of the actual daily expenditures of lower-class Cariocas can be taken as any guide, most poor people were eating far less than these numbers would indicate, spending somewhere around 1.60 cruzeiros per day. I arrived at these numbers by looking at the results of the 1938 study (see *Anuário Estatístico do Distrito Federal, 1941–45, 218*) and factoring in the inflation rates for food for an "average" middle-class Carioca family as calculated for a cost-of-living study by the Ministério do Trabalho, Indústria e Comércio. The same study, the results of which were also published in the *Anuário Estatístico do Distrito Federal,* concluded that an average middle-class Carioca family spent approximately 2,803.10 cruzeiros per month in 1941, or nearly twelve times the minimum wage of 240 cruzeiros per month. For more information on wages and living standards in Rio, see Lobo, *História*, vol. 2; and Lobo, ed., *Rio de Janeiro*.

212. All figures from Hochman, "Previdência." Tables for the *abono familiar* and minimum wage figures for Rio are from Moreira Cardoso, "Sindicalismo," who gleaned his statistics from the *Anuário Estatístico do Brasil* (1963).

213. The Legião Brasileira de Assistência (LBA) was founded to aid the families of Brazilian soldiers who had fought in World War II. Even before the war ended, however, the LBA, led by its founding president, Darcy Vargas, had begun to transform itself into Brazil's largest charitable organization. The Serviço do Obras Sociais (SOS) was founded in 1934 as a private nonprofit organization to help Rio de Janeiro's neediest residents; in the late 1930s and early 1940s, the SOS gradually forged close links with the municipal and federal governments, and, after the founding of the LBA, the two organizations collaborated closely in a number of municipal projects. Both organizations still exist today, although both had their heydays in the 1940s and 1950s. Information on the activities of both organizations can be found in the *Boletim da SOS,* copies of which still exist

for the years 1934–62. Statistics on private charitable organizations are from the *Resumo dos Boletins Mensais de Estatística do Distrito Federal, 1930–31* and from the *Anuário Estatístico do Distrito Federal,* 1942–46.

214. See the *Anuário Estatístico do Distrito Federal,* 1932–45. The vast majority of people served by these private institutions were children; a substantial number were also elderly or seriously ill, and a few groups targeted widowed or abandoned mothers. Only a few larger organizations sought to help poor individuals with no socially valid excuse for their poverty. Statistics are not available for later years.

215. See the *Anuário Estatístico do Distrito Federal,* 1942–46. See also Secretaria Geral de Saúde e Assistência, Departamento de Assistência Social, Albergue da Boa Vontade, "Mapa dos services prestados por esta dependência durante o ano de 1945," in Fundação Oswaldo Cruz archives, Vitor Tavares de Moura papers, série Medicina Social, dossiê Albergue da Boa Vontade e Fundação Leão XIII, caixa 1.

216. See the *Boletim da SOS,* 1934–62; the February 1962 issue contained a summary of the organization's activities since its founding in 1934. The SOS's capacity diminished quite dramatically over the course of the years in question, as its relationship with the LBA grew more distant and as federal and municipal subsidies shrank. Even during its heyday in the mid-1940s, however, the organization could not have dreamed of filling the city's needs; in 1944, for example, it was distributing an average of only 1,150 children's snacks and 534 kilograms of food per day.

217. Numbers for the early 1960s are entirely out of line with those in the rest of Brazil and are thus probably unreliable; it is possible that they were documenting individuals rather than individual acts of help, but it is impossible to know.

218. See Patterson, *America's Struggle*; Skocpol, *Protecting Soldiers*; and Pederson, *Family.*

219. Weinstein, *For Social Peace.*

220. See annual reports for the Albergue da Boa Vontade, Fundação Oswaldo Cruz archives, Vitor Tavares de Moura papers. See also the *Boletim da SOS.*

221. Vitor Tavares de Moura, undated report to the municipal director of the Department of Hygiene and Social Assistance and to the director of the Albergue da Boa Vontade, Fundação Oswaldo Cruz archives, Vitor Tavares de Moura papers, série Medicina Social, dossiê Albergue da Boa Vontade e Fundação Leão XIII, caixa 1.

222. Pamphlet published by the Casa do Pobre de Nossa Senhora de Copacabana, Rio de Janeiro, 1936, attached to a letter from Manoel de A. Castello Branco to President Vargas dated 9 December 1937, AN, records of the Secretaria da Presidência da República, série 17.4, caixa 123.

223. Proposal included with a letter from Laureana d'Oliveira Pereira dated 10 December 1935, AN, records of the Secretaria da Presidência da República, série 17.4, caixa 34. Oliveira Pereira was already the director of a more conventional charity for children called the Abrigo da Criança Pobre. Although a similar establishment was eventually organized in Rio, nothing seems to have resulted

directly from Oliveira Pereira's proposal. Vargas did read the letter personally, and his ministers lauded the idea behind the proposal, but the final response from the Ministry of Education and Public Health claimed that only the municipal government would be able to directly sponsor the Casa do Pobre, since the direct work of the federal government was limited to questions of public health and sanitation.

224. Syndicates were founded with legal grounding in the largely conservative 1944 rural syndicalization code, Decreto-Lei 7038 (10 November 1944). Rural laborers were formally invested with the sorts of rights set out in the CLT by the 1963 Estatuto do Trabalhador Rural, Lei 4215 (2 March 1963). There is some dispute regarding the law's impact, however. W. G. dos Santos, *Cidadania*, 33, argues that it was virtually null because the law was never funded. Welch, *The Seed*, argues that it accelerated changes in rural labor relations. Effective inclusion of rural workers in the social security system came in 1971. In 1972, domestic workers were brought in. Autonomous workers were included in 1973.

225. See Welch, *The Seed*.

226. See French, *Drowning*; French, *Brazilian Workers' ABC*; Wolfe, *Working Women*; and Fortes, "Revendo."

227. Unfortunately, the best evidence for these struggles—cases tried in the Justiça do Trabalho—has been routinely destroyed in Rio, and popular correspondence with Juscelino Kubitschek (the only such correspondence publicly available) does not contain any equivalent to the Vargas appeals.

228. The Estatuto do Trabalhador Rural, passed in 1963, formally extended guarantees given urban workers by the CLT to the countryside; in doing so, it effected the first major transformation in Vargas's labor system. The change was less complete than it might appear, though, since enforcement and financing remained precarious, and the law itself made distinctions between different kinds of rural workers (permanent versus itenerant, for example) that allowed a growing number of rural laborers to remain outside the system. Price controls and other measures aimed at keeping down the prices of essential goods (including public sale) came into being through laws 1521 and 1522, both of 26 December 1951.

229. See figure 1, above.

230. Moreira Cardoso, "Sindicalismo."

231. Ibid. (tables extracted from the *Anuário Estatístico do Brasil* (1941–45 through 1965).

232. No numbers exist for Rio alone; in Brazil as a whole, membership jumped from 1,912,172 in 1940 to 4,058,000 in 1960. See Coutinho and Salm, "Social Welfare," 244.

233. See chapters 5 and 6, this volume; see also Fischer, "'Quase Pretos.'"

234. See Fortes, "Revendo"; and French, *Drowning*.

235. Welch, *The Seed*; Abdias José Nascimento dos Santos, personal interview with the author, 27 November 2003.

236. Though the absolute number of jobs declared by employers in industry grew from 56,229 to 176,636 between 1920 and 1960 (and their percentage in the workforce climbed from around 11 percent to around 15 percent), by 1960 the percentage of workers who declared such professions had decreased from

27.5 percent to 20.2 percent. In that year, services replaced industry as the greatest single source of work in Rio, employing 23.7 percent of the workforce. Public employees followed closely, at about 21.4 percent, but that percentage dropped significantly after 1960.

237. Abdias José Nascimento dos Santos, personal interview with the author, 27 November 2003; Lúcio de Paula Bispo, personal interview with the author, 4 December 2003; Pandolfi and Grynszpan, *A favela fala.*

238. IBGE, *Estatísticas históricas do Brasil.* The real value of the minimum wage, after dropping sharply in the 1940s, was maintained by periodic readjustments in the 1950s and the early 1960s, only experiencing a permanent drop thereafter.

239. On the SENAI in São Paulo during these years, see Weinstein, *For Social Peace.*

240. Lúcio de Paula Bispo, personal interview with the author, 4 December 2003; Abdias José Nascimento dos Santos, personal interview with the author, 27 November 2003.

241. Odília dos Santos Gama, personal interview with the author, 2 December 2003.

242. Machado da Silva, "O significado."

243. Maria da Conceição Ferreira Pinto, personal interview with the author, November 1995. See also O'Gorman and Mulheres de Rocinha e Santa Marta, *Morro mulher.*

244. AJ, 2º TJ, processo 2115/1960, maço 424.

245. AJ, 2º TJ, processo 1450/1960, maço 416.

246. Zaluar, *A maquina.*

247. Cícero Nunes, "Inimigo do Trabalho," published in 1962 by Bandeirante Editora Musical and recorded by Jorge Veiga for RCA Victor; all spellings from the original. The *choro* was a sentimental older and whiter cousin of the samba; it originated in the late nineteenth century, the legend goes, in the northern suburbs and the Cidade Nova, and it was originally played by small groups of musicians, many of whom worked for the railroad or the postal service, who wished to give a Brazilian twist to the European polkas and waltzes popular at the time among Carioca high society. Based essentially on music of the flute, the violin, and the ukulele, the *choro* was often improvised, and it remains to this day the focus of nightlong sessions in some parts of Rio de Janeiro. Cícero Nunes, the composer of this *choro*, worked in various Carioca factories in the 1920s and 1930s and was also employed as a driver for a hospital. Jorge Veiga, who recorded it, was born in the Carioca suburbs and became known when, after working for years as a shoeshine man, a banana vendor, and an odd-jobber, he got a job painting the walls of a warehouse whose owner noticed his singing and connected him with one of Brazil's largest radio stations; see Marcondes, *Enciclopédia.* One phrase from the *choro* seems to have been taken from Wilson Batista and Henrique Alves's 1952 carnival *marcha* "Nasci Cansado," which began with the line "My father worked so much / That I was born / Already tired." The marcha continued in a similar vein: "Oh, boss / I am a finished man / My shack leaks / My suit is ruined / Oh, boss / I don't want to work any more / I am not like a crab / That only knows how to walk backwards" (cited in Matos, *Acertei*).

PART III: RIGHTS POVERTY IN THE CRIMINAL COURTS

1. There are few published records of the Morro da Formiga's early history. According to the 1933 building census, there were around 20 shacks on the streets adjacent to the settlement but no recognized streets on the *morro* itself; see Ministério do Trabalho, Indústria, e Comércio, Departamento de Estatística e Publicidade, *Estatística Predial do Distrito Federal, 1933*. This was probably not accurate, since the court case referred to here records ten independent witnesses from the *morro*, who are clearly only some of the area's residents (AN, 5a PCr, CF 70.9476). The 1950 favela census recorded over 600 residences there; see IBGE, Conselho Nacional de Estatística, Serviço Nacional de Recenseamento, *As Favelas do Distrito Federal e o Censo Demográfico de 1950*. The neighboring favelas of Borel and Salgueiro both owed much of their early growth to extralegal speculation that provided housing to workers employed in the various construction projects surrounding Rio de Janeiro's centennial independence celebration in 1922. Given the details of this dispute, it seems likely that Formiga followed a similar pattern. See Gomes, *As lutas*.

2. AN, 5a PCr, CF 70.9476.

3. Scattered evidence indicates that a disproportionate number of the "landlords" in the earliest generation of central and north-zone favelas were Portuguese or otherwise foreign-born. It is difficult, in the absence of systematic data, to know if this is a matter of truth or perception; the settlements' Brazilian residents may simply have resented the foreign landlords more, or the press may have been more likely to villainize them, drawing on slumlord stereotypes already common in the late nineteenth century. See Gomes, *As lutas*; see also chapters 7 and 8, this volume.

4. The conflict among the judicial, investigative, and repressive functions of Rio de Janeiro's police force dated to the mid-nineteenth century. Between 1841 and 1871, police chiefs and some of their subordinates could investigate, try, and judge certain misdemeanor cases without interference from judicial authorities. By 1929, their formal role was mostly restricted to initial fact finding and investigation; testimony given before police authorities was no longer considered fully reliable, and only prosecutors and judges had the right to indict suspects and judge their guilt or innocence. Misdemeanors (*contravenções*) were a partial exception: testimony in these cases was almost always gathered exclusively by the police, and indictments were practically automatic once the police forwarded the case to a judge. On the police in nineteenth-century Rio de Janeiro, see Holloway, *Policing Rio*. The best primary source for studying the daily functions of police *delegacias* in the twentieth century are the *livros de ocorrência,* log books used to record every notable occurrence. Marcos Bretas has based two studies on his reading of a sampling of these books; see Bretas, *A guerra*; and Bretas, "You Can't." In both studies, Bretas highlights the police forces' extrajudicial dispute-resolution functions; according to his statistics, cases brought to police attention that ever resulted in actual arrests rarely exceeded 20 percent in 1925; and in 1927, five of the seven districts he surveyed formally investigated fewer than 30 percent of the cases that came to their attention. Roberto Kant de Lima suggests

that Rio's police force continued as the principal arbiter of informal local disputes in the 1980s, especially among Rio's poorest classes; see "Legal Theory."

5. In my sample of police investigations and *livros de ocorrência*, this strategy seemed particularly important for women, who often resorted to police authority in order to halt male abuse but then refused to follow through and testify in a formal investigation. Women would also use the police to force men to marry young women whom they had "deflowered," or to settle neighborhood disputes. For men, such semi-formal recourse to the police was less common, important mainly in neighborhood conflicts with women or across classes—disputes that could not honorably be settled through physical fights.

6. *Código Penal dos Estados Unidos do Brasil (1890)*, title XI, *capítulo único*, article 317.

7. Ibid., article 315.

8. According to Brazilian law, in crimes considered part of the public domain (a category that included most common crimes, with the exception of cases related to sexual transgressions and assaults on individual honor), neither individual parties nor police authorities could drop the charges or end an official investigation. Both groups, however, exercised informal power to stifle an investigation: police authorities could delay cases to the point where the statute of limitations expired, or they could selectively lose track of witnesses, victims, and defendants; witnesses could refuse to appear before police authorities, or they could move without notifying the police. Witnesses could also recant or contradict their own damaging testimony once they were satisfied that the investigation itself constituted sufficient informal punishment.

9. See Valladares, *A invenção*, and also chapters 1 and 2, this volume.

10. On the history of Brazilian criminological thought in the early twentieth century, see Gomes da Cunha, "1933"; Carrara, *Crime*; and Fry, "Direito positivo."

11. Costallat, "A favela que eu vi," 33–34.

12. On crimes against female sexual honor, see Caulfield, *In Defense*; Abreu Esteves, *Meninas*; and Caulfield and Abreu Esteves, "50 Years."

13. For a fuller discussion of crimes against individual honor in Brazilian law and jurisprudence, see Fischer, "Slandering Citizens." For comparisons with Europe and the rest of Latin America, see note 69 to part II, above. For the classic formulation of honor in the Mediterranean world, see Pitt-Rivers, "Honor and Social Status." On Colonial Latin America, see Johnson and Lipsett-Rivera, eds., *The Faces of Honor*, especially the introduction and chapters by Geoffrey Spurling, Ann Twinam, Muriel Nazzari, Lyman L. Johnson, Sonya Lipsett-Rivera, and Sandra Lauderdale Graham.

14. The term "positivism" is a source of confusion for two reasons. First, the positivist school of penal law did not derive directly from the philosophical positivism of Auguste Comte, although there is a great deal of philosophical and methodological overlap between the two. Second, the positivist school of penal law has no relation with what legal scholars know as "juridical positivism" or "legal positivism." Although these terms are often, and sometimes mistakenly, used interchangeably, the latter two refer strictly to the current of late-eighteenth-

and early-nineteenth-century thought that held that so-called positive law should take precedence over natural law; for an explanation, see Bobbio, *O positivismo*, 22–23. Legal positivism is in many respects the intellectual inspiration for the modern civil law tradition, which codified the legal systems—rooted in canonical and Roman law—that govern most of the Western world, including Brazil. The term is often interchangeable with the term "classical law." But the positivist school of penal law (sometimes called the "new," "Italian," or "modern" school, and occasionally termed the "Lombrosian" or "anthropological" school), includes a rather diverse group of legal thinkers, the most important of whom are probably Cesare Lombroso, Enrico Ferri, and Raffaelle Garofalo, who drew their inspiration from nineteenth-century natural science and sociology. Over the course of the early twentieth century, positivist and neopositivist thought moved away from biological determinism and toward a belief in the psychological and social roots of crime. For contemporary discussions, see Barreto, *O crime*; Peixoto, *Criminologia*; Viveiros de Castro, *A nova escola*; and Lyra, *Novíssimas escolas*. For an excellent modern synthesis, see Álvarez, "Bacharéis"; see also Ribeiro, "Clássicos."

15. According to the classical tradition, individuals could be exempted from guilt only if it could be proven that they were somehow deprived of or incapable of exercising free will; thus, according to article 27, children younger than 9 years old, or those between 9 and 14 who were not capable of appreciating the criminality of their acts, were released from criminal responsibility. So were those who were senile; "natural imbeciles"; "those who were entirely deprived of their intelligence and their senses when they committed the crime"; those who committed a crime under threat of violence, or accidentally; and deaf-mutes. In addition, individuals who committed a crime either to avoid a greater evil or in legitimate defense of legal rights (their own or those of others) could be exempted from responsibility (article 32). On the differences between the classical and positivist schools of legal thought, see Fry, "Direito positivo"; and Fry and Carrara, "As vicissitudes."

16. The written law sometimes implicitly permitted such considerations. According to oblique language contained in the 1890 criminal code, for example, only an "honest" girl could be the victim of criminal offenses against her sexual honor, and the norms of criminal procedure dictated that witnesses could be disregarded as "suspect" or "defective" if they lacked a "good reputation." See Siqueira, *Curso*, articles 268–77.

17. Reciprocal insults were considered a purely private matter, according to article 322 of the 1890 penal code. When insults were provoked by some aggressive or unjust action by the insulted party, the severity of the charge was attenuated. See Macedo Soares, *Código penal*. For an excellent historical analysis of *injúria* laws in Brazil, see Hungria, *Comentários ao código penal*, vol. VI, article 140.

18. One of the more interesting aspects of the lawyer's claims involved a justification for the ditch digging. Despite the fact that Antônio's claim to *morro* land was questionable, the lawyer justified the ditch by referring to the Brazilian civil code, claiming that Antônio, as a property owner, was obligated to accept the

passage of waste waters through his property but had a right to defend his buildings from flooding or infiltration. In this way, without justifying his legal claim to property, Antônio claimed the legal rights of a property owner.

19. In my own survey of Carioca court cases in the late 1920s and early 1930s, Paixão appeared as a judge some 50 times; openly subjective criteria entered into his decisions only once, when he found a military official to be more responsible than a common citizen for being aware of arms-possession laws.

20. There is no automatic presumption of innocence in the Brazilian legal system. Although various legal scholars do argue that the advantage ought to go to the defendant in cases of doubt, Brazilian judges frequently justified their decisions with statements to the effect that a defendant was found guilty because he or she had been unable to prove his or her innocence definitively, and there is no legal mandate equivalent to "innocent until proven guilty." For a comparison of assumptions of guilt and innocence in the Brazilian and American criminal justice systems, see Kant de Lima, "Legal Theory," chap. 1.

21. In relative terms, a fine of 150 mil-reis was equivalent to one month's wages for a relatively well-compensated Rio de Janeiro textile worker in 1929. It is unlikely that many favela residents made much more than this; the domestic servants who left some record of their salaries in 251 criminal cases that I examined for the years 1929 and 1930—there were only a few—earned about half of this wage, while skilled laborers in construction and transportation could earn two to three times more. Information about textile workers' wages is from Lobo, *História*, vol. 2.

22. Bourdieu, "Rites as Acts." Bourdieu claims that a "rite of institution"—which could be anything from a school exam to a circumcision—is an act that "leads towards the consecration or legitimization of an arbitrary boundary, that is to say, it attempts to misrepresent the arbitrariness and presents the boundary as legitimate and natural." Such a rite is also, in Bourdieu's view, "an act of communication, but of a particular kind: it signifies to someone his identity, but at the same time as it expresses that identity and imposes it on him, it expresses it before everyone and authoritatively informs him of what he is and what he must be." In borrowing this notion here, I argue that while Brazilians of particular social classes, races, and ethnicities certainly had their own "rites of institution" after the end of the Brazilian Empire and before the 1930 revolution, very few were recognized at once by every sector of society and also by the institutions of the state. As I will argue below in relation to criminal law, and as I have argued in previous chapters in relation to laws governing work, property, and social welfare, one of the Vargas administration's legacies was the at least partially successful introduction of a number of bureaucratic "rites" that would reward individuals with a particular kind of status as "honorable citizens."

23. See the *Código Penal dos Estados Unidos do Brasil* (1890) and also the *Código do processo penal para o Districto Federal* (Decreto 16751, 31 December 1924). The most comprehensive commentaries on the penal code were written by Oscar de Macedo Soares (*Código penal*), and Galdino Siqueira (*Direito penal brasileiro*). In the early 1930s, as projects for a new penal code were being debated, appellate court judge Vicente Piragibe published a version of the 1890 code

that included all of the legal modifications made in the intervening decades; see Piragibe, *Consolidação das leis penais*. This became the official Brazilian criminal code in December 1932 and retained that status until the 1940 criminal code went into effect in 1942. Piragibe's edition is not commentated but does note the date of every modification. Cândido Mendes de Almeida's *Código do processo penal* (1925) is the best (and perhaps only) commentated edition of Rio's code of criminal procedure; Mendes de Almeida was a renowned jurist and president of the commission responsible for the processual code. For a complete retrospective of Brazilian criminal procedure, see Siqueira, *Curso*.

24. As I will argue further below, the question of the so-called individualization of criminal law was a central preoccupation of Brazilian positivist jurists in the first decades of the twentieth century. Many were particularly intrigued with three practical measures: "indeterminate" sentences, suspended sentences, and early release. For detailed discussions, see especially Moraes, *Problemas*; Peixoto, *Criminologia*; and Drummond, *Aspectos*.

25. *Código Penal dos Estados Unidos do Brasil* (1890), vol. I, title III, article 27. The code released children under the age of 9, as well as "natural imbeciles and those weakened by senility," from any criminal responsibility; similar status could be given to deaf-mutes and to minors between the ages of 9 and 14 if it could be shown that they were incapable of discerning the criminal nature of their acts. These provisions modified the 1830 criminal code only slightly. During the period when the 1890 code was in force, several modifications considerably broadened the definitions of these groups. In 1927, the special *Código de Menores* raised the age of criminal responsibility definitively to 14 and mandated the creation of an entirely separate court system for minors under the age of 18 as well as special treatment for those between the ages of 18 and 21. Another series of provisions, which culminated in 1921 with the inauguration of Rio's Manicômio Judicial, allowed for specific, separate treatment for the legally insane and also specified procedures for the legal determination of sanity. Both these modifications were seen at the time as explicit concessions to the positivist school. On the legal responsibility of the criminally insane in the first decades of the twentieth century, see Carrara, *Crime*; on the origins of the *Código de Menores*, see Álvarez, *Bacharéis*.

26. Mendes de Almeida, *Código do processo penal*, articles 59, 299, and 549.

27. The code of criminal procedure simply specified that for so-called private crimes (crimes against honor, sexual crimes, and property damage), complaints could be brought only by the offended party or the person who had legal authority to represent that party. According to the Brazilian civil code, however, married women were not authorized to represent themselves in a court of law; consequently, police, prosecutors, and judges frequently rejected the criminal complaints of married women who acted without the assistance of their husbands.

28. Mendes de Almeida, *Código do processo penal*, article 121.

29. Ibid., articles 661–66. On the humiliating nature of the identification process—and its importance as a marker, in and of itself, of "criminal tendencies"—see Gomes da Cunha, "The Stigma of Dishonor."

30. Mendes de Almeida, *Código do processo penal*, articles 101, 122, 125, 589, and 591. I will discuss the legal concept of vagrancy further below.

31. See Siqueira, *Direito penal brasileiro*; and Macedo Soares, *Código penal*.

32. See Siqueira, *Direito penal brasileiro*; Macedo Soares, *Código penal*; and Viveiros de Castro, *A nova escola*, 127–52.

33. Viveiros de Castro, *A nova escola*, 9–44.

34. For a concise argument against the admissibility of "passion," see Siqueira, *Direito penal brasileiro*, 386–89. For an exposition of positivist and classical arguments with respect to this issue, see Moraes, *Problemas*, 155–207. Moraes, in contrast to Siqueira, argues that the code mandates (erroneously, in his opinion) that individuals under the influence of any great passion be excused from criminal responsibility. A good example of the use of the passion argument in a concrete criminal defense can be found in Romeiro Neto, *O direito penal*.

35. *Código Penal dos Estados Unidos do Brasil* (1890), vol. I, title IV, articles 36–42.

36. Both early release and suspended sentences were originally authorized by Decreto 4577 (5 September 1922); the laws regulating the enforcement of both measures, however, were contained in Decreto 16655 (6 November 1924) and incorporated into Piragibe, *Consolidação das leis penais*.

37. The procedural rules governing early release were incorporated into the 1924 procedural code, articles 581–98. Suspended sentences were regulated by articles 567–80 of the procedural code.

38. Caulfield, *In Defense*.

39. Peixoto, *Criminologia*, 203–4. On vagrancy, see Gomes da Cunha, *Intenção*; Huggins, *From Slavery to Vagrancy*; Chalhoub, "Vadios e barões"; Holloway, *Policing Rio*; Kowarick, *Trabalho e vadiagem*; Flory, *Judge and Jury*.

40. Testimony in Brazilian police stations was given in the "inquisitorial" tradition, whereby defendants had no right to an attorney, and police officials posed all questions. Once a case proceeded to the trial phase, it was governed by the "accusatorial" tradition, whereby the defendant had the right to a lawyer, who would be present for all testimony. In this second phase, Brazilian criminal procedure still differed from common law in that questions to witnesses, defendants, and victims were posed first by the judge and only later by lawyers. The most succinct description of the formal features of Brazilian criminal trials after 1942 (and of their social significance) is Kant de Lima, "Cultura jurídica." For the rules governing criminal procedure before 1942, see the *Código do Processo Penal para o Distrito Federal* (1924); see also Siqueira, *Curso*.

41. There were also separate courts for minors.

42. Until 1941, the procedural rules governing the prosecution of private and public crimes alike were set by state codes of criminal procedure. For Rio in 1929, see Mendes de Almeida, *Código do processo penal*, chap. 1. Until 1941, the *pretorias* tried misdemeanors and relatively minor crimes, such as verbal *calúmnia* and *injúria*; offenses to public decency; trespassing; minor theft; traffic accidents; and physical assaults. They were also responsible for the first stage of judicial investigation for the most serious crimes, which would eventually be decided by

a jury. Each of the eight *pretorias* was responsible for a specific geographical area of the city. After the initial judicial investigation by the *pretoria*, the *Tribunal do Júri* tried cases involving homicide, death threats, and attempted bribery. The *varas* were responsible for judging everything else, and their cases were assigned randomly rather than geographically; see Decreto Municipal 16273 (1923). After 1941, the court system was simplified, with the *varas* responsible for judging all crimes except those involving death or attempted murder. See Decreto-Lei 3931 (31 December 1941). See also the *Código de Processo Penal* (1941); the most useful annotated edition is Azevedo Franco, *Código de processo penal anotado*.

43. This sort of work has also been undertaken recently to great effect with a basis in civil cases and wills. See Lewin, *Surprise Heirs*; Lauderdale Graham, *Caetana*; Mattos de Castro, *Das cores*; Motta, *Nas fronteiras*; Grinberg, *Liberata*; Lara, *Campos*; and Frank, *Dutra's World*.

44. See especially Sidney Chalhoub, Sueann Caulfield, and Olívia Gomes da Cunha.

45. See Caulfield, *In Defense*.

46. No one seems to know for sure just how many police inquiries and criminal trials passed through the Carioca justice system in the years around 1930. Statistics of variable quality do exist for the years before 1920, and there are complete data series for the early 1940s through the late 1960s, but what few figures detail Rio's justice system in the 1920s and 1930s paint an uneven and equivocal portrait. According to Marcos Bretas, reports by the chief of police estimated that prosecutions for crimes and misdemeanors between 1925 and 1928 varied between 4,759 and 12,727—statistics that differ so wildly that it is difficult to draw any conclusions from them. Bretas's analysis of daily police activity scarcely sheds more light. In his sample of seven police districts, average occurrences in 1927 ranged from only slightly over 0.5 per day in residential Santa Teresa to nearly 4.5 per day in downtown Santa Ana, and only two districts showed a relatively stable number of daily occurrences throughout the 1920s. Bretas estimates that the average number of daily occurrences across his sample ranged between 2.36 and 2.77 in the 1920s, but this does not indicate much about rates across Rio, since he included only the central districts, which presumably had greater population densities and occurrence rates. Still, if we take this as a high estimate, the 30 regular *delegacias* were dealing with somewhere between 25,840 and 30,330 individual complaints or reported criminal occurrences annually in the 1920s. Of these, according to Bretas's best estimates, fewer than 20 percent resulted in arrests, and somewhere around 29 percent—or between 7,494 and 8,796—resulted in official police investigations. According to Bretas, the most common crimes were physical assault (including traffic accidents), theft, and vagrancy. Although these are extremely rough estimates, they do generally conform to patterns that would emerge with improvements in official recordkeeping in the 1940s. See Bretas, "You Can't," 116.

47. My choice to include several years in the sample was based on a number of factors. First, since trials tended to drag on over many years, the precise date when a trial was initiated often has relatively little meaning. Second, police and judicial practices alike tended to depend a great deal on the individuals who were

in charge at any particular moment; in order to avoid the risk of exceptionalism, it seemed logical to look at a period rather than at a single year. Third, since the trials are organized in the archives only in rough chronological order, the burdensome task of retrieving trials with the appropriate geographical distribution would have proved much more difficult if I had limited myself to a single year.

48. These numbers are probably not exactly proportional to the overall distribution of inquiries, trials, and nonguilty verdicts in the Carioca justice system, where a somewhat smaller percentage of all defendants was probably found guilty. The percentage of police inquiries in the sample that ended without going to trial is probably particularly low, at least to judge from patterns drawn from the early 1940s. The distribution of the sample is due in part to the crimes represented, since many were misdemeanor cases that proceeded to trial almost automatically; it is also due to my interest in studying the judicial as well as the police phases of criminal cases.

49. Roughly 31 percent of my sample involved physical assault cases; 24 percent involved property crimes; 22 percent involved sexual crimes; around 8 percent involved vagrancy; 6 percent involved verbal assault; and the rest involved miscellaneous crimes including murder, mysterious death, resisting arrest, suicide, and black magic.

50. On gambling, see Chazkel, *Laws of Chance*.

51. It is often impossible to tell from trial records whether witnesses raised these issues spontaneously or because of official prompting; most of what appeared as testimony in the trial records was actually a string of responses to unrecorded official queries.

52. Paulo Ferreira Alves Junqueira was one of the few apparently well-off individuals in my sample who were arrested for vagrancy. The case is odd: he claimed that his arrest was in fact an act of vengeance carried out by corrupt police officers whom he had tried to purge from the forces when he was fighting for the 1930 revolution. His argument against the actual vagrancy charges, however, was based almost entirely on social class: Paulo's testimony before the judge was a slightly more elegant version of that given before police authorities upon his arrest. In the end, such arguments were to no avail; Paulo was not given the opportunity to present his documents (a blatant violation of procedural law), was convicted of vagrancy, and spent more than six months in prison. It may be that Paulo's family was not nearly so influential as he claimed—or that he in fact had only a distant connection to it. It may also be that this was in fact a case of police abuse and corruption. It is significant, however, that Paulo believed a class-based argument would have judicial validity.

53. Among many examples of such characterizations, see AN, 5a PCr, CF 70.10840 (*injúria*); AN, 7a VCr, caixa 10851/1931/55 (defloration); and AN, 1a PCr, caixa 2375/74 (physical assault).

54. Gomes da Cunha, *Intenção*.

55. AN, 8a VCr, caixa 2685/7-A. Caulfield, writing about the importance of race in defloration cases from the 1920s and 1930s, quotes a similar statement from an influential 1926 defloration verdict in which Judge Eurico Cruz lamented the defiling influences of dance halls and African-influenced music. As

in my sample, however, Caulfield found that judges, prosecutors, and attorneys rarely mentioned race explicitly; see Caulfield, *In Defense,* chap. 5.

56. AN, 8a PCr, 1932, 524; AN, 5a PCr, CF 70.10839.

57. The few cases involving open racial references that are cited by Caulfield, *In Defense,* also involved European natives; although so few cases are scant basis upon which to base any generalization, it does seem likely that race-based insults were more acceptable among Europeans than among Brazilians.

58. For an extended discussion, see Fischer, "'Quase Pretos.'"

59. For the most part, this conception of defensible honor conformed to well-established Mediterranean traditions; see note 13 to part III, above.

60. AN, 3a PCr, caixa 3658/18.

61. AN, 1a PCr, caixa 2390/201.

62. AN, 5a PCr, CF 70.10778.

63. AN, 5a PCr, CF 70.10545. It emerged over the course of the trial that Elvira's recent marriage to the defendant, Eduardo Rufino do Carmo, had resulted from his criminal prosecution for corruption of a minor (*Código Penal dos Estados Unidos do Brasil* (1890), article 266, no. 1). In light of this case, one wonders how often cases of defloration and corruption of a minor that ended in forced marriage actually advanced the interests of the offended girls and women.

64. AN, 6a PCr, CF 71.0485.

65. AN, 6a PCr, CF 71.0488; for a discussion of the definitions of "work" employed in this case, see page 145. Although both the prosecutor and the judge eventually accepted Octávio's assertions of mutual aggression—and although he was ultimately found not guilty—the degree to which his arguments about defending his right to work held sway remains unclear, since the judge made no mention of them in his decision. In this case as in many others, even the verdict itself is somewhat ambiguous, since Octávio spent nearly a month and a half imprisoned—much longer than the procedural code allowed in normal cases—while awaiting a decision, effectively suffering punishment without condemnation.

66. AN, 6a VCr, Caixa 1846/232.

67. AN, 5a PCr, CF 70.10766.

68. Lawyers most often cited police abuse, such as extraction of forced confessions, although they also sometimes pointed to illegal imprisonment, physical abuse, and procedural violations. Usually the lawyers' language indicated that such practices were widely known. The judges in my sample, however, never acknowledged them. They did occasionally release prisoners because they had spent much longer than legally allowed in jail before trial, although this in fact happened only in a small fraction of the cases in which imprisonment exceeded the limits mandated in the procedural code. Police abuse was widespread enough in Rio that even the academic and theoretical works of Carioca jurists acknowledged it from time to time; the best example is Peixoto, *Criminologia,* in which the author, while careful to note that police abuse existed throughout the world, recounted several examples of psychological and physical abuse. For accounts of police abuse in the nineteenth century, see Holloway, *Policing Rio.* For police abuse in the twentieth century, see Bretas, *You Can't*; and Gomes da Cunha, *Intenção.*

69. AN, 7a VCr, caixa 10859/1933/321.

70. See, for example, AN, 7a VCr, caixa 10851/1931/55.

71. See AN, 3a PCr, 3658/45; and AN, 1a PCr, 2390/592.

72. See AN, 5a PCr, CF 70.10765. See also AN, 5a PCr, CF 70.12381; AN, 1a PCr, caixa 2370/370; and AN, 7a VCr, caixa 10859/1932/77.

73. The renowned jurist Evaristo de Moraes argued for the validity of hunger or extreme economic need as a mitigator of criminal responsibility in theft cases; he noted, however, that the Brazilian criminal code did not, in the strictest of senses, allow the complete admissibility of such arguments. See Moraes, *Problemas*, 127–52.

74. Caulfield, *In Defense*, has written extensively about these issues, arguing that the stricter definition of defloration that emerged from the 1940 reform of the penal code reflected pressures placed on the law by the changing sexual mores of Rio's popular classes; my findings in this regard entirely echo hers. For a typical commentary on the subject from the late 1930s, see Drummond, *Aspectos*.

75. One example of a vagrancy case in which a defendant who argued that the law was illegitimate because some jobs were inherently itinerant in a slack economy (and who added, for good measure, that he was arrested on a Sunday and that no one had an obligation to work on a day of rest) can be found in AN, 5a PCr, CF 70.11263. For arguments that vagrancy arrests resulted from police vengeance, see AN, 5a PCr, CF 70.11640 and CF 70.11670. Three cases containing the argument that weapons were needed for work—one of which also notes that rural people had the custom of carrying knives—are AN, 5a PCr, CF 70.16291 and CF 70.11500, and AN, 3a PCr, caixa 3666/885. For two cases in which defendants argued that they carried knives in order to defend themselves because they either lived in or had reason to go to favelas, see AN, 5a PCr, CF 70.11269 and CF 70.11873.

76. The police report from one arms-possession case exemplified this language. Delegado (district chief) José de Oliveira Brandão called Reynaldo Bittencourt "um desordeiro incorrigivel" ("an incorrigible troublemaker") and said that his officers had stopped him because "tratando-se de um elemento pernicioso e nocivo à sociedade os policiais acharam de bom alvitre observal-o e notaram que no bolso de seu paletot se continha uma navalha de barba" ("seeing that the defendant is a dangerous element and a menace to society, the policemen thought it expedient to observe him and noticed that he had a straight-edge razor in his pocket"). Such language exactly replicated that found in countless other vagrancy and arms-possession accusations. In this case, as in numerous others (see Gomes da Cunha, *Intenção*), the police characterization apparently had more to do with the formal requirements of an arms-possession accusation than with the defendant himself. Over the course of the trial, it became clear that Bittencourt had never before been arrested or charged with a crime. See AN, 6a VCr, caixa 1846/232.

77. Abreu Esteves, *Meninas*, chap. 2.

78. Caulfield, *In Defense*, chap. 5.

79. Ribeiro, *Côr*.

80. Gomes da Cunha, *Intenção*.

81. The personal characteristics that were considered differed according to the type of analysis. For the cross-tabulations of the 1930s sample, I began with eleven commonly noted characteristics: region of birth, civil status, race, educational level, occupational level, employment status, housing type (shack, rooming house, apartment, and so on), neighborhood type (formal, informal, or mixed), access to legal counsel (considered only for cases that went to trial), prior arrest record, and possession of a state identification document (already, by the 1930s, an important marker of citizenship status). For the later sample, I added two categories: possession of the *carteira profissional* and each defendant's characterization in the police *vida pregressa*. For the logistic regressions, I necessarily reduced the number of factors considered, eliminating categories in order to maximize the predictive power of each model.

82. Because my sample included only 21 cases in which the defendant was female—a pattern typical of the criminal justice system as a whole—I did not include gender as an analytical category. Such analysis is sorely lacking, in relation both to defendants and to victims.

83. Small by statistical standards, my samples are nonetheless among the largest utilized so far in historical studies of Brazilian criminal justice.

84. The discussion that follows is a condensed discussion of statistical results. For a more extensive discussion of methodology, please see the statistical appendixes.

85. Although police and judges rarely acknowledged procedural violations in trial documents, such violations emerged in a variety of ways. On rare occasions, defense lawyers would point them out and demand action. More frequently, I was able to identify trial delays simply by looking at the dates in trial records and comparing them with the regulations set out in the procedural codes; illegally long pretrial imprisonments could be detected in the same way. Violations involving absent or incompetent lawyers were similarly easy to discern, and defendants and lawyers often brought complaints about police abuse directly to judges.

86. Caulfield, *In Defense*, reaches this conclusion.

87. For summaries of these criticisms, see Hungria, *Novas questões*; and Bicudo, *O direito*. See also Campos, *Exposição de motivos*. The most detailed and influential critiques of the 1890 code can be found in the explications of their commentators; see especially Siqueira, *Direito penal brasileiro*.

88. See Piragibe, *Consolidação das leis penais*; Costa e Silva, *Código penal*; and Siqueira, *Direito penal brasileiro*.

89. In his well-known *Exposição de motivos* for the 1940 law, Justice Minister Francisco Campos wrote: "In accordance with most modern codes, the project does not pray from orthodox primers, nor does it assume unconditional or irrevocable compromises with any of the schools or doctrines that claim correct solutions to our penal problems. Rather than adopting an extremist policy with regard to penal issues, the code is inclined toward a policy of transaction and conciliation. Within it, the classical postulates make common cause with the principles of the positivist school." The composition of the committee responsible for the 1940 penal code reflected Campos's eclectic vision: two of its most prominent members, Nelson Hungria and Roberto Lyra, were preeminent sympathizers

with, respectively, the classical and the positivist school. For their perspectives on the process through which the bill for the criminal code was written, see Hungria, *Comentários ao código penal*; Hungria, *Novas questões*; and Lyra, *Novíssimas escolas*.

90. *Código Penal de 1940*, article 76; *Lei das Contravenções Penais*, article 14.

91. *Código Penal de 1940*, article 77.

92. On changes in judges' rights and prerogatives, see the *Código de Processo Penal*, especially Campos' *Exposição de motivos*.

93. Campos, *Exposição de motivos* (for the *Código de Processo Penal*). The use of the *vida pregressa* represented yet another ameliorated version of a positivist theory. Rather than adopting the sort of proposals suggested in the Alcântara Machado project—which would have made the individualization of punishment dependent on the definitive categorization of each individual (as an "insane" criminal, a "habitual" criminal, and so on, following pseudoscientific Lombrosian models)—the authors of the criminal code chose to leave such evaluations to the less scientific but, they felt, ultimately more accurate discernment of individual magistrates.

94. For summaries of debates about the causes of criminality in the years immediately preceding the publication of the criminal code, see Carlos Barreto, *O crime*; see also the special edition of the *Revista Penal* dedicated to the proceedings of the 1936 Conferência Brasileira de Criminologia. For a lengthy exposition of the "modern" sociological influences on Brazilian criminology, see Lyra, *Novíssimas escolas*. For a rather more surprising analysis, offered by a prominent ideological rival of Lyra, see Hungria, "A criminalidade," about the social origins of racial variations in criminality rates. For a succinct but useful collection of thoughts about the causes of criminality that accurately reflects the range of Carioca judicial thought in the late 1940s, see the first issue of Roberto Lyra's *Revista Brasileira de Criminologia* (September–December 1947).

95. Campos, *Exposição de motivos* for the *Código de Processo Penal*.

96. *Código de processo penal*, title II, article 6, no. ix.

97. The universal "he" is repeated from the original and applies to all of the mostly male defendants who passed through the Carioca criminal justice system.

98. Saboia de Albuquerque, *Elucidário*. Deocleciano Saboia de Albuquerque was chief notary for the Special Vigilance Division of the Federal Department of Public Security (DFSP) in Rio de Janeiro.

99. For details about the second sample, see below.

100. AN, 20a VCr, caixa 1314/3533.

101. For a link between all of these factors and criminality, see Lyra, *Novíssimas escolas*.

102. AJ, TJ, caixa 397/3555/1960. For a description of one wealthy and well-educated but "calm, cold, and calculating" defendant who "lied easily," see AJ, TJ, caixa 517/2846/1958.

103. AJ, TJ, caixa 397/3208/1960.

104. See, for example, Arquivo da 20a VCr, processo 3333/1960, processo

2380/1959, processo 3098/1960, and processo 1314/3522; see also AN, 20a VCr, caixa 1314/3533 and caixa 1313/3530.

105. An explicit juridical discussion of police misuse of vagrancy statutes can be found in Judge Geraldo Irenêo Joffily's absolution of Aristeu Esteves da Silva in a 1958 vagrancy case in the 17a Vara Criminal; the decision, which quotes Rui Barbosa's comments on the dangers of the vagrancy statutes, is transcribed as part of the defense of José Damásio in AJ, 1a VCr, caixa 387/3066/1958.

106. AN, 20a VCr, caixa 1313/3526.

107. AN, 20a VCr, caixa 1300/2506, defendant Paulo Julião de Andrade.

108. AJ, TJ, caixa 423/1760/1961.

109. There are numerous inconsistencies in the citywide statistics. My research suggests that the numbers for the early 1940s are exaggeratedly low, and certain crimes—notably abortion—were systematically underreported; my sample contains more abortion cases from most of the years in the late 1950s and 1960s than the official statistics reported for the city as a whole. This underreporting may have been meant to disguise extremely low conviction rates in abortion cases.

110. This was due to a reorganization of the Carioca justice system. After 1950, the 20a Vara de Execuções Penais administered all cases with guilty verdicts. The court's records are relatively complete and are organized by defendants' names. But cases with non-guilty verdicts for all but jury crimes were left with the original courts and have either been destroyed or are unavailable to the public.

111. According to the 1960 census, 18 percent of Rio's population was illiterate.

112. *Crimes e Contravenções, 1942–59*, and my sample.

113. "Crimes against the popular economy" included violations of price controls, adulterations of food products, refusal to provide proper receipts, favoritism in buying and selling, and the like; such crimes were regulated by Lei 1521 (26 December 1951). There is as yet no study of these laws along the lines of Eduardo Elena's work on Argentina.

114. This may have been partially related to the ages of the defendants in my sample; younger Cariocas tended to be more literate, the average age in my sample was 31, and my cases included very few defendants over the age of 60.

115. Given the great attention with which it had been greeted in 1940, the *medida de segurança* ultimately had little effect on most defendants who passed through Carioca courtrooms; in effect, it turned into yet another measure used to repress "vagrants."

116. There are, as before, significant differences among crimes in this respect. Vagrancy, arms possession, and armed robbery seem to have the highest number of single, illiterate, dark-skinned defendants; theft, defloration, and murder have slightly more dark-skinned defendants than would be proportional with the general population, but they come closer to parity; and physical-assault defendants tend to be only slightly darker-skinned than the Carioca population as a whole. The correlations revealed in the statistical analysis of the sampled crimes as a

whole were, respectively, .59 between white skin tone and rates of archival, –.47 between whiteness and conviction rates, .79 between *sursis* and whiteness, and –.56 between whiteness and the *medida de segurança*. Nevertheless, a similar analysis of individual-case categories did not reveal much consistency.

117. AJ, TJ, caixa 391/2921/1958; AJ, TJ, caixa 414/900/1959.

118. AN, 20a VCr, caixa 1300/1591.

119. AJ, TJ, caixa 381/3017/1958, defendant Francisco Antônio da Silveira.

120. Often these criteria greatly resembled the social divisions that anthropologists such as Benjamin Penglase and Alba Zaluar have noted in contemporary favelas, dividing "workers" from "marginals," people with deep family ties to their communities from strangers, and those who respect local social norms from those who do not.

121. Arquivo da 20a Vara de Execuções Penais, caixa 2245/1959.

122. Arquivo da 20a Vara de Execuções Penais, caixa 2245/1959. For other examples, see AJ, TJ, caixa 397/3368/1960 (defendant Francisco Antônio dos Santos Veniciano); AJ, TJ, caixa 387/3066/1958 (defendant José Damásio); and AJ, TJ, caixa 392/3004/1959 (defendant Paulo Cabral de Barros). In both of the latter cases, petitions were submitted in favor of both the homicide victim and the defendant.

123. AN, 20a VCr, caixa 1312/5443; AJ, TJ, caixa 381/1213/1959.

124. This story was related by Judge Geraldo Irenêo Joffily of the 17a Vara Criminal and was transcribed as part of José Damásio's defense in AJ, 1a VCr, caixa 387/3066/1958. The case against the chief, Ary Leão Silva, was brought on 3 March 1959 in the 22a Vara Criminal.

125. For a literary iteration of this fear, see Azevedo, *O cortiço*; for more concrete instances, see Chalhoub, *Cidade febril*; Vaz, "Contribuição"; Benchimol, *Pereira Passos*; and Meade, *"Civilizing" Rio*.

126. See chapter 8, this volume.

127. See speech of 10 January 1956, published in *Anais da Câmara dos Deputados*, 1955–56, vol. III, 86–88.

128. Such raids were especially important in the late 1940s, right after the 1948 purge of communist politicians from elected office. For an example of police harassment of a communist sympathizer, see AN, 6a VCr, caixa 2173/8180; for an explicit link made by a civil policeman between communist sympathies and "marginality," see AJ, TJ, caixa 420/1647/1961 (defendant Aldemir da Silva Silvino).

129. For more detail, see chapter 8, this volume.

130. See the *Correio da Manhã*, 1–9 May 1948.

131. Geraldo Irenêo Joffily, 17a Vara judge in case involving defendant Aristeu Esteves da Silva, transcribed in AJ, TJ, caixa 387/3066/1958 (defendant José Damásio).

132. See minutes of "Reunião para decidir medidas policiais urgentes," 12 March 1963, held in the Carlos Lacerda archives, dossiê Gabinete/Correspondência, caixa 164.

133. Even in my small sample of jury cases from the 1950s and 1960s, I

came across four in which a defendant was murdered by police, who apparently were never punished for the crime. See AJ, TJ, caixa 392/3056/1959, caixa 424/2026/1962, caixa 424/2006/1962, and caixa 407/4155/1962.

134. A copy of the 36th police district's inquiry into the case is held in the Carlos Lacerda archives, dossiê Seção de Segurança Pública.

135. See speech of 10 January 1956, published in *Anais da Câmara dos Deputados*, 1955–56, vol. III, 86–88.

136. On the UTF, see chapter 8, this volume.

137. A document containing the Ministry of Justice's investigation of the allegation, though not the original complaint, can be found in the Fundação Getúlio Vargas, Alexandre Marcondes Filho papers, AMF 55/03.01/1.

138. See minutes of "Reunião para decidir medidas policiais urgentes," 12 March 1963, held in the Carlos Lacerda archives, dossiê Gabinete/Correspondência, caixa 164.

139. Though this book is extensively quoted in the article mentioned in note 140, below, I have never found a copy of it, and it is not in Licia do Prado Valladares's extensive bibliography (*Pensando as favelas cariocas*). If it exists, it would predate the more famous book by Carolina Maria de Jesus, *Child of the Dark*.

140. "Favelado toma consciência dos seus problemas e não quer a ajuda do govêrno," unattributed 1961 newspaper article found in the Carlos Lacerda archives, dossiê Gabinete/Correspondências, caixa 156.

141. See the discussion of Jacarezinho in chapter 8, this volume.

142. Abdias José Nascimento dos Santos, personal interview with the author, 27 November 2003.

143. See, for instance, a complaint brought in January 1954 by UTF lawyer Magarinos Torres regarding police raids in Borel, discussed in chapter 8, this volume.

144. Abdias José Nascimento dos Santos, personal interview with the author, December 2003. For a confirmation of the view that modern policemen do not know how to respect local distinctions, see Penglase, "To Live Here."

145. Odília dos Santos Gama, personal interview with the author, 2 December 2003.

146. "Uma favela que começa em Botafogo e termina em Laranjeiras," *O Globo*, 25 May 1948 (interview with Santa Marta resident Antônio José Lopes).

147. Abdias José Nascimento dos Santos, personal interview with the author, 27 November 2003.

148. For a somewhat idealized version of civil law mediation in Jacarezinho, see Souza Santos, "The Law."

149. Both Marcos Bretas and Roberto Kant de Lima call attention to police roles as informal mediators in minor disputes.

150. For instances of such silence, see AJ, TJ, caixa 424/2082/1963, caixa 419/1542/1962, caixa 387/2956/1959, and caixa 392/317/1959; see also AN, 6a VCR, caixa 2172/8675 (Hélio de Souza Campos).

Part IV: Owning the Illegal City

1. *Diário da Noite,* 18 December 1930.

2. Ibid.

3. On Maurício de Lacerda, see Corrêa, *O sertão carioca,* 183–84. Vicente Carino appears in newspaper accounts and court cases throughout his period, and a communist engineer by the name of Pedro Coutinho Filho would continue to represent squatters from Jacarepaguá and Guaratiba right into the 1950s; see "Lavradores do sertão carioca defendem seu direito à terra," *Imprensa Popular,* 10 August 1954.

4. See Mattos de Castro, *Das cores;* Naro, "Customary Rightholders"; and Motta, *Nas fronteiras.*

5. This was largely because of Euclides da Cunha's classic journalistic account of the war, *Os Sertões.* On the historical meanings of the *sertão* metaphor, see Trinidade Lima, *Um sertão;* on its relation to early perceptions of Rio's favelas, see Valladares, *A invenção.*

6. The term "supercivilized" is from Ricardo Palma's introduction to Corrêa, *O sertão carioca,* originally published in the *Diário Carioca* on 20 September 1932.

7. The most notable example is Corrêa, *O sertão carioca,* which paid homage in loving detail to the region's quickly vanishing pastoral life, invoking with nationalist pride such figures as the *pescadeiro,* the *machadeiro,* and the *cesteiro.*

8. Miguel Pereira coined the now famous phrase in 1916, quoted in Trinidade Lima and Hochmann, "Condenado pela raça," 24.

9. Recounted in Trinidade Lima, *Um Sertão,* 60.

10. "Far-West ou terra civilizada?," *A Batalha,* 16 December 1931.

11. Scholars such as Anthony Leeds and Janice Perlman long ago countered marginality theories by arguing that mid-century favelas had strong economic, social, and political ties to Rio; however, very few researchers have ever highlighted the degree to which outsiders have had abiding interests in the favelas' growth and survival. In this respect, Pereira da Silva, *Favelas Cariocas,* complements my own research.

12. For general discussions of Brazilian property law, see Cirne Lima, *Pequena história;* Costa Porto, *O sistema sesmarial;* Motta, *Nas fronteiras;* Mattos de Castro, *Das cores,* especially chap. 4; and Viotti da Costa, "Land Policies."

13. On land in Rio, see N. Santos, *As freguesias;* Costa Ferreira, *A cidade;* Fridman, *Donos;* and Pechman, "A gênese."

14. On the series of decrees that attempted to reassert this dimension of the sesmaria system, see Motta, *Nas fronteiras,* chap. 4.

15. See Motta, *Nas fronteiras.* Mattos de Castro gives a detailed analysis of why demarcation often worked against the perceived interests of large landholders (*Das cores,* chap. 4).

16. See Fridman, *Donos.*

17. The classic work on the relationship between land and patronal power is Martins, *O cativeiro.*

18. See Motta, *Nas fronteiras,* especially chap. 4.

19. See Mattos de Castro, *Das cores*, 82.

20. Ibid., 123.

21. Mattos de Castro, *Das cores,* 82; the remainder of her fourth chapter details this point.

22. Lei 601 (17 September 1850); for discussion, see Viotti da Costa, "Land Policies."

23. Viotti da Costa, "Land Policies"; Martins, *O cativeiro.*

24. On article 8, see Motta, *Nas fronteiras*; on widespread noncompliance with registration requirements, see Osório Silva, *Terras devolutas.*

25. See *Código Civil Brasileiro*, articles 550–53.

26. *Constituição da República do Brasil* (16 July 1934), title III, chap. II, article 113, no. 17.

27. This is similar to the situation described in São Paulo by Holston, "The Misrule of Law."

28. 2 June 1907, quoted in Almeida Abreu, "Reconstruindo."

29. AN, 3a PC, caixa 2415/262, dated 22 March 1934.

30. *Código Civil Brasileiro*, article 550: "The person who possesses a property as his own for 30 years, uninterrupted and unopposed, will acquire its dominion, independent of title or good faith, which in such cases is presumed; he may require a judge to pass a sentence so stating, which can serve as title for the purpose of legally registering the property."

31. "Mas 10 mil cariocas ameaçadas pelas picaretas da prefeitura," *Imprensa Popular*, 30 November 1952.

32. Nunes, *Favela,* 11.

33. In addition to those cited below, see the accounts collected in Varella, Bertazzo, and Jacques, *Maré.*

34. Lucíola de Jesus, personal interview conducted by Guaraci Gonçalves for the Favela Tem Memória project, 22 February 2005.

35. Salomão Pereira da Silva, personal interview conducted by Rita de Cássia for the Favela Tem Memória project, 16 July 2003.

36. Marina da Silva, personal interview conducted by Bete Silva for the Favela Tem Memória project, 31 August 2005.

37. References to gardens, fruit trees, and animals are common in most oral histories of early favelas; in official sources, they usually appear as offhand references, taken for granted as part of the favela landscape. See, for example, Fundação Leão XIII, *Morros e favelas,* 25; or Goulart, *Favelas,* 41. The photo collection held at the Arquivo Geral da Cidade do Rio de Janeiro confirms the rural aspect of many communities right through the 1960s.

38. The connection between rural origins and urban marginality was one of the staples of Latin American sociology for much of the 1950s and 1960s. For a summary (and rejection) of such views, see Perlman, *The Myth*. For a relatively mild version of the connection between rural origins and urban marginality in Brazil, see Sociedade de Análises Gráficas e Mecanográficas Aplicadas aos Complexos Sociais (SAGMACS), "Aspectos humanos"; for a more forceful argument, see Medina, *A favela* (Medina is one of the SAGMACS authors). For contemporary (and original) comment on the influence of the notion of rurality in the city, see Leeds, "O Brasil e o mito."

39. AN, 4a PC, maço 116, processo 5194, Emilio Antônio Turano vs. Ocupantes de um imóvel no morro do Salgueiro, 17 July 1933.

40. This provision first appeared in the 1934 constitution and was repeated in all that followed; see note 26 to part IV, above.

41. On the time of Rio's first building census, in 1933, Borel already had nearly 200 shacks; in 1948, when Rio's first favela census was published, that number of shacks had grown to more than 500, and probably housed about 2,000 people. Alemão's development came later, but by 1960 there were already more than 3,400 residents there, and debates about ownership of the *morro*'s lands had already been common in the early 1950s.

42. AN, records of the Secretaria da Presidência da República, série 17.7, caixa 41. The translation includes errors in spelling and grammar found in the original.

43. Fridman, *Donos*.

44. See, for instance, the story of Quintino Francisco Guedes, who claimed to have informally aquired land in Guaratiba from one Joaquim José de Lacerda in the late 1880s, and found it threatened by the Banco de Crédito Móvel's expulsions in 1931. His cousin, Antônio Guedes, was also expelled by the BCM from lands he had inherited without title from his father. Rio's 8a Pretoria Cível later nullified Antonio's expulsion. See "Far-West ou terra civilizada?," *A Batalha*, 16 December 1931; see also "A justiça reintegra tres 'posseiros' de Guaratiba vítimas das violências do Banco de Crédito Móvel," *A Batalha*, 17 March 1932.

45. See, for example, Apelação Cível 1088, apelante Mafalda Maria da Conceição, apelado Banco de Crédito Móvel, cited in final decision on Leopoldo Luiz dos Santos vs. Banco de Crédito Móvel, 4a Câmara da Corte de Apelação, reprinted in the *Jornal do Comércio*, 14–15 March 1932; see also Apelação Cível 1130, Manoel I. Botelho vs. Banco de Crédito Móvel, also cited in final decision on Leopoldo Luiz dos Santos vs. Banco de Crédito Móvel.

46. After the turn of the century, more of these agreements seem to have taken written form, even when all or most of the parties involved were illiterate—a movement that probably reflected owners' awareness of rising land values and the threat of *usucapião*.

47. This will be discussed further below in relation to Eduardo Duvivier's land claims in Copacabana/Leme, and in relation to the BCM's numerous land cases in Guaratiba.

48. These interpretations were based on the 1916 civil code, which granted specific rights to confirmed *posseiros*, among which were rights to any improvements made on the land (articles 516–19). The civil code also left room for indemnification for anyone who improved property that he or she did not legally occupy as a *posseiro* (article 547). For a discussion of the civil code and the rights accrued by *posseiros*, see Nascimento, *Posse*.

49. Estate of Manuel Luiz de Souza (represented by Alain Luiz de Souza) vs. Marcelino Martins et al., AN, 3a PC, 2440/1924, 29 June 1936.

50. This amount was somewhat less than what a poor family would have paid monthly for a shack in central Rio.

51. The practice of selling the rights to an inheritance was common enough not to attract any special notice in Brazil during this period. The most likely mo-

tive was avoidance of the lengthy legal process surrounding inheritance; heirs eager to cash in on homes and lands would often simply sell their presumed rights to property in lieu of the property itself. This could happen, as it did in this case, even among modest and scarcely literate people.

52. All quotations from original complaint, dated 29 June 1936, estate of Manuel Luiz de Souza (represented by Alain Luiz de Souza) vs. Marcelino Martins et al., AN, 3a PC, 2440/1924, 3–4.

53. The right to *reintegração de posse* was granted to all possessors by the 1916 civil code (article 499), so long as possession was taken by way of *esbulho*, or the violent, clandestine, or precarious usurpation of an object. See Nascimento, *Posse,* 200–204.

54. Estate of Manuel Luiz de Souza (represented by Alain Luiz de Souza) vs. Marcelino Martins et al., AN, 3a PC, 2440/1924, 7.

55. Testimony of José de Macedo Paes, 16 August 1936, ibid., 81–82.

56. Testimony of Souza's neighbor and fellow rural cultivator Adrino Francisco da Silva, 49; of his neighbor, the professional chauffeur Leonel Alves Machado, 23; and of his neighbor, the store clerk Ary Ferreira da Costa, 26, 16 August 1936, ibid., 83–88.

57. Testimony of Joaquim dos Santos Rodrigues, 30, a worker and Souza's neighbor, 6-29-1936, ibid., 15.

58. Lauderdale Graham, *House and Street,* 26.

59. Chalhoub, *Cidade febril,* 38–39.

60. See Karasch, *Slave Life,* on *quilombo* slave settlements in the hills (chap. 10), and on slaves who constructed such dwellings with their masters' permission (chap. 5, especially 186). On Leblon, see E. da Silva, *As camélias.* For a comparison with Santos, see M. Machado, "From Slave Rebels."

61. Ministério do Trabalho, Indústria, e Comércio, Departamento de Estatística e Publicidade, *Estatística Predial do Distrito Federal, 1933.*

62. Lauderdale Graham, *House and Street,* chap. 1; see also Karasch, *Slave Life,* chap. 3, especially 105, and chap. 5, 184–87.

63. Azevedo, *O cortiço.*

64. See chapter 1, this volume; see also Almeida Abreu, "Reconstruindo"; Vaz, "Contribuição."

65. See Vaz, "Contribuição."

66. The original public iteration of this often repeated history of the favelas' name seems to have come from Cruz, *Os morros.* On the wider links between Canudos and the early favelas, see Valladares, *A invenção.*

67. At mid-century, marginality theorists and their critics would vociferously debate the extent to which favela residents themselves were the "marginal" incarnations of a culture of poverty, but both groups underemphasized the extent to which the settlements themselves were fundamental to Rio's economies and political networks; neither point was lost on the politicians in Rio's municipal council. For a summary of these debates, see Leeds and Leeds, *A sociologia*; and Perlman, *The Myth.*

68. See Pereira da Silva, *Favelas Cariocas,* 123, quoting an article in the *Diário de Notícias,* 7 January 1938.

69. Conniff, *Urban Politics*, chaps. 3 and 4.
70. Cruz, *Os morros*, 13–14.
71. Letter dated 16 June 1934, AN, records of the Secretaria da Presidência da República, série 17.4, caixa 33, pasta 1934.
72. See chapter 3, this volume.
73. Letter dated 4 February 1942, Arquivo Geral da Cidade do Rio de Janeiro, Prefeitura do Distrito Federal, série Saúde e Assistência, 1937/45, caixa 203.
74. At least one of these letters has been preserved; in it, the writer speaks in the name of the residents, appealing for Vargas's help and affirming that the *moradores* are "poor Brazilians prepared to die for our beloved Brazil at any moment." See letter from José Moreira dos Santos dated 18 May 1942, AN, records of the Secretaria da Presidência da República, série 17.7, lata 402.
75. Letter dated 16 June 1934, AN, records of the Secretaria da Presidência da República, série 17.4, caixa 33, pasta 1934.
76. Instituto de Planejamento do Rio de Janeiro, "Cadastro das favelas do município do Rio de Janeiro," interviews conceded to IPLANRIO researchers by Felix Pereira da Silva and José Saraiva on the Morro do Escondidinho between 25 March 1981 and 11 August 1981, and by José Antônio da Felicidade and "Dona Argentina" on the Morro dos Prazeres between 19 March 1981 and 23 July 1981 (records held at the Instituto Municipal de Urbanismo Pereira Passos).
77. "Em Mangueira falta tudo," *O Mundo*, 9 December 1947.
78. See Souto Oliveira, *Favelas*, 157–58. For a more oblique version of the same story, see S. da Silva Pereira, "O serviço social," 14. See also Pino, *Family*. A 1949 article in *O Radical*, entitled "Com Getúlio, isto não aconteceu" and written in the midst of a new eviction threat, also stated that the favela's permanence was due to Getúlio Vargas's protection (20 May 1949). In a letter to Prefect Mendes de Morais, residents confirmed that the Legião Brasileira de Assistência had given them permission to settle on the site; the letter is printed in "Intenso Tumulto no Morro do Jacarezinho," *Diretrizes*, 22 October 1947. In a separate letter, a residents' committee claimed that the Vargas government had been close to granting them title in 1945 but never completed the transaction; see "35,000 pessôas ameaçadas de despejo," *O Radical*, 24 October 1947.
79. Remarks by Frota Aguiar, 18 May 1949, published in the *ACDF*, 1949, 290.
80. Conniff, *Urban Politics*, especially 107.
81. The Escola Humberto de Campos, in Mangueira; see ibid.
82. Pereira da Silva details some of Pedro Ernesto's early favela visits to São Carlos, Mangueira, and the Morro do Pinto, as reported in the *Jornal do Brasil* in 1933 and 1934. She also suggests that Ernesto was active in mediating between favela residents and companies that sought to remove them from their lands (*Favelas Cariocas*, 56 and note 110). Photos of the São Carlos visit are available at the Arquivo Geral da Cidade do Rio de Janeiro.
83. On samba and the morros, see Oliveira and Marcier, "A palavra."
84. Conniff, *Urban Politics*.
85. Henrique Dodsworth, "Favelas," *A Noite*, 17 October 1945. This article

appears in manuscript form among Vitor Tavares de Moura's personal papers; it is possible that he had a part in its composition. Fundação Oswaldo Cruz archives, Vitor Tavares de Moura papers, dossiê Produção Intelectual, caixa 2.

86. For the closest study of the actions of this commission, see Medeiros, "Atendimento."

87. On the Parques Proletários and the destruction of the Largo da Memória, see chapter 1, this volume.

88. For a good early expression of his views, see Tavares de Moura, "Favelas."

89. For the 1933 statistics, see Ministério do Trabalho, Indústria, e Comércio, Departamento de Estatística e Publicidade, *Estatística Predial do Distrito Federal, 1933*; for the yellow-fever estimates, see IBGE, Conselho Nacional de Estatística, Serviço Nacional de Recenseamento, *As Favelas do Distrito Federal e o Censo Demográfico de 1950*, 16.

90. Arquivo Geral da Cidade do Rio de Janeiro, Prefeitura do Distrito Federal, série Saúde e Assistência, caixa 191, letter dated 5 November 1940.

91. For the original census, see document addressed to "Exmo. Snr. Secretário Geral de Saúde e Assistência," Fundação Oswaldo Cruz archives, Vitor Tavares de Moura papers, série Parques Proletários e Favelas, caixa 1. The census notes the numbers of several houses that paid rent to the Ministério da Fazenda. For newspaper reports on the census, see "A Favela do Esqueleto," *Folha do Dia*, 20 December 1947; "Estão satisfeitos os moradores da 'Favela do Esqueleto,'" *Diário de Notícias*, 30 December 1947.

92. "500 famílias morando num único barracão," *Diretrizes*, 21 November 1947.

93. Arquivo Geral da Cidade do Rio de Janeiro, Prefeitura do Distrito Federal, série Saúde e Assistência, caixa 193, letter from SOS to Henrique Dodsworth dated 29 September 1944. On the SOS, see chapter 2, this volume; see also Conniff, *Urban Politics*, 124.

94. Arquivo Geral da Cidade do Rio de Janeiro, Prefeitura do Distrito Federal, série Saúde e Assistência, caixa 195, processo 5328/44. The file begins with a letter from Napoleão de Alencastro Guimarães to Henrique Dodsworth, 10 April 1944.

95. Speech by Gama Filho, 20 May 1949, published in the *ACDF*, 24 May 1949, 337. Gama Filho indicated that the EFCB was preventing residents from repairing their shacks, arguing that the company had only lent the extremely valuable land to the prefecture for one year and was now in need of it. In 1953, the EFCB finally did begin to evict residents from the area (then called Parque Arará), but full removal was blocked by vigorous protests from the residents (who at one point occupied the municipal council) and by careful politicking on the part of various council members. See *ACDF*, 26 March 1953.

96. Arquivo Geral da Cidade do Rio de Janeiro, Prefeitura do Distrito Federal, série Saúde e Assistência, caixa 195, protocolo 07863, letter from Atila dos Santos Couto to Henrique Dodsworth, 29 March 1945.

97. Report submitted to Moura by Jayme Maia Arruda, 13 June 1945, Ar-

quivo Geral da Cidade do Rio de Janeiro, Prefeitura do Distrito Federal, série Saúde e Assistência, caixa 195, protocolo 07863.

98. Requisition presented on 13 May 1947, published in the *ACDF,* 1947, vol. V, 9.

99. See letter from a committee of Jacarezinho residents to Municipal Secretary of Finance João Lima Filho, printed in "35,000 pessôas ameaçadas de despejo," *O Radical,* 24 October 1947.

100. Sagramor di Scuvero, speaking on 24 May 1949, *ACDF,* 25 May 1949, 352. For the reference to the plaza named for Professor Atila, see "Moradores de Jacarezinho desmascaram Geraldo Moreira," *Imprensa Popular,* 27 June 1954.

101. In this sense, as in others, the early favelas may have grown from business practices pioneered in the *cortiços.* According to various sources, many tenements—including the famous Cabeça de Porco, which gave birth upon its destruction to the Morro da Favela—had also been owned by families of considerable means.

102. On housing set up by the textile factories, see Lobo, Carvalho, and Stanley, *Questão hobitacional,* 80–81. On the Hospital Alemão, see letter from José Moreira dos Santos to Getúlio Vargas dated 18 May 1942 (AN, records of the Secretaria da Presidência da República, série 17.7, lata 402); see also a letter from Eulália Moreira Santos to Getúlio Vargas (Arquivo Geral da Cidade do Rio de Janeiro, série Saúde e Assistência, lata 203, 1942, no. 02801).

103. "No Morro dos Prazeres, a vida é um martírio," *O Mundo,* 15 May 1948.

104. Nóbrega Fernandes, *Escolas,* 70. In a 1928 contract, the widow, Julieta de Saião Lobato, showed clear awareness that shacks occupied the property, even detailing the property's contents shack by shack. The contract is reproduced in Pereira da Silva, *Favelas Cariocas,* 102–3; original in the AN, 30 Ofício de Notas, Livro de Escrituras 1092, 97–99, microfilm 010.169–79. The Companhia de Seguros Victória eventually purchased the property; for a detailed account of its rental practices, see a report from *agente social* Elias Marino da Silveira Lobo to Vitor Tavares de Moura, dated 24 April 1945 (Arquivo Geral da Cidade do Rio de Janeiro, Prefeitura do Distrito Federal, Saúde e Assistência, caixa 193, 2969/1945).

105. For a history of Wagner and his attempt to subdivide and sell much of Copacabana in the 1870s, see Gerson, *História.* Wagner also apparently attempted to build a tramway in the 1870s, and Decreto Federal 8914 (29 March 1883) details a contract (apparently never fulfilled) between the imperial government and Duvivier e Cia.—a company owned by Wagner's son-in-law and Eduardo's father—for an animal-powered streetcar line projected to run between Rio's center and Copacabana. This attempt to link transportation and real estate development followed the most successful business models of the period.

106. See "Eduardo Duvivier," in Alves de Abreu et. al., *Dicionário,* 1969.

107. On the evolution of middle-class and luxury apartments in the 1920s and 1930s, see Vaz, *Modernidade,* especially chaps. 3 and 4.

108. The company had aquired the lands in 1891 from Duvivier's maternal

grandfather, Alexander Wagner; the sale was registered in the 30 Ofício de Notas by Evaristo Valle de Barros and is affirmed in a subsequent sale record transcribed in several civil cases from the late 1920s and early 1930s, among them, Eduardo Duvivier vs. Antônio José de Carvalho, AN, 4a PC, 941/4304/1928, 12–16. For more on the company and its prominent associates, see Quieroz Ribeiro, *Dos cortiços.*

109. Quieroz Ribeiro, *Dos cortiços,* 225. For more on the deals reached between the company and the tram company, see Almeida Abreu, *Evolução,* 48, quoting N. Santos, *Meios,* 338–39.

110. Almeida Abreu puts the favela's origins sometime around 1907 ("Reconstruindo").

111. See Empresa de Construções Civis vs. Manoel dos Santos, Maria Luiza, José Manoel, and Albertina Amorim, 9 October 1916, AN, 4a PC, 72/3353; and Empresa de Construções Civis vs. Manoel Francisco de Souza et al., 17 May 1917, AN, 4a PC, 66/3109.

112. Empresa de Construções Civis vs. Dona Candida A. da Silva, 21 July 1926, AN, 4a PC.

113. See Eduardo Duvivier vs. Manoel Luiz da Silva, AN, 4a PC, 47/2717; Eduardo Duvivier vs. Honorato Lopes da Silva, AN, 4a PC, 68/3237; Eduardo Duvivier vs. Manoel do Sacramento, AN, 4a PC, 68/3236; and Eduardo Duvivier vs. Romualdo Antônio de Oliveira, AN, 4a PC, 68/3235.

114. That census listed only ten brick houses on the entire Morro de Babilônia, and it classified the *morro*'s remaining 64 structures as *casebres*; see Ministério do Trabalho, Indústria, e Comércio, Departamento de Estatística e Publicidade, *Estatística Predial do Distrito Federal, 1933,* 210, 223.

115. This full history is recounted in Decreto 24515 (30 June 1934); many of its details are corroborated in the 1891 contract by which Wagner sold the lands to the ECC. A subsequent statute, Decreto 1763 (10 November 1939) precisely delimited the army lands and ordered compensation for unwitting third-party purchasers, and a third measure, Decreto-Lei 4761 (30 September 1942) affixed compensation rates and listed all of the parties who would receive indemnification.

116. Decreto-Lei 4761 of (30 September 1942). One beneficiary was Vitorino Ferreira Amaro, who had contested one of the ECC's eviction suits in 1917; see Empresa de Construções Civis vs. Manoel Francisco de Souza et al., 17 May 1917, AN, 4a PCr, 66/3109. Manoel Francisco de Souza and José Soares de Souza were other *barraco* owners from the same case who may have been indemnified, but small discrepancies in the names make verification difficult. There are several other coincidences in last names, but these are too common to make it possible to verify people as members of the same families.

117. See Duvivier, "O problema da habitação," clipping held in FOC, Fundo VTM, Artigos, Caixa 03.

118. Odília dos Santos Gama, personal interview with the author, 2 December 2003. Other interviewees include Maria da Conceição Ferreira Pinto (Dona Filinha) and Lúcio de Paula Bispo.

119. These rents were of course steep for the workers themselves, but they

were roughly equivalent to what was charged in tenements, and they were much cheaper than formal houses or apartments; wage information from the América Fabril factory, compiled by Lobo in *Rio de Janeiro Operário*, 93 (table 2.4).

120. For sample rents and purchase prices for apartments in the late 1920s and early 1930s, see the scattered ads in Vaz, *Modernidade*.

121. In the mid-1940s, rents in most south-zone favelas were still 100–300 cruzeiros, and rents for shacks in some favelas were as low as 30 cruzeiros a month (see the Hospital Alemão case, cited above). The flat-fee method was quite common.

122. Undated report from Vitor Tavares de Moura to Municipal Secretary of Health and Social Welfare Jesuino de Albuquerque, Fundação Oswaldo Cruz archives, Vitor Tavares de Moura papers, série Parques Proletários e Favelas, caixa 1, 3.

123. See Almeida Abreu, "Reconstruindo," 37, quoting the *Correio da Manhã*, 17 October 1901.

124. See chapter 5, this volume. See also AN, 5a PCr, CF 70.9476, the criminal case from which the example is drawn.

125. "500 familias morando num único barracão," *Diretrizes*, 21 November 1947, 34–35.

126. In 1908, Salgueiro requested a copy of the certificate that dissolved a real estate company he had held with his brother, Joaquim Pires Alves Salgueiro. In that case, he appears to have owned property in the Cidade Nova and on what was then called the Rua Dona Feliciana; see AN, 1a VC, 373/3406. In 1913, Salgueiro's lawyer filed a *despejo* suit against Joaquim Esteves, an informal tenant of Salgueiro's on the *morro*, then known as the Morro do Trapicheiro. Esteves was 28 months late on his monthly rent of 22$000. Salgueiro, presenting a property tax receipt for the first half of 1913 as proof of ownership, prevailed in the case; see Domingos Alves Salgueiro vs. Joaquim Esteves, AN, 5a PC, 4182/33. In 1910, Salgueiro responded to a suit for back taxes on the same address; see AN, Juizo da Fazenda Municipal vs. Domingos Alves Salgueiro, 1910.

127. These suits were spurred by the competing claims of Emilio Turano, a notorious land grabber who claimed to have purchased a good portion of the Salgueiro lands in 1933. For more on Turano, and on the Salgueiro case, see below; for the record of his claim, see Emilio Antônio Turano vs. Ocupantes de um imóvel no morro do Salgueiro, 17 July 1933, AN, 4a PC, maço 116, processo 5194.

128. Pereira da Silva, *Favelas Cariocas*, 123 and note 236. See also a fuller description of this struggle, below.

129. Fundação Oswaldo Cruz archives, Vitor Tavares de Moura papers, série Parques Proletários e Favelas, caixa 1 (census reported on 13 January 1947).

130. Ibid., census reported on 26 April 1948.

131. See Decreto-Lei 7499 (27 April 1945). Accounts of the history of holding property in Catacumba vary. It is unlikely that Janice Perlman's account—which places original ownership with "The Baroness of Lagôa Rodrigo de Freitas" (sic) and ends with judicial conflict among the slaves she allegedly granted the lands to, her heirs, and an unnamed third party—is entirely reliable, principally be-

cause there was never a "Baroness of the Lagôa Rodrigo de Freitas" (Perlman, *The Myth*, pp. 24–25). Maria Lucia de Paula Petiz provides another judicial history in "A utilização" (2–3), citing a series of laws and disputes between the Federal government and the Empresa de Terrenos do Distrito Federal. Aside from a 1945 law, however, none of the legislation cited here seems to be specific to Catacumba. For more on the destruction of Catacumba, see Valladares, *Passa-se*; and E. Leeds, "Forms."

132. "500 famílias morando num único barracão," *Diretrizes*, 21 November 1947.

133. "Espaço vital no Morro de Jacarezinho," *O Globo*, 21 October 1947.

134. *O Globo*, 5 June 1948.

135. For example, Vitor Tavares de Moura's census of Esqueleto names a police sergeant, an official from the electric company, and a common resident who all furnished electricity to the *morro*; see census report submitted on 11 December 1947, Fundação Oswaldo Cruz archives, Vitor Tavares de Moura papers, série Parques Proletários e Favelas, caixa 1. The census of the Jockey Club favela from the same year points to three residents who charged for electricity; see census report submitted 14 July 1947, Fundação Oswaldo Cruz archives, Vitor Tavares de Moura papers, série Parques Proletários e Favelas, caixa 1. See also "'Pernambuco Come Gordo,' o manda-chuvas da favela," *Vanguarda*, 23 October 1947, which names two men who controlled electricity in the Barreira do Vasco favela.

136. "Uma favela que começa em Botafogo e termina em Laranjeiras," *O Globo*, 25 May 1948. For similar praise for *biroscas* from a politician, see José Carlos Machado Costa (PST), speaking in the city council on 12 June 1953, published in the *ACDF*, 1953, vol. 62, 423–24; Machado Costa argued that the *biroscas* were vital in providing goods in small quantities and extending credit "to odd-jobbers, washerwomen, and humble workers."

137. "'Pernambuco Come Gordo,' o manda-chuvas da favela," *Vanguarda*, 23 October 1947. The article was based in part on denunciations made by municipal councilwoman Sagramor di Scuveiro.

138. Lucio Cardoso, *Salgueiro*, 52.

139. Undated speech, Fundação Oswaldo Cruz archives, Vitor Tavares de Moura papers, dossiê Produção Intelectual, caixa 2, 3.

140. 8 January 1957, Fundação Oswaldo Cruz archives, Vitor Tavares de Moura papers, dossiê Produção Intelectual, caixa 2. The same brothers were profiled in a 1947 newspaper article, "4 irmãoes exploram a favela de Cantagalo," *Diário de Notícias*, 16 November 1947: "There exist there four brothers who exploit the shack industry, renting them for 300 cruzeiros a month and even more: they own dozens of shacks . . ."

141. See Tito Lívio, 6 May 1947, *ACDF*, 1947, vol. IV, 251–52.

142. For the details of Turano's career building, see below.

143. See Daniel Gonçalves vs. Aurélio Cunha, 1930, AN, 5a PC, 4184/6; and Daniel Gonçalves vs. Luiz Cachoeira, 18 August 1930, AN, 5a PC, 4184/50-A.

144. On the other *grileiros* who had controlled Borel before Gonçalves, see Gomes, *As lutas*. On Gonçalves's early rental of lands behind the tenement, see

AN, 5a PC, Daniel Gonçalves vs. Eugênio Luiz and Leocádio Luiz, 30 March 1931 (this is an eviction case for the rental of land behind the tenement rather than for a room within it).

145. Gomes, *As lutas,* 9–10.

146. See Sociedade Amante da Instrução vs. Jorge Chediac, AN, 3a PC.

147. For the latter accusation, see embargoes presented by José Rodrigues in Jorge Chediac vs. José Rodrigues, AN, 5a PC, 4053/33.

148. For discussion of these trends, see chapters 1 and 2, this volume.

149. For detailed accounts of early suburban development and the companies that carried it out, see Quieroz Ribeiro, *Dos cortiços,* especially chap. 6.

150. Leonardo Soares dos Santos, who has studied the convergence of urban and rural land movements in the 1940s–1960s, reaches a different conclusion; this may be because he did not consider earlier developments in the 1920s and 30s (Soares dos Santos, "Laços em Movimento," 8).

151. For a version of the story sympathetic to the legality of the bank's claims, see Corrêa, *O sertão carioca,* 183–84. For a detailed account of how the bank acquired the lands in the first place, see Fridman, *Donos,* 134–35.

152. Corrêa, *O sertão carioca.*

153. Without proof of a rental agreement, occupants could claim to be *posseiros* or could even make a case for *usucapião.*

154. Three of these cases (involving Miguel Fereira da Rosa, Leopoldo Luiz dos Santos, and Josefino Santos Mesquita) are referred to in a 1932 article printed in the communist daily *A Batalha* ("A justiça reintegra tres posseiros de Guaratiba, víctimas das violências do Banco de Crédito Móvel," 17 March 1932). It is possible that these were appellate court *acordões* 1786 and 1263. The entire text of Leopoldo Luiz dos Santos's appellate court decision (*acordão* 1198) was also printed, along with those of Manoel Isidro Botelho (*acordão* 1130) and Mafalda Maria da Conceição (*acordão* 1088), in the *Jornal do Comércio,* 14–15 March 1932.

155. Leopoldo Luiz dos Santos vs. Banco de Crédito Móvel, appellate court *acordão* 1198, 23 January 1931.

156. Caetano de Camorim's legendary thuggishness earned him a place in Corrêa's *O sertão carioca* (51–52). The BCI's shareholders sent Corrêa a note of complaint about his portrayal of the company, which he published in the book.

157. Corrêa presents an alternate version of this story, which lines up with the investigative report attached to Lima Soares's letter; he affirms that Sotello's widow was "barbaramente despejada" by Caetano and an associate (nicknamed Four Eyes) and claims that Sotello was in the hospital with a broken leg because of a train accident (*O sertão carioca,* 52).

158. Report from police chief Francisco Telles de Moraes, filed with *processo* begun by José de Lima Soares, 24 November 1931, AN, records of the Secretaria da Presidência da República, série 17.7, caixa 41.

159. The 24th district was the most frequently maligned by residents. The 26th was mainly condemned for inaction, and the 2d and 4th auxiliary districts were unbesmirched.

160. *ACDF,* 7 October 1950, 930, 970.

161. Family size gleaned from "Violências sobre violências," *A Batalha,* 18 December 1931; landholding history from Corte de Apelação, 3a and 4a Câmaras, *acordão* 1198, 23 January 1931.

162. *A Batalha,* 17 March 1932.

163. The areas involved in the most notorious of these conflicts, aside from those in Vargem Grande, Vargem Pequena, and Camorim, were the Fazenda Piai, in Sepetiba, and Fazenda Curicica, in the same region as the BCM conflicts. The land grabbers most frequently cited besides the BCM included the Lopes family, also said to have been involved in lotteries and the *jogo do bicho* (numbers game), and a rather mythical European with the surname Reinert.

164. For an explicit linking of the urban/rural question, see *ACDF* , 28 October 1948, 3224. For discussion of the rural question in the *sertão carioca,* see *ACDF,* 22 October 1948, 3107–8.

165. In 1950, for example, a judge ruled that the wealthy landowners had not proven territorial ownership of disputed lands on the Estrada dos Bandeirantes, in the same area as the BCM conflicts of the early 1930s (César Augusto da Fonseca et al. vs. Miguel Augusto et al., 12a VC, decision proferred 31 May 1950, published in *Diário da Câmara do Distrito Federal,* 15 August 1950, 973–75). The judge in the case, Rizzio Afonso Peixoto Bovendi, pointedly refused to grant the occupants *usucapião* rights, stating that the case was not the right forum, and that they had not proven their status as rural workers, which they needed to do if they were to claim rural *usucapião,* with a 10-year lead period rather than the longer 30 years required for urban land.

166. Figure of 90 percent from *Diário da Câmara do Distrito Federal,* 15 July 1950, 940. For legislation, see Lei Municipal 211/48 and Lei Municipal 671, sanctioned on 5 December 1951. For reference to Coutinho Filho, see "Lavradores do sertão carioca defendem seu direito à terra," *Imprensa Popular,* 10 August 1954.

167. Recreio dos Bandeirantes; controversy over land rights in Jacarepagua, Recreio, and Guaratiba has continued to be endemic into the twenty-first century.

168. Speech given 26 May 1948, published in the *ACDF,* 28 May 1948. On Breno da Silveira linking rural and favela land, see *ACDF* (1948), 2224.

169. See Fridman, *Donos,* 134–35.

170. This point, which is collaborated by the recent work of Maria Lais Pereira da Silva, flies in the face of much favela scholarship, which generally points to 1954 as the year when favela residents began to effectively organize themselves. See especially Trinidade Lima, "O movimento."

171. Nóbrega Fernandes, *Escolas,* 57.

172. See Pereira da Silva, *Favelas Cariocas,* 118–19.

173. This is generally traced to 1954 and the União de Trabalhadores Favelados. For the most nuanced version of this chronology, see Trinidade Lima, "O movimento."

174. Ibid., 199, quoting a *Diário de Notícias* report, 26 March 1944.

175. It is possible that this rural-urban connection came through lawyers and political supporters as well as through residents themselves; communist journal-

ists and lawyers, for example, were active in the Guaratiba and Jacarepaguá conflicts and may well have intervened in Salgueiro also. Trinidade Lima suggests that political radicalism was also quite common in the favelas during these years ("O movimento").

176. Cabral, *As escolas*, 87. Valentim's name is from Pereira da Silva, *Favelas Cariocas*, 199, quoting "Queria desalojar toda a população do Morro do Salgueiro," *Diário de Notícias*, 26 March 1944.

177. For the date of the decision and the name of the judge, see Cabral, *As escolas*, 87; for the content of the decision, see Pereira da Silva, *Favelas Cariocas*, 199–200, quoting the *Diário de Notícias*.

178. For a list of some other clients of Regadas, see Maria Antônia da Conceição's *usucapião* suit, 22 March 1934, AN, 3a PC, 2415/262.

179. Transcribed in Pereira da Silva, *Favelas Cariocas*, 124–25, quoting "Queria desalojar toda a população do Morro do Salgueiro," *Diário de Notícias*, 26 March 1944.

180. The auction was actually carried out on 28 February 1958; the buyer, a lawyer and real estate developer by the name of Fábio Kelly de Carvalho, promised to pay 3,100,000 cruzeiros for the hill and also told the press that he planned to build small houses and sell them to current residents; see "Vendido por 3 milhões e cem mil cruzeiros o Morro do Salgueiro," *Imprensa Popular*, 1 March 1958. Apparently, however, the sale never took effect: though residents mentioned to city officials in the early 1980s that a "Senhor Kelly" had once claimed the property, they said he had never been able to prove his claims in court, and that the Pastoral das Favelas was working out the land claim; see Instituto de Planejamento do Rio de Janeiro, "Cadastro das Favelas," interviews conducted by researchers from IPLANRIO with residents of the Morro de Salgueiro (records held at the Instituto Municipal de Urbanismo Pereira Passos).

181. According to communist city councilman Amarílio de Vasconcelos, the Carioca courts took a conscious decision not to grant the flood of eviction requests they received between 1945 and 1947. In 1947, however, that informal agreement came to an end, bringing many long-simmering cases to the fore.

182. These communities were Catacumba, Bonsuccesso/Avenida Brasil (probably the Baixa do Sapateiro), Jockey Clube, Tavares Bastos, Arará, Turano, Bangú, Jacarezinho, Areinha, Ferani (on the Rua Marques de Abrantes), Morro dos Macacos, Cantagalo, Assis Brasil (in Copacabana), Catumbi, Avenida Rio de Janeiro in Cajú, and the Morro do Vintém in Realengo.

183. On the Battle of Rio de Janeiro, see Pereira da Silva, *Favelas Cariocas*, 125–30. Surprisingly, given his later draconian stance, Lacerda in these years favored a sensitive and multitiered (though still top-down) approach to favela eradication; its clearest expression was a bill that he introduced to the city council in 1948 (Projeto-Lei 101/1948); see *ACDF*, 11 June 1948, 728–30.

184. "Despejaram os moradores e quebraram os barracos," *O Radical*, 30 December 1947; see also "Está sendo derrubada a favela do Catumbi," *Diário Carioca*, 30 December 1947.

185. "Macacos—Despejo," *O Globo*, 5 June 1948.

186. *Correio da Manhã*, 5 June 1948.

187. Joel Silveira, "Terror nas favelas," *Diário de Notícias*, 25 January 1948.

188. See, for example, "Rebelião nas favelas," *O Mundo*, 3 July 1948; "Está sendo destruido a 'favelinha' de Bonsuccesso," *A Noite*, 24 November 1947; "Cerca de dois mil pessôas ficarão desabrigadas," *O Globo*, 26 November 1947; "Despejaram os moradores e quebraram os barracos," *O Radical*, 20 December 1947; "Sessenta barracões destruidos," *Diário de Notícias*, 30 December 1947; and "Cinco mil moradores deixarão as favelas," *A Manhã*, 26 March 1948.

189. On relationships with lower-ranking officials, see, for example, "Uma favela que começa em Botafogo e termina nas Laranjeiras," *O Globo*, 25 May 1948, which documents the relationship between the Santa Marta favela and Gastão Vintens, the residents' "grande amigo" in the mayor's office.

190. For the organization's own account of its efforts, see Fundação Leão XIII, *Morros e favelas*.

191. See *ACDF*, 14 March 1947, vol. I, 172.

192. See "Rebelião nas favelas," *O Mundo*, 3 July 1948.

193. Speech given on 26 May 1947, published in the *ACDF*, 27 May 1947, vol. V, 288–89.

194. All of this information was provided by Antônio José Lopes to *O Globo*; see "Uma favela que começa em Botafogo e termina nas Laranjeiras," *O Globo*, 25 May 1948.

195. Santa Marta's relationship with Padre Veloso endured until his death in the 1980s, and its ties to the PUC and the NSA parish have endured to the present; for a sympathetic recounting, see Adair Rocha, *Cidade Cerzida*, chap. 2.

196. By 1948, the Fundação Leão XIII was active in Barreira do Vasco, São Carlos, Jacarezinho, Telégrafos, Salgueiro, and Praia do Pinto, in work that ranged from arranging basic sanitation and electricity to fomenting social and religious education to organizing neighborhood associations based in *centros de ação social*. By 1956, the organization's work had also expanded to Coruja e Alegria, Mangueira, Santo Antônio, Candelária, Tuiuti, Sumaré, Borel, Rocinha, Pavo/Pavãozinho, and Cantagalo.

197. On the early Catholic influence on favela neighborhood associations, see Trinidade Lima, "O movimento"; and Valladares, *A invenção*.

198. "Uma favela que começa em Botafogo e termina nas Laranjeiras," *O Globo*, 25 May 1948. It is likely, given the name, that Odilar was Antônio's brother, but it is not possible to verify this.

199. See, for example, *ACDF*, 7 October 1947, 2481.

200. "Nova ameaça do prefeito Tatuira contra a favela do Morro do Catumbi," *Tribuna Popular*, 6 March 1948.

201. "Uma líder da resistência do povo," *Tribuna Popular*, 11 March 1948.

202. *ACDF*, 13 July 1948, 1365; 15 July 1948, 1401.

203. "Rebelião nas favelas," *O Mundo*, 3 July 1948.

204. See, for example, all of the press coverage surrounding the Morro dos Macacos removal, as well as "Mil pessôas apelam para o Presidente Dutra," *O Radical*, 25 November 1947.

205. Petition from residents of the Praia do Pinto favela in Leblon to councilman Breno da Silveira, printed in the *ACDF,* 13 July 1948, 1367.

206. Interview with Pedro Paulino dos Santos, resident of a favela at 104–24 Avenida Rio de Janeiro, in "Cinco mil moradores deixarão as favelas," *A Manhã,* 26 March 1948.

207. Petition from residents of the Praia do Pinto favela in Leblon to councilman Breno da Silveira, *ACDF,* 13 July 1948, 1367.

208. "Rebelião nas favelas," *O Mundo,* 3 July 1948.

209. "Inquietos ante a ameaça de deportação," *Tribuna Popular,* 20 February 1948. The second quotation is from a washerwoman named Clotilde Cabral, whose husband worked in the Brahma Brewery.

210. "Uma líder da resistência do povo," *Tribuna Popular,* 11 March 1948.

211. "Rebelião nas favelas," *O Mundo,* 3 July 1948;

212. Petition from residents of the Praia do Pinto favela in Leblon to councilman Breno da Silveira and others, *ACDF,* 13 July 1948, 1367.

213. IBGE, Departamento de Censos, *Favelas do Estado de Guanabara: VII Recenseamento,* série especial, vol. 4.

214. See interview with resident Wilson da Silva in "Espaço vital no Morro do Jacarezinho," *O Globo,* 21 October 1947.

215. For further evidence on Almeida and the LBA's involvement, see letter written by inhabitants of Jacarezinho to Mendes de Morais, printed in "Intenso tumulto no Morro do Jacarezinho," *Diretrizes,* 22 October 1947.

216. *ACDF* 5 May 1949, 154–55. See also "Trinta dias para desocupar o Morro de Jacarezinho," *O Globo,* 22 October 1947. There are some references to other owners: in "Intenso tumulto no Morro do Jacarezinho" (*Diretrizes,* 22 October 1947) a reporter makes reference to a "Laboratório Lutécia"; and in 1951, council members mentioned the "Moinho Fluminense." It seems likely that Concordia sold parcels to these buyers.

217. See letter from a committee of Jacarezinho residents to Municipal Secretary of Finance João Lima Filho, "35,000 pessôas ameaçadas de despejo," *O Radical,* 24 October 1947.

218. Quotation from residents' letter to Mendes de Morais, printed in "Intenso Tumulto no Morro do Jacarezinho," *Diretrizes,* 22 October 1947. See also letter from a committee of Jacarezinho residents to Municipal Secretary of Finance João Lima Filho, "35,000 pessôas ameaçadas de despejo," *O Radical,* 24 October 1947.

219. Residents' letter to Mendes de Morais, "Intenso Tumulto no Morro do Jacarezinho," *Diretrizes,* 22 October 1947.

220. Breno Dália da Silveira traded his UDN affiliation for the PSB in 1951 and remained a leftist federal deputy until 1969, when his political rights were stripped under the military government's Institutional Act no. 5. The bills (270 and 272) that would have recognized Jacarezinho's streets both passed the council in October 1948 but seem never to have become law.

221. Fundação Leão XIII, *Morros e favelas.*

222. On the visit, see "Dutra na favela," *Vanguarda,* 5 August 1948; "Nen-

hum 'barraco' será demolido," *A Notícia,* 5 August 1948; "O presidente e as favelas," *O Jornal,* 6 August 1948; "Todos os favelados serão atendidos," *A Manhã,* 6 August 1948; "O Presidente e as favelas," *Gazeta de Notícias,* 7 August 1948; Carlos Cavalcanti, "Visita às Pelancas," *Diário da Noite,* 11 August 1948; "A favela do Jacarezinho," *Revista da Semana,* 14 August 1948.

223. This accusation that Moura was a UDN member and an anti-Getulista is from an article published in a blatantly partisan daily; see "Com Getúlio, isto não acontecia," *O Radical,* 20 May 1949. The note on materials comes from councilman Ari Barroso, *ACDF,* 17 May 1949, 290; according to Brazilian civil law, even people who could not establish a firm claim to legal possession (generally because they had occupied lands for less than a year) had a right to compensation for improvements.

224. See "Cidade maravilhosa," *O Radical,* 17 May 1949, reprinted in the *ACDF,* 18 May 1949, 294.

225. The mother of four provides a clue to possible disingenuousness; as it turns out, she was the wife of the very same man who was described a few days later, in another article, as politically well connected and prominent in the favela.

226. The passerby is also described as carrying a water can on his head, a posture usually (but not always) associated with those of African descent.

227. Projeto-Lei 76/1947 was the original Turano measure.

228. Breno da Silveira, *ACDF,* 17 May 1949, 291.

229. Frota Aguiar, ibid.

230. Frota Aguiar, *ACDF,* 18 May 1949, 302.

231. Breno da Silveira, speaking 19 May 1949, *ACDF,* 20 May 1949. See also "O caso da 'favela' de Jacarezinho," *Jornal do Brasil,* 19 May 1949; "Agradeceram ao chefe da polícia os moradores do Jacarezinho," *Diário Carioca,* 19 May 1949; and "O despejo em massa do Morro do Jacarezinho," *Correio da Manhã,* 19 May 1949.

232. For the standard early chronology on favela activism, see Parisse, *Favelas*; Leeds and Leeds, *A sociologia*; and Valla, *Educação.*

233. See Cotrim Neto, *ACDF,* vol. X, 2–11 July 1951, 233.

234. For the slow action on this second law, Bill 293-A from 1951, see *ACDF,* 25 May 1953, vol. 61, 234–38; see also *ACDF,* 27 April 1954, 372–73.

235. See Souto de Oliveira, *Favelas*; during these years, residents sent frequent requests for neighborhood improvements to the city council, and doubtless to other entities as well.

236. Veto on 27 October 1949, published in the *ACDF* (1949), 2436. Breno da Silveira, fearing the same sort of expulsion that was being attempted throughout the south-zone favelas, criticized the fact that the expropriation left the land in the hands of the prefecture; see *ACDF,* 20 September 1949, 1807.

237. "Jacarezinho, bairro abandonado," *Imprensa Popular,* 11 July 1954.

238. A copy of the rental contract can be found in Emilio Turano vs. Adelino da Fonseca, 1922; the contract was made in September 1921 with the guardian of the minor heirs of Manoel Fereira da Costa e Souza, the Barão da Formalição.

At the time, the hill was referred to as the Chácara do Vintém, and Turano paid 1:150,000.00 per month for the right to sublet it. Turano's original garantor was the owner of a shoe factory (AN, 5a PC, 4054/6).

239. The electricity business was described by Breno da Silveira on 7 July 1947 in the Câmara Municipal; see *ACDF*, 8 July 1947, 1159–60. In 1981 or 1982, the house at the top of the hill was described by Antônio Gonzaga da Silva, president of the residents' association, to interviewers from IPLANRIO; see Instituto de Planejamento do Rio de Janeiro, "Cadastro das Favelas" (records held at the Instituto Municipal de Urbanismo Pereira Passos). Barão de Itapegipe 319 was listed as Turano's home residence in a 1933 judicial case (Sizino Teles de Menezes vs. Emiliano Turano, AN, 3a PC, 2 February 1933), and councilman Paes Leme also said he had read the title, and that Turano had acquired the property in a 1923 purchase (*ACDF*, 14 October 1950, 1780). Breno da Silveira mentioned number 447 in a speech given on 18 August 1949, *ACDF*, 19 August 1949, 1376. Turano presented tax receipts for number 443 in a 1936 *despejo* case against his own *arrendatário*, Candida Barbosa (AN, 5a PC, Emilio Turano vs. Candida Barbosa, 1378/4045), and Pereira da Silva, *Favelas Cariocas*, note 219, uncovered a contract with a second *arrendatário* in 1942.

240. Speech by Breno da Silveira on 18 August 1949, *ACDF*, 19 August 1949.

241. See "Sobem aos morros os candidatos do asfalto," *Imprensa Popular*, 27 June 1954, in which the authors claim that the unofficial communist councilman Henrique Miranda had been involved in the local affairs of Liberdade/Turano since 1947.

242. According to his nephew, Edmundo, Calheiros Bomfim was a "comarada de militância" with Graciliano Ramos.

243. See the *Diário de Notícias*, 17 February 1946, cited in Pereira da Silva, *Favelas Cariocas*, 127.

244. Projeto-Lei 76/1947. The sambista Ary Barroso was the only noncommunist to sign on to the proposed law.

245. 1946 Constitution, article 141, no. 16, and article 156, no. 3.

246. The bill banning all evictions was Projeto-Lei 77/1947, which was shot down shortly after the expulsion of all communists from the Brazilian government on January 7, 1948.

247. Councilman Breno da Silveira pointed to negative decisions in the 13a and 14a Varas, and an article published in the *Tribuna da Imprensa* on 13 October 1950 also cited one in the 6a Vara. These cases, like others in the post-1945 period, can be found in the record books of the Varas, but access to them is effectively closed to researchers.

248. On events in late 1947, see "Turano e a polícia prometem novas violências hoje no Morro da Liberdade," *Tribuna Popular*, 23 December 1947. See also Joel Silveira, "Terror nas favelas," *Diário de Notícias*, 25 January 1948.

249. On the Tijuca neighbors' committee, see "Fundada uma comissão de ajuda ao Morro da Liberdade," *Tribuna Popular*, 24 December 1947. The criminal case was brought against Turano's son in law, José Bastos Ferreira, in the 13a

Vara Criminal, though its end result is unclear. On sporadic violence throughout 1948, see *O Mundo*, 14 April 1948; *A Folha do Povo*, 15 April 1948; *A Manhã*, 7 September 1948; and *Diretrizes*, 7 September 1948.

250. Fundação Leão XIII, *Morros e favelas*, lists Turano as being served by the Serviço Social São Sebastião of the Paróquia dos Padres Capuchinos. However, Turano was one of the few well-established favelas not to have been served by the Fundação Leão XIII itself during this early period, and there was no indication of active Catholic involvement in the *morro*'s land struggles.

251. Lei Municipal 359/1949.

252. See "Escándalo a vista: a desapropriação do Morro da Liberdade," *Tribuna da Imprena*, 13 October 1950.

253. Anésio Frota Aguiar, speech in the Câmara Municipal on 12 July 1950, *ACDF*, 13 July 1950, 1119. Another public health operation was carried out in the Baixa do Sapateiro, a swampy settlement near the Avenida Brasil.

254. The occupation occurred on 12 July 1950; See *ACDF*, 13 July 1950, 953.

255. Like the other post-1945 cases cited here, the Coroa case (from the 9a Vara Civil, Judge Martinho Garcez Neto presiding) is on the Vara's record books but not available for consultation; for details about it, see municipal council debates, especially for 11 July 1950, *ACDF*, 12 July 1950. For press coverage, see especially the left-wing *Imprensa Popular*, 10 July 1950, and the *Diário de Notícias*, 12 July 1950.

256. "The home is inviolable, whether it be a humble shack or one of the most noble palaces of the Zona Sul"; see *ACDF*, 12 July 1950, 939. For the bill, see Projeto-Lei 191/1950.

257. See Câmara Municipal debates of 7 August 1950, published in the *ACDF*, 8 August 1950, 1094, 1137. Breno da Silveira was the only signatory on both of these bills.

258. Both men had interesting connections to the deeper history of favelas and land issues in Rio. Vital, who began his career as a census official, had been responsible for the publication of the landmark 1933 building census, and Cardoso had been head of the 4th Auxiliary District of the Carioca civil police when residents of Jacarepaguá sought its aid during the violence of 1931–32.

259. See Trinidade Lima, "O movimento"; and Fundação Leão XIII, *Favelas*.

260. The PTB claimed nineteen members and substitutes; the UDN, eleven; and the PSD, seven. The PRT representatives included Antenor Marques, Antônio Costa da Silva, Aristides Saldanha, Ilizeu Alves de Oliveira (substitute), Henrique Aranha Miranda (substitute), and Milton José Lobato.

261. There were two members of the PSB active in the 1951–55 Câmara, Raymundo Magalhães Júnior and Urbano Lóes, but Lóes was Magalhães Júnior's substitute rather than a full member.

262. Marques, like other communists after 1948, was elected under the guise of the PRT.

263. *ACDF*, 1951, vol. III, 23–30 April, 287.

264. *ACDF*, 1952, vol. XXXI, 15–30 April, 541, 597.

265. See "Mais 10 mil cariocas ameaçadas pelas picaretas da prefeitura," *Imprensa Popular,* 30 November 1952.

266. On Arará, see *ACDF,* 26 March 1953, 378; residents came to the Câmara Municipal on that date and accused *guardas municipais* of previously taking bribes in order to spare them eviction. On the Rua Ati and the visit to the Câmara Municipal by a committee of its residents, see *ACDF,* 19 May 1953, vol. 61, 47 and 3 July 1953, vol. 64, 150.

267. For more on these bills, see chapter 2, this volume.

268. See complaint 1043.1954, sent to the 17th police district by Magarinos Torres Filho and 548 families from Borel, 2 February 1954, published in *Anais da Câmara dos Deputados,* 2 April 1954, vol. II, 211–19.

269. As on many points with regard to Borel, the memories of the *morro's* most complete chronicler, Manoel Gomes, clash somewhat with newspaper accounts and interviews done at the time of the events. Gomes relates this story in some detail, referring to the owners only as "Daniel" and "Pacheco" (*As lutas*). His version is reinforced by "4 vigilantes municipais ameaçam de desabrigo a 558 famílias" (*Tribuna da Imprensa,* 2 February 1954), which quotes "Cismiro de Tal" (probably Casemiro Pereira, who would become one of the residents' most outspoken activists) indicating Pacheco as the local rent collector and Gonçalves as a man whose name appeared on rent receipts but whom "poucos conheciam" (few had met).

270. See Gomes, *As lutas,* 13.

271. These buildings, according to Gomes, were nos. 1122 and 1212, near one of the structures that Daniel Gonçalves had sublet in the early 1930s. It is unclear whether they had also been managed by Gonçalves, or whether the same firm that employed him—owned by a Gonçalves who may have been Daniel's relative—was the one to sell the buildings. The information about the cessation of rent charges comes from "4 vigilantes municipais ameaçam de desabrigo a 558 famílias," *Tribuna da Imprensa,* 2 February 1954 (interview with "Cismiro de Tal").

272. The case was decided in the 13a Vara Cível.

273. See account given by residents in complaint 1043.1954, sent to the 17th police district by Magarinos Torres Filho and 548 famiiles from Borel, 2 February 1954, and published in the *ACDF,* 2 April 1954, 211–19.

274. See "Indignação no Morro do Borel," *Imprensa Popular,* 1 February 1954; "Terra de ninguém—vigilantes municipais ameaçam de desabrigo 558 familias," *A Folha da Imprensa,* 2 February 1954; and "Quatro mil favelados ameaçados de despejo," *A Notícia,* 2 February 1954.

275. According to the 1950 census, Borel's population that year was 3,873.

276. According to Nísia Trinidade Lima, whose master's thesis is the only comprehensive work on favela residents' mobilization after 1954, Magarinos Torres was suggested to one of the leaders of the Borel resistance ("Seu Izequiel") by a "pai do santo," to whom the residents had gone to ask for "proteção spiritual"; see Trinidade Lima, "O movimento," 106. Magarinos Torres's political sympathies would later become fuel for rancorous debate in the Câmara Municipal; see debates of 26 May 1954, *ACDF,* 27 May 1954, 729, 754.

277. Código Penal (1940), articles 344 and 350 no. 4. The entire sequence of complaints and police responses was reprinted in the *Anais da Câmara dos Deputados*, 1–20 April 1954, vol. II, 211–19.

278. See "4 vigilantes municipais ameaçam de desabrigo a 558 famílias," *Tribuna da Imprensa*, 2 February 1954. The chronology given here differs from some accounts of the *morro*'s struggles, most notably from one given on 14 November 2003 to Marcelo Monteiro by Mauriléia Januário, as reported on the Favela Tem Memória website. Januário claims that the residents' first encounter with Magarinos Torres was on 19 March 1954, but it is clear both from the criminal complaint and from the *Tribuna da Imprensa* article that this chronology is not correct. Manoel Gomes places all of these events in 1952 rather than 1954—an evident error of memory, since they are recorded in newspapers from the period as having taken place in 1954.

279. See photo caption on the first page of the *Imprensa Popular*, 6 February 1954.

280. Register of *ocorrência* for 11–12 February, 17th police district, published in the *Anais da Câmara dos Deputados*, 2 April 1954, vol. II, 211–19.

281. It was also, in theory, the municipal government's right under the 1937 building code.

282. Addition to complaint 1043.1954, sent to the 17th police district by Magarinos Torres Filho and 548 famiiles from Borel, 2 February 1954, and published in the *Anais da Câmara dos Deputados*, 2 April 1954, vol. II, 211–19.

283. "Para resistir a Vargas e ao prefeito," *Imprensa Popular*, 13 February 1954; see also *A Noite*, 13 February 1954.

284. "Moradores do Morro do Borel lutam contra a polícia e os grileiros," *Imprensa Popular*, 7 April 1954.

285. 26 March 1954, addition to complaint 1043.1954, sent to the 17th police district by Magarinos Torres Filho and 548 famiiles from Borel, 2 February 1954, and published in the *Anais da Câmara dos Deputados*, 2 April 1954, vol. II, 211–19.

286. Gomes, *As lutas*, 17.

287. "Moradores do Borel sob nova ameaça de despejo," *Imprensa Popular*, 3 April 1954.

288. Ibid.

289. Gomes, *As lutas*, 17.

290. "Moradores do Morro do Borel lutam contra a polícia e os grileiros," *Imprensa Popular*, 7 April 1954.

291. The chronology here is taken from "Moradores do Morro do Borel lutam contra a polícia e os grileiros," *Imprensa Popular*, 4-7-1954. It differs somewhat from Manoel Gomes' account, which puts the first large meeting with Magarinos Torres on April 19. The *Imprensa Popular*'s version is probably more accurate, as it was already reporting these events on 7 April. The content of the meeting is also somewhat unclear; Gomes claims that it was here that residents began to work with Torres, but police as well as press reports from as early as February show that this collaboration began several months earlier.

292. See, for example "Dispostos à resistência os moradores do Pasmado," *Impresa Popular,* 6 December 1952, which chronicles a visit for a committee of Catacumba's residents to the nearby community of Pasmado.

293. "Para combater a miséria e a grilagem," *Imprensa Popular,* 22 April 1954.

294. The plaintiff in the case was João Nogueira. Judge Hugo Auler had actually ruled in the residents' favor in the first instance, but his decision was overturned on appeal.

295. See speech by socialist Magalhães Júnior in the Câmara Municipal debates of 31 March 1954, published in the *ACDF,* 1 April 1954, 177. See also Frota Aguiar's intervention in the *Anais da Câmara dos Deputados,* 1 April 1954, vol. II, 87; and Breno Silveira's interventions, published in the *Anais da Câmara dos Deputados,* 2 April 1954, 164, 200–203, 208–9. For journalistic coverage, see "Usineiro e polícia despejam a favela Rua Ati," *Imprensa Popular,* 3 April 1954.

296. See Breno da Silveira's speech in the Federal Congress, 23 June 1954, published in the *Anais da Câmara dos Deputados,* vol. IX, 802.

297. *ACDF,* 23 April 1954, 339. The judicial case had been ruled on by Judge Ney Palmeira Cidade in the 9a Vara Cível. União's 1960 population was 3,860; it was not listed in the 1950 census.

298. "Dulcídio trama outro monstruoso despejo," *Imprensa Popular,* 23 April 1954. According to the 1950 census, the hill's population at that point had been 1,632, and in 1960 it would be 3,135. For an oral history of the morro of Timbau, see Ferreira dos Santos, *História,* quoted in Varella, Bertazzo, and Jacques, *Maré,* 25–27.

299. In 1960, Dendê's population stood at 2,211; it was not listed in the 1950 census.

300. "Nova derrubada de barracos no Timbau," *Imprensa Popular,* 16 June 1954; "Pagam os favelados aluguel até de Cr$300 e ainda assim, têm seus barracos arrasados por patrulhas do exército," *Imprensa Popular,* 19 June 1954; see also council debates of 15 June 1954, published in the *ACDF,* 16 June 1954, 930.

301. "Patrulhas do exército despejando favelados," *Imprensa Popular,* 15 June 1954; council debates of 15 June 1954, *ACDF,* 16 June 1954, 930; "Nova derrubada de barracos no Timbau," *Imprensa Popular,* 16 June 1954; Breno da Silveira, speech in the Federal Congress, published in the *Anais da Câmara dos Deputados,* 16 June 1954; "Pagam os favelados aluguel até de Cr$300 e ainda assim, têm seus barracos arrasados por patrulhas do exército," *Imprensa Popular,* 19 June 1954.

302. IBGE, Departamento de Censos, *Favelas do Estado de Guanabara: VII Recenseamento,* série especial, vol. 4.

303. Speech on 22 April 1954, *ACDF,* 23 April 1954, 339.

304. *Imprensa Popular,* 23 and 25 April 1954.

305. Speech on 26 April 1954, *ACDF,* 27 April 1954, 372.

306. Lei 794/1954 (5 May 1954) *ACDF,* 10 June 1954, 869.

307. *Imprensa Popular,* 30 April 1954.

308. "Cofraternizam-se para a luta, os favelados," *Imprensa Popular,* 5 May 1954.

309. "O morro quer a reeleição de Aristides Saldanha," *Imprensa Popular,* 8 May 1954. See also *Imprensa Popular,* 11 May 1954 (on Gávea); "Exploração eleitoral na favela do Jacarezinho," *Imprensa Popular,* 1 June 1954; and *Imprensa Popular,* 11 July 1954 (on Jacarezinho). Some time after the Santa Marta expropriation, the communist paper published a strident attack on Padre Veloso and his allies on the *morro;* see "'A festa da UTF aumentará nossa união,' dizem favelados de Santa Marta," *Imprensa Popular,* 15 October 1954.

310. *ACDF,* 8 June 1954, 829.

311. "Comício no morro de Santa Marta," *Imprensa Popular,* 9 June 1954.

312. Saldanha, speaking on 18 June 1954, published in the *ACDF,* 19 June 1954, 961. On the school, see Gomes, *As lutas,* though as always in this account the dates are somewhat uncertain.

313. "Reconstruiram o barraco derrubado pela polícia," *Imprensa Popular,* 23 June 1954.

314. "800 favelados lutam nas ruas pelo sagrado direito de um lar," *Imprensa Popular,* 23 June 1954.

315. *Correio da Manhã,* 24 June 1954.

316. Decision handed down in the 16a Vara Cível, 14 May 1954, published in the *ACDF,* 8 June 1954, 836–37.

317. See the debates of 26 May, where Couto de Souza aired these accusations, published in the *ACDF,* 27 May 1954, 729, 837. For a sensational version of Avelar's history, see "Lar Para Todos SA quer tomar o lar de todos," *Imprensa Popular,* 26 May 1954.

318. These were the descendants of a widow with the surname Brívio, whose executor (*inventariante*) was Jaime da Silva Rodrigues. See municipal council debates, 24 May 1954, published in the *ACDF,* 25 May 1954, 703.

319. Breno da Silveira, federal congressional debates of 23 June 1954, published in the *Anais da Câmara dos Deputados,* 24 June 1954, 802.

320. Raimundo Magalhães Júnior, debates of 25 June 1954, published in the *ACDF,* 26 June 1954, 1052.

321. Debates of 1 July 1954, published in the *ACDF,* 2 July 1954, 1083.

322. "Inédita no Brasil: 2 mil favelados ocupam a Câmara," *Imprensa Popular,* 2 July 1954.

323. "Transformada a Câmara dos Vereadores em hospedaria de favelados," *Correio da Manhã,* 2 July 1954.

324. "Inédita no Brasil: 2 mil favelados ocupam a câmara," *Imprensa Popular,* 2 July 1954.

325. "Transformada a Câmara dos Vereadores em hospedaria de favelados," *Correio da Manhã,* 2 July 1954.

326. Schumaher and Brazil, *Dicionário.*

327. Lei Municipal 797/1954.

328. See Roberto Morena's discourse in the Federal Congress, 6 October 1954, published in the *Anais da Câmara dos Deputados,* vol. XVII. See also "Os

moradores do morro do Borel impediram um novo despejo," *Imprensa Popular,* 7 October 1954.

329. "Marcado para hoje o despejo de Borel: favelados protestam," *Imprensa Popular,* 1 March 1955.

330. "Vão reunir-se em congresso os favelados cariocas," *Imprensa Popular,* 20 October 1954.

331. On the bill, see "Apresentará a UTF Projeto de Lei em favor dos moradores de favelas," *Imprensa Popular,* 13 October 1954.

332. "Marcado para hoje o despejo de Borel: favelados protestam," *Imprensa Popular,* 1 March 1955; numerous other articles followed in the same journal over the following weeks.

333. "O Morro do Borel é a nossa casa, daqui não sairemos," *Imprensa Popular,* 6 March 1955.

334. "Também o Morro da União sob a ameaça de despejo," *Imprensa Popular,* 4 March 1955.

335. See, respectively, "Populares Tiroteados por sicários policiais," *Imprensa Popular,* 9 March 1955; "Marcado para hoje o despejo de Borel: favelados protestam," *Imprensa Popular,* 1 March 1955; and "Nova vitória dos favelados," *Imprensa Popular,* 12 March 1955.

336. "Assinado decreto que susta o despejo do Borel," *Imprensa Popular,* 29 March 1955.

337. See, for example, a threatened eviction in Borel publicized in the Federal Congress by Bruzzi Mendonça in January 1956; speech given 27 January 1956, published in the *Anais da Câmara dos Deputados,* 1955–56, vol. VI, 128.

338. See debates of 29 June 1955, 5 July 1955, 5 August 1955, 9 September 1955, 13 September 1955, 14 September 1955, and 15 September 1955, all published in the *ACDF,* 30 June 1955, 6 July 1955, 6 August 1955, 10 September 1955, 14 September 1955, 15 September 1955, and 16 September 1955. In Vintém, the threat was the result of a high-court decision that, interestingly, reversed an earlier lower-court ruling in favor of the favela residents; see debates of 4 August 1948, *ACDF,* 5 August 1948, 2080.

339. Projeto-Lei 149/55, introduced on 4 August 1955 and passed on 15 September 1955; for the final version, see *ACDF,* 16 September 1955, 2082.

340. On Piai, see Câmara Municipal debates of 13 May 1956, *ACDF,* 14 May 1956. On Penha, see Câmara Municipal debates of 10 July 1956, *ACDF,* 11 July 1956. On the "Boogie-Woogie" favela, see debates of 16 July 1956, *ACDF,* 17 July 1956.

341. Moreira had been the frequent target of attacks for his political tactics in Jacarezinho, both from the communists—and especially the *Imprensa Popular*—and from more mainstream rivals, such as Edgard de Carvalho. Elizabeth Leeds, writing more about Moreira's later actions, argues that most residents of the north-zone favelas where she conducted fieldwork had a generally positive impression of Moreira; Nísia Verônica Trinidade Lima calls that interpretation into question.

342. See Câmara Municipal debates of 13 September 1955, published in the *ACDF* 14 September 1955, 2046.

343. On the genesis of such participatory urbanization, see Trinidade Lima, "O movimento"; for its most expressive manifestation, see J. A. Rios, "Operação Mutirão."

344. For the accusation of communism, see *ACDF,* 14 September 1955, 2047. One signal of the approximation was the fact that the communist *vereador* Waldemar Vianna, when asked by residents of Vintém for help in finding a lawyer, recommended Moreira, who saw no judicial solution but did attempt to negotiate another settlement. See debates of 29 June 1955, *ACDF,* 30 June 1955.

345. Projeto-Lei 32/1955. For full text, see debates of 5 July 1955, *ACDF,* 6 July 1955, 1260–61.

346. See debates of 6 July 1955, *ACDF,* 7 July 1955, 1260–61. This language anticipated by several years that of José Arthur Rios's Operação Mutirão in the early 1960s; for more on that, see chapter 2, this volume.

347. P-L 32/1955 did pass the Câmara in 1958.

348. Câmara Municipal discussion of 5 August 1955, *ACDF,* 6 August 1955.

349. Barroso, "Favelas." For a similar discussion, see Meuren, "Breves considerações," 463.

350. See *Anais da Câmara dos Deputados,* 3 February, 1956, vol. VII, 65. See also Bruzzi Mendonça's comments during the debates of 17 September 1956, published in *Diário do Congresso Nacional,* Seção I, 18 September 1956, 8318.

351. On Cardoso de Menezes, see Alves de Abreu et al., *Dicionário.*

352. Projeto-Lei 749/1955, eventually passed as 749-D. Most of the early debates played themselves out between late December 1955 and early February 1956. Ex-municipal councilman and former police chief Frota Aguiar also played an important role in these discussions.

353. Projeto-Lei 1/1956.

354. See, for instance, the decision in the 1954 Dendê case, brought up in the Câmara Municipal on 7 June 1954, and published in the *ACDF,* 8 June 1954, 836. On the nature of possessorial rights in general, see Nascimento, *Posse;* for one interpretation of favela residents' possessorial rights in the 1960s, see Conn, *The Squatters' Rights.*

355. Projeto de Lei do Senado 1/1956, Senator Moura Brasil, *Anais do Senado,* 3 January 1956, 23–25.

356. See congressional debates of 6 February 1956, published in *Anais da Câmara dos Deputados,* 7 February 1956, vol. VII, 290–91. Another amendment was also suggested that would have used the 50 million cruzeiros to expropriate favela lands rather than turning them over to the Cruzada de São Sebastião, but it was not adopted. See congressional debates of 6 February 1956, published in the *Anais da Câmara dos Deputados,* 1956, vol. VII, 289.

357. See congressional debates of 6 February 1956, published in the *Anais da Câmara dos Deputados,* 1956, vol. VII, 290–91.

358. See congressional debates of 17 September 1956, published in the *Diário do Congresso Nacional,* Seção I, 18 September 1956, 8319.

359. Lei 2875, signed into law by Juscelino Kubitschek (19 September 1956).

360. The introduction to the 1916 civil code required that "in applying the law, the judge will attend to the social ends to which it is directed and to the exigencies of the common good." Article 147 of the 1946 constitution declared "the use of private property will be conditioned by social well-being." For an explicit link between these articles and the Lei das Favelas, see Meuren, "Breves considerações."

361. This intention was clearly stated by Congressman Frota Aguiar in the congressional debates of 17 September 1956; see *Diário do Congresso Nacional*, 18 September 1956, 8318.

362. On both organizations, see chapter 2, this volume.

363. Decreto Municipal 374 (24 February 1961). This was revoked under the military government in 1965, but social service workers seem to have continued to invoke it even well after this date. Stephen Conn suggests that this decree was often enforced only loosely in the 1960s, given an appeals court ruling that supported owners' rights to collect something in exchange for leasing their land.

364. Meuren, "Breves considerações," 466. Meuren argues that the 1954 law, like every other Brazilian law, "revoked all dispositions contrary to it," and that the clauses of the rent law that governed evictions were among these; unless they were reestablished by law, there was no longer any legal mandate with which to evict favela residents. See also Conn, *The Squatters' Rights*.

365. See Conn, *The Squatters' Rights*, part 1.

366. Even Nísia Trinidade Lima, whose work with oral history and journalistic sources in the late 1980s gave unprecedented attention to the earlier period, wrote that "despite earlier struggles and associative movements, leaders point to the formation of the UTF of Borel as the great milestone of social struggles in the favelas"; see Trinidade Lima, "O movimento," 102–3.

367. Between 1962 and 1965, Lacerda's government, through the agency COHAB, "removed" thirteen entire favelas, most of which were tiny, but a few of which—Esqueleto, Pasmado, Bom Jesús, and Maria Angú—were home to between 200 and 2,000 families. COHAB also eliminated portions of sixteen other favelas, including 34 families from Turano, 366 from the combative Brás de Pina, and 253 from the Morro de São Carlos. Altogether, some 6,290 families, or 31,000 people, were affected; see Leeds and Leeds, *A sociologia*, 220.

368. See Trinidade Lima, "O movimento."

369. See Leeds and Leeds, *A sociologia*, 220; and Perlman, *The Myth*, 202.

370. "Marcado para hoje o despejo de Borel: favelados protestam," *Imprensa Popular*, 1 March 1955.

371. This seems to have eventually caused a rift between Magarinos Torres, who advocated the multilateral approach, and some of the ideological communists within Borel and the UTF; see Trinidade Lima, "O movimento."

EPILOGUE

1. Império Serrano, "E verás que um filho teu não foge à luta" (1996); the sociologist and activist Herbert de Souza ("Betinho") participated in the samba's performance. MV Bill, "Um Crioulo Revoltado Com Uma Arma" (2006).

2. Murilo de Carvalho, *Cidadania*.

3. For a specific manifestation of this, see Holston, "The Misrule of Law."

4. The senator was Benedita da Silva, a resident of the Chapeu Mangueira favela, on the same hill as Babilônia. On Rio's favela urbanization programs through the late 1990s, see Burgos, "Dos parques."

5. All of these events received ample press coverage; their respective dates were 23 July 1993, 29 August 1993, 12 June 2000, and 29 March 2005. On favela residents' views of police and drug lords, see Zaluar, *Integração*; Penglase, "To Live Here"; and Arias, *Drugs*.

6. José Cesário de Aguiar Filho (nicknamed Seu Pasqual), 76 (a resident of Praia do Ramos, part of the Maré favela complex in Rio's north suburbs), interview conducted by Claudio Pereira (himself from Maré) and Renata Siqueira for the Favela Tem Memória project, 4 November 2006; Seu Augusto Ribeiro da Silva, 74 (a resident of Rubens Vaz, Maré), interview conducted by Claudio Pereira for the Favela Tem Memória project, 15 April 2005; and Lucíola de Jesus, 104 (a Mangueira resident since her infancy and granddaughter of a slave), interview conducted by Guaraci Gonçalvez for the Favela Tem Memória project, 22 February 2005.

7. Marshall, "Citizenship," 8.

8. Holston, "Citizenship."

9. Murilo de Carvalho, *Cidadania*, 57.

10. Ibid., 110.

11. Ibid., 126.

12. Ibid., 110.

13. On slaves and the law, see Grinberg, *Liberata*; Chalhoub, *Visões*; and various articles contained in Lara and Mendonça, *Direitos e Justiças*.

14. Zaluar, *Integração*, especially chap. 10.

15. Leeds, "Cocaine."

16. MV Bill and Celso Athayde, *Falcão*.

STATISTICAL APPENDIXES

1. Because of organizational changes, the records that were once in the state judicial archives are now held by a private company and are accessible only through recourse to the judges of the individual courts. This represents a serious problem for researchers seeking to undertake this sort of investigation.

2. I am grateful to Nathan Wright for helping me to construct the initial logistic regression models, and for giving me an introduction to their interpretation. Thanks also to Christina Gómez for discussion of subsequent doubts and questions.

3. Tests for multicollinearity, however, proved negative, meaning that low statistical significance is not due to high levels of correlation between my independent variables.

Bibliography

Major Archives, Libraries, and Collections Consulted

Arquivo Geral da Cidade do Rio de Janeiro
  Iconographic collections, Henrique Dodsworth administration records
Arquivo da Polícia Civil, Rio de Janeiro
  Livros de ocorrência (log books), 1930–64
Arquivo da 20a Vara de Execuções Penais, Rio de Janeiro
  Judicial records from Rio de Janeiro's criminal courts, 1955–66
Arquivo do Serviço de Obras Sociais (SOS), Rio de Janeiro
Arquivo Judiciário, Rio de Janeiro
  Judicial records from Rio de Janeiro's Tribunais do Júri, 1930–66
Arquivo Nacional, Rio de Janeiro and Brasília
  Judicial records from Rio de Janeiro's civil and criminal courts, 1925–55
  Records of the Secretaria da Presidência da República, 1930–45
  Correio da Manhã archives
  Iconographic and miscellaneous smaller collections
Arquivo Público do Estado do Rio de Janeiro
  Political police records
Biblioteca Central do Gragoatá/Universidade Federal Fluminense (Niterói, Rio
  de Janeiro)
Biblioteca da Assembléia Legislativa do Estado do Rio de Janeiro
  Records of the Câmara Municipal, legal library
Biblioteca da Casa de Oswaldo Cruz, Rio de Janeiro
Biblioteca da Pontifícia Universidade Católica do Rio de Janeiro (PUC Rio)
Biblioteca do Instituto Brasileiro de Administração Municipal, Rio de Janeiro
Biblioteca do Instituto Universitário de Pesquisas do Rio de Janeiro
Biblioteca Nacional, Rio de Janeiro
  Periodicals, Books, Maps, Music, and Iconography
Biblioteca São Tomáz de Aquino do Convento dos Dominicanos do Leme
Carlos Lacerda archives, Biblioteca da Universidade de Brasília
Fundação Casa de Rui Barbosa, Rio de Janeiro
Fundação Getúlio Vargas (FGV)/Centro de Pesquisa e Documentação de História
  Contemporânea do Brasil (CPDOC), Rio de Janeiro

Fundação Instituto Brasileiro de Geografia e Estatística, Rio de Janeiro
  Vitor Tavares de Moura papers
Instituto de Planejamento do Rio de Janeiro (IPLANRIO)/Instituto Municipal de
  Urbanismo Pereira Passos, Rio de Janeiro
Northwestern University Library, Evanston, IL
Poder Judiciário do Estado do Rio de Janeiro
  Registry books for Rio's civil *varas*
Regenstein Library, University of Chicago, Chicago, IL
University of Michigan Library, Ann Arbor, MI
Widener Library, Harvard Law School Library, Graduate School of Design Library, Harvard University, Cambridge, MA

SERIAL PUBLICATIONS CONSULTED OR CITED

Anais da Câmara dos Deputados, 1946–59
Anais da Câmara do Distrito Federal, 1947–64
Anais do Conselho Municipal, 1914–36
Anais do Senado Federal, 1946–64
Anuário Estatístico do Brasil, 1936–65
Anuário Estatístico do Distrito Federal, 1937–60
Anuário Estatístico do Estado de Guanabara, 1960–64
Anuário Estatístico do Rio de Janeiro, 1959–60
A Batalha
Boletim Mensal de Estatística do Distrito Federal, 1930–37
Boletim do Ministério do Trabalho, Indústria e Comércio, 1934–60
Boletim do SOS, 1934–62
Correio da Manhã
Diário da Câmara do Distrito Federal, 1946–64
Diário Carioca
Diário da Justiça, 1930–64
Diário da Noite
Diário de Notícias
Diário do Congresso Nacional
Diário Oficial, 1930–64
Diretrizes
Folha do Dia
Folha da Imprensa
Folha do Povo
O Globo
Imprensa Popular
O Jornal
Jornal do Brasil
Jornal do Comércio
A Manhã
O Mundo
A Noite

A Notícia
Observador Econômico e Financeiro
O Radical
Revista da Semana
Tribuna da Imprensa
Tribuna Popular
Última Hora
Vanguarda

GOVERNMENT DOCUMENTS

Diretoria Geral de Estatística
   Recenseamento Geral da República dos Estados Unidos do Brasil, 31 de De-
      zembro de 1890 (Rio de Janeiro, 1895)
Instituto Brasileiro de Geografia e Estatística (IBGE)
   Recenseamento Geral do Brasil, 1 Septembro 1940 (Rio de Janeiro, 1943–)
   O Brasil em números (Rio de Janeiro, 1966)
   As Favelas do Distrito Federal e o Censo Demográfico de 1950, documentos
      censitários, série c, no. 9 (Rio de Janeiro, 1953)
   Favelas do Estado de Guanabara: VII Recenseamento, série especial, vol. 4
      (Rio de Janeiro, 1968)
   VI Recenseamento Geral do Brasil, 1950 (Rio de Janeiro, 1955)
   VII Recenseamento Geral do Brasil, 1960 (Rio de Janeiro, 1968)
   VIII Recenseamento Geral, 1970 (Rio de Janeiro, 1972–73)
   IX Recenseamento do Brasil, 1980 (Rio de Janeiro, 1982–83)
Ministério da Agricultura, Indústria e Comércio, Directoria Geral de Estatística
   Recenseamento do Brasil, 1 de Setembro de 1920 (Rio de Janeiro, 1924)
Ministério do Trabalho, Indústria e Comércio
   Levantamento do custo de vida no Brasil (Rio de Janeiro, 1946)
Ministério do Trabalho, Indústria e Comércio, Departamento de Estatística e
      Publicidade
   Estatística Predial do Distrito Federal, 1933 (Rio de Janeiro, 1935)
Prefeitura do Distrito Federal, Secretaria Geral do Interior e Segurança, Departa-
      mento de Geografia e Estatística
   Censo das Favelas (Rio de Janeiro, 1949)
República dos Estados Unidos do Brasil, Officina de Estatística
   Recenseamento do Rio de Janeiro (Distrito Federal), 20 de Setembro de 1906
      (Rio de Janeiro, 1907)

MAJOR LEGAL CODES CITED

Código Civil Brasileiro (1916)
Código de Obras do Distrito Federal (1937)
Código Penal do Brasil (1940)
Código Penal da República dos Estados Unidos do Brasil (1890)
Código de Processo Civil (1939)

Código de Processo Penal (1941)
Código de Processo Penal para o Distrito Federal (1924)
Consolidação das Leis do Trabalho (1943)
Decreto Federal 5156, Regulamento dos Serviços Sanitários a Cargo da União (8 March 1904)
Decreto Municipal 391, building code (10 February 1903)
Lei da Família (1941)
Lei de Inquilinato (1934, 1950, 1955)
Lei Orgânica da Previdência Social (1960)

INTERVIEWS CONDUCTED FOR ATTRIBUTION

Eliane Athayde
Lúcio de Paula Bispo
Odília dos Santos Gama
Maria da Conceição Ferreira Pinto (Dona Filinha)
Abdias José Nascimento dos Santos
Collection of interviews for the Favela Tem Memória project, http://www.favelatemmemoria.com.br

PRINTED PRIMARY AND SECONDARY SOURCES

All works are listed in the bibliography alphabetically by the author's final surname.

Abreu, Alzira Alves de, et al. *Dicionário histórico-biográfico brasileiro.* Rio de Janeiro: Fundação Getúlio Vargas/Centro de Pesquisa e Documentação de História Contemporânea do Brasil, 2001.

Abreu, Martha Campos. *O Império do divino: Festas religiosas e cultura popular no Rio de Janeiro, 1830–1900.* Rio de Janeiro: Nova Fronteira, 1999.

Abreu, Maurício de Almeida. "A cidade, a montanha, e a floresta." In Almeida Abreu, ed., *Natureza e sociedade no Rio de Janeiro.* Rio de Janeiro: Biblioteca Carioca, 1992.

———. *Evolução urbana do Rio de Janeiro,* 2d ed. Rio de Janeiro: Instituto de Planejamento do Rio de Janeiro/Jorge Zahar, 1988.

———. "Da habitação ao habitat: Uma interpretação geográfica da evolução da questão da habitação popular no Rio de Janeiro." Unpublished paper, Casa Fundação de Rui Barbosa, undated.

———. "Reconstruindo uma história esquecida: Origem e expansão inicial das favelas do Rio de Janeiro." *Espaço e Debates* 37 (1994), 34–46.

———, and Olga Bronstein. "Políticas públicas, estrutura urbana, e distribuição de população de baixa-renda na area metropolitana do Rio de Janeiro." Unpublished paper, Instituto Brasileiro de Administração Municipal, Nov. 1978.

Academia Carioca de Letras. *Aspectos do Distrito Federal.* Rio de Janeiro: Sauer, 1943.

Adamo, Sam C. "The Broken Promise: Race, Health, and Justice in Rio de Janeiro, 1890–1940." Ph.D. diss., University of New Mexico, 1983.

Agache, Alfred. *Rio de Janeiro; Extensão, remodelação, e embelezamento.* Paris: Foyer Brasilien, 1930.

Albuquerque, Deocleciano Saboia de. *Elucidário do inquérito policial.* Rio de Janeiro: Jacinto/Editora A Noite, 1945.

Alencar, Edigar de. *O carnaval carioca através da música.* Rio to Janeiro: Fco. Alves, 1979.

Almeida, Cândido Mendes de. *Código do processo penal para o Distrito Federal (Mandado executar pelo decreto n. 16751, de 31 de dezembro de 1924).* Rio de Janeiro: Imprensa Nacional, 1925.

Alonso, Annibal Martins. *Organização policial: história, legislação, administração.* Rio de Janeiro: Freitas Bastos, 1959.

Álvarez, Marcos César. *Bacharéis, criminologistas e juristas: Saber jurídico e nova escola penal no Brasil (1889–1930).* Ph.D. diss., Universidade de São Paulo, 1996.

Alves, Roque de Brito. *Uma interpretação da personalidade do delinquente.* Recife: Imprensa Universitária, 1958.

Alvito, Marcos. *As cores de Acari: Uma favela carioca.* Rio de Janeiro: Fundação Getúlio Vargas, 2001.

Andrews, George Reid. *Blacks and Whites in São Paulo, Brazil, 1888–1988.* Madison: University of Wisconsin Press, 1991.

Antunes, Dioclécio de Paranhos. "Transformações do quadro urbano e evolução do Rio de Janeiro." In Associação dos Geógrafos Brasileiros, Secção Regional do Rio de Janeiro, *Aspectos da geografia carioca.* Rio de Janeiro: Instituto Brasileiro de Geografia e Estatística, 1962.

Applebaum, Herbert. *The Concept of Work: Ancient, Medieval, and Modern.* Albany, N.Y.: SUNY Press, 1992.

Araujo, Américo Ribeiro de. *Sciência penitenciária positiva,* 2d ed. Rio de Janeiro: Leite Ribeiro, 1923.

Arias, Enrique Desmond. *Drugs and Democracy in Rio de Janeiro: Trafficking, Social Networks, and Public Security.* Chapel Hill: University of North Carolina Press, 2006.

Arrom, Sylvia. *Containing the Poor.* Durham, N.C.: Duke University Press, 2000.

Associação dos Geógrafos Brasileiros, Secção Regional do Rio de Janeiro. *Aspectos da geografia carioca.* Rio de Janeiro: Instituto Brasileiro de Geografia e Estatística, 1962.

Azevedo, Aluísio. *O cortiço.* Rio de Janeiro: Garnier, 1890.

Azevedo, Celia Maria Marinho de. *Onda negra, medo branco: O negro no imaginário das elites, século XIX.* Rio de Janeiro: Paz e Terra, 1987.

Azevedo, Thales de. *As elites de cor numa cidade brasileira: Um estudo de ascensão social e classes sociais e grupos de prestígio.* Paris: UNESCO, 1953.

Bacha, Edmar L., and Herbert S. Klein. *Social Change in Brazil, 1945–1985: The Incomplete Transition.* Albuquerque: University of New Mexico Press, 1989.

Backheuser, Everardo. "A faixa litorânea." In Everardo Backheuser, *A faixa litorânea do Brasil Meridional, hoje e ontem*. Rio de Janeiro: Besnard Frères, 1918.

———. "A geologia do Distrito Federal." *Anuário de Estatística da Cidade do Rio de Janeiro*. Rio de Janeiro, date unknown.

———. *Habitações populares: Relatório apresentado ao Exm. Senhor Doutor J. J. Seabra, Ministro da Justiça e Negócios Interiores*. Rio de Janeiro: Imprensa Nacional, 1906.

———. "Onde moram os pobres." *Renascença: Revista Mensal de Letras, Sciências e Artes* 13(2), 1905.

Bandeira, Manuel, and Carlos Drummond de Andrade. *Rio de Janeiro em prosa e verso*. Rio de Janeiro: José Olympio, 1965.

Barbot, Claude. "Favela: Problema de planejamento." *Notícias Municipais* 43 (Nov.–Dec. 1960).

Barreto, Carlos Xavier P. *O crime, o criminoso, e a pena*. Rio de Janeiro: A. Coelho Branco Filho, 1938.

Barreto, Lima. *Triste fim de Policarpo Quaresma*. Rio de Janeiro: Garnier, 1989 (originally published 1911).

Barreto, Paulo (João do Rio). *A alma encantadora das ruas*. Rio de Janeiro: Garnier, 1908.

Barroso, Manoel de Carvalho. "Favelas: Desapropriação impeditiva de despejo: Pagamento em apólices (parecer, 12-10-1956)." *Revista de Direito da Procuradoria Geral* 7 (1957), 509–14.

Batalha, Claudio H. M. "Formação da classe operária e projetos de identidade coletiva." In Jorge Ferreira and Lucília de Almeida Neves Delgado, eds. *O Brasil republicano*, vol. 1. Rio de Janeiro: Civilização Brasileira, 2003.

———. "A historiografia da classe operária no Brasil: Trajetórias e tendências." In Marcos Cezar Freitas (ed.), *Historiografia brasileira em perspectiva*. São Paulo: Contexto, 1998.

Beattie, Peter. *The Tribute of Blood: Army, Honor, Race, and Nation in Brazil, 1864–1945*. Durham, N.C.: Duke University Press, 2001.

Benchimol, Jaime Larry. *Dos micróbios aos mosquitos: febre amarela e a revolução pasteuriana no Brasil*. Rio de Janeiro: Editora Fiocruz, 1999.

———. *Pereira Passos: Um Haussmann tropical*. Rio de Janeiro: Biblioteca Carioca, 1990.

Bernardes, Lysia M. C. "Evolução da paisagem urbana do Rio de Janeiro até o início do século XX." In Associação dos Geógrafos Brasileiros, Secção Regional do Rio de Janeiro, *Aspectos da geografia carioca*. Rio de Janeiro: Instituto Brasileiro de Geografia e Estatística, 1962.

Bernardes, Nilo. "Notas sobre a ocupação humana da montanha no Estado de Guanabara." In Associação dos Geógrafos Brasileiros, Secção Regional do Rio de Janeiro, *Aspectos da geografia carioca*. Rio de Janeiro: Instituto Brasileiro de Geografia e Estatística, 1962.

Berry, Sara. "Debating the Land Question in Africa." *Comparative Studies in Society and History* 44 (Nov. 2002), 638–68.

Berson, Theodore. "The Favela: An Administrative Problem in Rio de Janeiro, 1933–1964." Unpublished paper, Nov. 1964.

Besse, Susan. *Restructuring Patriarchy: The Modernization of Gender Inequality in Brazil, 1914–1940*. Chapel Hill: North Carolina University Press, 1996.

Bicalho, Maria Fernanda. *A cidade e o império: O Rio de Janeiro no século XVIII*. Rio de Janeiro: Civilização Brasileira, 2003.

Bicudo, Hélio Perreira. *O direito e a justiça no Brasil*. São Paulo: Edições Símbolo, 1978.

Blay, Eva Alterman, ed. *A luta pelo espaço: Textos de sociologia urbana*. Petrópolis: Vozes, 1978.

Boaventura, Lúcia Miranda. "Crescimento Desigual: O bairro da Tijuca." Master's thesis, Universidade Federal Fluminense, 1986.

Bobbio, Norberto. *O positivismo jurídico: Lições de filosofia do direito*. Ed. Nello Morra. Trans. Márcio Pugliesi, Edson Bini, and Carlos E. Rodrigues. São Paulo: Ícone, 1995.

Bomeny, Helena. "Utopias de cidade: As capitais do modernismo." In Ângela Maria de Castro Gomes, ed., *O Brasil do JK*. Rio de Janeiro: Fundação Getúlio Vargas, 1991.

Bourdieu, Pierre. "Rites as Acts of Institution." In J. G. Peristiany and Julian Pitt-Rivers, eds., *Honor and Grace in Anthropology*. Cambridge: Cambridge University Press, 1992.

Borges, Dain. "Brazilian Social Thought of the 1930s." *Luso-Brazilian Review* 31:2 (1994), 137–52.

———. *The Family in Bahia, Brazil: 1870–1945*. Stanford, Calif.: Stanford University Press, 1992.

———. "'Puffy, Ugly, Slothful and Inert': Degeneration in Brazilian Social Thought, 1880–1940." *Journal of Latin American Studies* 25:2 (1993), 235–57.

Bracet, Heitor. "O registro civil das pessoas naturais." *Revista Brasileira de Estatística* 30–31 (Apr.–Sept. 1947), 363–72.

Brandão, Ana Maria de Paiva Macedo. "As alterações climáticas na área metropolitana do Rio de Janeiro: Uma provável influência do crescimento urbano." In Almeida Abreu, ed., *Natureza e sociedade no Rio de Janeiro*. Rio de Janeiro: Biblioteca Carioca, 1992.

Brasil. Departamento de Imprensa e Propaganda. *O Brasil dos nossos dias*. Rio de Janeiro: Imprensa Nacional, 1940.

———. *Os grandes problemas nacionais*. Rio de Janeiro: Imprensa Nacional, 1942.

Bretas, Marcos. *A guerra das ruas: povo e polícia na cidade do Rio de Janeiro*, Rio de Janeiro: Arquivo Nacional, 1997.

———. "You Can't! The Daily Exercise of Police Authority in Rio de Janeiro, 1907–1930." Ph.D. diss., The Open University, 1995.

Brito, Juares Guimarães, Lília da Rocha Bastos, and Célio José Alves. "Tres favelas cariocas: Mata Machado, Morro União, Brás de Pina—levantamento socioeconômico." Unpublished paper, Department of Research, School of Sociology, Pontifícia Universidade Católica do Rio de Janeiro, 1967.

Britto, Lemos. *Os sistemas penitenciárias do Brasil*. Rio de Janeiro: Imprensa Nacional, 1924.

Bruant, Catherine. "Donat Alfred Agache: urbanismo, uma sociologia aplicada." In Luiz César Quieroz de Ribeiro and Robert Pechman, eds., *Cidade, povo e nação*. Rio de Janeiro: Civilização Brasileira, 1996.

Burgos, Marcelo Baumann. "Cidade, territórios e cidadania." *Dados: Revista de Ciências Sociais* 48:1 (2005), 189–222.

———. "Dos parques proletários ao Favela-Bairro: As políticas públicas nas favelas do Rio de Janeiro." In Alba Zaluar and Marcos Alvito, eds., *Um século de favela*. Rio de Janeiro: Fundação Getúlio Vargas, 1998.

Burke, Peter, ed. *New Perspectives on Historical Writing*. University Park: Pennsylvania State University Press, 1991.

Burns, E. Bradford. *A History of Brazil*, 3d ed. New York: Columbia University Press, 1993.

Butler, Kim. *Freedoms Given, Freedoms Won*. New Brunswick, N.J.: Rutgers University Press, 1998.

Cabral, Sérgio. *As escolas de samba do Rio de Janeiro*. Rio de Janeiro: Lumiar, 1996.

Caldeira, Teresa P. R. *City of Walls*. Berkeley: University of California Press, 2000.

———, and James Holston. "Democracy and Violence in Brazil." *Comparative Studies in Society and History* 41:4 (1999), 691–729.

Campos, Francisco. *Exposição de motivos* (for the 1940 criminal code). Rio de Janeiro: José Olympio, 1940.

———. *Exposição de motivos* (for the 1942 *Código de Processo Penal*)

Cancelli, Elizabeth. *O mundo da violência: A polícia da era Vargas*. Brasília: Universidade de Brasília, 1993.

Cardoso, Adalberto Moreira. "Sindicalismo, trabalho e emprego." In Wanderley Guilherme dos Santos and Marcelo de Paiva Abreu, eds., *Estatísticas do século XX*. Rio de Janeiro: Instituto Brasileiro de Geografia e Estatística, 2003.

Cardoso, Lúcio. *Salgueiro*. Rio de Janeiro: José Olympio, 1935.

Carone, Edgard. *O Centro Industrial do Rio de Janeiro e a sua importante participação na economia nacional (1827–1977)*. Rio de Janeiro: O Centro Industrial do Rio de Janeiro, 1978.

Carrara, Sérgio. *Crime e loucura: O aparecimento do manicômio judiciário na passagem do século*. Rio de Janeiro: Universidade do Estado do Rio de Janeiro, 1998.

———. "A sciência e a doutrina da identificação no Brasil." *Religião e Sociedade* 15:1 (1990), 83–105.

Carvalho, Astrogildes Feiteira Delgado de. *História da cidade do Rio de Janeiro*. Rio de Janeiro: Biblioteca Carioca, 1990.

Carvalho, Eduardo Guimarães de. *O negócio da terra: A questão fundiária e a justiça*. Rio de Janeiro: Universidade Federal do Rio de Janeiro, 1991.

Carvalho, José Murilo de. *Os bestializados: O Rio de Janeiro e a república que não foi*. São Paulo: Cia. das Letras, 1987.

——. *Cidadania no Brasil: O longo caminho*. Rio de Janeiro: Civilização Brasileira, 2001.

——. "A política de terras no Império: Uma não-decisão." Unpublished paper, Biblioteca do Instituto Universitário de Pesquisas do Rio de Janeiro.

——. "República de cidadanias." *Revista de Ciências Sociais* 28:2 (1985), 143–61.

Carvalho, Ladário de. "A alimentação do operário." *Boletim do Ministério do Trabalho, Indústria, e Comércio*, Nov. 1935, 86–90.

Carvalho, Lia de Aquino. *Habitações populares*, 2d ed. Rio de Janeiro: Biblioteca Carioca, 1995.

Castro, Hebe Maria Mattos de. *Das cores do silêncio: Os significados da liberdade no sudeste escravista—Brasil século XIX*. Rio de Janeiro: Arquivo Nacional, 1995.

Castro, Josué de. *Geografia da fome*, 2d ed. Rio de Janeiro: O Cruzeiro, 1946.

——. *O problema da alimentação no Brasil*. São Paulo: Editora Nacional, 1934.

——. *Salário mínimo*. Rio de Janeiro: Departamento de Estatística e Publicidade, 1935.

Castro, Francisco José Viveiros de. *Os delitos contra a honra da mulher*, 4th ed. Rio de Janeiro: Freitas Bastos, 1942.

——. *Jurisprudência criminal*. Rio de Janeiro: Garnier, 1900.

——. *A nova escola penal*, 2d ed. Rio de Janeiro: Jacinto Ribeiro dos Santos, 1913.

Caulfield, Sueann. *In Defense of Honor: Sexual Morality, Modernity, and Nation in Early Twentieth-Century Brazil*. Durham, N.C.: Duke University Press, 2000.

——, and Martha de Abreu Esteves. "50 Years of Virginity in Rio de Janeiro: Sexual Politics and Gender Roles in Juridical and Popular Discourse, 1890–1940." *Luso-Brazilian Review* 30:1 (1993), 47–84.

Caulfield, Sueann, Sarah Chambers, and Lara Putnam, eds. *Honor, Status and the Law in Modern Latin America*. Durham, N.C.: Duke University Press, 2005.

Cavalcanti, Sandra. Interview with Carlos Eduardo Sarmento and Marly Motta. In Américo Freire and Lúcia Lippi Oliveira, *Capítulos da memória do urbanismo carioca*. Rio de Janeiro: Fundação Getúlio Vargas, 2002.

——. *Rio: Viver ou morrer*. Rio de Janeiro: Expressão e Cultura, 1978.

Chalhoub, Sidney. *Cidade febril: Cortiços e epidemias na Corte Imperial*. São Paulo: Cia. das Letras, 1996.

——. "Diálogos políticos em Machado de Assis." In Sidney Chalhoub and Leonardo Affonso de M. Pereira, eds., *A história contada: Capítulos de história social da literatura no Brasil*. Rio de Janeiro: Nova Fronteira, 1998.

——. "The Politics of Silence: Race and Citizenship in Nineteenth-Century Brazil." *Slavery and Abolition* 27:1 (2006), 73–87.

——. *Trabalho, lar e botequim*, 2d ed. Campinas, São Paulo: UNICAMP, 2001.

———. "Vadios e barões no ocaso do Império." *Estudos Ibero Americanos* 9:1–2 (1983).

———. *Visões da liberdade: Uma história das últimas décadas da escravidão na Corte*. São Paulo: Cia. das Letras, 1990.

Chazkel, Amy. "Laws of Chance: The *Jogo do Bicho* and the Making of Urban Public Life in Brazil, 1880–1968." Ph.D. diss., Yale University, 2002.

Chevalier, Louis. *Laboring Classes and Dangerous Classes in Paris during the First Half of the Nineteenth Century*. Princeton, N.J.: Princeton University Press, 1973.

Coaracy, Vivaldo. *Memórias da cidade do Rio de Janeiro*. Rio de Janeiro: José Olympio, 1955.

Coelho, Edmundo Campos. "A administração da justiça criminal no Rio de Janeiro, 1942–1967." *Dados: Revista de Ciências Sociais* 29:1 (1986), 61–81.

Cohen, Lisbeth. *Making a New Deal: Industrial Workers in Chicago, 1919–1939*. Cambridge: Cambridge University Press, 1990.

Comissão Nacional de Bem-Estar Social, Subcomissão de Habitação e Favelas. *Favelas e habitação popular, relatório preliminar*. Rio de Janeiro, 1954.

Companhia Industrial Santa Fé. *A questão do Morro de Santo Antonio: Collectânea de notícias, pareceres e documentos*. Rio de Janeiro: Mandarino e Molinari, 1937.

Conn, Stephen. *The Squatters' Rights of Favelados*. Cuernavaca: Centro Intercultural de Documentación, 1969.

Conniff, Michael L. *Urban Politics in Brazil: The Rise of Populism, 1925–1945*. Pittsburgh, Pa.: University of Pittsburgh Press, 1981.

Corrêa, Armando Magalhães. *O sertão carioca*. Rio de Janeiro: Imprensa Nacional, 1936.

Cortes, Geraldo de Menezes. *Favelas*. Rio de Janeiro: Imprensa Nacional, 1959.

Costa, Emilia Viotti da. *The Brazilian Empire: Myths and Histories*. Chicago: Dorsey Press, 1985.

———. "Land Policies: The Land Law, 1850, and the Homestead Act, 1862." In Emilia Viotti da Costa, *The Brazilian Empire: Myths and Histories*. Chicago: Dorsey Press, 1985.

Costa e Silva, Antônio José da. *Código penal*. Rio de Janeiro: Editora Nacional, 1938 (originally published 1930).

Costallat, Benjamim. *Mistérios do Rio*. Rio de Janeiro: Flôres & Mano, 1931.

———. "A favela que eu vi." In Benjamim Costallat, *Mistérios do Rio*. Rio de Janeiro: Flôres & Mano, 1931.

Coutinho, Maurício C., and Cláudio Salm. "Social Welfare." In Edmar L. Bacha and Herbert S. Klein, *Social Change in Brazil, 1945–1985: The Incomplete Transition*. Albuquerque: University of New Mexico Press, 1989.

Cruls, Gastão. *Aparência do Rio de Janeiro*. Rio de Janeiro: José Olympio, 1949.

Cruz, H. Dias da. *Os morros cariocas no novo regime: Notas de reportagem*. Rio de Janeiro: Gráfica Olímpica, 1941.

Cruzada São Sebastião. "Duas experiências de promoção humana: Bairro São

Sebastião, Favela do Rádio Nacional." Paper presented at the third Congresso Brasileiro de Serviço Social, Rio de Janeiro, Oct. 1965.

Cunha, Euclides da. *Os sertões*. Rio de Janeiro: Laemmert, 1902.

Cunha, Maria Clementina Pereira. *Ecos da fólia: Uma história social do carnaval carioca entre 1880 e 1920*. São Paulo: Cia. das Letras, 2001.

Cunha, Olívia Maria Gomes da. "1933: Um ano em que fizemos contatos." *Revista USP* 28 (Dec.–Feb. 1995–96), 142–63.

———. *Intenção e gesto: Pessoa, côr e a produção cotidiana da (in)diferença no Rio de Janeiro*. Rio de Janeiro: Arquivo Nacional, 2002.

———. "The Stigma of Dishonor: Individual Records, Criminal Files, and Identification in Rio de Janeiro, 1903–1940." In Sueann Caulfield, Sarah Chambers, and Lara Putnam, eds., *Honor, Status and the Law in Modern Latin America*. Durham, N.C.: Duke University Press, 2005.

Dantas, Mercedes. *A força nacionalizadora do Estado Novo*. Rio de Janeiro: Departamento de Imprensa e Propaganda, 1942.

D'Araujo, Maria Celina, ed. *As instituições brasileiras da era Vargas*. Rio de Janeiro: Editora Universitária da UERJ (EdUERJ) and Fundação Getúlio Vargas, 1999.

Dávila, Jerry. *Diploma of Whiteness: Race and Social Policy in Brazil, 1917–1945*. Durham, N.C.: Duke University Press, 2003.

Dean, Warren. *The Industrialization of São Paulo*. Austin: University of Texas Press, 1969.

———. *Rio Claro: A Brazilian Plantation System, 1820–1920*. Stanford, Calif.: Stanford University Press, 1976.

Deniz, Eli. *Voto e máquina política: Patronagem e clientelismo no Rio de Janeiro*. Rio de Janeiro: Paz e Terra, 1982.

Dodsworth, Henrique. *A Avenida Presidente Vargas: Aspectos urbanísticos, financeiros e administrativos de sua realização*. Rio de Janeiro: Jornal do Comércio, 1955.

Domíngues, Aurélio. *Manual prático da identificação*. Recife: M. Campos e Cia., 1933.

Drummond, José de Magalhães. *Aspectos do problema penal brasileiro*. Rio de Janeiro: Sfreddo & Gravina, 1940.

———. *Estudos de psychologia, criminologia, e direito penal*. Rio de Janeiro: Revista Forense, 1938.

Duarte, José. *Comentários à lei das contravenções penais*. Rio de Janeiro: Revista Forense, 1944.

Durand-Lasserve, Alain, and Lauren Royston. *Holding Their Ground: Secure Land Tenure for the Urban Poor in Developing Countries*. London: Earthscan Publications, 2002.

Edmundo, Luiz. *O Rio de Janeiro do meu tempo*. Rio de Janeiro: Imprensa Nacional, 1938.

Elena, Eduardo. "Peronist Consumer Politics and the Problem of Domesticating Markets in Argentina, 1943–1955." *Hispanic American Historical Review* 87:1 (2007), 111–49.

Elia, Francisco Carlos da Fonseca. "A questão habitacional no Rio de Janeiro da Primeira República, 1889–1930." Master's thesis, Universidade Federal Fluminense, 1984.

Epstein, David G. *Brasília: Plan and Reality*. Berkeley: University of California Press, 1973.

Esteves, Martha de Abreu. *Meninas perdidas: Os populares e o cotidiano do amor no Rio de Janeiro da Belle Epoque*. Rio de Janeiro: Paz e Terra, 1989.

Fausto, Boris, ed. *Crime e codidiano: A criminalidade em São Paulo (1880–1924)*. São Paulo: Editora da Universidade de São Paulo (EdUSP), 1999.

———. *História geral da civilização brasileira*. São Paulo: DIFEL, 1985.

Fernandes, Edésio, ed. *Direito urbanístico e política urbana no Brasil*. Belo Horizonte: Del Rey, 2000.

———, and Ann Varley, eds. *Illegal Cities: Law and Urban Change in Developing Countries*. London: Zed Books, 1998.

Fernandes, Nelson da Nóbrega. *Escolas de samba: Sujeitos celebrantes e objetos celebrados*. Rio de Janeiro: Coleção Memória Carioca, 2001.

Ferreira, Aurélio Buarque de Holanda. *Novo dicionário da língua portuguesa*. Rio de Janeiro: Nova Fronteira, 1986.

Ferreira, João da Costa. *A cidade do Rio de Janeiro e seu termo: Ensaio urbanológico*. Rio de Janeiro: Imprensa Nacional, 1933.

Ferreira, Jorge Luiz. "A cultura política dos trabalhadores no primeiro governo Vargas." *Estudos Históricos* 6 (1990).

———. "O nome e a coisa: o populismo na política brasileira." In Jorge Luiz Ferreira, ed., *O populismo e sua história*. Rio de Janeiro: Civilização Brasileira, 2001.

———, ed. *O populismo e sua história*. Rio de Janeiro: Civilização Brasileira, 2001.

———. *Prisioneiros do Mito: cultura e imaginário político dos comunistas no Brasil (1930–1956)*. Rio de Janerio: Editora Universidade Federal Fluminense (EdUFF)/ Mauad, 2002.

———. *Trabalhadores do Brasil: o imaginário popular*. Rio de Janeiro: Fundação Getúlio Vargas, 1997.

———, and Lucília de Almeida Neves Delgado, eds. *O Brasil republicano*. Rio de Janeiro: Civilização Brasileira, 2003.

Ferreira, Jurandyr Pires, ed. *Enciclopédia dos municípios brasileiros*, vol. 23. Rio de Janeiro: Instituto Brasileiro de Geografia e Estatística, 1960.

Ferreira, Marieta de Moraes, ed. *Rio de Janeiro: Uma cidade na história*. Rio de Janeiro: Fundação Getúlio Vargas, 2000.

Ferri, Enrico. *Criminal Sociology*. Trans. Joseph I. Kelly. Boston: Little, Brown, 1917.

———. *The Positive School of Criminology*. Trans. Ernest Untrermann. Chicago: C. H. Kerr & Co., 1912.

Fischer, Brodwyn. "Direitos por lei, ou leis por direito? Pobreza e ambigüidade legal no Estado Novo." In Silvia Lara and Joseli Maria Nunes Mendonça, eds., *Direitos e justiças no Brasil: Histórias plurais*. Campinas: UNICAMP/ CECULT, 2006.

―――. "'Quase Pretos de Tão Pobres?' Race and Social Discrimination in Rio de Janeiro's Criminal Courts." *Latin American Research Review* 39:1 (2004).

―――. "Slandering Citizens: Insults, Class, and Social Legitimacy in Rio de Janeiro's Criminal Courts." In Sueann Caulfield, Sarah Chambers, and Lara Putnam, eds., *Honor, Status and the Law in Modern Latin America*. Durham, N.C.: Duke University Press, 2005.

Flory, Thomas. *Judge and Jury in Imperial Brazil, 1808–1871*. Austin: University of Texas Press, 1981.

Fontaine, Pierre-Michel. *Race, Class and Power in Brazil*. Los Angeles: Center for Afro American Studies, University of California, 1985.

Fortes, Alexandre. *Na luta por direitos*. Campinas: UNICAMP, 1999.

―――. "Revendo a legalização dos sindicatos: Metalúrgicos de Porto Alegre (1931–1945)." In Alexandre Fortes, *Na luta por direitos*. Campinas: UNICAMP, 1999.

―――. "Trabalhadores e populismo: Novos conturnos de um velho debate." Unpublished paper, 2003.

Foucault, Michel. *Discipline and Punish: The Birth of the Prison*. New York: Vintage, 1979.

Franco, Angela Maria de Paiva. "Vila Aliança: Atuação de serviço social num programa de habitação." Trabalho de conclusão de curso, School of Social Service, Pontifícia Universidade Católica do Rio de Janeiro, 1965.

Franco, Ary Azevedo. *Código de processo penal anotado*. Rio de Janeiro: Jacinto, 1942.

Frank, Zephyr. *Dutra's World: Wealth and Family in Nineteenth-Century Rio de Janeiro*. Albuquerque: University of New Mexico Press, 2004.

Freire, Américo, and Lúcia Lippi Oliveira. *Capítulos da memória do urbanismo carioca*. Rio de Janeiro: Fundação Getúlio Vargas, 2002.

Freitas, Marcos Cezar de, and Laura de Mello e Souza, *Historiografia brasileira em perspectiva*. São Paulo: Contexto, 1998.

Freitas Filho, Almir Pita. "A industrialização no Rio de Janeiro, 1930–1945 (indústria e industriais no antigo Distrito Federal)." Master's thesis, Universidade Federal Fluminense, 1986.

French, John D. *The Brazilian Workers' ABC: Class Conflict and Alliances in Modern São Paulo*. Chapel Hill: University of North Carolina Press, 1991.

―――. *Drowning in Laws*. Chapel Hill: University of North Carolina Press, 2004.

Freyre, Gilberto. *The Mansions and the Shanties*. Trans. Harriet de Onís. New York: Knopf, 1963.

―――. *The Masters and the Slaves: A Study in the Development of Brazilian Civilization*. Trans. Samuel Putnam. New York: Knopf, 1956.

―――. *Order and Progress*. Trans. Rod W. Horton. New York: Knopf, 1970.

Fridman, Fania. *Donos do Rio no nome do rei*. Rio de Janeiro: Jorge Zahar, 1999.

Fry, Peter. "Color and the Rule of Law in Brazil." In Juan E. Méndez, Guillermo O'Donnell, and Paulo Sérgio Pinheiro, eds., *The (Un)Rule of Law and the Un-*

derprivileged in Latin America. Notre Dame, Ind.: University of Notre Dame Press, 1999.

———. "Direito positivo versus direito clássico: A psicologização do crime no Brasil no pensamento de Heitor Carrilho." In Servulo A. Figueira, ed., *Cultura e psicanálise*. São Paulo: Brasiliense, 1985.

———. "Febrónio Índio do Brasil: Onde cruzam a psiquiatria, a profecia, a homosexualidade e a lei." In Alexandre Eulalio, ed., *Caminhos cruzados*. São Paulo: Brasiliense,1982.

———, and Sérgio Carrara. "As vicissitudes do liberalismo no direito penal brasileiro." *Revista Brasileira de Ciências Sociais* 1:2 (1986), 48–54.

Fundação Leão XIII. *Favelas: Um compromiso que vamos resgatar*. Rio de Janeiro: Fundação Leão XIII, 1962.

———. *Morros e favelas: Como trabalha a Fundação Leão XIII*. Rio de Janeiro: Imprensa Naval, 1955.

Galvão, Maria do Carmo Corrêia. "Aspectos da geografia agrária do sertão carioca." In Associação dos Geógrafos Brasileiros, Secção Regional do Rio de Janeiro, *Aspectos da geografia carioca*. Rio de Janeiro: Instituto Brasileiro de Geografia e Estatística, 1962.

Gancho, Cândida Vilares. *A posse da terra*. São Paulo: Atica, 1991.

Garrioch, David. *Neighborhood and Community in Paris, 1740–1790*. Cambridge: Cambridge University Press, 1986.

———. "Verbal Insults in Eighteenth-Century Paris." In Peter Burke and Roy Porter, eds., *The Social History of Language*. Cambridge: Cambridge University Press, 1987.

Gawryszewski, Alberto. "Administração Pedro Ernesto: Rio de Janeiro (DF), 1931–36." Master's thesis, Universidade Federal Fluminense, 1988.

Gay, Peter. *Popular Organization and Democracy in Rio de Janeiro: A Tale of Two Favelas*. Philadelphia: Temple University Press, 1994.

Geiger, Pedro Pinchas. "Esbôço da estrutura urbana da área metropolitana do Rio de Janeiro." In Associação dos Geógrafos Brasileiros, Secção Regional do Rio de Janeiro, *Aspectos da geografia carioca*. Rio de Janeiro: Instituto Brasileiro de Geografia e Estatística, 1962.

Geremek, Bronislaw. *Poverty: A History*. London: Basil Blackwell, 1994.

Gerson, Brasil. *História das ruas do Rio*, 5th ed. Rio de Janeiro: Lacerda, 2000.

Gilbert, Alan. *The Latin American City*, London: LAB, 1994.

———, and Peter M. Ward. *Housing, the State and the Poor: Policy and Practice in Three Latin American Cities*. Cambridge: Cambridge University Press, 1985.

Gomes, Ângela Maria de Castro. *O Brasil do JK*. Rio de Janeiro: Fundação Getúlio Vargas, 1991.

———. *Burguesia e trabalho: Política e legislação social no Brasil, 1917–1937*. Rio de Janeiro: Editora Campus, 1979.

———. "A construção do homem novo: O trabalhador brasileiro." In Lúcia Lippi Oliveira, Mônica Pimenta Velloso, and Ângela Maria de Castro Gomes, eds., *Estado Novo: Ideologia e poder*. Rio de Janeiro: Zahar, 1982.

————. *A invenção do trabalhismo*, 2d ed. Rio de Janeiro: Relume Dumará, 1994.

————. "O populismo e as ciências sociais no Brasil: Notas sobre a trajetória de um conceito." In Jorge Luiz Ferreira, ed., *O populismo e sua história*. Rio de Janeiro: Civilização Brasileira, 2001.

————. "Temas clássicos, temas novos, perspectivas renovadoras." In Ângela Maria Carneiro Araújo, ed., *Trabalho, cultura, e cidadania: um balanço da história social brasileira*. São Paulo: Scritta, 1997.

————. *Trabalho e previdência: Sessenta anos em debate*. Rio de Janeiro: Fundação Getúlio Vargas, 1992.

Gomes, Flávio dos Santos. *A hidra e os pântanos: Mocambos, quilombos, e communidades de fugitivos no Brasil*. São Paulo: Universidade Estadual Paulista (UNESP), 2005.

————, and Olívia Maria Gomes da Cunha. *Quase cidadão: Histórias e antropologias da pós-emancipação no Brasil*. Rio de Janeiro: Fundação Getúlio Vargas, 2007.

Gomes, Manoel. *As lutas do povo do Borel*. Rio de Janeiro: Edições Muro, 1980.

Gotkowitz, Laura. "Trading Insults: Honor, Violence, and the Gendered Culture of Commerce in Cochabamba, Bolivia, 1870s–1950s." *Hispanic American Historical Review* 83:1 (2003), 83–118.

Gottdiener, Mark. *The Social Production of Urban Space*. Austin: University of Texas Press, 1985.

Goulart, José Alípio. *Favelas do Distrito Federal*. Rio de Janeiro: Ministério da Agricultura, Serviço de Informação Agrícola, 1957.

Graham, Richard. *Patronage and Politics in Nineteenth-Century Brazil*. Stanford, Calif.: Stanford University Press, 1994.

Grinberg, Keila. *O fiador dos brasileiros: Cidadania, escravidão e direito civil no tempo de Antônio Pereira Rebouças*. Rio de Janeiro: Civilização Brasileira, 2002.

————. *Liberata, a lei da ambigüidade: As ações de liberdade da Corte de Apelação do Rio de Janeiro no século XIX*. Rio de Janeiro: Relume Dumará, 1994.

Guillermoprieto, Alma. *Samba*. New York: Vintage, 1991.

Guimarães, Alberto Passos. "As favelas do Distrito Federal e o recenseamento de 1950." *Revista Brasileira de Estatística* 14:55 (July–Sept. 1953), 250–78.

Guimarães, Antônio Sérgio Alfredo. "Côr, classes e *status* nos estudos de Pierson, Azevedo e Harris na Bahia, 1940–1960." In Marcos Chor Maio e Ricardo Ventura Santos, eds., *Raça, ciência e sociedade*. Rio de Janeiro: Fiocruz/CCBB, 1996.

Gusmão, Chrysolito de. *Dos crimes sexuais*, 4th ed. Rio de Janeiro: Freitas Bastos, 1954.

Hagopian, Frances. "Latin American Citizenship and Democratic Theory." In Joseph S. Tulchin and Meg Ruthenburg, eds., *Citizenship in Latin America*. Boulder/London: Lynne Rienner, 2007.

Hahner, June E. *Poverty and Politics: The Urban Poor in Brazil, 1870–1970.* Albuquerque: University of New Mexico Press, 1986.

Hanchard, Michael George. *Orpheus and Power: The Movimento Negro of Rio de Janeiro and São Paulo, Brazil, 1945–1988.* Princeton, N.J.: Princeton University Press, 1994.

Hartog, Hendrik. "Pigs and Positivism." *Wisconsin Law Review* 4 (1985), 899–935.

Harvey, David. *Social Justice and the City.* Baltimore, Md.: Johns Hopkins University Press, 1973.

Hasenbalg, Carlos. *Discriminação e desigualdades raciais no Brasil.* Rio de Janeiro: Graal, 1979.

Hochman, Gilberto. "Os cardeais da previdência social: Gênese e consolidação de uma elite burocrática." *Dados: Revista de Ciências Sociais* 35:3 (1992), 371–401.

———. *A era do saneamento.* São Paulo: HUCITEC-ANPOCS, 1998.

———. "Previdência e assistência social nos anuários estatísticos do Brasil." In Wanderley Guilherme dos Santos and Marcelo de Paiva Abreu, eds., *Estatísticas do século XX.* Rio de Janeiro: Instituto Brasileiro de Geografia e Estatística, 2003.

Holloway, Thomas. "'A Healthy Terror': Police Repression of *Capoeiras* in Nineteenth-Century Rio de Janeiro." *Hispanic American Historical Review* 69:4 (1989), 637–76.

———. *Policing Rio de Janeiro: Repression and Resistance in a Nineteenth-Century City.* Stanford, Calif.: Stanford University Press, 1993.

Holston, James. *Cities and Citizenship.* Durham, N.C.: Duke University Press, 1999.

———. "Citizenship in Disjunctive Democracies." In Joseph S. Tulchin and Meg Ruthenburg, eds., *Citizenship in Latin America.* Boulder/London: Lynne Rienner, 2007.

———. "The Misrule of Law: Land and Usurpation in Brazil." *Comparative Sudies in Society and History* 33:4 (1991), 695–725.

———. *The Modernist City: An Anthropological Critique of Brasília.* Chicago: University of Chicago Press, 1989.

Hobsbawm, E. J. *Nations and Nationalism Since 1780: Programme, Myth, Reality.* Cambridge: Cambridge University Press, 1990.

Huggins, Martha Knisely. *From Slavery to Vagrancy in Brazil: Crime and Social Control in the Third World.* New Brunswick, N.J.: Rutgers University Press, 1985.

———. *Vigilantism and the State in Modern Latin America.* New York: Praeger, 1991.

Humphrey, John. *Capitalist Control and Workers' Struggle in the Brazilian Auto Industry.* Princeton, N.J.: Princeton University Press, 1982.

Hungria, Nelson. *Comentários ao código penal.* Rio de Janeiro: Forense, 1942.

———. "A Criminalidade dos homens de côr no Brasil." *Revista Forense* 48:134 (1951), 21–30.

————. *Novas questões jurídico-penais*. Rio de Janeiro: Editora Nacional de Direito, 1945.

Ignatiev, Noel. *How the Irish Became White*. New York: Routledge, 1995.

Iliffe, John. *The African Poor: A History*. Cambridge: Cambridge University Press, 1987.

Instituto Brasileiro de Geografia e Estatística. "Atividades e posições na ocupação nos diversos grupos de côr da população do Distrito Federal." In Instituto Brasileiro de Geografia e Estatística, *Pesquisa sobre os diversos grupos de côr nas populações do estado de São Paulo e do Distrito Federal*. Rio de Janeiro: Instituto Brasileiro de Geografia e Estatística,1951.

————. *Enciclopédia dos municípios brasileiros*. Rio de Janeiro: Instituto Brasileiro de Geografia e Estatística, 1958.

————. *Estatísticas históricas do Brasil*. Rio de Janeiro: Instituto Brasileiro de Geografia e Estatística, 1990.

Instituto de Pesquisa e Estudos do Mercado. *Favelas e favelados do Distrito Federal*. Rio de Janeiro: Instituto de Pesquisa e Estudos do Mercado, 1957.

————. *A vida mental dos favelados*. Rio de Janeiro: Instituto de Pesquisa e Estudos do Mercado, 1958.

Instituto de Planejamento do Rio de Janeiro (IPLANRIO). "Cadastro das favelas do Município do Rio de Janeiro" (unpublished reports held in IPLANRIO's archives).

————. *Morar na metrópole: Ensaios sobre habitação popular no Rio de Janeiro*. Rio de Janeiro: Instituto de Planejamento do Rio de Janeiro, 1988.

James, Daniel. *Resistance and Integration*. Cambridge: Cambridge University Press, 1988.

Jardim, Germano Gonçalves. "Os recenseamentos e a estatística do estado conjugal." *Revista Brasileira de Estatística* 10:57 (1954).

Jesús, Carolina Maria de. *Bitita's Diary: The Childhood Memoirs of Carolina Maria de Jesus*. Ed. Robert Levine. Trans. Emanuelle Oliveira and Beth Joan Vinkler. Armonk, NY: M. E. Sharpe, 1998.

Johnson, Lyman L. "Dangerous Words, Provocative Gestures, and Violent Acts: The Disputed Hierarchies of Plebeian Life in Colonial Buenos Aires." In Lyman L. Johnson and Sonya Lipsett-Rivera, eds., *The Faces of Honor: Sex, Shame, and Violence in Colonial Latin America*. Albuquerque: University of New Mexico Press, 1998.

————, and Sonya Lipsett-Rivera, eds. *The Faces of Honor: Sex, Shame, and Violence in Colonial Latin America*. Albuquerque: University of New Mexico Press, 1998.

Jones, Gareth Stedman. *Languages of Class: Studies in English Working-Class History, 1832–1982*. Cambridge: Cambridge University Press, 1983.

————. *Outcast London: A Study in the Relationship Between Classes in Victorian Society*. Oxford: Oxford University Press, 1971.

Karasch, Mary. *Slave Life in Rio de Janeiro, 1808–1850*. Princeton, N.J.: Princeton University Press, 1987.

Katzman, Martin T. "Urbanization since 1945." In Edmar L. Bacha and Herbert

S. Klein, *Social Change in Brazil, 1945–1985: The Incomplete Transition*. Albuquerque: University of New Mexico Press, 1989.

Katznelson, Ira, and Aristide Zolberg. *Working-Class Formation: Nineteenth-Century Patterns in Western Europe and the United States*. Princeton, N.J.: Princeton University Press, 1986.

Kogut, Edy Luiz. *Análise económica do fenômeno demográfico no Brasil*. Trans. Geni Hirata. Rio de Janeiro: Fundação Getúlio Vargas, 1976.

Kowarick, Lúcio. *As lutas sociais e a cidade: São Paulo, passado e presente*. Rio de Janeiro: Paz eTerra, 1988.

———. *Trabalho e vadiagem: A origem do trabalho livre no Brasil*. São Paulo: Brasiliense, 1994.

Lacerda, Carlos. "Batalha do Rio" (series), *Correio da Manhã*, May 1948.

Lacombe, Mercedes Dantas. *A força nacionalizadora do Estado Novo*. Rio de Janeiro: Departamento de Imprensa e Propaganda, 1942.

Lara, Silvia. *Campos da violência: Escravos e senhores na Capitania de Rio de Janeiro, 1750–1808*. Rio de Janeiro: Paz e Terra, 1988.

———, and Joseli Maria Nunes Mendonça, eds. *Direitos e justiças no Brasil: Histórias plurais*. Campinas: UNICAMP/CECULT, 2006.

Lauderdale Graham, Sandra. *Caetana Says No: Women's Stories from a Brazilian Slave Society*. Cambridge: Cambridge University Press, 2002.

———. *House and Street: The Domestic World of Servants and Masters in 19th-Century Rio de Janeiro*. Austin: University of Texas Press, 1988.

Leal, Maria da Glória de Faria. "A construção do espaço urbano carioca no Estado Novo: A indústria da construção civil." Master's thesis, Universidade Federal Fluminense, 1987.

Leeds, Anthony. "O Brasil e o mito da ruralidade urbana: Experiência urbana, trabalho e valores nas 'áreas invadidas' do Rio de Janeiro e de Lima." In Anthony Leeds and Elizabeth Leeds, *A sociologia do Brasil urbano*. Rio de Janeiro: Zahar, 1977.

———. "Favelas e comunidade política." In Anthony Leeds and Elizabeth Leeds, *A sociologia do Brasil urbano*. Rio de Janeiro: Zahar, 1977.

———, and Elizabeth Leeds. *A sociologia do Brasil urbano*. Rio de Janeiro: Zahar, 1977.

Leeds, Elizabeth. "Cocaine and Parallel Polities in the Brazilian Urban Periphery: Constraints on Local Level Democratization." *Latin American Research Review* 31:3 (1996).

———. "Forms of 'Squatment' Political Organization: The Politics of Control in Brazil." Master's thesis, University of Texas at Austin, 1972.

Leff, Nathaniel H. *The Brazilian Capital Goods Industry, 1929–1964*. Cambridge, Mass.: Harvard University Press, 1968.

Lenharo, Alcir. *Sacralização da política*. Campinas: UNICAMP, 1986.

Levine, Robert. *Father of the Poor: Vargas and His Era*. Cambridge: Cambridge University Press, 1998.

———. *Vale of Tears: Revisiting the Canudos Massacre in Northeastern Brazil, 1893–1897*. Berkeley: University of California Press, 1992.

———. *The Vargas Regime: The Critical Years, 1934–38*. New York: Columbia University Press, 1970.

Lewin, Linda, *Surprise Heirs*. Stanford, Calif.: Stanford University Press, 2003.

Levy, Maria Barbara. *A indústria do Rio de Janeiro através de suas sociedades anônimas*. Rio de Janeiro: Universidade Federal do Rio de Janeiro, 1994.

Lima, Evelyn Furkim Werneck. *Avenida Presidente Vargas: Uma drástica cirurgia*. Rio de Janeiro: Biblioteca Carioca, 1990.

Lima, Nísia Verônica Trinidade. "O movimento de favelados do Rio de Janeiro: Políticas do estado e lutas sociais, 1954–1973." Master's thesis, Instituto Universitário de Pesquisas do Rio de Janeiro, 1989.

———. *Um sertão chamado Brasil*. Rio de Janeiro: Revan/Instituto Universitário de Pesquisas do Rio de Janeiro, 1999.

———, and Gilberto Hochman. "Condenado pela raça, absolvido pela medicina: O Brasil descoberto pelo movimento sanitarista da Primeira República." In Marcos Chor Maio e Ricardo Ventura Santos, eds., *Raça, ciência e sociedade*. Rio de Janeiro: Fiocruz/CCBB, 1996.

Lima, Roberto Kant de. "Constituição, direitos humanos e processo penal: Quem cala, consente?" *Dados: Revista de Ciências Sociais* 33:3 (1990).

———. "Cultura jurídica e práticas policiais: a tradição inquisitorial." *Revista Brasileira de Ciências Sociais* 10:4 (1989).

———. "Legal Theory and Judicial Practice: Paradoxes of Police Work in Rio de Janeiro City." Ph.D. diss., Harvard University, 1986.

———. "Ordem pública e pública desordem: Modelos processuais de controle social em uma perspectiva comparada." *Anuário Antropológico* 88 (1991).

Lima, Ruy Cirne. *Pequena história territorial do Brasil: Sesmarias e terras devolutas*, 2d ed. Pôrto Alegre: Livraria Sulina, 1954.

Lima e Silva, Leopoldo de. "Alimentação e trabalho." *Boletim do Ministério do Trabalho, Indústria, e Comércio*, Nov. 1936, 301–20.

Lima e Silva, Ruy Maurício de. "Iluminação e gás." In Fernando Nascimento Silva, ed., *Rio de Janeiro em seus quatrocentos anos: Formação e desenvolvimento da cidade*. Rio de Janeiro: Distribuidora Récord, 1965.

Lobo, Eulália Maria Lahmeyer. "Condições de vida dos artesãos e do operariado no Rio de Janeiro da década de 1880 a 1920." *Nova Americana* 4 (1981).

———. *História do Rio de Janeiro: Do capital comercial ao capital industrial e financeiro*. Rio de Janeiro: IBMEC, 1978.

———, ed. *Rio de Janeiro operário: Natureza do estado, conjuntura econômica, condições de vida e consciência de classe*. Rio de Janeiro: Access, 1992.

———, Lia A. Carvalho, and Myrian Stanley. *Questão hobitacional e o movimento operário*. Rio de Janeiro: Universidade Federal do Rio de Janeiro, 1989.

Lombroso, Cesare. *Crime: Its Causes and Remedies*. Trans. Henry P. Horton. Montclair, N.J.: Patterson Smith, 1968.

Lopes, Valdecir Freire. "Duas favelas do Distrito Federal." *Revista Brasileira dos Municípios* 8:32 (1955), 283–98.

Lovell, Peggy, ed. *Desigualdade racial no Brasil contemporâneo*. Belo Horizonte: CEDEPLAR/FACE/UFMG, 1991.

Ludwig, Armin K. *Brazil: A Handbook of Historical Statistics*. Boston: G. K. Hall, 1985.

Lyra, Roberto. *Novíssimas escolas penais*. Rio de Janeiro: Borsoi, 1956.

Macedo, Roberto. *Henrique Dodsworth*. Rio de Janeiro: Serviço de Documentação, Departamento Administrativo do Serviço Público, 1955.

Machado, José de Alcântara. *Para a história da reforma penal brasileira*. Rio de Janeiro: Freitas Bastos, 1941.

———. "O projeto do código criminal perante a crítica." *Revista da Faculdade de Direito da USP* 35:1 (1939), 39–96.

Machado, Maria Helena. "From Slave Rebels to Strikebreakers: The Quilombo of Jabaquara and the Problem of Citizenship in Late-Nineteenth-Century Brazil." *Hispanic American Historical Review* 86:2 (2006), 247–74.

Machado Neto, A. L. *História das idéias jurídicas no Brasil*. São Paulo: Grijalbo, 1969.

Maggie, Yvonne. "'Aqueles a quem foi negada a côr do dia': As categorias côr e raça na cultura brasileira." In Marcos Chor Maio e Ricardo Ventura Santos, eds., *Raça, ciência e sociedade*. Rio de Janeiro: Fiocruz/CCBB, 1996.

———. *Medo do feitiço: Relações entre magia e poder no Brasil*. Rio de Janeiro: Arquivo Nacional, 1992.

Marcondes, Marco Antônio. *Enciclopédia da música brasileira: Erudita, folclórica, popular*. São Paulo: Art Editora, 1977.

Marshall, T. H. "Citizenship and Social Class." In T. H. Marshall, *Citizenship and Social Class and other Essays*. Cambridge: Cambridge University Press, 1950.

Martine, George. *Formación de la familia y marginalidad urbana en Rio de Janeiro*. Santiago, Chile: Centro Latinoamericano de demografía, 1975.

Martins, José de Souza. *O cativeiro da terra*. São Paulo: Hucitec, 1986.

Marx, Anthony. *Making Race and Nation*. Cambridge: Cambridge University Press, 1998.

Marx, Karl. *Capital: A Critique of Political Economy*. Trans. Ernest Mandel. New York: Vintage, 1977.

Matos, Claudia. *Acertei no milhar: Samba e malandragem no tempo de Getúlio*. Rio de Janeiro: Paz e Terra, 1982.

Matta, Roberto da. *Carnivals, Malandros, and Heroes: An Interpretation of the Brazilian Dilemma*. Trans. John Drury. Notre Dame, Ind.: University of Notre Dame Press, 1991.

———. *A casa e a rua: Espaço, cidadania, mulher e morte no Brasil*. Rio de Janeiro: Brasiliense, 1991.

———. "Pedro Malasartes and the Paradoxes of Roguery," in *Carnivals, Malandros, and Heroes: An Interpretation of the Brazilian Dilemma*. Trans. John Drury. Notre Dame, Ind.: University of Notre Dame Press, 1991, 198–238.

Mayhew, Henry. *London Labour and the London Poor*. London: C. Griffin and Co., 1861.

McCann, Bryan. "Carlos Lacerda: Rise and Fall of a Middle-Class Populist in 1950s Brazil." *Hispanic American Historical Review* 83:4 (2003), 661–96.

————. *Hello, Hello Brazil: Popular Music in the Making of Modern Brazil.* Durham, N.C.: Duke University Press, 2004.

McDowall, Duncan. *The Light: Brazilian Traction, Light, and Power Company Limited, 1899–1945.* Toronto: University of Toronto Press, 1988.

Meade, Teresa. *"Civilizing" Rio: Reform and Resistance in a Brazilian City, 1889–1930.* University Park, Pa.: Pennsylvania State University Press, 1997.

Medeiros, Lídia Alice. "Atendimento à pobreza durante a era Vargas, do Albergue da Boa Vontade aos Parques Proletários: A atuação do Dr. Victor Tavares de Moura (1935–1945)." Master's thesis, Universidade do Estado do Rio de Janeiro, 2002.

Medeyros, J. Paulo de. *Getúlio Vargas, o reformador social.* Rio de Janeiro: Departamento de Imprensa e Propaganda, 1941.

Medina, Carlos Alberto de. *A favela e o demagogo.* Rio de Janeiro: Livraria Martins, 1965.

Méndez, Juan E., Guillermo O'Donnell, and Paulo Sérgio Pinheiro, eds. *The (Un)Rule of Law and the Underprivileged in Latin America.* Notre Dame, Ind.: University of Notre Dame Press, 1999.

Merrick, Thomas W., and Douglas H. Graham. *Population and Economic Development in Brazil: 1800 to the Present.* Baltimore, Md.: Johns Hopkins University Press, 1979.

Merriman, John M. *The Margins of City Life: Explorations on the French Urban Frontier, 1815–1851.* Oxford: Oxford University Press, 1991.

Merryman, John Henry. *The Civil Law Tradition: An Introduction to the Legal Systems of Western Europe and Latin America.* Stanford, Calif.: Stanford University Press, 1985.

Meuren, Waldir. "Breves considerações sôbre a lei das favelas." *Revista Forense* 186 (Nov.–Dec. 1959), 462–67.

Moogke, Peter N. "'Thieving Buggers' and 'Stupid Sluts': Insults and Popular Culture in New France." *William and Mary Quarterly* 36:4 (1979), 524–47.

Moraes, Evaristo de. *Problemas de direito penal e de psychologia criminal,* 2d ed. Rio de Janeiro: Pimenta de Mello, 1927.

Morais, Fernando. *Olga: A vida de Olga Benário Prestes, judia comunista entregue a Hitler pelo governo Vargas.* São Paulo: Alfa-Omega, 1985.

Morris, Fred B., and Gerald F. Pyle. "The Social Environment of Rio de Janeiro in 1960." *Economic Geography* 47:2 (1971).

Morse, Richard. *From Community to Metropolis: A Biography of São Paulo, Brazil.* New York: Octagon, 1974.

————, and Jorge E. Hardoy, eds. *Rethinking the Latin American City.* Washington, D.C./Baltimore, Md.: Woodrow Wilson Center Press/Johns Hopkins University Press, 1992.

Mortara, Giorgio. "Os estudos demográficos no Brasil." In Ministério da Educação e Cultura, *Decimália.* Rio de Janeiro: Ministério da Educação e Cultura, Biblioteca Nacional, 1959.

Moscoso, Alexandre. "Alimentação e o salário mínimo." *Boletim do Ministério do Trabalho, Indústria, e Comércio,* June 1936, 69–77.

———. "A alimentação do trabalhador nacional." *Boletim do Ministério do Trabalho, Indústria, e Comércio,* Feb., 1937, 114–34.

———. "O problema alimentar." *Boletim do Ministério do Trabalho, Indústria, e Comércio,* May 1937, 117–40.

Motta, Márcia Maria Menendes. *Nas fronteiras do poder: Conflito e direito à terra no Brasil do século XIX.* Rio de Janeiro: Vício da Leitura, 1998.

Moura, Margarida Maria. *Os deserdados da terra.* Rio de Janeiro: Bertrand Brasil, 1988.

Moura, Roberto. *Tia Ciata e a pequena África no Rio de Janeiro.* Rio de Janeiro: Biblioteca Carioca, 1995.

Moura, Vitor Tavares de. "Favelas do Distrito Federal." In Academia Carioca de Letras, *Aspectos do Distrito Federal.* Rio de Janeiro: Sauer, 1943.

———. *Relatório sobre o problema das favelas.* Report to the Secretário de Saúde e Assistência, Rio de Janeiro, 1940.

Moya, José. *Cousins and Strangers.* Berkeley: University of California Press, 1998.

MV Bill and Celso Athayde. *Falcão: Meninos do tráfico.* Rio de Janeiro: Objetiva, 2006.

Nascimento, Tupinambá Miguel Castro de. *Posse e propriedade,* 2d ed. Porto Alegre: Livraria do Advogado, 2000.

Naro, Nancy Priscilla Smith. "Customary Rightholders and Legal Claimants to Land in Rio de Janeiro, 1870–1890." *The Americas* 48:4 (1992), 485–517.

Needell, Jeffrey D. *A Tropical Belle Epoque: Elite Culture and Society in Turn-of-the-Century Rio de Janeiro.* New York: Cambridge University Press, 1987.

Nobles, Melissa. *Shades of Citizenship: Race and the Census in Modern Politics.* Stanford, Calif.: Stanford University Press, 2000.

Nonato, José Antônio, and Nubia Melhem Santos, eds. *Era uma vez o Morro do Castelo.* Rio de Janeiro: IPHAN, 2000.

Norton, Mary Beth. "Gender and Defamation in Seventeenth-Century Maryland." *William and Mary Quarterly* 44:1 (1987), 3–39.

Nunes, Guida. *Catumbi: Rebelião de um povo traído.* Petrópolis: Vozes, 1978.

———. *Favela: Resistência pelo direito de viver.* Petrópolis: Vozes, 1980.

O'Gorman, Frances, and mulheres de Rocinha e Santa Marta. *Morro mulher.* São Paulo: FASE/Edições Paulinas, 1984.

Oliveira, Antônio de, and Eulália Maria Lahmeyer Lobo. "O Estado Novo e o sindicato corporativista." In Eulália Maria Lahmeyer Lobo, ed., *Rio de Janeiro operário: Natureza do estado, conjuntura econômica, condições de vida e consciência de classe.* Rio de Janeiro: Access, 1992.

Oliveira, Jane Souto de. *Favelas do Rio de Janeiro.* Rio de Janeiro: Fundação Instituto Brasileiro de Geografia e Estatística (FIBGE), 1983.

———, and Maria Hortense Marcier. "A palavra é favela." In Alba Zaluar and Marcos Alvito, eds., *Um século de favela.* Rio de Janeiro: Fundação Getúlio Vargas, 1998.

Oliveira, Lúcia Lippi. "O Ambiente intelectual dos anos 30." Unpublished paper, date unknown.

———, ed. *Cidade: história e desafios.* Rio de Janeiro: Fundação Getúlio Vargas, 2002.

———, Mônica Pimenta Velloso, and Ângela Maria Castro Gomes, eds. *Estado Novo: Ideologia e poder.* Rio de Janeiro: Zahar, 1982.

Oliveira, Ney dos Santos. "Parque proletário da Gávea: Uma experiência de habitação popular." Master's thesis, Universidade Federal do Rio de Janeiro, 1981.

Pacheco, Maria Stella Bezerra. "Uma experiência de desenvolvimento e organização de comunidade no Parque Proletário Provisório no. 3." Undergraduate thesis, Pontifícia Universidade Católica do Rio de Janeiro, 1962.

Pacheco, Moema de Poli T. "A questão da côr nas relações de um grupo de baixa renda." *Estudos Afro-Asiáticos* 14 (1987), 85–97.

Pandolfi, Dulce, José Murilo de Carvalho, Leandro Piquet Carneiro, and Mário Grynszpan, eds. *Cidadania, justiça e violência.* Rio de Janeiro: Fundação Getúlio Vargas, 1999.

Pandolfi, Dulce, and Mário Grynszpan. *A favela fala.* Rio de Janeiro: Fundação Getúlio Vargas, 2003.

———. "Poder público e favelas: uma relação delicada." In Lúcia Lippi Oliveira, ed., *Cidade: história e desafios.* Rio de Janeiro: Fundação Getúlio Vargas, 2002.

Paoli, Maria Célia. "Trabalhadores e cidadania: Experiência do mundo público na história do Brasil moderno." *Estudos Avançados* 3:7 (1989), 40–66.

———. "Os trabalhadores urbanos na fala dos outros." In José Sérgio Leite Lopes, ed., *Cultura e identidade operária: Aspectos da classe trabalhadora.* Rio de Janeiro: Universidade Federal do Rio de Janeiro–PROED, 1987.

———, and Eder Sader. "Sobre 'classes populares' no pensamento sociológico brasileiro." In Ruth Cardoso, ed., *A aventura antropológica: Teoria e pesquisa,* vol. 1. Rio de Janeiro: Paz e Terra, 1986.

Parisse, Luciano. "Bibliografia cronológica sobre a favela do Rio de Janeiro a partir de 1940." *América Latina* 12:3 (1969).

———. *Favelas do Rio de Janeiro: Evolução—sentido.* Rio de Janeiro: Centro Nacional de Pesquisas Habitacionais, Pontifícia Universidade Católica do Rio de Janeiro, 1969.

Patai, Daphne. *Brazilian Women Speak: Contemporary Life Stories.* New Brunswick, N.J.: Rutgers University Press, 1988.

Patterson, James T. *America's Struggle against Poverty, 1900–1985.* Cambridge, Mass.: Harvard University Press, 1986.

Paula, Antônio de. *Do direito policial.* Rio de Janeiro: Editora A Noite, c. 1948.

Pechman, Roberto Moisés. "A gênese do mercado urbano de terras, a produção de moradias e a formação dos subúrbios no Rio de Janeiro." Master's thesis, Universidade Federal do Rio de Janeiro, 1985.

———. *Olhares sobre a cidade.* Rio de Janeiro: Universidade Federal do Rio de Janeiro, 1994.

Pederson, Susan. *Family, Dependence, and the Origins of the Welfare State: Britain and France, 1914–1945.* Cambridge: Cambridge University Press, 1993.

Peixoto, Afrânio. *Criminologia,* 4th ed. São Paulo: Saraiva, 1953.

Penglase, Benjamin. "To Live Here You Have to Know How to Live." Ph.D. diss., Harvard University, 2002.

Pereira, Carlos Alberto Messeder, ed. *A invenção do Brasil moderno: Medicina, educação e engenharia nos anos 20–30*. Rio de Janeiro: Rocco, 1994.

Pereira, Leonardo Affonso de Miranda. *O carnaval das letras*. Rio de Janeiro: Biblioteca Carioca, 1994.

Pereira, Margareth da Silva. "Pensando a metrópole moderna: Os planos de Agache e Le Corbusier para o Rio de Janeiro." In Luiz César Quieroz de Ribeiro and Robert Pechman, eds., *Cidade, povo e nação*. Rio de Janeiro: Civilização Brasileira, 1996.

Pereira, Silvia Baptista da Silva. "O serviço social e a urbanização da favela do Jacarezinho." Trabalho de Conclusão de Curso, School of Social Service, Pontifícia Universidade Católica do Rio de Janeiro, 1965.

Perlman, Janice E. *The Myth of Marginality: Urban Poverty and Politics in Rio de Janeiro*. Berkeley: University of California Press, 1976.

Petiz, Maria Lúcia de Paula. "A utilização do método de D.O.C. num programa de melhoramentos físicos na favela da Catacumba." Trabalho de Conclusão de Curso, School of Social Service, Pontifícia Universidade Católica do Rio de Janeiro, Rio, 1963.

Piccato, Pablo. *City of Suspects*. Durham, N.C.: Duke University Press, 2001.

Pimenta, João Augusto de Mattos. *Para a remodelação do Rio de Janeiro*. Rio de Janeiro, 1926. Unpublished ms.

Pinheiro, Paulo Sérgio. "Democratic Governance, Violence, and the (Un)rule of Law." *Daedalus* 129:12 (2000), 119–43.

———. "O proletariado industrial na Primeira República." In Boris Fausto, ed., *História geral da civilização brasileira*, vol. 9. São Paulo: DIFEL, 1985.

Pino, Julio César. *Family and Favela: The Reproduction of Poverty in Rio de Janeiro*. Westport, Conn.: Greenwood Press, 1997.

Pinto, Maria Novaes. "A cidade do Rio de Janeiro: Evolução física e humana." *Revista Brasileira de Geografia* 27:2 (1965).

Pinto, L. A. Costa. *O Negro no Rio de Janeiro: Relações raciais numa sociedade em mudança*, 2d ed. Rio de Janeiro: Universidade Federal do Rio de Janeiro, 1998.

Piragibe, Vicente. *Consolidação das leis penais*. Rio de Janeiro: Saraiva, 1932.

Pitt-Rivers, Julian. "Honor and Social Status." In J. G. Peristiany, *Honor and Shame: The Values of Mediterranean Society*. Chicago: University of Chicago Press, 1966.

Porto, José da Costa. *O Sistema sesmarial no Brasil*. Brasília: Universidade Federal de Brasília, 1979.

Porto, Rubens. "O problema da habitação operária." *Boletim do Ministério do Trabalho, Indústria e Comércio* 35 (July 1937).

Putnam, Lara Elizabeth. "Sex and Standing in the Streets of Port Limón, Costa Rica, 1890–1935." In Sueann Caulfield, Sarah Chambers, and Lara Putnam, eds., *Honor, Status and the Law in Modern Latin America*. Durham, N.C.: Duke University Press, 2005.

Reichmann, Rebecca, ed. *Race in Contemporary Brazil*. University Park, Pa.: Pennsylvania State University Press, 1999.

Reis, José de Oliveira. "As administrações municipais e o desenvolvimento urbano." In Fernando Nascimento Silva, ed., *Rio de Janeiro em seus quatrocentos anos: Formação e desenvolvimento da cidade*. Rio de Janeiro: Récord, 1965.

———. *O Rio de Janeiro e seus prefeitos: Evolução urbanística da cidade*. Rio de Janeiro: Prefeitura da Cidade do Rio de Janeiro, 1977.

Rezende, Vera. *Planejamento urbano e ideologia*. Rio de Janeiro: Civilização Brasileira, 1982.

———. "Planos e regulação urbanística: A dimensão normativa das intervenções na cidade do Rio de Janeiro." In Lúcia Lippi Oliveira, ed., *Cidade: História e desafios*. Rio de Janeiro: Fundação Getúlio Vargas, 2002.

Ribeiro, Gladys. *A liberdade em construção*. Rio de Janeiro: Relume Dumará, 2002.

Ribeiro, Leonidio, W. Berardinelli, and Isaac Brown. "Estudo biotypológico de negros e mulatos brasileiros normaes e delinquentes." In Gilberto Freyre, ed., *Estudos Afro-brasileiros: Trabalhos apresentados ao 1o Congresso afro-brasileiro do Recife, 1934*. Rio de Janeiro: Ariel, 1935–37.

Ribeiro, Luiz Cesar de Quieroz. *Dos cortiços aos condomínios fechados: As formas de produção de moradia na cidade do Rio de Janeiro*. Rio de Janeiro: Civilização Brasileira, 1996.

———, and Robert Pechman, eds. *Cidade, povo e nação*. Rio de Janeiro: Civilização Brasileira, 1996.

Ribeiro Filho, Carlos Antônio Costa. "Clássicos e positivistas no moderno direito penal brasileiro: Uma interpretação sociológica." In Carlos Alberto Messeder Pereira, ed., *A invenção do Brasil moderno: Medicina, educação e engenharia nos anos 20–30*. Rio de Janeiro: Rocco, 1994.

———. *Côr e criminalidade: Estudo e análise da justiça no Rio de Janeiro (1900–1930)*. Rio de Janeiro: Universidade Federal do Rio de Janeiro, 1995.

Rios, Ana Lugão, and Hebe Mattos. *Memórias do cativeiro: Família, trabalho e cidadania na pós-abolição*. Rio de Janeiro: Civilização Brasileira, 2005.

Rios, José Arthur. Interview with Lúcia Lippi Oliveira and Marly Motta. In Américo Freire and Lúcia Lippi Oliveira, *Capítulos da memória do urbanismo carioca*. Rio de Janeiro: Fundação Getúlio Vargas, 2002.

———. "Operação Mutirão." Unpublished paper, date unknown.

———. "Remover ou urbanizar favelas." *Debates Sociais* 4:7 (1968).

Rios, Maria Monteiro Machado de. "O desenvolvimentismo e as favelas." In Victor Valla, ed., *Educação e favela*. Rio de Janeiro: Vozes, 1986.

Rocha, Adair Leonardo. *Cidade cerzida: A costura da cidadania no Morro Santa Marta*. Rio de Janeiro: Relume Dumará, 2000.

Rocha, Oswaldo Porto. *A era das demolições: A cidade do Rio de Janeiro, 1870–1920*, 2d ed. Rio de Janeiro, 1995.

Rodrigues, Raymundo Nina. *As raças humanas e a responsibilidade penal no Brasil*. Salvador: Aguiar & Souza, 1957.

Romeiro Neto, João. *O direito penal nos casos concretos*. Rio de Janeiro: A. Coelho Branco, 1939.

Roxo, Estélio Emanuel de Alencar, and Manoel Ferreira. "O saneamento do meio físico." In Fernando Nascimento Silva, ed., *Rio de Janeiro em seus quatrocentos anos: Formação e desenvolvimento da cidade.* Rio de Janeiro: Récord, 1965.

Sá, Paulo. "Abonos familiares." *Boletim do Ministério de Trabalho, Indústria e Comércio,* 1936, 285–300 (originally presented at a conference titled Primeira Semana de Acção Social do Rio de Janeiro).

Salvatore, Ricardo D., and Carlos Aguirre. *The Birth of the Penitentiary in Latin America: Essays on Criminology, Prison Reform, and Social Control, 1830–1940.* Austin: University of Texas Press, 1996.

Sampaio, Carlos. *Idéias e impressões.* Rio de Janeiro: Gazeta da Bolsa, 1929.

Santos, Boaventura de Souza. "The Law of the Oppressed: The Construction and Reproduction of Legality in Pasargada." *Law and Society Review* 12:1 (1977), 5–126.

Santos, Carlos Nelson Ferreira dos. *História do Morro do Timbau.* Rio de Janeiro: UFF, 1983.

———. *Movimentos urbanos no Rio de Janeiro.* Rio de Janeiro: Zahar, 1981.

Santos, Leonardo Soares dos. "Laços em movimento: As relações dos pequenos lavradores do Sertão Carioca com outros movimentos sociais (1945–1964)." Paper presented at the Colóquio Agrário, Universidade Federal Fluminense, Nov. 19, 2005.

Santos, Francisco Agenor Noronha. *As freguesias do Rio antigo.* Rio de Janeiro: Edições O Cruzeiro, 1965.

———. *Meios de transporte no Rio de Janeiro: História e legislação.* Rio de Janeiro: Jornal do Commercio, 1934.

Santos, Wanderley Guilherme dos. *Cidadania e justiça: A política social na ordem brasileira.* Rio de Janeiro: Campus, 1979.

———. *Razões da desordem.* Rio de Janeiro: Rocco, 1992.

———. *Votos e partidos. Almanaque de dados eleitorais: Brasil e outros países.* Rio de Janeiro: Fundação Getúlio Vargas/Fundação de Amparo à Pesquisa do Estado do Rio de Janeiro, 2002.

———, and Marcelo de Paiva Abreu, eds. *Estatísticas do século XX.* Rio de Janeiro: Instituto Brasileiro de Geografia e Estatística, 2003.

Schultz, Kirsten. *Tropical Versailles: Empire, Monarchy, and the Portuguese Court in Rio de Janeiro, 1808–1821.* New York: Routledge, 2001.

Schumaher, Schuma, and Érico Vital Brazil. *Dicionário Mulheres do Brasil: De 1500 até a atualidade.* Rio de Janeiro: Zahar, 2000.

Schwarcz, Lilia Moritz. *O Espetáculo das raças: Cientistas, instituições, e questão racial no Brasil, 1870–1930.* São Paulo: Cia. das Letras, 1993.

———, and Renato da Silva Quieroz, eds. *Raça e diversidade.* São Paulo: Editora da Universidade de São Paulo (EdUSP), 1997.

Schwartzman, Simon, Helena Maria Bousquet Bomeny, and Vanda Maria Ribeiro Costa. *Tempos de Capanema.* São Paulo/Rio de Janeiro: Editora da Universidade de São Paulo (EdUSP)/Paz e Terra, 1984.

Scobie, James. *Buenos Aires: Plaza to Suburb, 1870–1910.* New York: Oxford University Press, 1974.

Scott, Rebecca, and Michael Zeuske. "Property in Writing, Property on the Ground: Pigs, Horses, Land, and Citizenship in the Aftermath of Slavery, Cuba, 1880–1909." *Comparative Studies in Society and History* 44 (Oct. 2002).

Sevcenko, Nicolau. "A capital irradiante: Técnica, ritmos e ritos do Rio." In Nicolau Sevcenko, ed., *História da vida privada no Brasil. República: Da Belle Epoque à era do rádio.* São Paulo: Cia. Das Letras, 1998.

Shapiro, Ann-Louise. *Housing the Poor of Paris, 1850–1902.* Madison: University of Wisconsin Press, 1985.

Shaw, Lisa. *The Social History of the Brazilian Samba.* Aldershot/Burlington: Ashgate Publishing, 1999.

Sheriff, Robin. *Dreaming Equality.* New Brunswick, N.J.: Rutgers University Press, 2001.

———. "Exposing Silence as Cultural Censorship: A Brazilian Case." *American Anthropologist* 102:1 (2000).

Silva, Eduardo da. *As camélias do Leblon e a abolição da escravatura.* São Paulo: Cia. das Letras, 2003.

———. *Prince of the People: The Life and Times of a Brazilian Free Man of Colour.* London: Verso, 1993.

Silva, Fernando Nascimento, ed. *Rio de Janeiro em seus quatrocentos anos: Formação e desenvolvimento da cidade.* Rio de Janeiro: Récord, 1965.

Silva, Fernando Teixeira da, and Hélio da Costa. "Trabalhadores urbanos e populismo: Um balanço dos estudos recentes." In Jorge Luiz Fereira, ed., *O populismo e sua história.* Rio de Janeiro: Civilização Brasileira, 2001.

Silva, Lígia Osório. *Terras devolutas e latifúndio: Efeitos da lei de 1850.* Campinas: UNICAMP, 1996.

Silva, Lúcia. "A Trajetória de Alfred Donat Agache no Brasil." In Luiz César Quieroz Ribeiro and Robert Pechman, eds., *Cidade, povo e nação.* Rio de Janeiro: Civilização Brasileira, 1996.

Silva, Luiz Antônio Machado da. "A Continuidade do 'problema da favela.'" In Lúcia Lippi Oliveira, ed., *Cidade: história e desafios.* Rio de Janeiro: Fundação Getúlio Vargas, 2002.

———. "O significado do botequim." *América Latina* 12:3 (1969), 160–82.

Silva, Maria Hortência de Nascimento. "Impressões de uma assistente social sobre o trabalho em favela." Rio de Janeiro: Prefeitura do DF, Secretaria de Saúde e Assistência, Instituto Social, 1941.

Silva, Maria Lais Pereira da. *Favelas cariocas, 1930–1964.* Rio de Janeiro: Contraponto, 2005.

———. *Os transportes coletivos na cidade do Rio de Janeiro.* Rio de Janeiro: Biblioteca Carioca, 1992.

Silva, Rosauro Mariano da. "A luta pela agua." In Fernando Nascimento Silva, ed., *Rio de Janeiro em seus quatrocentos anos: Formação e desenvolvimento da cidade.* Rio de Janeiro: Récord, 1965.

Siqueira, Galdino. *Curso de processo criminal.* São Paulo: Livraria Magalhães, 1924.

———. *Direito penal brasileiro.* Rio de Janeiro: J. Ribeiro dos Santos, 1921.

Skidmore, Thomas E. *Black into White: Race and Nationality in Brazilian Thought.* Durham, N.C.: Duke University Press, 1993.

———. *Politics in Brazil.* New York: Oxford University Press, 1967.

Skocpol, Theda. *Protecting Soldiers and Mothers: The Political Origins of Social Policy in the United States.* Cambridge, Mass.: Harvard University Press, 1992.

Soares, Carlos Eugênio Líbano. *A capoeira escrava e outras tradições rebeldes no Rio de Janeiro (1808–1850).* Campinas: UNICAMP, 2001.

———. *A negregada instituição: Os capoieras no Rio de Janeiro.* Rio de Janeiro: Biblioteca Carioca, 1994.

Soares, Maria Therezinha de Segadas. "Fisonomia e estrutura do Rio de Janeiro." *Revista Brasileira de Geografia* 27:3 (1965), 329–85.

Soares, Oscar de Macedo. *Código penal da República dos Estados Unidos do Brasil, commentado por Oscar de Macedo Soares.* Rio de Janeiro/Paris: Garnier, 1910.

Sociedade de Análises Gráficas e Mecanográficas Aplicadas aos Complexos Sociais (SAGMACS). "Aspectos humanos da favela carioca." *Estado de São Paulo,* Apr. 13 and 15, 1960.

Soihet, Rachel. *Condição feminina e formas de violência: Mulheres pobres e ordem urbana, 1890–1920.* Rio de Janeiro: Forense Universitária, 1989.

Soto, Hernando de. *The Other Path.* New York: Basic Books, 2002.

Souto Maior, Mário. *Dicionário do palavrão e termos afins,* 6th ed. Rio de Janeiro: Record, 1988.

Souza, Laura de Mello e. *Desclassificados de ouro: A pobreza mineira no século XVIII.* Rio de Janeiro: Graal, 1982.

Starr, June, and Jane F. Collier, eds. *History and Power in the Study of Law: New Directions in Legal Anthropology.* Ithaca, N.Y.: Cornell University Press, 1989.

Stepan, Nancy. *Beginnings of Brazilian Science: Oswaldo Cruz, Medical Research, and Policy, 1890–1920.* New York: Science History Publications, 1976.

Stilgoe, John. *Metropolitan Corridor: Railroads and the American Scene.* New Haven, Conn.: Yale University Press, 1983.

Stuckenbruck, Denise Cabral. *O Rio de Janeiro em questão: O plano Agache e o ideário reformista dos anos 20.* Rio de Janeiro: Observatório de Políticas Urbanas e Gestão Municipal, 1996.

Tati, Miécio. *O mundo de Machado de Assis.* Rio de Janeiro: Biblioteca Carioca, 1995.

Telles, Edward E. "Industrialization and Racial Inequality in Employment: The Brazilian Example." *American Sociological Review* 59 (Feb. 1994), 46–63.

———. *Race in Another America: The Significance of Skin Color in Brazil.* Princeton, N.J.: Princeton University Press, 2004.

———. "Who Gets Formal Sector Jobs? Determinants of Formal-Informal Participation in Brazilian Metropolitan Areas." *Work and Occupations* 19:2 (1992), 108–27.

Thompson, E. P. *The Making of the English Working Class.* New York: Vintage, 1966.

——. *Whigs and Hunters*. New York: Pantheon, 1975.

Tôrres, Laura Bogado. "Parque proletário provisório no. 1." Trabalho de conclusão de curso, School of Social Service, Pontifícia Universidade Católica do Rio de Janeiro, 1953.

Tulchin, Joseph S., and Meg Ruthenburg, eds. *Citizenship in Latin America*. Boulder/London: Lynne Rienner, 2007.

Twine, Frances Winddance. *Racism in a Racial Democracy*. New Brunswick, N.J.: Rutgers University Press, 1998.

União Pro-Melhoramentos dos Moradores da Rocinha. *Varal de lembranças*. Rio de Janeiro: Tempo e Presença, 1983.

Valla, Victor, ed. *Educação e favela*. Rio de Janeiro: Vozes, 1986.

Valladares, Licia do Prado. "A gênese da favela carioca: A produção anterior às ciências sociais." *Revista Brasileira de Ciências Sociais* 15:44 (2000), 5–34.

——. *Habitação em questão*. Rio de Janeiro: Zahar, 1979.

——. *A invenção da favela: Do mito de origem a favela.com*. Rio de Janeiro: Fundação Getúlio Vargas, 2005.

——. "A luta pela terra no Brasil urbano: Reflexões em torno de alguns casos." Unpublished paper, date unknown.

——. *Passa-se uma casa*. Rio de Janeiro: Zahar, 1978.

——. *Pensando as favelas do Rio de Janeiro, 1906–2000: Uma bibliografia analítica*, Rio de Janeiro: URBANDATA-Brasil/Relume Dumará, 2003.

Valle e Silva, Nelson do. "Côr e processo de realização sócio-econômica." In Nelson do Valle e Silva and Carlos Hasenbalg, eds., *Estrutura social, mobilidade e raça*. São Paulo/Rio de Janeiro: Vértice, 1988.

——. "Uma nota sobre 'raça social' no Brasil." *Estudos Afro-Asiáticos* 26 (Sept. 1994), 67–80.

——, and Carlos Hasenbalg, eds. *Estrutura social, mobilidade e raça*. São Paulo/Rio de Janeiro: Vértice, 1988.

——. *Relações raciais no Brasil contemporâneo*. Rio de Janeiro: Rio Fundo, 1992.

Varella, Drauzio, Ivaldo Bertazzo, and Paola Berenstein Jacques. *Maré: Vida na favela*. Rio de Janeiro: Casa da Palavra, 2002.

Vargas, Getúlio Dornelles. *Diário*, Rio de Janeiro: Fundação Getúlio Vargas, 1995.

——. *O governo trabalhista no Brasil*, vols. 1 and 2. Rio de Janeiro: José Olympio, 1954.

——. *A nova política do Brasil*. Rio de Janeiro: José Olympio, 1938–46.

——. *Todos são necessários uns aos outros*. Rio de Janeiro: Departamento de Imprensa e Propaganda, 1941 ("speech to the workers of Brazil," May 1, 1941).

——. *Unidade moral e unidade econômica da nacionalidade*. Rio de Janeiro: Departamento de Imprensa e Propaganda, 1940 ("speech to the conservative and proletarian classes," November 10, 1940).

Vaz, Lilian Fessler. "Contribuição ao estudo da produção e transformação do espaço da habitação popular: As habitações coletivas no Rio antigo." Master's thesis, Universidade Federal do Rio de Janeiro, 1985.

————. *Modernidade e moradia: Habitação coletiva no Rio de Janeiro, séculos XIX e XX*. Rio de Janeiro: 7 Letras, 2002.

————. "Notas sobre o Cabeça de Porco." *Revista do Rio de Janeiro* 1:2 (1986), 29–35.

Velho, Gilberto. *A utopia urbana: Um estudo de antropologia social*, 5th ed. Rio de Janeiro: Zahar, 1989.

Velloso, Cleto Seabra. "A alimentação do povo brasileiro." *Boletim do Ministério do Trabalho, Indústria, e Comércio* 32 (Apr. 1937), 278–90.

Velloso, Monica Pimenta. "A dupla face de Jano: Romantismo e populismo." In Ângela Maria de Castro Gomes, ed., *O Brasil do JK*. Rio de Janeiro: Fundação Getúlio Vargas, 1991.

Ventura, Zeunir. *Cidade partida*. São Paulo: Cia. Das Letras, 1994.

Vianna, Hermano. *O mistério do samba*. Rio de Janeiro: Zahar/Universidade Federal do Rio de Janeiro, 1995.

Vianna, Luiz Fernando. *Geografia carioca do samba*. Rio de Janeiro: Casa da Palavra, 2004.

Vianna, Francisco José de Oliveira. *Evolução do povo brasileiro*. São Paulo: Monteiro Lobato e Cia., 1923.

Vieira, Luis Fernando. *Sambas da Mangueira*. Rio de Janeiro: Revan, 1998.

Vianna, Luiz Werneck. "Estudos sobre sindicalismo e movimento operário: Resenha de algumas tendências." *Dados: Revista de Ciências Sociais* 17 (1978), 9–24.

Weffort, Francisco. *O populismo na política brasileira*. Rio de Janeiro: Paz e Terra, 1980.

Weinstein, Barbara. *For Social Peace in Brazil: Industrialists and the Remaking of the Working Class in São Paulo, 1920–1964*. Chapel Hill, N.C.: University of North Carolina Press, 1996.

Welch, Cliff. *The Seed Was Planted*. University Park, Pa.: Pennsylvania State University Press, 1999.

Western, John. *Outcast Cape Town*. Berkeley: University of California Press, 1996.

Williams, Daryle. *Culture Wars in Brazil: The First Vargas Regime, 1930–1945*. Durham, N.C.: Duke University Press, 2001.

Wolfe, Joel. "'Father of the Poor' or 'Mother of the Rich?': Getúlio Vargas, Industrial Workers, and Constructions of Class, Gender, and Populism in São Paulo, 1930–1954." *Radical History Review* 58 (Jan. 1994), 81–111.

————. "The Faustian Bargain Not Made: Getúlio Vargas and Brazil's Industrial Workers, 1930–1945." *Luso-Brazilian Review* 31:2 (1994), 77–95.

————. *Working Women, Working Men: São Paulo and the Rise of Brazil's Industrial Working Class, 1900–1955*. Durham, N.C.: Duke University Press, 1993.

Wood, Charles H., and José Alberto Magno de Carvalho. *The Demography of Inequality in Brazil*. Cambridge: Cambridge University Press, 1988.

Zaluar, Alba. *Integração perversa: Pobreza e tráfico de drogas*. Rio de Janeiro: Fundação Getúlio Vargas, 2004.

————. *A Máquina e a revolta.* São Paulo: Brasiliense, 1985.

————, and Marcos Alvito, eds. *Um século de favela.* Rio de Janeiro: Fundação Getúlio Vargas, 1998.

Zylberberg, Sónia. *Morro da Providência: Memórias da "favella."* Rio de Janeiro: Prefeitura da Cidade do Rio de Janeiro, 1992.

Index